Third Edition

GENDER ROLES

A Sociological Perspective

Linda L. Lindsey
Maryville University—St. Louis

With a joint chapter by
Sandra Christie
Fact Finders, Inc.

Prentice Hall, Upper Saddle River, New Jersey 07458

Library of Congress Cataloging-in-Publication Data

LINDSEY, LINDA L.
   Gender roles: a sociological perspective / Linda L. Lindsey.—
3rd ed.
   p. cm.
   Includes bibliographical references and index.
   ISBN 0-13-533621-X
   1. Sex role. 2. Sex role—United States. I. Title.
HQ1075.L564   1997
305.3—dc20   96-38322

Editorial director: *Charlyce Jones Owen*
Editor-in-chief: *Nancy Roberts*
Associate editor: *Sharon Chambliss*
Production editor: *Edie Rike*r
Cover design: *Kiwi Design*
Buyer: *Bob Anderson*
Director of marketing: *Gina Sluss*
Editorial assistant: *Pat Naturale*

This book was set in 10/12 New Baskerville by East End Publishing Services
and was printed and bound by Courier Companies, Inc. The cover was printed by
Phoenix Color Corp.

© 1997 by Prentice-Hall, Inc.
Simon & Schuster / A Viacom Company
Upper Saddle River, New Jersey 07458

Printed in the United States of America

10   9   8   7   6   5   4

ISBN   0-13-533621-X

Prentice-Hall International (UK) Limited, *London*
Prentice-Hall of Australia Pty. Limited, *Sydney*
Prentice-Hall Canada Inc., *Toronto*
Prentice-Hall Hispanoamericana, S.A., *Mexico*
Prentice-Hall of India Private Limited, *New Delhi*
Prentice-Hall of Japan, Inc., *Tokyo*
Simon & Schuster Asia Pte. Ltd., *Singapore*
Editora Prentice-Hall do Brasil, Ltda., *Rio de Janeiro*

CONTENTS

PART II
GENDER ROLES, MARRIAGE, AND THE FAMILY

Chapter 8
Gender and Family Relations

Chapter 9
Men and Masculinity

PART III
GENDER ROLES: FOCUS ON SOCIAL INSTITUTIONS

PREFACE

It is truly amazing to witness the dramatic, ongoing expansion of the topic of gender roles in society and how the explosion of gender-related research has literally served to shape many disciplines. From both a teaching and a research perspective the topic of gender has moved from the margins to the center of these disciplines, and sociology is no exception. The third edition of this book takes into account the multitude of new material on gender, especially as associated with multicultural and global issues. Scholarship in the area has expanded so rapidly and has become so theoretically and empirically sophisticated that it is now time to introduce students to some of the complex, important issues emerging from this scholarship.

In assembling this edition I recognized that a recurrent theme surfaced in almost every piece of material I reviewed. Simply stated, the theme revolves around the question, "but what about me?" This edition earnestly attempts to capture the experiences of specific groups of people and the intricacies of their gendered lives as related to, for example, issues of class, race, and culture. Recent research on women at midlife is a special focus. This means that material had to be carefully chosen to accurately represent the groups involved as well as be both specific and general at the same time. This edition also expands on the contributions of other disciplines as they impinge on the sociology of gender roles. Thus only a fraction of the abundant, almost overwhelming, gender-related information can be adequately presented. While these tasks are formidable, they are manageable, especially when employing a sociological perspective. Throughout the text students will find a solid sociological foundation that links the diverse information. These tasks are also gratifying in that they clearly demonstrate the continued activity, enthusiasm, and keen interest in the areas of gender roles and women's issues.

This text is written primarily for students in courses on the sociology of gender or sex roles. It is also useful as a text for those studying the sociology of the family, psychology of women, and women's or men's studies. For those who have not been exposed to the sociological perspective, the opening chapter provides an overview of the major sociological theories (functionalism, conflict, and symbolic interaction) and concepts and demonstrates how they can be used in explaining the sometimes contradictory research on gender issues. These theories are applied throughout the text to show students not only how the sociological perspective provides a logical framework for approaching a host of gender topics, but also how different theories explain the same research. Both introductory and advanced students should find this approach useful.

Part I provides insight from other disciplines, particularly biology, psychology, and history as they have influenced thinking on gender roles and the creation of beliefs about women and men, masculinity and femininity. This edition expands considerably on health-related themes, specifically addressing the issue of multiple roles on women's health and well-being. Considering the vast amount of new research on women in development and the impact of the U.N. Conference on Women in Beijing, global issues are highlighted in many chapters. The chapter on global perspectives has been considerably updated to account for more of the intricacies in examining both the similarities and differences of women in selected countries and regions of the world. The theme of the productive roles of women in their unpaid capacity is introduced in this section and carried throughout the text.

The sociological perspective dominates the balance of the book. Part II focuses on marriage and the family and accents the newest research on love, mate selection, and changing family structure and functions. It is attendant to the theme of family variety in a multicultural context. This section also demonstrates how traditional definitions of masculinity and men's roles are being challenged, and how they are responding to these challenges as well as to the changing roles of women. Finally, Part III looks at the continuities and changes in the social institutions, including the economy, education, religion, the media, and politics, and it suggests future trends related to gender roles. The "gendered" nature of the media is emphasized as influencing all the social institutions. Chapter 10, which focuses on workplace issues, is jointly written by Sandra Christie, who is chief executive officer of a market research firm. As a sociologist and business executive, Sandy combines sociological analysis with her work in management and the corporate world to present a unique view of the world of paid employment.

It is expected that this text will provide opportunities for students to explore a variety of gender role issues and how these impact their personal, academic, and professional lives. When social change affects our attitudes and behaviors regarding the roles that men and women are supposed to play, we find ourselves confronted with challenges to our traditional ways of thinking and doing. We may eagerly pursue new directions or stubbornly resist them. In either scenario, our decisions will be wiser if we understand the myth and reality associated with gender issues, whether related to our relationships, homes, schools, or workplaces.

For both women and men the topic of gender roles is definitely a controversial one. You will be confronted with ideas that reinforce as well as challenge your thinking about women and men and masculinity and femininity. An objective of this book is to raise your level of consciousness about what you take for granted concerning gender. However, once you have grappled with the research, confronted the stereotypes, and selected the theory you consider most reasonable in explaining gender issues, you will have gained a greater understanding of our "gendered" world. And perhaps of equal importance, you will have gained insight about the other half of humanity.

The completion of this edition relied on the time and talent of many people. My editors at Prentice Hall, Nancy Roberts and Sharon Chambliss, have given me continued encouragement throughout the long process. My production editor, Edie Riker, ensured that the manuscript was clear and accurate. Murray Fisher did an outstanding job in creating an index that will serve the needs of students and others who will find this text very useful for research purposes. Those who have read and critiqued various chapters: Kristine Gunsaulus-Musick, University of Northern Colorado; Jane I. Johnson, Southwest Texas State University; and Polly F. Radosh, Western Illinois University; Willie Melton, Michigan Technological University; Edith Graber, University of Missouri–St. Louis; and Linda Pitelka, Maryville University. I am very indebted to them. Others who provided research assistance, and kept me well supplied with the most current material have been extremely helpful. In this regard I would particularly like to thank Linda Pitelka, Willie Melton, Staley Hitchcock, Edith Graber, and Riane Eisler. The administration and staff at Maryville University and Washington University's Social Thought and Analysis Program provided much needed support services and leave time. I thank Juanita Aycock, Carol Trauth, Pat Scott, Anita Bledsoe, Pat Thro, and Keith Lovin in this respect. Finally, I would like to thank my friends Cheryl Hazel, Joe Overton, Diana Dierberg, Bill Nagel and Dick Stellway and the staff of the St. Louis Bread Company in Kirkwood for the much appreciated encouragement to finish this edition.

Linda L. Lindsey
St. Louis, Missouri

To Robert Houston Lindsey (1920-1961)
and Ruth Weimert Lindsey

CHAPTER 1

THE SOCIOLOGY OF GENDER
Theoretical Perspectives
and Feminist Frameworks

> All causes, social and natural, combine to make it unlikely that women
> should be collectively rebellious to the power of men. They are so far in a
> position different from all other subject classes, that their masters require
> something more from them than actual service. Men do not want solely the
> obedience of women, they want their sentiments.
> —John Stuart Mill, *The Subjection of Women* (1869)

The study of gender roles has emerged as one of the most important trends in
the discipline of sociology in the last half century. From being a marginal concern, the sociology of gender is now a central feature of the discipline. This
text will document how sociological theory and research have aided our
understanding of how gender shapes our lives, our perspectives, and our
behavior. That understanding is enhanced by investigating both the links
between sociology and other disciplines as well as concepts which illuminate
gender relations, such as race and social class. Sociology is interested in how
human behavior is shaped by group life. Although our social relations are
ordered in a variety of ways, gender is a key component of this ordering. With
more and more research now suggesting that all social relations are "gendered" in some manner, not only is sociological theory being modified, but the
discipline itself is also being reshaped. Gender issues have provided at least two
important avenues for contemporary sociology. As Maynard (1990:270)
asserts, the first is the development of gender awareness and a serious attempt
to make up for the earlier neglect of the female experience in empirical sociology. The second is to introduce new subjects for sociological inquiry. These
concerns are "new" because they have been previously ignored or viewed as
inconsequential. Such material has extended both the study of gender roles
and the scope of sociology as a discipline.

BASIC SOCIOLOGICAL CONCEPTS

Every society places its members into a series of categories which determines
how members will be defined and treated. These social categories or positions are known as **statuses**, and they become major organizing referents for
how we relate to other people. We acquire our statuses by achievement,
through our own efforts, or by ascription as we are born into them or assume
them involuntarily at some other point in the life cycle. We each occupy a
number of statuses simultaneously, such as mother, daughter, attorney,
patient, and passenger. Acquired by ascription, the status of female or male
is a **master status** in that it is one which will affect almost every aspect of our
lives. A status is simply a position within a social system and should not be
confused with rank or prestige. In this sense, then, there are high-prestige

statuses as well as low-prestige statuses. For example, in American society, a physician occupies a status which is ranked higher in prestige than a secretary. All societies categorize members by status and then rank these statuses in some fashion, thereby creating a system of **social stratification**. To date, there has been no society where the status of female is consistently ranked higher than that of male.

The expected behavior associated with any given status is referred to as a **role**. As the dynamic aspect of status, roles are defined and structured around the privileges and responsibilities the status is seen to possess. Females and males, mothers and fathers, and daughters and sons are all statuses with different role requirements attached to them. Generally, the status of mother calls for expected roles involving love, nurturing, self-sacrifice, and availability. The status of father calls for expected roles of breadwinner, disciplinarian, and ultimate decision maker in the household. Societies will allow for a degree of flexibility in acting out roles, but in times of rapid social change, the acceptable limits are in a state of flux and redefinition, producing uncertainty about what the appropriate role behavior should be. For instance, the largest increase in labor force participation involves mothers who have preschool children. In acting out the roles of mother and employee, women are expected to be available at given times. Unless new limits are set which provide for a greater range of acceptable role behavior, these roles inevitably compete with one another.

The concepts of status and role are key components of the social structure and are necessary in helping us organize our lives in a consistent, predictable manner. In combination with the **norms** or shared rules of behavior established by society, we have prescribed methods of acting and associating with others. Yet there is an insidious side to this kind of predictable world. When expected role behavior becomes rigidly defined, an individual's freedom of action is severely compromised. This is often associated with the development of **stereotypes**, defined as oversimplified conceptions that people who belong to the same group or category share certain traits in common. Although stereotyping can be used positively, it is most often considered in the negative sense and used to justify discriminatory behavior against members of a given group. The categories of male and female are stereotyped such that members of the category are assumed to possess certain characteristics by virtue of their biological categories. This results in **sexism**, the belief that one category, female, is inferior to the other, male. While males are not immune to the negative consequences of sexism, females experience it firsthand since it permeates all levels of our social institutions. This belief in inferiority is then used to justify and legitimize the discriminatory behavior directed primarily toward females.

Sexism is perpetuated by systems of **patriarchy** where male-dominated structures and social arrangements elaborate the oppression of women. Patriarchy almost by definition also exhibits **androcentrism**, meaning male-centered. In consort with patriarchy androcentrism assumes that male norms operate throughout all social institutions and become the standard to which all persons adhere. For example, men's greater power to control words means that until recently history has been recorded from the perspective of half of humanity. What women have written and talked about has been marginalized. As the oldest social institution, the family is seen as the place where patriarchy originated and eventually reproduced throughout society. While patriarchal systems are universal, they are no longer seen as inevitable. As will be demonstrated, this is substantiated by evidence suggesting that other models, including societies based more on a gender partnership, predated patriarchy.

DISTINGUISHING SEX AND GENDER

The terms *sex* and *gender* now have much confusion associated with their usage. Overall, the term **sex** is considered in light of the biological aspects of a person, involving characteristics which differentiate females and males by chromosomal, anatomical, reproductive, hormonal, and other physiological characteristics. **Gender** involves those social, cultural, and psychological aspects linked to males and females through particular social contexts. What a given society defines as masculine or feminine is a component of gender. Given this distinction, sex is viewed as an ascribed status and gender as an achieved one.

This relatively simple distinction is deceptive in that it implies either-or categories which are unambiguous. Certainly the status of sex is less likely to be altered than that of gender. Yet even here there are those who believe they have been born with the "wrong" body and will undergo sex change surgery to allow their gender identity to be consistent with their biological sex. From their perspective, only by becoming a transsexual can psychological harmony be realized. **Sexual orientation**, or the manner in which people experience sexual pleasure or achieve sexual arousal, also varies. Males who have a sexual orientation for other males are also likely to consider themselves very masculine.

These issues will be addressed more fully later but are mentioned here to highlight the problems of terminology. And as will be demonstrated throughout this book, gender itself is learned, is not immutable, has changed over time, and varies considerably in different cultures. Therefore, it is reasonable to view gender, in particular, as a continuum of characteristics which an individual may demonstrate, regardless of biological sex. When the word "role" is added to either sex or gender, the confusion of terminology may increase. Role is essentially a sociological or social psychological concept which can be misleading when combined with the biological concept of sex. The term **sex role**, then, may convey myths or misinformation about males and females from both the biological and sociocultural components. On the other hand, the addition of the word "role" to sex or gender can also simplify discussion of the abundance of research which uses the terms sex and gender interchangeably anyway. Whereas there has been a marked increase and option in the literature for the use of the terms gender and gender roles, references to sex roles per se still abound. Journals like *Sex Roles* and *Gender & Society* deal with theoretical and research issues involving the interplay of many variables, including the biological and sociocultural.

Gender roles are defined as those expected attitudes and behaviors which a society associates with each sex. These include the rights and responsibilities that are normative for the sexes in a given society. To maintain a focus on the sociocultural component, this book will show a preference for the terms gender and gender role, rather than sex and sex role. However, research will be referred to which does not follow this convention and which is stated in the style of a specific author. The key term is *role*, which places the reference squarely on the sociocultural level.

SOCIOLOGICAL THEORY

In order to explain gender roles in any society, some type of organizing framework is necessary. A theoretical perspective guides the research process and
then provides a means for interpreting the collected data. In essence, a theory is an explanation. More specifically, formal theories consist of sets of logically interrelated propositions which seek to explain a group of facts, phe-
nomena, or an entire class of empirical events. For instance, data indicate that
women, compared with men, are more likely to be segregated in lower-paying
jobs which offer fewer opportunities for professional growth and advancement. As will become evident, such data can be explained differently according to a given theoretical perspective. The issue of gender crosses many disciplines, and certain models from biology, psychology, anthropology, and
history are referred to throughout the text. However, since sociological concepts provide the basic framework for addressing the topic, sociological theory will dominate. What follows is how gender roles may be explained from the
three major theoretical models in sociology (see Table 1-1 for a summary).

Functionalism

Functionalism, also known as structural-functional thought, begins with
the premise that society is made up of interdependent parts, each of which contributes to the functioning of the whole. Functionalists seek to identify the basic
elements or parts of society, determine the functions these parts play, and then
consider how the entire society operates or functions. The basic question of functional analysis is how any given element of social structure contributes to the stability of the whole. What is the social function of any structural element?
Functionalism, then, attempts to discover the consequences of any given pattern.

Modern functionalism views society as a system of integrated or interdependent parts. Social systems remain stable because they have built-in mechanisms of control. In the event of societal disruption and dysfunction, these
mechanisms restore the system's equilibrium. Change is gradual and in the
long run the system accommodates itself to it and what was once disruptive
now becomes institutionalized. Society remains integrated because its members agree on a certain set of values. The value system is the most stable element of the social system. With its emphasis on harmony and stability, which
are tied to strong value consensus, functionalism assumes that the system is
always working toward equilibrium. Problems and conflict may arise, but they
are temporary in nature and not indicative of an impaired social system.

In terms of gender roles, functionalists would argue that in preindustrial societies, such as those which depended on hunting and gathering, men and
women fulfilled different roles and took on different tasks because it was most
useful or functional for society for them to do so. As hunters, men were frequently away from home and, hence, centered their lives around the responsibility of bringing food to the family. Since a woman's mobility is more limited by pregnancy, childbirth, and nursing, it was functional for her to spend
more time near the home and take care of household and child-rearing tasks.
Once established, this division of labor carried through to developing and
developed societies. Even though women may also have been involved in agricultural production or were gatherers in their own right, they were still largely dependent on men for food and protection. The dominant role assumed by
men, in turn, created a pattern where male activities come to be more highly

TABLE 1-1 The Three Major Theoretical Paradigms: A Summary

Theoretical Paradigm	Image of Society	Illustrative Questions
Functionalism	A system of interrelated parts that is relatively stable; each part has functional consequences for the operation of society as a whole	How is society integrated? What are the major parts of society? How are these parts inter–related? What are the consequences of each for the operation of society?
Social conflict	A system characterized by social inequality; any part of society benefits some categories of people more than others; conflict-based social inequality promotes social change	How is society divided? What are major patterns of social inequality? How do some categories of people attempt to protect their privileges? How do other categories of people attempt to improve their social position?
Symbolic interaction	An ongoing process of social interaction in specific settings based on symbolic communication; individual perceptions of reality are variable and changing	How is society experienced? How do human beings in interaction generate, sustain, and change social patterns? How do individuals attempt to shape the reality perceived by others? How does individual behavior change from one situation to another?

Source: Adapted from Macionis, 1995:23.

valued than female ones. Thus, the pattern becomes institutionalized and difficult to change; it rests on a belief that gender stratification is inevitable due to biological sex differences.

Classical functionalism dictates a similar set of principles when applied to gender roles in the modern family as well. There is less disruption and competition, thus more harmony and stability, when spouses assume complementary and specialized roles (Parsons and Bales, 1955; Parsons, 1966). When the husband-father takes on the **instrumental role**, he helps to maintain the basic social and physical integrity of the family by providing food and shelter and linking the family to the world outside the home. When the wife-mother takes on the **expressive role**, she helps cement relationships, provides the emotional support and nurturing qualities which sustain the family unit, and ensures that the household runs smoothly. When deviation from these roles occurs or when they overlap to a great extent, the family system is propelled into a temporary state of disequilibrium. Functionalism maintains that the system will eventually return to a balanced state, but that disruption may have been avoided if traditional gender roles had been followed in the first place. A functionalist would argue, for instance, that gender role ambiguity is a major element in divorce.

It should be obvious from this that functionalism tends to be inherently conservative in its orientation and does not account for a variety of existing family systems which can be said to be functional for the families themselves as well as society. As detailed in Chapter 8, contemporary families and household units are immensely adaptable and exhibit a diversity of patterns and circumstances. Single parents, for example, are required to carry out numerous roles which are nontraditional from a functionalist perspective, and many successfully combine instrumental and expressive roles.

Ideally, social scientific theories are expected to be objective and value-neutral. Even if this ideal is achieved, theories can still be employed to support a specific position or viewpoint. Ideologically, functionalism has been used as a justification for the persistence of male dominance and overall gender stratification. Functional analyses of the family were developed and popularized in the 1950s when a nation, weary of war, latched onto traditional versions of family life and attempted to reestablish not just a prewar, but a pre-Depression existence. Functionalism would support what Abramovitz (1988) refers to as a traditional, white middle-class family ethic that includes a constellation of family patterns emphasizing the male household head as breadwinner, the subordination of women and children in the family, and reproduction, child care, and socialization as female responsibilities. Women function outside the home only as a reserve labor force. This alignment of marketplace and family assures patriarchal control, with socialization patterns legitimizing its perpetuation. And since this family ethic is based on assumed white middle-class patterns, it may not apply to poor women or women of color who are less likely to separate the family and economic spheres. Functionalist views of gender and the family have not kept pace with the rapid social change which is altering them; hence its explanations of contemporary patterns suffer accordingly.

To its credit, functionalism does offer a reasonably sound explanation for the origin of gender role differentiation and demonstrates the functional utility of assigning tasks on the basis of gender in those societies where children are viewed as necessary to maintain the economic integrity of the family unit. In contemporary industrialized societies, large families are actually dysfunctional and the family itself is no longer a unit of economic production. Families may be maintained without the previous rigid division of labor, which means that specialization of tasks within families, especially by gender, are now more dysfunctional than functional. For example, women who are relegated to family roles which they see as restrictive are unhappier in their marriages. In this argument functionalist terminology is used to explain how a division of labor based on gender arose, but it has difficulty analyzing the current diversity of family patterns and marital roles. As will be demonstrated, research also consistently demonstrates that despite the tension associated with multiple roles in the home and workplace, women report high levels of gratification, self-esteem, status security, and personally enriched lives.

This is compatible with Johnson's (1993a) argument that functionalism recognizes that strain exists when there is a sharp differentiation between the public and private sphere (work and family), particularly for the "feminine" role. Neofunctionalism accounts for the multiple levels where gender relations are operative—biological, psychological, social, and cultural. A functionalist examination of their interdependence allows us to understand how female subordination and male superiority become reproduced throughout society.

Conflict Theory

Emanating from the nineteenth-century writings of Karl Marx (1848/ 1964; 1867–1895/1967), conflict theory is based on the assumption that society is a stage where struggles for power and dominance are acted out. These struggles occur among social classes which compete for control over the means of production and the distribution of resources. It was Marx's collaborator, Friedrich Engels (1884/1942), who applied these assumptions to the family. He argued that primitive societies were essentially egalitarian because there was no surplus generated; hence no private property. Once private property emerged, capitalistic institutions developed and power came to be consolidated in the hands of a few men. As far as the family is concerned, the master-slave or exploiter-exploited relationships which occur in broader society between the bourgeoisie (owners) and proletariat (workers) can be translated into the household. After the introduction of private property and the advent of capitalism, a woman's domestic labor "no longer counted beside the acquisition of the necessities of life by the man; the latter was everything, the former an unimportant extra." The household is an autocracy with the husband's supremacy unquestioned. "The emancipation of woman will only be possible when women can take part in production on a large, social scale, and domestic work no longer claims but an insignificant amount of her time" (Engels, 1884/1942:41– 43).

Later conflict theorists such as Dahrendorf (1959) and Collins (1975; 1979) have refined original Marxian assertions to reflect contemporary patterns. Conflict is not simply based on class struggle and the tensions between owner and worker or employer and employee but occurs among many other groups as well. These include parents and children, husbands and wives, the young or middle aged and the elderly, the handicapped and nonhandicapped, physicians and patients, males and females, and any other groups that can be defined as a minority or majority—the list is infinite. Smelser (1981:14) states that modern conflict theory makes the following assumptions:

1. The main features of society are change, conflict, and coercion.
2. Social structure is based on the dominance of some groups by others.
3. Each group in society has a set of common interests, whether its members are aware of it or not.
4. When people become aware of their common interests, they may become a social class.
5. The intensity of class conflict depends on the presence of certain political and social conditions (e.g., freedom to form coalitions), on the distribution of authority and rewards, and on the openness of the class system.

To apply the contemporary conflict framework to gender stratification, class can be redefined to mean groups who have access to and differential control over scarce resources such as authority and political power, in addition to economic power. In simple terms, men have an economic advantage over women, and this provides the basis for gender inequality. A man's superior economic position carries over from the society at large to the family. Unless domestic labor is given some kind of monetary value or, as Engels believed, unless women are not tied to domestic roles, male dominance over women will be perpetuated. This perspective is evident in Shelton and Firestone's (1989) research on the impact of household labor on the gender gap in earnings. They find that household responsibilities directly affect earnings but are also linked to occupational location, work experience, and number of hours worked per week. This indicates that to understand the gender gap in earnings, it is necessary to examine the impact of women's unpaid labor on their paid work.

Conflict theory, especially the Marxian variety, has been criticized for its overemphasis on the economic basis of inequality and its contention that conflict, competition, and tension are inevitable between certain groups. It tends to dismiss the consensus families may show in how they structure family roles and allocate tasks on the basis of more traditional views. It is also clear from cross-cultural research that women's paid employment is not the panacea envisioned by Engels to overcome male dominance in our social institutions. Finally, there is a conspiratorial element which emerges when conflict theory becomes associated with the idea that men as a group are consciously organized to keep women "in their place." A number of social forces, many of them unorganized or unintended, come into play when explaining gender stratification. As with functionalism's inherent conservative bias, conflict theory must certainly be seen as exhibiting a bias toward change. This bias is perhaps less of a criticism for conflict theory, especially if stripped of some of its Marxian baggage, than functionalism, since most people are now uncomfortable with specific patterns of gender stratification and the sexism which results. Ideologically, it is easier today to justify change if that change is not viewed as individually and socially damaging. It is likely that toleration levels for overt sexism will lessen, as has occurred with overt racism.

Symbolic Interaction

Unlike functionalism and conflict theory which approach gender roles from a broad societal or institutional view, symbolic interaction, also called the interactionist perspective, takes a narrower, social psychological frame of reference. The interactionist model is based on the assumption that society is created and maintained through the interaction of its members and how its members negotiate and define reality. In this sense, reality is what members agree to be reality. Gender, therefore, is a social construction based on society's agreement that people called males or females are imbued with certain traits defined as masculine or feminine. Society is continually being built and rebuilt through interaction and negotiation, and as Denzin (1993:203) suggests, terms like "gender" must be found in the meanings people bring to this category of experience.

This process of negotiation is expressed in William I. Thomas's (1931/1966) classic statement, which is now referred to as the Thomas theorem: A situation defined as real is real in its consequences. As developed by George Herbert Mead (1934), symbolic interaction is interested in those meanings people attach to their own behavior as well as the behavior of others. Interaction occurs in a patterned, structured way because people can agree on the meaning of shared symbols, such as words, written language, signs, and gestures. Group members respond to each other on the basis of shared meanings and expectations for behavior. Thus people do not react automatically to one another. Instead they carefully choose among a number of options depending upon the specific situation. Once symbols are learned and internalized, it may appear that the interaction process is more or less spontaneous, but symbolic interactionists are quick to point out that a rational, individually determined series of actions is still occurring.

A variation of symbolic interaction theory, known as dramaturgical analysis, is especially meaningful when considering gender roles. The active role which individuals take in guiding their behavior is maximized if interaction is seen to occur on a kind of social stage. Associated with the writings of Erving Goffman (1959; 1963; 1971), **dramaturgy** maintains that when people attempt to create a certain impression, they actually assume various roles in a performance which others will evaluate. Each encounter with another person allows for a myriad of roles to be performed. As on a stage, settings can be constructed to convey the best possible impression with the hope of achieving a desired set of results. While Goffman contends that gender displays are in essence socially scripted and conventionalized expressions of gender, he would still support symbolic interaction's assumption that they are optional, fluid, and almost situationally specific. West and Zimmerman (1987:130) argue that this emphasis obscures the effects of gender on a wide range of activities. An overall symbolic interaction perspective is still applied here, but they state that, although it is plausible to suggest that gender displays are optional, "it does not seem plausible to say that we have the option of being seen by others as female or male." Symbolic interaction theory becomes problematic when its emphasis on choices based on interpretive cues in specific circumstances limits how gendered behavior may be generalized.

The utility of symbolic interaction and its dramaturgical subset can be seen in how romance and attractiveness are culturally constructed. The cultural model of romance is not a series of rules, but one of interpretation—a meaning system that is continually negotiated. In their longitudinal study of a sample of women with strong academic records and career aspirations, Holland and Eisenhart (1990) employ a cultural model predicated on a taken-for-granted world where men and women are evaluated on their attractiveness. For example, if the woman is more attractive than the man, then he treats her especially well; if she is the less attractive, she lowers her expectations for good treatment. Reinforced by rewards providing intimacy, both physical and emotional, and peer prestige, men and women interact in identifiable patterns. A woman's prestige is especially tied to her appeal to men, since men set the standard for women's attractiveness. The authors argue that although on the surface ideas of attractiveness appear to place men and women on equal footing, men's prestige can be derived easier from other domains. This study of these bright and privileged women shows that less than one-third met their own expectations. Educated for romance, they ended up with "intense involvements in heterosexual romantic relationships, marginalized career identities, and inferior preparation for breadwinning roles."

With some variation, these kinds of scripts are performed daily in a host of settings. Gender roles are highly structured by one set of scripts designed for males and another designed for females. Although within each script a range of behavior options is permitted, the likely result is that the gender roles themselves promote competition, alienation, rejection, and a lack of self-disclosure. As exemplified by symbolic interaction, the theme that traditional gender roles are stultifying and limit opportunities for meaningful encounters for both men and women will be a consistent one throughout the text.

A more sophisticated model of gender-related behaviors which combines concepts from symbolic interaction and broader social psychology is offered by Deaux and Major (1987), who propose that actions are influenced by the expectations of perceivers, self-systems of the target, and situational cues. This interaction-based approach allows for the prediction of both stable and variable gender differences in behavior and emphasizes what symbolic interactionists consider crucial in the explanation, the setting in which the behavior occurs. Gender thus becomes a "component of ongoing interactions in which perceivers emit expectancies, targets (selves) negotiate their own identities," and 'in which the context of the interaction shapes the resultant behavior (Deaux and Major, 1987:369). Their model points to the complexity of gender-linked expectations and provides a useful framework for analyzing data from a variety of situations.

Linking Gender, Race, and Class

In the political arena, the issue of diversity will be a theme that carries us into the next century. It will also allow for broader-based theory building in sociology as we seriously begin to integrate ideas about gender, class, and race. The gender-class-race construct originated with black feminism in the 1960s (Daly, 1993). Since then it has been incorporated into the discourse of all the social sciences and has offered many interdisciplinary leads for theory building. Conflict theory, particularly as related to both race and gender in social stratification, provides perhaps the most successful integrative potential in this regard. The task is to synthesize where appropriate but still account for how we are differentiated. As Lorde (1992:402) notes, there are very real differences between us in age, race, and sex, but the failure to recognize them and to examine their distortions continues to separate us. A related issue is that when one category gains ascendence, it is often embraced by those looking for simple solutions to complex problems, such as in the media and political arenas, and in turn discourages further research, hence understanding of the linkages.

Research on the poverty of older women is a case in point. One theme of this text is that women are at heightened risk for poverty because of gender-related issues, but that the risk increases for certain categories of women, such as single parents, women of color, and elderly women living alone. The "feminization of poverty" theme reverberates throughout the social sciences, has been picked up by the media, and has become a defining characteristic of national and global poverty. While gender is clearly a critical factor in explaining much poverty, Dressel (1994) argues that authors tend to ignore the "inextricable link between race and social class," particularly as it affects older women. Patriarchy is not discounted but needs to be viewed in the context of racial oppression as well. A focus on gender assumes that women of color have separate political interests from men of color. The desire to build coalitions among women who are diverse in background may be further compromised because the primacy of gender means that only some will benefit from the selective targeting of limited resources (Dressel, 1994:118).

Class differences must also be added here. White, middle-class feminists focus on the oppression of women but have difficulty recognizing the privileges that come with their race and class. According to Collins (1996), oppression is full of contradictions. To understand its impact, the daunting task is to suggest new categories of analysis that are inclusive of race, class, and gender as distinctive yet interlocking categories of oppression. But these barriers must be transcended by building coalitions to bring about social change. The sociological insight is that privilege is a structural, institutionalized characteristic rather than simply an individual one. A women's movement which 30 years ago did not fully understand the implications of how we are alike and how we are different on all these dimensions remains less unified today.

Another way to approach the complexity of similarity yet difference is to view gender, race, and class as comparable mechanisms for producing social inequality. They are experienced simultaneously by individuals with different intersecting systems of relationship and meaning. They are combined with other relevant categories of experience, such as age, region, religion, and sexual orientation (Andersen and Collins, 1995). The colonization experienced by women in the developing world needs to be added to this list as well. At some level all can produce inequality—through both privilege and oppression. While the impact of the oppression needs to be acknowledged, there is a danger in ranking them (Moraga, 1995). It implies, too, that the seeds of dissention are sown when one form of oppression is seen as more "important" than another. Indicative of a conflict theory orientation, Collins (1995:493) notes the problem of dealing with oppression in its multitude of forms.

> It is one thing to say that manipulating "difference" comprises one effective tactic used by dominant groups to maintain control. . . . It's quite another to wring one's hands about the "problem of difference," laying the groundwork for handling differences as the real problem, instead of the power relations that construct difference.

The goal, then is to understand how gender, race, and class as social categories simultaneously work together. As a subset of symbolic interaction, **ethnomethodology** demonstrates how we create and share our understandings of social life, The categories of gender, race, and class are first socially constructed but then take on the properties of objective reality. West and Fenstermaker (1995) argue that the category of sex (male and female) serves only as an "indicator" of sex but does not depend on it. Society will construct a world of two sexes and then through negotiation and agreement will determine the appropriate traits associated with each. The new category of gender emerges, "not merely as an individual attribute but something that is accomplished in interaction with others" (West and Fenstermaker, 1995:21). The "doing" of gender occurs. From a broader symbolic interaction perspective, the same can be said for the "doing" of race or the "doing" of class. The authors believe this serves two purposes: an understanding of how important categories of social life, such as gender, are socially constructed, and how the most profound divisions of society are legitimated and maintained.

It is possible to celebrate diversity and unity at the same time. As bell hooks (1992:444) argues, women and men must share a common understanding and definition of feminism if a mass-based political movement is to occur. She suggests that feminism can be broadly defined as "a movement to end sexism and sexist oppression." With this goal in mind, men and women can then bring their differing perspectives together on how the goal can be reached. When women come together, they also need to understand how race and class impact their relations with individual men. The bonding process will be more complex, but "this broader discussion might enable the sharing of perspectives and strategies for change that would enrich rather than diminish our understanding of gender" (Hooks, 1992:445).

FEMINISM AND SOCIOLOGICAL THEORY

Another theoretical issue involves the movement toward a new sociological paradigm based on feminist theory. As should be evident from the critique of the dominant theories, the emerging paradigm will find it easier to incorporate some sociological perspectives more than others. For example, if structural functionalism is to be part of a new synthesis, it must come to grips with a view of the family and gender role socialization which is oppressive for both genders, but particularly for women (Wallace, 1989:12). Yet to dismiss functionalism as irrelevant for a new paradigm ignores its other contributions, such as how Parsons's model of social change and his definition of progress can be applied to an analysis of the women's movement and the evolution of feminist thinking (Johnson, 1989). When considering theory from a conflict and minority group perspective, the task may be easier. One promising direction is to focus on power relations from the standpoint of women located within a variety of social structures who are "ruled" and who lack the resources to seriously challenge or alter the existing arrangement. A symbolic interaction view may be linked to this by determining how these women must manage their behavior in gender-appropriate ways but also maintain a sense of personal integrity. According to Stacey and Thorne (1985) a new feminist paradigm in sociology would transform existing conceptual frameworks and provide a better understanding for empirical work in such areas as sex segregation of labor, the patriarchal family, and sexual violence.

Unlike other theories which purport to explain inequality, Chafetz (1988:5) argues that a theory is feminist if it can be used to challenge a status quo that is disadvantageous to women. Although there is disagreement as to what should be encompassed in feminist theory, she suggests that three elements are important:

1. Gender comprises a central focus or subject matter.
2. Gender relations are viewed as a problem, in that they are tied to inequity, contradiction, or strain.
3. Gender relations are not natural or immutable; they are a product of sociocultural and historical forces.

While these elements can provide the foundation for feminist theory building, they also provide key linkages with dominant themes in sociological theory. As Acker (1989:78) argues, the emergence of a new sociological paradigm based on feminist theory will create dissent and strain and may limit its acceptance within relevant disciplines because, in essence, it will challenge traditional explanations and create power struggles related to intellectual dominance. A truly integrative theory will draw together "conceptual pieces into a web of ideas that transcend patriarchal theory building" (Ollenburger and Moore, 1992:36). As such, the very process will inevitably create ferment. But I agree with Wallace's assessment (1989:15) that theoretical synthesis can occur and that feminist theory offers a powerful new perspective in sociology. Sociology will benefit from the intellectual ferment already created by feminist theory.

A final issue in addressing feminist theory involves how to conveniently segment and summarize a host of historical and intellectual traditions that have been referred to as feminist. Feminism is cyclical, and what was viewed as radical in the 1960s is seen as much more mainstream in the 1990s by the public, the media, and those women and men who define themselves as feminists. The multiple approaches to feminism reflect sociocultural and demographic diversity and point to the heterogeneity of feminist thought found in postindustrial societies and the developing world. This very diversity indicates that categories of feminism are also not mutually exclusive.

FEMINIST FRAMEWORKS

Theory has been defined as an explanation for empirical events or data. Science assumes that theories are to be as unbiased or objective as possible, thereby contributing to the knowledge and understanding of the empirical world but without the entanglements of personal judgment or one's own values. In the late nineteenth century, German sociologist Max Weber argued that sociology as a science must be value-free, differing from earlier writers such as Marx, who advocated that science and reform or revolution could and should be successfully combined (Weber, 1946). Today scientists are still grappling with the impact of values on theory building and data analysis, but there is tacit agreement that the ideal of objectivity must at least be kept in mind during any scientific investigation. Although values are never eliminated in research, their potential impact on results needs to be considered. For this reason, the term value-freedom has been replaced by value-specification, the stating of one's values at the outset in order to recognize potential sources of bias. Even here there is a problem because it assumes we are (already) aware of our own values and biases.

This issue of objectivity is involved in any theory, but more so in feminist theories because, by definition, feminism involves the opposition to the sexism and patriarchy inherent in most societies. Bolstered by feminist theory, the woman's movement has been organized to change the existing and what is believed to be unjustified social structure. Feminist theory provides the ideological framework for addressing women's inferior social position and the social, political, and economic discrimination which perpetuate it. Some scientists may argue that to join the term *feminist* with *theory* is contradictory since the former is supposedly ideologically based and opposes the objectivity assumed in the latter. This argument, I believe, is too narrow and unrealistically views the canon of objectivity in science. The three sociological theories outlined earlier also contain ideological components but have not been completely rejected as a result. Although feminist theories may be more explicit in their value orientation, as we shall see, they can be viewed as modifications and extensions of the major sociological perspectives, especially as related to conflict theory.

According to Sylvester (1995:941), at present feminist theorizing is marked by several interlocking and simultaneous tendencies. The first sees feminism as having ongoing philosophical and identity differences. Absence of consensus is defended as appropriate to the current era and as fueling necessary debate. The second tendency expresses concern about issues of power and solidarity that such fragmentation generates. The third accounts for both solidarity and fragmentation. While there are a myriad of subsets, the following classification provides an overview of what may be described as the main branches of feminism with each branch rooted in, or compatible with, certain theoretical perspectives.

Liberal Feminism

Liberal feminism, also called egalitarian feminism, is considered the most moderate branch and is based on the simple proposition that all people are created equal and should not be denied equality of opportunity because of gender. Liberal feminism is based on the Enlightenment tenets of faith in rationality, a belief that women and men have the same rational faculties, a belief in education as the means to change and transform society, and a belief in the doctrine of natural rights (Donovan, 1985:8). This is articulated in John Stuart Mill's (1869) *The Subjection of Women*, with his statement that "what is now called the nature of women is an eminently artificial thing—the result of forced oppression in some directions, unnatural stimulation in others." Therefore, if men and women are ontologically similar, the rights of men should also be extended to include women.

As the statement of purpose at the beginning of the chapter suggests, the National Organization of Women is part of this branch. The moderate approach of the liberal feminist model would allow for working with men and an incorporation of men into the ranks of the feminist movement, since both genders benefit by the elimination of sexism. Women need to be integrated into a wider array of roles, including employment outside the home, and men need to assume greater responsibility for domestic tasks. Whereas assimilation is a key to this approach, it concentrates more on the assimilation and eventual acceptance of females in the world of males than males in the world of females. Critics would charge that it places a greater value on the activities of men, hence implicitly undervalues women's traditional roles.

By working within a system which is seen as pluralistic with no single group dominating, women can organize and compete with other groups. Demands will be met if mobilization is effective and pressure is efficiently wielded (Deckard, 1983:463). Liberal feminists believe it is not necessary to have a complete restructuring of society but merely to alter it enough to incorporate women into other meaningful and equitable roles. This view tends to be adopted by professional, middle-class women who place a high value on education and achievement. Because these women would be more likely to have a greater range of economic resources, they can better compete with men for desirable social positions and employment opportunities. Liberal feminism thus appeals to "mainstream" women who have no disagreement with the overall structure of the present social system, only that it should be nonsexist.

Many liberal feminists may also embrace "cultural feminism" with its focus on empowering women through emphasizing the positive qualities that are associated with women's roles such as nurturing, caring, cooperation, and connectedness to others (Worell, 1996:360). The issue of how much women are alike and how much they are different is highlighted in this emphasis. Although it does not constitute a separate branch of feminism per se, the debate around the "degree of gender difference or similarity" has allowed cultural feminism to become incorporated in all the feminist branches at some level.

Socialist/Marxist Feminism

This feminist framework is indicative of the conventional Marx-Engels model previously described which suggests that the inferior position of women is linked to a class-based capitalistic system and the family structure within such a system. Socialist feminism argues that sexism is functional for capitalism because it is supported by the unpaid labor of women who also function as a reserve labor force only when needed. If paid, women work for low wages, which results in high corporate profits. Unpaid household labor is necessary for the reproduction and maintenance of the work force. The nuclear family, with the husband as sole supporter of the wife and children, also stabilizes a capitalist society. The wife is first economically dependent on her husband, but this soon turns into emotional dependence and passivity (Deckard, 1983:451). She is fearful of loss of economic security, so he retains complete power over her.

Unlike liberal feminism, the socialist view maintains that in order to free women, as well as the laborers who are exploited by the owners of the means of production, the capitalistic economic system needs to be changed. Sexism and economic oppression are mutually reinforcing, so a socialist revolution is needed to change both. Marx provided a plan for a society where private property would be abolished and principles of collectivization in the workplace would be in effect. Engels called for the need to collectivize household labor and child rearing, thereby freeing women to pursue economic roles outside the home (Donovan, 1985). The family itself would not be destroyed, but the functions the family now performs would be socially altered.

Socialist feminism appeals to working-class women and those who feel disenfranchised from the economic opportunities in capitalism. It has made a great deal of headway in Latin America and has served as a powerful rallying point for women in other developing nations. It is perhaps ironic, however, that its expression in the former Soviet Union has been demonstrated more by Marx and less by Engels. As will be discussed in Chapter 6, women continue to carry the heavy burden of unpaid household labor while also functioning in the paid labor force. Many contemporary socialist feminists believe that unencumbered entry into the labor force must occur, but that housework must be socialized as well; otherwise women will find themselves with two jobs. Regardless of Marxian rhetoric, this is apparently what has happened in the former Soviet Union.

Although socialist feminism is explicitly tied to Marxist theory, MacKinnon (1982) argues that they still need to be analytically distinct. Whereas Marxist theory focuses on property and material conditions to build an ideology, feminism focuses on sexuality and gender. As MacKinnon states, "sexuality is to feminism what work is to Marxism" (1982:515). Hartmann (1993) asserts that men and women retain interest in their own gender group so that it remains unclear if the socialism being struggled for is the same for both men and women. A humane socialism requires consensus on what the new society should be and would require men to renounce their privileges as men. This is congruent with criticisms of a specifically Marxist variety of feminism that emphasize class over either gender or race in analyzing stratification systems in capitalist societies (Castro, 1990:3). Despite the differences in terminology, both strains of thought would agree that fundamental changes are required in the institutions of the economy and the family if women's equality is to be achieved.

Radical Feminism

Radical feminist theory came to fruition during the late 1960s and early 1970s when a group of women who were working in the civil rights and anti-war movement "became aware of their own oppression through the treatment they received from their male cohorts." Donovan recounts that during an anti-inauguration rally in 1959, when women attempted to present their feminist position, not only were they booed, laughed at, and catcalled to by men in the audience, but also some men went as far as yelling out obscenities to the women on the stage. The radical feminist model thus originated as a reaction against the theories, organizational structures, and personal styles of the male "New Left" (Donovan, 1985:141). This also resulted in the rebirth of the women's movement in America. It is interesting that history repeated itself in that the roots of American feminism can be traced to the men who denied women any real leadership in the antislavery movement. The patronizing attitudes of the men of that era provided the catalyst for women to recognize gender-based oppression and then organize to challenge it. A century later it happened again.

Contemporary radical feminists view sexism as being at the core of patriarchal society, with all its social institutions reflecting this reality. They focus on the patriarchal family as a critical system of domination, more important than a woman's subordination in the paid labor force (Shelton and Agger, 1993). However, since society is made up of interdependent parts which are inextricable, it would be virtually impossible to attack sexism in any meaningful way. This differs from liberal feminism, which sees the system as perfectible. Women's oppression stems from male domination, so if men are the problem, institutional change of the socialist variety will not overcome it. The alternative path for women is to be different than men. The measure of a woman is judged according to her correspondence, or lack thereof, from man (MacKinnon, 1993). The measure of a woman would be other women. Therefore, women must create their own separate institutions and sever their relationships with men. Through the establishment of women-centered institutions, women will come to rely on other women and not on men. The extreme version of radical feminism calls for the ending of heterosexual relationships. A society will emerge where the female virtues of nurturance, sharing, and intuition will dominate in a woman-identified world.

Certainly there is less agreement among the adherents of radical feminism than the other models. A blueprint for the total restructuring of society has yet to be worked out or agreed upon, especially concerning the future role for men in a woman-identified world. The conviction that male supremacy functions as the defining characteristic of a society which oppresses women unifies the disparate elements of radical feminism.

Multicultural and Global Feminism

While it may not be recognized as a distinct feminist framework or branch of feminism, multicultural and global feminism explicitly acknowledges the impact of the intersection of gender with race, class, and issues of colonization and exploitation of women in the developing world. Global feminism is a movement of people working for change across and regardless of national boundaries which themselves are expressions of patriarchy. The world is interdependent and becoming more so. Global feminism contends that no woman is free until the conditions which oppress women worldwide are eliminated (Bunch, 1993:249). Multicultural feminism is attendant to the specific cultural elements and historical conditions which serve to maintain oppression. In Latin America, for instance, military regimes have devised specific patterns of punishment and sexual enslavement for women actively resisting or fighting dictatorial governments (Bunster-Bunalto, 1993). Asian-American women are confronting the historical, cultural, and structural barriers that have hindered political activism. As women and as women of color they face cultural dilemmas related to obedience versus independence, collective (or familial) versus individual interest, fatalism versus change, and self-control versus self-expression or spontaneity (Chow, 1993).

It is clear that all the branches or varieties of feminism are dealing with the linkages of gender with other relevant social categories. Members of specific communities negotiate gender construction according to their own situations of institutionalized oppression (Stack, 1994). Different feminisms result from these constructions. They are always in a state of transition and will be modified according to the newer research and understanding coming out of academic circles as well as to their own experiments and experiences in translating feminism into their daily lives.

A final note must be made about why feminism is considered the "f-word." Feminism is a movement to end the oppression of women. It uses women's understandings, perceptions, and experiences in strategies to deal with and overcome oppression. It embraces political goals which offer gender equality. Research consistently shows that the public is supportive of the goals of feminism and a majority of American women agree that feminism has altered their lives for the better (Kaminer, 1993; Mandel, 1995; Women's Equality Poll, 1995). Yet there is hesitation and even downright refusal to identify oneself as a feminist, even among those women who work in women's groups which have explicit feminist goals. We have already seen that feminism is not a homogenous movement. A theme of this text is that diversity and disagreement occur side by side with unity and consensus.

Because feminism *has* empowered women, the dialogue has also changed. Passivity has been replaced by open and critical debate among women and men who both agree and disagree with feminism as well as between feminists. This debate is intellectually stimulating, necessary and in itself further empowering. Inclusiveness fuels disagreement. The critical point is that feminists can agree to disagree. There are many feminisms and many themes of feminist thought and as Worell (1996:361) points out, "although we have joined a common parade, we do not all march to the same music." We will see that all the media have a great deal of influence in reinforcing gender role stereotypes, and the feminist stereotype is no exception. Both agreement and the value of disagreement are ignored or even ridiculed by the media. The question becomes "how to project feminist power in an era when feminisms parade their differences against a backdrop of backlash" (Sylvester, 1995:943). While all sides are represented, the erroneous impression is that feminism has split into irreconcilable warring factions. Racist comments are unacceptable in the media. Sexist comments are acceptable. The unfavorable light feminists are cast into by the media is not going unchallenged. It may be that the back-lash against feminism is a sign that goals are being reached and real power shifts are occurring. A growing number of young women are interested in women's issues (Henneberger, 1994), and I suspect that the feminist label will eventually be seen as compatible with their concerns.

According to Wolfe (1993a:3), the critics charge that *all* feminism is puri-tanical, man-hating, and obsessed with defining women as victims, something which the media are quick to point out. Victim feminism sees women as "sex-ually pure and mystically nurturing" and focuses on their powerlessness against oppressive men. Wolfe suggests another approach, "power feminism," which sees women as no better or worse than men but which "lays claim to equality simply because women are entitled to it." As such, victim feminism may have been a necessary but disheartening stage to rally around at one point in the longer quest for gender equality.

A NONGENDERED SOCIAL ORDER?

Each of these feminist frameworks begins with the notion that gender has pro-vided an integral basis for social organization, and each offers a glimpse of society where this organization can be modified. None suggests that gender is to be eliminated entirely from a social order. Lorber (1986:567) contends that if gender is a social construction and that if the relations between men and women are essentially social relations, "what is socially constructed can be reconstructed, and social relations can be rearranged." Thus a social order without gender as an organizing principle is possible. The construct of gender rests on the physiological and biological dichotomy of the sexes which is then extended to other social realms, but Lorber demonstrates that this assertion is in fact debatable. And as this text will continually point out, evidence from biology, psychology, and sociology suggests that the division of humanity into two distinct, mutually exclusive categories is both unrealistic in the scientific sense and unproductive or inhibiting in the social sense.

The concept of **androgyny** refers to the integration of characteristics defined as feminine with those defined as masculine. A new model emerges which maintains that it is possible, and desirable, for people to express both masculine and feminine qualities since they exist in varying degrees within each of us anyway. In gender measurements this translates to a person scoring high on both active-instrumental traits (the masculine dimension) and nur-turing-expressive traits (the feminine dimension). Androgyny allows for flexi-bility in the statuses we possess and gives us greater adaptability to the variety of situations we must confront. For example, an androgynous person can be an empathic listener to a friend's problem, an assertive leader mobilizing a group, or a sensitive boss who must fire an employee (Basow, 1996:83). Ideally, androgyny eliminates the restrictions imposed by gender roles and increases opportunities to develop to our fullest potential.

While offering one of the first liberating views of gender, and as discussed in Chapter 3, the notion of androgyny has since been criticized for its ambi-guity, lack of definitional rigor, inability to predict across races, and, perhaps most important, as being yet another canon by which we must all be measured (Trebilcot, 1977; Cook, 1985; Archer, 1989; Binion, 1990; Basow, 1996). A truly biting indictment of what androgyny supposedly portrays comes from radical feminist Mary Daly (1990:397), who contends that attempts to combine the patriarchal concepts of masculinity and femininity expresses only "pseudo-wholeness in its combination of distorted gender descriptions." She asserts that what was eventually realized was "combining the 'halves' offered to consciousness by patriarchal language results in something more like a hole than a whole." In Daly's terms, androgyny adds nothing to the completeness of our beings but actually detracts from it.

To continue with a theme of this chapter, such criticisms create needed intellectual ferment. Androgyny still provides an alternative to images of men and women based on traditional gender roles. Androgyny is also useful in reconciling the ideological currents of the feminist movement and providing the broadest possible base for consensus—the kind of approach as previously outlined by bell hooks (1992). As Castro (1990:163) contends, an androgynous approach to feminism would support the

> fundamental principle of defining people as human beings and not as members of one or the other sex. For feminism to remain consistent with its own principles, it must recognize the logic of the notion that if women are equal to men, then men are also equal to women.

The theories and concepts presented here, and the visions of society which they suggest, are offered as tools to be used in approaching the following chapters and the diverse array of issues related to gender roles you will be confronting. Each has its own insight and explanation for any given issue. As these issues are addressed, consider which perspective you believe to be most realistic. It is hoped that at the conclusion of this book you will have developed a perspective on gender roles which is most meaningful to you.

CHAPTER 2

GENDER ROLE DEVELOPMENT
Biological and Psychological Perspectives

> There are a large number of women whose brains are closer in size to those of gorillas than to the most developed male brains. This inferiority is so obvious that no one can contest it for a moment. . . . all psychologists who have studied the intelligence of women . . . recognize today that they represent the most inferior forms of human evolution and that they are closer to children and savages than to an adult, civilized man.
> —Gustave LeBon, 1879 (quoted in Gould, 1981:10–45)

> It must be stated that conceptual thought is exclusive to the masculine intellect. Her skull is also smaller than man's; and so, of course, is her brain.
> —T. Lang, 1971 (cited in Tavris, 1996:336)

The argument used against equality between males and females is essentially a biological one. As the above quotes demonstrate, even totally opposite biological observations have been used to justify the same conclusion—women are inferior to men. The explosion of research on issues of sex and gender worldwide has provided a multitude of evidence demonstrating that culture is a greater barrier to equality than biology. When desire and talent are combined with opportunity and encouragement, people can move with relative ease into the "traditional" gender role of the other. When such movement becomes widespread, gender distinctions are blurred. Decades of research have made it empirically clear that the benefits of equality for everyone, males and females alike, far outweigh the disadvantages. But patriarchy persists and biological reasons for its persistence abound. The fact that males remain in the most powerful positions is justified as the natural outcome of biological differences. It is difficult to deny the factual basis for the benefits of equality. The trump card that is cunningly played by those who oppose it is the inevitable statement that, "you can't deny biology; it's only natural that women and men have different roles." The almost ruthless objectivity associated with what is seen as clearly "natural" dictates that the sexes, which therefore extend to the genders, are destined to inequality by virtue of biological differences which mandate different gender roles.

Certainly males and females are different. Patterns of differentiation between the sexes include not only the physiological component but the sociocultural, attitudinal, and behavioral realms as well. Are these differences significant enough to suggest that patriarchy is inevitable? Do the differences outweigh the similarities? What role does biology play in determining these differences? An examination of the theory and research generated by these questions will help shed light on the "it's only natural" argument. This argument is in fact an extension of the nature versus nurture, or heredity versus environment, debate. Since this chapter focuses on biological issues concerning males and females, the term most used in referring to these categories is (the) "sexes."

MARGARET MEAD

Famed anthropologist Margaret Mead was interested in exploring such issues when she journeyed to New Guinea in the 1930s. Her original belief in the biological basis of gender roles was overridden by her work among three tribes which clearly supported the notion that cultural conditioning had a massive impact when comparing the sexes in terms of behavior (Mead, 1935). She found that among the gentle, peace-loving Arapesh, for example, both men and women exhibited the qualities of nurturance and compliance. A society which knew little about warfare, the Arapesh spent their time gardening, hunting, and child rearing. What American society would define as maternal behavior extended to both men and women. The joy of child rearing and simply being around children meant that child-care responsibilities were eagerly assumed by men as well as women, a task from which the Arapesh derived immense satisfaction. Children grew up to mirror these patterns and learned to become as responsive and cooperative as their parents, with a willingness to subordinate themselves to the needs of those who are younger and weaker (Mead, 1935:124). Mead concluded that in this tribe, the personalities of females and males were not sharply distinguished by gender.

The fierce Mundugumor, on the other hand, exhibited characteristics which we would associate with males, such as competitiveness, strong independence, and even violence at times. Children were barely tolerated, left to their own devices as early in life as possible and taught to be hostile and suspicious of others. Both mothers and fathers demonstrated little in the way of tenderness toward their children, with physical punishment being the common mode for assuring that children learned and adhered to family and tribal rules. Children quickly understood that success in this community was measured by aggression, with violence as the acceptable, expected solution to many problems. Since both males and females demonstrated these traits, the Mundugumor, like the Arapesh, did not differentiate personality in terms of gender. It may be argued that even by American standards of masculinity, the Mundugumor represented the extreme. As Mead points out, however, the traits she described as typical of both sexes would be viewed as definitive characteristics of males in American society.

Finally, the Tchumbuli demonstrated what we would call reverse gender roles. This tribe consisted of practical, efficient, and unadorned women and passive, vain, and catty men who took pleasure in decorating themselves and preparing the ceremonial rituals and festivities for the tribe. Through their fishing, weaving, and trading activities, the women were the economic providers, while the men remained close to the village and practiced their dancing and art. Women enjoyed the company of other women, while the men strived to gain their attention and affection. While the women accepted this situation with tolerance and humor, they were apt to view men more as boys than as peers.

Mead concluded that what we define as masculine and feminine are culturally rather than biologically determined. If "it is natural" that women and men act in ways according to biology, then such cross-cultural differences should not be manifest. It is granted that the gender roles described here are aberrant compared with the majority of societies, that they are presented as generalizations, and that they have likely been modified a half-century later. Yet if biology is considered the cause of certain behavior patterns associated with the sexes, it should have caused the men and women in these cultures to act similarly. After we examine the impact of biology on the sexes, we will return to this point.

Since Mead's work continues to be used as an anthropological standard on gender differences, it is presented here in some detail. We know today that gender roles vary within a narrower range than suggested by Mead's research in New Guinea, but "her message that gender constitutes an arena of great variability in human experience has borne out under empirical evidence" (LeVine, 1990:5). In fact, LeVine states that contemporary evidence demonstrates that no existing theory could have generated the immense variety of meanings attached to being male and female. It is precisely such variation which has led many scholars to question accepted perspectives regarding femininity and masculinity (Maccoby, 1987; Reinisch et al., 1987). We can identify biological differences and similarities between female and male, but to determine how these relate to what is considered masculine and feminine the world over is exceedingly difficult.

THE HORMONE PUZZLE

Since the biological differences between men and women have become so politicized, it is important to understand the subtle but profound interaction between hormonal and psychosocial factors in behavior. Of the two types of sex chromosomes, X and Y, both sexes have at least one X chromosome. Females possess two X chromosomes while males have one X and one Y chromosome. It is the lack or presence of the Y chromosome which determines if the baby will be a male or female. That the X chromosome has a larger genetic background than the Y chromosome is advantageous to females with their XX chromosomes. The extra X chromosome is associated with a superior immune system and lower female mortality at all stages of the life cycle. All of our other chromosomes are similar in form, differing only in our individual hereditary identities (Woldow, 1996).

Such comments concerning the chromosomal basis of the sexes are widely accepted and leave little room for controversy. When discussing the sex hormones, however, the roles they play in sexual development and behavior are less clear. This has generated heated debates about their impact, especially in relation to the physiology of behavior and gender role socialization. Hormones are internal secretions produced by the endocrine glands that are carried by the blood throughout the body, which affect target cells in other organs. Both sexes possess the same hormones, but they differ in the amounts secreted. For example, the dominant female hormone, estrogen, is produced in larger quantities by the ovaries, but in smaller quantities by the testes. The male hormone, testosterone, is produced in larger quantities by the testes and smaller quantities by the ovaries. The endocrine differences between males and females are not absolute but differ along a continuum of variation, with most males being significantly different than most females (Woldow, 1996).

We know that sex hormones have two key functions which must be considered together. They shape the development of the brain and sex organs and then determine how these organs will be activated. Because hormones provide an organization function for the body, their activational effects will be different for the sexes. For example, during fetal development when certain tissues are highly sensitive to hormones, the secretion of testosterone both masculinizes and defeminizes key cellular structures throughout the brain and reproductive organs. Because the ovaries are more quiescent during this stage, the female phenotype is less susceptible to hormonal influences (McEwen, 1990:35). This also indicates that the fetus first starts to develop female organs but later masculinizes itself under the influence of testosterone, if it possesses a Y chromosome. As Christen (1991:29) states, "the male can be regarded as a female transformed by testosterone." According to McEwen (1990:36), "the processes of masculinization and the development of sex differences are continuing ones, influenced by later activity of the hormones *as well as* individual experiences" (emphasis added).

Can Sex Reassignment Be Successful?

A series of classic studies on sexual anomalies conducted by Money and Ehrhardt (1972) have provided clues to help disentangle various elements of the biological basis of sex differences. The impact of hormones on sexual development has been studied on infants who were born with sexual anomalies due to the fact their mothers had excessive or impaired hormone production during the second or third month of their pregnancies (Money and Ehrhardt, 1972). The *androgen sensitivity syndrome* occurs when a genetic male, due to a metabolic error, is born with female genitalia; he develops female secondary sex characteristics in puberty and still has functioning testes which produce ineffective androgens. For genetic females, the *andrenogenital syndrome* occurs when abnormal amounts of androgens are secreted, thus masculinizing the female genitalia. This may result in the infant being born with a penis, empty scrotum, some degree of labial fusion, and/or an enlarged clitoris. Similarly, male external organs may develop on a genetic female if the mother is given progestin, a synthetic substitute for progesterone, to prevent miscarriage, and *progestin-induced hermaphroditism* occurs.

Research on the hormonal basis of such anomalies helps to clarify the process of sexual development. From a sociological viewpoint, it allows a rare opportunity to study the physiological-behavioral link and to understand the important distinction between the biological aspect of sex and the sociocultural-psychological aspect of gender role. Children born with these conditions are referred to as **hermaphrodites**. They possess ambiguous genital structures, have external genitalia different from their genetic sex, or are inconsistent in terms of their sex hormones. The principle of **sexual dimorphism**, the separation of the sexes into two distinct morphologic and later psychologic forms, is violated. Assigned one sex at birth, the child's "true" sex is often discovered later. Depending on when in the child's development this discovery is made makes a crucial difference in psychological adjustment. Money and Ehrhardt (1972) suggest that sex reassignment has a greater likelihood of success if it occurs by age three, or four at the latest. Both language acquisition and gender identity are occurring, with the child beginning to develop the first sense of self. Once gender identity becomes stabilized, attempting to change it would be emotionally traumatic.

While the cultural power of adopting a single gender identity is profound, there are some who move freely as "mixed" in either biological sex or gender identity. Many native American tribes, primarily in western North America and the Plains, have recognized that sex and gender are not always the same. The cross-gender role of biological females who perform the duties associated with males was an accepted role (Blackwood, 1984). There is also the role of "berdache," a title conferred on biological males who exhibit non-masculine characteristics. Williams (1996:73) reports that a berdache holds an accepted social status, especially as related to tribal mythology. A berdache may act as a mediator between men and women and between the physical and spiritual realms (Roscoe, 1992). Rather than being viewed as deviants or misfits, such people may be bestowed with honor and power.

Consider, too, the case of a hermaphrodite named Emma, described in a medical volume in 1937, who grew up as a female but who possessed a penis-size clitoris and a vagina. She was attracted to and sexually involved with females during her teens but married a man (Fausto-Sterling, 1996). Emma did not have any sexual pleasure with her husband so kept several girlfriends on the side. She at times expressed a wish to be a man, a medical possibility even at that time. But she was quite aware that her vagina was her meal ticket. As she said to her physician, "My husband supports me well, and even though I don't have any sexual pleasure with him, I do have lots with my girlfriends" (quoted in Fausto-Sterling, 1996:70–71). Emma's apparent comfort with her hermaphrodite status also demonstrates that the principle of sexual dimorphism is itself not completely value-free. Biological sex and gender identity, as well as the categories which make them up, are not separate, opposite, and immutable. There is considerable overlap, with people such as Emma and the berdache adjusting to the overlap quite well.

The difficulty in separating the biological and cultural determinants of sex and gender is demonstrated by what is now a famous case described by Money and Ehrhardt (1972) involving sex reassignment of a 17-month-old genetic male, one of a pair of identical male twins. During a circumcision procedure at seven months, the electrical current used to remove the foreskin was set too high, which resulted in the loss of the entire penis. Ten months later the agonized parents decided to raise him as a girl. Reconstructive surgery with the creation of a vagina began the process which would be followed by hormonal and estrogen therapy at puberty.

The determination of the parents in this endeavor coupled with a strong definition of appropriate roles for the sexes were responsible for this re-creation. By age five, the twins were demonstrating almost stereotypical gender roles. Preferences in terms of clothing, toys, and activities were differentiated by gender. She was being prepared for a life of domesticity, helping her mother with housework and encouraged in female occupational goals. Her brother was being introduced to the challenges of another world outside the home, with stereotypical preferences for occupational goals such as fireman and policeman (Money and Ehrhardt, 1972:219). Is this indicative of successful reassignment?

A follow-up of the twin girl at age 13 when she was first seen by a new set of psychiatrists suggested she demonstrated "significant psychological problems relative to her role as a female." She had a masculine gait, was teased by other children for her unfeminine characteristics, and believed that boys have a better life and that it is easier to be a boy than a girl (Diamond, 1982:185). Although it is unclear how much the twin knew of the original sex assignment, eventually the choice was made to reconstruct a penis. As an adult, he prefers females as sexual partners (Unger and Crawford, 1992:220). How can we evaluate the "success" of sex reassignment surgery at 17 months and a reversion to the biological sex in late adolescence?

Considering the uniqueness of the situation, there are several approaches to the question. First, even with the hormonal therapy, the effects of her first biological sex could not be completely altered. Second, because of strong cultural definitions of what girls and boys are supposed to be and do, those who do not physically or behaviorally conform are most vulnerable, especially during early adolescence when peer groups take precedence in childhood development. As we shall see in the next chapter, however, gender role socialization has allowed for greater flexibility for girls, with more latitude than for boys in dress and behavior. It is likely that the parents of the twin attempted to create an almost stereotypical girl, encouraging and rewarding feminine traits. A masculine gait on a girl who is "supposed" to act feminine—exceedingly so by contemporary standards—would be cause for confusion, frustration, and potential ridicule. To some extent the conversion may have been too successful, especially at the point when this girl realized she could never fulfill her ultimate role, that of biological mother. In this sense, then, she *should* be confused.

Because of medical technology not possible 20 years before, here was an individual who now had a choice. The powerful and culturally understandable preference for maleness succeeded. While it is apparent that the later information on the psychological development of the twin questions the belief that gender identity is basically learned, neither can this thesis be rejected. Studies of hermaphrodites with the same physical conditions, for example, have been successfully assigned to different genders (Tavris and Wade, 1984). We shall see that since cogent arguments for both cultural and biological influences on gender identity can be offered, in the final analysis both sets of factors need to be taken into account.

Aggression

The debate on the influence of hormones versus socialization is further complicated when studies of aggression in females and males are considered. In most species, including primates, males are more aggressive than females. In an extensive research review by Maccoby and Jacklin (1974) on human sex differences in aggression, the evidence suggests that the higher aggression in males is apparent by about age two. Three years later Frodi and her colleagues (1977) reviewed several hundred experimental studies on aggression in adult males and females and likewise found essentially the same pattern. However, over half of these studies (61 percent) did not demonstrate the higher male aggressiveness under all conditions. Overall, girls and boys are about equal in learned aggressiveness, but boys are likely to carry out the aggression in a physical way whereas girls prefer verbal confrontation (Archer and Westeman, 1981; Eagly and Steffen, 1986). A number of animal studies have linked testosterone to increases in aggression, and in humans correlations have been found between a high testosterone level and committing violent crimes (Kreutz and Rose, 1972; Joslyn, 1973; Petersen, 1980:46; Kimble, 1990:409; Christen, 1991:39-40).

Yet we cannot conclude that the male hormone testosterone is the crucial variable in explaining these findings. First, most animal studies are done on rats. It is not possible to conclude scientifically that humans would react similarly. There is simply no consistent research support for the testosterone-aggression link in humans (Björkqvist, 1994). Second, while experimental procedures on certain animals may suggest causal connections, research with humans is at best correlational. Recent research by Björkqvist and Niemelä (1992) points out that whether males or females are more aggressive depends on the type of aggression and the situation in which it occurs. Studies on the biology of aggression and literature reviews on the topic reveal serious theoretical and methodological flaws (Epstein, 1991). Third, sociocultural determinants of aggression are powerful. There are different standards regarding the appropriateness of aggressive behavior and they are learned early in life (Huesmann, 1994). Males and females experience anger differently but expression of it is associated with being male. Men may feel pressured to act aggressively when publicly challenged. Because it is a socially undesirable emotion for females, they may feel embarrassed to aggress under the same circumstances (Campbell et al., 1992; Geer and Shields, 1996).

However tentative their conclusions, these studies often make their way into the popular press and the notion that males are somehow biologically programmed for aggression becomes reinforced. The fact that testosterone may increase aggression but aggression also increases testosterone is overlooked. The social situation is extremely influential in physiological response. The differences between the sexes in aggression are real but not very large (Eagly and Steffen, 1986). What exaggerates the differences is the cultural belief that the higher male testosterone level causes them to be more aggressive. The belief continues in part because it is a politically useful myth (Adams, 1992). The differences cannot be accounted for by either socialization *or* biology (Eron, 1992; Fraczek, 1992; Rabbie et al., 1992). If there is a biological predisposition in males toward aggression, it is mediated by social influences.

Hormones and Motherhood

On the female side, the hormonal argument has been used in postulating the existence of a maternal instinct. Animal behavior studies implicating the "female" hormones of estrogen, progesterone, and prolactin which are elicited during pregnancy and after labor are used in support (Beal, 1994). Rossi (1977) argues that types of mother-infant interaction such as cradling the infant on the left so it is soothed by the "maternal heartbeat familiar in uterine life" suggest the presence of unlearned responses. Since only women bear and nurse children and men possess the androgens which are seen as inhibiting the formation of this instinct, it has been only recently that the concept has been challenged at all (Rothman, 1991).

The idea of a maternal instinct is not supported. As Shields (1984:269) points out, while there is little scientific value to be gained from denying the existence of unlearned responses to the young, we cannot suppose that adult reactions are not based on learning. Socialization of females maximizes attachment to the young, while for males it is minimized. Some women suffer from postpartum depression and may even reject the child. The fact that most women eagerly respond to their infants and readily take on the caretaking role is due to many factors, including the expectation that this will occur anyway because of a lifetime of socialization for these very roles. A woman's nurturing behavior will be heightened when she is in immediate contact with her newborn, even the first minutes after birth, but parental love emerges within the first week of the birth through repeated exposure to the infant (Maccoby and Jacklin, 1974; Klaus and Kennell, 1983). However, a study by Robson and Kumar (1980) finds that 40 percent of new mothers were so exhausted by the birth experience that their first reaction to the newborn was indifference!

The birth experience will undoubtedly create a special bond of mother to child which cannot be experienced by even the father. This does not mean, however, that hormones will make one parent better or more nurturing than the other. Male gender typing probably plays a larger role in the process than androgens. Consider Mead's (1935) study of the gentle Arapesh where both sexes enjoyed child-care responsibilities. A study in Fiji by Basow (1984) also confirms that infant care can be a rewarding joint effort, especially if gender typing is low. If these two cultures were studied in isolation, it might be concluded that there was a parenting instinct shared by both sexes. Hormones are unnecessary for the emotional bonds established and the excitement and arousal human fathers experience at the birth of their babies. Fathers have intense interest in their newborns and the capacity for nurturance. Research sadly concludes that its expression is thwarted by gender stereotypes suggesting that such behavior is inappropriate for men, including new fathers (Beal, 1994).

The influence of hormones on human behavior is somewhat puzzling, and the research is equivocal at times. But it can be suggested that even if hormones predispose the sexes to different behavior, societal factors will ultimately activate this behavior. There is a growing consensus among social and behavioral scientists that human development is a mosaic of biological inheritance and social experience (Epstein, 1991:85). Overall, the relationship between hormones and distinctive social behavior exhibited by the two sexes is one of mutual interaction.

IN SICKNESS AND HEALTH

Biology and culture again come into play when viewing males and females on numerous health-related characteristics. Biologically speaking, women are definitely not the weaker sex. A clear and consistent inverse pattern emerges in gender differences in mortality (death) and morbidity (sickness). Women have higher morbidity rates but live longer than men; men have lower morbidity rates but do not live as long as women. In the United States females can expect to outlive males on an average of seven years. As Figure 2-1 and Table 2-1 indicate, not only is life expectancy lower for males, but mortality levels for each of the 15 leading causes of death are higher for males. Ten of these leading causes of death show differentials in which death rates for males are at least 1.5 times those for females. When race is factored in for life expectancy, both black and white females still have a clear advantage.

The female advantage in longevity holds globally as well (see Table 2-2). The highest overall life expectancy is found in Japan, where men can expect to live to age 75 and women to age 81. The current elderly population throughout the world is predominantly female. In less than a decade many countries will have only five men to every ten women over the age of 80 (Myers, 1992; Taeuber and Rosenwaike, 1992). The female advantage is narrower in the developing world. The typical pattern is that development will increase the life expectancy rate for both males and females, but that females will show

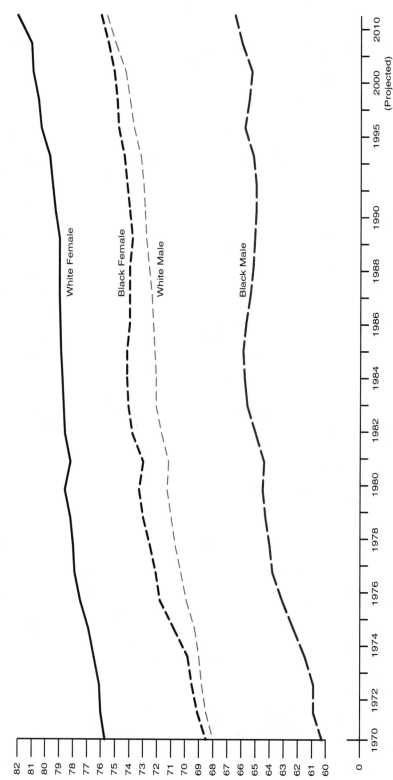

FIGURE 2–1. Life Expectancy by Sex and Race, 1970 to 1995 and Projections for 2000 and 2010

Sources: National Center for Health Statistics, *Monthly Vital Statistics Report,* 1993, 41(7S):5; U.S. Bureau of the Census, *Statistical Abstract of the United States,* 1995. Adapted from Table No. 114:86.

TABLE 2-1 Ratio of Male to Female Age-Adjusted Death Rates for the 15 Leading Causes of Death

All causes		1.74
1	Diseases of heart	1.90
2	Malignant neoplasms, including neoplasms of lymphatic and hematopoietic tissues	1.48
3	Cerebrovascular diseases	1.18
4	Accidents and adverse effects	2.66
	Motor vehicle accidents	2.46
	All other accidents and adverse effects	3.01
5	Chronic obstructive pulmonary diseases and allied conditions	1.85
6	Pneumonia and influenza	1.68
7	Diabetes mellitus	1.11
8	Suicide	4.22
9	Chronic liver disease and cirrhosis	2.30
10	Human immunodeficiency virus infection	8.43
11	Homicide and legal intervention	3.88
12	Nephritis, nephrotic syndrome, and nephrosis	1.50
13	Septicemia	1.40
14	Atherosclerosis	1.33
15	Certain conditions originating in the perinatal period	1.25

Source: National Center for Health Statistics, 1993, *Monthly Vital Statistics Report*, 41(7S):5.

greater gains. As development proceeds, males should catch up slightly (Gray, 1993; World Health Organization, 1995).

But even in poor countries such as Mali, Sri Lanka, and Jamaica, life expectancy is still higher for females (Gray, 1993). As discussed in Chapter 3, poverty combines with sex-selective abortion and neglect and abandonment of female infants and girls in many parts of the world. Of the 500,000 maternal deaths that occur every year, 99 percent occur in developing countries and most of these are preventable with primary health care intervention (World Health Organization, 1995). Given this reality, the overall female advantage in mortality is astounding.

Health surveys and data compiled from various mortality studies repeatedly demonstrate that women have higher overall rates of physical illness, physician visits, and disability days, but men succumb earlier to virtually all causes of mortality (Wingard, 1984; Stillion, 1985; Verbrugge, 1985, 1989; Veevers and Gee, 1986; Jacklin, 1989; Cockerham, 1995). The 1990s witnessed for the first time mortality data which show all three nondisease causes of death (accidents, suicides, and homicides) in the top-ten list (Table 2-2). Compared to females, the death rate for males in accidents is over two and a half times more, and about four times more for suicide and homicide (National Center for Health Statistics, 1993a). After reviewing the research in these areas, we will consider the biological and sociocultural explanation of these differences.

Males have higher mortality rates at every stage of life. The fact that females possess an additional X chromosome apparently contributes to their biological advantage. Even at the prenatal stage, spontaneous abortions of male fetuses are more likely to occur, with overall male fetal deaths approximately 12 percent greater than female. Males are also afflicted with a whole range of genetic disorders much less common in females such as myopia, night

TABLE 2–2 Life Expectancy Rates by Sex, Selected Countries*

	Male	Female
Developing World		
Africa		
Algeria	65.7	66.3
Egypt	62.8	66.3
Mali	55.2	58.6
Nigeria	48.8	52.0
Rwanda	45.1	47.7
Somalia	45.4	48.6
South Africa	60.0	66.0
Zambia	50.7	53.0
South America		
Argentina	65.4	72.7
Bolivia	57.7	61.0
Brazil	64.0	68.6
Chile	68.5	75.5
Peru	62.7	66.5
Asia		
Afghanistan	43.0	44.0
China	66.7	70.4
India	55.4	55.6
Philippines	63.1	66.7
Middle East		
Kuwait	64.6	72.7
Iran	58.3	59.7
Saudi Arabia	68.3	71.4
Yemen	49.9	50.4
Developed World		
Australia	73.9	80.9
Canada	74.9	81.2
France	73.3	81.5
Germany	72.9	79.4
Italy	72.3	80.9
Japan	76.6	83.0
Norway	74.2	80.3
Sweden	75.5	80.8
Switzerland	74.7	81.4
United Kingdom	73.6	79.0
United States	72.8	79.7

*Information, based on most recent data available, ranges from 1990 to 1995.
Sources: Demographic Yearbook 1993, New York: United Nations, 1995; Organization for Economic Cooperation and Development, *OECD Health Data,* 1995; *Japan 1996: An International Comparison,* Tokyo: Keizai Koho Center.

blindness, hemophilia, absence of central incisor teeth, icthyosis (scalelike skin), juvenile glaucoma, progressive deafness, and a white occipital lock of hair. The first year of life is the most vulnerable time for both sexes, but infant mortality rates are higher for males (Waldron, 1988; Strickland, 1989; Verbrugge and Wingard, 1991).

Mortality rates are calculated relatively easily since they are dependent upon generally objective criteria, with most nations having conventional rules for reporting and measuring the incidence of death. **Morbidity**, referring to the amount of illness in a population, involves more difficult measurement. By using available statistics, researchers are relying on cases of reported or treated disease, which may underestimate its incidence. Even household surveys are not always accurate because illness is in part a subjective experience. Many people do not recognize their own sickness, may recognize it but refuse to acknowledge it by altering their behavior by taking off work or seeing a physician, or prefer to treat themselves. This is particularly true of mental illness. These cautions are important in examining gender-related morbidity data.

One of the most striking features of these data is the trend of females to report physical and mental disorders and use health services more than males. There appears to be a gradual emergence of morbidity that is especially noticeable between the ages of 7-15 in female adolescents who report higher levels of asthma, migraine headaches, and neurotic disorders than males. Health service utilization rates mirror this trend (Sweeting, 1995). Morbidity differentials between the sexes are realized in types of diseases, with females more likely to suffer limitations due to acute conditions, while for males limitations are due to chronic conditions. But these data are more meaningful when we examine specific acute and chronic conditions. Women report higher rates of acute and transient illness, such as colds, headaches, and infectious and digestive diseases but also have a higher prevalence of nonfatal chronic conditions such as arthritis, anemia, and sinusitis. Men have lower overall acute illnesses, but higher prevalence of chronic conditions which are life-threatening and associated with long-term disability, such as heart disease, atherosclerosis, lung cancer, and emphysema (Verbrugge, 1985; Verbrugge and Wingard, 1991; National Center for Health Statistics, 1993b). Men have the highest rates of cancer at the youngest and oldest ages and are 1.5 times more likely to die from it than females (Cockerham, 1995:41).

Health and the Workplace

There are interesting findings when morbidity rates are considered for women who work outside the home. Employed women have better physical and psychological health than nonemployed women (Verbrugge, 1989; Nelson and Hitt, 1992). Type of work is a critical factor.

Clerical women have the best overall health profile, with low rates of injury, fewer limitations due to chronic conditions, and average use of health services (Verbrugge, 1984). Clerical workers are not exempt from hazards, however, with negative health effects showing up perhaps twenty years later. Offices can take on factorylike qualities. Radiation exposure, chemical fumes from toners, stencil fluid, and liquid eraser, poor ventilation, and excessive noise are hazards which can lead to mental and physical fatigue, vomiting, visual problems, and confusion. The negative health effects of sedentary work are well documented, and include muscular and orthopedic problems, weight gain and fluid retention. Rather than changing the conditions that contribute to the health problems, employers often attempt to exclude women from certain jobs, especially if their reproductive systems are at risk (Love, 1978; Paul et al., 1989; Bureau of National Affairs, 1989; Klein, 1991). Professional women describe their jobs as stressful, but clerical and other lower-level workers are more likely to report stress-related illnesses, such as headaches and insomnia (Glenn and Feldberg, 1995). Occupational health hazards for women are different than for men. Risk factors for men are more immediate and associated with higher exposure to dangerous activities, such as crime and fire fighting, coal mining, bridge building, and other hazardous construction work.

Despite these observations, women who work outside the home in any occupational classification have better health than housewives. A study by LaCroix and Haynes (1987) finds that being employed is the strongest correlate of good health for women. In fact, paid employment actually improves the health of married and unmarried women, particularly if they also hold positive attitudes toward employment. And compared to working men, when health problems do occur, they are less severe and shorter in duration. Working in itself is no more stressful for women than men (Sloan, 1985; Repetti et al., 1989). Important factors that influence this are powerlessness, which is unhealthy for both men and women, and multiple roles involving work and family life which, as we shall see, may actually be beneficial to health.

Women, Health, and Disease

As mentioned in the previous section males are more prone to certain illness and injury categories in which women tend to be exempt. Similarly, women are more prone to ailments men do not get, with most related to their reproductive systems. When women get sexually transmitted diseases (STDs) such as herpes or gonorrhea, the risks are greater than for men. Infertility and cancer can result. Osteoporosis and toxic shock syndrome are women's diseases. Menstruation has been viewed as a disease of women and historically with suspicion, scorn, and fear. In some contemporary cultures the menstruating woman is forbidden to mingle with others and must undergo ritual purification at the conclusion of her cycle (Delaney et al., 1988). The medical literature has viewed this normal physical process as a pathology which victimizes women (Martin, 1994a). The myths associated with it have not been dispelled, even in the health care and scientific community.

The recent research on premenstrual syndrome (PMS) may be used to challenge some of these myths, but depending on the political overtones and how this research is interpreted, a backlash can occur. As Fausto-Sterling (1993) points out, credible research that even defines, much less analyzes, PMS is difficult to find. There are many faces of PMS that are variously defined by health professionals, researchers, and women themselves (Figert, 1995). Correlational research has linked PMS to fluctuations in hormones, especially estrogen, which is seen to influence anxiety, depression, and other behavioral changes. Other studies find no consistent hormonal abnormalities of the few women who are diagnosed with PMS (Schmidt et al., 1991; Rothman and Caschetta, 1995).

To infer that hormones cause mood changes is not justified. While about 40 percent of all women experience some premenstrual *symptoms*, such as water retention and cramping, only 2 to 10 percent experience severe to disabling symptoms that may be defined as premenstrual *syndrome* (Hoyenga and Hoyenga, 1993:191). Also, it is virtually impossible to separate out the cultural components of what it means to be a menstruating woman (Hoyenga and Hoyenga, 1993). The whole notion of PMS is still equivocal, but the acceptance of its legitimacy by some health care professionals has aided those women who experience great physical and psychological difficulty with their periods. These women have been turned away from a male-dominated health care system with vague, paternalistic assurances that it is all in their heads.

On the other hand, by virtue of their postpubescent and premenopausal age, where most employed women fall, a PMS diagnosis could mean being passed over for promotion or employment in certain jobs where emotional stability is deemed critical. And if women are excused from inappropriate or even criminal behavior because they have PMS, it reinforces the myth that women are not fit for important positions and even permanently impaired because once a month their judgment is unreliable. Only now a so-called scientific basis is used to justify the outcome. While a few women may be impaired, the vast majority are not. As McElhiney (1993a:105) notes, "women must understand the double bind they may find themselves in if they attribute changes in their behavior to PMS."

It is interesting, too, that research is now suggesting that males have relatively large hormonal cycles that are associated with changes in mood, cognitive task performance, and sexual activities (Parlee, 1982; Klaiber et al., 1982; Hoyenga and Hoyenga, 1993). Would they be seen as emotionally vulnerable on their jobs if testosterone levels fluctuated in a patterned way? Gloria Steinem (1993:447) takes a humorous look at this when she asks what would happen if men could menstruate.

> Men would brag about how long and how much. Young boys would talk about it as the envied beginning of manhood . . . Doctors would research little about heart attacks, from which men are hormonally protected, but everything about cramps. Sanitary supplies would be federally funded and free.

Few women experience PMS, and research findings should be interpreted optimistically for those who do. We need to be most diligent in monitoring how the PMS research is being conducted and how the results are ultimately used.

Menopause is also imbued with misinformation and cultural stereotypes. During menopause women report symptoms of irritability, depression, headaches, or the infamous hot flashes. However, like PMS, most symptoms are not disabling. The severe distress accompanying menopause is experienced by only about 10 percent of women. No data support the relationship of the physical symptoms of menopause to serious depression in women, although some women report concerns about loss of their reproductive role (Dickson, 1990; Fausto-Sterling, 1993). As Hyde (1991) notes, when considering the psychological factors, menopause is probably not as bad as adolescence in a woman's life.

Yet much of the medical establishment conforms to the belief advocated by Robert Wilson (1966) in his influential book *Feminine Forever* that menopause is a "disease of estrogen deficiency" treatable by estrogen replacement therapy (ERT). He views menopausal women as unstable "castrates," creating untold misery in the form of alcoholism, drug addiction, and broken homes because of their estrogen starvation (cited in Fausto-Sterling, 1993:336). Consider the happily-ever-after scenario of the menopausal woman who goes to her gynecologist:

> After weighing the risks of therapy against its benefits, patient and doctor decide on ERT. She begins taking it three to six months after her last period, and will continue to do so for up to ten years, perhaps indefinitely. . . . She soon returns to her premenopausal hormonal state. Her physical distress vanishes and her mental state improves. She may not be perennially 39, but in a sense, she can be 49 forever. (Gallagher, 1987a:51)

The jury is still out on risks and benefits of ERT. Benefits include protection against osteoporosis, or loss of bone calcium, and heart disease. The risks are linked to preexisting uterine and breast cancers and blood clots (Bergkvist et al., 1989; Hunt et al., 1990; Hoyenga and Hoyenga, 1993).

In a compelling argument against the view of menopause as a disease which produces psychologically unstable women, Fausto-Sterling (1993) asks if its effects are so unbearable that women may prefer to increase the risk of cancer, even slightly, than suffer the daily discomforts encountered during this time. From this medical standard, women are seen as being encumbered with inescapable distress caused by raging hormones throughout life. ERT can be said to play on the fears of the aging woman and a loss of her fertility in a society which worships youth. While it may be successfully prescribed for *some* women, the view of many medical practitioners is that *most* women would benefit from it. McFarlane (1996) calls for a feminist view of menopause which focuses on it as a normal developmental process which provides women accurate information to make educated choices concerning treatment.

There are serious health effects in striving for youth and beauty. In women this has translated to a tremendous increase in eating disorders, especially **anorexia nervosa**, a disease of self-induced severe weight loss. A variant of this is **bulimia**, where girls will alternate between binge eating and purging. The incidence rates of these "fear of fat" diseases have steadily increased since the 1950s. They will affect 1 in 200 girls and young women, mostly between the ages of 12 and 25, of which 10 to 15 percent will die (U.S. Public Health Service, 1985; Travis, 1993; Russell, 1995a). During puberty, when a girl begins to worry about attractiveness, there is an average weight gain of about 24 pounds. This fat spurt occurs at the exact time she would like to have a thin, leggish, and almost boyish figure. The problem is that her idea of a desirable weight is highly unrealistic (Beal,1994:240). As discussed later, a girl's self-esteem plummets during her early teenage years. The weight issue is a major factor in this.

Anorexia can be described as a *culture bound syndrome* since it was first associated with norms and beliefs unique to American society. However, the power of the media has extended such norms to other societies so that eating disorders might now be called diseases of "Westernization." As the Duchess of Windsor reportedly said over a half century ago, "you can never be too rich or too thin." American and European physicians have recorded cases of eating disorders since the nineteenth century. There is evidence that many noted women had eating disorders, including Queen Victoria, Eleanor Roosevelt, Indira Gandhi, and Anna Freud (Silverstein and Perlick, 1995). Today cases are steadily increasing in the developing world and are also showing up in male patients (Simon and Hughes, 1985; Travis, 1993; Russell, 1995a;

Silverman, 1995; Silverstein and Perlick, 1995). In terms of race, the norm of bodily dissatisfaction has been subscribed to mostly by white women. African-American women are significantly more satisfied with their bodies (Harris, 1994). However, recent research is suggesting a steady increase in eating disorders among both African-American and Hispanic women (Thompson, 1994). A feminist theory of eating problems is proposed by Thompson (1992), who suggests that they can be identified as survival strategies for coping with issues related to the oppressions of race, class, and gender. The focus on appearance is shifted to one which portrays such disorders as survival strategies women use to take care of themselves in coping with these oppressions. This model could be used as a basis for therapeutic interventions with these populations.

Obsession with thinness is definitely media based. Fashion models and movie and television stars have gotten progressively thinner throughout this century. Beauty contestants average well below the national norm and almost 20 percent lower than ideal weight (Silverstein et al., 1986; Russell, 1995b:94). Adolescent girls are particularly vulnerable to media messages that equate thinness with not only attractiveness, but also with competence, allure, and professional success (Brumberg, 1988; Silverstein and Perlick, 1995). Chronic dieting and excessive physical exercise are reinforced by other messages telling the public that over half of us are overweight. The health and diet industries bolster these beliefs. From a conflict theory perspective, this has resulted in a form of **medicalization**, where medical control over parts of one's life is legitimized (Conrad and Schneider, 1990). Combined with cosmetic surgery, the social pressure for thinness now has a billion dollar industry supporting it.

For both men and women the use of alcohol and other drugs, including caffeine and nicotine, is culturally acceptable, but gender differences in morbidity rates to these usages are evident. More men than women use alcohol throughout their lives and alcoholism is higher among men. But women suffer more from both its acute and chronic effects. Fetal alcohol syndrome (FAS) is linked to congenital heart defects, defective joints, mental retardation, and low birthweight of infants (Paludi, 1992). Alcohol is a critical factor in rape and spouse abuse, with homicide an all too frequent outcome.

A pattern of men being involved with illicit drugs and women with licit ones continues to hold true. Twice as many men use marijuana and other illicit drugs, but for women, the most common addiction is nicotine from cigarette smoking (U.S. Public Health Service, 1985). Although there has been a general overall decrease in smoking for both sexes, the percentage decline for females has been smaller (National Center for Health Statistics, 1993b). By the beginning of the twenty-first century the overall smoking rate for females is estimated to exceed that for males. This is largely due to the cohort of teenage girls who are now smoking at higher rates than boys of comparable ages. Another factor is that while both younger men and women attempt to quit smoking at about equal rates, women are substantially more concerned about weight gain (Pirie et al., 1991:324). Although men still exceed women in mortality for lung cancer, rates of this disease have doubled for women since the 1950s (National Center for Health Statistics, 1993b).

As men turn to alcohol to cope with stressful situations, women turn to prescribed drugs, particularly psychoactive ones. Current prevalence rates for those who take both over-the-counter and prescribed drugs, mostly sedatives and minor tranquilizers, are double for women. Consistent with the process of medicalization, alternative modes of treatment remain unexplored when a pill or capsule seems a legitimate solution to a physical or emotional problem. Compared to men, women are more likely to receive a drug for a psychological problem. This has resulted in the frequent abuse and misuse of prescription drugs (Goode, 1989; Cafferata and Meyers, 1990; Ettorre, 1992; Doyal, 1995).

Global Focus: Women and AIDS

Less than a decade ago discussions of Acquired Immune Deficiency Syndrome (AIDS) focused on the high mortality rate of men with the disease. In the United States today it is the leading killer of men between the ages of 25 and 44, with the highest percentage among gay males. Changes in sexual behavior in this group may show some leveling off of the disease. New infections are increasing fastest in inner city populations of poor African-Americans and Hispanics. Women now make up 11 percent of U.S. AIDS cases and over half of these are African-American women (Lewis, 1995). It is spreading fast into the heterosexual population, with women becoming its most likely victims. In the United States, women as a percentage of AIDS cases rose from 7 to 18 percent between 1985 and 1994, with a 10 percent increase in 1992 alone (World Health Organization, 1995). It is becoming apparent that race, class, and gender are the multiple jeopardies that increase AIDS risk among women (Osmond et al., 1993).

The rapid spread of AIDS worldwide and the patterns that have been produced by this spread have transformed AIDS into a woman's disease. The World Health Organization (1995) reports that women worldwide are becoming infected with the HIV (AIDS) virus at faster rates than men and at the turn of the century, the number of annual number of AIDS cases for women will equal or exceed that of men. Women now represent 50 percent of all new HIV infections and half of these occur in women ages 15 to 24. Most of these women are monogamous. In Sao Paulo, Brazil the ratio of male-to-female infection rose from 42-to-1 in 1985 to 2-to-1 in 1995. In Bangkok, Thailand virtually all prostitutes are infected and in Northern Thailand 8 percent of women who simply work in antenatal clinics are infected. The most staggering numbers are in Africa, where 6.5 million have the AIDS virus. The largest number are in Sub-Saharan Africa, where 10 percent of the population in the five countries of Malawi, Rwanda, Uganda, Zambia, and Zimbabwe are infected, with 25 percent infection rates in some of the large cities. To date AIDS means a death sentence. Yet the cultures with the highest infection rates are the ones where women have little power to alter the sexual habits in their own families.

Women are more vulnerable to infection because of cultural norms which restrict power in all areas of life—from their families, to educational opportunities, to the legal systems. In Africa and much of the developing world, AIDS is a family disease. The most common route of transmission is heterosexual. Men pass it to their wives who pass it to their infants and children. Children born to HIV mothers have a 14 to 45 percent chance of contracting the virus and are likely to lose their mothers during childhood, and most of these women do not even know they are infected (Heymann, 1995). The condom is presently the most effective preventive measure against the sexual transmission of

AIDS, but many women are culturally restricted from suggesting it. It may be seen as an indication of her infidelity and is perceived by the man as defiance or insolence (Erben, 1995:26). In a seminar on AIDS in Nigeria a woman stood up to ask how she could get her husband, whom she knew had other sexual partners, to wear a condom. The question brought shock, embarrassment, and silence (Esu-Williams, 1995). Despite the grave consequences of AIDS, the fact that she could not get help from even the women there shows the difficulty in altering cultural norms regarding sexuality.

The symbolic interaction perspective emphasizes that sexuality is socially constructed. Young (1994) states that it is necessary to understand the different forms of sexual expression and sexual meanings to fight the AIDS epidemic. In terms of sexual practices, the vulnerable position of women must be recognized. Prevention efforts are undermined when they focus only on women by making them solely responsible for risk reduction. Prevention of AIDS among heterosexuals requires the realization that traditional gender role socialization runs counter to safer sexual practices (Campbell, 1995). AIDS prevention must go hand in hand with greater equity. Conflict theory recognizes that improving both women's economic and social status makes them less vulnerable to AIDS. An empowerment focus which provides women with a "repossession" of their bodies is necessary (Carovano, 1994:265). In the short run they can mobilize power by organizing. For example, the Zimbabwe Women's AIDS Support Network has helped give women the confidence to fight AIDS in a society where they have little control over the sexual behavior of men (Erben, 1995:27). In Latino cultures where the Catholic Church is a formidable barrier against change in sexual habits and traditional family practices, women have capitalized on the worldwide movement for access to safe contraception and family planning. Women's organizations are increasing awareness "that the sexual relationship is one that empowers people at different levels" (Araujo et al., 1995).

The AIDS crisis, particularly as it affects women, reflects what sociology would call a functionalist challenge. In fighting AIDS, traditional values which restrict women are compromised. There is visible strain on the social order. But more social disequilibrium (disorder) will occur if AIDS is left unchecked by isolating its victims and denying the grim reality of men's sexual power over women. It also denies the vulnerability and responsibility of the broader population. The increase of AIDS in the world is a threat to everyone.

Mental Health

The fact that women are the primary users of licit drugs, especially psychoactive ones, is a critical issue when examining gender differences in morbidity rates related to mental illness and depression among different categories of women. Some of the data are inconsistent due to the difficulty in gathering such data at all, as well as the changing definitions of what constitutes various disorders. Mental health professionals may diagnose and label the same person differently. However, data since the 1950s suggest that there are some distinct differences between men and women on certain indicators of mental illness. While there appear to be no significant differences in overall *rate* of mental disorder, there are consistent differences in *type*. Women are more likely to suffer from affective and anxiety disorders, while men are more likely to suffer from personality disorders (Chino and Funabiki, 1984; Carson et al., 1988; Mechanic, 1989; Williams, 1993; Cockerham, 1995). Women attempt suicide three to four times more often than men, but men choose more lethal means and are more likely to succeed (Sanborn, 1990).

Marital status is a key variable in mental health. Overall, it is better to be married. For men, it is much better to be married. Single men have the highest mortality and morbidity rates for both physical and mental disorders. Never-married, divorced, and single men have higher rates of mental illness when compared to all marital categories of women (American Psychological Association, 1985; Gallagher, 1987b). Marriage appears to be an important buffer against mental illness, but married women suffer more mental health problems than married men (Bernard, 1972; Gove and Tudor, 1973; Steil and Turetsky, 1987; Rosenfield, 1989).

A puzzling finding occurs when considering single women. Gallagher (1987b) reports that married women have higher depression rates than single, widowed, or divorced women. And, as discussed earlier, since working outside the home contributes to better psychological and physical health, single women would appear to be better off since, by necessity, they must have paid employment. In her classic study, Bernard (1972) noted that single women show up as mentally healthier than both married women and unmarried men. But these data also need to be viewed with the consideration that some single parents fall into the single category and some into the never-married. The female single parent is at higher risk for all areas of morbidity. This category of women constitutes the fastest growing poverty segment in the nation, with poverty the single most important variable in nutrition, housing, life chances, and psychological well-being (Belle, 1990). Their problems are exacerbated by lack of education and job skills, with many dependent on welfare. Thus when socioeconomic factors are added to the mental health picture, gender and marital status lose some of their explanatory power. Women experience mental health problems differently depending on their socioeconomic status (Walters, 1993). More data are needed to determine the prevalence of mental illness among financially secure and at-risk single women who may or may not be single parents.

Overall, these findings of gender differences in mortality and morbidity rates can be explained by biological and cultural dimensions. On the biological side, the immunological superiority of the second X chromosome is apparently at work. Women may have higher morbidity rates, but they are likely to recover from the same sicknesses that kill or disable men. In almost every society, women outlive men. Considering the oppression and extreme hardship of a life of physical labor which women especially in developing societies must endure, this finding is all the more remarkable. There are also clear social and cultural determinants of these patterns, most often associated with gender role socialization. Females are taught as young girls to be sensitive to their bodies and be aware of changes in bodily states and physical processes. They openly express their concerns to the health care community. Thus the number of physician visits are higher. By the same token, they are more likely to take advantage of the new directions for preventive health and self-care. This is demonstrated by lowered mortality rates for breast and ovarian cancer. There are some encouraging signs that for physical health at least, men may be seeking more preventive services. For example, mortality rates for prostate cancer have been positively influenced through early detection.

When symptoms emerge, women are more likely than men to admit to them and seek help, especially for emotional distress. The classic functionalist view of the **sick role** (Parsons, 1951) describes those behaviors which are socially expected of a sick person according to prevailing norms. Like other roles it consists of privileges and obligations. It can be an acceptable role, but since it allows the person to be temporarily exempt from social responsibilities, sick people are expected to return to a healthy state of functioning as soon as possible. The judgment of vulnerability associated with the sick role makes it more culturally appropriate for women. Psychological distress continues to be seen as less role-appropriate for men and therefore more likely to be socially proscribed. When men maintain an exterior of emotional toughness (Kimmel, 1992) in times of emotional trauma, it is difficult for them to get the psychological help they may desperately need. This is also reflected in rates for diseases that may have been arrested if detected and treated sooner. An exception to this for physical health is the common cold, where men are more likely to overrate their symptoms compared to women (Macintyre, 1993). As will be discussed in Chapter 9, however, there are lethal consequences of a rigid male gender role which denies helpseeking behavior.

Role flexibility allows women to be less constrained in seeking help for psychological distress. They maintain a larger social support network which helps mitigate problems related to mental illness, especially depression (Vilhjalmsson, 1993; Turner, 1994). On the negative side, there is not only a bias toward diagnosing depression in women by male psychiatrists, but "therapy" often entails a prescription for a psychoactive drug, which does not address the problem for which help was sought in the first place (Loring and Powell, 1988; Cockerham, 1995).

Several possibilities for other gender role determinants for the higher levels of depression among women have been offered. The traditional female role may be a mental health liability. Using the Bem Sex Role Inventory, Rendely and her colleagues (1984) find that homemakers who are defined as more masculine or androgynous have fewer symptoms of depression and anxiety. Earlier studies by Gove (1972) and Gove and Tudor (1973) confirm that the frustrating position of the traditional woman, bound to housewifery and child care, is linked with poorer mental health in women and is a reflection of a secondary status that restricts them to passive and dependent roles. Later research confirms that the traditional female role is associated with more chronic conditions, less energy, a sense of helplessness and isolation (Repetti and Crosby, 1984; Nolen-Hoeksema, 1990; Helson and Picano, 1990; Anson et al., 1993). Depression results in women who feel pressured to conform to roles with which they are unhappy.

Multiple Roles and Mental Health

The second critical variable in mental health is employment. We have already shown that employment outside the home is a major determinant of good physical and mental health. Paid employment is associated with reduced depression among both husbands and wives (Glass and Fujimoto, 1994). Work has an intrinsic value that enhances self-esteem, life satisfaction, and overall psychological well-being (Quick et al., 1992). From a functionalist viewpoint, this value is intensified in cultures such as America where a work ethic is deemed essential to smooth societal functioning as well as individual identity. The impact of work is seen in Sigmund Freud's answer to the question of what a "normal" person should do well. For Freud, normal psychological functioning emphasizes work and family (Quick et al., 1992). The ideal is to create an environment where work and family are not opposed to one another (Lobel, 1991).

Achieving this ideal is becoming more difficult, especially for women. The dual-earner household is the norm and one which is voluntarily chosen by the majority of couples. There is some controversy about the effects of work roles on the mental health of a woman or her family (Simon, 1995). Work is not a psychological jungle and a rewarding career actually shields a woman against pressures encountered at home (Darnton, 1985). Contrary to what we might expect, multiple roles which include marriage, children, and satisfying work are associated with better health, enhanced self-esteem, and lower rates of depression. A satisfying career is optimized when domestic responsibilities are shared by one's spouse (Crosby, 1982; Adelmann, 1994; Bullers, 1994; Hong and Seltzer, 1995). This is especially true when women perceive that their family and paid work roles offer autonomy (Pugliesi, 1995; Reisine and Fifield, 1995). Caregiving to the elderly and others adds to the hidden work and multiple roles of women, but here, too, gratification and other positive psychological outcomes are reported (Krause et al., 1992; Moen et al., 1995). Roles which enhance personal control are psychologically healthy for women. These studies support the "role accumulation" hypothesis which stresses the positive outcome of occupying multiple roles (Thoits, 1986; 1992).

On the other hand, the mental health advantages of multiple roles are fewer for women compared to men, particularly since work and family roles hold different meanings for men and women (Simon, 1995). The "role overload" hypothesis suggests that family and employment put women into two full-time jobs which may contribute to psychological problems (Roberts and O'Keefe, 1981; Nolen-Hoeksema, 1990; Steil, 1995). Overall, the homemaker role by itself or the homemaker, worker, and single-parent roles in combination appear to be the most stressful. A study of 2,300 working women by Wolfe and Haverman (1983) shows that the added burdens of child care and housework contribute to health problems. Higher rates of illness occur for women with children when compared with employed women without children. Their jobs did not influence the amount of time they devote to their children or homes. Added to this are the unique stressors women face in the workplace, including gender discrimination and stereotyping (Nelson and Hitt, 1992).

Although it is difficult to sort out all these variables, we can conclude that multiple family and work roles are most beneficial for women when they maintain a sense of autonomy in these roles and when they are supported by other family members, especially their partners or spouses. Presently research points to the greater benefits of multiple roles (the role accumulation hypothesis) rather than to the stresses associated with role overload.

Finally, explanations of the mental health differences between men and women must also account for how therapists respond differentially to their male and female patients. One of the first warnings that therapy in itself may not be in a woman's best interest comes from Chesler's (1972) assertion that a masculine standard of mental health may be detrimental to women. A series of what are now classic studies conducted in the 1970s examined gender role stereotyping among mental health professionals, including psychologists, psychiatrists, and social workers (Broverman et al., 1970, 1972; Nowacki and Poe,

1973). In general they demonstrated that, like the broader lay public, psychotherapists hold different conceptions of mental health for men and women. When asked to describe a mature, competent, and socially healthy adult, their judgment was skewed in the direction of traditional gender role expectations. They were more likely to assign those traits characteristic of a healthy adult to a healthy man than to a healthy woman. A double standard of health emerges. For a woman, health involves adjusting to her environment, even though this adjustment may not be socially desirable and healthy for a mature adult. Therapy may also reinforce dependency and helplessness if they are seen as part of the feminine role. Males are not immune to labeling either. By virtue of the definitions inherent in the traditional male role, their complaints may be overlooked or minimized when they should be seriously regarded.

Progress has been made. Phillips and Gilroy (1985) find no significant relationship between social desirability of traits and gender role stereotypes. In confirming these conclusions, Poole and Tapley (1988:270) state that since clinical psychologists do not hold vastly different expectations for males and females, the convention of labeling poles on psychological tests as "masculine" and "feminine" seems outdated and misleading. Clinicians expect that both women and men adjust their behavior to the environment. Brems and Schlottmann (1988:13) find that while there are differences found by therapists-in-training in the perception of healthy men and women, they are of no clinical significance as indicators of psychopathology. Today, positive traits are chosen for healthy persons, regardless of gender. Sexism in therapy has not been eradicated. But the devaluation of women as patients is slowly being eroded as women take more responsibility for themselves and as the male ideology in mental health care is confronted.

THE WOMEN'S HEALTH MOVEMENT

The women's health movement has emerged as a challenge to mainstream modern medicine, which is dominated by attitudes and practices not in the best interest of a large segment of the population it is supposed to serve. Blatantly sexist attitudes regarding the sexual inferiority of women still run rampant in this system. The movement is helping to empower women with the belief that alternatives to traditional health care are not only possible, but beneficial. Women are encouraged to take an active role in all phases of health and health care. According to Zimmerman (1987:443-44), a fundamental assumption of the movement is that women have not had control over their bodies or their health. This is demonstrated by an androcentric system that governs health policy, planning, legislation, delivery of services, and the important clinical roles that determine the creation of health knowledge. The specific etiology, diagnosis, and treatment of diseases in women is based on a male-dominated system where actions can be harmful to the health and well-being of women.

Challenging Gender Bias in Research

A major example has been the virtual absence of female participants in clinical trials involving drug research and experiments in advanced medical technology. Androcentric medicine insists that biological differences between men and women have major, inescapable health consequences, but then routinely conducts research using only male subjects. Male is the medical norm.

Consider the truly infamous federally funded study which examined the effects of diet on breast cancer. Only *men* were used as sample subjects! (Tavris, 1996). What is known about the natural history of diseases and their treatment in men is inapplicable to women. Evidence suggests that gender bias has flawed some medical research (Rosser, 1994). This bias in research extends to areas such as lack of analysis of study results by gender, scarcity of interdisciplinary research, inadequate funding for research on diseases primarily affecting women, and lack of female researchers (Giudice, 1991; Keville, 1993). In countering these trends there also needs to be the recognition that when women *are* used as research subjects, they are likely to be white and middle class (Rothman and Caschetta, 1995). The interplay of race and class in particular must be account-ed for to make findings applicable to a diverse population of women.

Research on heart disease and AIDS are notable examples where the exclusion of women in clinical trials are ominous. Two widely publicized stud-ies on the effect of low doses of aspirin and the risk of heart attack were con-ducted using study samples of 12,866 general subjects and 22,071 physicians, respectively. All subjects in both studies were male (Steering Committee of the Physician's Health Study, 1989; Rosser, 1994). The reduced heart attack risk that emerged from this research was considered so spectacular that the public was made aware of the potential results before the findings were published. These findings cannot be generalized to women, in part because the role of estrogen needs to be considered. And as Healy (1991) notes, the exclusion of women in research reinforces the notion that heart disease is primarily a male affliction. It is still the leading cause of death among women and women have greater risk in the year following the first heart attack than men. Women receive less aggressive cardiac care than men (Young and Kahana, 1993). As for AIDS, research has not kept up with its spread among women. There have been no published natural histories of women with HIV infection, although 1994 witnessed the first phase of a long-term study (Driscoll et al., 1994; Institute of Medicine, 1994). This delay has resulted in the denial of benefits and programs to women because the Centers for Disease Control (CDC) do not include women's conditions in their "official" list of what characteristics constitute AIDS (Institute of Medicine, 1994).

Women are taking a much more active role in their health care. In addressing these and other health-related issues, several organizations, such as the Society for the Advancement of Women's Health Research, Caucus for Women's Issues, the National Women's Health Network, and the Office of Research on Women's Health of the National Institutes of Health, have emerged as advocates to publicize and influence health policies (Giudice, 1991; Dan, 1994; Institute of Medicine, 1994). More women are entering the health care field as physicians, especially as gynecologists, hospital administra-tors, clinical psychologists, and other mental health therapists. Nurses are assuming more responsibility in decision-making processes. The concept of a health care team tied to a holistic health perspective has helped in this regard. All this provides impetus for change.

Midwives and Medicine

This section ends with an example that brings together many gender-related issues in health. It is discussed from a sociological conflict perspective. Until the mid-nineteenth century childbirth in America was usually assisted by midwives who believed that nature was adequate and intervention, especially with instruments, was dangerous. Medical training at that time also accepted the view that "nonintervention is the cornerstone of midwifery." Although the belief in the naturalness of birth was accepted, midwifery, soon to be called obstetrics, moved in the opposite direction with greater reliance on intervention and the use of "aids" to control natural processes (Wertz and Wertz, 1990). Despite all the evidence that deliveries attended by midwives were safe for both mother and child (Rothman and Caschetta, 1995), by the early twentieth century midwifery was virtually eliminated in the United States.

Until the American Medical Association gained control over all medical licensing, physicians and midwives were in direct competition for patients and fees (Rothman and Caschetta, 1995). Indeed, recent research is showing that obstetricians are again resisting the private practice of nurse-midwives because it will lead to renewed competition for healthy and paying clients (Langton, 1994). With medicalization gradually taking hold, midwives were characterized by the new medical establishment as ignorant, meddlesome, and unscientific, yet they were denied access to becoming physicians. The belief that a dissecting room and hospital were no places for a woman was widespread. It would harm her "delicate feelings" and "refined sensibility" and she would see things that would "taint her moral character" (Wertz and Wertz, 1990:153). It is interesting that female nurses were absolved of these concerns.

Although women's practice of midwifery is ancient and continues worldwide, once childbirth became medicalized, women were seen as unsuited for independent medical roles. This attitude is reflected by the editor of the *Journal of the American Medical Association* in 1900: "When a critical case demands independent action and fearless judgment, man's success depends on his virile courage which the normal woman does not have or is expected to have" (Mumford, 1983:273). Even before midwives lost their status as independent practitioners, they became more marginalized and found themselves restricted to working with poor and immigrant women. Doctors also believed that middle- and upper-class women had more difficult deliveries, hence needed more intervention than robust farm women (Wertz and Wertz, 1990).

Today there are indications that the "adequacy of nature" is making a comeback. Although major restrictions limit their practice roles, nurse-midwives are growing in number. As uneasy alliance is being forged by some obstetricians who deliver high-risk babies and do more costly Caesarian sections and nurse-midwives who are attracting those who desire a more natural birthing experience. Even with an oversupply, the high incomes of obstetricians are guaranteed and gains are made in professional autonomy and respectability of nurse-midwives (Little, 1982; Radosh, 1986).

The roller coaster ride of midwifery in the United States has not ended. But the return of the nurse-midwife indicates that an era of de-medicalization with an emphasis on holistic health is being ushered in. Kornblum and Smith (1994:132) suggest that American medicine is finally catching up to the feminist movement in its support of midwifery, natural childbirth, and home delivery. Rothman (1994:133-34) calls for empowering midwives to "enable them to practice midwifery as a fully autonomous profession." Similar to what is characteristic of the women's health movement, midwives offer an alternative ideology that can be translated into an alternative view of procreation. It is fascinating that this alternative view is also an ancient one.

THEORIES AND EVIDENCE

Explaining gender patterns in mortality and morbidity must realistically take into account biology and society, physiology, and culture. Several theories have been advanced which offer some explanations for these patterns. These are more formal and integrated perspectives than most of those suggested above. Based on the criticisms which have been leveled at these theories, they have achieved varying degrees of success.

Recognize, too, that each theory carries with it the baggage from the discipline with which it originates. This will necessarily limit its scope and applicability. The following theoretical overviews summarize the contributions made to the area of gender roles related to biology. As we shall see, these contributions have added to our understanding of the connections between biology and society but at the same time generated a great deal of controversy which has not yet been resolved.

Freud: Anatomy Is Destiny

The impact of Sigmund Freud (1856–1939) on medical science, psychology, and the social sciences has been profound. There was no systematic psychology as a discipline before Freud. He was the first to tie a specific theory of development to a therapeutic intervention strategy, that of psychoanalysis, which he founded. Although almost a century of empirical research on the foundations of Freud's work has produced more questions than answers and more inconsistencies than agreement, he remains a strong influence on the contemporary intellectual climate in a variety of disciplines.

For Freud, the fact that a boy possesses a penis and a girl does not is the overriding element in his theory of sexual development. It is between the ages of three and six that children recognize the anatomical distinction separating the sexes. This is also the stage in life where gratification is focused on the genitals and when masturbation and sexual curiosity increase for both girls and boys. As identified by Freud, this is the *phallic* stage, where the clitoris is the area of greatest sexual pleasure for the girl as is the penis for the boy.

Sexual pleasure notwithstanding, the girl comes to believe that the male penis, unlike the barely noticeable clitoris, is a symbol of power denied to her. Penis envy results, which "reaches its highest point in the consequently important wish that she should also be a boy" (Freud, in Brill, 1962). Her mother is inferior in her eyes because she, too, does not have a penis and is rejected. The girl's *libido*, or sexual energy, is transferred to her father, and he becomes the love-object. This is called the Electra complex by later writers. The resolution occurs when the girl's wish for a penis is replaced by her wish for a child. A male child is even more desirable since he brings the longed-for penis with him. In this way, the female child eventually learns to identify with her mother. In addition, clitoral stimulation is abandoned for vaginal penetration, which is proclaimed as a sign of adult maturity for women.

It is during the phallic stage when the boy's libido is transferred to his mother, with his father becoming the rival for his mother's affections. This is termed the Oedipus complex. In his discovery that girls do not have a penis, he develops "castration anxiety," or the fear he will be deprived of the prized organ. This is the stage of the greatest turmoil and distress for the young boy as he works, unconsciously, to resolve the Oedipus complex. He eventually overcomes the underlying fear involved, identifies with the father and his masculinity, reduces his incestuous desires for the mother, and is later ushered into psychosexual maturity.

For boys the fear and distress experienced during this time are productive in that they lead to the development of a strong superego, which for Freud is the highest attainable mark of human mental evolution (Freud, in Brill, 1962). Conscience and morality, the very hallmarks of civilization, are produced with strong superegos. Girls, on the other hand, have weaker superegos, since resolution of the Electra complex occurs through envy rather than fear. They experience less psychic conflict than boys which leaves its mark on later personality development. This explains why women are more envious, jealous, narcissistic, and passive than men. Indeed, biology is destiny for Freud. The anatomical distinction leaves ineradicable marks on both sexes, but particularly for the female.

It is understandable why Freud has come under serious attack by feminists, especially with his unabashed statements on female sexual inferiority. His ideas were no doubt conditioned by the Victorian society in which he lived and worked, a society which espoused strict gender differentiation based on traditional roles of homemaker and breadwinner in a patriarchal world. The empirical work to support his theories has been inconclusive at best, with some of his ideas of sexuality disproven, such as the vagina being the "true" center of female sexuality.

It is impossible to dismiss the inherent sexism in Freudian theory, but Williams (1987:39) notes that Freud himself cautioned repeatedly that many of his statements were tentative and needed confirmation. Even Kate Millett (1995:61), who views psychoanalytic theory as demonstrating unreasoned, anti-woman bias, states that "the most unfortunate effects of vulgar Freudianism far exceeded the intentions of Freud himself." Perhaps his own qualifications for his theories have been lost in the eager scramble to formulate rigorous scientific theories of personality. He wrote at a time when the fledgling discipline of psychology needed scientific bolstering to increase its credibility. Given a patriarchal scientific community where assumptions about men and women often go unquestioned, it is easy to see how Freud was severely criticized for his notions on infantile sexuality and the psychosexual stages but gained more quiet acceptance for his comments concerning the biologically inferior design of females.

Feminist scholars and therapists who are supportive of certain Freudian constructs and therapeutic techniques, particularly the successes of psychoanalysis for some patients, must come to grips with these criticisms. Mitchell (1974) implies that some Freudian concepts are not incompatible with feminism and that to dismiss Freud completely because of his sexist statements would be counterproductive for those women who are helped by psychoanalysis. In support of this, Rose (1983) argues that while psychoanalysis is not a theory oriented to the social change feminism desires, it at least allows us insight into the process itself and how it is a politicized process. Freud began the process of examining how gender roles are acquired, and psychoanalytic feminism provides the arena for analyzing the construction of gender and its effects on women, including women's subordination (Daugherty and Lees, 1988; Elliot, 1991; Slipp, 1995). As an example, Benjamin (1988:5) notes that it is Freud who provides us with the basis for "seeing domination as a problem not so much of human nature as of human relationships—the interaction between psyche and social life." She uses feminist criticism and reinterpretation of psychoanalytic theory to view the problem of domination from this unique perspective.

As a feminist, Chodorow (1978, 1993) integrates psychoanalytic and sociological theory. She posits that since in most cultures it is women who do the child care, mothers produce daughters who then desire to mother. Mothering thus reproduces itself. Sons are produced who devalue women for these very roles. Penis envy occurs because women, even young girls, recognize the power of males, so it is natural to desire this kind of power. There is nothing inherently biologically superior about this. Yet it is the ability of the girl to maintain her identification with her mother that achieves the desirable traits of empathy and connectedness. In this sense, there is a positive resolution of the Oedipus complex, which Freud overlooked, ignored, or rejected from his male-biased view.

There are both conflicts and compatibilities of psychodynamic (Freudian) and feminist theories and efforts to integrate the perspectives are incomplete (Daugherty and Lees, 1988). Feminists are searching for an androgynous theoretical and therapeutic model to supplant the traditional, often Freudian-based, androcentric approach (Ganley, 1988). This model would encompass feminist therapy appropriate for both male and female clients. With the required reinterpretation and empirical justification, it is possible that neo-Freudian scholars may be able to use Freud's insights for the benefit, rather than the degradation, of women.

Sociobiology

As Freud wrote on biological determinism a century ago, a new form has emerged in the writings of contemporary sociobiologists who use evolutionary theory as a foundation for their work. Within this framework, evolutionary theory can be applied to both animals and humans. The fundamental assertion of sociobiology is that we are structured by nature with a desire to ensure that our individual genes pass to future generations. This is the motivating factor in almost all human behavior. More specifically, some sociobiologists believe that the principles of evolution will allow for a greater understanding of how our social behaviors developed. We can look to natural selection to find adaptive behaviors which can determine why males are aggressive, why females do child care, and why sex inequality where males are dominant occurs worldwide.

E. O. Wilson (1975, 1978), the leading sociobiologist, maintains that it is such behaviors which allowed for species survival. Aggressiveness, for example, allowed humans to successfully compete with the other wild animals who shared our primeval environment. Males are aggressive, too, in their competition between themselves for females who then decide with whom they will mate. Regardless of the immense variability of cultures, humans share certain traits in common. Human males and females are also differentiated by certain shared traits. The cultural universal of an incest taboo is used to provide the greatest support for sociobiology. Beyond this, most social scientists find no way to empirically link genes to specific behavior.

The sociobiological argument for women assuming the child-care role maintains that a mother will always know her own child, whereas this is not always the case with the father. It is adaptive for the mother to care for the child to ensure the continuation of her own genes. Sociobiologists see male and female human natures as extraordinarily different from one another. Each sex has evolved attributes which will increase its reproductive interests. Promiscuity in males is explained with the same reasoning. Whereas women are extremely selective in choice of their sexual partners, men will spread their sperm as widely as possible (Barash, 1982; Dovidio et al., 1991). Men can actually increase their reproductive success in this manner. This suggests that male sexuality is so different from female sexuality that sexual deviation by males from the norms is understandable. It is an outcome of evolutionary history rooted in biology. For both sexes, therefore, these behaviors are adaptive. Even the double standard is thus packaged and explained.

Bonding is one manifestation of our common history. Sociobiologists argue that the mother-infant bond is strong, invariable, necessary for the well-being of the child, and precedes all other types of bonds in time. Excessive separation of mother and child is devastating. "Nature is ruthless about this" (Tiger and Fox, 1971:64). Males bond, too, but to one another, originally for defense and hunting. Species survival was dependent upon these two bonds. That men and women eventually become segregated from each other and inhabit two different worlds is a natural consequence of these bonding patterns. Contemporary gender roles thus reflect this evolutionary heritage.

Besides the lack of empirical support for its assertions, sociobiology has not had a great following among either social scientists or other sociobiologists who prefer to keep sociobiology, as it was originally developed, in the area of animal research. Wilson's (1975) formulations were based on insect life. Inferences from animal studies are methodologically and theoretically unwarranted. Empirical testing of sociobiology is impossible, and the theory itself is based on faulty assumptions and stereotypes regarding male and female human behavior.

Feminist criticism centers on the fact that sociobiology is an androcentric perspective that ignores research which contradicts its view. Our nearest evolutionary ancestors are the chimpanzees. Most sociobiologists ignore the female chimpanzee because she is notoriously promiscuous. Second, sexual selection in sociobiology emphasizes competition and aggression in males but ignores the other half of the process in which females make choices among males (Hyde, 1991). Feminist sociobiologists point out that females can be sexually aggressive and competitive and males can nurture and be passive. Among animals and people, females do not just stand by and wait for the most successful males to come along and mate (Hrdy, 1986; Hubbard, 1994). As Hyde (1991) notes, this could be used to an argument for human females as being more intelligent, more perceptive, or more powerful in controlling human males. This is not to say that productive leads involving human social behavior are impossible (Nielsen, 1994), only that there must be recognition that leaping into the human arena is tenuous at best. In a review of research on the biology of gender, developmental biologist Fausto-Sterling (1985) concludes that what we consider to be results of biology are really reflections of culture. And even here we cannot clearly mark their boundaries.

More importantly, biological determinism ushers in social and political conservatism. If something is defined as "natural," then to tamper with it is to cause frightening, unforeseen consequences. Sociobiology provides a rationalization for a continuing patriarchal system which serves to subordinate women or even other men who do not meet the rigid evolutionary standards set forth. In essence, biological deterministic theories, like any other deterministic theories, are overwhelmingly weak in their inability to account for the immense variation in human cultures as well as the rapid pace of social change.

HUMAN SEXUALITY

Major assaults on the biological determinism inherent in beliefs about sexuality and the sexes were led by the pioneering work of Kinsey and his associates (1948, 1953) and Masters and Johnson (1966, 1970). Until fairly recently, beliefs about human sexuality have been shrouded in myth and superstition, encumbering serious research. Just as Freud shocked the scientific and then the lay world with his assertions on sexuality, Kinsey had similar results upon revealing his data on sexual behavior.

Portions of the original data were at first dismissed as inaccurate and suffering from methodological flaws when it reported sexual activities vastly different from the supposed norms. It is interesting how science questions research on its methodology and scrutinizes it more than usual when it is reluctant to accept findings which go against long-held beliefs and practices. This shows how vulnerable science itself can be and calls into question some of its tenets concerning objectivity. Yet in the long run the Kinsey studies have been integrated into the literature on human sexuality, especially as replications have stood the test of time.

There are definite gender differences related to masturbation. Kinsey discovered that about 92 percent of males and 58 percent of females engage in masturbation to orgasm. Females also begin to masturbate to orgasm at later ages than males, often for the first time in their twenties and thirties. Later data by Hunt (1974) and Hyde (1991) suggest that this has not changed significantly since Kinsey's original research. Both sexes may be starting earlier, but girls are still later than boys in this regard. An interesting finding emerges on unmarried females who have sexual intercourse and may not masturbate.

In orgasm achieved during intercourse, males and females also differ. Men are much more likely to have orgasm than are women. Kinsey found that over one-third of married women never had an orgasm prior to marriage and that one-third of married women never have orgasm. The Hunt (1974) data show that this has decreased to approximately 10 to 15 percent of women. It is likely that the new openness in expressing sexual concerns, gaining from the wealth of information on sex techniques now available, and a loosening of the double standard are responsible for these statistics. Indeed, in therapeutic and educational contexts, women are being encouraged to discover themselves sexually as a way of achieving greater satisfaction with their partners as well as gaining a sense of sexual independence (LoPiccolo and Stock, 1986; Dodson, 1987).

Males continue to have fewer problems than females in achieving orgasm. The fact that females are less consistent with this may account for some of the male-female difference in desire for intercourse. Husbands generally would like more frequent intercourse than their wives, particularly early in the marriage. Later in life, this trend may be reversed. As women experience greater comfort and respond with less anxiety, the desire for intercourse may be heightened. In addition, orgasm should occur more often. A lifetime of socialization which suggests that women, who are later wives, are not sexual beings but are responding to their husbands because of duty rather than desire is difficult to alter. Research finds that unmarried women who masturbate and engage in "heavy petting" report more guilt and less satisfaction than unmarried women who engage in sexual intercourse (Davidson and Moore, 1994). We know that sexual activities of a pleasurable nature are conditioned by prevalent attitudes.

Another example relates to sexuality and the elderly, where the issue has been ignored or denigrated. For the elderly sexuality is invisible because it is associated with youth and virility. It is denigrated because older people are considered to be sexless. If men show sexual interest they are labeled as lechers or "dirty old men." A woman's sexuality is judged by her roles as child bearer and mother. Once these roles are completed she is expected to retreat to a sexless existence. From a symbolic interaction perspective, such negative labeling can create a self-fulfilling prophecy which will discourage the elderly from actively engaging in sexual activity. This can occur despite the fact that sexual desire remains strong and willing and able partners are available.

Men and women do age differently in terms of sexuality. Consistent with negative labeling, Masters and Johnson's (1970) pioneering research suggests that, especially among elderly men, sexual ability declines when psychological barriers such as performance anxiety due to physical changes intrude. His wife believes his "failure" is a rejection of her. This perpetuates a cycle of less sex, leading to less interest in sex, leading to both physical and psychological distance between the couple. Widows are at a greater disadvantage than widowers since age and gender role barriers reduce their options for acceptable sex partners. The irony is that it is easier to cope with the problem if society assumes they are not supposed to be sexually active anyway. As attitudes regarding women as sexual beings change and become less restrictive, they should be reflected both in frequency of intercourse, sexual satisfaction, and orgasm at all life stages.

In terms of premarital sexuality, the Kinsey (1953) data reported that only one-fourth of the women born before 1900 had experienced premarital coitus. One decade later, the rate for women had doubled. When age is considered, one-third of young women reported they had premarital sex by age 25 in the Kinsey study. A dramatic increase again one decade later showed that the figure had risen to 81 percent. For males it remained consistently high for both samples, with 95 percent of the males under the age of 25 reporting premarital coitus (Hunt, 1974). Today, premarital sexual experiences for both women and men is the norm and college in particular brings with it the expectation that intercourse will occur. Research also shows that almost 90 percent of college females are sexually experienced—a persistent pattern for almost 20 years (Elliott and Morse, 1989; DeBuono et al., 1990; Nathanson, 1991; Miller et al., 1993). This is reflected in Moffatt's (1989) study of college students with the conclusion that premarital sexual chastity was "almost [as] dead as the dodo."

A gender-based sexual double standard still exists for attitudes, but it is eroding for behavior. A woman will have fewer sex partners than a man and will plan for her first intercourse. Women are more likely to assume a person-centered approach to sex with men whom they love or to whom they feel committed in some way. However, females are increasingly reporting that they have sex and multiple sex partners without emotional involvement (Lottes, 1993). A man more likely adopts a body-centered approach to intercourse, with his first experiences with a woman who is a pick-up or a casual date (Miller et al., 1993). But when compared with women, men are still not as likely to be criticized for intercourse (Williams and Jacoby, 1989). Concern for contracting sexually transmitted diseases, especially AIDS, will affect the *number* of partners but have less of an impact on the *rate* of premarital sex per se. Fear rather than guilt is the issue here. This implies, too, that the term "premarital sex" is outdated. A better term would be "nonmarital sex" since it does not suggest either long-term commitment or emotional involvement. Finally, if the double standard vanishes, it does not necessarily reflect an advancement for women. The result is no significant gender difference in either frequency of nonmarital sexual intercourse or emotional involvement with one's partner(s). Given the potential risks related to health, unplanned pregnancy, and sexual violence, gender parity in this instance is likely to be detrimental to women.

Other challenges to ideas about sexuality, female sexuality in particular, continued with the work of Masters and Johnson (1966, 1970) on the physiology of sexual response and treatment approaches to sexual dysfunction. Whereas Freud attributed vaginal orgasm to the mature female, he discounted the clitoral orgasm as indicative of immaturity since it was practiced by children. Masters and Johnson show that physiologically, orgasms are the same, regardless of how they are reached. It is the clitoris which serves a purely sexual function and contributes the most to female sexual pleasure.

The clitoris is also responsible for allowing women to be multiorgasmic. Even the Kinsey (1953) data showed that 14 percent of the women sampled had achieved multiple orgasms. Perhaps this was so against accepted notions about women that the incredulous scientific community rejected the findings on methodological grounds. Males, on the other hand, have a single orgasm. After orgasm they experience a resolution and immediately go into a refractory period, during which they cannot sustain an erection. A myth related to male sexuality involves size of the penis. Organ size is unrelated to male capability or satisfaction of one's partner.

For women, age and pregnancy are also related to sexuality and orgasm. Women tend to grow in their sexual activities and have satisfying sexual experiences later in life, peaking later and perhaps outdistancing men. Time is not a deterrent to female sexuality, although for both sexes there must be a regular pattern of activities to sustain sexual expression into old age. Pregnant women have an increased potential for orgasm and sexual responsiveness during their second trimester. Contrary to the myths that pregnancy reduces interest in sex in women or that it is somehow harmful to the developing fetus later in the pregnancy, the evidence does not support these beliefs. It is only in the two months following delivery that sexual responsiveness in a woman may be compromised and this, too, will vary depending on the extent of the recovery (Hyde, 1991:280). We know now that pregnancy does not necessarily inhibit, and may actually enhance, a woman's sexual responsiveness.

These data support the idea that a sexual revolution has occurred. Sexual *evolution* may be a better term since the changes have been gradual and noticeable over a long period of time (Scanzoni and Scanzoni, 1988). This evolution became apparent in the 1920s when a shift in attitudes toward sexuality was noticed.

Despite this shift, a double standard which reinforces a woman's passivity during the heterosexual sex act continues. Steedman (1993) states that the "discovery" of the potential for female orgasm has occurred in a climate of masculine dominance. Women and men believe her orgasm is a sign of his success as a lover and both are asked to accept a code of social passivity for women during coitus. Her sexual pleasure is compromised when his "manhood" is at stake. As pointed out by Masters and Johnson almost 30 years ago, cultural barriers inhibit sexual pleasure. Traditional gender roles are dysfunctional for sexual pleasure.

NATURE VERSUS NURTURE: THE POLITICS OF BIOLOGY

Research which uniformly demonstrates the advantages leading to greater female longevity has been used to support the contention that women are clearly biologically stronger than men. Montagu (1974) uses the Kinsey and Masters and Johnson findings to present a view that women are not only the superior sex but are really more valuable than men because they maintain the species during a child's crucial developmental stages. From a sociobiological standpoint, Montagu uses the idea of adaptive strategies to suggest that women are more necessary than men. In this way, he literally turns around earlier interpretations of women as passive beings who are sexually and biologically inferior. He presents the case that men suffer from a biological inferiority complex because they cannot conceive children. Their womb envy is compensated for by a drive to work and to produce in other areas. This is evident in their use of language. According to Montagu, when a man is proud of something, he says, "that's my baby." He conceives an idea and then gives birth to it (cited in Dunn, 1986). Freudian and sociobiological explanations are used in women's behalf. Such arguments might also be evoked in light of recent research at the University of Pennsylvania suggesting that men's brains shrink as they grow older, which slows their response time and contributes to loss of memory. Women do not experience this brain shrinkage (*St. Louis Post-Dispatch*, 1996a).

Though Montagu believes women are the superior sex biologically, he takes issue with the idea that natural superiority implies social inequality. We have seen that differences between the sexes (genders), both perceived and real, have been used to subordinate women. It is unreasonable to substitute the ancient myth of female inferiority for another equally untenable myth.

Let us return to our original question of nature versus nurture, of heredity versus environment, of biology versus society. All the evidence points to the impact of both in explaining the differences between the sexes. Deterministic theories which either dismiss or fail to account for biology *and* society are doomed as useful explanatory models in science. For example, feminist scholars like Alice Rossi (1984) are critical of social scientific explanations which deny or overlook the influence of a woman's biological makeup in explaining the bond between mother and child. Some biological differences must be accepted as givens. The problem, according to Bem (1996:11), is that there is too much of a focus on biological difference and not enough on the "institutionalized androcentrism" that transforms male-female differences into female disadvantage. The popular press takes hold of the sex difference theme and soon people believe that men have "math genes" and women have "caring genes" that destine them to certain roles. Regardless of the critical reasoning that debunks biological determinism, "there is, at present, no aspect of social or individual life that is not claimed for the genes" (Lewontin, 1994). Gender stereotypes are again biologically reinforced.

Biological arguments are consistently drawn upon to justify gender inequality and the continued oppression of women. It has been shown that these arguments are ideologically embraced but not empirically sound. This book proceeds with the understanding that there are biologically conditioning elements which differentiate the sexes. However, the similarities outweigh the differences. As Lorber (1996:103) states, "gendered people do not emerge from physiology or hormones" but from the social order. As detailed in the next chapter, learning and socialization mitigate the differences that do exist. As a sociologist I am biased in favor of theories that are rooted in sociocultural factors in explaining gender roles, which take into account a range of variables, and which imply that the potential for women and men to achieve in any direction they desire is virtually unlimited.

GENDER ROLE DEVELOPMENT
The Socialization Process

> Girls play at being pretty, but boys play cars.
> Boys don't clean house and girls don't get dirty.
> Boys stay outside as long as they want, but girls can't.
> Boys don't play hopscotch. Girls don't play rough or get sweaty.
> Girls are cute and harmless and don't get as muddy as boys.
> —Comments from seven- and eight-year-olds when asked "How are
> boys and girls different?" (cited in Freedman, 1995:401)

These comments demonstrate that as early as second grade, children have strong ideas about what boys and girls are supposed to do and be. They embrace and even celebrate smaller gender differences, in turn obscuring larger gender similarities. From the moment a girl infant is wrapped in a pink blanket and a boy infant in a blue one, gender role development begins. The colors of pink and blue are among the first indicators used by a society to distinguish female from male. As these infants grow, other cultural artifacts will assure that this distinction remains intact. Girls will be given dolls to diaper and tiny stoves on which to cook pretend meals. Boys will construct buildings with miniature tools and wage war with toy guns and tanks. In the teen and young adult years, although both may spend their money on records, girls buy cosmetics and clothes while boys buy sports equipment and stereo components. The incredible power of gender role socialization is largely responsible for such behavior. Pink and blue begin this lifelong process.

CULTURE AND SOCIALIZATION

Socialization can be defined as the lifelong process through which individuals learn their culture, develop their human potential, and become functioning members of society. As a critical process in social life, socialization requires social interaction. As the ways of a particular society are learned, personality is also shaped. This simple definition does not do justice to the profound impact of socialization. Not only is an understanding of what is entailed in this process needed, but we must also recognize that it is our culture which molds our beliefs and behaviors about male and female, masculine and feminine.

A **culture** involves the total way of life of a given society. It includes both material aspects, such as buildings and books, as well as nonmaterial aspects such as religion and roles. Our culture defines which behavior patterns are considered appropriate. Indeed, culture encompasses all that we have developed and acquired as human beings, with each generation transmitting essential cultural elements to the next generation through socialization. Cultures are organized through **social institutions** which ensure that basic needs are met and societal functions are carried out. Thus each social institution is organized around a defined need. For example, the institution of the family is responsible for childhood socialization which continues with the institution of education. Other institutions include religion, government, the economy, and an evolving leisure and recreational institution with a media focus. As we are socialized into our culture, we begin to understand that males and females are expected to be different in many ways. Gender roles are differentiated in American culture according to workplace, leisure activities, dress, possessions, language, demeanor, reading material, college major, and even degree of sexual experience and pleasure. The list is seemingly endless.

In each of these areas, our culture dictates expectations and actions which differ according to gender. To choose another course of action, to deviate from the accepted norm, may mean risking social disapproval. Conformity becomes a matter of providing cultural mechanisms for **social control**. Every society has mechanisms to ensure that its members act in normative, generally approved ways. In many societies, when a woman asks a man for a date or a married couple decides to reverse occupational and household roles, they become vulnerable to a number of social control mechanisms which may include ridicule, loss of friends and family support, or exclusion from certain social circles.

Social control remains effective particularly when socialization processes encourage the perpetuation of stereotyped portrayals of the genders. As already noted, a stereotype is a category which assumes that certain characteristics can be attributed to individuals simply on the basis of their group membership. Although they are general, exaggerated, often inaccurate, and usually unfavorable, stereotypes are extremely difficult to dislodge. To a large extent, stereotypes are useful in that it would be impossible to enter every situation with a completely new perspective. As Kornblum and Julian (1995:268) note, we build up mental pictures of various groups and then define all members of the group according to these images, regardless of individual differences.

As classification devices, stereotypes in and of themselves are not necessarily negative. Stereotypical thinking becomes insidious when individuals are damaged because they are defined in terms of assumed group characteristics. If we stereotype women as passive, an individual woman may be passed over for a job requiring leadership ability. Her own individual ability in terms of job leadership is not even considered due to the stereotype given to her gender as a whole. A man may be denied custody of his child on the basis of stereotypes of both genders which view women as inherently more qualified to raise children and men as incompetent in this regard. This case also suggests that stereotypical thinking about gender can be so pervasive that legal processes are not immune. As with other categories, gender role stereotypes emerge through socialization and are reinforced through social control.

From this discussion, it might appear that socialization is so powerful and all-encompassing that we are like little robots molded by our culture, who succumb to prescribed gender role behaviors uncritically. If this were so, gender role change would not be evident. To argue that the automatons of one generation produce their own carbon copies in the next ignores two important facts. First, socialization is an uneven process which takes place on many fronts, with different agents. We are socialized by parents, siblings, peers, teachers, the media, and all the social institutions. We all know of women who are independent, achievement oriented, and admired. There are men who are esteemed precisely because of their effectiveness with, and caring toward, young children.

Second, we live in a diverse, heterogeneous society made up of numerous **subcultures** which may exhibit gender role patterns at variance with the dominant culture's norms, attitudes, behavior, and lifestyle. Numerous subcultures exist in contemporary industrialized societies, indicating their degree of heterogeneity. Subcultures may be based on many factors, including race, ethnicity, social class, or common interest. Age-based subcultures are also important since they emerge at points in the life course which are strongly defined according to gender role norms. For example, age peers in elementary school determine criteria for prestige which in turn impacts self-esteem, achievement motivation, and even academic success. A boy defined as effeminate has much to lose in this regard. At the other end of the age spectrum, the elderly, too, are not immune to such rankings. Both widows and widowers who would like to begin dating again risk social disapproval by peers who accept cultural stereotypes that negatively define sexual activity for older adults in general.

Social Class and Race Patterns

In terms of social class, research shows that gender roles are more flexible in middle-class families than in working- and lower-class families (Mc-Broom, 1981; Brooks-Gunn, 1986; Lackey, 1989; Lips, 1995). This pattern is particularly shaped in homes which have career-oriented middle-class mothers. Boys and girls from these homes are offered less stereotypical gender role choices in behavioral expectations and career development and hold more egalitarian attitudes. (Betz, 1993; Tuck et al., 1994). However, research is less clear as to what specific variable accounts for this pattern. Boys from middle-class homes are more achievement oriented than are girls. White middle-class women are described by college students in more stereotypical ways than black women in general. And families who move upward in social mobility are more likely to embrace traditional gender roles (Lips, 1993). It may be that race, mother's employment, and social mobility are more important than social class in forming gender attitudes. And since social class itself is multidimensional and determined by factors such as these, it is difficult to sort out the direction of causation.

Race as an added variable complicates the gender role socialization portrait, but it does provide important explanatory leads. Research indicates that African-Americans are less stereotyped than whites in behavioral expectations according to gender. Black women are esteemed for their independence and strength, black girls with nontraditional gender role training have high achievement motivation, and black children are socialized into views of gender which are less rigid (Bardwell et al., 1986; Binion, 1990; Lips, 1995; Houston and Wood, 1996). This is consistent with research showing that African-American males and females are more androgynous than whites of both genders (DeLeon, 1993). Examples of expressions of androgyny come from studies showing that black males are less likely to report that housework is divided unfairly than are white males and that they have high levels of participation in child care (Hossain and Roopnarine, 1993; John et al., 1995).

Although it at first seems contradictory, other evidence suggests that African-American women encourage independence and self-reliance in their daughters but also socialize them to accept traditional female roles. Compared to white parents, black parents express a greater level of concern that their girls be feminine and their boys be masculine (Dugger, 1991). Carr and Mednick (1988) report that traditional gender role training among black male preschoolers leads to higher achievement motivation. These studies are congruent with research indicating that African-Americans may actually have higher levels of gender role stereotyping than whites (Price-Bonham and Skeen, 1982). Perhaps one way of resolving this issue is to consider the historical pattern of gender role configuration in the African-American subculture. As will be discussed in Chapter 8, black families have a high regard for the independence and initiative of African-American women. In this sense, the "traditional" gender role of women is one of strength rather than weakness. Likewise, black children are socialized with a view of gender that is less polarized when compared to whites (McAdoo, 1990; Dugger, 1991). Male and female are not "opposite" human beings who have completely different normative expectations. Nurturing men and assertive women are encouraged. The research is inconsistent only when race and class are conceptually separated and when white, middle-class standards of masculinity and femininity are applied to the African-American experience.

For some Hispanic populations (Puerto Rican and Mexican-American) the data show stronger support for a female role that is more deferential and subordinate than with either African-Americans or whites and one which places motherhood above all else (Garcia, 1991; Lips, 1995). This role is reinforced by powerful religious socialization within Hispanic subcultures which promotes women's subservience to men (Anzaldua, 1995). What is interesting about data such as these is that in terms of gender roles, Hispanic men in both populations do not demonstrate "excessive" masculinity by the standards of broader American culture. For the Puerto Rican group, DeLeon (1993) explains that cultural values of familism, nurturance, and concern for others buffer hypermasculinity. For the Mexican-American group, Zinn (1989) suggests that close family patterns represent adaptations to a society which keeps these men in economically marginal positions. Hispanic women of all subcultures are challenging conventional images through organizing, often with men, through writing, and through economic resources gained from working outside the home (Valcarcel, 1994; Almquist, 1995). These challenges will provide seeds for socializing the next generation of Hispanic youth.

This research demonstrates the impact of the intersection of race, class, and gender on socialization. Despite a great deal of new data on gender relations of minority women and men, most research continues to use middle-class and college student samples, mostly with white subjects or where race is not a separate variable. It is becoming increasingly evident that many of the apparent discrepancies in the data can be explained by recognizing that the variables of gender, race, and class are not simply additive but interactional. Second, gender role socialization is multidimensional and must account for many factors, such as demographics, including other minority statuses, social institutions, and personality. Finally, research clearly suggests that masculinity and femininity are simply not theoretically useful if they continue to be polarized. As discussed earlier, this has implications for the usefulness of the concept of androgyny itself in that it may implicitly accept this polarization.

The concepts reviewed here are important for understanding the process of gender role development. Socialization is a continual, lifelong process with various requirements designated as appropriate at certain age levels. **Primary socialization**, beginning in the family, allows the child to acquire what is necessary to fit into society, especially language and acceptable skills for social interaction. **Continuing socialization** provides the basis for the varied roles an individual will fill throughout life. Socialization is directional, with various paths and patterns appearing along the way. Three major theories have emerged which help explain this process as well as the development of our gender identities: social learning, cognitive development, and gender schema theories.

THEORIES OF SOCIALIZATION

Social Learning Theory

As a modification of behaviorism or reinforcement theory, social learning theory considers socialization in terms of rewards and punishments. Specifically, social learning theory is concerned with the way children model behavior they view in others, such as aggression, cooperation, selfishness, and sharing. The child gains approval for appropriate behavior or is reprimanded for doing what is deemed inappropriate. Toilet training, table manners, and grooming habits are so determined. As with other behaviors, gender roles are learned directly through reprimands and rewards and indirectly through observation and imitation (Bandura and Walters, 1963; Mischel, 1966; Bandura, 1986). Imitation or modeling initially appears to be spontaneous in children, but through the reinforcement process specific patterns of behavior soon develop.

The logic is simple. Differential reinforcement occurs for doing either "girl" or "boy" things. In anticipating the consequences of girl or boy behavior, the child learns to get the label applied to herself or himself that is associated with rewards. This becomes the basis for gender identity. An awareness develops that the two sexes behave differently and that two gender roles are proper. As parents, teachers, and peers model gender role behavior during the critical primary socialization years, children imitate accordingly. Continued reinforcement of the valued gender identity results. Thus the assumption is that "knowledge about gender roles either precedes or is acquired at the same time as gender identity" (Intons-Peterson, 1988:40). In contrast to the psychoanalytic perspective (see Chapter 2), social learning theory is not interested in biological influences, unconscious motivation, or other internal processes but views gender socialization solely in terms of environmental influences.

Some of the earliest research on social learning theory and gender socialization was conducted by Lynn (1959, 1969) to account for the seeming difficulty that boys encounter in gender role socialization. Lynn asserts that during the first years of primary socialization, the father is not likely to be available as much as the mother. And when the father is home, the contact is qualitatively different from contact with the mother in terms of intimacy. Using even stronger terms, Levy (1989:12) maintains that it is the mother who provides the basis for *all* subsequent learning in the child. In general, male role models in early childhood are scarce and boys must somehow manage to put together a definition of masculinity based on incomplete information.

They are often told what they should not do rather than what they should do. The classic examples are "big boys don't cry" and "boys shouldn't act like sissies." Girls have an easier time in this regard because of the continuous contact with the mother and the relative ease of using her as a model.

Lynn (1969) further contends that it is the lack of exposure to males at an early age that leads boys to view masculinity in a stereotyped manner. This may explain why the male role is considered to be the more inflexible one and why males remain insecure about their gender identity. The consequences of this narrow view of masculinity are many. Male peer groups encourage the belief that aggression and toughness are virtues. Males exhibit hostility toward both females and homosexuals, and cross-gender behavior in boys ("sissies") is viewed more negatively than when it occurs in girls ("tomboys"), with women more accepting of cross-gender children than men (Carter and McCloskey, 1983; Fagot, 1985; Martin, 1990; Miedzian, 1991). Men's fear of ridicule propels them to exaggerate antihomosexual and sexist remarks to ensure that others do not get "the wrong idea" concerning their masculinity (Kimmel, 1994). Although this research does not confirm that modeling per se is responsible for gender role acquisition, it does indicate that gender-appropriate behavior is strongly associated with social approval. Although laden with uncertainty and inflexibility, the boy prefers the masculine role. He learns that his role is the more desirable one, bringing with it more self-esteem.

It would also be a mistake to conclude, however, that the socialization path for girls is easy simply because of the greater availability of her mother during early childhood. Even young children are bombarded with stimuli which suggest that higher worth, prestige, and rewards are accorded to males. Boys can embrace the gender roles which flow from these messages. Girls, on the other hand, are offered gender roles associated with less worth and must model behavior that may be held in lower esteem. Gender expectations lead to a preference for characteristic masculine behavior. Subordinate roles are offered to girls which encourage dependence and deference (Geis, 1993). Remember the twin from the last chapter who, when given a choice, chose to be a male? If modeling and reinforcement are such enticements to behavior as social learning theory suggests, a girl would understandably become quite anxious about being encouraged to perform roles held in lower esteem. But regardless of societal evaluation, girls, like boys, soon learn to prefer their own role. It may be that this preference is augmented by the advantage of flexibility and less consistent reinforcement offered by the girl's role compared to that of the boy's.

In the most general sense, social learning theory has provided the foundation for a great deal of research on socialization, especially when it is combined with a symbolic interaction perspective emphasizing the importance of role playing. Evidence for a broad social learning approach to socialization comes from a variety of research topics. As will be discussed, gender role stereotyping and behavior increase with age. Mothers and fathers demonstrate different role expectations in child rearing, and both peers and teachers differentially reward males and females based on gender role concepts (Langlois and Downs, 1980; Snow et al., 1983; Block, 1984; Fagot, 1984; Lips, 1995). While there is now a substantial body of evidence supporting the social learning hypothesis of differential reinforcement, Weitzman (1984:162) suggests that research still has not measured the numerous subtle ways parents communicate their gender expectations to children.

Certainly imitation and rewards are important, but social learning theory fails to account for the fact that even if socialization is not a random process, it is far from being a consistent one. A girl may be rewarded for a masculine activity, such as excelling in sports, but she retains other aspects of her feminine role. In an early review of research, Maccoby and Jacklin (1974) conclude that it is age rather than sex which is more likely to determine parental behavior. The main exception to this generalization is that boys are given less flexibility than girls, especially in terms of clothing and toys. This does support the notion that boys experience greater pressure to conform than girls. They also maintain that modeling is more complex than social learning would propose and later research backs this up (Raskin and Israel, 1981; Lott and Maluso, 1993; Beal, 1994). Children may not necessarily model the same-sex parents, or they may choose other opposite-sex models outside the family. Parents are also socialized by their children and may use them as barometers of contemporary, changing gender roles.

For social learning theory to be strengthened, several items must be considered. It must account for the often immense individual variation in the genders. Likewise it needs to assess the variety of cultural and subcultural influences which children experience, such as the single-parent family or in ethnic communities where siblings and adults take on a range of nontraditional roles. Since children observe the type and frequency of tasks performed by males and females, they will form an impression of which behaviors are gender appropriate. Divorce has created a scope of family structures. Consider the gender socialization consequences of parental role reversal when today about 5 percent of nonresident parents are mothers instead of fathers (Depner, 1993). Related to this, lastly, is the criticism that social learning views children as passive, buffeted by rewards and punishments aimed at instilling in them a sense of who they are and what they should do. Children are not merely passive recipients of adult socialization (Davidman, 1995). Social learning theory ignores their active participation in the socialization experience as well as any differences in level of cognitive ability.

Cognitive Development Theory

Cognitive development theory offers another view of the process of gender role socialization, which is based on Piaget's (1950, 1954) assertion that the child's reality is different from that of the adult. The child's level of understanding of the world varies with the stage of cognitive development. Simply stated, the mind matures through interaction with the environment. Unlike social learning theory, the child takes an active role in structuring the world. Lawrence Kohlberg (1966), who formulated this model, claims that children learn their gender roles according to their level of cognitive development, and their degree of comprehension of the world.

In Kohlberg's view (1966), one of the earliest ways a child organizes reality is through the self, which becomes the highly valued component of the child's existence. That which is associated with the self becomes valued as well. Although children do not recognize the permanence of their gender until between the ages of five and seven, by age three they begin to self-identify by gender and accurately apply gender-related labels to themselves and often to others (Kessler and McKenna, 1978). Though they are too young to understand that all people can be so labeled, this is the beginning of gender identity. By age six the girl knows she is a girl and will remain one, and only then, Kohlberg asserts, is a gender identity said to be developed. Since these developments occur at about the same point in time, gender identity becomes a central part of the self, invested with strong emotional attachment. Individual differences in gender roles are accounted for by the different experiences of children. Since in part children subsequently perceive these experiences based on reinforcement, there is some consistency with social learning theory.

Once gender identity is developed, much behavior is organized around it. It is at this point when children actively seek models which are labeled as boy or girl or female or male, and identification with the same-sex parent may occur. Now that the child understands his or her own gender, behavior will be consistent with the understanding of that label. As Kohlberg (1966:89) states, social learning theory contrasts with cognitive theory which sees the sequence as "I am a boy, therefore I want to do boy things, therefore the opportunity to do boy things (and to gain approval for doing them) is rewarding." And because of the active process on the part of the child, it is also a theory involving self-socialization. As Serbin and her colleagues (1993) point out, reinforcements are important, but the child is essentially directed by the need to perform roles congruent with his or her own sense of self. In integrating ideas from social learning and cognitive development theories, Bussey and Bandura (1992) have formulated what they refer to as a "social cognitive theory of gender self-regulation." Gender constancy motivates children to seek out social interactions where they can learn gender appropriate behavior.

Like social learning theory, the cognitive development model cannot account for the whole of gender role socialization. It has been criticized because of Kohlberg's exclusive use of male samples, which makes generalizations to females tenuous at best. More damaging is its failure to explain the underlying mechanisms of cognitive development and the methodological difficulty of testing the hypothesis that gender identity is a prerequisite to gender constancy and other information about gender roles (Intons-Peterson, 1988:44). However, some cautious empirical support for this notion is offered by Martin and Little (1990), who studied the gender concepts of children, ages three to five. They conclude that while gender understanding is necessary for children to learn about gender stereotypes and to show sex-typed preferences, such knowledge need only be rudimentary. The more critical factor here appears to be gender stability. "Once children can accurately label the sexes, they begin to form gender stereotypes and their behavior is influenced by these gender-associated expectations" (Martin and Little, 1990:1438). Regardless, this is supportive of cognitive development theory in that gender understanding contributes to the sex-typing process.

Other studies also offer some substantiation for the theory. Children, especially boys, value their gender highly, prefer same-gender individuals, and give gender role-related reasons for their preferences (Zuckerman and Sayre, 1982; Cann and Palmer, 1986; Etaugh and Duits, 1990). Leahy and Shirk (1984:289) find that as age increases, there is an increasing agreement with adult stereotypes, which indicates that children "develop the ability to classify characteristics by gender." And in a test to measure cognitive maturity on children ages three to six, Coker (1984) observes that performance improves with age on gender concepts. Both boys and girls learn the gender concepts in the same sequence, and measures of cognitive maturity are "positively related to performance on the gender concept tasks" (Coker, 1984:19).

Gender Schema Theory

Elements of cognitive development theory are incorporated into a newer theory of gender role development that uses information-processing models. **Gender schema theory** states that once the child learns appropriate cultural definitions of gender, this becomes the key structure around which all other information is organized (Bem, 1981, 1983). This is compatible with cognitive development theory in two major ways. First, a *schema* is a cognitive structure which helps to interpret perceptions of the world and second, before a schema can be formulated and gender-related information processed appropriately, children must be at the cognitive level to accurately identify gender. When a girl learns that the cultural prescription for femininity includes politeness and kindness, these are incorporated into her emerging gender schema, and she adjusts her behavior accordingly. With such a schema providing both pre-scriptions and proscriptions, it not only impacts behavior but can also pro-foundly influence one's sense of self-esteem. Adequacy as a person becomes tied to adequacy in matching behavior to gender schema.

As children develop their gender schema, they increasingly use them as key organizing perspectives. Martin and Halverson (1981) argue that the in-group ("own-sex") schema develops first and is more complex and detailed than the out-group ("other-sex") schema. Using an in-group schema, children assimilate new information, plan activities, and choose roles. This helps to explain why first the child's world and then the adult's world become so dif-ferentiated by, and associated with, gender. Most important, an understanding of gender schema may help us understand why it is so difficult to dislodge gen-der stereotypical thinking.

Whereas Bem believes that androgynous people and those possessing few traits associated with their own sex would be more gender *aschematic*, other theorists assert that *all* people are gender schematic, including androgynous people since they still identify masculine and feminine traits within themselves (Crane and Markus, 1982; Markus et al., 1982). The only exception would be undifferentiated people who contend their traits are not largely associated with gender at all.

Bem (1983) concludes from her research with adults that people who are the most sex-typed are also those who process new information on the basis of gender differences. In cultures that rigidly adhere to attitudes emphasizing gender differentiation, gender schemas are likely to be complex and elabo-rate. Martin and Halverson's (1981, 1983) research with children suggests that the order in which gender concepts are acquired is gender identity, own-sex schema, and other-sex schema. They also indicate that gender schema appear to have an impact on the memory of young children. While a study by Fried-man and Pines (1991) on gender-related childhood memories does not use an explicit gender schema model, they find that men's memories were more active and women's more emotional. They state that these may reflect actual differences between the genders in childhood experiences or may result from a process of memory selection that reflect different gender-related experi-ences as adults. For example, think about any recent class discussion when someone tries later to remember who made a certain comment. Ample research evidence suggests that if we misremember, it is more likely to be a within-sex mistake rather than a between-sex mistake (Cross and Markus, 1993:61). It is also easier to remember activities and people when they are gender stereotyped than when they are not. Our memories are better for information consistent with gender schema (Fiske et al., 1991; Burn, 1996).

A study by Fagot and Leinbach (1989) demonstrates that the gender schema of parents impact how they behave toward their children and, in turn, how this influences their development. Finally, Mullen's (1990) research with second graders indicates that they associate symbols of nature with the concept of female and symbols of culture with the concept of male. She supports Bem's contention that in American culture such a classification is part of the network of gender associations we learn to accept. As she states, the realm of nature is thought to be less controllable, less predictable, and less rational, but more balanced, more whole, and more nurturant—characteristics associated with females. The male artifact (culture) domain is associated with an opposite set of characteristics (Mullen, 1990:585). In all of these scenarios, a case can be made that gender schema information processing is salient.

More recent work by Bem (1993) on gender socialization provides another track for gender schema theory which accounts for the cultural impact on gender acquisition. Every culture contains assumptions about behavior that are contained throughout its social institutions and within the personalities of individuals. She refers to these as "cultural lenses." A sociological view would liken these lenses to societal values, beliefs, and norms. She suggests that in American culture, three gender lenses are most prominent: gender polarization, androcentrism, and biological essentialism. As already discussed, these are the shared beliefs that females and males are fundamentally different and opposite beings, that males are superior to females, and that biology produces natural, hence inevitable, gender roles. Despite the massive evidence against gender polarization and biological essentialism, the beliefs persist. I would assert that these in turn justify androcentrism as a societal value. In essence, they become another set of gender schemas in which to organize behavior. Bem notes that children accept them without recognizing that alternatives are possible. Later they cannot envision their society (or any other for that matter) organized according to a different set of gender schema.

It is clear that in the process of developing our gender identities, we construct various gender schema. In bridging the gap between sociological and psychological approaches to gender role socialization, gender schema theory offers a viable alternative. Gender schema theory assumes that "individuals interact with their environments, actively constructing mental structures to represent their awareness of the events around them" (Intons-Peterson, 1988:48). Since this is also a core component of symbolic interaction theory, it provides a basis for additional interdisciplinary work on the socialization process. Bem's (1993) idea of gender lenses is another interdisciplinary path which offers connections to macrolevel sociology. Functionalism would be interested in the identification of core cultural and subcultural gender lenses in terms of implications for social order and social change. Monitoring gender schema change over time provides insights as to their functional and dysfunctional consequences for society as a whole. More data are needed before these models can be rigorously evaluated.

In general, all of these theories offer productive avenues for explanations of gender role socialization. At this point a truly integrative theory which incorporates the basic elements of each model has yet to be delineated. Basow (1992) declares that

> such a coordinated explanation would include an active role for children in developing concepts of masculinity and femininity and in organizing their world consistent with their level of cognitive development. In this process, differential treatment by primary socializing agents and observation of different models all add to the information the child gathers about appropriate gender behaviors.

At a minimum, the models reviewed here will allow us to assess some of the research on gender role socialization. We now turn to those "primary socializing agents" which have a critical impact on our gender roles.

AGENTS OF SOCIALIZATION

Since socialization is a continuing process carried through to old age, there are many points in life where it occurs. The agents of socialization are numerous and include a wide variety of informal and formal situations and institutions. Gender role socialization is a component in each of these. The focus here will be on those agents that carry the most influence in determining our gender roles, especially as related to primary socialization.

The Family

The family is by far the most significant agent of socialization. Even when social change increases opportunities for socialization in other institutions, the family maintains the major responsibility for socializing the child during those critical first years of life. Here the child gains a sense of self, learns language, and begins to understand norms of interaction with parents, siblings, and significant others in her or his life. Clearly gender role socialization is pervasive.

The strength of gender role expectations is suggested in an important early study by Rubin and his colleagues (1974) which finds that sex-typing of infants by parents begins on the day of the child's birth. Though both parents are likely to describe sons as strong, firm, and alert, and daughters as delicate, soft, and awkward, fathers are more stereotyped in their assessments. These findings are especially revealing in light of the fact that the infants did not differ in any health-related aspects, such as weight or length. With gender role stereotyping evident on day one of life, it is easier to explain why parents hold such different expectations for their sons and daughters. Research continues to document that parents differentiate between daughters and sons on a number of dimensions. Data from parents (as well as other adults) demonstrate that they engage in more physical, rougher play with their infant and toddler sons (MacDonald and Parke, 1986; Ross and Taylor, 1989), describe male babies as big and tough and female babies as cheerful and gentle (Stern and Karraker, 1989), believe that girls require more help than boys (Snow et al., 1983), and encourage closer physical proximity with toddler daughters (Bronstein, 1988). It is important to note, too, that fathers are significantly more likely than mothers to differentiate between their sons and daughters and to encourage more traditional, gender-specific behavior in their sons (Roopnarine, 1986; Fagot and Leinbach, 1995; Hardesty et al., 1995).

Studies overall support Block's (1984) belief that boys develop "wings" which permit them to explore realms outside the home while girls develop "roots" which tend to anchor them. Girls are encouraged in activities which keep them closer to their homes and families while boys are provided more opportunities for play and other activities away from home and independent of adult supervision, a finding which holds in both Western and non-Western cultures (Erwin, 1993). Consistent with cognitive development theory, Josephs and colleagues (1992) argue that the sources of self-esteem differ by gender. The socialization process encourages gender appropriate norms dictating separation and independence for males and connection and interdependence for females with self-esteem measured accordingly. While Dick is allowed to cross the street, use scissors, or go to a friend's house by himself, Jane must wait until she is older.

If parents are defining their newborns within 24 hours of birth, it could be hypothesized that knowledge of the sex of the fetus could also prompt gender-typed responses. Through medical advances such as ultrasound and amniocentesis, the sex of the fetus can be known months before birth. Would a woman carrying a male fetus behave differently than if she were carrying a female? If newborn males are described as hardy and strong, would the mother herself be more active or less cautious in her daily activities prior to the birth of her son? Would she exhibit more protective behavior if she believes that the daughter she will deliver is fragile and delicate? Such questions remain unanswered and focus on the mother's behavior. A recent study looks at how fetal ultrasound has increased the involvement of the expectant father in pregnancy. Sandelowski (1994:232) contends that this procedure has allowed men access to a "female world from which they have been excluded by virtue of their limited biological role in reproduction." It serves as a technological means that has made the mother's and father's relationship to the fetus as more equal. Will more "equal access" to the fetus, especially by fathers, impact parenting roles? Would it serve to lessen or heighten traditional gender role socialization? Again, the implications for socialization need to be explored.

Do You Want a Boy or a Girl?   We do know that preferences for one gender over the other are strong. Parents indicate that their first concern is for having a healthy baby. Beyond this, most couples prefer male over female children, especially if it is a first or only child, a finding that remains true from American studies conducted since the 1930s and from available evidence throughout much of the world (Williamson, 1976; Fidell et al., 1979; Gilroy and Steinbacher, 1983; Moen, 1991; Beal, 1994). In examining data from 1985 and 1988 on college students who were asked the question "If you could have only one child, which one would you prefer?" Pooler (1991) finds one important exception. While 80 percent of male students in both survey years prefer a male child, showing an even stronger preference than in earlier studies, a majority of female students (54 percent in 1985 and 58 percent in 1988) prefer a female child. Pooler argues that it is the difference in role expectations men and women have for wives and mothers which explains this change. While college women believe women can maintain some independence so as not to be completely defined by their roles as wife and mother, college men are in much less agreement. These women are aware of the potential conflict in retaining a sense of self while shouldering most parenting responsibilities.

Given this scenario, a daughter may have a closer relationship with the mother, be more nurturant, and be viewed as easier to raise than a boy (Pooler, 1991). The irony here is that while women strive to maintain a sense of independence, they may inadvertently foster gender-typing of their children.

Global Focus: Preference for Sons in Asia Favoritism is strongest where gender stratification is a dominant feature, such as in traditional or less technologically developed cultures, and where it is bolstered by religious beliefs, inheritance norms, and naming customs. A family name may be "lost" if there is no son to carry it on. Centuries of tradition in Chinese cultures continue today, especially in rural areas, where women remain essentially nameless. Watson's (1993) ethnographic research carried out in the Hong Kong New Territories demonstrates the significance of such customs. Patriarchal values which trace the family name only through male lines combine with marriage customs which require women to move into the household of their husbands. Inheritance laws keep women economically dependent on their new families. Confucian ideals which give complete authority to the males, especially the oldest males, bolster these patterns. Village land is owned by the (male) lineage and private, male landlords (Watson, 1985). Women are always outsiders and will remain so. The naming ceremony at the birth of a boy usually involves a banquet and festivities as elaborate as the family can afford. Unlike boys, a girl's naming meets with little celebration, especially since she loses it at marriage. She is never identified as an individual, but only in kin or category terms, such as "old woman." According to Watson (1993:121), all males worry about the quality of their names and those of their sons, but women are excluded from this discourse "because in adulthood they are not named, nor do they name others." Daughters are temporary commodities. Chinese proverbs such as "Raising a daughter is like weeding another man's garden" and "The best daughter isn't worth as much as a splayfooted son" continue to be quoted and attest to the strength of preference for sons (Carmody, 1989:97).

Son preference pervades many Asian cultures, including Taiwan, Hong Kong, Korea, (Mainland) China, India, Pakistan, and Bangladesh. It persists in rural and urban areas and among Muslims, Hindus, Buddhists, Confucians, and those who practice more noninstitutionalized forms of spirituality. The consequences of son preference are profound. Research has documented a major shift in the sex ratio which increasingly favors males. From 1981–1989 it rose from 107.8 to 113.8 in China and from 1980–1992, it rose from 103.9 to 114 (Park and Cho, 1995). Return to the discussion in Chapter 2 about the biological protection of the XX chromosome and the overall life expectancy rates which should naturally favor females. It is clear from research that the high sex ratio, particularly of firstborn children, is due to factors related to son preference. These include underreporting of female births, female infanticide, neglect of female infants and girls, and abortion of female fetuses (Miller, 1981; Johansson and Nygren, 1991; Zeng et al., 1993; Lloyd, 1994; Park and Cho, 1995). Sex-choice technology followed by abortion appears to be the preferred method to ensure the outcome.

In India, female infanticide and neglect are tied to the economic survival of the family which is dependent on the number of sons and the control of the number of daughters, who are regarded as financial liabilities (Miller, 1993). As in China, when a woman (or girl) marries, she moves to the village of her husband and into his household. She is expected to bring money and goods in the form of a dowry to help offset the expenses associated with her upkeep. When dowries are considered too paltry by the groom's family or the groom himself, the torture and death of the bride can occur. After a long dormant period, dowry abuse is increasing among all castes in India (Black, 1991; Teays, 1991). In most cases the women are doused with kerosene and set on fire, in what is supposed to look like a cooking accident (CBS, 1993). These are only the reported cases. Unreported dowry deaths are included in figures indicating that over 22 million women are simply "missing" (Breakaway, 1995). CBS reports that this figure includes cases of abuse, neglect, abortion, and infanticide and is especially true in north and east India. Recent surveys indicate that the risk of dying between the ages of 1 and 5 is 43 percent higher for girls than for boys (U.S. Agency for International Development, 1994). India represents one of the largest sex-based mortality differences in the world.

In addition to the human rights issues involved, the changing sex ratio has social and economic implications. Korea is predicting a serious shortage of brides, a fact which may be ultimately beneficial in raising the status of women. Offsetting this, however, is that large families, which have fewer resources overall, consist mainly of girls, while small families consist mainly of boys. Daughters, who are already discriminated against for traditional reasons, will be in a worse position than sons (Blake, 1989; Park and Cho, 1995). Economic issues are also involved. Preference for males is mitigated in areas where females are used extensively in agricultural labor, especially subsistence farming (Charlton, 1984; Kishor, 1993). This is a factor in explaining a more equitable sex ratio in parts of south India.

In the struggle to curb a burgeoning population, couples in Mainland China are now restricted to having only one child, risking severe penalties if they do not comply. Given the heritage of patriarchy in China and regardless of governmental efforts to the contrary, reports of female infanticide are widespread. Again, programs which monitor population trends continue to report that selective abortion of almost exclusively female fetuses is common in Asia, particularly in China (Charlton, 1984; *Asia-Pacific Population and Policy,* 1995a). The consequences of the one-child policy will be discussed in detail in Chapter 5, but suffice it to say here, it has reinforced the preference for sons. Despite egalitarian ideology, the improvements in health care, and the recent outlawing of sex screening of fetuses, the preference for sons in China, indeed in much of Asia, has dire consequences for the well-being of daughters.

Gendered Childhood: Toys, Clothes, and Games   Socialization, now perhaps initiated before birth, continues once the proud parents leave the hospital with their daughter or son. In most societies, the first artifacts acquired by the infant are toys and clothes. In anticipating the arrival of the newborn, friends and relatives choose gifts which are neutral to avoid embarrassing themselves or the expectant parents by colors or toys which suggest the "wrong" gender. Teddy bears and clothing in colors other than pink or blue are safe selections in this regard. Parents may have originally decorated the child's room to accommodate either gender. But within weeks after the arrival of the infant, such rooms are transformed and easily recognizable as belonging to a boy or a girl.

Color-coded and gender-typed clothing of infants and children is almost universal. A study by Shakin and colleagues (1985) finds that over 90 percent of infants observed in a shopping mall could be readily categorized by sex according to the characteristics of their clothing. Pink and yellow on girls were contrasted sharply by blue and red on boys. While jeans and slacks for school and casual wear are now more common than dresses, girls' clothing is likely to be in pastels with embroidered hearts and flowers as adornments. Since slacks for girls often do not have pockets, the purse becomes a necessity. Boys in sweatshirts have superhero and athletic motifs while girls wear those depicting female television characters or nature scenes. It is interesting that pictures of outstanding male athletes are typically represented in nonathletic clothing for boys, and sometimes for girls, but it is rare to find female athletes so depicted. Gender-oriented clothing provides the initial labels to ensure that children are responded to "appropriately."

Along with clothing, toys carry a formidable force for socialization. A clothing-toy link is especially true for girls who buy "fashions" for their dolls. Considering that over 250 million Barbie™ dolls have been sold in the last 25 years and that over 20 million outfits are bought for these dolls every year, the seeds for a clothing addiction in girls are sown early (Freedman, 1995). Toys for girls encourage domesticity, interpersonal closeness, and a social orientation while boys receive not only more categories of toys but ones which are more complex, more expensive, and foster self-reliance and problem solving (Rheingold and Cook, 1975; Hughes, 1994; Leaper, 1994). Studies continue to document not only the persistence and preferences children and parents have for gender-typed toys but also the differential messages that are sent to children who play with the toys (Peretti and Sydney, 1985; Stoneman et al., 1986; Miller, 1987; Caldera et al., 1989; Etaugh and Liss, 1992). Children's advertisements in catalogues and on television reinforce gender typing in toys. On your next outing to any store which sells toys, note how aisles and shelves are stocked and categorized according to gender and how the pictures on the boxes suggest how girls and boys are using the toys in question. Little Jane uses her tea set to have a party for her dolls, most likely in her room, while same-age Dick is experimenting with baseball or racing trucks outside in the mud. Certainly these kinds of toys encourage higher levels of physical activity in boys. Parental expectations are tied to the kinds of toys they provide to their children.

Yet it might be argued that while boys are more vibrant physically, girls are more imaginative in their play. At an early age both Jane and Dick are given toys which require less imagination to use. But as they get older they acquire toys which encourage more imagination, pretense, and role taking. By age two, there is a decrease in pretense of boys while girls' pretense increases. Pretend play is developed early in girls so that by the age of 18 months, they are actually staging their manner of play, while boys are not (Sutton-Smith, 1979). In examining these findings, Sutton-Smith (1979) is not as optimistic about the implications. Though girls are more imaginative than boys in the play of early childhood, after age seven the reverse holds true. Girls stage one type of activity, having to do with dolls and playing house, thereby assuming a caretaking, domestic role. Toys given to girls bolster this pattern. If boys are restricted in any way, it is in the lack of encouragement in staging activities suggestive of later domestic roles. Girls script their play around role taking in realistic settings, such as playing house. Boys script their play around more fantastic scenarios, such as superheroes (Leaper, 1994).

Research on the physical environments of infants and young children confirms that gender typing remains dominant in early childhood (Pomerleau et al., 1990). Boys receive more sports equipment, tools, and vehicles; girls receive dolls, fictional characters, and child's furniture. Girls have pink and multicolored clothes and pink pacifiers; boys have red, white, and blue clothing and blue pacifiers. As the authors state, "parents and other adults still encourage sex-typed play by selecting different toys for female and male children, even before the child can express her or his own preferences" (Pomerleau et al., 1990:365).

Gendered Parenting Styles Toy selection represents one of many instances of gender role socialization in early childhood. Suggestive of social learning theory, even infants receive reinforcement for behavior which is gender appropriate, and children as young as age two have already developed a strong sense of gender roles. Based on these early experiences, older children expect their parents to respond to them differentially (Culp et al., 1983). In an analysis using stories depicting children experiencing interpersonal conflict, 8- to 12- year-olds expect parents to respond according to traditional instrumental-expressive gender role stereotypes (Dino et al., 1984:709). This study would be consistent with cognitive development theory by indicating that the development of gender role identity is linked to children's perception of adult behavior. The cycle repeats as parents respond to their children based on their stereotyped beliefs about which gender is naturally suited to certain domains. Research by Eccles and her colleagues (1990:197) definitely indicates that parents perceive the competencies of their children in such areas as math, English, and sports in terms of their children's gender and that these influences are independent of any real differences in the children's competencies. Beginning in early childhood, later socialization experiences in school impact the occupational activities males and females pursue.

Regardless of the awareness of parents, there are clear differences between men and women in role expectations concerning child rearing. Children of all ages are more frequently seen with women than men (Hoffman and Teyber, 1985). Mothers assume caretaking roles, talk to their children, and stay closer to them than fathers (Fagot, 1984). This research also demonstrates that children younger than age four do not elicit different types of play behavior from male and female adults and that both parents are responsive to their infants. When gender of parent is a predictor of how they behave toward their children, as would be expected, fathers are much more involved with their sons and tend to concentrate on instrumental support and activities. Mothers tend to be more supportive in the traditional, affective sense, regardless of their children's gender, demonstrating a pattern of gender intensification that increases with age (Starreis, 1994; Crouter et al., 1995).

The primary socialization experiences in the family provide the basis for gender role identity in later life. According to symbolic interactionists, even with the shift in gender role patterns we are now witnessing, our responses will be based on these early family influences. This does not mean that the gender role change will cease, but that its degree of acceptance will be assessed by how we were first socialized. In reviewing the research, Weitzman (1979:3-4) states:

> Sex role socialization begins before the child is even aware of a sexual identity: before he or she can have an internal motive for conforming to sex role standards. It also indicates that cultural assumptions about what is "natural" for a boy

or for a girl are so deeply ingrained that parents may treat their children differentially without even being aware of it.

Peers and Preferences

As children get older, they are gradually introduced to the world outside of the family. We have seen that patterns established in the family are already gender role oriented, with children soon realizing that the same holds true for what awaits them with their peers. Parents initiate the first relationships for their children, with these often developing into later friendships chosen by the children themselves. Two- and three- year-olds delight in playing with their same-age companions, and parents are not compelled to separate them by gender at this early age. As school age approaches, however, this situation radically changes.

Activities, games, and play are strongly related to gender roles and become important aspects of socialization. These are definitely seen when a brother and sister play together. When Jane pressures Dick into playing house, she is inevitably the mommy and he is the daddy. Or she can convince him to be the pupil while she takes the role of teacher and relishes the prospect of scolding him for his disruptive classroom behavior. On the other hand, if brother Dick coerces Jane into a game of catch, he bemoans her awkwardness and ridicules her lack of skill. What would social learning theory say about the likelihood of Jane's gaining expertise in catch? Games such as these are usually short-lived, dissolve into conflict, and are dependent upon the availability of same-gender peers with whom siblings would rather play.

Peer play activities socialize children in other ways as well. The games of boys are more complex, competitive, rule-governed, and allow for more role differentiation and a larger number of participants than games played by girls (Lever, 1978; Corsaro and Eder, 1990; Ignico and Mead, 1990). Girls play ordered games, like hopscotch or jump rope, in groups of two or three, with a minimum of competitiveness. The stereotype that generally associates competitive behavior with masculinity but not with femininity is consistently supported by research (King et al., 1991). In an indictment of this, Harragan (1977:49-50) almost bitterly concludes that

> girls' games teach meaningless mumbo-jumbo—vague generalities or pre-game mutual agreements about "what we'll play"—while falsely implying that these blurry self-guides are typical of real world rules.

Beginning in the family with siblings, and then in other peer groups, games reserved for Dick *or* Jane continue into the school environment. We will view the consequences of this later.

Both cognitive development and social learning theory emphasize the importance of peer interaction in the socialization process. Gender segregation and the influence of peer groups increase throughout the school years, exerting powerful influences on children. As would be suggested by the research on games, boys interact in larger groups and have more extensive peer relationships, with girls having more intensive ones (Corsaro and Eder, 1990; Moore and Boldero, 1991; O'Connor, 1992). Peer intimacy should thus be easier for girls. This is consistent with much research demonstrating that self-disclosure, intimacy, and trust are higher for women, especially between female best-friend pairs (Buhrke and Fuqua, 1987; Dolgin et al., 1991; Johnson, 1996). Rotenberg (1984:956) hypothesizes that after children gain a pattern of same-sex relationships, these relationships are reinforced through a same-sex pattern of trust. A lesser degree of trust could then inhibit later cross-sex friendships. Gender boundaries are monitored and enforced by peers (Maccoby, 1994). The worlds of male and female are further divided.

Socialization into gender identity is nurtured through peers, with gender-appropriate behaviors reinforced in a similar manner. When children interact, reinforcement for same-gender peers occurs more frequently than with other-gender peers. Boys in particular are tenacious in their gender role attitudes and exhibit strong masculine preferences through preadolescence (Brinn et al., 1984). These preferences result in the increase of gender segregation throughout childhood. A major consequence of this is that "boys and girls will meet in adolescence virtually as strangers, having learned different styles of interaction" (Fagot, 1994:62). Adulthood may soften the stereotypes, but the preferences persist. Consistent with symbolic interactionist thinking, early peer and family influences can counter later attempts at resocialization.

Television

Television is a powerful source of socialization, especially in the child's early years. This observation is empirically justified considering that a child may spend up to one-third of the day watching TV. It sets standards of behavior, provides role models, and communicates expectations in a host of areas, particularly regarding the family. When television images are reinforced by the other mass media, like movies, magazines, and popular songs, the impact on socialization is substantial. Chapter 14 will document how the mass media view the genders, but here we will offer an overview of the influence of television programming directed at children.

Television teaches. Studies of children as young as two years of age copy what they see on TV, with imitation increasing through the elementary school years (Comstock and Paik, 1991; Wood et al., 1991). Television encourages modeling. Children identify with same-gender characters. Boys identify with characters possessing physical strength and girls with those who are physically attractive (Reeves and Miller, 1978; Evans, 1993). Television is gender stereotyped. Gender role portrayals in shows which are deemed acceptable for children emphasize stereotyped female roles. In cartoons, men and male characters outnumber women and female characters almost five to one (Signorielli, 1991). Cartoons influence girls in their beliefs about female roles. Pollitt (1991:22) finds that cartoons are either all-male or have a lone female in a "little sister" relationship. Boys determine the storyline and the code of values for the group. Girls are only defined in relation to the boys. Television influences self-image. Implicit in Saturday morning TV is the idea that boys are more significant persons than girls, if only by the sheer number of male characters compared to female. This is bolstered by television's consistent and stubborn portrayal of female characters existing only as appendages to males.

The research is conclusive that children's television is sexist as well as gender stereotyped. Contrary to reality, children are presented with severely limited portrayals of women and men. In a major study of commercial children's TV programs, Barcus (1983) distinguishes several patterns. Children see more males in significant roles. Females constitute only 22 percent of all characters and are likely to be found in minor roles with little responsibility for characters and are likely to be found in minor roles with little responsibility for the outcome of the story (Barcus, 1983:39). Few characters who work outside the home are female, and these are in clerical or student positions. Men, on the other hand, are in a variety of occupations, notably professional ones, such as attorney, physician, and scientist. As we approach the turn of the century, despite massive real-world changes in gender roles, the world of television persists in these stereotyped and sexist images (Hansen and Hansen, 1988; Alcock and Robson, 1990; Gerbner, 1993b; Kahan and Norris, 1994). Biological attributes and physical characteristics are continually emphasized as justification for television's portrayal of male and female roles.

Television themes can also be differentiated according to how the genders are portrayed. In prime-time television men are often portrayed as tough, aggressive, and competitive and women as interpersonally sensitive. Women who work outside the home are far less likely than men to be depicted in roles requiring decision making or corporate and political leadership (VandeBerg and Streckfuss, 1992). Females pursue goals related to altruism, home, and family. Self-preservation is an important female goal, too, because female characters are likely to be the targets of threats and violence. Male goals are headed by self-indulgence, wealth, revenge, and expressions of hatred (Barcus, 1983:49-50). Interestingly, women are more likely to achieve their goals when compared to men. This is not an inconsistent finding if we realize that the goals of women are traditional and socially acceptable. The outcome is not as optimistic for those television women who step into a "man's world."

Children's television is supported by commercials aimed at products for children, mainly toys and sugared cereal. Before television transformed the family, advertising for children's items was aimed primarily at adults. The child consumer audience characterizes the contemporary toy industry (Jackson, 1994a). Today children are more likely than adults to actually watch the commercials (Schneider, 1989). Advertisers orient children to the idea that products are waiting to be bought at local stores and that to do without them is an unfortunate hardship. Commercials are blatant in creating desires for toys encouraging domesticity in girls and high activity in boys.

Parents who resist pressure from their children to buy these products or find that the products children want are unavailable are made to feel guilty, by advertisers and children alike. Remember the frantic search several years in a row for Cabbage Patch™ dolls and Power Rangers™ by parents who feared a disappointed child during holidays or on his or her birthday? Picture, too, the angry exchanges we have encountered between parent and child in front of the toy, candy, or cereal displays. Parents searching for nonstereotyped toy alternatives may feel demoralized when the offer of a tea set to their son or a truck to their daughter is met with resistance. Tantalized by television, what the child desires is within reach. For toys, the desire is likely to be gender role-oriented. The parent stands in between. Who is likely to give up the fight first?

School

Family life paves the way for the next major agent of continuing socialization, the educational institution. The intimacy and spontaneity of the family are replaced by an environment valuing impersonal evaluation and rewards based on competition and scholastic success. For the next 12 to 20 years school will play a critical role in the lives of most people. We will view this institution's impact on the genders fully in Chapter 12. Note here, however, that regardless of intent, schools are not immune to gender role stereotyping and actually serve to foster it.

Teachers who honestly believe they are treating boys and girls similarly are unaware that they are perpetuating sexist notions. When Jane is ignored or not reprimanded for disruptive behavior, is encouraged in her verbal but not mathematical abilities, or is given textbooks which show her that women are housewives at best, or literally invisible at worst, gender role stereotyping continues. Dick discovers his rowdiness will gain attention from his female elementary school teacher, that he can aspire to any occupation except nurse or secretary, and that he is rewarded for his athletic skills during competitive games at recess. Unlike Jane who may begrudgingly be admired by engaging in "tomboy" behavior, Dick is loathe to even investigate school-related activities deemed typical for girls lest he be called a "sissy." A decade of research on students of all grade levels conducted by Sadker and Sadker (1994) brings this point home. Their study asked: What would it be like to become a member of the "opposite sex"? Both boys and girls prefer their own gender, but girls find the prospect intriguing, interesting, and were willing to try it out for a while. As girls write: "I will be able to be almost anything I want" or "I will make more money now that I am a boy." Boys, on the other hand, find it appalling, disgusting, and humiliating. Comments from two sixth-grade boys suggest the intensity of these feelings: "My teachers would treat me like a little hairy pig-headed girl," and at the extreme: "If I were turned into a girl today I would kill myself" (Sadker and Sadker, 1994:83).

Educational institutions are given the responsibility for ensuring that children are trained in the ways of society so that they can eventually assume the positions necessary for the maintenance of society. Schools provide experiences which offer technical competence as well as the learning of values and norms appropriate to the culture. American culture believes that competition, initiative, independence, and individualism are values to be sought, and schools are expected to advocate these values. We have already seen how these values are associated more with masculinity than femininity. From a functionalist viewpoint, schools are critical ways of bringing a diverse society together through the acceptance of a common value system.

Unfortunately, many schools unwittingly socialize children into acquiring one set of values, to the virtual exclusion of the other. Stereotypical thinking assumes that in filling breadwinning roles, boys will need to be taught the value of competitiveness; in filling domestic roles, girls will need to be taught the value of nurturance. Though both may be positive traits, they are limited to, or truly accepted by, only one gender. As schools begin the task of first discovering and then working to eliminate sexist practices, differential gender role socialization can be effectively altered.

ANDROGYNY IN SOCIALIZATION

We have seen that socialization is neither consistent nor uniform. Though its agents are diverse, patterns of gender roles still emerge. Children are taught that girls and boys should exhibit behavior that is either feminine or masculine. But major contradictions arise in this process. Girls climb trees, excel in mathematics, and aspire to become professors. These same girls are concerned about physical attractiveness, career achievement, finding the right husband, and raising a family. Boys enjoy cooking, like to play with children, and are not ashamed to demonstrate their emotions. These same boys are concerned about physical attractiveness, career achievement, finding the right wife, and raising a family. Yet they have all been socialized by similar routes.

It is apparent that our views of masculinity and femininity need to shift in the direction of reality. These terms are not the opposite of one another. Consider the concept of androgyny, as discussed in Chapter 1. In an early view of the concept, Bem (1974) argues that many people exhibit androgyny, which combines or reconciles traits considered to be feminine or masculine. She has designed an attitude scale, the Bem Sex Role Inventory, which demonstrates that both men and women can score high or low on either set of traits or have a combination of them. Work with the inventory is revealing that large numbers of androgynous people do indeed exist. Biological sex is not an issue here. People know and accept their maleness or femaleness, but gender role flexibility is much more evident. As the situation demands, behavior can be adapted. By not being confined to rigid gender roles based on presumptuous notions of masculinity and femininity, people can respond according to their desires and abilities. Androgyny would certainly encourage this. Block (1984:159) contends that parents who manifest androgynous identification tend to be less stereotyped in notions of masculinity and femininity and offer a wider range of behavioral and attitudinal possibilities to their children.

However, as mentioned earlier, the concept of androgyny has been criticized. It suggests that people can be defined according to a range of gendered behavior and then classified accordingly. This in itself may be indicative of stereotypical thinking. In a revision of her earlier view, Bem (1985:222) now argues that "society should stop projecting gender into situations irrelevant to genitalia." But she also recognizes that cultures will continue to define what is masculine and feminine. Men and women may be culturally defined as androgynous because they are nurturing, sensitive, and cooperative as well as assertive, ambitious, and competitive (Bem, 1993). A gender-neutral model for socialization that is oriented toward a range of positive traits for both females and males has yet to be developed. Until then, an androgynous model provides at least an alternative that allows acceptance of gender "inappropriate" behaviors.

The research literature also suggests that efforts aimed at counter-stereotyping are particularly successful when modeling techniques are employed, especially with children ages four to ten (Katz, 1986). As would be expected, intervention strategies are more effective with girls. A related study finds that when children observe gender atraditional behavior and then also observe positive consequences of the behavior, they were more likely to imitate it, implying that stereotyped behavior can be altered (Katz and Walsh, 1991). What is perhaps more revealing in this study is that the most atraditional behavior from children was elicited from male examiners. It can be argued that as men in particular move toward greater androgyny, they can exert a major influence on the socialization process.

Androgyny recognizes that socialization into two nonoverlapping gender roles is not a productive way of encouraging behavior that must be readily adapted to a changing society. Society as well as the individual is demanding more. Agents of socialization must be altered to meet this demand. Consider this dictum as we now discuss the role of language as another powerful socialization agent.

CHAPTER 4

LANGUAGE AND SOCIALIZATION

> . . . to boldly go where no *man* has gone before.
> —Capt. James Kirk, *Star Trek*

> . . . to boldly go where no *one* has gone before.
> —Capt. Jean-Luc Picard, *Star Trek, The Next Generation*

> I don't like being called "sir". . . I prefer "Captain."
> —Capt. Kathryn Janeway, *Star Trek, Voyager*

Language exerts a commanding force in socialization. Primary socialization literally bombards children with mountains of information and learning they must effectively assimilate. This process includes mastering the rules and complexities of the society's language, both its verbal and nonverbal components. Language reflects culture and is shaped by it; therefore, it is fundamental to our understanding of gender roles. Once we learn language, we have a great deal of knowledge about how the culture defines the two genders. The problem is that this knowledge must be discovered because language itself is taken for granted. As we shall see, it is for this reason that language is such a powerful element in determining our gender roles. For speakers of English, unless specifically designated, everyone begins as a man. As suggested by two decades of research on American English usage, all people are male until proven female.

THE GENERIC MYTH

We begin with the idea that the English language constantly focuses attention on gender. Nowhere is this more evident than when the word *man* is used to exclude woman and then used generically to include her. This is demonstrated when anthropologists speak of culture as manmade or the evolution of mankind. Other examples may be less clear, such as referring to a voter as the typical "man on the street" or finding "the right man for the job." Are women included as voters or workers? But more often the word is used to distinguish man from woman, such as in the phrases "it's a man's world" and "this is man's work." The word is definitely ambiguous and may be subject to interpretation even within one context. In each instance of usage, it is unclear where women belong, but it implies that they are somehow "part" of man. Sometimes no interpretation is necessary. At a wedding ceremony when a couple is pronounced "man and wife," she becomes defined as his. In learning language, children are also taught that the genders are valued differently. Not only is language use ambiguous, it is discriminatory as well. As quoted by Miller and Swift (1991b:257), George Orwell might have put it this way, "all men are equal but men are more equal than women."

It is awkward to change language to make it more precise. If "man" is supposed to refer to "woman," then "he" is also supposed to mean "she." Because English does not have a neutral singular pronoun, *he* is seen as the generic norm, with *she* as the exception. A doctor is *he* and a nurse is *she*. More neutral designations are also "he" words. A consumer, writer, patient, or parent is seen as he. In reality, many, if not most, of these people are women. But women are linguistically excluded. Now we see that language is ambiguous, discriminatory, *and* inaccurate. Thus the generic use of *he* is presumed to include all the *shes* it linguistically encompasses. It is quite clear from research, however, that this is not the case.

A study by Switzer (1990) finds that adults are likely to develop masculine imagery for neutral words, with men doing so more than women. This is consistent with gender schema theory in which gender-related information is more easily incorporated into in-group (own-sex) schema. Through early adolescence children parallel adults in their response to generics. While generics are *intended* to be neutral, both girls and boys report primarily male, sex-specific imagery when hearing generic terms. An example is provided by Richardson (1996:421) of an eight-year-old girl who interrupts her reading of "The Story of the Caveman" to ask how we got here without cavewomen. This is consistent with research suggesting that the inclusive humanity which we supposedly find in the generic use of *man, men,* and *he* is illusory. When such words are used, people visualize male and interpret the reference as male rather than male *and* female (Martyna, 1983; Hamilton, 1988; Harrigan and Lucic, 1988; Khosroshahi, 1989; Miller, 1994). Male imagery is promoted at the expense of female imagery. The power of generics in imagery is also reflected in research showing that when women are exposed to feminine generics, they report feelings of pride, freedom, importance, superiority, and power (Adamsky, 1981). The effects of *he/man* language have considerable significance in the process of socialization.

This also means that since the use of male generics gives more prominence and visibility to men, language contributes to a woman's invisibility. In Spender's (1993:409) view, it is a step in ensuring that in thought and reality "it is the males who become the foreground while females become the blurred and often indecipherable background." From a conflict theory perspective, the structure and vocabulary of English have been fashioned by men and they retain the power to name and to leave unnamed. When an encyclopedia states that "man is the highest form of life on earth" and that "his superior intelligence has enabled man to achieve things impossible for other animals, the response of a young boy is likely to be 'wow!' while the response of a girl to the same information is 'who?', does that mean me, too?" (Miller and Swift, 1993:73). While some still insist that the word "man" is a clear, concise, and universal reference to mean "person," the mass of evidence is squarely against this view (Miller and Swift, 1993:74). Considering that in a lifetime the average American speaker and listener of English will be subject to over one million usages of just the *he* prescriptive (MacKay, 1983), the implications for equity issues are profound.

To avoid sexism, many writers use he/she, she or he, s/he, or they to convey the fact that both genders are being discussed. This is cumbersome but one way around the problem. Another suggestion had been to adopt a "true" generic pronoun that is gender neutral. Data from a study by Harrigan and Lucic (1988) show that many people are aware of the gender bias in language and state that they would try to incorporate a new or invented gender-indefinite pronoun or even create new terms altogether. For instance, some colleges are experimenting with different words to replace the "freshman" term for entering students. The term has been called archaic and an artifact of a bygone era that is inconsistent with curricula that examine race, class, and gender issues. The designation "first-year student" was introduced on many campuses in the 1980s and has gained a great deal of informal acceptance. Colison (1993:442) cites students and administrators who say its use is enforced by general sentiment. Calling someone a "freshman" is like calling a woman a "girl."

When attempts to introduce language change are met with resistance, the change is often seen as artificially imposed rather than naturally evolving. An example from linguistic history may counter this argument. The use of "he" as the "correct" pronoun for referring to a single human being of indeterminate sex came into usage during the eighteenth century. Formerly, "they" *or* "he" *or* "she" were considered the proper choices. Several powerful grammarians of the period were disdainful that "they" was a plural word used to describe a single entity and so prescribed "he" as a legitimate substitute (Adams and Ware, 1995:334, n. 15). In 1850 the British Parliament passed a law declaring that "in all acts words importing the masculine gender shall be deemed and taken to include females" (Miller, 1994:268). In both instances language change occurred by fiat, not through "natural" evolution. Its acceptance rested on cultural definitions which gave males more worth than females. In order to make language more gender-neutral today, that worth is being questioned. The term "politically correct" is used to convey such a viewpoint. It sarcastically implies that people are now required to change acceptable terminology on frivolous, inconsequential, and unreasonable grounds.

While the singular versus plural issue may have been historically resolved, we now have a term that is presumed to be both generic (he = he and she) and nongeneric (he = he). Although the earlier usage may not have been awkward to use and not as grammatically sound, it was certainly more accurate. Not only did language change "artificially," it also created a great deal of interpretive problems.

Titles and Occupations

Linguistic sexism abounds in how titles and occupations are designated. We write Dear Sir or Dear Mr. Jones even if we are unsure of the gender of the addressee, especially if it is a business letter. After all, business*men* are seen as the likely occupants of these positions. The same can be said for chair*men*, fore*men*, congress*men*, news*men*, and garbage*men*. Physicians, attorneys, and astronauts are men. Nurses, teachers, and secretaries are women. If either gender deviates occupationally and enters a nontraditional field, we add linguistic markers to designate this remarkable fact. The media, too, are grappling with these issues and remain extraordinarily inconsistent in use of generics. In a cursory reading of only two sections of a Sunday newspaper, actor Jamie Lee

Curtis is referred to as a pitch*man* for pantyhose and two pictures of different women who are heading charitable events appear on the same page and are referred to as chairman in one caption and chairwoman in the other. The simpler, nonsexist and preferred designation would be "chair" of the event (Dames, 1996; Levins, 1996). For children, meaning may be assigned to words quite differently than what the adult assumes the child understands. There is the example of the child who was disappointed that the "dog doctor" was not a dog at all (Miller and Swift, 1993:71). Children use linguistic markers frequently in referring to females in traditionally male roles or males in traditionally female roles. What emerges is the idea of a female doctor, lady spaceman, or male secretary.

When women enter predominantly male occupations, there is usually little attention given to how they are so named. A woman may become an engineer and be referred to as a female engineer lest people mistakenly think most engineers are women. The male occupation becomes linguistically protected by invasion from females. However, when males begin to enter predominantly female occupations in greater numbers, a language shift occurs rather quickly. While women are still the majority of elementary teachers, the fact that more men are in the field now makes the use of *she* as a label a subject of controversy. The point is that it is now incorrect and improper to refer to teachers as *she* when more than a token number of men enter the occupation (Miller and Swift, 1991a:37). The same can be said for stewardesses now being called flight attendants. Females will soon become a majority of pharmacists, but the generic *he* will certainly be retained in referring to them as a group.

Another linguistic marker involves adding appendages or suffixes to words to show where women "belong" occupationally. A poet becomes a poet-*ess* and an usher an usher*ette*. Again, women are defined as a kind of male appendage that are the exceptions to the male-as-norm rule— imitators not to be taken seriously. This is what acclaimed performer Whoopi Goldberg means when she states: "I am an actor and I do not mean actress. Actresses are sort of cute, you know? What I do is not cute" (Russo, 1986:9).

Titles assure that women remain a part of men. We address men as Mr. but have a major concern for the marital status of women. Miller and Swift (1991a:108) argue that this simple distinction historically served a double purpose for men. Information was conveyed regarding a woman's sexual availability and pressure was on the single woman to think about marriage since she was categorized with the young and inexperienced. Traditionally, Miss and Mrs. are considered the acceptable titles for women, who are defined according to their relationship with a man. Any time a woman fills out a form where she must check either "Miss" or "Mrs." she is conveying personal information not required of men.

To counter this titular sexism, Ms. has been offered as a substitute for a standard form of address for both married and unmarried women who want to be recognized as individuals or who believe that their marital status is private information that they may or may not choose to convey to others. Although it is becoming more acceptable in business and academia, language change does not come easily, and the use of Ms. has also been accompanied by ridicule and contempt as well as misuse. The tenacity of believing that women should be identified according to their relationship with men is demonstrated by those who use it to refer to divorced women in spite of its intended neutrality (Ehrlich and King, 1993). Editors bemoan its style, while ignoring its precision. It has only been in the last decade that *The New York Times* and the Associated Press style guides have finally agreed to use Ms. at the insistence of women who preferred the title (Stewart et al., 1990; Erlich and King, 1993). Miller and Swift (1991a) believe it is not a question of style but of politics. Patriarchy is assaulted and another double standard is questioned.

While Ms. is gaining acceptance and gets around the problem of marriage as a linguistic marker, its usage is still equivocal. Women may be perceived as dishonest if they are thought to be deliberately concealing something (Connor et al., 1986). On the other hand, women who use Ms. are also seen as having higher self-esteem, being more outspoken, intelligent, competitive, reliable, and successful, and having the overall qualities of a manager. Today there is more public acceptance of the title (Connor et al., 1986; Adams and Ware, 1995). When an opposition speaker of the New York Equal Rights Amendment (ERA) addressed Senator Karen Burstein, an ERA supporter, an agitated digression on whether to address her as Miss, Mrs., or Ms. ensued. Burstein quietly diverted the tumult by suggesting, "Perhaps it would be easier if you addressed me as Senator" (cited in Miller and Swift, 1991a:109).

What's In a Name?

A simple one-word answer to this question is "identity." While a name symbolically links us to our past and provides us a sense of self-definition, in most Western cultures a girl is socialized to accept the fact that her name can literally be abandoned. Upon marriage a woman can lose her complete name and be called someone different. Jane Smith becomes Mrs. Richard Jones. The new name and title will alter the earlier identity legally, socially, and even psychologically. Mrs. Jones is now linguistically encompassed by her husband. Even without legal sanction, the belief that women and children should take their husbands' and fathers' surnames is adhered to strongly (Intons-Peterson and Crawford, 1985).

The change in status from single person to wife or husband carries with it other linguistic conventions. Newspaper articles often identify women of accomplishment according to their husbands' names, such as Mrs. Richard Jones, rather than even Jane Jones. In dictionaries of famous people, women are typically listed with male names even if the males did not contribute to the reasons the women are in the dictionary at all. How many of us are aware that Mrs. George Palmer Putnam is Amelia Earhart, Charlotte Brontë is Mrs. Arthur B. Nicholls, and Harriet Beecher Stowe is the sister of Henry Ward Beecher? According to how Nilsen (1993:162) interprets her study, the editors felt it "was almost indecent to let a respectable woman's name march unaccompanied across the pages of a dictionary."

It is also permissible to append a name normally given to a boy to refer to a girl. Paul becomes Pauline, Christopher becomes Christine, and Gene or Jean becomes Jeanette. A boy's name will often be used to designate girls, especially in shortened form. Pat, Lee, Dale, Chris, and Kelly are examples. But when a boy's name is "taken over" by girls, it quickly falls into disfavor as a continuing name for boys. Shirley, Marion, and Beverly were originally boys' names which quickly lost their appeal once they were routinely given to girls (Nilsen, 1993).

Another linguistic dimension involves the ordering and placement of names and titles. Husband and wife, Mr. and Mrs., and Dr. and Mrs. give prominence to men. If she is a doctor and he is not, Dr. and Mr. would not be used, and if they are both doctors, Dr. and Dr. would not be a form of address. In 1553, a Mr. Wilson was evidently the first to insist that it is more "natural" to place the man before the woman and later grammarians took this precedence for granted. Men should take "pride of place" since the male gender is the "worthier" gender (Miller, 1994:268). An exception to this ordering rule is bride and groom, but considering that her wedding is viewed as the most important event in the life of a woman, this is understandable. Her wedding day, the bridal party, bridesmaids, mother and father of the bride, and giving the bride away indicate that the status of bride*groom* is really secondary in the whole affair.

LINGUISTIC DEROGATION

English is hostile to women. It denigrates, debases, and defines women in often derogatory sexual terms. Research indicates that there are several hundred sexually related terms for women and only a handful for men and that these terms are used almost exclusively by men (Bernard, 1981; Baker, 1993). While men might consider the use of such terms as standard and nonpejorative because of their insulting connotation and association with playthings and animals, women do not typically identify themselves with this language (Baker, 1993:67). Only a few of the numerous examples include broad, chick, doll, bitch, whore, babe, wench, fox, vixen, tramp, and slut. When men want to insult other men, they typically use many of these same terms. And consider the connotations of "mistress," and "madam" as opposed to the male counterparts of "master" and "lord." Females are sexual beings and males are superior beings. The word "girl" suggests both child and prostitute. It would be insulting for grown men to be called boys but we routinely refer to grown women as girls. College students take for granted the "guys-girls" distinction so that males do not have to be referred to as "boys." In this manner, linguistic practice routinely implies that females are immature, helpless, and incapable. Males are complete beings who readily take on adult qualities and females are sexual childlike objects who linguistically retain an immature status throughout their lives.

Over time English words for women acquire debased or obscene references. Henley (1989:60) points out that words such as lady, dame, madam, and mistress originally were neutral or positive designations for women. The masculine counterpart terms of lord, baronet, sir, and master escaped pejoration. The word pair *spinster/bachelor* suggests another instance. Which word would be selected to fill in the following blank?: "They were always careful to have at least one attractive _____ at their parties." Also, when a man chooses to remain unmarried, he is a "confirmed" bachelor. As Saprio (1994:289-90) indicates, both these examples show that positive terms for an adult, unmarried female are unavailable. Once a word becomes associated with women, semantic characteristics congruent with social stereotypes of women as a group also emerge (Smith, 1985:48). If women occupy a secondary position in society, stereotyped language continues to reinforce this placement.

Language trivializes women. The phrases "women's work," "women's place," and "wine, women, and song" suggest this. And when the word *lady* is substituted for *woman* in other contexts, an effective mechanism for implicit ridicule occurs. The nonseriousness of the "lady" designation is demonstrated by substituting it for "women" in the following organizations: National Organization for Women; Harvard Medical School Committee on the Status of Women, and Black Women's Community Development Foundation. Substitute it in the following titles: *The Subjugation of Women* by John S. Mill; *The Emancipation of Women* by V.I. Lenin, and *Vindication of the Rights of Women* by Mary Wollstonecraft (Bosmajian, 1995:390). A lady dentist or lady artist is the frivolous exception to the male-as-norm rule. If man and woman connote sexual and human maturity (Richardson, 1996:422), the term *lady* minimizes the "adultness" of females. A wife or child may be referred to as "the little lady" of the house. When the term *woman* is used in this context, an adjective often accompanies it, serving to bolster the childlike reference. Thus we have "the little woman." Given its insulting nature, it is not surprising that the male equivalent term is nonexistent. As we raise our linguistic consciousness, such references will likely be abandoned. Until then, women must continue to internalize a language that is belittling to them.

GENDERED LANGUAGE USAGE

We are socialized into the language of our culture. In addition, since women and men occupy different subcultures, and subcultures are also differentiated according to how language is used, it is reasonable to conclude that the genders would exhibit distinctive language patterns. Beginning with the pioneering work of Lakoff (1975), it is now well documented that women and men communicate on the basis of language which is to a large extent differentiated according to gender.

Female Register

Linguists use the term "register" to indicate a variety of language defined according to its use in social situations (Crystal, 1985). Registers are gendered in that males and females who share the same formal language, such as English, also exhibit different styles of communicative interaction, including grammatical constructions, word choice, and nonverbal communication. They are socialized into both a shared linguistic system as well as separate feminine and masculine speech communities. While the focus here is on female register and the communication patterns associated with it, the male patterns are implied.

Lakoff's (1975) early work was the first to systematically document important aspects of female register. First, women use more qualifiers than men. These words hedge or soften statements that are mostly evaluative in nature. Rather than describing a person, particularly a friend, as "shy," the words "sort of," "kind of," or "somewhat" may be inserted to soften the statement. A more blatant qualifier is when the sentence already begins with words which make it questionable. "This may be incorrect, but," is an example. Second, tag questions are typically used by women. This means that after making a statement, there follows a question relating to that statement. "I enjoyed the concert, didn't you?" or "It's a beautiful day, isn't it?" Less assertive than declaratory statements, tag questions assume that women must ask permission for their feelings, likes, or dislikes. Use of qualifiers and tag questions may suggest that women are uncertain, tentative, or equivocal in what they are saying. They are also used as a defense against potential criticism. Consider the impact of the following statements that use both qualifiers and tag questions in the same sentences:

I guess this is correct, don't you?
This sort of makes sense. Does it to you?
I kind of liked the movie. What do you think?

Another form of female register is the use of intensifiers, and what Lakoff (1975) refers to as "empty" adjectives or adverbs. Some of these could be contained in a word list which is distinctively female. "This is a divine party," "Such a darling room," or "I think croissants are absolutely heavenly" serve as examples. A study by McMillan and her colleagues (1977) indicates that in group discussions women use six times more intensifiers than men. While men may use a modicum of intensifiers, an exclusive pattern for women is that they often literally intensify the intensifier by heavily emphasizing and elongating the word. In describing a fine dining experience, for example, both men and women may say "it was so wonderful" but women will draw out and accent the adverb to become "it was so-o-o-o wonderful." An emotional overtone is added to a simple declarative sentence. Other word choices may add to this pattern. In areas which are important to role prescriptions, women's vocabulary is more complex and descriptive than men's. Women express a greater range of words for colors, textures, food, and cooking. They are able to describe complex interpersonal relationships and emotional characteristics of themselves and others using a greater variety of words and communication styles that are adapted to the setting, a pattern which is supported cross-culturally. When parents talk to their children about emotional aspects of events, they use a greater number of "emotion" words with daughters than with sons. Specialized vocabularies emerge from specialized roles (Kuebli and Fivish, 1992; Sapiro, 1994; Flannagan and Hardee, 1994; Flannagan et al., 1995; De Lange, 1995). This indicates that topic is an important factor in determining which aspects of female register are manifest.

Finally, female register includes forms of speaking that are more polite and indirect. Coupled with the use of tag questions, women's speech appears much more polite than men's. By keeping the conversation open, asking for further direction, and not imposing one's views on another, polite requests rather than forced obedience result (Lakoff, 1991:294). While men use imperatives with greater frequency ("Answer the phone"), women will make polite requests ("Please answer the phone" or "Will you please answer the phone?"). In studying verbal interaction between parents and children, Bellinger and Gleason (1982) show that fathers produce more directives phrased as imperatives than mothers. Both men and women share the same stereotypes about what is considered "polite" speech (Kemper, 1984). Women should never speak like men—in what they say and how they say it.

Socialization into language forbids profanity in general, but more so for females. Men tell "dirty" jokes, and women are often the targets of them. When women do not laugh at the jokes so as not to participate in their own denigration, they are told that "I was only joking," or "Can't you take a joke?" and accused of having no sense of humor (Crawford, 1995:135). Males believe profanity demonstrates social power and, interestingly, can be used to make them socially acceptable (Selnow, 1985). While both men and women use expletives, women not only use them less frequently but also still maintain a degree of politeness when uttering them. They also use substitute expletives that are deemed more acceptable. In spilling coffee on herself in front of other people, a woman's angry and embarrassed response may be "Oh darn!" or "Oh shoot!" The stronger expletives men would more likely use are obvious. This is consistent with my earlier research (Lindsey, 1974) on African-American children who use verbal duels called "playing the dozens" to assert dominance and gain respect from their peers. While girls are adept at verbal duelling, boys do so with much stronger expletives and profanities, and rarely will a girl and boy challenge one another. Playing the dozens is a gender-specific game. The game often ends for boys when physical fights ensue. For children of both races, boys begin to use profanity earlier than girls. These verbal duels in childhood may be useful for African-American women in adulthood. As mentioned below, men have an assumed right to interrupt women and subordinates. When challenges to these conversational tactics occur, men are more likely to sustain the challenge, with women giving in to men's conversational control. However, white males and African-American females sustain speech challenges and are much more likely to hold their conversational grounds than white females (Adams, 1980; Smith-Lovin and Brody, 1989).

Interruptions, Talkativeness, and Friendship

Men interrupt women more than women interrupt men, especially if it is used to change topics (Eakins and Eakins, 1978; West and Zimmerman, 1983; 1985; Mulac et al., 1988; McConnell-Ginet, 1989). Typically, interruption is viewed as an attempt to dominate and control a conversation by asserting one's right to speak at the expense of another. From a conflict perspective, men's interruption of women is an indication of differential power which asserts that it is the "right" for a superior to interrupt a subordinate. This is reflected in research which demonstrates that parents and adults, as superiors, frequently interrupt children, their subordinates (West and Zimmerman, 1977). When women interrupt conversations, they do so mainly to indicate interest in what is being talked about, to respond, and show support (Stewart et al., 1990). However, some studies find that dominance differences are related more to conversational context rather than gender per se. Kimble and Musgrove (1988) show that men dominate women in arguments but that women's visual behavior during the argument is more dominant. Also, structured conversations are more likely to be dominated by men, with women exerting more control of free discussion (Kimble et al., 1981).

Overall, the evidence suggests that in mixed-gender conversations males dominate females. This is an indication of differential power, and contrary to the stereotype, it also implies that men are more talkative than women. In mixed-gender groups, research consistently reveals a higher degree of male talkativeness. In classroom interaction at all educational levels, male students talk more and for longer periods than female students (Brooks, 1982; Spender, 1989; Crawford and MacLeod, 1990). In arguments men talk more than women opponents (Kimble and Musgrove, 1988) and in structured conversations where expertise is an ingredient, male "experts" talk more than female "experts" (Leeft-Pellegrini, 1980). The research clearly suggests that when males and females are conversing, men do the bulk of the talking. But the perception that women are the more talkative gender persists. Spender's (1989) research finds that even when men outspeak women by margins of two to three times longer, the men feel they did not have a fair share of conversation. This relates to the belief that women, like children, should be seen but not heard. According to Spender (1989:9), "quite simply, if a woman is expected to be quiet, then any woman who opens her mouth can be accused of being talkative."

While males dominate in amount of verbal output in mixed-gender groups, when they are with other males and want to encourage or maintain a friendship, they engage in activities, such as sports, poker, or fishing. These are "active" friendships which tend to discourage lengthy conversations but encourage time together (Arliss, 1991; Inman, 1996). Yet they can provide avenues to discuss more serious matters. Whereas women use more open, free-flowing conversations as a bonding source, and appreciate self-disclosing information, men feel uncomfortable in this regard. Women tend to like both men and women who self-disclose but men do not (Petty and Mirels, 1981). "Safe" topics like sports and politics dissuade men from revealing details of their personal lives to one another. When comparing talk within same-gender groups, women talk more frequently and for longer periods of time, enjoy the conversation more, converse on a wider variety of topics and consider talk as a preferable social activity (Coates, 1988; Tannen, 1990; West, 1994; Wood, 1994; Johnson, 1996). Findings such as these are expected since women's friendships and interpersonal intimacy are cultivated in conversation (Walker, 1994; Johnson, 1996). It is in these same-gender contexts, where power and domination are inconsequential and efforts at bonding are ongoing, that female talkativeness is higher than males'.

In building relationships between men and women, gendered communication patterns also appear. Women often report that after a relationship "takes hold," the couple does not communicate as well as they did earlier on. As she attempts to draw him out with more talk, he appears to silently resist. Women often feel that the lack of communication indicates that the relationship is failing or that he has lost interest in her. In marriage, women are more likely to view problems in communication and other relational dynamics more than men (Bruess and Pearson, 1996:62). But as Tannen (1990:83) points out, the woman has had practice all her life "in verbalizing her thoughts and feelings in private conversations with people she is close to; all his life he has had practice in dismissing and keeping them to himself." Women are socialized to be more attuned to relational issues. Men are socialized to be more attuned to accomplish instrumental objectives. Compared to women, men give minimal response cues (Wood, 1993, 1994). Therefore, it is no wonder that they assess their relationship differently in terms of communication.

When we see groups of two or three women in a restaurant engaged in lengthy conversation long after they have eaten, young girls who are best friends intently and quietly conversing in their rooms, or female teens talking on the phone for hours, we are apt to suggest that they are engaging in "gossip." In fact, the term is used almost exclusively to indicate a specific kind of talk engaged in by females—talk that is viewed by some, especially males, as negative and pointless. If gossip is defined as talking about others or oneself by revealing personal information, women may gossip more than men. Men gossip about others and do reveal personal information about *these* people, but they talk about *themselves* without doing so. Such patterns are predictable given women's higher degree of self-disclosure. Yet, in a study of students, Levin and Arluke (1985) show that there are no significant differences in derogatory tones of gossip but that men gossip, about distant acquaintances and celebrities while women gossip about close friends and family. Both genders gossip about dating, sex, and personal appearance.

Revealing personal information is what cements friendships between females. In gossip begins friendship. As Tannen (1990:97) states:

> Telling details of others' lives is partly the result of women's telling their friends details of their own lives. These details become gossip when the friend to whom they are told repeats them to someone else—presumably another friend.

Thus telling secrets, sometimes referred to as gossip, is evidence of friendship, especially for women. It is talk between women in their common roles. According to Arliss' (1991:50) review of research on what women and men talk about, several trends are clear. Men today report that women are a frequently discussed topic, whereas previously they talked more about other men. Both men and women talk about work and sexual partners. In examining this research, a caution must be added about what constitutes talk and gossip. The term can also be used to mean talk between women in their roles as women and the common experiences they share. At various life stages gossip is important for women, especially for young mothers (see Coates, 1988). In this sense, gossip is functional for women. I would argue that gender differences in gossip, if there are any, depend on which aspect of gossip is being investigated. If men "talk" and women "gossip" but are conversing on similar topics in the same manner, it is apparent that what separates the two is simply the gender stereotype associated with gossip. Gossip defines women but not men.

NONVERBAL COMMUNICATION

The language we verbalize expresses only one part of ourselves. Communication also occurs nonverbally, often conveying messages in a more forceful manner than if spoken. Besides bodily movement, posture, and general demeanor, sometimes referred to as **kinesics**, nonverbals include eye contact, use of personal space, and touching. Table 4-1 summarizes ways in which nonverbal behavior carries messages of power and domination. Overall, women are better at expressing themselves nonverbally and appear to be more accurate in understanding the nonverbal messages of others. Although power imbalances explain part of this, the context of women's socialization emphasizing relationship building is a major factor (Henley, 1977:13; Fugita et al., 1980; Wood, 1993).

Facial Expressions and Eye Contact

In decoding nonverbal cues, not only do women rely more on facial information than do men (Noeller, 1980), but women also exhibit a greater variety of facial expressions. For example, women smile more often than men (Halberstadt and Saitta, 1987). As a test of this, take a look at your high school yearbook. Smiling may be an indication of socialization into the traditional feminine role which teaches girls that they should be demure, attractive, and "aiming to please." Since boys are socialized to resist displays of emotion, the masked emotion in facial restraint is congruent with that learning. The notable exception to this pattern is anger. Since the expression of anger is culturally proscribed for females, anger may be masked by another emotional display, such as crying, which is more acceptable (Ekman et al., 1980). However, in contexts such as the workplace, when a woman's anger results in tears, she is judged as weak. If she does not confront the aggressor, she can be exploited.

TABLE 4-1 Examples of Gestures of Power and Prestige

Nonverbal Behaviors	Behaviors between Status Equals		Behaviors between Status Nonequals		Behaviors between Men and Women	
	Intimate	Non-intimate	Used by Superior	Used by Subordinate	By Men	By Women
Address	Familiar	Polite	Familiar	Polite	Familiar?*	Polite?*
Demeanor	Informal	Circumspect	Informal	Circumspect	Informal	Circumspect
Posture	Relaxed	Tense (less relaxed)	Relaxed	Tense	Relaxed	Tense
Personal space	Closeness	Distance	Closeness (option)	Distance	Closeness	Distance
Time†	Long	Short	Long (option)	Short	Long*	Short?*
Touching	Touch	Don't touch	Touch (option)	Don't touch	Touch	Don't touch
Eye contact	Establish	Avoid	Stare, ignore	Avert eyes, watch	Stare, ignore	Avert eyes, watch
Facial expression	Smile?*	Don't smile?*	Don't smile	Smile	Don't smile	Smile
Emotional expression	Show	Hide	Hide	Show	Hide	Show
Self-disclosure	Disclose	Don't disclose	Don't disclose	Disclose	Don't disclose	Disclose

*Behavior not known.
†Who waits for whom; who determines the length of the encounter; who ends the conversation, and so forth.
Source: Nancy M. Henley, *Body Politics: Power, Sex, and Nonverbal Communication.* © 1977, p. 181. Reprinted by permission of Prentice Hall, Inc., Englewood Cliffs, NJ.

If she counters the anger with a verbal barrage, she is too aggressive. While overt expressions of anger may be discouraged for both male and female employees, there are differential consequences for the genders.

Research clearly shows that women engage in more eye contact than men. This may counter another stereotype that a woman modestly averts her eyes from the gaze of an adoring man. In both same-gender and other-gender conversational pairs, women will look at the other person more and retain longer eye contact, a pattern found in children as young as two years old (Podrouzek and Furrow, 1988; Tannen, 1994). Eye contact can be an indication that the gazer is subordinate to the gazee. An employee is anxiously watchful of her or his employer in order to determine what follows next in their interactive situation. Superiors expect subordinates to be prepared in this regard. An alternative interpretation may view higher amounts of eye contact as assertive with the assumption that strength rather than meekness is being communicated. Women may capitalize on this nonverbal behavior and use it to gain a measure of prestige. Again, the context of the communication must be considered.

Touch and Personal Space

The dimensions of status and sexual intimacy are issues in touching. Men touch women more than women touch men (Henley, 1975), and women are touched more often than men overall (Stier and Hall, 1984). Subordinates are touched by superiors, such as a hand on the shoulder or pat on the back. These are not necessarily sexual in connotation. But when women flight attendants and bartenders are pinched and poked while on the job and when a man nudges and fondles a status equal in the office, sexual overtones cannot be dismissed. Cases of sexual harassment have called attention to the fact that women do not appreciate such acts and feel threatened by them, especially if the "toucher" is a boss or superior. Women will likely view touch as harassing when men use it to establish power (Poire et al., 1992). Forden (1981) finds that when women touch men, the men are viewed as passive. The message that is conveyed is that the toucher is in the dominant position.

Men, on the other hand, rarely touch one another, especially in what would be seen as an emotional display. While we are accustomed to the exuberant behavior of male athletes during sports events, which often involve fairly intimate displays of physical contact, these, too, appear to have limits. Soccer players were admonished by the International Federation in Zurich that their exultant outbursts of jumping on top of one another, kissing, and embracing were excessive and inappropriate. They were reminded to "behave like adults" (cited in Parlee, 1989:14). Women hug each other after a long absence, while men are more likely to shake hands or give a quick squeeze on the shoulder.

Men are more protective of their personal space and guard against territorial invasions by others. In his pioneering work on personal space, anthropologist Edward Hall (1966) found that in American culture there is a sense of personal distance, reserved for friends and acquaintances, which extends from about one and a half to four feet, while intimate distance, for intimate personal contacts, extends to 18 inches. Men invade intimate and personal space of women more than the reverse, and this invasion is more tolerated by the women. The space privilege of males is taken for granted throughout American culture. The next time you are on an airplane or at a movie, note the gender differences in access to the arms of the seat. Even in our homes, a woman's personal space is more limited. An office or study primarily used by the husband may be off-limits to the rest of the family. Wives, especially when they are also mothers, rarely "own" such space. Not only are spaces gendered, but evidence suggests that this has a bearing on gender inequity. Research in Britain, the United States, and several nonindustrial societies posits that gendered spaces restrict women from access to valued knowledge, whether in the home, educational institutions, or the workplace. When considering limited walking or standing space, women yield their space more readily than men, especially if the person who is approaching is a man (Arliss, 1991:110). Men retreat when women come as close to them as they do to women and loudly protest if other men come as close to them as they do to women (Richardson, 1988:25).

GLOBAL FOCUS: THE LANGUAGE OF JAPANESE WOMEN

In the last two decades a flurry of research has documented the existence and consequences of female register in English. For speakers of Japanese, although its consequences have only recently been investigated, the language of women has been recognized as a separate social dialect for at least 100 years. Its origins can be traced as far back as the eighth century (Ide and McGloin, 1990; Takahara, 1991). One of the most important novels in all of Japanese literature, *The Tale of Genji*, was written in 1016 by a woman, Lady Murasaki, in women's language. According to Ide and McGloin (1990:i), "Japanese women's language of today may be viewed as a manifestation of language used in women's quarters since nearly a thousand years ago."

As in English, Japanese female register has distinctive linguistic patterns in terms of lexicon (vocabulary), topic choice, phonology (sound and intonation), and styles of discourse. Unlike English, there are syntactic or grammatical forms used exclusively by women. This means there are numerous forms for which men and women use entirely different terms and that rules governing the ways word are combined to form sentences can differ according to gender of the speaker. Shibamoto (1985) has documented some of these important distinctions. For example, the words for "box lunch," "chopsticks," and "book" differ depending on if they are spoken by a female or male. Special terms of self-reference and address through different sets of first- and second-person pronouns distinguish speakers by gender. Female speakers may avoid second-person pronouns ("you") entirely. They also refrain from vulgar language. In terms of phonology, female speech is associated with a higher and greater range of pitch than male speech. Females speak a larger proportion of their sentences with rising intonation, a characteristic considered representative of the greater emotionalism of female speech. Most important are the numerous studies on gender-related syntax in Japanese focusing on the end of the sentence where the differences are most evident.

Choice of verb endings are particularly constrained by gender of the speaker (Shibamoto, 1985:60). Women are obliged to select endings which have the effect of rendering their sentences ambiguous, indirect, tentative, and less assertive. With gender distinctions built directly into the syntax, women's speech is not derived from female applications to (supposedly) gender-neutral grammar as it is in English (Takahara, 1991:61).

One of the most consistent findings on Japanese women's speech is that it is formal and polite, evidenced in part by usage of the honorific and humiliative forms of speech much more frequently than men's and in a variety of conversational contexts (Reynolds, 1985; Takahara, 1986; Kittredge, 1987; Ide and McGloin, 1990; Smith, 1992). Women also use fewer demonstratives and interrogatives—assertions and requests—and construct them differently from men when they are used (Takahara, 1991). In conversations, women speak of different things than men and say things differently when they converse about the same topic. The following is an abbreviated example cited by Shibamoto (1985:48-49):

FEMALE VERSION
My what a splendid garden you have here—the lawn is so nice and big. It's certainly wonderful, isn't it?
Oh no, not at all, we don't take care of it at all any more, so it simply doesn't look as nice as we would like it to.

MALE VERSION
It's a nice garden, isn't it?
Un.

When these styles of discourse are combined with the formal linguistic features of Japanese women's language, the image of a Japanese woman that emerges is one who is not assertive, overly polite, formal, and tentative in her speech (Reynolds, 1990). The consequences of these speech forms are linked to social powerlessness, especially in the public domain, and put women at a disadvantage when they venture into roles outside the home. Smith (1992) argues that Japanese women who are in positions of authority in nontraditional settings experience linguistic conflict when they attempt to defeminize their speech. A good example is provided by Reynolds (1990) of the female school principal. As a principal she cannot display linguistic traits indicative of women which give the impression she is indecisive or indirect in her talk. But at the same time she cannot be as authoritative as her male counterpart. She must not be too informal with teachers or with other principals, the majority of whom are male. If she defeminizes (or masculinizes) her speech too much, she may be perceived as a threat to the established norms of society.

Research by Von Hassell (1993) on the life histories of Issei (first-generation Japanese-American women) demonstrates the same conflict. Their role is to maintain family harmony but also to work or manage businesses, all the time living up to the image of the proper woman. They do not want their daughters to adopt cultural traits which would interfere with their success in the United States. Such traits could include the linguistic deference typical of Japanese women. Japanese language has a great impact on the way in which Japanese women live. According to Reynolds (1990:141),

> Attempts to remove the boundary between the male/female speech division inevitably ends in failure, as a result of self-restraint on the part of female speakers who foresee social punishment. It appears that the way women are supposed to talk has changed little; the norm functions as a conservative force.

Despite these observations, there are indications that women are adopting linguistic strategies to deal with linguistic conflict. One method is to adopt the speech patterns that are successful in the home for use outside the home (Smith, 1992), especially since these are ones with which many Japanese resonate. The Issei women in Von Hassell's (1993:549) study uses various linguistic devices, including silence, that "created the least conflict in order to have a cover behind which they could act and exert some modicum of power, at least in the realm of the family." Another is to defeminize speech within limits and then gradually expand the limits, creating new linguistic norms. When any individual woman challenges the linguistic system, the seeds for changes in female speech are sewn. This is the classic conflict theory application. Reynolds (1990:141) states that there is a ripple effect of conflict that can "generate the energy necessary to undermine the traditional division of the language."

A final thought is to use the politeness norm to the advantage of women. Styles of discourse in Japan stress politeness for both men and women and reflect ancient traditions of a hierarchal society where social rankings persist as a defining cultural characteristic. The language of the Japanese workplace is one which stresses cooperation and consensus. This is indicative of cultural communication strategies which are purposely designed to be noncommittal, imprecise, and conflict-evasive in order to indirectly achieve cooperation (Takahara, 1991). If Japanese female register allows women to be more proficient in these, they may be adopted for those nontraditional roles which place high value on them anyway (Lindsey, 1992). As Takahara (1991:84) suggests, "the language of women is for female speakers, but the language of courtesy is for all within the Japanese speech community."

EXPLAINING GENDERED LANGUAGE: DOMINANCE AND DIFFERENCE

This discussion has revealed two major patterns of explanation related to gendered language. Lakoff (1975) was influential in arguing that gender differentiated language is a reflection of women's subordinate status. The conflict-theoretical perspective would explain the use of equivocation, tag questions, hedges, and conversational cooperativeness as determined by the power differences between males and females. Girls and women are forced to adopt language patterns which keep them from acting as independent or nonsubordinate agents. This "dominance model" has gained a great deal of research attention and has prompted investigations of the power associated with language usage (Coates, 1993; Eckert and McConnell-Ginet, 1994). But it also implies that male speech is associated with superiority and female speech with inferiority. "Women are disadvantaged relative to men by a basically inferior, less forceful 'women's language' which they learn through socialization" (Henley and Kramarae, 1994:385).

Feminist reinterpretations of the dominance model are emphasizing women's power in using men's speech to their advantage and developing alternative explanations for the ways they interact (Mills, 1995; Freeman and McElhinny, 1996). Depending on the context, the language of cooperation and consensus may be more beneficial than the language of competition and control. A manager in the boardroom adjusts her language to the situation at hand. Research finds that in courtroom debate female expert witnesses exhibit few forms of female register (Erickson et al., 1977). As Adams and Ware (1995:339) point out, it is wrong to assume that such forms of speech are always weak and tentative and that "a woman's utterance may be defined as weak just because a woman is doing the talking." If female register is associated with powerlessness, it occurs in a society that appears to value consensus less than competition, and connection less than independence. Linguistic patterns are reflected accordingly.

While women use language to negotiate relationships and environments and establish connections, men converse to maintain independence and status in a society which is hierarchical, especially in the workplace (Tannen, 1990). As Tannen suggests, men do "report-talk" and women do "rapport-talk." This is indicative of the second approach emerging from our discussion of gendered language, referred to as the "difference" or "dual-culture model." According to this approach, the interactional styles of women and men are separate but equal. If girls and boys are raised in separate subcultures, miscommunication occurs not because of male power but because of lack of cultural understanding. West (1994) argues that gender differences in conversational topics, for example, are determined in part by the opportunities to express whatever interests they have. The context of the conversation is the critical factor.

The dual-culture model avoids women-blaming or female deficit in language. It stresses flexibility and choice. The reason for misunderstanding is due to "incompatible styles, not unscrupulous motivations" (Crawford, 1995: 93). In our increasingly multicultured environments, it alerts us to be sensitive to the backgrounds, characteristics, and cultural cues of all speakers. This model is compatible with a symbolic interaction view in its emphasis on interpersonal communication styles that can be negotiated. Language as a symbol shapes our perception of reality. We redefine that reality by altering language. As described above, what is named or left unnamed influences our perceptions.

Gender differences in conversational topics persist but are getting smaller over time (Bischoping, 1993). Although gender differences cut across context, on many verbal and nonverbal behaviors, girls and boys are more alike than different (Kolaric and Galambos, 1995). Because gender stereotypes continue, small but significant gender-related differences in language remain identifiable (Ferber, 1995). This research would support the dual-culture model but also indicates that there may be less separation in the speech communities of males and females. The choice between the dominance or difference models in explaining gendered language is perhaps a false one. Dominance suggests a victimization theme. Difference, while supposedly value-neutral, can lead to inequity. As Freeman and McElhinny (1996:242) note, to determine the best strategy for achieving equity, more contexualized and localized studies of interaction are needed.

IMPACT OF LINGUISTIC SEXISM

It is evident that verbal and nonverbal elements of our language view the genders unequally. When discussing language change, it is expected that one will encounter remarks like "so what?" Words are not seen as important in gender role change, even by those who fervently work on other issues involving women, such as equal pay or domestic violence. What answers do we give? Several are suggested. Language pervades all areas of our lives. Once learned, language influences our perceptions of what is proper, accepted, and expected. When we hear the words "man" and "he," we conjure up male images. Alternative images of women in traditionally male occupations, for example, are never expressed. Bem and Bem (1970) speak to the power of an ideology they define as nonconscious because alternative beliefs and attitudes about women remain unimagined. Language supports a nonconscious ideology concerning the genders. There is much evidence to indicate that the use of masculine generics, for example, makes it difficult to see females in a mental representation or imagery (Hamilton, 1988:796).

This chapter has documented how language subtly, and not so subtly, transmits sexist notions. Research is replete showing that the use of masculine generics can bias one's cognitions, with males displaying greater bias than females (Hamilton, 1988); that those who use sexist language in written form are also likely to use it in oral form on some responses (McMinn et al., 1990); that the use of the generic masculine pronoun differentially affects the self-esteem of the reader (Henley et al., 1985); and that ambiguous interpretation of masculine generics can be harmful to both men and women (Martyna, 1983; Hamilton et al., 1994). During early childhood socialization, boys internalize masculine generics as part of a continuum that applies throughout the animate world. Their own sense of well-being is linked to that world. When girls begin to expand their environments, they have no such set of referents. For a girl "not to experience a recurring violation of reality, she must look upon a familiar symbol for herself as something different and apart from the symbol used for animate beings in general" (Miller and Swift, 1991a:34). In a thorough review of the research on gender bias in language in general and the use of the masculine generic in particular, Henley (1989:68) argues that the direction of evidence on the detrimental effects is clear: Much damage is being done.

Another answer, flowing from the dominance model, is that words assert position and power. Sexist language is primary and produces sexist thought (Hyde, 1984:705), thus bolstering the notion of female inferiority in a world of male superiority. As that world changes to accommodate newer, egalitarian roles, language needs to reflect these. Accuracy and precision are gained. Finally, language learning produces a double bind for women who are socialized into believing they must always speak politely and refrain from "man talk." Women's language is associated with maintaining femininity. But since the language they use deprecates, ignores, and stereotypes women, women may be internalizing beliefs that they are lesser persons. High femininity in young girls is also associated with lower self-esteem (Sears, 1990). Sexist language functions as a primary shaper of attitudes, and as MacKay (1983) notes, the masculine generic resembles a highly effective propaganda technique. Language learning in girls may be the counterpart for the difficulty boys may experience in gaining a sense of their identity from incomplete information they are offered during primary socialization. In either case, the socialization road is not easy.

CHAPTER 5

WESTERN HISTORY AND THE CREATION OF GENDER ROLES

> The recognition that we had been denied our history came to many of us as
> a staggering flash of insight, which altered our consciousness irretrievably.
> —Gerda Lerner (1996:8)

Reflecting an egalitarian model far ahead of its time, in 1801 an anonymous author wrote in the *Female Advocate,* an American publication: "Why ought the one half of mankind, to vault and lord it over the other?" (cited in Woloch, 1992:ix). Identifying a critical need to explore the other half of humankind, the field of women's history has rapidly expanded. It is impossible to understand the present without reference to the past. Historians say that they search for a "usable past," for a record which will clarify and give meaning to the present (Carlson, 1990:81). In order to explain the differential status of women and men in contemporary society, it is necessary to examine the impact of powerful historical forces that have created gendered attitudes. Only recently has scholarly work started to scrutinize the past with the goal of uncovering the hidden elements of a woman's history. As we shall see, such a history is vastly different than the centuries of discourse on the status of women that focuses on women's proper roles in society.

These discourses date back to the earliest writings of the Greek philosophers and center on debates about women's place, women's souls, and women's suitability for domestic functions. Writings of this type were used, and often continue to be used, to justify a patriarchal status quo. What is clear is that the centuries of debate on "women's themes" do not constitute a women's history. Citing pioneer women's historian Mary Ritter Beard, Keller (1990:3) states that in the 2,500 years history has been written, most male writers overlooked the histories of females. In historical writing, the whole of human experience has been dominated by the political, economic, and military exploits of an elite and usually powerful group of men. As this chapter will illustrate, throughout history women have assumed a myriad of critical domestic and extra-domestic roles, many of which have been ignored or relegated to inconsequential historical footnotes.

PLACING WOMEN IN HISTORY

The revitalized women's movement of the 1960s provided the catalyst for the independent field of women's history to emerge. Although there is a general agreement as to what is *not* women's history, scholars do not agree on what it should or must include in terms of approach, content, and boundaries. There is broad consensus, however, that since women and men experience the world around them in qualitatively different ways, the starting point must be on those very experiences (Riley, 1986; Daniel, 1987; Berkin, 1989; Keller, 1990).

In other words, women's history must ask why women have a fundamentally "different historical experience from men" (Daniel, 1987:2).

Since women have essentially been left out of historical writing, the first attempts at reclaiming their historical place centered on combing the chronicles for appropriate figures to demonstrate that female notables of similar authority and ability to males existed (Miles, 1989:xii). If there was Peter the Great, there was also Katherine the Great. As Lerner (1996:2) notes, this "women worthies" or "compensatory history" approach is the history of exceptional, even deviant, women and does not provide much information about the impact of women's activities to society in general. In "contribution history" women's contributions to specific social movements are explored, but their activities are judged not only by their effects on the movement but also by standards defined by men. Most important, these kinds of histories do not describe the experience of the masses of women who still remain invisible to the historical record (Lerner, 1996).

This does not mean that we cannot take pride in the achievements of notable women; only that this kind of focus parallels previously accepted historical tradition which also ignores the "nonelites" of any society, both men and women of classes and races defined as marginal to society as a whole. Such groups are now being historically rediscovered, with the notion that an inclusive approach to the past must account for their lives and cultures. Along with such groups, a balanced history which makes women visible is an affirmation of identity. According to Carlson (1990:79), "the usual way of doing history is incomplete" and since "the male world is the point of reference for traditional history . . . females become peripheral."

In considering the different approaches to women's history, another critical factor is the race-class-gender link. If a women's history emerges from the notion of patriarchy and the dynamics leading to the power of men over women, it glosses over the power relations between women, especially those due to social class. Despite the fact that the relation of gender to power is the foundation of women's history, African-American women historians are reticent to use the male/female dichotomy and find that it is impossible to separate race and gender. Higginbotham (1992:273) suggests that gender-based dichotomies can lead to a false homogenizing of women. "Gender and class preclude a monolithic black community as well" (Higginbotham, 1996:19). This perspective admonishes us to recognize that claims to a homogeneous womanhood remain unconfirmed for women of different races, regions, socioeconomic backgrounds, and sexual orientations. Related to this is the concern that when the historical experiences of women of color become chronicled, they may be acknowledged according to race, but only with a biracial—black and white—focus. While the rejection of the notion of a universal and homogenous female experience attests to the rapid growth of interest and sound scholarship in women's history, other elements are still missing. Ruiz and DuBois (1994:xiii) contend that a multicultural framework should be adopted because it explores simultaneously the interplay of many races and cultures and provides what may be the only way to organize a truly inclusive history of women. As women's history becomes both more sophisticated and mainstreamed, white feminist scholars must account for these dimensions and work to overcome a narrowness of vision (Riley, 1986; Higginbotham, 1992).

Rather than attempting a full historical reckoning of women's history, the intent here is to offer an overview of certain historical periods which have been important in influencing attitudes and subsequent behavior concerning the genders. In general, we will focus on Western society and the paths which lead to American women and men. This history will illustrate the impact of **misogyny**, the disdain or hatred of women, and their subjection and oppression. This reflects the first of two important themes of women's history that will be overviewed here. The first is related to power, patriarchy, and the subjection of women, a theme which emerges as central to all feminist scholarship on women, regardless of discipline.

However, the women-as-victim theme will be countered by stories of courage, survival, and achievement that reveal an alternative view. The alternative view indicates that although women's history is still at an early developmental stage, it has issued a formidable challenge to traditional thinking on gender roles. Bock (1996) maintains that feminist historical scholarship has challenged gender dichotomies related to nature versus nurture, work versus family, and private versus public spheres of men and women. This is similar to what has occurred in sociology. It reflects the interdisciplinary elements evident in social history, where the theories and methods of sociology are applied to understanding the linkage between social and historial patterns. Using the framework provided by Ruiz and DuBois (1994), I would suggest an additional dichotomy, unicultural versus multicultural. This dichotomy reflects the second theme which gives recognition to the race-class-gender intersection as well as other critical cultural components, such as region and religion. Consistent with the discussion in Chapter 3, culture is used in the broadest sense both to highlight diversity and to provide for more inclusiveness in women's historical record.

This kind of approach has several objectives. First, the roots of patriarchy will be discovered in a format which is manageable. Second, misconceptions about the roles of women and attitudes toward these roles will become evident. An acknowledgment of such misconceptions has implications for contemporary social change. Third, it is a history of "most women," a massive group who have been historically ignored but who have profoundly impacted their societies and who responded to multiple oppressions in a variety of ways. As such, it represents the field of social history, which approaches social change by connecting larger social structures with everyday life and experiences (Elliott, 1994:45). Finally, this overview has a consciousness-raising objective because a discovery of an alternative historical account allows us to become aware of our culturally determined prejudices and stereotypes. **Her-story** allows for a balance to the historical record.

CLASSICAL SOCIETIES

The foundation of Western culture is ultimately traced to the Greek and Roman societies of classical antiquity. Western civilization is rooted in the literature, art, philosophy, politics, and religion of a time that extends from the Bronze Age (about 3000 to 1200 B.C.E) through the reign of Justinian (565 C.E.). In particular, the period between 800 B.C.E. and 600 C.E. witnessed spectacular achievements for humanity. With the achievements came ideological convictions which persist in modified form today. The dark side of classical societies was laced with war, slavery, deadly competitions, and a brutal existence for much of the population. Inhabiting another portion of this cordoned-off world was democracy, literacy, grace, and beauty. These opposites serve as a framework from which to view the role of women. Like the societies themselves, the evidence concerning women's roles is also contradictory.

The Glory That Was Greece

The Greek view of women varies according to the time and place involved. Greek literature is replete with references to the matriarchal society of Amazons. Though shrouded in mystery, Greek mythology saw the Amazons as female warriors, capable with a bow, who had little need of men except as sexual partners. Greek heroes were sent to the distant land on the border of the barbarian world to test their strength against the Amazons. Since the Amazons invariably lost, and eventually were raped by or married to the heroes sent to defeat them, some feminist historians associate these myths with reinforcing historical ideas that male dominance is inevitable (Miles, 1989:32). On the other hand, too much evidence exists to dismiss the stories outright (Kleinbaum, 1990). We know that throughout Asia Minor and the Mediterranean during this period there are innumerable references to physically strong women who were leaders and soldiers. The admiration for the skills of these warrior women is used to support the belief that ancient Greek women were held in higher esteem than women of later times. And, regardless of its historical accuracy, as Kleinbaum (1990:107) indicates, "The Amazon image proves empowering to all women."

Whether Amazonian society or the myths surrounding it indicate that matriarchy also existed is debatable. Archaeological material from the Neolithic to the Early Bronze Age period immediately predating the birth of Greek civilization provides massive evidence of matrilineal inheritance, the sexual freedom of women, the goddess as supreme deity, and the power of priestesses and queens (Gimbutas, 1989; 1991). Eisler (1988) argues that in these ancient societies neither matriarchy nor patriarchy was the norm. In her view, the inference that if women have high status, then men must inevitably have low status does not necessarily follow. An egalitarian or partnership society is also possible. The egalitarian zenith was reached in the goddess-worshipping culture of Minoan Crete. It is defined by cultural historians as a "high civilization" because of its art, social complexity, peaceful prosperity, and degree of technological sophistication. The social structure of Minoan Crete, Eisler (1995:85) contends, conformed to a partnership model with a key part of that partnership a free and equal sexual relationship between men and women. This is consistent with Miles' (1989) assertion that at the birth of civilization women enjoyed more freedom, including sexual freedom, and less restraint on their "modesty." Judd's (1990) analysis of the mythology of such cultures, which points to the absence of warfare, private property, class structure, violence, and rape would support this kind of model. Referred to as the Golden Age, the mythology bolsters the view of a society where gender stratification was unknown.

Over time, a matrilineal system based on judging descent from the female line was replaced by a patrilineal system. As more fully documented in Chapter 12, the goddesses who dominated the ancient world lost their central position as gods were added to religious imagery. The earlier maternal religion lost its ascendance as patriarchal theology was grafted onto it. Patriarchy eventually prevailed. However, patriarchy did not completely dislodge the revered goddess from later Greek mythology. This points to the main realm where the women of ancient Greece maintained a degree of power and prestige.

But except for religion, most of the Greek world saw women as inferior in political, social, and legal realms. The Amazon legends and goddess images have helped to perpetuate the idea that Greece revered women. Plato called for girls to be educated in the same manner as boys with equal opportunities open to them to become rulers. As Wender (1984) notes, Plato believed that a superior woman was better than an inferior man. In the *Republic* he states that "there is not one of those pursuits by which the city is ordered which belongs to women as women, or to men as men; but natural aptitudes are equally distributed in both kinds of creatures." This supposed an enlightened image of women that does not take into account Plato's disdain, even antipathy, of women. In championing the democratic state, Plato was a pragmatist as well as a misogynist. An inferior class of uneducated women might work against the principles of democracy. This is one reason why Plato championed the emancipation of women. Women may "naturally participate in all occupations," Plato continues, "but in all women are weaker than men" (cited in Ashton-Jones and Olson, 1991:155).

It is Aristotle rather than Plato who is more representative of the Greek view of women. In his *Politics*, Aristotle explicitly states that a husband should rule over his wife and children. If slaves are naturally meant to be ruled by free men, then women are naturally meant to be ruled by men. Otherwise, the "natural" order would be violated:

> Man is full in movement, creative in politics, business and culture. Woman, on the other hand, is passive. She stays at home, as is her nature. She is matter, waiting to be formed by the active male principle . . . Man consequently plays a major part in reproduction; the woman is merely the passive incubator of his seed. (cited in Miles, 1989:47)

And since the active elements of nature are on a higher level than the passive, they are more divine. This may be why Aristotle believed women's souls were impotent and in need of supervision.

The women of Athens can be realistically described as chattels. At one point in Greek history, even a wife's child-bearing responsibilities could be acceptably taken over by concubines (Arthur, 1984), which lowered the wife's already subordinate status. Divorce was rare but possible. As a group, women were classified as minors, along with children and slaves. Aristotle speaks of a propertyless man who could not afford slaves but who could use his wife or children in their place (De St. Croix, 1993). Husbands and male kin literally held the power of life and death over women. Some upper-class women enjoyed privileges associated with wealth and were left to their own devices while their husbands were away at war or serving the state in some other way. Considering the plight of most women of the time, these women achieved a measure of independence in their households if only because of the absence of their husbands. But Athenian repression of women was so strong, even wealth could not compensate for the disadvantages of gender. From a conflict perspective De St. Croix (1993:148) maintains that the class position of a citizen woman belonging to the highest class is determined by her gender, "by the fact that she belonged to the *class* of women." Her male relatives would be property owners but she would be devoid of property rights. As a woman, therefore, her class position is greatly inferior to theirs. In Marxian terms, women are an exploited class, regardless of the socioeconomic class to which they belong.

Athenian society did not tolerate women in public places except at funerals and all female festivals, so for the most part they remained secluded in their homes. Athenian households were further segregated. Women had special quarters that were designed to restrict freedom of movement and to keep close supervision over their sexual activities. Supervision was so strong that evidence suggests Athens established a formal police force to monitor and "protect" the chastity of women (Keuls, 1993).

The few women who did become successful in this world of men were of two groups. One group consisted of those women who practiced political intrigue behind the scenes to help elevate their sons or husbands to positions of power. The second group were the hetairai, or high-level courtesans whose wit, charm, and talent men admired. When pederasty was in vogue, men sought boys or other young men for their sexual and intellectual pleasure. By the fourth century B.C.E. Athenian men rediscovered women, but not their wives, because they had no desire to become "family men." The uneducated wives could not compete with the social skills and cultural knowledge exhibited by the hetairai, who were often thoroughly trained for their work when they were girls. Tannahill (1980:100-101) remarks that "as throughout most of history, courtesans had a better time than wives."

The subordinate position of Athenian women extended to most of the Greek world. However, when comparing Athens to Sparta, some differences can be ascertained. Sparta practiced male infanticide when newborns were deemed unfit enough to become warriors. Whether girls were killed is unclear. Regardless, it cannot be said that male infanticide indicated a higher regard for females in Sparta. It is significant only to the extent that Sparta was organized and continually mobilized for war, a fact which did influence the role of Spartan women. If Athenian men were separated from their wives by war, the situation was magnified in Sparta, in that Sparta was either always at war or preparing for it. Army life effectively separated husband and wife until he reached the age of 30. These years of separation, marked by infrequent visits by their husbands, essentially allowed the wives to develop some talent and capability of their own.

While the men were away, the women enjoyed a certain amount of freedom. Although the woman's responsibility was to bear male children who would become warriors, girls also were to be physically fit. Gymnastic training to promote both fitness and beauty was encouraged. Compared to Athens, young unmarried Spartan women enjoyed a higher degree of freedom. Euripides, an Athenian, commented on this scandalous state of affairs:

> The daughters of Sparta are never at home! They mingle with the young men in wrestling matches, their clothes cast off, their hips all naked. It's shameful! (cited in Miles, 1989:31)

In addition to physical activities, citizen women were expected to manage the household and all the associated properties. Women retained control of their dowries and were able to inherit property. In comparison to Athens, the free women of Sparta had more privileges if only because they were left alone much of the time. But in the context of the period as a whole, the vast majority of women existed in a legal and social world which viewed them in terms of their fathers, brothers, and husbands. Subordination and suppression of women was the rule.

The Grandeur That Was Rome

The founding of Rome by Romulus, traditionally dated at 753 B.C.E., led to an empire which lasted until it was finally overrun by invading Germanic tribes in the fifth century C.E. The Roman Empire evolved and adapted to the political, social, and cultural forces of the times and in turn influenced these very forces. Changes in gender roles mirrored the fortunes and woes of the empire. The prerogatives of women in later Rome contrasted sharply with the rights of women in the early days of the republic. It is true that women remained subservient to men and cannot be portrayed separately from the men who dominated and controlled them. But compared to the Greeks, Roman women achieved an astonishing amount of freedom.

Early Rome granted the eldest man in a family, the **pater familias**, absolute power over all family members, male and female alike. His authority could extend to death sentences for errant family members and selling his children into slavery to recoup the economic losses of a family. Daughters remained under the authority of a pater familias throughout their lives, but sons could be emancipated after his death. Even after marriage, the father or uncle or brother still had the status of pater familias for women, which meant the husbands could exercise only a limited amount of control over wives.

The absolute authority of the pater familias may have in the long run helped women. The right of guardianship brought with it a great deal of responsibility. A daughter's dowry, training, and education had to be considered early in life. If she married into a family with uncertain financial assets, the possibility existed that she and her new family could become a continued economic liability. The pater familias exercised extreme caution in assuring the appropriate match for the women under his guardianship. This system allowed for total power of the pater familias, but it also caused a great burden for that very power to be maintained. By the first century C.E. legislation was passed which allowed a freewoman to be emancipated from a male guardian if she bore three children. The roles of childbearer and mother were primary, but they allowed for a measure of independence later in life. Considering that at some level Rome was always involved in warfare, a declining birth rate was an alarming reality. The abandonment of the pater familias rule functioned to decrease the economic burden women caused for the family. Emancipation in exchange for babies was an additional latent function.

Unlike the Greeks, the Romans recognized a wider role for women. Religious life still retained vestiges of goddess worship, and women shared in the supervision of the religious cult of the household. The comparative power women held in the religious life of the empire is reflected in the highly revered Vestal Virgins who symbolized society's economic and moral well-being. Though open only to a select few, these women took on roles of great public importance. Roman women in general, however, knew that their lives would be carried out as wives and mothers. But wives also carried out the business of the family while their husbands were on military duty. These roles gradually extended so that it became common for women to buy and sell property as well as inherit it and participate in the broader economic life of the society (Gimbutas, 1991).

Their expertise was both praised and criticized, especially as women amassed fortunes in their own names. The necessity for economic decision making led to a much less secluded lifestyle. The Greeks would have been astounded to see women in public roles and seated with men at dinner parties. Although most women remained illiterate, even the upper-class women who had the most independence, they experienced other gains including greater opportunities for learning, especially in music and dancing. These women challenged a system where they were chained to their husbands or fathers, eventually gaining the right to divorce.

Freedom is relative. Roman society allowed a few women of higher social standing privileges unheard of in Greek society. Religion was the one area where women exercised much control, but with few exceptions religious dominance did not expand into other realms. The emancipated woman was a rarity even in Roman times. That a sexual double standard existed is unquestionable. Women may have been more visible but they were definitely not autonomous. Rome was a brutal, slave-based society where a dominator model of male control over women and the control of "superior" men over "inferior men" regulated all existence at all levels, whether personal, familial, national, or international (Eisler, 1995:123). When compared to almost any free males in Rome, the most assertive, independent, and visible women were still in bondage to men.

THE MIDDLE AGES

When the Roman emperor Constantine reigned, between 306 and 337 C.E., the empire was already in the throes of disintegration. Regardless of the religious overtones, Constantine's decision to wed the empire to Christianity was politically astute, since Christianity seemed to offer an integrative force in a period where the empire's decline was accelerating. Constantine's foresight on the impact of Christianity was remarkable. He did not envision, however, that the collapse of Rome itself would be instrumental in allowing Christianity to gain a firm grip on Europe that lasted throughout the Middle Ages. And even the Renaissance combined with feudalism did not radically diminish this powerful hold. Christianity profoundly influenced the role of women. Compared to the preclassical era, women's status in the classical era markedly deteriorated. This already bleak situation was considerably worsened when Christianity dominated Europe during the Middle Ages.

Christianity

To its credit, the Church, in the form of a few monasteries and abbeys, became the repository of Greek and Roman knowledge that surely would have been lost during the sacking, looting, and general chaos following the disintegration of the Empire. The decline of a literate population left reading, writing, and education as a whole in the hands of the Church. The power of literacy and the lack of literate critics permitted the Church to become the unreproachable source of knowledge and interpretation in all realms. The Church's view of life was seen as absolute.

If certain sentiments of the early Church had persisted, Christianity might not have taken on such misogynous overtones. Extending from Jewish tradition, the belief in the spiritual equality of the genders offered new visions of and to women. The ministry of Jesus included women in significant roles, thus demonstrating that spiritual equality could be actualized even in the steadfastly patriarchal society of the time. Also, the Church recognized that women provided valuable charitable, evangelistic, and teaching services which were advantages to the fledgling institution. Some positions of leadership in the hierarchy were open to women and served as models for women who might choose a religious life. The convent also served as a useful occupation for some women, particularly of the upper classes, who were unsuited for marriage. It also provided a place of education for selected girls. Whereas the convent may have offered different opportunities for women, the measure of independence that they achieved in becoming nuns was eventually viewed with suspicion. Education for nuns eroded and with more restrictions put on women's ownership of land, it was increasingly difficult to found new convents, and existing ones later came under the management of male friars. In discussing this distrust of the independent woman, Weitz (1995) points out that in Catholic Europe nuns were stripped of their autonomy and in Protestant Europe women were left without a socially acceptable alternative to marriage.

But misogyny eventually dominated as the Church came to rely heavily on the writings of those who adopted a traditional view of women. With Old Testament restrictions on women elevated, women remained excluded from the covenant community (Lerner, 1995b). Biblical interpretations consistent with a cultural belief of the inferiority of women and placing the blame squarely on Eve for the fall of humanity became the unquestioned norm.

Christianity also changed the attitudes about marriage and divorce. Unlike in classical society, marriage could not be dissolved. Since divorce was unobtainable, women may have benefited if only for the fact that they could not be easily abandoned for whatever transgressions, real or imagined, their husbands attributed to them. Whereas childlessness was grounds for marital dissolution throughout history, even this was no longer an acceptable cause. However undesirable the marriage, the marriage was inviolable in the eyes of the Church.

With the medieval Church as a backdrop, misogyny during the late Middle Ages created an outgrowth for one of the most brutal periods of history concerning women—the time of the witch hunts. It was the woman who deviated from the norm, especially regarding gender roles, who generated the greatest distrust. If she remained unmarried, was married but barren, or was viewed as independent or powerful, she was often denounced as being a witch (Unger and Crawford, 1992:503). The power of the Church was directly related to the poverty of the people. Women who were economically dependent on their roles as healer, midwife and counselor were particular targets of the witch hunts. Such women were admired for their expertise and sought out by the communities in which they practiced their professions. They were transformed into witches who symbolized evil and the wrath of God (Barstow, 1994).

Female power was on trial but so also was the fear of female sexuality, reinforced by Christian theology's view that sexual passion in women is irrational and potentially chaotic (Reineke, 1995). Eighty percent of the victims of the European witch hunts were women. It displayed an eruption of misogyny that remains unparalleled in Western history (Ruth, 1995:78).

Accused of sexual impurity and in order to appease God's anger, thousands of women were burned as witches, confessing to anything their tormentors suggested. Although confession meant death at the stake, the horrible tortures used to extract confessions were impossible to endure, and it was common for women to publicly confess to such absurdities as eating the hearts of unbaptized babies and having intercourse with the devil (Tannahill, 1980). Daly's (1975:187-88) scathing comments on the witch craze, evidenced not only by her words but also her refusal to capitalize specific words, speaks to the attitude that slaughtering women meant doing God's will.

> Since the demonologies accused witches of lewd acts, their male persecutors were perfectly "justified" in destroying them. To this end, the good sons of the holy father projected their fantasies on the accused women. . . . Since their obscene "acts" were performed with the devil, god's enemy, their christian killer could feel totally religious and righteous.

Although this view is caustic, it cannot be denied that the medieval Church's attitudes about women played a prominent role in sanctioning the witch craze.

Feudalism

In the feudal system where war was always a possibility, serfs and their families were protected by lords who in turn expected their serfs to fight when called upon. All serfs owed their lives to the lord of the manor, and the wives of serfs owed their lives to their husbands. The lack of respect for serfs in general and their wives in particular is indicated by a custom which allowed the lord to test the virginity of the serf's new bride on their wedding night.

Women of noble standing fared somewhat better in that they were valued for their role in extending the power of the family lineage through arranged marriages, though here, too, the lord of the manor had to grant permission for any marriage. The young unmarried woman was a property worth guarding, with her virginity as a marketable commodity (Lucas, 1983:85). Her marriage would serve the purposes of uniting two houses and providing an heir.

At marriage, the bride would be given in exchange for a dowry of money or jewelry, and in some places, the custom required her to kneel in front of her husband-to-be to symbolize his power over her (Lucas, 1983:87). As her husband was controlled by the lord of the estate, she was to be controlled by her lord and husband. In this way, whether serf or noble, feudal wives had much in common.

The Renaissance

The last 300 years of medieval Europe, which included the Renaissance and Reformation, were years of ferment and change extending into realms which included women. Although more control by male religious orders was established, convents were often viewed as the sanctuaries where women could write on religious subjects, as well as be poets and dramatists. Educated aristocratic women became patrons of literature and art, many of them as authors in their own right. Lucas (1983:179) also notes that these noble women set the standard for patrons of the arts for the centuries to follow. A few literate women of noble blood were accorded a certain amount of prestige for their accomplishments. But other forces were at work which kept traditional images of women from being seriously challenged.

With the Reformation came the startling notion that a church hierarchy may actually exclude people from worship. Preaching a theology of liberation from a Church charged with becoming too restrictive, Martin Luther advocated opening Christianity to everyone on the basis of faith alone. Critical of Aquinas's view that women are imperfect, or in essence "botched males," Luther argued that those who accuse her of this are in themselves monsters and should recognize that she, too, is a creature made by God. The Reformation, so it appeared, offered an opportunity to present different interpretations of Christianity in regard to the genders.

This was not to be the case. Luther himself presents a paradox. Women may not be "botched males," but he still believed they were inferior to men. Though woman is a "beautiful handiwork of God," she does "not equal the dignity and glory of the male" (quoted in Maclean, 1980:10). Theological statements of the time abound with themes of superior man and inferior woman.

Carmody (1989:175-76) points out several of these: Woman is subordinate to man because she bears greater responsibility for the curse that came with original sin; women are to provide men both procreation and companionship; the natural order assigns women only those functions that correspond to her sexual and procreative organs; adulterous women should be stoned to death but not unfaithful husbands. In all, a woman was positive but never superior, only because of her maternal role, and inferior in all else. Thus, as the Reformation reverberated throughout the Western world, no dramatic changes relative to the Christian image of women occurred.

The Renaissance generated the rebirth of art, literature, and music in a world that was becoming transformed by commerce, communication, and the growth of cities. As a force in people's lives, Christianity now competed with others, especially education. More men and some women became literate, opening up intellectual life which had been closed to most except clergy and nobility. Women made some economic headway by working in shops or producing products in the home for later sale. As money replaced barter systems and manufacturing increased, a new class of citizens emerged who were not dependent on either agriculture or a feudal lord for protection.

Like other periods in history, the Renaissance presents contradictory evidence about women. The question of whether women had a Renaissance depends on the answer to other questions: Which women? Where were they located? What was their social class? Rose (1986) mentions scholars who state that cultural traits like courtly love, which dates from the twelfth century, long before the Renaissance, provide evidence for some female power and prestige among noble women. Historians have scoured the 100 years (1580-1680) of this "Golden Age" for records of female notables, and many have been discovered or rediscovered (Kloek, 1994). As testimonies to intellect, talent, and stature, women poets, artists, artisans, and musicians abounded.

While they provide an image of the past which is affirming to women, they remain, as always, a witness to extraordinary rather than ordinary women of the day. Social history provides a more inclusive view, and from this several plausible conclusions can be drawn. The Renaissance witnessed women in more diverse roles. Many women, particularly lower-class women, migrated to the expanding cities and were employed as servants, barmaids, fish mongers, textile workers, and peat carriers, to name a few. More educated women established themselves as actresses and midwives. While a woman was protected from financial destitution by marriage, a surplus of women in European cities such as Amsterdam may have made marriage unattainable, but less disastrous, if she was employed. Prostitution also burgeoned during this period (Carlson, 1994; De Baar, 1994; Kloek et al., 1994; Van De Pol, 1994). Compared to wives and unmarried women (spinsters), widows in England enjoyed the most freedom since they could inherit property and were free to continue their husbands' businesses (Prior, 1994). But misogyny continued to govern Europe. Any women who ventured outside of prescribed gender roles found themselves in precarious positions, both socially and economically.

THE AMERICAN EXPERIENCE

Women's history and American social history are fundamentally intertwined, an association that has been advantageous for the growth of both areas. Since social history focuses on previously neglected groups, such as minorities and the working classes, women are brought in as part of that cohort. But until recently, the interest in women has been largely confined to issues related to the attainment of legal rights, such as the suffrage movement. Only in the last two decades has women's history in America come into its own not only for its subject matter but also as a way of reframing American history as a whole. Kerber and De Hart (1991:5) suggest that this new women's history issues three challenges: to reexamine gendered social relations, to reconstruct many historical generalizations, and to reconfigure historical narrative. Similar to what is occurring in sociology with the emergence of a new sociological paradigm based on the infusion of feminist theory, these challenges from women's history are laying the foundation for a paradigm shift in history.

The First American Women

As a prelude to this paradigm shift, women's history is bringing to the surface a range of taken-for-granted assumptions about women in America. While it so obvious that the first American women were native American women, this fact has been virtually ignored by historians. And in those instances when it was not ignored, stereotyped and inaccurate portrayals based on European, Christian, patriarchal beliefs prevailed.

Prior to colonization, in the fifteenth and sixteenth centuries, there were at least 2,000 native American languages, representing such cultural diversity that Europeans appear to be homogeneous (Evans, 1991:31). Given such tribal diversity, it is certainly difficult to generalize about the status of native American women as a group. However, the archeological and historical record, the latter based mainly on diaries, letters, and some ethnographic descriptions from the period, allows some reliable conclusions, especially for coastal and midwestern tribes, such as the Seneca of western New York, the Algonquins distributed along the Atlantic Coast, and a number of Iroquoian tribes scattered throughout the territories east of the Mississippi River.

Overall, accounts of American Indian women during this period can be interpreted in many ways, and much of this is dependent on their particular tribe. A missionary view of American Indian women on the Eastern shores during the 1600s saw them as beasts of burden, slaves, and "poor creatures who endure all the misfortunes of life" (Riley, 1986:28). This led to a negative and stereotypical "squaw" image that was perpetuated by zealous missionaries who saw native Americans in general as primitive savages. This image contrasts sharply with the historical record.

The old tribal systems were characterized by complementarity, balance, and functional separation of gender roles. While gender segregation was the norm in most spheres of life, it provided women a great deal of autonomy, especially given the value placed on women's economic, political, and artistic skills (Kuhlmann, 1996). The success of the system depended upon balanced and harmonious functioning of the whole (Allen, 1995). The work of both men and women was viewed as functionally necessary to survival, so even if a hierarchy existed related to leadership, one group would not be valued or, more importantly, devalued, in comparison to the other. In sociology this would be recognized as the ideal functionalist model, void of judgments which define inferiority or superiority based on the tasks performed. Many tribal units were matrilineal and matrilocal, a man living in the home belonging to his wife's family. Women were farmers and retained control over their agricultural products, feeding hungry settlers with their surpluses and influencing warfare and trade with the settlers through the power to distribute economic resources (Jensen, 1994; Perdue, 1994). About 1600, the constitution of the Iroquois Confederation guaranteed women the sole right to regulate war and peace (Rediscovering American Women, 1995:455). They were also tribal leaders, many who represented gynocratic systems based on egalitarianism, reciprocity, and complementarity (Allen, 1986; LaFromboise et al., 1990). Allen (1995) states that this is not a contradiction in terms, but believes that egalitarianism is not possible unless gynocracy is at its base. She notes that the Iroquoian gynocracy was referred to as a "petticoat government" by John Adair. Among Virginia Indians, women often held the highest authority in their tribes, and were recognized as such by white colonists. As Lebsock (1990) notes, "the English, fresh from the reign of Elizabeth I (1558-1603), knew a queen when they saw one." A European perspective based on patriarchal assumptions would of course envision systems using hierarchal imagery. The notion of gynocratic egalitarianism, is consistent with what Lerner (1995b:20) refers to as a new angle of vision for women's history: "Only when women's vision is equal with men's vision, do we perceive the true relations of the whole and the inner connectedness of the parts."

Another significant source of authority and status for native American women was through their roles as religious leaders and healers, creating a most powerful entity when roles of shaman and warleader coincided (Joe and Miller, 1994; Woloch, 1994). Spiritual role assignments were so important that in some tribes, the gods were women (Daly, 1994). In North American creation myths, women are the mediators between the supernatural and earthly worlds. Men and women sought spiritual understanding through individual quests for vision. Again, the worlds of men and women were rigidly separated. Fasting and seclusion, especially during menstruation, were part of a woman's spiritual quest (Evans: 1991). Menstruating women were believed to be dangerously powerful and potentially harmful to hunting and could drain the spiritual power of men, so they would withdraw to menstrual huts outside of the villages during thus time. Is this interpreted as taboo and banishment? In answering this, Evans (1991:33) suggests that they likely welcomed the respite and saw it as an opportunity for meditation, spiritual growth, and the enjoyment of the company of other women. The balanced and cooperative functionalist system represented by these practices would serve to enhance gender solidarity.

Colonization and its accompanying Christianity were the most disruptive forces in both these ancient tribal patterns and, by extension, the stature of women. The Iroquois Confederacy provided an image to the Europeans for a self-ruling inclusive democracy. But female participation in a democracy that was economically based on matrilineal-matrilocal clans was mystifying to them (Evans, 1991). With increased European contact, women were gradually stripped of tribal political power and economic assets, becoming more defined, hence confined, by their domestic roles. They began to look more and more like their subordinated European sisters. Christianity further eroded their powerful religious roles. The impact of Christianity on native American women continues to be debated among historians. There is evidence from the writings of Father Le Jeune in 1633 about the tribes living on the St. Lawrence River that women were the major obstacles to tribal conversion. They resisted being baptized and allowing their children to be educated at mission schools run by Catholic Jesuits. The women were accused of being independent and not obeying their husbands, and under Jesuit influence, the men believed that the women were the cause of their misfortunes and kept the "demons" among them (Devans, 1996:25). This indicates that women were acutely aware that conversion to Christianity brought with it severe role restrictions.

On the other hand, New England and Puritan missionaries, especially the Quakers, had greater success with women. If change was gradual and the Indians could retain key cultural elements, the belief was they would willingly accept the Christian message. This Christian Gospel did not obliterate native culture but "offered membership in God's tribe," and attracted women by "honoring their traditional tasks and rewarding their special abilities." (Rhonda, 1996). The culture could remain simultaneously Christian and Indian. Although historians disagree on the extent of native American women's resistance to Christianity, most scholars now accept the fact that these women had a high standing in precontact societies (Norton and Alexander, 1996a:21).

The Colonial Era

The first white settlers in America were searching for a kind of religious freedom that had been denied expression in the Old World. The Puritans sought to practice a brand of Christianity unencumbered by bureaucratic or doctrinal traditions which they believed hampered the expression of humanity's devotion to God. As with the Reformation, religious change was advocated, but the Puritans felt such change was impossible, given the political and theological climate of England and the Old World. Yet in challenging the old order, the Puritans retained traditional beliefs about women.

The Christian assumption of male superiority carried easily into the New World. Males were subordinate to God as females were subordinate to males. Puritan settlements such as the Massachusetts Bay Colony extracted a high degree of religious conformity which was considered necessary to the well-being and survival of the community. The Puritan community existed on the basis of obedience to the civil and moral law of the Old Testament as defined by the clergy. Social harmony and order were praised; any deviation from what these clerics sanctioned was seen to threaten the entire social fabric (Carlson, 1990:92). What complicated this picture was that Puritanism placed spiritual power in the individual, thus cultivating women's spiritual autonomy and religious development but within the confines of a rigid patriarchal family (Koehler, 1991). In 1637 Anne Hutchinson was banished from the Puritan colony of Massachusetts Bay for criticizing the minister's sermons, holding separate meetings for men and women who were of similar mind, and as indicated by documents from her trial, for challenging gender roles by not fulfilling her ordained womanly role (Kerber and De Hart, 1991; Koehler, 1991).

Along with the threat of banishment, the convenient accusation of witchcraft kept potentially ambitious women in tow. An epidemic of witchcraft persecutions ravaged the Puritan colonies, fueled by images of independent and disobedient women who defied authority. The infamous Salem witch trials of 1690 to 1693 occurred when a few adolescent girls and young women accused hundreds of older women of bewitching them. Invariably the older women were viewed as aggressive and threatening, out of character with the submissive women who knew their "proper place" in the Puritan community (Norton and Alexander, 1996a:46). Considering that this community was strictly organized around hierarchy and order, it was easy to condemn people who did not accept biologically ordained places in this order. Family relationships of many accused witches were marked by conflict. Women were brought to court for witchcraft for "railing" at their husbands or "speaking harsh things" against them (Demos, 1996:59). Perhaps more important, Karlsen (1991) indicates that there was an economic rationale to witchcraft. Many women condemned as witches had no male heirs in their immediate families and could potentially inherit larger portions of their fathers' or husbands' estates. These women were "aberrations in a society designed to keep property in the hands of men." Ultimately, an inheritance could also produce more economically independent women. Overall, being burned as a witch was a convenient way to rid the colony of its aberrations, foil challenges to gender norms, and maintain the desired social order.

Since religion extended to all areas of life and only men could be citizens, women were denied any public expression. When married, colonial women entered a legal status known as "civil death." Based on English Common Law the marital union meant that she could not vote, own property, sue or be sued, administer estates, sign contracts, or keep her children in the event of divorce. She had some control over property she brought to the marriage and could inherit property at the death of her husband but could not sell it. Marriage was sacrosanct but divorce was possible, particularly in cases of adultery or desertion. These arrangements ensured family harmony and prevented the community from taking over the responsibility of destitute women (Woloch, 1992). The community was divided into public and domestic spheres. Though women had essential tasks in the domestic area, Puritan men still controlled both spheres.

The other side of the picture saw Puritan men being required not only to provide for the economic and physical needs of the family, but also to love their wives. The revolutionary idea that love and marriage must be connected was historically significant because until this time marriage was simply seen as an economic necessity. If the couple happened to love one another, so much the better.

The ideal family was patriarchal and marriage, while based on love, fit into a family power structure which required a wife's obedience to her husband. From a writer in 1712, the well-ordered family is described with a strong dose of biblical imagery.

> The duty of love is mutual. The husband's government ought to be gentle and easy, and the wive's obedience ready and cheerful . . . though he governs her, he must not treat her as a servant, but as his own flesh; he must love her as himself. (Stout, 1986:134)

Much of the contemporary world would look at the Puritans with wonder in that love as a basis for marriage is rare for the majority of the globe.

Puritan women were also valued in part because they were so scarce. Most settlers were male and because many colonies were literally wiped out by disease or starvation, the colonists knew that it was vital to repopulate or see their religious visions doomed. Besides providing domestic services and children, women were deemed essential to build a foundation for a stable social order. Though wives were valuable, when it came to starvation, patriarchy prevailed, as the following excerpt from a Jamestown, Virginia, historical record documents.

> And one amongst the rest did kill his wife, powdered (salted) her, and had eaten part of her before it was known, for which he was executed, as he well deserved. Now whether she was better roasted, boiled, or cabonadoed (grilled), I know not, but of such a dish as powdered wife I never heard of. (quoted in Frey and Morton, 1986:40)

In addition, women were important for their economic productivity within the family. Family survival, hence community survival, was tied to the efforts of both men and women. But planting gardens, weaving, canning, and candle and soap making contributed to the family's economic fortunes, and these tasks were largely confined to women. Subsistence living was the rule, but surplus products could be bartered or sold. The family was the basic social unit for the colonists, and women were integral to its well-being.

Historians are at odds about the prestige of women during this era (Carr and Walsh, 1989; Koehler, 1989, 1991; Grob and Billias, 1992). Since there were far fewer immigrant women than men and women were considered valuable, leads some to suggest that the colonial period was a "golden age" for women. Although the colonists came to the New World with patriarchal ideas, adapting to the harshness of the environment required the modification of many beliefs. Strict adherence to gender roles was impossible for survival. Women were economically productive and of necessity had to have expanded roles. Outside the home women could be found engaging in merchant, trading, and crafts functions. And while English Common Law intruded into the colonies, it was often circumvented.

If a golden age existed, it had clearly declined by the late eighteenth century. The family lost its centrality as the economic unit in society, to be replaced by a wider marketplace dominated by men. Women's work was once again confined to activities which were not income-producing. Colonial women became more dependent on their families for how their lives were defined. The American economy did not allow many opportunities for women to be wage earners, with increased resistance to women, who more out of necessity than desire, sought work in enterprises not strictly viewed as within the family realm. The crucial element, however, is that Puritan ideology was based on the assumption of female inferiority and subordination which was never really questioned throughout the colonial period. In all, the colonial environment was a modified version of Old World notions about women. The thesis that between the seventeenth and nineteenth centuries a status decline occurred for women from a golden age (in the colonial period) is still contested. It is partly resolved by Norton (1984), who argues that while there was no "golden age," political participation and education enhanced women's autonomy during the Revolutionary era. These changes kindled public discourse on women's roles that served as a catalyst for later gender role change.

The Victorians: The Cult of True Womanhood

The struggle for survival faced by the colonists gradually diminished as they prospered on farms and in shops. As judged by economic contributions to the family, a woman's productive role lessened, and she became occupied with solely domestic tasks, like housekeeping and child rearing. By the nineteenth century her world had changed considerably. Victorian examples of womanhood made their way into magazines and novels directed toward women. Despite an undercurrent of liberal feminism that was fermenting during this period, periodicals targeted to middle-class women presented them with the ideology of domestic femininity (Cantor, 1993). More and more women achieved literacy, and what they did read admonished them to be "True Women," and assume the cardinal virtues of piety, purity, submissiveness, and domesticity (Lystra, 1989; Welter, 1996). These were the standards upon which society would judge them and which they would judge themselves.

Tied completely to her family, the middle-class woman found herself with time on her hands, which was a luxury not shared by her colonial sisters. The reality of idleness was transformed into gentility, an ideal for which many families strived. This gentility was accompanied by attitudes which put women on pedestals that literally made them out of reach. Women were to be protected from the harshness of the world outside the home. Protectionism in reality meant repression. Victorian femininity meant that a woman was sexually, socially, and politically repressed. The doctrine of separate spheres for the activities of women and men became firmly entrenched in the American consciousness.

The strength of the cult of "True Womanhood" was generally effective in silencing many of the voices of feminism which were being heard in Europe and America also during the Victorian era. From pulpits throughout America, women were told that happiness and power could be found in their own homes, with society being disrupted if they chose to listen to voices calling them to other spheres (Welter, 1996). Supposedly, a woman did have a choice to define her rights and roles either inside or outside the home. Welter (1996:122) quotes the Rev. Mr. Stearns in this regard:

> Yours is to determine whether the beautiful order of society. . . . shall continue as it has been (or whether) society shall break up and become a chaos of disjointed and unsightly elements.

The "True Woman" was not to be swayed by so-called reformers speaking of other rights. In such an atmosphere, what real choice did women have? It is also interesting to consider these ideals for women over a century ago in light of contemporary arguments against extending greater rights to women. Perhaps history may be repeating itself in this regard.

The Victorian era conjures up images of rigidity and repression which cannot be denied, but explorations into women's history are providing alternative views. Lystra (1989) demonstrates that middle-class Victorian America exhibited marked sexual expression and erotic intensity through the private correspondence of lovers. Her analysis of this intimate correspondence from the perspective of Victorian social conventions is sociologically a symbolic interaction approach. Romantic love and sexual expression flourished at a time when public prudery was the norm. Though hidden, this intimate reality is also culturally significant. "The system of ideas and behavior commonly referred to as romantic love provided one significant means of integrating private and public worlds" (Lystra, 1989:6). Since one's "true" self was disclosed in this correspondence, it can be argued that women gained a sense of mastery not allowed in other parts of their lives.

Other historical research confirms that women exercised active control in adapting conditions of their domestic lives to meet their personal needs. While the patriarchal family remained firmly entrenched and basic gender inequities intruded into domestic life, Victorian women were able to achieve a modicum of autonomy (Sklar, 1991). Gender role segregation produces gender solidarity which is nurtured by the emotional segregation of men and women. This allowed for the existence of a female world where a supportive, intimate network of female friendships and intimacy could grow. Smith-Rosenberg (1985; 1996) argues that this secretive world created an autonomous female culture serving to empower women. Contemporary functionalism would suggest that a focus on the rigidity associated with the Victorian era and the "True Woman" model overlooks the latent functions these very patterns served for women.

Frontier Life

Idleness was impossible on the frontier. Victorian America extolled the gentility and supposed frailness of middle-class women. Frontier society would have been disdainful of these very traits. As with the colonial era, women were valued for their work both inside and outside the home. During the early frontier expansion, women were scarce; yet colonial society never seriously questioned the notion of woman's inferiority; hence, her relative status remains unclear. Through the hardship and deprivation of frontier life combined with less adherence to religious proscriptions concerning gender, it is evident that the pioneer woman achieved a degree of freedom and respect unlike previous periods of America's brief history.

The frontier experience began with the grueling trip west which often took six months to complete. Faced with the deprivation of the trail, surviving the trip often meant that the normal sexual division of labor was suspended, with both women and older children filling expanded roles. Yet rather than viewing the situation as an opportunity for male-female equality, diaries from these women suggest that they saw themselves as invaders of a male domain. Although few women who emigrated west on the Oregon or Overland Trails came from the northeastern middle classes where the cult of "True Womanhood" reached its zenith, they were not immune to it either. In the journey west, women and men maintained separate worlds of existence as much as possible. Women created a specific female culture based on their roles of motherhood, healer, and nurse, but Faragher (1996:207) states, trail life precluded sustained interaction and deep attachments to other women. Whereas men used the trip to fulfill dreams of "camaraderie, action and achievement," many women found the experience lonely and isolating.

While life on the trail and later settlement in the West threw their domestic roles in a state of disarray, women appeared reluctant to redefine their boundaries to create anything but a temporary alteration of affairs. Although women often shared work and had overlapping functions with their fathers and husbands, gender remained the key variable in determining their duties and interests, and this meant that the primary focus of their lives was domestic (Riley, 1988, 1991).

It is not safe to conclude from this, however, that frontier women should be categorized as primarily passive. Myres (1988) suggests that they exhibited a spirit of nonconformity, adventure, and adaptation. Frontier settlements saw the necessity of woman's labor not being confined to the home. Child rearing was often left to siblings as wives worked in the fields with their husbands. Subsistence farming required that as many goods as possible be produced and consumed within the home. Women took the major responsibility in this area. Isolated farms, prairie loneliness, and the daily harshness of frontier living generated the understanding that men and women, wives and husbands, depended on one another for not only physical but emotional survival. This understanding served to elevate the status of women. Popular images of women as saints in sunbonnets, madonnas of the prairies, and pioneer mothers abounded during the era of westward expansion as well as accounts of the deprivation, ardor, and premature aging associated with frontier life (Riley, 1988:1). Moynihan and her colleagues (1990) note that the diaries and letters of pioneer women demonstrate that the continuities of Victorian domesticity existed side by side with newer roles and that both interpretations are reasonable.

Stratton's (1981) accounts of women who emigrated to the Kansas frontier during the latter part of the nineteenth century provide testimony to their critical roles and how they withstood and accepted them. Using diaries, letters, and other autobiographical statements of these pioneer women, actual experiences and reminiscences are recorded. A daughter recalls the birth of her brother on a day when her father had made an all-day trip to town for wood. Her mother was alone with two babies, no neighbors, and no doctor, when the stork arrived.

> So my brave mother got the baby clothes together on a chair by the bed, water and scissors . . . drew a bucket of fresh water from a sixty-foot well; made some bread-and-butter sandwiches; set out some milk for the babies. . . So at about noon the stork left a fine baby boy. . . My mother, having fainted a number of times in her attempt to dress the baby, had succeeded at last; and when my father came in he found a very uncomfortable but brave and thankful mother, thankful that he had returned home with the precious wood, and that she and the baby were alright. (quoted in Stratton, 1981:87)

Such accounts are characteristic rather than exceptional. They speak of women who, with their families, endured prairie fires, locusts, droughts, disease, and the ever-present loneliness. Most did not return to their homes in the East, but accepted their new life with stoicism and a hope for making their own farm an economic success. Through hundreds of excerpts from diaries, letters, and oral histories, a number of writers have provided a picture of matter-of-fact women who adapted to, and did not seem to begrudge, their frontier existence (Stratton, 1981; Norwood, 1988; Moynihan et al., 1990).

This is not meant to idealize the brutal existence many pioneer women confronted. It is only to point out that adversity was apparently an important ingredient in bringing men and women together more equitably on the frontier, even if the participants themselves failed to recognize that alterations in gender roles were occurring. As with other times in history, frontier life undeniably demonstrates that a woman's contributions are as important as a man's. In this case, however, her contributions enhanced her status, a fact which has been recognized earlier by historians.

Industrialization

An interesting incongruity in American history is that as the cult of domesticity gained ascendance, the first mass movement of white women into industrial employment was also occurring. From the founding of America, women have always participated in the world of paid labor and could not be completely circumscribed by their domestic roles. When teachers or shopkeepers or planters or traders were needed and men were unavailable, women were encouraged to fill these roles. Industrial expansion during the nineteenth century required an entirely new class of workers. Faced with a shortage of males who continued to farm, industrialists convinced women that even if they were too weak for agriculture, work in the mills could suit their temperaments, was good for them, and good for the country. For the less marriageable, factory work saved them from pauperism. The Civil War and its aftermath accelerated the need for women in industry (Woloch, 1992). Thousands of women and many children answered the call.

By the latter part of the century, the shift from an agricultural to an urban industrialized economy in the nation was accelerating. New definitions of work recognized that the family was no longer a critical unit of production and that work was to be performed for wages at other locations outside home and farm. By the turn of the century, agriculture required less than 10 percent of America's labor power with 20 percent of all women in the United States over the age 16 employed outside the home (Balanoff, 1990:611). These women were young, single, or the wives and daughters of working-class families whose income was necessary to keep the family out of poverty. As Balanoff (1990:611) states, married women worked only out of dire necessity, often driven into the labor market by widowhood.

More specifically, it was the middle-class married woman who again was expected to devote her time and talents to the emotional well-being of the family. This was happening at the very time when labor-saving products and appliances began to be introduced to the home. By 1900, the realization that housework and child care were no longer a full-time occupation led to more leisure, boredom, and restlessness for women who were discouraged from seeking paid employment outside the home. This led to two important results. First, many middle-class women became involved in social reform work, including the growing feminist movement. Second, the already existing schism between working-class and middle-class women widened (Ogden, 1986; Daniel, 1987; O'Neill, 1989; Carlson, 1990). As we shall see, to date this schism has not been completely mended.

The working-class woman was confronted with different issues, the basic one being subsistence. Industrial growth increasingly demanded an abundance of cheap labor and looked to poorer women and immigrants to take on this load. The urbanizing Eastern states accommodated the flood of immigrants who settled in areas close to the factories, mines, and mills in which they worked, often creating a ghettolike atmosphere cutting them off from wider society. By the beginning of the twentieth century, 25 percent of unmarried immigrant women worked outside the home in comparison to 15 percent of native-born women, with the immigrant women overrepresented in unskilled labor activities (Banner, 1984:61). African-American women worked on farms and as domestics because factory labor was, for the most part, closed to them in the North. In the South, there was an oversupply of black female labor which made their position worse. In 1912 a black woman working as a domestic reported that she had to tolerate low wages and could not rely on labor unions of any kind because there "would be hundreds of other Negroes right on the spot to take their places" (Woloch, 1994).

The working conditions faced by women, and many men, were appalling, even by the standards of the day. Banner (1984:67-69) and Wertheimer and Nelson (1989) point out that unsanitary conditions, no rest breaks, not being allowed to sit down, ten-hour work days with a half-day on Saturday, and grueling, rote tasks were characteristic. In combination with an unsafe environment where machines had no safety guards and buildings were poorly ventilated and lacked fire escapes, it is understandable why job-related injuries and deaths skyrocketed. In 1911, the Triangle Shirtwaist Company in New York caught on fire, killing 146 workers, many of them woman. Doors were kept locked so that workers could be inspected before they left for possible possession of company merchandise, and what fire escapes were available were in need of repair and buckled under the pressure of those fleeing the fire (Wertheimer and Nelson, 1989:321).

The garment industry was notorious in its treatment of lower-level workers. A system of subcontracting finishing work to people, primarily immigrant women, became common. Women would work in what came to be called sweatshops, in basements and workrooms of low-rent tenement apartments, thereby saving the company much in the way of production costs (Banner, 1984:67). What made an already dismal situation worse was that it was necessary for workers to purchase their own equipment which would then require years of arduous labor to pay off.

When men and women were employed in the same factories, women took less prestigious jobs and were paid less. Men resisted being employed with women in the same job. The fact that the genders were segregated by type of activity led to a stratification system which justified the lower wages paid to women. Women rarely resisted the system since they moved in and out of the labor force at the discretion of others. Since both women and their employers viewed employment as temporary, gender segregation of jobs not only perpetuated low wages but also kept women out of training programs and demands for job-related benefits (Kemp, 1994:157). As we will see in Chapter 14, the nineteenth-century roots of gender typing in jobs has carried over to today in the debate over comparable worth.

The scandalous conditions under which people worked generated much sympathy nationally and created a ripe atmosphere for unions to flourish, with major growth occurring from the 1870s through World War I. Union activist Mary Harris ("Mother") Jones reported on the horrendous plight of women and children in industry, "condemned to slave daily in the washroom (of breweries) in wet shoes, and wet clothes . . . in the vile smell of sour beer, lifting cases . . . weighing from 100 to 150 pounds" (Woloch, 1994:238). In 1881 the Knights of Labor was opened for women and blacks, calling for equal pay for equal work. In 1885, 2,500 women members of the Knights of Labor endured a six-month strike marked by violence in Yonkers, New York, at a mill where they worked as carpet weavers. The International Ladies' Garment Workers Union (ILGWU) gained recognition in many shops as a result of a strike which lasted through the winter of 1909 and involved 20,000 shirtwaist workers throughout the city, most of whom were women. With the support of the Women's Trade Union League and public outrage from the Triangle Shirtwaist Company fire, legislation was passed requiring more stringent safety and inspection codes for factories.

But compared to the union movement involving men, women's attempts to unionize were not nearly as successful. For both men and women, the courts, employers, police, and often the public were not supportive of union efforts. Many unions still refused to admit women, and even with an official policy urging equal pay to women, the most powerful union, the American Federation of Labor (AFL), was unwilling to exert the pressure necessary for its affiliates to conform to the rule. The AFL was also becoming a union of skilled crafts workers made up exclusively of men, and there was fear that the success of the union would be diluted if it took on the numerous women still in the ranks of the unskilled. Originally welcoming women as members, a period of economic recession saw members of the Knights of Labor competing with one another for scarce jobs. Women were no longer welcomed with open arms. In 1895, only 5 percent of all union members were female, and by 1900 only 3 percent of all women who worked in factories were unionized (Wertheimer and Nelson, 1989:319; Banner, 1984:72).

The ILGWU had become the third largest affiliate of the AFL by 1913 (Banner, 1984:71), and it did capitalize on the power that was being wielded by the AFL itself. But because men and women were segregated by job, the unions representing women had less success. Unionization was obstructed by men's fears of job competition and the tenacious belief that women's place was in the home (Kessler-Harris, 1991). By 1900, women represented half the membership of unions in five industries (women's clothing, gloves, hats, shirtwaist and laundry, and tobacco), and they earned about half of what men earned; black women earned half of what was made by white women.

The characteristics of the female labor force also made unionization efforts difficult. Work for women was unstable, temporary, and subject to economic ups and downs. In jobs performed by both genders men were given preference in slack periods, and women were laid off. Young women worked until marriage, which was the preferred exit out of the factories and into a middle-class life style. Overall, unions were most helpful to women when they were allowed to join with men. Unions of women workers tended to be small, more isolated, and financially weak, although they did provide opportunities for women to develop both leadership skills and agendas representing their own interests (Wertheimer and Nelson, 1989:321).

Women have tended to advance more in the labor force during periods of growth as well as in periods of war. During the Civil War women served as nurses, clerks, and copyists and produced uniforms and munitions needed. World War I also saw an expansion of job opportunities both in Britain and the United States. Government campaigns to rally support for war, its supply needs, and women's labor force participation have been seen throughout American history. World War I was also the first war where women in America and Europe were actively recruited for military service (Schneider and Schneider, 1994). After the war British women who had worked in engineering; on buses, railways, and trams; in the services; and in government offices were dismissed and expected to return home. Those who persisted on jobs were often labeled as hussies or as women who stole men's jobs (Beddoe, 1989:3). Such statements were also echoed in the United States. Public support for the war effort made the transition to the labor force easier for women who, if they had a choice, had not previously considered working outside the home. In most instances, however, women were summarily dismissed after the men returned.

While women who ventured outside the home were caught in conflicting roles, it is apparent that both industrialization and war were the catalysts for creating the "new woman" of the 1920s. Lamenting the demise of the "True Woman," her new counterpart was both hailed and damned as she strove for equality with men. She "entered the 1920s with high expectations, ready for challenge and for choice" (Brown, 1987:30-31,47). The flapper era saw a loosening of sexual and social restraint. Searching for independence from parents and excitement from one another, working women migrated to cities, seeking each other out in the crowded boarding houses in which they lived. Meyerowitz (1990:150) asserts that these furnished rooms created new peer-oriented subcultures where women charted sexual terrain that other women later followed. While retaining a separate political sphere from men, many of these new woman worked for social and legal change. Prosperity, hope, and the formation of an identity that included extra-domestic activities led many of these women to pursue feminist causes.

In less than a decade, much of this hope was dashed. The rule that scarce jobs go to men first continued through the Depression. Job segregation and the belief that there was "women's work" and "men's work" ironically protected the jobs of women who worked as waitresses, domestics, or clerks. Rather than accepting the loss of prestige that would be associated with doing a "woman's" job, some men abandoned their families because they were no longer breadwinners. In those instances where a job was not defined completely in gender terms, such as teacher, it was rare to see a woman either obtain it or keep it if a man could be employed instead.

In general, industrialization saw women make steady headway in the world of paid employment. Older attitudes about women's functions in the family continued to compete with the needs of an expanding economy. But the precedent for women working outside the home gained strength and was nurtured by gradual public acceptance for newer roles. Once the industrial era established this trend, it was World War II that provided the most important catalyst for expanding employment options.

World War II

Historically war has been an impetus for positive social change that otherwise might not have occurred or would have occurred at a much slower pace. War suspends notions of what is considered typical or conventional and throws people into novel situations which, in turn, sensitizes them to an awareness of potential never dreamed possible. This happens on and off the actual battlefield.

Women have consistently taken on expanded roles in wartime, by choice as well as necessity. As shown in this chapter, throughout history we see women managing the affairs of home, farm, and business while their husbands, sons, or brothers were away for extended periods. Considering, too, that the history of the world has been marked by frequent and prolonged periods of war, the roles women assumed were essential for social equilibrium. Usually these newer roles have been short-lived, with the prewar social order swiftly reestablished when the men returned home. Although this was indeed the case with World War II, it can also be stated that this particular war profoundly influenced American women involved in the war effort to the extent that its liberating effects not only endured but were also consequential for the next generation of women. The impact was seen most in the areas of employment and family.

When America officially entered the war in 1941, government leaders quickly recognized that victory depended upon the total commitment of the nation. One task of the Office of War Information (OWI) was to constantly monitor public opinion to determine the degree of commitment and willingness to sacrifice for the war. Accustomed to men taking the lead in both politics and war, women were less enthusiastic about the war and less receptive to military themes and national and international events regarding the war than were men (Campbell, 1984:6-7). Because women were socialized into values related to domesticity, the war was simply more remote for them. Within a few months of Pearl Harbor, when patriotism was at its height, a concerted national policy to fully mobilize the civilian population in the war effort was initiated. Much of this policy was focused on women.

The powerful War Production Board (WPC) and War Manpower Commission (WMC) were set up to convert to a wartime economy, coordinate labor for the various sectors of the economy, and allocate workers for both war and civilian production. The booming wartime economy literally ended the Depression almost overnight. It soon became apparent to these agencies that the war machine required uninterrupted production schedules through an increased labor supply. Women were essential in filling the roles in the war production industry as the men were called into military service. An efficient propaganda program was put into effect which prompted women to respond to the employment needs of a nation at war.

The battle abroad could only be won if women would recognize their patriotic duty to become employed on the home front. After the Depression years, the higher pay and better working conditions offered in the war industry found many women eagerly seeking work in all areas. When jobs became available again, women were first hired in positions where women had previously worked, as clerks or semiskilled laborers in factories producing uniforms or foodstuffs. The higher pay for work in defense plants enticed many women to apply for jobs, but they found themselves rebuffed.

At first, defense employers were reluctant to hire women, even if it meant paying men overtime or creating shortages in production. And when plants were converted from civilian to war production, thousands of women lost their jobs and were replaced by men. As Hartmann (1982:54-55) notes, women were also likely to be excluded from government training programs though there was official acknowledgment that women could be efficient and versatile employees. If implemented over a long period, such a policy would have had disastrous consequences for the war effort.

As labor shortages reached crisis proportions, job training for women and opportunities in almost all phases of defense work dramatically increased. Within six months after Pearl Harbor, employers indicated a willingness to hire women in a variety of semiskilled, professional, and managerial jobs. OWI was responsible for "selling" the war to women and created images of defense work as exciting, even glamorous, and economically rewarding. Campaigns appealed to patriotism and guilt for slacking off when the war effort needed women. "Rosie the Riveter," popularized through a wartime song, became the new home front heroine. She represented the millions of women who worked at munitions plants, foundries, and quarries as lumberjacks, shipbuilders, and plumbers. OWI met with success in recruitment for the civilian labor force as well as for induction into the armed services. Women's corps of all branches of the military were formed during World War II, and by January 1944, over 100,000 women joined (Mathis, 1994). The employment of women reached its wartime peak in July 1944, when 19 million women were employed, an increase of over 5 million from 1941 (Clive, 1989:360-61).

Once the gender barrier eroded, women's opportunities in the war industry advanced, with less regard also paid to age, marital status, and race. However, preferences were given to women who were white, single, and younger. The war allowed African-American women access to employment in defense plants, which significantly decreased their reliance on agricultural and domestic labor. Employment prospects for both black men and women were increased by defense contracts, which contained clauses prohibiting racial discrimination. However, some companies refused to hire African-American women throughout the war. Labor shortages increased their numbers but they were hired for the lowest-level jobs and unless they were protected by a union, were paid less than either white women or black men (Anderson, 1996). The mixed feelings of this situation—patriotism and pride along with disenchantment—are poignantly expressed by an African-American woman who worked in a defense plant.

> I'm not fooling myself about this war. Victory won't mean victory for Democracy—yet. But that will come later. . . . maybe a hundred years later. But doing my share today, I'm keeping a place for some brown woman tomorrow. (Johnson, 1943/1996)

As the war continued and the demand for defense workers grew, the demographic balance of the female labor force shifted considerably so that both older and married women were recruited, with some industries reporting an even division between single and married workers (Daniel, 1987; Clive, 1989). Near the end of the war married women outnumbered single women in the labor force.

The new encouragement for married women to enter the labor force challenged a society which firmly believed that a mother's place was at home with her children. By the close of the war, 32 percent of women who worked in the major defense centers had children under the age of 14 (Campbell, 1984:82). Day-care centers, foster home programs, and other variations of child care were developed throughout the country. By suggesting that defense production was tied to provisions for child care, day-care services increased dramatically. The Federal Works Agency administered a program which, at its height, enrolled 130,000 children in over 3,000 centers (Hartmann, 1982:59; Martin, 1991).

Rather than viewing such options as a menace to children and an indictment for their mothers, such provisions were praised for allowing mothers of younger children to enter the work force where they were sorely needed. Campbell (1984:82) suggests that the lure the government used was to assure mothers that their children would be well looked after. Overall, day-care centers were not that abundant and were used by relatively few employed mothers, with most relying on friends and relatives for child care. Some women remained suspicious of organized day care and preferred to remain unemployed rather than believe the media campaigns. The key issue here is that when women were needed for industry, innovative strategies were developed to help them in their quest for adequate day care. Also, the suspension of traditional beliefs combined with an effective media and government propaganda program allowed a nation to view day care, at least for a time, as a virtuous and acceptable choice. Although mothers were working in defense plants, for the most part their children were not regarded as being socially, physically, or psychologically at risk as a result.

The earlier reluctance to employ women at all, especially married women, for the heavy industry of war, was replaced by an understanding that women could, and actually should, shoulder more of the responsibility for the war effort. But a paradox remained. The men were doing battle overseas to protect the cherished values of home and family, and yet these very values were potentially being threatened by the kinds of roles in which women found themselves. To get around this problem, another propaganda campaign suggested that women were in it only "for the duration," and they would reassume their domestic duties after the war, gladly giving up their jobs to the returning men. This would supposedly alleviate any problems of joblessness for the men. Of course, female unemployment was never an issue. Devotion to country meant the sacrifice of temporarily becoming employed for pay, with the home held up as where women would and should want to be. And to a great extent, this belief was accepted by both men and women after the war.

The ideal for which the war was fought, country and family, remained unshaken. Romantic visions of resumed, postwar lives as wives and mothers abounded during the war, alongside the images of capable women working in defense plants. Hovering in the wings during the war years, the cult of the home made a triumphant comeback to entice even the most reluctant women out of the labor force. For some women who remained in the labor force, a return to prewar job segregation caused mobilization and protest. But with no fully articulated class consciousness or feminist movement to bolster them, they had no real basis for a sustained challenge to the system (Gabin, 1989; Milkman, 1991:220-21).

The conversion to a peacetime economy was accelerated with soaring marriage and birth rates. Labor-saving devices and technological innovations were introduced which revolutionized housekeeping but did not allow for a lessening of a woman's domestic responsibilities. Whereas the wartime media appealed to a woman's efficiency in the home to keep her productive in the defense plants, propaganda after the war concentrated on homemaking roles (Mathis, 1994) and higher standards of excellence for them. In addition, wives were made responsible for the psychological adjustment their husbands had to undergo with the return to civilian life. This meant that her needs were to be subordinated to his. Women were cautioned to be sensitive, responsive, and above all, feminine, since this is what civilian life meant for men.

It is apparent from this that the new roles for women created during the war existed alongside traditional beliefs concerning their primary domestic duties. The view that World War II represented a watershed in the experience of American women is shared by several historians, while others argue that continuity and persistence of gender roles was the reality (Campbell, 1984; Kaledin, 1984; Daniel, 1987; O'Neill, 1989). The women themselves were divided in their postwar plans. Although many enjoyed the work, they saw it as temporary and only for the duration of the war. Many women who gained a sense of independence from their wartime jobs were bitter when postwar cutbacks forced them out of the labor force (Gabin, 1989). Single women, war widows, and those who had to support themselves anyway had no choice but to continue to work. The loss of pay and respect during the postwar years weighed heavily on many women.

While the debate continues, it is impossible to ignore the liberating effects of World War II on women because the war itself contributed to broad social changes in American society. The seeds of social change were planted during the war and took root in an atmosphere of economic growth. Campbell (1984:237) points out that recovery from the Depression, greater equality in the distribution of income, and urban expansion affected both women and men. Home and family remained integral to women's aspirations, but a doctrine of the spheres which had effectively separated women from any other outside existence was doomed after the war. In all, the roots of the sociocultural trends of the 1950s and 1960s can be traced to the war years.

Attitudes do not change as quickly as behavior. Efforts that sought to restrict the nondomestic roles and activities of women in the postwar years relied on beliefs about biological determinism which were difficult to reject. Throughout history we have seen scores of women who have successfully broadened narrow role definitions. But World War II provided models for gender role change on such a grand scale that women's accomplishments could not be conveniently relegated to a forgotten footnote in history. Contemporary women and men alike must contend with theories of biological destiny and other beliefs which seek to bolster the older gender role system. Yet such attitudes must inevitably erode in the face of massive evidence which contradicts these assumptions. The progress made by women during the war coupled with rapid postwar social and economic changes provided the framework for the reemergence of the women's movement in the United States.

THE WOMEN'S MOVEMENT

> In the new code of laws....I desire you would remember the ladies and be more generous and favorable to them than your ancestors. (Abigail Adams, March 31, 1776)

Abigail Adams wrote to her husband John when he was attending the Second Continental Congress and cautioned him that if the ladies were ignored and denied the rights for which the Revolutionary War was being fought, they would eventually create a revolution of their own. She believed that women could not be bound by laws which they had no hand in creating. Abigail Adams persisted in her quest with additional letters to her husband and her friends. To John Adams she also wrote:

> That your sex is naturally tyrannical is a truth so thoroughly established as to admit of no dispute; but such of you as wish to be happy, willingly give up the harsh title of master for the more tender and endearing one of friend. Then put it out of the power of the vicious and the lawless to use us with cruelty and indignity and impunity . . . so whilst you are proclaiming peace and good will to men, emancipation for all nations, you insist on retaining an absolute power over wives. But you must remember that arbitrary power is like most other things which are hard, very liable to be broken. (Abigail Adams, in Norton and Alexander, 1996a:77)

John Adams, later to become the nation's second president, dismissed these warnings while helping to draft humanistic documents which proclaimed that all men are created equal. As he wrote to Abigail, "As to your extraordinary Code of Laws, I cannot but laugh . . .We know better than to repeal our masculine system" (John Adams in Norton and Alexander, 1996a:77). For the Founding *Fathers*, the business at hand was to build the infrastructure for an enduring democracy. That this democracy denied basic rights to females, as well as to blacks, was overlooked by most. The challenges which did emerge from a few individuals, even from such influential women as Abigail Adams, did not provide the momentum for any kind of organized protest. While Abigail Adams did accurately predict that women would themselves ferment another revolution, it took another half century before it would be actualized at all in America.

Two other events served as important ingredients for the rise of feminism and the beginnings of a woman's movement in the United States. The French Revolution's ideals of liberty and equality inspired the Declaration of the Rights of Man in 1789. A reply by Olympe de Gouges came two years later with the Declaration of the Rights of Woman, where she declared that "woman is born free and her rights are the same as those of man" and that "the law be an expression of the general will" and "all citizens, men and women alike" participate in making it (cited in Deckard, 1983:207). For the first time, humanistic standards were applied explicitly to both genders. More importantly, the democratic fervor which was sweeping France and influencing other parts of Europe and England created an atmosphere where such radical writings were at least considered. It is likely that had such a work appeared first in America, it would have been rejected, dismissed, and buried.

Second, in 1792, English writer and activist Mary Wollstonecraft wrote what was to become the bible of the feminist movement, *The Vindication of the Rights of Woman*. In this remarkable work, Wollstonecraft argues that ideals of equality should be applied to both genders, and that it is only in bodily strength where a man has a natural superiority over a woman:

> Not only the virtue but the knowledge of the two sexes should be the same in nature, if not in degree, and that women, considered not only as moral, but rational creatures, ought to endeavor to acquire human virtues (or perfections) by the same means as men, instead of being educated like a fanciful kind of half being. (Wollstonecraft, in Hardt, 1982)

She maintained that women must strengthen their minds, become friends to their husbands, and not be dependent on them. When women are kept ignorant and passive, not only do their children suffer but society as a whole will be weakened. In advocating full partnership with men, Wollstonecraft explicitly called for a "revolution in female manners" to make women part of the human species by reforming themselves and then the world.

> Let women share the rights and she will emulate the virtues of man; for she must grow more perfect when emancipated. . . . (Wollstonecraft, in Hardt, 1982:409)

The Early Movement: 1830 to 1890

As mentioned earlier, the Industrial Revolution altered society through a drastic reorganization of the process of production. By the 1830s, women found themselves working for low wages in factories under dismal conditions. When manufacturing altered home production of items such as soap, bread, candles, and clothing, middle-class women lost much economic power. Whereas factory women used unions as vehicles for organized protest, middle-class women realized that their aims could best be met through opportunities for higher education and political rights. In both instances, these women had different class-based ambitions and used divergent strategies to meet their needs. But unique to American history, they organized into their respective groups as women meeting the needs of women.

The issue of economics generated the stimulus for working-class and middle-class women to first organize. But the major catalyst for the woman's movement was ostensibly humanistic in orientation and provided an outlet for mostly middle-class women who had the time and money to participate in a social cause. It was only during the latter suffrage movement that more women of both classes joined together for a common goal. Before suffrage became the rallying point for women, slavery was the issue. When Wollstonecraft was calling for the emancipation of women, many women were already playing a critical role in the abolitionist movement to emancipate the blacks from slavery.

It soon became apparent to the women who worked in the antislavery movement that they were not on the same political level as the male abolitionists. Women abolitionists were often not allowed to make public speeches, and with the formation of the American Anti-Slavery Society in 1833, they were denied the right to sign its Declaration of Purposes. When the World Anti-Slavery Convention met in London in 1840, women members of the American delegation, including Lucretia Mott and Elizabeth Cady Stanton, had to sit in the galleries and could not participate in any of the proceedings. They became painfully conscious of the fact that slavery had to do with gender as well as race.

Women abolitionists began to speak more openly about women's rights to the extent that their male comrades feared the antislavery issue would be weakened. As progressive as the abolitionist movement was, the inherent sexism of the day served to divide and alienate its members. While continuing their work for antislavery, women were also now more vocal about legislative reforms related to family rights, divorce, women's property and temperance issues and how they affected home and society (Bolt, 1993; Rose, 1996). Recognizing that the inferior status of women needed to be urgently addressed, the first Woman's Rights Convention was held in Seneca Falls, New York, in

1848, an event hailed as the birth of the women's movement in the United States.

The Seneca Falls Convention approved a Declaration of Sentiments modeled after the Declaration of Independence, which listed the forms of discrimination women had to endure, and which they vowed to eliminate. The following examples (cited in Hole and Levine, 1995:480) from the declaration demonstrate the continuities of the past and present concerns of women.

1. We hold these truths to be self-evident: that all men and women are created equal; that they are endowed by their Creator with certain inalienable rights; that among these are life, liberty and the pursuit of happiness.
2. The history of mankind is a history of repeated injuries and usurpations on the part of man toward woman, having in direct object the establishment of an absolute tyranny over her.
3. He has compelled her to submit to laws, in the formation of which she has no voice.
4. He has made her, if married, in the eye of the law, civilly dead.
5. He has monopolized nearly all the profitable employments, and from those she is permitted to follow, she receives but a scanty remuneration. He closes against her all the avenues to wealth and distinction which he considers most honorable to himself. As a teacher of theology, medicine or law, she is not known.
6. He has endeavored, in every way he could, to destroy her confidence in her own powers, to lessen her self-respect, and to make her willing to lead a dependent and abject life.

This listing of the discriminatory practices against women was accepted by the convention as well as eleven of the twelve resolutions aimed at ending such practices. Whereas it was agreed that women had to submit to laws they did not help create, there was not unanimous agreement about whether they should seek the vote. History has given the Seneca Falls meeting the distinction of originating the suffrage movement, but the suffrage resolution was passed only by a small majority. Although the early women's movement has become synonymous with suffrage, this was the very issue which initially split its supporters. Perhaps difficult to understand by today's standards, many women believed that equality was possible without the vote.

The following years saw conventions for women's rights being held throughout the North and West. Since abolition was part of its platform, the movement itself never spread to the South before the Civil War. During the war, activities on the behalf of women per se were dormant, but they emerged in earnest soon after. Even with no national agenda, disagreements as to strategy, and run by a few women who had the strength and spare time to work for its causes, the movement grew in strength. Deckard (1983:253) credits three outstanding women and their unique talents for this growth: Lucy Stone, the movement's most gifted orator; Elizabeth Cady Stanton, philosopher and program writer; and Susan B. Anthony, the organizing genius. They spoke on social, economic, and legal issues affecting women and pressed for reforms in such areas as education, wages, organized labor, child welfare, and inheritance.

As the movement grew, so did its opponents. First as abolitionists, then as feminists, and always as women, the movement was despised and ridiculed by many. By the standards of the day, what were seen as militant methods fueled opposition. The ever-present verbal abuse at women's rallies (Sherr, 1995) along with the threat of mob violence caused some supporters to advocate less militancy and even to downgrade the importance of the vote. Again, the ranks of the movement were divided so that by the end of the Civil War it was split into two factions.

Although both factions agreed on the need to get the vote, they were split on questions related to ideology and strategy. In 1869 two organizations were formed. Susan B. Anthony and Elizabeth Cady Stanton founded the National Woman Suffrage Association (NWSA). NWSA did not admit men, was considered militant in tactics, focused on issues which were controversial such as husband-wife relations, and worked for the vote in order to achieve other rights for women. Enfranchisement, then, was seen as a means to a greater end.

The second organization, the American Woman Suffrage Association (AWSA), led by Lucy Stone and Julia Howe, was more moderate in character, attracting many middle- and upper-class women. Concentrating on making the suffrage question more mainstream, the AWSA refrained from addressing issues thought to be controversial, such as marriage and religion (Hole and Levine, 1995). The primary goal of AWSA was to work within each state to achieve the vote. Wyoming was the first state to grant the vote to women, doing so in 1869, for a pragmatic rather than strictly democratic reason. Women were scarce in the territory and it was felt that the right to vote would encourage more migrants to the area. Wyoming was almost not granted statehood because Southern congressmen argued that the states did not have the right to grant suffrage. But as Deckard (1983:262) explains, since the legislature was elected in part by the vote of women, they stated that Wyoming "will remain out of the Union for a hundred years rather than come in without the women." By a small margin Wyoming was admitted to the Union in 1890.

AWSA strategies eventually brought in many proponents to the movement, with suffrage gaining the respectability it needed to attract a broader base of support. In the meantime, NWSA increasingly turned its attention to suffrage and campaigned for political and legal rights. In 1890, the two groups merged to form the National American Woman Suffrage Association (NAWSA). One unfortunate consequence of the merging and the gain in "respectability" was that the organization became isolated from the plight of black women, immigrant women, and working-class women in general. African-American women worked diligently in the suffrage movement but were acutely aware that a double standard existed for black and white women suffragists. Black suffragists called on their white sisters in the movement to "put aside their prejudices and allow black women, burdened by both sexism and racism, to gain political equality" (Terborg-Penn, 1991:133). Their words were largely unheeded. The exclusion of these potential allies at the turn of the century impacted the movement for the next half century. As discussed later, it is only as we approach the next century that it can be said that the schism has narrowed considerably.

The Nineteenth Amendment

The next 30 years saw renewed energies for passage of a suffrage amendment, though NAWSA actually accomplished very little. Strategies deemed as too radical were disavowed, militant members were expelled, conservatism set in, and a crisis in leadership occurred. Some of the expelled faction joined a group founded by militant suffragist Alice Paul in 1913. Embracing the tactics of the more militant English suffrage movement, Paul headed the Congressional Union, later known as the Woman's Party, and used mass demonstrations to bring the constitutional amendment to America's public consciousness. In the meantime, Carrie Chapman Catt became president of NAWSA and in 1915 began a rigorous suffrage campaign. NAWSA continued distributing leaflets, lobbying, and speaking to numerous influential organizations. Woman's Party members held rallies, went on hunger strikes, and used other unorthodox, and definitely unfeminine, means. Although the tactics varied, the common goal was passage of a suffrage amendment that had been introduced and defeated in every session of Congress since 1878.

By the end of World War I, the idea of giving the vote to women had widespread public support. In 1919 the Nineteenth Amendment was passed by a vote of 304 to 90 in the House and 56 to 25 in the Senate. But the struggle would not be over until two-thirds of the states ratified it. On August 26, 1920, by only two votes, the amendment was ratified in Tennessee making the Nineteenth Amendment part of the Constitution.

The Contemporary Movement

Once the right to vote was gained, feminism literally died in the United States for the next 40 years. The end of the arduous campaign resulting in ratification of the Nineteenth Amendment found some feminists insisting that broader social reforms, rather than narrower feminist goals, were now necessary, since political equality had been achieved. Others, including Alice Paul, called for passage of the Equal Rights Amendment (ERA) which would prohibit all forms of discrimination against women. The ERA was first introduced in Congress in 1923, but even by this time the unity of support for a specific cause had been dissolved. Coupled with the Depression and a conservative national mood, most activism for women's issues was abandoned. It was not until after World War II that the women's movement emerged again on a national scale. The reawakening of feminism was encouraged by three major events. First, President John Kennedy established the Commission on the Status of Women in 1961. The Commission issued a report documenting the inferior position of women in the United States and set up a citizen's advisory council and state commissions to deal with the problems addressed in the report. Second, in 1963 Betty Friedan published her landmark work, *The Feminine Mystique.* In this book, Friedan argues that women are given no road to fulfillment other than wife and mother. They have no identity apart from their families, find themselves unhappy, and cannot even name their problem. By restrictive roles and a society that condones and applauds such restrictions, women are beginning to voice their unhappiness. "It is no longer possible to ignore that voice, to dismiss the desperation of so many American women" (Friedan, 1963:21). The second-class status of women which was pointed to in the Kennedy report was bolstered by Friedan's assertions and research.

The third event heralding the return of feminism was the founding of the National Organization for Women (NOW) in 1966, with Betty Friedan serving as its first president. These events are not in isolation from one another. Many of the women first met when they worked on state commissions set up after the Kennedy report. They were also unhappy with the progress being made on their recommendations and felt that a separate effort to deal with issues related to women was important. The creation of NOW can be viewed as an indirect result of the Commission on the Status of Women.

It is important to remember that NOW was formed during the turbulent 1960s, an era of heightened political activism and social consciousness. The drive to organize women occurred during a time when African-Americans, native Americans, Hispanics, poor people, students, and anti-Vietnam war activists were also competing for public attention through mass demonstrations for their respective causes. In comparison to many of the organizations which were spawned as a result of these causes, including other women's groups, NOW was, and is, much more moderate in its approach. Perhaps NOW's ability to survive into the twenty-first century as a viable organization can be tied to its mainstream emphasis.

White, college-educated, middle-class women were attracted to NOW and became the base for its original growth. The disadvantage was that a top-down structure was created, and this in itself tended to limit diversity (Freeman, 1995a). Although NOW remains hierarchically organized with a national body and formal constitution, its semiautonomous local chapters have aided its growth and diversity. In the decades since its founding, NOW's membership has expanded considerably, bringing in more nonprofessional and younger women and women of color. This is vital to the ultimate success of feminism in America. A feminist consciousness among African-American women, for example, can only be nurtured through a framework that also addresses the ideology of racism existing in America (Terrelonge, 1995). It has also become more controversial, adopting a more flamboyant style.

In 1967 the first NOW national conference adopted a Bill of Rights, which included support for the adoption of an Equal Rights Amendment to the Constitution, women's full right to work at all types of jobs, maternity leave rights, and the right of women to control their reproductive lives. As suggested by these goals, NOW has a wide orientation in terms of areas of interest affecting women, but with a focus on political tactics to achieve these goals. Using a traditional organizational format, other groups were also founded during the 1960s and 1970s and have more specialized interest areas but with a similar focus on tactics. Thus, in addition to NOW, the moderate branch of the movement generated the Women's Equity Action League (WEAL), which seeks to enact legislation that is not as gender-specific, and the National Women's Political Caucus (NWPC), which promotes women as candidates for public office.

The second branch of the movement consisted of a more diverse array of women and still remains more radical in orientation. Many shunned the structure of organizations like NOW, believing that such a formal hierarchy could inhibit individual expression. This branch was made up of younger women and women who had been involved with the other social movements of the time, especially the civil rights movement. Unlike NOW, some groups excluded men from their ranks, others worked solely for reproductive rights, and many came together simply under the banner of sisterhood for the purpose of consciousness-raising and dialogue (Freeman, 1995a). Attitude change at one level can help serve broader social change later. Whatever issue spawned such groups, solidarity with other women is a critical byproduct.

The two branches of the movement which developed in the 1960s are still evident today, although there is some overlap in membership. The belief in passage of the Equal Rights Amendment (ERA) is what all factions can agree on, and they have worked for this effort to varying degrees with a variety of approaches. The political impact of ERA will be discussed in Chapter 14. ERA's importance in this context has to do with keeping the movement alive and its serving as a unifying force. As judged by the failure to gain the necessary two-thirds of the states for ratification before the legal deadline expired, the movement has not been successful. But considering that NOW was able to lobby to extend the 1979 deadline by three years, an unprecedented move by Congress, it was obvious that the movement was still a viable force in the 1980s. Until its ratification, ERA will continue to be a focus of activity for the movement. After ratification, concern will likely shift to issues relating to its enforcement.

Other activities remain on the agenda for the women's movement, many which are international in scope. On both the national and global levels, this movement has impacted millions of women and men worldwide. Although much of this discussion relates to issues which have been divisive for the women's movement in America, divisiveness is being bridged. The next chapter will demonstrate that the diversity of women worldwide has actually been conducive for a strong global feminist movement.

CHAPTER 6

GLOBAL PERSPECTIVES ON GENDER

Development, if not engendered, is endangered.
—United Nations Development Program (1995)

THE UNITED NATIONS CONFERENCES ON WOMEN

In its Charter of 1945, the United Nations announced its commitment to the equality of women and men. The year 1975 was declared as International Women's Year and the years 1976 to 1985 were recognized by the United Nations (UN) General Assembly as the UN Decade for Women. Official conferences to mark the decade and work on a global agenda of women's issues were held in Mexico City in 1975, Copenhagen, Denmark in 1980, and Nairobi, Kenya in 1985. Under the banner of "equality, development and peace," each conference assessed the progress of commitments made on behalf of women by various nations.

Alongside each official UN conference ran a parallel one, a forum consisting of hundreds of nongovernmental organizations (NGOs) which brought women from all over the world and all walks of life together. These "grassroots" organizations represented a wide diversity of opinions and agendas. Inclusiveness brings dissent and the conferences were marked by political, religious, and economic factionalism, which, unfortunately, became media highlights. A concerted effort by conservative groups to discredit and interrupt the proceedings also occurred. Many women who attended the NGO Forum in Copenhagen were discouraged by the amount of friction which appeared to separate rather than unify women. Some women felt that the Copenhagen conference became politicized because the focus was on issues detracting from what they shared in common, especially as related to the intersection of class and race with gender (Cagatay et al., 1989). The understanding that feminism must address issues relevant to women in the developing world led to a greater acceptance of diverse perspectives and priorities. By Nairobi, then, much of the friction dissipated as dialogue opened and consensus was reached. As Cagatay and colleagues (1989:468) note, a central change from Copenhagen was the "widespread recognition that political issues are women's issues, and that the women's movement is fundamentally a political movement."

The gains in political astuteness were clearly evident a decade later. In 1995, the international women's movement took center stage when Beijing, China hosted the largest UN conference in history. With an attendance estimated at 50,000, Beijing was historic not only in terms of numbers, but also because the woman's agenda moved from the margin to the center of global debate. NGOs throughout the world are dedicated to making the vision of empowerment for women and girls offered in Beijing a global reality (Mann, 1996). After overviewing gender roles from a global perspective, it will become clear that Beijing served as a watershed for the women's movement worldwide (see Box 6-1, p. 158). Even with the inevitable backlash with which any movement for social change must contend, the women's movement has been successful in sending its message throughout the world. This message is that women's inferior status will no longer be ignored, that women's rights are human rights, and that nations will be held accountable for their progress, or lack thereof, in ending gender inequality.

There have been major advances in reducing the gender gap in human capabilities. In two areas, education and health, the gap has been halved in the last 20 years (Crossette, 1995a). However, data from governmental and private sources concerning the state of the world's women continue to document inequality and its consequences (Beyani, 1995; UNHCR, 1995; United Nations Development Program, 1995). These include the following:

1. Women represent 70 percent of the 1.3 billion people worldwide who live in poverty.
2. If women's unpaid work in the household was given economic value, it would add an estimated one-third ($4 trillion) to the world's annual economic product. When wage discrimination is added, the figure rises to $11 trillion.
3. Women grow half the food of the world but own hardly any land.
4. More than two-thirds of the 960 million illiterate adults worldwide are women.
5. About one-third of all households in the developing world are headed by women.
6. Most of the world's 17 to 20 million refugees are women and their dependent children. Sexual violence and exploitation of female refugees are frequent in refugee camps throughout the world.
7. Ninety percent of all countries have organizations that promote the advancement of women, but women make up only 10 percent of the world's legislative seats.

Overall, the underlying cause of the inequality of women is that their primary roles are domestic in nature, those of mother, wife, and homemaker, and although these roles are vital to the well-being of society, they are undervalued and unpaid. Yet such roles consume half of the time and energy of women.

This chapter will overview specific aspects of the position of women in selected countries, primarily in the developing world. It will emphasize those cultural patterns which serve as defining gender markers. Even with such a limited focus, the task is almost insurmountable. It is written with the understanding that generalizations are necessary and a myriad of exceptions exist. However, one objective is to illustrate that not only do women share similar statuses throughout the world but also that these statuses are similarly evaluated. How they confront, acknowledge, or deal with issues relating to inequality is culturally determined.

WOMEN IN DEVELOPMENT

The role of women in economic development has emerged as a major issue within the last two decades. The argument that development has an adverse effect on women, and often leads to their impoverishment and exploitation, is well documented (Boserup, 1970; Dixon-Mueller, 1985; Kandityoti, 1985; Waring, 1988; Afshar, 1991; Lindsey, 1994, 1996a). According to Norris (1992:183), the scenario is a relatively simple one: "As development proceeds, women are denied access to productive resources and new technologies," which in turn, "serves to lower their relative, if not absolute productivity." This is particularly true for those women in rural areas whose nondomestic work is particularly true for those women in rural areas whose nondomestic work consists of subsistence farming. Although subsistence farming is defined as less valuable because it does not produce cash income, it has provided women with a measure of respect and control over an essential productive process. Many farms are female-managed even if they are not female-owned.

Yet the traditional economic definition of labor is consistent with the view that only those functions which create a surplus for profit in the marketplace are considered aspects of productive work. Thus as Waring (1988:30) suggests, the international economic system imposes a reality which excludes the majority of work women perform, such as child care, domestic labor, and subsistence farming.

Since the subsistence farming roles of women have been de-emphasized if not ignored in evaluating labor force activities in the Third World, development policies have also largely ignored their contributions as well. Such policies are designed to upgrade the economic standards of families by concentrating on the assumed male head of household, who is seen as the breadwinner, with his dependent wife in the homemaker role. It is reasoned that by improving the employment situation of the husband, the entire family would also be upgraded. Ahmad and Loutfi (1985:5) state that this is a "ridiculous" urban middle-class model that is supposed to benefit women in developing countries but does quite the opposite. By failing to acknowledge the varied productive roles of rural women, many development programs have not only fallen short, but have also actually undermined the fragile nature of the subsistence activities of these women. A simple example of this is the introduction of mechanization to oxen and plow or hoe agriculture. This technology may decrease the workload of men who now produce cash crops or who seek employment elsewhere, but it increases the burden of women who do not have the technology available to them, who lose male help in their remaining subsistence farming, and who lose control over agricultural activities as a whole if farmland is converted to cash crops.

Other problems which contribute to women's impoverishment during development include the loss of traditional crafts and goods (often cash activities of women) through imports of manufactured goods and the dependence formerly self-sufficient communities now face as a result of commercialization and cash crop farming. Given their transition to specialized agriculture, one or two seasons of drought can impoverish an entire region. In these situations the men often migrate to cities in search of employment, leaving women with few if any resources to maintain the economic integrity of the family.

There is growing recognition among policy planners that development must take serious notice of all the productive roles of rural women. Most important is that any development project must be informed by an analysis of the gender-based division of labor in the specific cultural context (Lindsey, 1994). The development literature is replete with cases of microenterprise programs which have helped women become successful entrepreneurs (Vickers, 1991; McDonnell et al., 1993; Young et al., 1993). Success is linked to the acceptance of broader definitions of labor that account for the productive economic activities of the informal sector which comprise the majority of work women perform, such as subsistence farming, home handicraft production, and child care. Armed with the proper "credentials," women now have access to credit, technology, and training programs previously denied to them. Women are increasingly being included in development efforts at all levels, a strategy which has met with great success (Brydon and Chant, 1989; Overholt et al., 1991; Young et al., 1993).

A sociologically informed model of women in development (WID) can offer planners useful leads to help explain, understand, and then design appropriate development projects. I believe that at least four elements should be included in any WID model (Lindsey, 1995). First, it must be informed by sociological theory and take into account the global stratification system which keeps the developing world in an economic dependent position. As Afshar (1991) argues, it is important to understand that capitalism and colonialism intertwine to shape the economic structures that ultimately shape the subordination of women. Second, since the strength of sociological theory for development planning is only as useful as how it is translated into practice, sound methodology must be employed with a feedback loop to further nurture and refine theory. The theory-practice link is necessary for both sociology and those who use sociology in development planning. Fieldwork informs policy and in turn forces a rethinking of basic social science concepts (Billson, 1994:7). Third, it should be interdisciplinary in scope and capitalize on the rich conceptual and empirical work throughout the social sciences that inform different segments of the development process. Sociologists, economists, and anthropologists need to talk to one another, to practitioners who work in development, and most important, to the community which will be impacted by development decisions.

Fourth, a WID model should explicitly adopt a feminist perspective which emphasizes women's empowerment. When combined with sociological theory, this would be subsumed under a conflict perspective since it issues a challenge to the patriarchal status quo. Empowerment was a key element in the Platform of Action adopted at the UN Conference in Beijing. Research clearly documents that women's empowerment and the gender equity it entails are associated with an enhanced quality of life for women, their families, and their communities (Eisler et al., 1995; Lindsey, 1996b).

Development projects which neglect gender analysis and ignore broader definitions of production are both unrealistic and unsuccessful. Gender disparities are being increasingly recognized for what they are, "unacceptable injustices and serious constraints to the achievement of sustainable people-centered development" (SIDA, 1995). The focus here has been on the agricultural role of women, but all the daily child-care and household production activities should also be included. These productive activities are necessary for family survival in much of the world. This livelihood must be protected, extended, or realistically evaluated and modified. At a minimum it must be acknowledged.

RUSSIA

The collapse of the Soviet Union was heralded with the belief that a true democratization of the world would now seriously begin. Former Soviet Premier Mikhail Gorbachev's policies of *glasnost* ("openness") combined with *perestroika* ("restructuring") were determined to be the key elements that would transform the Soviet Union into a democratic free-market nation. Yet even he could not predict that a relatively short period of massive change would crumble his vision to retain the actual union of republics under the Soviet banner but within a democratic framework. It is important to recognize that while the former republics, including Russia, are in the throes of drafting or redrafting constitutions, it is the gender-related areas which appear to have the least priority.

The former Soviet constitution stated: "Women and men have equal rights." One of the first mandates of the Lenin regime in 1917 to 1918 was to upgrade women's position in the new society by abolishing all forms of discrimination against women which were inherent in tsarist Russia. This meant that women were to have full equality in educational and employment opportunities, family and property rights, and competition for administrative offices. However, while women made up almost half of the deputies in state legislatures and were well represented in the trade unions, the most influential national political positions from the Politburo to the Central Committee of the party were essentially devoid of women (Browning, 1985:207; Moses, 1986:389). Regardless of the formal commitment, this was the case since the founding of the USSR. The old adage of "the higher the position, the fewer the women" readily applied to the equality-conscious former Soviet Union. As a result, Mamonova (1994) contends that the rhetoric of equality has served to mask women's continued oppression.

In terms of paid labor, the former USSR had the largest percentage of women in the labor force than any other industrial society. This remains the case in Russia today where paid employment is virtually universal for women. Unemployed women will be reemployed. Compared to Western women, although Russian women have much higher representation in law, medicine, and engineering as well as in the skilled trades, such as metalworking and construction, they are overrepresented in low-paying and menial jobs and underrepresented in managerial jobs. Most are engaged in industrial or manual work, and this is despite negligible educational differences between women and men (Mamonova, 1984; Peers, 1985; Shapiro, 1992). The official doctrine of equal pay for equal work exists, but women make less money than men, even in the professions, and even if more highly qualified than men (Mamonova, 1984:3; Peers, 1985:122). Under the communists, the average female worker earned two-thirds of the average male income, but the postcommunist erosion continues for women. Women who work now earn less than half of what men average (Gray, 1990a; Hockstader, 1995). In the restructured economy white-collar and professional jobs are growing in prestige and garnering higher salaries. But with women already entrenched in unskilled jobs and within a gender-based system of job segregation, for the foreseeable future they will reap fewer benefits from perestroika.

Gender inequity in the labor force is clearly evident in contemporary Russia, a trend which persists when considering unemployment as well. Economic restructuring, the need to move workers out of heavy industry and create a service sector, and the call for a reduced government bureaucracy have had a heavy toll on women (Clements, 1994). Female unemployment has reached an all-time high and at the same time unemployment benefits have considerably eroded. In examining this trend, a paradox unfolds. Women who have lost their jobs are likely to be professionals, technical specialists, managers, and white-collar workers who would seem to be the most marketable in a new service-oriented economy. Professionals make up the ranks of the employed, the majority of whom are women. Of the 10 percent of manual workers who are the unemployed, the numbers of men and women are roughly equal. Khotkina (1994:101) asserts that women are competing with men for those better jobs with better working conditions. Women who cannot withstand the competition from men are ousted precisely from specialized jobs, since men are "not interested in competing with women for manual or heavy jobs or for work which is injurious to health." In this instance, gender equity in education has worked as a detriment against being employed in the very jobs for which they have been trained and where they could contribute to what Russia desires in terms of economic growth.

The inequity between men and women is most evident in agricultural production. During the Soviet reign women did almost all the labor associated with private agricultural plots when they were made available (Dodge and Feshbach, 1992). During the grueling transition period to a free-market economy, women may see opportunities to both produce food for their families and receive a profit for excess production. In line with worldwide trends, subsistence farming for pre- and post-Soviet women has been beneficial. It remains to be seen if these women will have a repeat of the experiences of other women, mostly in the developing world, where a move to cash crops translates into a severe loss of economic opportunity.

Russian women working in industry are probably the daughters and granddaughters of peasants who migrated to the cities to take factory jobs when they could no longer be supported on the land and when the burgeoning industrial economy demanded an expanded labor force. The peasant rhythm of life was different for women. Women brought different life and work experiences, different aspirations, and different expectations. While land was not individually owned, it was controlled by men. Women had rights to their dowries and some household goods which they brought with them to the patrilocal family upon marriage. All peasant life—values, obligations, and rewards—revolved around the land and the male attributes associated with it (Glickman, 1992). Abandoning the land did not mean abandoning the cultural attributes surrounding it. Critical aspects of traditional peasant culture were translated to life in the city and to employment in industry. These factors have profoundly impacted contemporary Russian women.

The glaring disparity between men and women in labor force activities can thus be partly explained by a unique combination of ideological factors. Family barriers that impose a double burden on women, hindering career advancement, remain formidable. As in the West, men have not taken on an equal share of domestic duties when their wives, sisters, and mothers are also in the paid labor force. The situation is particularly acute for rural women who suffer most from "the double shift"—the second shift of household labor following work outside the home (Bridger, 1992:271). Traditional views of family roles, coupled by a chronic labor shortage in rural areas, serve to maintain this situation, which has been heightened by the chaos generated by the collapse of the former state-controlled economy.

The dilemma faced by the new regime is that there is alarm over a falling birth rate and the increased preference for smaller families but a need for women workers in some areas. Professional women are being pushed out of the labor force and manual workers are still in demand. The economy could not withstand a mass exodus of women from the ranks of the paid labor force.

But measures which were designed to encourage the health and well-being of the mother and her child while at the same time maintaining a high level of national productivity have diminished, such as day-care facilities, preferential housing, inclusive prenatal and pediatric health care, and liberal pregnancy leaves. Another confounding factor is that while many Russian women do not want to have large families, only 18 percent have access to birth control. Abortion rates, therefore, are very high. Official figures show that women have one to two abortions for every birth, but that when illegal abortions are taken into account, including teen pregnancy, the number rises to an incredible eight abortions for every birth (Mamonova, 1994).

Despite the fact that women will take on all the domestic responsibilities, the prospect of marriage and children, albeit a small family, is a high priority and may even be increasing, especially among rural women. Allott (1985) and Bridger (1992) mention that rural women are more preoccupied with romance and appear to accept the far from egalitarian arrangement that will likely emerge after marriage. Recent data suggest that Russian women, regardless of occupation, are more family oriented than men and continue to place a high value on child-rearing activities (Goodwin and Emelyanova, 1995). They may be agricultural workers, professionals, or clerks, but their main concern is to be married and raise a family.

The falling birth rate and the view that the family is disintegrating have prompted authorities to actually promote the "woman as homemaker image." Gray (1991) states that there is this "masculinized woman," one who is striving for equality, who is being blamed for social problems related to changes in the family such as divorce, juvenile delinquency, abandoned children, and drug abuse. While women are also needed in the labor force and as income earners for their families, there is still no reprieve from social disapproval. In fact, the tendency toward bolstering gender stereotypes is increasing, fueled by media images reinforcing these beliefs. Women lament the lost manliness of modern men and men in turn reproach women for their lack of femininity (Lipovskaya, 1994:129). Labor officials openly state that women should stay home and take care of children as working will take good jobs away from deserving men (Hockstader, 1995). And the media routinely run stories that both women and the workplace suffer when women work outside the home (Klimenkova, 1994:15).

Women themselves are torn by how to deal with *peregruzhenost* ("overburdening"). In interviewing hundreds of women, Gray (1991:306) cites this as a recurrent complaint, especially in light of figures which suggest that on the average husbands have 30 hours more free time per week than wives. Yet these very women say they control everything in their households, with this control verging on tyranny. This is not the image of passive women dominated by men but literally the opposite, at least in their homes. Men, then, become weak and withdraw from home and family. Perhaps the question becomes how one defines egalitarianism in these homes. This superior woman image has also nurtured the belief that men are lazier by nature and provides an understanding of the Russian proverb "women can do everything; men can do the rest" (Gray, 1990a).

The picture that is emerging suggests that in the upheaval after communist rule, women are facing a number of difficult issues. Perestroika has not altered sexual inequality, but glasnost has at least opened discussion on the plight of women, particularly rural women (Gray, 1990a; Bridger, 1992:294).

Glasnost played an important role in making the women's movement mainstream and allowing women to speak out on a variety of issues, and as they do so their criticisms become more penetrating. The increasing belief is that women have been manipulated throughout Russian history and must now hear their own voices (Clements 1994:127). Women are expressing their dissatisfaction with their plight in a number of ways, such as when rural women abandon agriculture to find better employment in cities. In addition, glasnost has rekindled a feminist spirit that has been hidden but not buried. For instance, the former Soviet government was unsuccessful in campaigns to halt the underground publications of dissident feminist writers who sought to expose the problems women faced. There is a growing recognition that a democratic society must concern itself with gender equity in a meaningful way. The revival of feminism is less about the backlash to get "unneeded" women out of the labor force. According to Posadskaya (1994:169)

> After decades of political silence the independent women's movement in Russia is an attempt by women to speak out in their own voice: on their own behalf, concerning those problems that women themselves consider the most important. This . . . is the essence . . . of contemporary Russian feminism, even if women themselves are not familiar with the word.

As disheartening as it sounds to Western feminists, many Russian women would agree with the words of a distraught wife, who is also a psychologist, that "the principal function of a women's movement in this country would be to quiet our women down (and) make them more capable of reassuring their men" (Gray, 1991:307). This is not incompatible with what many men see as the future for Russia. If the Russian economy is a hundred years behind America's, women must be patient until things get better, and then they will be able to depend on their husbands again for support (Khanga, 1991). Women believe that if it takes decades to catch up to the West, they can wait to do so. Their ability to cope has sustained them through all the catastrophes of Soviet history. As put by one woman, "We'd like bigger apartments. We'd like more women in the legislatures. We'd like men to treat us better. But we can wait. We're used to it" (Clements, 1994:143). Feminism in Russia must also shed the image that it is not so different from communist ideology (Risman, 1991). Glasnost has opened up critical analysis of problems faced by women but, to date, there is insufficient government support to answer the problems identified (Bridger, 1992:223). The ironic twist to democratization in Russia, in the short term at least, may be an eroding of women's rights.

CHINA

Even before the revolution which elevated Mao Tse Tung to head of the new People's Republic of China, the Chinese Communist Party (CCP) had recognized that women were valuable allies in building socialism. In order for the peasant revolution to maintain its momentum or hold ground during the construction of a new regime, it was believed that women's issues must be given priority. Since women were inextricably bound to an ancient, oppressive, and seemingly immutable family structure, this was the area that was given highest priority. However, as Johnson (1986:440) points out, the CCP's promotion of women's rights and family reform continues to be tied to other more immediate priorities, such as economic development.

Official government policies aimed at increasing labor force participation have proceeded with the argument that if women gain in the economic sphere, they will also gain in the family. As outlined in Chapter 1, whereas Karl Marx articulated the structure of classical social conflict theory, it was Friedrich Engels who carried this approach specifically to the family. For Engels, the family is the basic source of women's oppression. As wives, mothers, and daughters, women take on the proletariat role, as compared to the bourgeoisie role assumed by men. The patriarchal family is a microcosm of a larger, oppressive capitalistic society. By this reasoning, therefore, once women expand their roles outside the family to become an economically productive part of the new socialist system, their servility to men will cease. Popularized as the "liberation through labor" ideal, the improvement of the economic status of women continues as the foundation for achieving gender equality (*Situation of Chinese Women*, 1994). Family reform would inevitably follow. Let us review the record of Chinese family reform since the revolution.

The traditional Chinese family was based on Confucian principles that gave complete authority to males, particularly to the oldest males. The family was patriarchal, patrilineal, and patrilocal. In Confucian classic writings, females are seen as inferior by nature, emotional, unintelligent, jealous, indiscreet, narrow-minded, and capable of seducing the most innocent male (Guisso, 1981). Given such negative views, it is not surprising that the movements of women were severely curtailed and that legal proscriptions would reflect these values. A woman's marriage was arranged; she could not normally inherit property, would move into her husband's household at marriage, and had to survive under the unquestioned authority of her husband, his father, and his grandfather, as well as other assorted male relatives. A female hierarchy also existed, with her mother-in-law exercising much control, including being beaten or sold for disobedience or for running away. In all, the bride would occupy the lowest rung in the domestic hierarchy of the traditional Chinese family.

Running at all was impossible for those women who endured the technique of footbinding, which could reduce a foot to as small as three inches. Dating to the early part of the twelfth century, this crippling procedure was more likely to be practiced on women from the upper classes who did not have to work in heavy manual labor or in the fields. Besides becoming a status symbol and eventually being elevated to a prerequisite for marriage among the upper classes, footbinding ensured that women remained passive and under the control of men. Indeed, for the family and hence Confucian society to function smoothly, the subordination of women was required and practices like footbinding helped ensure this.

The only real option for women to gain any semblance of prestige was to produce sons. Not only was inheritance and the family name jeopardized if there were no male heirs, the ancient practice of ancestor worship could not continue. People could exist only by virtue of ancestors and would then continue to live on in the spirit world at their own deaths. Ancestors were powerful and could bless or curse a family, so offerings and prayers had to be bestowed frequently. A woman could gain ancestral status only through her husband and sons. Without male descendants she could have no afterlife. Chinese women who trace their family trees back three thousand years cannot find any women on them. Dismal indeed were the prospects of a wife who conceived no male children or who remained unmarried or a childless widow. With so many obstacles to confront and overcome, it is understandable why suicide was seen as an acceptable solution to many peasant and gentry women (Wolf, 1985). It was better to die with honor than to bring disgrace to a husband's family for not bearing sons.

The Marriage Law of 1950 abolished many of the practices which had oppressed women in the traditional Chinese family. The fundamental principle on which the new law was based was free-choice marriage. It was expected that this would lay the foundation for releasing women from their abysmal existence in feudal marriage and alter the belief that for thousands of years regarded men as superior to women (*Fortnightly Review,* 1995). Not only did both genders gain equal rights to divorce, but marriages had to be monogamous; bigamy and other forms of plural marriage, as well as concubinage, were abolished. Also eliminated were child betrothal, bride prices, and any restrictions placed on the remarriage of widows.

In 1980 another marriage law was passed that did not make substantial changes but merely updated some of the details of the older law. The 1980 law specifically mentions the rights of both genders. Some important ones are the prohibition of marriage upon arbitrary decision by any third party; the equal status of husband and wife in the home; and the provision that both husband and wife have the freedom to engage in production, to work, to study, and to participate in social activities with neither party allowed to restrain or interfere with the other. Data indicate that between half and three-quarters of marriages are free choice, decided by husband and wife themselves (*Situation of Chinese Women,* 1995; Zi, 1995:86). Although these data do not report the use of matchmakers, it is probable that this group includes some form of arranged meetings, either through parents or matchmakers. By abolishing many of the blatant abuses existing in the feudal Chinese family, the two marriage laws have been beneficial to women, especially for rural women.

But these successes must be tempered with the cultural realities of an ancient patriarchal society as well as other official policies which have undermined equality for women in China. For example, free-choice marriages assume that the conditions are right for young people to meet and develop relationships. Cultural restrictions on girls' activities combined with lack of privacy, overcrowding, and no private automobiles make reliance on arranged meetings and matchmakers an acceptable alternative, regardless of the marriage laws. Engel (1995:66) notes that the Chinese family is remarkably stable in its resistance to change despite government efforts to the contrary. However, while the past invades the present, conjugal relationships are more common and the nuclear family, especially in urban areas, is replacing the extended patrilocal family.

China is still a rural country with the vast majority of its population existing in villages oriented to a life based on farming and strong family ties. Despite the massive campaigns to create marriages and families based on egalitarian principles, this ideal is far from the reality. Kin customs pervade, and parents of potential partners still wield much authority in arranging marriages. A patrilocal extended family structure continues to put the new bride at a disadvantage. Since daughters will marry and move to the home of their husbands, often in another village, the preference for sons continues. Parents know that daughters are only temporary commodities. Ancient Chinese proverbs, such as "Raising a daughter is like weeding another man's field" and "The best daughter isn't worth a splayfooted son," continue to be quoted and attest to the strength of the preference for sons (Carmody, 1989:97).

In rural China, women are valued for their domestic work and are not as likely as men to work outside the home for pay. Even agricultural work, which women routinely perform, is often not paid in money but in agricultural products. When money is received, it is collectively maintained, so even if women are bringing in other sources of income, it goes to the household which is under the control of the men. The male head of household usually collects all monies from family members. In all, the strength of the traditional family has continued to make women into a dependent class, even for those women who are nominally heads of household because of the absence of husbands who leave the village for work in the city (Wolf, 1985; Croll, 1995).

Females now make up about half of the Chinese labor force. In rural areas the employment rate of women is 76 percent compared to 87 percent for men. In urban areas there are no differences in employment rates of men and women, with both at 97 percent (*Beijing Review*, 1995). While women are expected to work outside the home, they work in gender differentiated jobs and are paid less than men. And when rural women do work for pay, the gender disparity in income is even greater. These facts are more revealing in light of statistics which indicate that the educational attainment of Chinese women has risen dramatically from virtual illiteracy 50 years ago (*Women and Men in China*, 1995). It is clear, however, that employment and income do not match the higher educational levels of contemporary Chinese women. Although the government is officially committed to women's equality, it has not devised legal or administrative mechanisms to enforce it in the workplace. As such, urban women remain in transient, low-paying, and subordinate jobs (Honig and Hershatter, 1988:337).

As noted in Chapter 3 the extent of ancient traditions which put a premium on sons and devalue daughters has taken a more ominous turn. Official government policy has focused on upgrading the status of women. Simultaneously, they have introduced a stringent campaign to reduce population growth in a country of over a billion people. These two goals have disastrously collided with one another. In 1978, a new family program was initiated which demanded that families should have no more than one child. Whereas China has had other programs to curb its rate of population growth, the one-child policy is unique in that enforcement has been much more uniform and even severe for noncompliance. Massive public campaigns have been conducted to make prospective parents aware of the incentives or penalties related to the policy. The program of incentives has become standardized throughout most of China so that couples receive one-child certificates which entitle them and their child to an annual cash subsidy. For subsequent children, an "excess child levy" is imposed on a couple's income as compensation for the extra burden placed on the state in educating and feeding the extra children. What makes these sanctions more punitive is that rewards for the single child must be returned with the birth of the second. If a woman with a one-child certificate gets pregnant again, she is encouraged to have an abortion. If she refuses she would lose her bonus, be left out of the next wage increase, and be scorned by her fellow workers. Male sterilization is no option since it is seen to "weaken" men. The baby is inside her body so she is to blame (Wolf, 1993:349).

The policy has had more of an effect on urban than rural families. Although there has been a decline in the birth rate in rural areas, rural families are units of production as well as consumption, and there is the continual necessity for agricultural laborers. Peasant communities recognize that they have power in this regard and continue to welcome two or three children per couple. In addition, enforcement of the new one-child law is much weaker in rural areas. And since the farm family has the ability to produce food, if sanctions are applied, they are not nearly as detrimental when compared to the smaller urban family which exists as a less powerful unit of production.

Most important, the one-child policy has reinforced the preference for sons in all areas. Strong vestiges of ancestor worship remain with many still believing that there can be no descendants without a son. With one child as the option, that child had better be a male. Female infanticide has been practiced in China for centuries, but it diminished considerably in the decades after the Chinese revolution in 1949. Egalitarian ideology, the outlawing of sex screening, and the improvement in health care notwithstanding, incidents of female infanticide are increasing. It is a case of unintended effects of public policy and the limits of government coercion (Kristof, 1993; Croll, 1995). In a culture which prides itself on large families, the one-child program is likely to be the most unpopular policy in contemporary China.

On the other hand, Hong (1987:317) argues that latent functions of a one-child policy include reducing the significance of patrilineal heritage and encouraging women to make nontraditional career choices. In addition, research suggests that the one-child policy will ultimately improve the status of women and make daughters more valued overall (Davis-Friedman, 1985; Yu et al., 1990). Two questions thus remain unanswered. What type of governmental intervention is necessary to seek the cooperation of a reluctant populace? And, if the policy is fully implemented, what will be the long-term effect on issues related to gender equity? At this point, the one-child policy in contemporary China suggests dire consequences for females.

INDIA

As with other developing nations, India is confronting challenges that threaten its economic, hence its political, stability. By the turn of the century India's population is expected to reach the one billion mark. After China, it is the world's second most populous nation. Considering the staggering problems related to population growth, land and food shortage, unemployment, and a growing disparity between poverty and wealth, India must look to all segments of its very heterogeneous society for solutions. Opportunities for women are perhaps the major factor in the solution of many of these problems. Yet, as noted by Duley (1986:128), economic planners have barely acknowledged this reality.

India is similar to Western nations in that its history reflects apparent inconsistencies when considering the role of women. Goddess images, important female religious occupations, and critical economic roles for women in the pre-Vedic and Vedic eras (2500 to 300 B.C.E.) demonstrate that they had some degree of prestige and were not completely reduced to chattel (Jayakar, 1987). With the ascendance of Hinduism and the beginnings of technology, it appears that this kind of prestige was lost. As discussed in Chapter 12, Indian women share a parallel religious history with women of the West.

Women's freedom and status become severely compromised when religion gains an institutional foothold. Patriarchy and religion have continued to go hand in hand.

By the beginning of the first century, India had gone through a period of decentralization of the authority of the various Indian states. High-caste Brahmin scholars were powerful enough to interpret the ancient Smitris ("laws"). Duley (1986:136) suggests that by this time the "Laws of Manu" enveloped India and demonstrated the extent to which the position of women had deteriorated. Manu made a woman completely dependent on a man (husband, father, or son) and decreed women were naturally seducers of men. Manu also forbade widow remarriage and, in fact, reduced a widow's status to such a lowly extreme that *suttee*, or widow burning, gradually took hold. Faced with a life of derision, and abandonment, who can say if these widows voluntarily chose the fate of becoming a suttee? The Laws of Manu not only demonstrate "the polarized male perception of the female" but were used to both legitimate gender inequality and protect the interests of the ruling Brahmin class (Mitter, 1991:87).

By the nineteenth century, new ideas concerning the status of women began to emerge in India, and the roots of a reform movement took shape. The more blatant aspects of the inhumane treatment of women were attacked, such as child marriage, lack of property rights, purdah, and the dismal condition of widows who were forbidden to remarry. D'Souza and Natarajan (1986:361) indicate that reformers believed that such customs were responsible for the condition of women and that through education, women would make better wives and mothers. Though raising the status of some women, reformers still accepted the notion that a woman's life was within her family. And the vast majority of rural and lower-caste women remain untouched by the reforms. This is reinforced by data which show that divorce in contemporary India poses a greater hardship on women. Factors responsible for this include women's continued economic dependence on men, cultural beliefs about women and marriage, and the patriarchal organization of the Indian joint (extended) family (Amato, 1994).

The first serious questioning of women's roles came with Mahatma Gandhi, who felt that women were not only essential to India's quest for independence, but also that social justice demanded their equality. Given the nationalist sentiment and the charisma of Gandhi, women of all castes and regions flocked to the independence movement, assuming leadership roles and participating in all manners of political dissent. Gandhi's vision was shared by Jawaharlal Nehru, who wanted men and women to have equal places in society. As the first prime minister of India, and against much opposition, Nehru pushed through legislation that gave women the rights of inheritance and divorce, as well as the right to vote (D'Souza and Natarajan, 1986:363). But as with the reforms a century before, the effect was minimal for the majority of women. A strong women's movement in India worked for gender equality 30 years before independence. But its effectiveness was curtailed by agendas set by British colonialists and Indian nationalists who only supported women on issues when their interests happened to coincide (Liddle and Joshi, 1986:39-40). The overall effect was, and to a large extent continues to be, that the vast majority of Indian women have not seen the effects of a woman's movement on their daily lives.

The Nehru factor in Indian politics has been played out politically since independence. Nehru's daughter, Indira Gandhi, succeeded to the post of prime minister in 1966 because she was a member of the Nehru dynasty and because her party believed they could control her. Her skill and strength proved them wrong. She was politically astute, using her gender as an asset rather than a liability. She identified herself as a member of the oppressed but also appealed to those looking for a mother-goddess figure, so imbued in the Hindu tradition (cited in D'Souza and Natarajan, 1986:373). Until her assassination, Indira Gandhi ruled with an authoritarian hand for 16 years.

Though Indira Gandhi certainly served as a symbol for women who aspired to other than traditional roles, it must be said that her own commitment to elevating the position of women in India is far from realized. A very few educated women exist among millions who are illiterate. And when compared to the masses of unskilled female laborers in India, most of whom work in agriculture, professional women comprise only a tiny minority. Although there has been an expansion of female employment in general, this has not offset the decrease in the employment of unskilled women. Duley (1986:211) states that throughout this century there has been a steady decline in the overall employment of women. Today the bulk of women workers are found in the "unorganized sector," most as landless agricultural laborers, street vendors, day workers, and those who are employed in village and cottage industries.

In principle, as modernization and development extend into rural areas, the population as a whole should benefit. But the WID trend where the position of women deteriorates with development can also be demonstrated in the case of India, especially regarding health and reproduction. Despite modernization, higher mortality and lower life expectancy rates exist for women in many areas of India and have actually widened in the last century (U.S. Agency for International Development, 1994). And similar to China, the sex ratio in India is declining. Son preference contributes to higher mortality rates for females than males, with female infants less likely to receive the necessities for survival in poverty-ridden households. As documented in Chapter 3, these data are highly unusual when considering that in almost every country in the world, the sex ratio indicates a marginally higher proportion of women. Frequent and excessive childbearing also severely compromises the health of women. Knowledge of family planning is almost universal and women want to limit the number of children, but they remain unaware of methods that would enable them to space births, with only 6 percent using any spacing method. The most widely used method of contraception is female sterilization, with one-fourth of married women unaware of male sterilization as a modern contraception device (*Asia-Pacific Population and Policy*, 1995b).

The neglect of girls and the lesser amount of attention they receive are also linked to a strong dowry tradition in India. In highly stratified societies like India, dowries, like other property, are a means of social mobility where men use rights over women to compete for social status (McCreery, 1993). We saw the deadly consequences of dowry and son preference on females in Chapter 3.

Finally, the sex ratio is more equitable in the hundreds of villages off the major highways in India which serve as prostitute towns for truck drivers and men in neighboring villages. Girls are socialized early to put on makeup and go out to earn money to support the family. In these towns the girls are clean and well-fed and boys are not. An explosion of AIDS has hit such towns throughout India where over 600,000 Indians are positive for HIV. Research on these women suggests that most have never heard of AIDS or seen a condom (*Asia-Pacific Population and Policy,* 1995c). But even if informed, the fatalistic attitude about their lives persists. "What can we do?" asks one young prostitute. "We have to earn a living. The choice is dying of AIDS or dying of starvation" (Roy, 1994).

There are some signs that the situation of women in India will be given more serious attention and that the government is willing to make greater strides in putting democratic principles into practice. In the area of health, programs are underway which are designed to combine traditional and modern medicine in a way that is acceptable to the rural population. Village midwives are being trained in techniques of delivery suitable for rural conditions and are also providing prenatal care. Since women are responsible for the health care of the children, any program that can offer them more acceptable solutions in dealing with the diseases which rampage a family will be embraced. Although suspicious of intrusions into their traditional ways of thinking about health, village women are no longer summarily rejecting allopathic, or "modern" Western medicine (Lindsey, 1982, 1983). When programs take into account traditional beliefs and cultural practices, women in particular will benefit. The long-term results should show up in reduced infant and maternal mortality rates.

The Indian Council of Social Science Research has suggested that when compared to the total female population, only a small number of urban, middle-class women have actually realized the advantages of development. When development brings any form of mechanization or technological "advance," women are routinely bypassed. For example, women can do the backbreaking work of hauling sand and cement baskets on their heads but are not allowed to lay bricks; they can sweep gutters but not drive trucks equipped with sweepers; they can cultivate with hand hoes but not drive tractors (Gargan, 1991:A2). To be successful, development goals must address patriarchal attitudes which perpetuate the belief that women are incapable of moving beyond traditionally circumscribed boundaries. And to extend these efforts to the rural and poor population of women, priorities in employment, health, and education are essential.

A five-year plan which specifically addresses the issues of excessive female mortality and low literacy rates of women was recently adopted. Through their efforts on social and welfare measures, women's organizations are increasingly being drawn into the political process, with political parties beginning to recognize the importance of the woman's vote. Training is a component of this process as well. Outreach programs for poor, marginalized producer women are enhancing their empowerment and self-reliance. Family-owned microenterprises in India are more productive when women have joint decision making with men. At the community level, they are starting to participate in and influence decisions in local self-governing bodies and for the first time are exerting their voting rights at all levels (*Udyogini,* 1995). Organizations such as SEWA (Self-Employed Women's Association) are offering union membership to women who pick up paper and scraps from the streets for recycling, jobs men do not consider to be real work. SEWA's women have seen their incomes increase, with that income put back into their family for education, health care, and birth control.

Studies show that men use extra income for alcohol, cigarettes, and personal items (Bumiller, 1995a). Alcohol use by their spouses is the culprit for many of India's most repressed women, where poverty and wife battering are some of its consequences. To combat this and other problems, with support from international nongovernmental organizations Indian women have launched what is considered to be the first large-scale grass-roots women's movement in the country's history (Moore and Anderson, 1993). In contrast to reformist peasant movements where gender inequality is reinforced, movements that focus solely on women and are organized by women are more beneficial for women's empowerment (Roy, 1993). Although a concerted government effort is necessary to even begin to approach Mahatma Gandhi's vision of an egalitarian society, Indian women are beginning to challenge the rigid cultural codes of their countries. Politicians take notice when existing legal rights are translated into action.

JAPAN

In overviewing Japanese gender roles, one immediately confronts what first appears to be a series of paradoxes. During World War II, Japanese and American women had much in common in that both groups assumed major responsibility for the functioning of the domestic economy, yet were denied leadership positions in the government and industries who relied upon their services. After Japan's surrender in 1945, Occupation forces were determined to set down a policy that would ensure that a democratic system would emerge which would be compatible with a Japanese cultural climate. Japan's remarkable advances in economic growth, health, higher education, and overall prosperity attest to the spectacular success of the experiment in guided social change introduced during the Occupation. In congruence with this, there has been major attitudinal change regarding equality of human relationships, particularly those involving women and men (Suzuki, 1991:246). It can be argued that the single largest beneficiary of this experiment was the Japanese woman.

Occupation policy was also dictated by the provisions of the Potsdam Declaration, July 26, 1945, which mandated that democratic tendencies among the Japanese people be strengthened and that freedom of speech, religion, and respect for the fundamental human rights be ensured (Pharr, 1981). With the enactment of the new Showa Constitution on May 3, 1947, five articles provided for rights of women. Included are the assurances of equality under the law with no discrimination because of race, creed, sex, social status, or family origin; universal adult suffrage; equal education based on ability (which meant that women would be admitted to national universities); permission for women to run for public office; and marriage based on the mutual consent of both parties (Sugisaki, 1986: 110; Hisae, 1989).

Although legal guarantees are only valid through stringent enforcement, Japanese women in 1947 in essence had greater rights than American women, since their new constitution explicitly provided for gender equality. A similar statement of equality is embodied in the Equal Rights Amendment to the United States Constitution, but this has yet to be passed.

The legal assurances of equality had their greatest impact on Japanese employment practices beginning with the Occupation. Laws were enacted that guaranteed women protection from long work hours as well as maternity and menstrual leave and emphasized that a new Japan required the strong support of women as the producers and socializers of the next generation (White, 1991). It is obvious today that such laws serve to inhibit women's advancement and stereotype women as less physically capable than men. Yet it took 30 years before the disparity was acknowledged. The Equal Employment Opportunity Law was passed in 1986, which calls for equal pay and other improvements in hiring and working conditions. Unfortunately, with no provisions for violation, many employers simply do not adhere to the law. While some changes have occurred in terms of overt and blatant discrimination, the law does not have enough power to prevent gender-based personnel policies and clearly cannot tackle the monumental problems of indirect discrimination (Lam, 1993). Statistics underestimate the extent of discrimination against women in the workplace, especially those interested in pursuing management or professional careers. Despite two decades of litigation, employment discrimination has been "stark and uncompromising" in recruitment and promotion of women (Upham, 1987:127).

Like women throughout the world, women in the Japanese labor force are constrained by restrictive and stereotyped gender roles. Though they make up almost half of the work force, they are concentrated in lower-level jobs and earn much less than the average male. Women are rapidly advancing in educational opportunities, but they are virtually excluded from management positions in most Japanese firms (Saso, 1990; Lo, 1990). Sugisaki (1986:122) considers it a paradox that Japanese working women continue to suffer both overt and hidden discrimination when their contributions make possible Japan's viability as a world economic power. The flexibility associated with female employment makes it easy to hire or fire women depending on the success of the company and keeps women as part of a peripheral labor force (Kawashima, 1987). It also helps counterbalance permanent employment for men (White, 1991). In explaining this paradox, Sugisaki (1986:122), suggests that an ancient, rigid system of male supremacy cannot be rapidly changed and that men remain unaware of their privileged position or its attendant discrimination. Women may also not recognize the true extent of discrimination, and even if they do, they often subscribe to cultural principles dictating quiet, unassuming behavior for women.

Japanese women are entering paid employment in increasing numbers, and now make up over 40 percent of the total labor force with most of the increase due to part-time workers who return after an absence during childbearing and child rearing. In comparison to other industrialized nations, Japan is unusual in that both women's labor force activity and fertility actually declined between 1950 and 1976 (Osawa, 1988). The more common pattern, as in the United States, is that a lower fertility rate is associated with higher labor force participation, especially among educated women. Osawa (1988:644) suggests that "this may reflect increased demand for child quality by more highly educated mothers."

Tied to women's strong cultural beliefs that their goal in life is to bear children, this trend is not surprising. A women's role is ranked as mother first and wife second (Usui, 1991). Employment is not even considered in the ranking hierarchy. This expectation is so strong that it is virtually impossible for employed women with preschoolers to escape social judgment if anything is amiss at home when she is at work. This cultural ideology makes the mother "solely and totally responsible for the well-being of her children" (Fujita, 1989:90). The principle of segregation into different spheres puts a greater burden on her when compared to her American counterpart. There is virtually no overlap between domestic and occupational roles.

To compensate somewhat, professional women may employ substitute housewives or rely on their mothers who live with or near them. Such an arrangement provides no assurances of equality nor does it eradicate role overload. But it does allow some measure of occupational success for women who refuse to give up the domestic sphere of mother and wife. In speaking of the contemporary Japanese woman, Copeland (1992:101) notes that a woman's sphere of activities may have been broadened, but motherhood is still the essence of her social identity.

Oddly enough, in a country which erects massive cultural obstacles for women in the labor force, a model system of nursery schools has emerged. This may be one response to the concern that Japan's birth rate has plummeted far below the level needed for population replacement (Atoh, 1994). Japan has the lowest fertility rate (1.5) and highest life expectancy rate (83 for women and 76.6 for men) in the world (*Nikkei Weekly*, 1993; *Japan,* 1996). Despite barriers to employment, more women are making dramatic strides in education, and embarking on careers. This bolsters the pattern for delaying marriage and having fewer children (Atoh, 1994). To entice those who would like to remain in the workplace into marriage and childbearing, the unprecedented step of day care may be made available (Kristof, 1995). The shortage of eligible brides is also reflected in the emergence of "groom schools" where men learn to polish their social skills to attract women into matrimony (Chang, 1990). Unlike in the United States, this is a facet of an expanding marriage industry catering primarily to men and one in which women retain a high degree of power in the process of mate selection (Nagao, 1993).

Another paradox presents itself when considering the role of women in the Japanese family. Postwar changes concerning women saw laws which no longer regarded them as incompetent. Parental consent was abolished as a condition for marriage beyond a certain age; divorce could be obtained by mutual consent, and in a divorce, property would now be divided between husband and wife (Sugisaki, 1986: 116). It would appear, therefore, that such laws were to augment her lowly status in the family. Herein lies the paradox. On the one hand Japanese women are depicted as relegated to domestic drudgery, stripped of power, and expected to be "demurely submissive, coquettishly feminine and hopelessly removed from the attainment of self-fulfillment" (Lebra, 1984:ix). But this stands in opposition to a strong tradition of decision making in the family to the extent that the Japanese housewife is viewed as being in full control of domestic life with almost unlimited autonomy (Sugisaki, 1986; Iwao, 1993).

Lebra's (1984) extensive study of Japanese women living in a prosperous city sheds light on this paradox. Her literature review finds that women are role-specialized in the domestic area, are socially and symbolically (among various forms) segregated by gender, and are inferior in terms of most measures, such as esteem, power, honor, privilege, and authority. Thus women as a group are defined by the principles of domesticity, seclusion, and inferiority, although individual women can be placed at some point along a continuum for each element (Lebra, 1984:2). If inferiority is assigned to women in certain spheres, it is balanced somewhat by the powers of their domestic role.

In Japan, "being a woman is virtually synonymous with being a mother" (cited in Copeland, 1992). Mothers are revered, almost idealized by their children. But child rearing is associated with hardship, so women are discouraged from having large families. Iwao (1993:133) asserts that children are not reared for independence because the mother's role may be compromised. The more dependent the child, the more indispensable the mother. Husbands, too, assume a childlike dependence on their wives. Lebra (1984:133–34) states that this may be characteristic of patriarchy, but the wife then receives leverage to make her services indispensable. A husband who is domestically astute and does household chores deprives his wife of domestic matriarchy. Nowhere is domestic matriarchy more in evidence than in how the household expenses are divided. While it is expected that the husband is the provider, in most instances, the wife maintains full control over the financial management of the household. Paradoxically, his authority is demonstrated when he hands over his paycheck to her. In this sense patriarchy and matriarchy are reciprocal. Earning the money is his responsibility. Managing the money is hers.

Who is the "average" Japanese woman? Surveys suggest that the portrait is of a person who values family life and will sacrifice for it; who is unwilling to divorce even in an unsatisfactory marriage; who believes she is discriminated against in both society as well as in the family; but who is also proud of her decision-making family role, especially in financial matters. She is also more egalitarian and more individualistic in her role values than in the 1970s (Sugisaki, 1986:122; Suzuki, 1991:257). She is likely to have worked outside the home until her first child is born and then to return to the labor force when the oldest child enters high school. In her homemaker role, she is a professional and enjoys the status associated with being a "good wife and wise mother" (Hendry, 1993). Mariko, a 44-year-old middle-class Tokyo suburban woman with three children, two part-time jobs, and a disengaged husband, exemplifies this pattern. In a moving ethnographic case study of Mariko, Bumiller (1995b:289) provides us insight into the life of a Japanese woman.

> It was a Japanese life, a woman's life, no worse and no better than so many others, a life spent largely in reaction to children, to a husband, to sick parents. Even on a good day Mariko knew how hard it was to get out in front of her life, to do the few things she wanted to do, to feel a sense of accomplishment, to have fun . . . . Her children were getting older and would soon be gone, just in time, it seemed, for her to turn around and be a parent to her parents.

It is probable that as women achieve higher levels of education and social change continues, the principle of seclusion into separate domestic and occupational spheres will also be weakened. It is unlikely, however, that these women will disavow what they perceive as their basic domestic responsibilities.

Women in Japan have been vital in bringing their country to economic prominence in the world, in achieving a high standard of living, and in amassing perhaps the best overall health record of any nation, particularly in terms of low infant mortality and high life expectancy rates. Legal reform has paved the way for challenges to the ancient patriarchal model in Japan. Reform has proceeded through elements of feminist activism which have linked disparate women's and citizen groups under a common banner, but compared to the women's movements in other countries, mass-based feminism in Japan is still at an embryonic stage (Mackie, 1988; Garon, 1993). Social norms which pro-

pelled a woman into early marriage are eroding so that there is more toleration of women staying single (Fujiwara, 1994). Women are demanding
expanded roles and greater autonomy for those roles, more than men, at this
point, would like to see (Tanifuji, 1995). Rising expectations and the wish to
improve one's lot in life will provide the basis for future reforms aimed at
equalizing the positions of women and men.

LATIN AMERICA

While Latin America exhibits a great deal of diversity in terms of ecology, politics, and culture, certain common features, such as a rigid class structure, the
prevalence of Catholicism, and a colonial heritage from Spain and Portugal,
help to define the region. Knudson and Weil (1988:14) suggest that Latin
American women also demonstrate this diversity but "share common problems and strengths which both unite and divide them." Although there has
been a marked improvement in the overall situation of Latin American
women, a gender gap in all status indicators persists.

As suggested in Chapter 8, the socialization of men and women in Latin
America hinges on the concepts of *machismo* and *marianismo*, which are viewed
as mutually exclusive beliefs which separate the genders. Derived from the
Spanish word *macho* ("male"), machismo is associated with ideological and
physical control of women (Cubitt, 1988). It embodies a cult of virility emphasizing sexual aggressiveness, courage, intransigence, and competition between
men and sexual prowess, aggression, and arrogance between men and women.
Machismo allows for male dominance in the household and is invoked to
restrict socioeconomic, sexual, and other lifestyle choices of women. It has
been associated with the legitimation of violence against women as well as compromised physical and mental health among men, and an ideological mechanism to reproduce male privilege (Cubitt, 1988; Casas et al., 1994). Marianismo embodies a cult of female spiritual superiority which suggests that women
are morally stronger than men. Reinforced by teachings of the Roman
Catholic Church, marianismo is associated with the glorification of and spiritual verification of motherhood, a stoic acceptance of one's earthly lot with the
hope of heavenly reward, and the endurance of an unhappy marriage. Unlike
men, the moral superiority of women maintains that hardship is suffered in
silence. It has evolved as a nearly universal model of behavior for Latin American women (Ehlers, 1993).

These rigid images are more indicative of the mestizo people of mixed
Indian and Spanish descent. Before the Spanish conquest there was apparently more egalitarianism and role complementarity between men and
women, with women assuming important economic positions (Scott, 1986;
Cubitt, 1988). The conquistadors brought views of women stemming from Old
World religious and feudal attitudes. Marianismo and machismo eventually
became entrenched in the New World. Although this ideology survives today,
Ehler's (1993) research on Guatemalan wives argues that women's behavior is
not merely a response to machismo but a survival strategy emerging from
female economic, political, and social dependence on men. From a conflict
perspective, gender relations shift with the material conditions of women's
lives.

This research also confirms the link between gender and development.
Subsistence farming and other economically productive activities of women

deteriorate and economic degradation accelerates when males enter external labor markets and receive cash income. Women are often abandoned by men and enter into fragile and temporary alliances with other men for the same reasons they originally wed—for money and children (Ehlers, 1993:319). Thus in addition to religion and the survival of feudal attitudes, economic factors remain important in explaining the inferior position of women in Latin American cultures. Except for certain regions, most notably in Brazil and Argentina, Latin America remains underdeveloped after almost 500 years of European colonization and the establishment of independent republics in the nineteenth century. Underdevelopment can be approached through dependency theory, which looks at the unequal relationships between Latin America and world markets. Dependency theory can be used to explain how processes of change have specifically affected women in Latin America. Unequal opportunities due to fluctuations in world markets negatively influence the region anyway, but the effects on women are disastrous.

The transformation from subsistence farming to commercial agriculture hastens this process. Both psychologically and monetarily, women lose ground as a result. When women take nonagricultural jobs, their economic returns are very low. In expanding industrial centers, work is segmented by gender and women work in low-paying, nonunion, dead-end jobs. Development issues are also intricately tied to the innumerable economic crises and political transitions that have occurred in Latin America. Not only are women and children the most vulnerable by inroads on the subsistence economy, but in response to debt burdens, governments cut welfare budgets first. Since state policy and agricultural reform are not gender neutral but, indeed, serve to diminish the status of rural women, Latin American women have engaged in collective action to ensure survival (Nash, 1990). Unlike Indian women who are hindered in gender equity by peasant reform movements (Roy, 1994), such tactics for Latin American women allow them to become more politically astute and form both a class and gender consciousness.

The plight of the majority of Latin American women who are in poverty is contrasted sharply with upper- and upper-middle-class women who may be professionals or who are part of the elite leisure class. Career women are supported by their husbands, parents, and other bolsters which allow them to combine professional and family roles. The irony here is that professional success is to a large extent dependent upon the hiring of domestic help. Domestics provide services which help to blunt the impact of a career on the family. Domestic servants in Latin America represent the majority of female wage earners. There is considerable disagreement about whether working as a servant provides a channel for upward mobility or whether it allows for a more rigid stratification system based on class (Jelin, 1977; Chant, 1987; Miller, 1991; Radcliffe and Westwood, 1993). This is a prime example of the intersection of class and gender and the difficulty of separating their relative influence in explaining the role and status of many Latin American women. As Beneria and Roldan (1987:10) note, it may be analytically possible to distinguish class and gender at the theoretical level, but in practice they cannot be easily disentangled.

It would appear that the ideology of marianismo combined with jobs offering limited economic rewards reinforce gender stereotypes, suggesting that Latin American women are passive and dependent. Marianismo assumes that since women are relegated to the home, any influence they achieve is from this source. When venturing into other uncertain arenas, they risk loss of respect. But other studies are questioning such logic. Research indicates that Latin American women are engaged in a variety of political activities, are organizing for social and economic change, and exert considerable influence within their households (Babb, 1990; Jelin, 1991; Miller, 1991; Fisher, 1993; Brooke, 1994). NGO initiatives resulting from the United Nations Conference on Women in Beijing include pressing governments to review family planning and birth control issues. Both politically and culturally Latin America is solidly linked to the Catholic Church. Peru, for example, has collided with the Vatican with its new policy to disseminate birth control material throughout the population. While women and their families will certainly benefit from this, it is also in response to the doubling of Peru's population since 1960, about half of whom live in extreme poverty , and a fertility rate of 6.2 among women with little or no education (Mann, 1995a). The appointment of women to top level cabinet posts in Peru (Escobar, 1994) has provided more political clout to implement state-supported family planning efforts.

Nicaragua has followed suit with official government policy now stating that reproductive health, sex education, and services in family planning will be available to women. While continuing to condemn abortion to prevent pregnancy and for population control, Nicaragua recognizes a woman's right to decide on when and how frequently she will have children (*Bolsa de Mujeres,* 1995). These positions have been advocated in spite of the Church's insistence that practicing birth control is "a grave sin" (Mann, 1995a). Political influence for Latin American women has previously been exercised mostly within informal settings and in regard to accepted cultural norms which have not seriously challenged gender role differentiation. The influence of NGOs is changing this pattern.

Feminist scholars and political activists in Latin America also have yet to resolve the issue of whether class conflict is the critical issue which serves to perpetuate the lowly status of women. The question becomes whether feminist theory needs to focus attention on class or gender as the key factor. Jacquette (1986:246) states that Latin American feminists are now declaring both categories as valid and "that efforts to liberate women are consistent with and reinforce the class struggle." In sociological terms, this is congruent with a strong conflict theory orientation within the socialist/Marxist branch of feminism which suggests that patriarchy influences women to continue to uphold a system which perpetuates their inferior position.

ISRAEL

Issues of gender equality have been salient in Israel since its new beginnings as an independent nation. We are aware of impressive experiments which are designed to minimize traditional forms of gender stratification, such as in the military and on the kibbutz. The rise of Golda Meier to the highest political position in the fledgling state is another often-cited instance in how far women can progress. Legislatively, women in Israel have achieved what women in the United States continue to fight for, like maternity leave and equal opportunities with men in education and employment.

Yet despite impressive gains and the internalization of an egalitarian gender role ideology, feminists contend that gender equality in Israel is illusory

(Lorber, 1993). Myths of gender equality are traced to the socialist egalitarian rhetoric before the modern founding of Israel. These myths are perpetuated but institutionalized gender discrimination prevails (Swirski and Safir, 1991). In this manner, the system which informally serves to limit the choices of women remains intact. As Boneparth (1986) suggests, alongside the egalitarian ideal and all the improvements which favor increasing the status of women, "the overwhelming thrust of Israeli public policy is toward reinforcing women's traditional roles." Part of this stems from the fact that Israeli society is organized around the principle of the family as the dominant institution and the family as the cradle of Jewish heritage. As such, the Jewish family is tied to ancient religious traditions which are unquestionably patriarchal in nature. The family is what defines the woman's role. She may contribute to the social and economic life of the community, but her family life takes precedence above all else (Boneparth, 1986:125-26).

It may seem contradictory that a patriarchal family structure reinforced by seemingly immutable religious beliefs could give rise to an experiment in collectivization, the *kibbutz*, which literally calls for a radical departure from the traditional gender division of labor in the family. On the surface at least, the kibbutz represents an effort at eliminating distinctions between the work of men and the work of women, with men sharing in child care and women working in agriculture and construction. It also redefines the structure of the family to be more collective in organization. Since attempts to raise children communally increased women's dissatisfaction with kibbutz life, the practice has been essentially halted. While the kibbutz "family" is neither extended nor completely nuclear, within a collective organization it is taking on more "nuclearlike" structural characteristics.

The kibbutz is oriented to children, with child rearing seen as a serious task which must not be left to haphazard arrangements. From infancy on, the child spends most time with his or her peers and lives in the children's house. On the Sabbath the children usually spend the day with their parents. Teachers and nurses do most of the socialization of the children. Although children do not live with, or for the most part are not raised by, their biological parents, the parents are still critical to their development. Children know who their parents are, identify with them as such, and derive security, love, and affection from them. Ideally, such an arrangement would free both parents from child-care responsibilities which would in turn allow them to work for the betterment of the community as a whole, performing a variety of other critical functions. Again, based on the principle of gender equality, it is assumed that there is no substantial differentiation between the roles performed by women and men.

These principles, however, have not been transformed into reality. Even from the beginning, the kibbutz population has represented only a small group (less than 4 percent) of Israeli society. But this group has been extremely influential and its representation in the political, military, economic, agricultural, and artistic life is far greater than its actual numbers. From pioneering origins where economic survival was uncertain, most kibbutzim have become middle class. The early kibbutzim were characterized by role sharing and a minimization of gender differentiation. Women and men did each other's work, at least by the standards of other parts of the society. Today, however, this has changed considerably. Once financial stability and numbers sufficient for survival were assured, gender stratification accelerated (Agassi, 1989; Neuman, 1991). Women function almost exclusively as child-care workers, nurses, teachers, and kitchen workers. It is only when children reach high school that they will probably see male teachers. It is at this point when they begin to work directly in the economy of the kibbutz. The early ideal of equal sharing of work has been steadily assaulted and is on the verge of elimination in many kibbutzim.

While it is clear that the contemporary kibbutz is marked by gender division in work roles, especially related to child care, there are many who find such divisions unacceptable. This may explain the fact that women are more likely to leave the kibbutz than men, both after arriving there as adults or being born there (Jacobsen, 1994:413). Carmody (1989:154) notes that both industrialization and the women's movement are challenging the self-perpetuating lower positions assigned to women in kibbutzim. Although social stratification clearly exists on the kibbutz, the ideology of gender emancipation has allowed for a structure which enables some women to be free of gender-related tasks and roles (Anson et al., 1990:214-15). It is not a call to return to the "pioneer" days but rather a recognition that they must find ways to augment principles of equal opportunity and the development of full human potential on the kibbutz.

Beyond the kibbutz, when considering the position of women in Israeli society as a whole, family roles are still primary. In particular, religious schools inculcate a religious-based conception of womanhood that is shaped by both "divine" law and the male world (Rapoport, 1995). But smaller family size and increased female labor force participation offer women alternatives to domestic roles. Money matters, even for professional women. Data on female Israeli physicians indicate that compared to women who earn more than their husbands, women who earn less hold more traditional gender role attitudes, attribute less importance to their own career success, and express satisfaction in their ability to combine work and family roles (Izraeli, 1994). Public policy overall has not significantly helped with the burdens women must face in carrying out these dual roles and women's groups are at odds over how much to press the government for constitutional guarantees of rights for women (Lorber, 1993). To counter ancient traditionalism which hampers gender equity, the policy-making process must be used to translate the needs of women into effective and culturally acceptable legislation.

THE MUSLIM WORLD

To the Westerner, the Muslim world represents conflicting images and attitudes. On the one hand, the oil-rich nations have created better living standards and enhanced educational and job opportunities for their inhabitants. On the other hand, as Islamic nations, efforts at development occur within a unique socioreligious framework which Westerners view with both curiosity and suspicion. Nowhere do these conflicting images emerge more forcefully than when viewing women in Arab cultures.

Given the stereotypes surrounding Islam, it is surprising for many to discover that Islam first developed as both a new religion and as a movement toward social reform which was specifically aimed at challenging and ultimately changing the lowly status of women. Pre-Islamic Arabian men had the right of unlimited polygamy, and a husband could end any one of his marriages as he saw fit. Women could be bought, sold, or inherited. Their lowly position contributed to the common practice of female infanticide. With Islam came a specific legal status for women. A woman's dowry became her sole property, she could inherit and own property, become a guardian of minors, and even enter into a business or trade. Polygamy was now restricted to four wives, who, according to the Koran, the holy book of Islam, had to be treated equally (Ahmed, 1992; Cleveland, 1994).

But the letter and the spirit of the law are different matters. Reforms are possible only in the context of a culture's willingness to undergo change and endure stressful transitions. This has simply not been the case in the Arab world. Regardless of the position of women in the pre-Islamic world, the Koran has continued to be used as a moral rationale for restricting women. A resurgence of religious fundamentalism has bolstered Koranic interpretations which have sanctioned women's inferior status.

Islamic legal reform has many advocates, and interpretations can provide Koranic evidence for upgrading the position of women. But reformist counterattacks are losing ground in the current era which is becoming known as the "Islamization" movement (Zakaria, 1986; Salman, 1987; Zenie-Ziegler, 1988; Hossain, 1995; Kamal, 1995). What this means is that Islamic societies are retreating to the "old ways" when modernization is seen as threatening a more traditional way of life. These religious forces view religion and state as inseparable and believe that all laws, governing both public and private issues, must have a religious basis. The most extreme version of this movement is seen in Iran, but elements can be found in most Arab cultures as well as other Islamic societies, such as Pakistan (Lindsey, 1988). Although Iran is not an Arab culture, it shares a strong Islamic orientation with its Arab neighbors. Indeed, it can be said that Islamic fundamentalism has reached its height in this non-Arab society. Countermodernization is selective, with certain ideas and technologies being accepted while others are rejected (Lindsey, 1984). When a countermodernization movement occurs, women are likely to be its victims rather than its beneficiaries.

Iran

The case of Iran provides the best example of how countermodernization can serve to restrict women. What is startling about the overthrow of the Shah of Iran in 1979 and the establishment of the Islamic regime under the Ayatollah Khomeini is that women were a major force in propelling the Ayatollah to power. As sentiment against the oppression and exploitation under the Shah grew, women also became more politically active. Women took to the streets in anti-Shah demonstrations in mass numbers. At a time when the veil was becoming a remnant of the past, women actually embraced it as a symbol of solidarity against the Shah. The images of veiled women protesting in mass demonstrations shocked many. It seemed to contradict the liberal view of women which was supposedly a hallmark of the Shah's regime.

Actually, the veil served several purposes. It prevented the easy identification of the protesters which could make them targets of the secret police (the dreaded "Savak"), and it was a gesture against what many felt to be the excessive Westernization of Iran. Modern transformation hastens the loss of Islamic identity. When that identity is linked to the female, by restoring the veil as the Islamic marker, broader identity is also restored (Najmabadi, 1993). It may be that the veil was seen by women as a symbol of solidarity which was to be discarded or worn at will after the fall of the Shah. Tabari (1982:6) suggests that many women believed that under the new leadership the sacrifices and militancy they showed would be rewarded and that the religious leaders would concede that rights for women should be extended. These would include greater opportunities for education and employment, as well as concessions granting them more self-determination in their domestic roles.

Khomeini's own position during the anti-Shah movement increased women's support for him. Though remaining rather indefinite about the role of women, he opposed the idea of women-as-object and saw a woman is a man's equal: "She and he are free to choose their lives and their occupations." He stated that the "Shah's regime has destroyed the freedom of women as well as men" (cited in Sanasarian, 1982:117). The new republic would not oppress women, according to Khomeini, and with such words, women flocked to his movement. Less than a month after the ousting of the Shah, illusions of equality were shattered. Since then, the new regime has systematically undermined the freedom of women. Legislation was enacted to alter gender relations so they would not resemble anything like those existing in the West. The Islamic Republic emphasized that the family was rooted in the "precious foundation of motherhood," and that male and female roles are separate and distinctive, which bolstered the desirability of gender segregation in public places. The minimum legal age for girls to marry was lowered from 18 to 13 and now to 9 (Tohidi, 1991; Moghadam, 1995). An extreme example of loss of freedom is loss of life. Some women under the Khomeini regime have been executed for adultery and prostitution (Brydon and Chant, 1989:32). No longer was the veil a symbol of militant solidarity. In the eyes of many, it has become a symbol of oppression.

With Khomeini's death, the new regime has continued a policy intent on "restoring" women to their primary role, that of domestic responsibility. Both women and men were compelled by religious righteousness to work in overthrowing the Shah. Once this succeeded, a woman's religious duty demanded that she concentrate on domestic roles, and as a result, women have been literally pushed out of public life and into the home. It is likely that many women would have embraced domestic roles anyway, but with the new regime options in other realms became severely circumscribed. Islam is invoked to deny reproductive choice, educational opportunity, and paid employment for women (Tohidi, 1991; Obermeyer, 1994). In order to bolster a ruinous economy and divorce itself from its pariah status internationally, Iran has recently made tentative overtures to the West. To date, however, women's issues have not been a priority in their agendas. The last decade has witnessed a continual eroding of women's freedoms. Women are now separated from most public life. The walls that surround them are many: the walls of their homes, the walls of illiteracy, and the walls of the veil.

This is not to say that attempts at reform have been silenced completely. But even reformists must work within definitions of an "Islamic identity" accepted by the regime. Both reformist and fundamentalist Islamic women appear to accept the following ideological components of this identity:

1. Women are equal to but dissimilar from men.
2. Western values are a corruptive menace to be avoided by women.

Reformists also add the idea that complementarity does not mean superiority or inferiority, but it does imply separate but equal (Sanasarian, 1986:214-15). Working from such interpretations, reform has not made great strides. The Iranian resistance movement has elevated a woman, Marysam Rajavi, as Iran's president in exile. She would serve as interim president for six months if the mullahs in Iran were overthrown. She wears an Islamic headscarf, does not shake hands with men, but believes that there must be a separation of mosque and state in future Iran. As such, she has the support of many women, intellectuals and members of the exiled Iranian community (Iranian Resistance, 1994). Her husband heads a National Liberation Army based in Iraq. It remains to be seen if she is indeed the leader the resistance movement makes her out to be or if she is being used as a figurehead to attract needed Western support. There are many parallels with this movement and the revolution to overthrow the Shah, so many women who support the resistance movement express caution at the motives of its leadership.

Under the present regime, there is no possibility for a women's movement to emerge. However, the economic crisis in Iran has prompted many women to find employment outside the home. Since women do have the right to run for public office in Iran, they have actually gained several parliamentary seats (Sciolino, 1992). Although economic reasons, which are acceptable, rather than feminist reasons, which are unacceptable, are cited for these changes, it is clear that women on the whole can benefit. Finally, there are signs that feminism is active among the Iranian exiles and that they may ultimately help influence at least a modicum of rebirth of feminist ideology within the country.

The Arab Middle East

Iran is at one end of a continuum of women in the Muslim world. Other Muslim countries must be considered in light of their own unique traditions, beliefs, and interpretations of Islam regarding women. Mernissi (1987) contends that there are no real effective models for women's liberation which can appeal to Muslim women. They are either too Western or too pre-Islamic. Islamic societies are based on fairly rigid definitions of family which serve as the focus for societal organization. Tampering with these definitions brings fear that social chaos will result. This means that the traditional male-female and master-slave relationship existing in Islamic families which exclude love as a male weakness are accepted (Mernissi, 1987:174).

On the other hand, Islam regards women as potentially powerful, influential, and aggressive, images which can serve as empowering to women. In their quest for modernization, women are embracing but also testing traditional norms. In Saudi Arabia women run investment firms, manage shops, and are employed in hospitals. Most businesses are still gender segregated, but opportunities for employment for educated women are offered (Siddiqi, 1993). They see themselves as pioneers who are ignoring rules in the hope that changing needs will reshape their roles as women. As one women states, "The worst thing you can do in the Arab world is ask for permission. It will always be no" (Boustany, 1994). By stretching the narrow limits of male-dominated Saudi society, they endure public criticism, but believe that change will eventually come (LeMoyne, 1990). In Egypt an elite strata of middle-class professional women have overcome societal pressures and religious taboos to attain success outside the home. Influences on them are both modern—Western capitalism and socialist egalitarian ideology—and traditional—the images of formidable females such as Queen Nefertiti and the Prophet Muhammad's strong-willed wife Khadija (Murphy, 1993).

Research in Arab cultures as diverse as Jordan, Saudi Arabia, Kuwait, and Palestine has suggested that the role and status of women are being influenced by even small gains in health, literacy, and political reform (Rishmawi, 1986; Sanad and Tessler, 1988; Shami et al., 1990; *Jordan Issues and Perspectives*, 1993; MacLean, 1993; Ambah, 1995). Even with the severe separatist policies against women in effect in Saudi Arabia, the Gulf War provided opportunities to demonstrate that women from other cultures could be competent, interested, and successful in a variety of nondomestic roles. As we have seen throughout history, war is latently functional for altering perceptions of women.

North Africa: Female Genital Mutilation

The extent of women's liberation in the Arab Muslim world is debatable and must be approached according to the political and social structure within each society. Islam is not uniform across Muslim societies so women's roles in those societies cannot be approached simply by viewing laws and interpretations of religious texts (Kandiyoti, 1991). However, these societies are linked in their views of women by certain cultural practices. While the veil may be a symbol of oppression from a feminist viewpoint, other customs suggest an even more frightening reality. It is the practice of female genital mutilation which has stirred global debate. Though predating Islam, this practice is still found in parts of the Middle East and it is most pervasive in North Africa and some sub-Saharan regions. Estimates of the total number of females who have had this operation range from 80 to 100 million, including 4 to 5 million children as young as five years of age. It is practiced widely among both Muslims and Coptic Christians, among the wealthy and the poor, and in both urban and rural areas (Kouba and Muasher, 1985; Gruenbaum, 1993; Rushwan, 1995).

Female genital mutilation (FGM) refers to a variety of genital operations, which are essentially designed to eliminate any erotic pleasure and ensure a girl's virginity, hence her marriageability. Often referred to as female circumcision, it is *not* the counterpart of male circumcision so is actually a misnomer. There are three types of operations which young girls can undergo and which vary according to region and country. There is the partial clitoridectomy, sometimes referred to as the Sunna circumcision, where excision of the clitoral hood is done. The Sunna variety is both the mildest and least common and may not physically impair the woman's sex life but is associated with psychological trauma. The second type, practiced mainly in Egypt, is when a full clitoridectomy occurs. Scar tissue may result which is so extensive that the vaginal opening itself is covered, which necessitates a second operation. The third, and most radical type, is infibulation or pharaonic circumcision, which consists of a full clitoridectomy and excision of the labia minora plus the inner walls of the labia majora. It is practiced mostly notably in Sudan, Somalia, and parts of Ethiopia. After infibulations, the two sides of the vulva are partially sliced off or scraped raw and then sewn together with catgut. A small opening is left for the release of urine and menstrual blood. These operations are extensively performed without anesthetics and in unsanitary conditions. The last two types are the most prevalent forms (Toubia, 1986; Zenie-Ziegler, 1988; Gruenbaum, 1993; Rushwan, 1995).

The effects of these mutilations are many, ranging from psychological trauma, to hemorrhage, septicemia (blood poisoning), pain during intercourse, lack of sexual pleasure, and death from infections or complications during childbirth. The practice continues because it ensures female chastity by making intercourse practically impossible or extremely painful until the vaginal opening is slit immediately before marriage. Fidelity after marriage is also protected by eliminating sexual pleasure. In interviews with rural Egyptian women Zenie-Ziegler (1988:95) finds that, since it is keeping with traditional values, they do not see it as an infringement on their rights. In their segregationist world, they accept the view that "the pleasures of sex are reserved for men, and the dignity of childbirth and motherhood for women." They will perpetuate the practice with their own daughters. The isolation and circumscribed, nonoverlapping gender roles explain why 80 percent of Sudanese girls are still infibulated, although the government has made all but the Sunna circumcision illegal (Brydon and Chant, 1989:30–31). Regardless of how it is justified, it is a grim reminder of the subjugation of women.

Consider the case of an Egyptian woman who recalled her own "circumcision" at the age of six when she was roughly taken from her bed and found a hand clapped over her mouth to prevent her from screaming.

> It looked as though some thieves had broken into my room and kidnapped me from my bed . . . I realized that my thighs had been pulled wide apart . . . gripped by steel fingers . . . Then suddenly a sharp metallic edge seemed to drop between my thighs and there cut off a piece of flesh from my body. I screamed with pain despite the tight hand held over my mouth . . . I saw a red pool of blood around my hips. I did not know what they had cut off from my body . . . I just wept, and called out to my mother for help. But the worst shock of all was when I looked around and found her standing by my side . . . right in the midst of these strangers, talking to them and smiling at them, as though they had not participated in slaughtering her daughter just a few moments ago. They carried me to my bed. I saw them catch hold of my sister, who was two years younger. (el Saadawi, 1980:7-8, cited in Minces, 1982:52-53)

FGM also continues because it is part of a complex sociocultural arrangement of female subjugation in strongly patriarchal societies. Even with its untraceable past, until recently it has remained untouched as part of the cultural core of the identity of traditional people (Gruenbaum, 1993). The practice came to the forefront of women's issues during the United Nations Conference on Women in Copenhagen in 1980, and created a wedge between African and Western women. Viewed as a unique and functional cultural practice serving critical needs, especially the marriageability of daughters, African women felt they were being unfairly criticized. In addition, women who perform the procedure, such as traditional birth attendants, derive both prestige and income from it. Efforts to abolish it must deal directly with the local situation and the impact on the lives of those women as well. However, dialogue remained open and by the next UN conference in Nairobi, women were discussing its cultural connotations in a less confrontive manner. By Beijing in

1995, consensus emerged among African and non-African women that viewed FGM as a violation of human rights. Traditionally, women's rights have been treated as separate and not taken as seriously as human rights (Bunch, 1994). Under the banner that women's rights are human rights, practices such as FGM could no longer withstand the argument that changes cannot or should not occur because of cultural interference. More important, African women felt empowered to seriously challenge the practice and to get political support for the challenge. As a result, some countries, such as Nigeria and Ghana, have issued legal mandates against it, and it has been used as grounds for asylum in the United States (Burstyn, 1996). Previously women feared that their daughters could not be married without being "circumcised." When entire villages do not allow their girls to undergo the procedure, men must look for marriage partners elsewhere or marry uncircumcised women. Women's empowerment now suggests the latter.

It is unfair to regard this procedure as the defining characteristic of an entire region, but it calls attention to the issue of cultural change through women's empowerment. It also serves as an example of symbolic interaction's emphasis on definition of the situation. Female circumcision was linguistically transformed into female genital mutilation. It was then framed as a human rights violation rather than a form of cultural interference. The new definition of the situation became the reality and the practice has been seriously challenged, curtailed, and, in some places, eliminated.

SCANDINAVIA: NORWAY AND SWEDEN

When compared to gender roles in the developing world and the gendered nature of its poverty, the Scandinavian countries of Northern Europe stand in sharp contrast. By every measure of overall human development as well as those used to assess equality between men and women, all the Scandinavian nations are consistently ranked the highest (Eisler et al., 1995; United Nations Development Program, 1995). Norway and Sweden in particular provide the global standard for gender egalitarian models.

Norway has essentially reached it goal of political parity with 40 percent of it legislative seats held by women, including long-time prime minister Grö Harlem Brundtland (Ciabattari, 1996a). In 1993 all three candidates for prime minister were women. This demonstrates the clear association between political power and gender equality. Women have clout when they are represented by other women in the legislative bodies of their nations.

The objective of gender political parity has been an aim of the Norwegian government for many years. Norway has essentially embraced the sociological perspective with its understanding that gender permeates our lives in countless ways and that decisions which on the surface appear to be gender neutral may have a different impact on women than on men. Their goal is to mainstream the gender perspective into all public activities. As we will see in Chapter 14, unlike the United States which uses measures such as Affirmative Action and comparable worth to make up for deficiencies, mainstreaming assures that the gender concern is incorporated from the outset. This does not mean that attention is exclusively directed toward women's concerns, values, and experiences. The goal is equality and the gender perspective promotes it. As viewed by the Norwegian government, "the long-term objective is that the gender perspective shall be an automatic reflex and influence all important decisions" (Mainstreaming, 1995). In order to understand how the structure of social institutions and everyday life are influenced by gender, all public servants acquire knowledge of the gender perspective.

Norway recognizes that gender roles will not be eliminated and there is no attempt to do so. Women and men have different priorities and organize their lives differently, such as through vocational preferences, consumer patterns, and leisure activities. Such differences, however, should not be grounds for unequal access to social benefits and economic resources. The gender perspective assures that the different behaviors and aspirations of women and men will be equally favored in the organization and governing of Norway (Mainstreaming, 1995). For example, parental leave for new fathers has been in existence for over two decades. A high priority on the political agenda is to make it easier for parents with young children to combine family with work responsibilities outside the home (*Gender Equality in Norway*, 1994). As we shall see in the next two chapters, this is probably the key issue impacting American men and women and their families.

The most notable progress of mainstreaming the gender perspective has been in politics, and in the fields of child and family policies which incorporate the reality of women's unpaid domestic work. However, despite women's increased levels of education and training, equal pay has yet to be attained because "women's work" remains consistently undervalued. In addition, and reflecting a worldwide pattern, women are paid less than men when they enter male occupations. Recent data on women farmers in Norway show that while they are equal to men in formal status, "important aspects of the existing gender system are being preserved." These young women farmers continue to take the responsibility for domestic work, but their farming income is viewed as less important for the household than their husbands', and, compared to male farmers, their farm income is less (Haugen and Brandth, 1994:206). However, the authors suggest that they represent a new type of women in farming and are striving to show that their talent in operating farms is comparable to that of a man's. As such, they will be the role models for the next generation of farming women.

Sexual violence is another matter of critical concern with which Norway is dealing, not just with the provision of more shelters, but with more preventive measures. Attention is also directed to the situation of Norway's minority indigenous groups, such as the Sami, who are disadvantaged on a number of quality of life indicators compared to the rest of Norwegians. The Gender Equality Act was passed in 1977 and, except for the internal life of churches, covers all areas of society. While the aims of the law are still not fully realized in Norway, monumental progress has been made as Norway continues its efforts to mainstream the gender perspective (*Gender Equality in Norway*, 1994).

Like Norway, Sweden's trend toward gender equality has been advanced with legislative changes and an increased number of women in elective office, where Sweden also has about 40 percent women in legislative seats (Ciabattari, 1996a). But Sweden is unique in that egalitarian principles are being advocated through an emphasis on gender role change in males, especially as it relates to the family. Sweden has gone farther than any other government in stipulating that economic support and daily care and nurturing of children is the equal responsibility of both parents. The prime minister of Sweden has stated that men have great stakes in gender equality, and more examples need to be set "before men at large become the good partners for modern feminism and before women become partners in men's search beyond the old traditional role" (Carllson, 1995:8).

From as early as 1966, legislation has been passed in Sweden for a wide array of innovative programs to improve the economic status of women outside the home and the child-rearing capabilities of men. While data continue to indicate that mothers still assume the bulk of domestic work and the physical tasks associated with child care, there have been notable changes in men's nurturing familial roles, particularly related to emotional caregiving (Sandqvist, 1987; Kalleberg and Rosenfeld, 1990; Haas, 1993). However, similar to men in the United States, Swedish men espouse attitudes about participation in child care that are "more egalitarian than the division of labor they actually practiced" (Haas, 1993:249). Although Haas asserts that the gender revolution in Sweden is stalled by the failure of fathers to assume equal responsibility in the home, the fact that Swedes hold very egalitarian attitudes overall is a step toward gender equity. Political priorities will continue to bolster this objective.

An example of how public policy can impact attitudes about parenting is the birth experience itself. Sweden was one of the first countries that offered an expectant father the opportunity to be present at the birth of his child. Men's accounts of these experiences are understandably filled with detail, emotion, positive feelings, and the firm conviction that this is the greatest experience that connects the couple as partners and as parents (Swedin, 1995). But Sweden is unique in that is provides for men to be "trained" as fathers, both before and after the birth of their children. Generous paternity leave, mentoring with other fathers, and a host of educational and training programs allow fathers to take advantage of new parenthood. While still voluntary, more men are eager to pursue what has been called "new fatherliness" (Swedin, 1995). As advocated by the head of one of Sweden's largest industrial companies, fathering and the importance of a man's presence for his children are the strongest reasons for men "to battle against the magnetic attraction of their jobs" (Westerberg, 1995). In accordance with the United Nations Convention on the Rights of the Child, Sweden has accepted the belief that the child has a right to both its parents. Sweden has translated that right into public policy.

Compared to most of the world, particularly the developing world, gender equity in Norway and Sweden is dramatically advanced. While there are social and psychological alterations that accompany gender role change, it is the monetary cost that is currently creating most upheaval. The costly array of social and welfare benefits that Norway and Sweden provide to their citizens are extraordinary from an American perspective. Although these benefits have translated into overall well-being and an enhanced quality of life, it is unclear if this path will continue to be followed. Like benefits associated with health care, gender equity initiatives will be scrutinized carefully to determine their cost effectiveness. It is doubtful that there will be a major retreat from efforts aimed at reducing gender disparity, but the reduction of funds for these efforts is a real possibility. Regardless, Norway and Sweden still stand as powerful national role models in the move toward global gender equality.

BOX 6–1   The Legacy of Beijing: A Personal Perspective

It is not surprising that, in covering the largest gathering of women in history, the United Nations Conference on Women in Beijing, international media attention focused on controversy and conflict rather than the more pervasive atmosphere of unity and support which emerged from the conference. The Beijing gathering and the parallel NGO Forum in nearby Huairou represent landmark developments in global understanding and cooperation among women of the world.

As addressed in a number of sessions at the conference, women represent a glaring blindspot for the media. News outlets in many countries, including the United States, too often approach women's issues with stereotypes, misconceptions, and biased data. And when addressing a public believed to relish controversy, the seeds for reinforcing these stereotypes continue to be sewn. Yet the truly remarkable events in Beijing managed to alter this trend.

Even while attending the conference, many of us were acutely aware that the international media were dwelling on issues which generated the most controversy, especially religious fundamentalism, with frequent staged demonstrations by those representing conservative groups. The Iranian delegation of fully veiled women and their male "escorts" provided the media with much camera time. Their efforts were met by what I would describe as "bemused toleration" by most women. But the international media would willingly toddle behind with cameras and microphones and report on the nightly news that religious fundamentalism was tearing the conference apart.

This could not be further from the truth. While religious fundamentalism was certainly one of many controversial topics, the NGO Forum was remarkable in its ability to bring women of all faiths to engage in dialogue over matters which impacted their daily lives—including issues of reproduction, parenting, family violence, and health and well-being—all of which have religious overtones. Many workshops brought together women of all religious and spiritual traditions. When politics, religion, and cultural tradition were met head on, as between Palestinian and Israeli women or between African and other women who did and did not accept FGM, toleration and understanding emerged in an atmosphere of open dialogue. What became clear, however, is that the die is cast against religious fundamentalism when religion is used to restrict women's human rights. In a presentation I gave on this topic, I argued that religious fundamentalism can be recast so that it becomes liberating rather than restrictive and used as a weapon *against* sexism and *for* empowerment.

The norm of the NGO Forum sessions was to ensure that everyone had the opportunity to voice opinions, and in most cases there was not complete unity. While such inclusiveness may be at the root of controversy when people "agree to disagree," the stage is set for a better understanding of the issues and more toleration of dissenting opinion.

What is the legacy of Beijing? I speak from the perspective of attending the gatherings in Copenhagen and Nairobi as well as Beijing. The previous conferences were more divisive, but also smaller, less inclusive, and with fewer women on the organizing bodies or official delegations. While the Beijing conference was racked with negative international media attention, Chinese obstructionism, logistical nightmares, and inadequate facilities, the ability and perseverance of the women who attended and worked to get the Platform of Action adopted were nothing short of spectacular. As Hillary Rodham Clinton stated in her address to the Forum, "NGOs are where the action is." With thousands of NGOs as watchdogs, governments will be held accountable for the pledges made to women and their families throughout the world through the ratified UN document. This document addressed 12 critical areas of concern and outlined action steps to be taken in implementing objectives. For example, the number one issue was women's poverty. Action steps for this issue included calling for gender-sensitive economic policies, placing economic value on women's unpaid work, and increasing education and training programs for poor women.

It is clear that this gathering of women in Beijing attests to the recognition that women's empowerment is beneficial to everyone, and that, despite misconceptions in the media, global sisterhood has emerged as a reality that cannot be denied.

CHAPTER 7

LOVE AND MARRIAGE IN CONTEMPORARY SOCIETY

> His attachment to her must be imaginary. But still he would be her husband. Without thinking highly of either men or of matrimony, marriage had always been her object; it was the only honourable provision for well-educated young women of small fortune, and however uncertain of giving happiness, must be her pleasant preservative from want.
>
> —Jane Austin, *Pride and Prejudice* (1813)

The story of Cinderella promotes love and marriage as an escape from a world of drudgery and lack of fulfillment into one of enchantment and "living happily ever after." Indeed, the term "Cinderella story" has now come to symbolize the lives of those few fortunate, and always beautiful, women who have gone from rags to riches, when the right prince comes along. At the turn of the new century, the 1949 Disney version of Cinderella is still alive and well. Instead of a cartoon prince we have Richard Gere carrying Debra Winger and Julia Roberts away from their pre-princess lives as factory worker in *An Officer and a Gentleman* and as prostitute in *Pretty Woman*. As Kelley (1994) suggests, the movie *Pretty Woman* is modern in its openness toward sexuality but reinforces the "sexist dreams and social values of the past." This chapter will examine the empirical reality associated with some of these media images.

We are so accustomed to the notion that love and marriage are inseparable and that romantic love is the primary determinant for marriage that it is rather startling to realize these concepts have been paired only since the nineteenth century in the United States. The ideal of passionate love existed prior to this, but until recently in Western history, love was not seen as a basis, especially not *the* basis, for marriage. In many parts of the contemporary world, the selection of a spouse is in the hands of marriage brokers, parents, other relatives, or matchmakers whose qualifications are respected by the family and community. The belief that love should be a significant factor in assessing a potential marriage partner is gaining popularity throughout the world, but initially it was a unique phenomenon associated with America.

LOVE

The poets and philosophers who sang the praises of courtly love during the feudal era elevated love to something unattainable in marriage. The ladies of the court would bestow gifts, blessings, and an occasional kiss on suitors who would do battle or endure hardships for such prizes. Love which would eventuate in sexual passion was unseemly, even discouraged. Courtly love was reserved for the highborn, almost a game to be played, and thereby excluded the vast majority of the population who did not have the luxury of games.

Marriage, on the other hand, was an obligation. While the aristocracy glorified the romantic ideals of courtly love, they were expected to simultaneously marry and raise children. A rigid stratification system could be threatened if passionate love served as a realistic alternative for choosing a mate. Marriage was a practical and economic arrangement which influenced kinship ties, lineage, and inheritance. Since power, property, and privilege are affected, marriage could not be taken lightly. Marriage was the mundane but necessary alternative to the enchantment and passion of feudal romance. Issues related to personal fulfillment and incompatibility were irrelevant. The decision was a rational rather than a romantic one.

The Puritan era ushered in the revolutionary idea that love and marriage should be tied. This was a radical departure from early Church teachings which warned men that even to look on their wives with lust made them adulterers. Now good Christian husbands and wives were admonished to love one another. If love was not the reason for marriage, it was expected to flourish later. Theories of family development emphasizing a functionalist approach would support this expectation, and it is confirmed by some research on arranged marriages (Jamieson, 1994; Myers, 1996). Parental control leading to approval of marriage partners remained the norm, but the fact that love should play a part in the process became etched into the fledgling American consciousness.

Marriage as a purely rational event was eroded by dramatic social changes. A political climate receptive to egalitarian attitudes was bolstered by the Industrial Revolution which almost mandated a further leveling of stratification and less separation between the genders. As women moved into the world of paid employment, their economic power increased. Social change combined with economic assets enhanced choices for both genders, but particularly for women. By the 1890s couples began to be influenced by the idea that marriages could be companionate (Roberts, 1994:137). Responsibilities that had formerly been under the control of one or the other spouse began to be shared.

Murstein (1986:21) states that the improved status of women in combination with opportunities for youth to interact, privacy for such interaction, and sufficient leisure time were the conditions that needed to be met before romantic love could truly blossom. By the beginning of the twentieth century, these conditions had been met. Love and marriage, with the assumption of freedom of choosing a marriage partner, have since become inextricably bound.

Friends and Lovers

> I fell in love with him at first sight.
> Then why didn't you marry him?
> Oh, I saw him again afterwards.
> (Anonymous. Quoted in Mullan, 1984:226)

Since love is such a complex emotion and so difficult to define to everyone's satisfaction, it is easy to understand why it is encumbered with folklore, superstition, and myth. Love is extolled for its virtue and damned for its jealousy. Euphoria, joy, depression, restlessness, anger, and fear are all words used to describe love.

The love for a friend, sibling, parent, or child is certainly different from the feelings accompanying romantic love and the strong emotional attachments it engenders, but distinguishing among the different kinds of love is exceedingly complicated. In comparing love and friendship, for example, Davis (1985) develops three broad clusters of characteristics. The profile of friendship, especially "best" friends, includes enjoyment, acceptance, trust, respect, mutual assistance, confiding, understanding, and spontaneity. For love, we must add passion (fascination and preoccupation with the lover, exclusiveness, and sexual desire) and caring (giving the utmost and being a champion or advocate for the lover).

The distinction between romantic and other varieties of love includes what the ancient Greeks viewed as *eros*, or the physical, sexual component of love; *agape*, its spiritual and altruistic component; *philos*, the love of deep and enduring friendships; and *nomos*, subjugation of the will and allegiance to the love object, metaphorically as to God (Hendrick and Hendrick, 1992a). Although we assume that romantic love would ideally include all of these components, *agape* and *philos* are also indicative of other kinds of love relationships, such as the love between friends or siblings and parents and children. What is interesting is that while the sexual dimension of eros is the very component which is critical in distinguishing romantic love from friendship, it is also its most selfish aspect. The need for sexual gratification may counter the altruism entailed in idealized, but accepted, beliefs about romance. As we shall see, this is an important element in male and female views of love.

When men and women are compared in terms of the gender of their best friends with the explicit indication that it is not a romantic relationship, Davis finds that 27 percent of subjects listed someone of the other sex. When extended to close friends, 56 percent of the men and 44 percent of the women nominated at least one person of the other sex (Davis, 1985:26). Perhaps because the passion dimension lurks behind cross-gender friendships and liking may turn into loving, as discussed in Chapter 3, research consistently reports that same-gender friends are more intimate, stable, and emotionally supportive (Davis, 1985; Wright and Scanlon, 1991; Rawlins, 1993). Early socialization emphasizes patterns of gender segregation which contribute to the vulnerability of enduring cross-gender friendships (Leaper, 1994). Media images reinforce these patterns. Cross-gender friendships are doomed by romance. In the movie *When Harry Met Sally*, Billy Crystal (Harry), "proves his own point that men and women can't be continuing friends" since he marries Sally at the end of the movie. In the reverse, but less common, direction, Jerry and Elaine from *Seinfeld* move from a romantic to a platonic relationship. In citing these examples, West and colleagues (1996) say there are formidable barriers to the formation and endurance of close cross-gender friendships, but that they can be rich and rewarding. Rather than discounting or ignoring the sexual attraction that may also linger in the background, it can add "spice" to a very special relationship (Ambrose, 1989). Overall, it is clear that our ideas about love are dependent on whom we are considering as the object or target of our affection, whether it be a spouse, sex partner, sibling, child, best friend, or parent.

Overall, the clusters differentiate the spouse-lover from the best-close friend, particularly for the passion cluster, but there are exceptions. Spouse-lovers would more likely give the utmost, but best-close friends are likely to be advocates or champions of each other to the same degree. And the hypothesis that there are few differences between best-close friends and spouse-lovers in terms of enjoyment of each other's company is not supported. Davis (1985:25) suspects this may be an indication that a greater range of human needs can be met by a love relationship. This is also consistent with gender role socialization patterns that prescribe instrumental and goal-oriented friendships for males and expressive and emotion-centered friendships for females (Duck and Wright, 1993). From a symbolic interaction perspective, same-gender friendships are enhanced and stabilized when each party accepts the role definitions attached to gender.

Since many, if not most, of the qualities related to close friendship are also reported in research on romantic love, it is the sexual component that must be added to distinguish the two (Rubin, 1973; Hatfield, 1988; Aron and Aron, 1991; Hendrick and Hendrick, 1995). According to Sternberg's (1988) theory, love is a triangle formed by three interlocking elements: intimacy, passion, and commitment. Through open communication, intimacy brings with it emotional warmth and bonding. Physiological arousal and sexual desire are part of the passion component, where feelings of romance take precedence. Commitment involves the choice to continue and maintain the love relationship. All relationships undergo change and transformation, so each vertex of the triangle will not be equal, but if there is too much mismatch among the components, the theory would predict the relationship to fail. When gender role socialization is added to the picture, we can envision increased difficulty in maintaining equal vertexes.

Love Myths

Regardless of its definition, romantic love is idealized in the United States. We are literally bombarded with romantic stimuli throughout our lives which serve to reinforce these idealizations. The most complicated of emotions has produced a range of myths which demonstrate how we romanticize love. To the extent that these myths carry over into our beliefs and behaviors related to gender roles, marriage, and the family, romanticization can have dire consequences.

The myth that love conquers all is a pervasive one. The "all" that is supposedly conquered involves the problems and obstacles inherent in daily living. By idealizing the love-object, problems are even more difficult to solve. Total agreement with another person's views on problem solving is impossible. Lamm (1980, cited in Mullan, 1984:227) notes that romantic love offers a paradox. Idealization requires remoteness to be maintained, but intimacy evaporates remoteness. One's partner cannot fulfill all needs and make all problems disappear. Love does not conquer all, even for a short time.

Love is blind. This myth asserts that true love will dissolve social boundaries and that anyone has the potential for becoming the romantic love object. The belief that "it doesn't matter, as long as I love her/him" is operating here. As we shall see, the process of mate selection and the love that it supposedly encompasses are very structured. We are socialized to fall in love at certain times in our lives and with certain categories of people. Rubenstein's (1983:45) data show that everyone has faith in romance. An amazing 96 percent agree with this. But love is conditioned by a number of social and demographic variables that exert a tremendous influence on us. Both genders are susceptible to these influences, but to a different degree.

The idea that falling in love is part of a structured and rational process counters another myth—that people fall in love at first sight. Physical attractiveness is certainly a critical variable during the first encounter and provides the initial impression. Until verbal interaction occurs, information comes indirectly from the person's overall appearance. The "love at first sight" myth is bolstered by what psychologists refer to as the **halo effect**. This means that people who are attractive are assumed to possess more desirable qualities than those who are less attractive. Beauty and good looks are associated with other positive characteristics, such as goodness, competence, warmth, and sensitivity (Eagly et al., 1991; Feingold, 1992; Perkins and Lerner, 1995). Although it is evident that initial attraction based on appearance is more important in chance encounters such as on airplanes or at one-time events, love requires ongoing, sustained interaction. As a prerequisite to love, interpersonal attraction is enhanced by the **mere exposure effect**. Simply by being frequently exposed to a person increases our liking for that person. Familiarity does not breed contempt, it breeds liking. This explains why college dormitories are major marriage markets where love can flourish. It also explains why the adage that "absence makes the heart grow founder" is incorrect. Its opposite, "out of sight, out of mind," is more empirically justified.

Women are the romantic sex/gender. They are believed to be starry-eyed and to fall in love easily. This belief is associated with the stereotyped idea that since women are more emotional, women succumb faster to romance, hence love. A number of studies have shattered this myth. Men express a higher level of romantic love than women and fall in love earlier and harder than women (Fengler, 1974; Lester et al., 1984; Hatfield and Sprecher, 1986; Brehm, 1992). Overall, men are found to be more idealistic and romantic in their attitudes toward love, with women being more cautious, pragmatic, and realistic (Lester, 1985; Rubin et al., 1991).

However, when women make the decision to fall in love, they exceed men in levels of emotion and euphoria. Women are defined as the experts who will work harder and sacrifice more to maintain the relationship (Wood, 1994; Hite, 1995). In Sternberg's (1988) theory of love, women attach greater importance to the commitment vertex of the triangle. For women, the rational behavior eventually leads to the romantic idealism characterizing love in America. It is at the passionate first stage of love where men are more romantic.

Sex without love is now not only normative but also acceptable. This myth is fueled by a sexual revolution replete with statistics indicating that, as discussed in Chapter 2, nonmarital sex is an American universal. It also assumes the virtual disappearance of the double standard, with women engaging in sex with partners to whom they are not necessarily attracted. However, Rubenstein (1983:40) finds that in comparing a 1969 survey with one done in the 1980s, both men and women actually express a higher degree of sexual conservatism. While gender differences regarding love and sex are converging to some extent (Rabine, 1985), the figures still suggest the double standard is operating with 29 percent of the men and 44 percent of the women believing sex without love is unenjoyable or unacceptable. And even if there are no changes in current levels of sexual "escapades," both genders continue to subscribe to the belief that love is the prerequisite for marriage (Simpson et al., 1986; Hendrick and Hendrick, 1992b; Benokraitis, 1996). The much publicized study on American sexual attitudes and practices by Michael et al. (1994) reports that the most frequent and physically satisfying sex occurs for married people and very committed live-in lovers. Sex in more fulfilling because love attributes, such as caring and commitment, characterize the relationship.

Unlike the other love myths, the permissiveness without affection belief has partial support. This is understood in the context of a continuing, but eroding, double standard in terms of the behavioral but not the attitudinal dimension. Specific nonmarital sexual patterns, especially premarital sex, are the norm. Research indicates that women believe they are not handicapped in romantic involvements with men because of roles that are supposed to be more submissive or sacrificing, that attractiveness is more important than pragmatics, such as income, in romance, and that they are at least willing to become involved with another person regardless of their current relationship (Heiss, 1991; Seal et al., 1994; Desrochers, 1995). But what we say and what we do often differ. Although women engage in nonmarital sex, it is less frequent than men, occurs later in the relationship, and is more likely to occur once commitment and love messages (but not necessarily marriage messages) are given by the man (Davidson et al., 1994; Mongeau et al., 1994). Traditional gender role orientations intrude when women in nonmarital sexual encounters report more frequent sex and more sexual pleasure than in the past, an indication of the erosion of the double standard, but also that they feel guilty about it, an indication of the continuing double standard. Sex without love or outside of marriage may be normative in terms of behavior, but it is still unacceptable as an expressed value.

Given the difficulty of defining love in all its dimensions, the final myth is perhaps easier to understand. The opposite of love is not hate. If its opposite can be said to exist, it is not hate, but indifference.

Androgynous Love

The openness and sharing that most would agree are important components of love serve to separate women and men in the later stages of love and marriage. Gender role socialization commands that masculinity be associated with lack of vulnerability. One becomes vulnerable through self-disclosure; therefore, to love fully is to self-disclose fully. At the beginning of a romantic relationship, men are likely to have higher levels of self-disclosure than later. Yet as the relationship continues, even into marriage, men become the silent partners where women are expecting more responsiveness. Female partners become resentful and irritated when men appear unwilling to express thoughts and feelings. Hite (1995:247) states that it is this lack of emotional equality which is the greatest stumbling block to love in relationships. In a study of married couples, Whitbourne and Ebmeyer (1990:15) find that when husbands lack the potential to be intimate and are uncomfortable in exposing themselves to the "intense emotionality of a long-term close relationship," the wives themselves are not only less well adjusted in their marriages, but their own capacity for intimacy becomes compromised (Beach and Tesser, 1988; Fowers, 1991). Overall, couples with a highly intimate husband are better adjusted. Whereas women express a greater need for intimacy, it is the man's behavior that appears to set the direction for intimacy-related behavior in relationships.

Cancian (1986; 1987) maintains love is so identified with emotional expression and self-disclosure, in which women are supposedly more skilled, that we often disregard the instrumental and physical aspects which men prefer. Men are viewed as incompetent at loving because romantic love ideals overlook the instrumental, pragmatic dimension, thereby giving more weight to the expressive. A male deficit model which defines women as "relationship experts" has led to an incomplete and overly feminized perspective of love.

For relationships to become more loving for women and men is to reject "polarized gender roles and [to] integrate 'masculine' and 'feminine' styles of love" (Cancian, 1986:693). She proposes an alternative, androgynous view on love which assumes that both the instrumental and expressive dimensions are represented and combined in meaningful ways. If love and loving are gender-typed, androgyny should overcome the imposed limitations. Coleman and Ganong (1985) provide an empirical test for the idea of androgynous love. They hypothesize that androgynous individuals would experience love differently than gender-typed individuals. The findings indicate that neither masculine nor feminine gender roles are as conducive to experiencing and expressing love as is an androgynous gender role orientation, that gender role orientation is a better predictor of love behavior than is biological sex, and that gender-typed persons are less able to love (Coleman and Ganong, 1985:175).

The idea of androgynous love provides an escape from traditional gender-typing where love and loving become compromised. Nonetheless, remember that androgyny itself assumes the existence of gender stereotyped roles. Wood (1994:183) proposes an alternative paths model which agrees that men and women differ in interaction styles, but it does not presume men are lacking in either emotional depth or a desire for intimacy. The paths for men and women are different, but equally valid. More empirical work is necessary to determine if a model of androgynous love or alternate paths becomes the preferred conceptual basis for understanding the complex emotion of love. Regardless, we sustain the belief that we marry for love and that love can last a lifetime. Rubenstein (1983:45) concludes that romance does not flourish, love does not survive, and marriages do not work. Unrealistic gendered expectations contribute to this.

It is apparent that women and men differ on attitudes and behavior surrounding the notion of romantic love and that traditional gender roles jeopardize love and loving. The relationship script for women has called for a passive role that eventually allows them to exchange sex for commitment. The relationship script for men has called for activity and sexual conquest (Knox and Schacht, 1991:51-52). Although both scripts are in the throes of change, the courtship game still functions according to gender role stereotypes. Moving toward an androgynous love ideal may overcome some of the barriers existing between the genders. Loving relationships that endure the harshness of the "unromantic" world may result.

MATE SELECTION

In the United States we encourage the ideology of romantic love and adhere to it as the basis for mate selection, the sentiment being shared by both genders. Love may be viewed as a panacea, but prior to making a marriage commitment, prospective mates are carefully scrutinized on a number of characteristics deemed important. As already indicated, in pursuing the objective of a marriage partner, love itself becomes structured by an array of social and demographic factors.

The sociological literature on the family fully documents the impact of **homogamy**, the likelihood of becoming attracted to and marrying someone similar to yourself (Buss and Barnes, 1986; Zinn and Eitzen 1990; Strong and DeVault, 1992; Eshleman, 1994). Similarity in terms of age, race, religion, socioeconomic status (SES), and a host of attitudinal and other sociocultural variables strengthens the role of homogamy in mate selection. The result is **assortive mating**, where coupling occurs based on similarity rather than chance.

Though considered nonaffective in nature, that is, not tied to the emotional expressiveness and highly charged romanticism entailed in love, these variables are more likely to predict mate selection than the more prized notion of romantic love per se. It is these nonaffective elements which help to determine with whom we will likely fall in love. The fact remains that romantic love is tempered by a market approach to mate selection. This results in a process that appears to be radically different from the ideology surrounding it (Melton and Lindsey, 1987).

Gender Differences

Gender differences in heterosexual romantic love continue when a prospective spouse is considered. Since men score higher on romanticism scales than women and fall in love earlier than women, women are the pragmatists, at least at the beginning of the whole mate selection process. This caution is justified because marriage for women will become a major determinant of their future social status. The tradition that women have been expected to achieve their greatest source of fulfillment in marriage and motherhood roles continues even as they succeed in careers and opportunities outside the home.

Thus homogamy is filtered by the trend of **hypergamy**, where women tend to marry men of higher social and economic status. This provides the conventional channel through which women have gained upward mobility. Women prefer men who are well educated and have the financial resources and earning capacity necessary for assuming responsibility for a family (Melton and Lindsey, 1987; Hatfield and Sprecher, 1986; Murstein, 1991). This corresponds to Melton and Thomas's (1976) research on attitudes of college students showing that females differ from males in that they place a greater value on the instrumental qualities of a prospective mate, such as working, saving, paying bills, and maintaining the basic physical integrity of the family unit. Reflective of a functionalist model, Buss and Barnes (1986:569) argue that traditional socialization practices support structural differences of this type and are used to instill role-appropriate values of males and females.

Men, on the other hand, value physical attractiveness much more than women and consider it an important characteristic for a potential spouse, especially for ambitious, upwardly mobile men (Hatfield and Sprecher, 1986; Lott, 1994). A cursory look at the kinds of advertisements found in newspapers and magazines devoted to singles looking for dating partners emphasizes this, with the sought-after "beautiful and slender" women typifying these ads. A study of personal ads by Smith and his colleagues (1990) confirms this observation. They find that females most often seek "interpersonal understanding" in a date while males seek physical attractiveness and thinness. Physical attractiveness in women increases their probability of being married and appears to be more important than masculine attractiveness for such traits as popularity, number of dates, and perception of having a favorable set of personality characteristics (cited in Murstein, 1986:37–39). Men's preoccupation with physical attractiveness cuts across both race and social class and is implicated in reasons why men fall in love sooner than women (Lott, 1994:134).

As Murstein (1986:39) points out, men do not have to be as attractive as women because men possess greater status and power in our society. Added to this is the economically subservient role in which many women find themselves. Physical attractiveness can be a bargaining tool for economic security. With women excluded from power, they are viewed by themselves and men alike as objects of exchange. In terms that take on a degrading connotation, physical beauty enhances the value of women as sex objects. Buss and Barnes (1986:569) state that attractiveness is an important means for designating relative value among exchange commodities.

The impact of the feminist movement and the increased economic integrity of women could alter these patterns somewhat. It is evident that many women are choosing to remain single, in part because they have the economic capability and self-assurance to do so. But in a study where we compared college students' attitudes toward prospective mates in the 1980s with those in the 1970s, we find that value preferences are not radically different (Melton and Lindsey, 1987). Females continue to place a greater emphasis on instrumental behaviors whereas males place substantially more emphasis on sexual and physical attractiveness. And for both females and males, the mean instrumental index score is higher for the contemporary groups of college students.

Our study is particularly surprising since the sample is made up of a high proportion of women who are pursuing nontraditional academic curricula, such as engineering and pharmacy, where earnings potential and professional advancement are quite high relative to other career possibilities. The research is conclusive that college women indicate that they want to successfully combine a career with marriage and children. Perhaps it is at those points of interruption for childbearing and/or child rearing where they see themselves as even temporarily economically dependent on their husbands, which mandates their emphasis on instrumental qualities. Also, both genders may view the current job market as extremely competitive and recognize that their mates must reinforce the economic stability of the family (Melton and Lindsey, 1987). This would explain the higher instrumental index for the contemporary males as compared to the earlier male group.

Age and Race

Age is a key variable which influences mate selection. Most people marry others near to their own ages. As we would expect, when gender differences do occur, the combination of the somewhat older man with the somewhat younger woman is the pattern. In later or remarriages, age differences are likely to be greater, but usually favoring the same younger woman-older man pattern. The major reversal of this trend is that elderly women who remarry after widowhood are likely to marry men younger than themselves.

Age at first marriage is legally controlled, with some states still allowing earlier marriages for females than for males. There is no state which has a legal marriage age for females which is higher than for males. There has been a steady rise in age at first marriage for both men and women since 1970. By the mid-1990s, the typical first-time bride was about three and one-half years older

(24.6) compared to her 1970s counterpart (20.8). For men the current median age is 26.6 (U.S. Bureau of the Census, 1995). What is revealing is the fact that the median age is now the highest for women than at any time since 1900. Role differences and socialization factors between the genders readily explain these trends. Men are discouraged from marrying too soon because they must gain the education and job skills necessary to support a family. Women, who have traditionally been socialized for domestic roles, are not as bound. The contemporary trend where both genders marry later is likely to continue, but it should be more pronounced for women. With women now representing over half of all college students and the increasing numbers of women entering the labor force, age at first marriage for women may eventually approach that of men.

Educational institutions that are age-stratified through high school and continue for the most part through college will maintain age homogamy in mate selection, especially for "traditional age" students. Hypergamy will also function to support the younger woman-older man trend. However, a mini-trend has appeared which indicates that the younger man-older woman marriage is becoming more acceptable, most common among the elderly. Generally, elderly widows are at a disadvantage for a homogamous remarriage because men marry younger women at all life stages and women outlive men on the average of about 7.5 years. However, new role models for women, success in economic spheres, divorce and remarriage, the marriage squeeze (discussed later), and less constraint from family and society will likely accelerate the pattern for all but the youngest women.

Of all the major demographic variables, homogamy is strongest concerning race, with interracial marriages fairly infrequent. Although all legal blocks to interracial marriage had been removed by 1967 in the United States, sociocultural norms continue to strongly discourage it, especially marriages involving African-Americans and whites. According to the U.S. Bureau of the Census (1995), between 1970 and 1990 the number of interracial marriages more than doubled. But even with the continued increase, by the mid-1990s, interracial marriages still represent only 2.3 percent of all marriages. Of these, about one-half of 1 percent are African-American/white marriages. The remainder are between whites and nonblacks, especially Asians. Of significance here is that about 70 percent of the African-American/white marriages consist of a white wife and black husband. When comparing race and class in these marriages, the data generally, but tentatively, support homogamy in socioeconomic status (SES) (Gadberry and Dodder, 1993; Kalmijn, 1993). If hypergamy is evident in these marriages, the trend would be that the woman is of a lower SES than the man. The idea behind hypergamy in this instance is that the wife compensates for her lower SES and the husband compensates for his lower-valued caste. Both parties marry "up" in this sense.

Though explanations for the white female-black male pattern in interracial marriage are unclear, Murstein (1986) suggests that homogamy is the factor of overriding importance. When African-Americans and whites become attracted to one another, it is for reasons similar to white-white or black-black marriages. When asked about the impact of race on his marriage, a white man who married an African-American woman, responded that "from the beginning I was surprised less by how important race was than how important it wasn't" (Tartakov and Tartakov, 1994:148). The main mitigating factor is that race is weighted to the advantage of whites so that blacks must possess some desirable characteristics seen as better than the whites who are available. This is consistent with other research on the low incidence of black-white marriages relative to other racial intermarriage. Roberts (1994:73) maintains that "most whites place blacks at the bottom of the racial and ethnic hierarchy," with greater social stigma attached to "Negro genes and known ancestry" than to "Mongoloid or Amerindian ancestry." This is supported by data indicating that in 1970 one-third of all Indians were married to non-Indians, but a decade later the percentage increased to 50 percent (Thorton, 1988:237).

The Marriage Squeeze

We have seen that age homogamy is strong and that most people marry for the first time in their early to mid 20s. But age at first marriage for both women and men is inevitably affected by a number of circumstances, including the proportion of marriage-age men and women who are available and who fit other normative categories. When there is an unbalanced ratio of marriage-age men to marriage-age women, a **marriage squeeze** is said to exist, with one or the other gender having a more limited pool of potential marriage partners. There are both demographic and sociocultural explanations for these patterns. Changing birth rates, male and female mortality rates, war, marriage and divorce trends, attitudes to premarital sex, and economic trends are some of the factors which influence the development of a marriage squeeze.

Because of a declining birth rate, in regard to a common pattern where a 26-year-old male marries a 23-year-old female, Eshleman (1994) states that males in the 1990s through to the turn of the century will face a shortage of women, just as they did in the 1950s. This reverses the situation of the 1980s where women faced a shortage of men. Eshleman (1994:246-47) explains the situation as follows:

1. The 1950s marriage squeeze resulted from a decline of births during the Depression (1920s-1930s). More men were born in 1930 than women born in 1933, causing a smaller pool of younger women. A marriage squeeze existed for men.
2. The 1980s marriage sqeeze resulted from an increased number of births after World War II (the baby boom years). More women were born in 1950 than men born in 1940, causing a larger pool of younger women. A marriage squeeze existed for women.

Given the sharp decline of birth rates in the 1960s and 1970s, this suggests that a 1990s-turn of the new century male marriage squeeze currently exists. Marriage rates for younger men and women, those in their 20s and early 30s, and age differences between mates will be examined over the next decade to determine if this prediction is empirically verified.

If younger men are caught in a current marriage sqeeze, the same is true for women at midlife. The trends of women marrying men two to three years older than themselves combined with higher male mortality rates and economic independence for women help explain this. Widows make up a large portion of the single-women-living-alone category, but the proportion of single women at the prime marrying age is steadily increasing.

Perhaps for the first time in modern society, women are caught in a paradox which both restricts and enlarges their choices for marriage. They are restricted in the number of what they deem to be eligible partners precisely because of their own successes outside the confines of domestic life. Women, like men, want to eventually marry. But women are less likely than in the past to marry simply for financial security. They can afford to be more choosy in mate selection, and even postpone marriage until career opportunities are realized.

The result of this flexibility narrows the range of partners when these women are ready to seriously consider the permanency of marriage. It is at this point when singleness may be chosen as the preferred lifestyle because they find that they cannot realistically settle for those single men who are "left," as it were. Hypergamy results in two groups of people who may be squeezed out of the marriage market. These are the highly educated, economically success-ful women and the poorly educated, lower SES men.

In viewing all the factors related to the marriage squeeze, remember that demographic trends provide only a portion of the explanation for mate selec-tion. More powerful sociocultural factors determine who are the "acceptable" partners for marriage. The marriage squeeze itself is a byproduct of these influences, of which gender role norms is perhaps its most important. As these are altered, the marriage squeeze also fluctuates. In this sense, symbolic inter-action would view the marriage squeeze not as an objectively determined demographic process, but a socially constructed one. This is clearly the case when race is factored in.

When considering African-American women as a separate subgroup, the marriage squeeze is even more prominent. As demonstrated in Chapter 2, life expectancy rates are lowest for black males, in comparison to white males and all females. According to the U.S. Bureau of the Census, for blacks, women outnumber men at about age 18; for whites it is at age 32. For every ten college educated African-American women, there are fewer than two men within what are considered to be eligible age groups (Goldman et al., 1984). This signifi-cantly restricts the field of eligibles for black women, making homogamy on a number of variables less likely to occur. As a result, in comparison to white women, black women are more likely to marry men who are older, of a lower educational level, and have been previously married. Other patterns for African-Americans as a group show that age at first marriage is lower and rate of marital dissolution is higher than for non-Hispanic whites (Ortiz, 1994; U.S. Bureau of the Census, 1995).

Homogamy related to age, education, and previous marriage are more predictive of marital stability than when there are major discrepancies in these variables for any couple. When lack of homogamy is tied to additional stresses such as coping with prejudice, and lower levels of economic attainment, we can see how African-American marriages are at higher risk than white ones in terms of divorce. A marriage squeeze that requires many black women to select mates who are significantly different than themselves may influence overall marital stability.

The marriage squeeze may be responsible for the hard choices that all women must make. For many, this can mean whether to marry at all or forego childbearing altogether. It can be hypothesized that when women in their 30s or 40s do marry, they may find it less satisfactory because they are unwilling to give up motherhood. However, given the options of marrying later in life and the advantages and disadvantage of "settling," singleness is now being embraced by confident women who see it as a positive alternative to marriage. After examining traditional marriage in terms of the genders, we will return to this point.

GENDER ROLES IN MARRIAGE

Marriage in American society is both idealized and faced with apprehension. Images of loving couples with contented children coexist with those of abandonment, violence, and the potential of divorce. Regardless of the perception or the reality, the vast majority of us eagerly seek marriage and will marry at some point in our lives. However, shifts in gender roles have altered our views of marriage and the family. Attitude change is manifest not only in marriage per se, but also in the emergence of a variety of lifestyles which are viable options for those seeking alternatives to what they define as traditional marriage.

Views of Marriage and the Family: Functionalism and Conflict

Functionalism argues that marriage and eventual parenting are good for society and the individual couple. The family system provides critical benefits, including orderly procreation, regulation of sexual behavior, socialization of the children, economic cooperation, conferring status on its members, personality formation, protection and security, and the expression of affection, to name but a few benefits. Companionship and ego support of family members, especially husband and wife, are enhanced.

Functionalism assumes that the family system operates best when husband and wife do not overlap roles. When marital roles are specialized, the efficiency of the family unit is maximized. If one partner takes on the roles typically prescribed to the other, dissension in the marriage and disruption of the system are likely results. For these functions to be effectively carried out, a stable family unit, which in turn maintains a stable society, is necessary. This is the argument that is used when attention turns to social problems that are both the causes and consequences of family change, such as increases in divorce, the number of unwed parents, and domestic violence. Functionalism emphasizes that change in other social institutions, such as the economy, has a major impact on stable family functioning. To its credit, functionalism highlights the continued, critical role of the family as the key social institution responsible for carrying out functions no other social institution can perform to the same extent. On the other hand, functionalism has difficulty explaining either the development of alternative family forms or how the so-called traditional family has managed to successfully adapt its family functioning in the face of massive social change.

Conflict theories view marriage and the family as made up of individuals who possess differing amounts of resources and power, and who have individual interests to consider and defend. It is conflict and change and not order and harmony that family systems demonstrate. In the traditional family where patriarchy is unquestioned, women are dominated by men. Only when women gain greater economic power will the system be significantly altered. Thus, conflict theory assumes that women and wives should explore and experiment not only with roles which have been the prerogative of men and husbands in the past, but also with alternative visions of the family which may suggest new roles for family members. In this view, traditional marriage must change. On the other hand, conflict theory has had difficulty in addressing the continued inequality in the family when women are also working outside the home. Adherents to both functionalist and conflict views of marriage and the family will find merit in the following arguments.

In Defense of the Traditional Family

What is traditional? If a family is viewed as traditional, it is because it combines certain normative characteristics involving roles of family members and living arrangements. The idea of a nuclear family is usually considered in this traditional sense. The **nuclear family** consists of wife, husband, and their dependent children who live together, apart from other relatives, in their own residence. In the "traditional" nuclear family, tasks are divided so that the husband is the sole breadwinner with the wife maintaining the responsibility for domestic tasks, including child care. Ideologically it assumes a patriarchal model in which ultimate decision making rests with the husband. Family values and behaviors supportive of this ideology include affectively close family members who maintain strong ties with kin who live near, respect of parental authority, and sexuality and childbirth within the confines of stable marriages (Anderson, 1994a). Most important, traditional gender roles function to maintain separate spheres for wives and husbands. This is the functionalist ideal and the structural model which we assume is the most prevalent.

Many are surprised to learn that in the United States, in terms of both structure and function, this model emerged primarily during the Industrial Revolution and is far from the norm today. And Coontz (1992) states the values that were supposedly part of this model are mostly idealized fiction. Recall that intimacy, love, and even friendship between spouses is a rather recent phenomenon. As will be documented in Chapter 8, nostalgia is expressed for a family form that was *never* the American norm. Considering the last 30 years, the factor that has had the greatest impact on family structure and functioning is the massive increase in labor force participation of women, especially married women with young children. Sixty percent of all women and over half of all married women are in the paid labor force, either full or part time. The labor force participation rate of married women with children under the age of six was at 60 percent by the early 1990s. Most employed mothers work full time and the proportion who do has increased even among women with preschoolers. Nearly 70 percent of employed mothers who have children under age three work full time (Costello and Stone, 1994:302-3; Wright, 1995). The traditional nuclear family where one earner is present (likely to be the husband) and children are still living at home consisted of only 13 percent of households as far back as 1977 (Ramey, 1978; U.S. Bureau of the Census, 1989, 1995). With more women reentering the labor force as part-time employees, the "Leave It to Beaver" family of sole breadwinning husband, breadbaking wife, and their at-home children under the age of 18 is at about the 10 percent level (U.S. Bureau of the Census, 1995, 1996). As more women with preschoolers enter the labor force and as couples delay having children, this figure is likely to decline even further. The family model that many believe to be the norm simply does not fit the reality.

Regardless of the structural changes in the American family, arguments in defending the idealized model are pervasive. These are particularly in response to feminist approaches calling for changes in the worlds of paid labor and marital roles. At one extreme we have people like Phyllis Schlafly (1981) who maintain that women who work outside the home take away jobs from males, sabotage family stability, and undermine motherhood. She disregards the one-third of American households which are made up of single parents and divorced, separated, single, and widowed people living alone. Most of these are women. They do not have the luxury to decide whether to work outside of the home or not. In order not to undermine their families, themselves or, ultimately, broader society, they must be employed.

Perhaps because the 1970s witnessed the first real thrust of a unified, and for some, frightening, women's movement, arguments similar to Schlafly's proliferated. At that time she was supported by another of her ilk, Marabel Morgan (1973:80), who argued that if marital conflict occurs, the wife should always give in to her husband because, after all, "God planned for woman to be under her husband's rule." Morgan's plan for marital bliss was to become the "total woman," where wives are to cater to their husbands' needs, thereby minimizing the possibilities of two egos in conflict. Notice the functionalist overtones of this approach. She insisted that a woman should not be subservient but that a "wife should be under her own husband's leadership" (Morgan, 1973:81). If her plan is meticulously followed, communication is opened and the wife gets what she wants, whether it be a fur coat or a vacation in the Bahamas. What else could a wife possibly want? Morgan ignores the fact that if the wife gains anything through these tactics, it is through manipulation and deceit. And candidates for "total women" do not work outside the home.

Others of the period defended traditional marriage on the grounds that there is no other relationship possible which gives a woman as much happiness, pleasure, fulfillment, or purpose. Sakol and Goldberg (1975:1975) state that feminism has attacked marriage and that feminists are "those same people who would take our babies away from us and put them in state nurseries so that we could march off to work in the mines." While careers for married women are possible, they are not preferable. They believe it is better "to be taken care of" in the home since jobs are boring and difficult. They conclude with the assertion that "marriage remains the most wonderful institution devised by man (yes, we'll even let the men take credit for it)" (Sakol and Goldberg, 1975:38). Conflict theory would ironically agree with this. Patriarchy assumes a system men would devise and then control.

These convictions concerning marriage date back over two decades. They ignore the social changes that were already evident concerning gender roles at that time. Recent views maintain the same derisive tone but are more sophisticated in that to some degree they account for the labor force participation of women. For example, Davidson (1988) is perplexed by the beliefs that men desire women who can balance family and career and that women themselves want to have both. She states that she does not know such women and cannot understand how women can successfully split themselves between home and marketplace. Feminist action has taught that "sacrificing one for the other does not satisfy, but having both together simultaneously is so difficult that no one I know has found anything but the most quirky and incomplete solution" (Davidson, 1988:102). She says men are tired of "leathery career women" and while they do not fear them, they "prefer the other kind." Apparently the "other kind" either are not leathery or do not have careers. Women, too, are yearning for a "vanished simplicity" of life. Apparently, career and family do not make one whole. That wholeness comes with the birth of a child (Davidson, 1988:105-6).

In at attempt to strip the traditional marriage of its ideological components, Ruth (1995) asserts that it comes down to a simple husband-wife pact: Through his income he is required to provide the physical necessities of life. In return she provides care of the home and family. Unlike the traditional husband who has a role-world outside the home, the traditional wife is unified in her role. The married woman doesn't *do* housewifing, she *is* a housewife. Interor intrarole conflict do not exist. The patriarchal wife "yields her own individual identity" and commits her life to the needs of the family (Ruth, 1995:215). This can equate to regaining the "vanished simplicity of life" that Davidson (1988) longs for.

While these viewpoints are not representative of the cross section of the American public, they do express the sentiment of many who are grappling with the impact of massive social change on the family. What is clear is that when difficulties are experienced through role change, the "solution" is for women to return to those roles on which the traditional family are based. In functionalist terms, the system returns to a state of equilibrium. This is explicit in Carlson's (1995) call for a family political agenda which has an intellectual task in reviving and extending the historical sociological interpretation of the family and a social and personal task of rebuilding a traditionalist society. Sociological functionalism is used as the theoretical and, more important, the ideological justification for this agenda.

The functionalist perspective was implicit in the 1992 and 1996 presidential elections in which the "family values" theme became a politically explosive issue. Former Vice-President Dan Quayle exemplified this viewpoint with his concern that society is threatened because the basic values inherent in the traditional family are being eroded. Pat Buchanan and others echoed these sentiments throughout the 1996 presidential campaign. The "breakdown of the family" was an ongoing focus, and as argued in the past, the traditional family is being threatened by feminism. Family restorationists use social science evidence to bolster their claims that society is doomed unless the traditional family makes a viable comeback. Unfortunately, as Skolnick and Rosencrantz (1995:9) note, "the family restorationists' values have colored their reading of the evidence," since the research literature does not support their statements regarding the "consequences of family structure or some of the drastic policies they propose to change it." This will become clear as we review the evidence related to changes in both family function and structure. What is interesting is that fear of the disintegration of the family has been expressed since the founding of America, with New England settlers bemoaning lack of parental responsibility and loss of respect for authority among children (Mintz and Kellogg, 1988; Coontz, 1992).

Families are undergoing a transition to more companionate models based on depth in the relationship as well as individual autonomy. Nuclear families can malfunction during the transitional period. Rather than recognizing the potential advantages of this change, defenders of the "old ways" surface and adamantly attack what they see as the perpetrators of the change, namely the women's movement. The nuclear model need not be abandoned as an ideal, but some of its traditional arrangements need to be seriously questioned. If spouses are viewed as co-leaders or partners where, ideally at least, neither has clear domination over the other, then the nuclear family still functions, is stable, but has changed. The definition of nuclear family is too limited to encompass the many new kinds of households and living arrangements which are emerging. The contemporary reality is that nuclear families coexist with other varieties in networks of social relationships where services traditionally associated with family life are being rendered (Litwak and Kulis, 1987). A more inclusive definition of a modified nuclear family that may not include marriage partners could take into account such varieties, especially single-parent households. Apparently politicians are unaware that, in dealing with problems of classification, the U.S. Bureau of the Census has essentially adopted this modified view by defining a family as "a group of two persons or more related by birth, marriage, or adoption and residing together."

Either by choice or circumstance, family structure has been altered to meet conditions of social change. When major change affecting the roles of its members also occur within the new, modified nuclear family, it becomes essentially nontraditional. Structural change has occurred. Functional change related to family roles has lagged behind.

The Case against Traditional Marriage

While there is support for traditional marriage and family arrangements, much opposition exists. Opposing views center on evidence pointing to the inequality of wives and husbands and how that inequality has dire consequences for the family unit as a whole as well as the individuals within it. In the early 1900s, activist and author Emma Goldman (1910/1995) issued an attack on the insurance pact a woman and man make in a patriarchal marriage. Marriage is an economic arrangement where a woman pays her insurance premium by "giving up her name, her privacy, her self-respect, her very life." Marriage insurance condemns her to lifelong dependency. A man pays his toll, but he is less limited than his wife. "He feels his chains more in an economic sense." She uses divorce statistics to show "that marriage is a failure none but the very stupid will deny." Dante's motto applies to marriage: "Ye who enter here leave all hope behind" (Goldman, 1910/1995:502-3).

The 1970s produced the first "modern" versions of these kind of arguments. At one extreme is Kathrin Perutz (1972) whose book title says it all—*Marriage Is Hell.* The expectations of marriage, she asserts, transform it into a "ghetto of lunacy" with an attempt at an impossible union where indignation, individuality, egoism, and pride must be compromised. With marriage comes an end to self-development and an unnatural death of the spirit. Modern Western marriage is the perfection of hypocrisy; it is not a decision but a fate (Perutz, 1975:47, 49). Women in particular are pushed into that fate, with all but the "philosophically hardy or the unasked" getting married. Bird (1975) backs up the case against marriage for women by suggesting that in areas such as credit, social life, and job opportunities, married women lose.

Moving from the ideological to the empirical level, there is much evidence demonstrating that the husband's marriage is different than the wife's. At the height of the women's movement Jessie Bernard (1972) found that when husbands and wives were asked identical questions about their marriages, the replies were quite different. Although it was assumed that perceptions would differ on items regarding general happiness or feelings of romance, Bernard (1972:198) reported that when even basic facts on frequency of sexual relations, household tasks, and decision making were viewed, the couple appeared to be speaking about two different marriages. Contrary to what one would expect, differences increased with the length of the marriage.

The next quarter century of research on marital satisfaction and family roles continues to support these conclusions. Although both wives and husbands say they are happy in their marriages, males as a group are more likely to be satisfied with their marriages and families than are females as a group. Females make more adjustments in their marriages than males. A key factor is the extent that wife and husband share expectations regarding traditional gender roles (Glass, 1988,1992; Fowers, 1991; Wilkie, 1993). Marital quality decreases for wives and husbands who hold divergent views, such as when the authority granted to the husband in a sole-provider role is questioned by a wife who now contributes income (Chesser, 1991; Lye and Biblarz, 1993). When wives adopt less traditional gender role attitudes, their perceived marital quality goes down. When husbands adopt less traditional attitudes, it goes up (Amato and Booth, 1995:58). Bowen and Orthner (1983:223) show that marriages with the lowest evaluation of marital satisfaction are those with a traditional husband and a "modern" wife.

The quality of the marital relationship is enhanced for employed women who work for more than financial rewards but has mixed results for men (Spade, 1994). A study of older women who provided direct services (such as entertaining, volunteering, and bookkeeping) which enhanced their husbands' careers, reports varying satisfaction with that involvement. Almost all the women (94 percent) who pursued paid careers during this life stage say they would choose the same pattern again, in contrast to only 58 percent of the homemakers and 27 percent of those who worked only for needed income (Pavalko and Elder, 1993:561). There are no gender differences in relationship satisfaction when comparing male physicians and female physicians with children, an important finding considering the excessively high career and family demands faced by these women (Grant and Simpson, 1994). This is consistent with other research showing that occupational factors are less important in perceptions of marital quality than is the perception of fairness about those roles (Blair, 1993). Overall, research suggests that marital quality is enhanced when women pursue alternative roles and that these roles are perceived to augment the family. What emerges is a traditional family with nontraditional roles. Implications for this pattern are discussed later.

Marriage is beneficial to men. When comparing married to unmarried men on psychological, physical, and social well-being, the married come out far superior. Review Chapter 2 for the general conclusions concerning gender differentials in health. Married women, especially homemakers, suffer more psychological disability, depression, and anxiety than married men (Doyal, 1995). And comparing never-married women to never-married men, the women do well and the men do poorly, with almost twice as many of the men having mental health impairments (Zinn and Eitzen, 1990:271). Although there is cultural support for men complaining about their marriages as if they were "roped into it," marriage, especially traditional marriage, is the preferred lifestyle for men (Schoenberg, 1993:121). This is confirmed by statistics indicating that while wives are twice as likely to seek divorce than husbands, both divorced and widowed men are more likely to remarry (London and Wilson, 1988; U.S. Public Health Service, 1989).

If wives are deprived of satisfactory expectations in marriage, it is primarily due to a broader social system which strongly influences what occurs in individual marriages and families. The subordination of wife to husband mimics what exists outside the home. From a conflict perspective, the interaction is similar to discrimination patterns experienced by other minority groups. The power of gender role socialization has seduced the husband into the oppressor role just as surely as the wife has inherited the oppressed role (Alsbrook, 1976:522). Once those roles are accepted, the group that benefits most by them, men, will jealously guard and protect its monopoly (Fishman, 1982).

Marriage is not the culprit in this scenario. Both men and women want to be married and couples continue to give their marriages high marks in satisfaction and personal fulfillment. The most frequent and enduring reason for a happy marriage is having a generally positive attitude toward one's spouse (Lauer and Lauer, 1991). The culprit is the "traditional" part that seems inextricably linked to marriage as a whole. In traditional marriages as defined here, the castelike status of husband and wife serves to separate rather than cement the marital relationship. Women in unequal relationships pay significant costs in terms of career achievement, loss of leisure, and impaired well-being (Steil, 1995:159). Men and women say they both benefit from equal relationships.

If the women's movement raised the consciousness of young single women to reexamine their relationships with men, it would seem that their eventual marriages would demonstrate less traditionality. This is only true in a minority of marriages. When husbands and wives both hold nontraditional attitudes about family life, they are also less satisfied with their marriages (Lye and Biblarz, 1993:157). Fleming's (1986) study on American wives sheds light on why traditional marriage appears to triumph. She states that "it is clear in 1986 that the brides of the 70s may not have been deferential to men, but were deferential to marriage" (Fleming, 1986:32). Powerful socialization factors pull women and men into marital roles and expectations which are difficult to discard.

Housewives and Housework

The housewife image is bombarded with contradictions. Historically, the traditional housewife role has been associated with a fulfillment of the American dream for women (Grambs, 1991). On one hand it is seen as the height of a woman's aspirations, a deliberate choice which gives her the maximum amount of pride and satisfaction. She can be expressive, creative, and autonomous. In an early study of London housewives, Oakley (1974) found that even if women felt that housework itself was less gratifying, they were generally happy as housewives. On the other hand, housewifery is relegated to a low-prestige status in the eyes of many, especially more educated women, another finding of the Oakley study. Women may express satisfaction in what they are doing as housewives and mothers, but they feel it is a devalued position overall. This is of major importance given research consistently reporting that women in all household situations do more housework than men, but that the gender gap is widest for married women (South and Spitze, 1994).

There are several factors which contribute to this feeling. First, a woman must continually be on call to the demands of her husband and children. Her needs are often given the lowest priority. As suggested above, she is exclusively attached to and sacrifices for her family, becomes more securely bound to it, and unlike her husband and children has fewer roles that are nonhome related. Second, the demands and time spent on the homemaker role have not decreased to any great extent, even with those wonderful appliances to make household tasks less time consuming (Ogden, 1986; VanEvery, 1995). When housework time includes child care and related tasks, the time significantly increases. Baking cupcakes for an elementary school party is part of the housework and cooking time, but added to this is the time spent at the party itself.

A conflict perspective explains the most important reasons for the devaluation of the housewife role: It is not a paid role. Women carry out vital services to their families and society but receive no definitive remuneration. This ignores the homemaker's economic contributions in managing household resources, creating and maintaining the labor force, and serving as an auxiliary labor force (Sapiro, 1994; Lindsey, 1996c). As Strong and DeVault (1992:367) note, "if homemakers were paid the going rate for their work, they would earn over $50,000 annually." When the husband is the sole wage earner, those wages are distributed in a variety of ways. Some wives receive their husband's paychecks and determine how the money will be apportioned; other wives receive "allowances" from their husbands which go toward household expenses. Regardless of the myriad of ways the money is spent, she has not "earned" it in the same way he does. This perspective supports the power or resource hypothesis which assumes that since housework is undesirable, it will be "performed disproportionately by those who lack resources to enforce sharing or purchase substitutes" (Spitze, 1986:691).

This contributes to the burden of dependency experienced by many housewives. Fleming (1986) cites the case of one wife who believes that when a man outearns his wife, he is in charge. If the woman is a full-time housewife, he is likely to be more dominant. His dominance is conducive to her dependency. To a very large extent, his paycheck becomes the controlling factor in her life. Many women who do not work outside the home and find themselves in conflict-ridden, psychologically debilitating marriages see no alternative but to remain where they are. Financial and psychological dependency go hand in hand.

Although housewifery suggests that housework and child care are the woman's primary responsibility, men are expected to take on some of these chores. But studies consistently document that both homemakers and employed wives spend as much as 50 percent more time on household chores (Coltrane and Ishii-Kuntz, 1992; Shelton and John, 1993). Lawn care, house repairs, plumbing and electrical work, and automobile maintenance are the conventional household tasks that husbands assume. Tasks may be specialized by the marital partners, but men are doing their fair share, so the argument goes, especially since he is working all day. The implication here is that what she is doing all day falls into some other amorphous category. This argument also neglects the fact that the domestic tasks assumed by men are usually specific to a project, such as car repair, or are seasonally related, such as lawn care. The routinized, mundane, and ongoing tasks such as laundry, cleaning, child maintenance (as distinct from child care), and cooking are defined as the responsibility of the woman. The reality is that the old adage where "men may work from sun to sun, but women's work is never done" holds true.

The full-time homemaker is caught in a struggle to positively affirm her housewife role at a time when women's labor force participation is mushrooming. While she derives a measure of satisfaction from this role, her well-being is conditioned by how her role is socially defined (Thompson and Walker, 1989; VanEvery, 1995). Homemakers who have the social and familial support necessary to counteract the boredom and loneliness they may experience as housewives will be more satisfied in their roles (Rubenstein and Shaver, 1982; Shehan et al., 1986:415).

A related issue is how patriarchy functions to undermine *all* women, whether they are homemakers or employed for pay. The homemaker role may be devalued, but this is the very role which women are expected to enthusiastically embrace. Women who work outside the home are held accountable for anything that may be construed as going awry because of their nondomestic roles. From a feminist view, patriarchy inserts a wedge of suspicion and finger pointing which encourages dependency for the homemaker and guilt for women who work for pay. The system and the marital arrangements within it which encourage these behaviors need to be altered.

The housewife role is obviously an ambiguous one. Regardless of how it is valued, the primary role responsibilities of the housewife involve housework and child care. Some specialized task sharing occurs between husbands and wives, but her full-time housewife status minimizes his contributions overall. Beyond gender, the key variable in household work allocation and general marital satisfaction is whether the wife also has some kind of paid employment.

Marriage and Dual-Earner Couples

Housework. The movement of women into the paid labor force has profoundly influenced not only their drive toward greater equality but also impacted the other social institutions, particularly the family. The focus of most research on this impact has to do with wives' employment, marital satisfaction, and division of household labor.

It is logical to assume that lack of time for household duties normally assigned to the wife would cause the husband to take on significantly more of these tasks. A classic study conducted by Blood and Wolfe (1960:63) concluded that husbands feel obligated to take on an appreciably larger share of the housework when their wives are also working. However, when attitudes are matched with behavior, this has not occurred. Data find that if the husband seems to do a larger proportion of household tasks it is because the absolute level of his wife's household work goes down, not because his actually increases (Coverman, 1989). It is exceedingly difficult for a woman who works 40 hours a week outside the home to add another 40 or 50 inside. This gives no respite from work. Therefore, she leaves certain tasks uncompleted, and husbands do not complete them. This research is representative of conclusions drawn from empirical work on the topic.

Such research usually starts with the logical assumption that a married woman's labor force activity translates into more equitable domestic role sharing with her spouse. An examination of 30 years of data finds this to be logically true but empirically false. In the 1970s, a husband's contribution to domestic work remained very small (Vanek, 1974; Walker and Woods, 1976;

Berk and Berk, 1979). By the 1980s, some research showed a slight increase in time spent on household tasks by husbands, but wives assumed the major responsibility, including child care or arranging for it (Geerken and Gove, 1983; Maret and Finlay, 1984; Pleck, 1985; Coverman, 1989). The same pattern is reproduced in the 1990s (Coltrane and Ishii-Kuntz, 1992; VanEvery, 1995). And as expected, wives are less satisfied when their husbands' share of domestic labor is taken up by child care and traditional male chores, perceiving the division of household labor as unjust (Benin and Agostinelli, 1988; Lennon and Rosenfield, 1994). Women clearly are aware that when a man "helps out" his wife in the home, it is not an indication of true task sharing. Women employed full time walk into their homes after work and begin a second shift (Hochschild, 1989). They may be referred to occupationally as attorney, physician, or administrator, but the role of homemaker is still a salient one and persists for employed wives.

Task sharing in two-earner families is also mediated by several other variables, such as income contribution of each partner, the social class, ethnicity, the number and ages of children, and the couple's gender role ideology. Different subgroups of dual-earner families distribute tasks differently and show a greater involvement on the part of the husband. Middle-class wives may decrease their housework because they can afford to hire domestic help. Mothers of all social classes have more difficulty balancing work and family roles, but professional couples have more control over how these roles can be balanced (Duxbury and Higgins, 1995). And it can be tentatively concluded that compared to white men, men in African-American, Mexican-American, and Puerto Rican dual-earner families take on a greater share of household activities (Roopnarine and Ahmeduzzaman, 1993; Herrera et al., 1995; John et al., 1995). Finally, it's good for men to get involved in housework. They have happier marriages, better physical health, less anxiety, and even better sex lives than men who don't (Rubin, 1983; AtKisson, 1995).

Despite the continued overload of dual-earner women on household tasks, this research does suggest at least the beginnings of a trend for more domestic role sharing. The provider role remains a salient one for men. But men are showing "greater acceptance of women's employment as well as their own involvement in family roles" (Willinger, 1993:127). A cultural lag between expressed attitudes and translation to behavior in the home is indicated. To restate an important point: The family does not exist independently from the other social institutions. As Pleck (1985:155) states, how a family allocates its work and arranges its role structure "is a complex response to its social and economic environment."

Balancing Employment and Family. The impact of the employed wife carrying the load for household and child-care responsibilities has tremendous consequences for her career success. This section uses the term dual *earner* rather than dual *career* because it indicates that although many couples have paid employment, they do not necessarily have "meaningful" careers. Jobs interfere with family in a different way than careers. A higher degree of commitment and personal sacrifice is associated with career orientation along with the assumption that a developmental sequence will characterize one's career path. Women who have careers but still take on the bulk of the household labor find it difficult to achieve beyond a certain level. Studies also suggest that a woman's career achievement is compromised by the belief that a husband's career is more important than the wife's (Skinner, 1984; Giele, 1988). It is much more likely, for example, that the family will relocate for his career advancement rather than hers. Married men in particular still adhere strongly to traditional attitudes regarding (gendered) breadwinning responsibilities (Wilkie, 1993).

The success stories of women who apparently "have it all"—great marriages, wonderful children, rewarding careers—are replete. Nelton and Berney (1987) report that women in business are in a second wave of progress, moving up the corporate ladder or advancing through their own business enterprises. They have found ways to favorably reconcile problems between career and family, such as purchasing services allowing for career mobility. Some adjustments are made by the husband, but the wife has to grapple with the changes the family will undergo.

These women are the exception to the rule. The rule is that women may combine work and marriage successfully, but they are severely compromised in their quest for career ascendance by marital and family obligations. The pull toward the wife and mother role is so great that many women, possibly even most, will not abdicate what they see as their primary responsibility, even if it means giving up career opportunities. Home-based businesses, part-time work, and employment offering flexible work time are compromises women use to balance their roles. Research shows, however, careers are either put on hold, change directions, or abruptly end, and levels of housework and child care increase (Silver, 1993; Silver and Goldscheider, 1994; Wharton, 1994). Any career commitment is severely compromised by the intrusion of the traditional role. It is not that these women are shirking their professional duties. It simply means that career mobility declines, specifically in comparison to men who are not constrained by domestic encroachments in the workplace (Shelton, 1992). Many favor an overall balance between career and family life rather than having what they would define as excessively high levels of professional involvement (Stratham et al., 1987:119).

We have already seen that employment has beneficial effects for women's overall well-being. Even with the multiple role experienced by all marital categories of employed women, they are the healthiest and feel better about themselves than full-time homemakers (Barnett and Rivers, 1995). Marital satisfaction is also enhanced. Indeed, some research indicates that currently employed wives as well as those formerly employed have higher life satisfaction as they get older, when compared to the never-employed wives (Freudiger, 1983:218).

The research is less clear for husbands of wives who work outside the home. Some men feel threatened by a wife who is also employed. For instance, Crosby (1987) asserts that even though wives are now likely to be employed, many husbands are reluctant to share the provider role. He may feel less control as she gains more independence outside the home. When wives earn more than their husbands, relationships can become strained. Husbands may like the fact that their wives are employed, but feel it is important that they earn more (Hiller and Philliber, 1991:139). Another possibility is that if his wife is working solely out of economic necessity, his breadwinner role is assaulted, and he sees his masculinity in jeopardy.

The age of the husband is a critical factor in evaluating the dual-earner marriage. Men in their 30s, 40s, and 50s who have employed wives have lower levels of self-esteem than men in their 20s. Rubin (1983:72) points out that these younger men have grown up with different expectations concerning work and family and are more likely to see the breadwinner role as only one of several important to them. College-age men are expressing more egalitarian attitudes toward sharing the provider role (Wilkie, 1993). These are the men willing to assume more of the child-care and household tasks in their homes.

For the dual-career marriage, there has been slow progress toward egalitarianism on the behavioral level but more rapid progress on the attitudinal level. Both in economic and symbolic terms, the power associated with traditional family functions is responsible for this level of change. Employed women continue to place a higher priority on gendered household behavior, articulated as an ethical dilemma between equity and care (Stohs, 1994). It is resolved in favor of care (of the home) even if associated with costs in the workplace.

NEW MARRIAGE FORMS

Commuter Marriage

The dual-location couple is not new. Men and women who serve in the armed forces, for example, have homes maintained by their spouses thousands of miles away and see them during leaves determined by the military. Almost all of the home-maintainers, however, are women. What is new is a dual-career couple evolving into a dual-location couple for reasons of the wife's, rather than the husband's career. Historically, the common pattern is for the woman, literally, to follow her man from city to city as he advances up the career ladder. The rarely challenged expectation is for her own career, if she has one, to be secondary to his. Today, many wives are unwilling to abdicate their careers if a move is required and the couple is determined to maintain the marital relationship. The commuter marriage emerges. The estimated one million commuter marriages generally consist of highly educated and highly paid spouses who may see one another only on weekends or as infrequently as once a month, but who may maintain these arrangements for several years (Rhodes and Rhodes, 1984; Rindfuss and Stephen, 1990).

The gains in career may be offset by the stress of living in two locations with only periodic time together. Self-sufficiency and independence are enhanced, but loss of emotional support and dissatisfaction with family life increase. When the couple has been married longer, have children who are already launched, and where one partner is already established and successful in his/her career, there is less stress in following the regimen associated with a commuter marriage (Gross, 1980; Bunker et al., 1992).

Earlier career subordination on the part of the wife leads to unhappiness and stress that the eventual commuter marriage helps overcome. The following comments by commuter wives sum up this orientation to work and career:

> I go to pieces when I don't work. I get bored when I am not working. We probably work too hard and occasionally feel guilty about it. But we're not the kind of people who can just relax.
>
> I want to feel I am accomplishing something. It's important to work. And I suppose I do because I want to do it. I think it is FUN! (Gerstel and Gross, 1984:32)

About 90 percent of the commuter husbands strongly support the professional activities of their wives, as indicated in these comments:

I want her to do it only because she wants to, not because I want her to.

I like her to work. I've always encouraged her to work. It makes her more interesting to me. I couldn't even imagine not being with a professional woman. There is just no way the woman who is my wife could be a housewife. (Gerstel and Gross, 1984:36-37)

The stress in dealing with the logistics of a commuter marriage is difficult to resolve. But comments like these suggest that the marriage is not likely to sustain itself if career ascendancy on the part of the husband stifles that of the wife. The guilt and regret commuter couples feel when they are not together is due to the fact they accept the standard of career success while at the same time accepting most assumptions regarding marriage and the family (Gerstel and Gross, 1984:200). This again demonstrates the impact of traditional views of marriage, even in one of the most nontraditional marriage alternatives.

Egalitarian Marriage

Traditional marriage is almost by definition a closed marriage, where the couple exists as a fused entity, but where they lead separate existences. In their popular but controversial book published at the height of the women's movement, George and Nena O'Neill (1972) argued that a closed marriage is based on the faulty assumption that two people can be all things to one another, with each fulfilling the other's emotional, psychological, intellectual, and physical needs. The open marriage is an alternative form resting on the belief that each spouse can maintain a joint as well as separate existence within the marriage. Options remain open for the couple to grow as individuals (O'Neill and O'Neill, 1972:54).

Since the open marriage concept argues for enhancement in marriage through altering, almost condemning, traditional marital roles, it would seem the ideal alternative to couples seeking an escape from the confines of gender roles. But because the book did not necessarily rule out finding sexual gratification outside the marriage, it drew much criticism. Is finding a companion to go to the opera because your wife/husband does not like opera, different from finding a companion who becomes a sexual partner because your wife/husband is not meeting your needs? Since few marriages, open or otherwise, are devoid of gender roles, it is likely to be the wives who find themselves most compromised in this regard. Five years later Nena O'Neill (1977) reevaluated the original concept based on the feedback from numerous couples who found it difficult to achieve the flexibility entailed in the idea, particularly if sexual permissiveness is involved. American couples continue to express strong disapproval for extramarital relationships (Michael et al., 1995). It is undoubtedly better to view open marriage as an early effort toward a more egalitarian alternative which provides a range of choices for couples restrained by traditional gender roles.

Egalitarianism in marriage is strongly associated with employment opportunities for women. When wives contribute financially to the maintenance of the family, they also gain a greater amount of decision-making power. It is the relative power of husband to wife which has bolstered the patriarchal nature of marriage and the broader society. A more equitable arrangement in society will eventually carry over to the family. We have seen that dual-career/earner marriages are not necessarily equal ones because wives retain most household and child-care tasks. Yet these are the very marriages which are moving in the direction of egalitarianism.

As the term denotes, the egalitarian marriage is one which is no longer tied to traditional beliefs about gender roles. Household tasks are divided by skill and desire, rather than what is seen as a masculine or feminine duty. She may enjoy lawn maintenance and he may enjoy cooking. The undesirable chores, such as cleaning or laundry, are equitably distributed. It is the sharing of the domestic chores which creates the most difficulty for the egalitarian couple, because they, too, have been socialized into a world of traditional marriage and family patterns where gender roles continue to intrude. While egalitarian attitudes regarding issues of career and child rearing are consistent with behavior, it is clear that the marriage will not be truly egalitarian until husbands participate equally in housework.

Regardless of the problems which the egalitarian model might bring, the benefits are overriding. Marital satisfaction is increased because communication and sharing are also enhanced. Using the term "peer marriage," Schwartz (1994a) describes such satisfaction as part of an overriding, empathic friendship couples report when traditional marriage patterns are suspended. This carries over to an improvement in parent-child relations since both spouses share the burden and the joy of child rearing. The benefits accrue to children who learn that both parents are nurturers who demonstrate their love and support.

In their study of successful marriages in which partners are equal, Vannoy-Hiller and Philliber (1989:142-43) suggest that the key to success has been that both partners "express honest feelings and find the compromises that work for them." Although competition erodes support for one another, this study also suggests that marital success is conditioned by a perceived balance of costs and rewards. When high-achieving career women find an imbalance, such as with domestic chores, marital quality suffers. Competition may not be beneficial but conflict can be. Conflict is not necessarily negative in relationships and may actually have functional consequences. In a study of college students at different stages in premarital relationships, higher levels of love and movement toward marriage are associated with increases in conflict (Sprecher and Felmlee, 1993). An erosion of traditional gender roles at the premarital stage should have some carryover effects in the marriage.

It is clear that attitudes about the roles of husbands and wives in marriage are shifting toward an egalitarian model. The ultimate goal remains elusive. Attitudes about marital equality have not yet been translated into actual behavior. Research is unanimous in the conclusion that gender equity in the workplace has not occurred in the home, especially once children arrive (Perkins and DeMeis, 1996). It is the vital area of gender roles in marriage that needs to be significantly altered if the egalitarian ideal is ever to be achieved.

EMERGING LIFESTYLES

The Singlehood Alternative

The marriage mandate for both genders remains very strong. The vast majority of most people expect to be married. But the percent of never-married people continues to increase, especially for women (U.S. Bureau of the Census, 1995). The availability of eligible partners and the marriage squeeze do not account for this trend. Market conditions offering either mate surpluses or deficits have little to do with women's willingness to marry men with dissimilar characteristics (Lichter et al., 1995). The cultural meanings of marriage and the forces of attraction propelling people into marriage are major factors (Qian and Preston, 1993; Nock, 1995).

Many young people no longer view marriage as necessarily better than remaining single (Thornton and Freedman, 1986:30). The shift in opinion of singlehood as a legitimate status is in marked contrast to earlier beliefs which viewed failure to marry as not only undesirable but indicative of personal or social faults. For the first time, the choice not to marry is being seen as appropriate for some. At the very least, the debasement associated with remaining single has significantly eroded. As Kephart and Jedlicka (1991:342) note, the stigma once attached to the never-married and divorced is no longer true, and the successful woman who prefers career to marriage is often envied rather than stigmatized. This is also reflective of research showing that the number of single people who report that they are "very happy" has steadily increased, with a slight decline in the number of married people saying this (Glenn and Weaver, 1988).

Because men conventionally have been the initiators in marriage proposals, it has been assumed that only unattractive or undesirable women would not marry. She is the lonely spinster; he is the carefree bachelor who must be wary of single women who are interested in matrimony. Even as initiators, the image of a man snagged into marriage by a woman in hot pursuit has been a popular one. The media perpetrate images of women doomed to singlehood by a marriage squeeze and feeling desperate since their biological clocks for motherhood are ticking away. Faludi (1996) points to media reports that the woes of single women are self-generated and that a spinster boom is impending. Good looks and good jobs do not translate into marriage. As Faludi (1996:391) indicates, the "man shortage" is "a moral comeuppance for independent-minded women who expected too much." The media condemn these women for the sins of greed and pride. Men, on the other hand, emerge unscathed by these media accounts.

These are stereotypes that are simply untrue. We have seen that it is better for men to be married than remain single. They are healthier, happier, and live longer if they marry. Women seem to get along better without men than vice versa. And compared to single men, single women are happier and more satisfied with their lives. Even George Gilder, the avowed champion of traditional marital and gender roles, laments the single status for men. "Unless he can marry, he is often destined to a Hobbesean life—solitary, poor, nasty, brutish and short" (Gilder, 1974:31).

Single people now have many of the benefits formerly reserved for the married, including options for parenthood (Wolfe, 1993b). The highly educated woman who is financially independent is the likely candidate for life as a single person. As mentioned earlier, they are increasingly choosing to remain single than to marry heterogamously. Interestingly, there are no significant differences between men and women in terms of what they like and dislike about being single. They enjoy its mobility and freedom and the social options it affords but must contend with periods of loneliness and the problems and uncertainties of the "dating grind" (Simenauer and Carroll, 1982). Yet it is apparent that contemporary singlehood now represents opportunities for choice and happiness for a significant subset of the American population who may reject marriage and any permanent and/or exclusive sexual relationship.

Cohabitation

A couple living together without marriage was cause for condemnation, even in the recent past. The whispers, innuendos, and raised eyebrows accompanying this living arrangement have all but disappeared as more and more couples choose cohabitation as a preferred lifestyle, whether they intend to marry later or not. Social support does vary, however, in that peers are more accepting than family members. While parents may not express discomfort with the arrangement openly, they usually breathe a sigh of relief if the couple marries. The dramatic increase in the rate of cohabitation and its choice as a permanent lifestyle for some may be responsible for a slight decrease in the marriage rate (Bumpess et al., 1991).

Cohabitant households have risen steadily, from about one-half million in 1970 to over five times that today (U.S. Bureau of the Census, 1995). This has led to the creation of a formal term to categorize this group. These people are designated as domestic partners or POSSLQs, People of the Opposite Sex Sharing Living Quarters. While POSSLQs represent the largest segment of cohabitants, the term does not account for all such households. The U.S. Census Bureau arrives at the number merely by counting households where an unmarried male and female reside. It is clear that many couples do not report the arrangement or maintain separate addresses even while cohabiting. And since cohabitation assumes that a sexual relationship is also involved, same-sex couples should also be included. Eshleman (1994:288) expands the definition of cohabitation to mean "a sitaution where two adults of the same or opposite sexes who are not married to each other, either by ceremony or by common law, occupy the same dwelling." Even after excluding same-sex heterosexual roommates, the total POSSLQ population has now topped three million (U.S. Bureau of the Census, 1995).

POSSLQ arrangements continue to be popular among college students, with data indicating that this population views such arrangements as preparation for later marriage (Thornton, 1988; Macklin, 1988). On the other hand, the POSSLQ numbers are increasing in other populations as well. As early as 1970, a full 75 percent of cohabiting couples under age 25 were *not* enrolled in college, and today it has increased to 80 percent (Glick and Norton, 1977; U.S. Bureau of the Census, 1995). Other significant subsets of the cohabiting population include persons over age 65, those legally married to someone other than with whom they live, divorced people, and couples with children present, this last segment representing almost 40 percent of all POSSLQs (Bumpess et al., 1991; Spanier, 1991). While the numbers within these groups show some fluctuation, it is quite clear that POSSLQs are much more than a passing phenomenon and involve a significant cross section of the population. In this sense, POSSLQ signals a "new normative pattern in courtship" that for many couples may become institutionalized as the stage between dating and marriage (Gwartney-Gibs, 1990:129). However, as a stage, it is highly unlikely that it will replace marriage as the preferred lifestyle.

In reviewing the literature on cohabitants compared to married couples, Newcomb (1982:146) finds that the emotional closeness and perception of roles do not differ and that as a screening device for later marriage, traditional courtship patterns work just as well. Contrary to what may be expected from the idea that the realities of living together prepares the couple for marriage, the traditional patterns may actually work better. Some research concludes that cohabitants who marry have lower marital satisfaction and adjustment, lower commitment to marriage, and divorce rates that are higher than or equal those of noncohabitants (Watson, 1986; DeMaris and Rao, 1992; Thompson and Colella, 1992). Another factor working against marital happiness for this group includes previous cohabitation with someone other than the current spouse. Stets (1993) suggests that this may predispose the couple to problems that come from the failed past relationships. If a divorce occurs, previous cohabitants are likely to cohabit again (Wu, 1995). These are the same factors cited for the failure of second and third marriages and demonstrate that cohabitation has a degree of emotional intensity comparable to that in a legal marriage. If cohabitation becomes a normative stage in the mate selection process, the differences between those who live together before marriage and those who do not are likely to disappear. As Schoen (1990) argues, the earlier cohabitants are at greater risk. They were the pioneers of the movement and would incur the liabilities associated with it, especially with much lower social support.

Differences between the genders in terms of cohabitation occur on a number of fronts. First, men who may have cohabited themselves express stronger preferences than women for a marital partner who has not done so, suggesting that there is yet another "marriage market" issue that is gender related (Nock, 1995). Second, although married females do more housework than cohabiting females, the latter still take on the greater burden for housework than cohabiting males (Stafford et al., 1977; Shelton and John, 1993). Third, money is rarely pooled, which has the advantage of financial independence, but the couple gives precedence to the man's career over the woman's (Kotkin, 1983; Blumstein and Schwartz, 1983). This is critical when taking into account data indicating that cohabiting women view themselves as independent, competitive, and managerial. Thus if the relationship dissolves, women are more likely to cite infringement on personal freedom as a reason (Macklin, 1988:68). The exception to this is that cohabitants not planning to marry are essentially egalitarian, but the males in these relationships are also less successful in career attainment than other cohabiting males (Kotkin, 1983:975). And if cohabiting is assumed to be a trial marriage, women are more committed to it than men. Women look to the arrangement as security which will come through later marriage, whereas men are more likely to view it as an alternative to marriage and as a means of sexual gratification (Jackson, 1983; Macklin, 1988).

Considering these findings, it is somewhat surprising to witness an ever-increasing population of cohabitants. Perhaps they are drawn to the idealism that is inherent in an arrangement which, on the surface at least, offers more benefits than liabilities. But the benefits appear to erode as cohabiting time increases. Indeed, the California Supreme Court decision in the famous *Marvin* v. *Marvin* case where a "palimony" suit brought against actor Lee Marvin by his cohabiting partner of seven years demonstrates that their relationship was in essence a marriage anyway. Rulings such as this would lead one to question why cohabiting would offer as positive an option as marriage, at least in the eyes of the law. Data from the next generation of cohabitants are needed to determine the overall consequences related to gender role change, marital satisfaction, and divorce.

Extramarital Relationships

Extramarital relationships, once routinely described as adultery, but now commonly referred to as affairs, take on a myriad of forms. These arrangements are extremely varied, involve different degrees of openness, and include married as well as single people. Estimates of secret extramarital relationships for married people range from 65 to 70 percent for men and 45 to 65 percent for women (Stayton, 1984:4). Hite's (1994) data report even a higher estimate for men at 72 percent today. When considering only the sexual component, the original Kinsey et al. (1953) data indicate that 50 percent of males and 26 percent of females engaged in extramarital coitus by age 40. By 1975, the figure for women had increased to 38 percent (Atwater, 1982:16). And perhaps most revealing is that today, wives under the age of 30 engage in extramarital relations slightly more often than their husbands, and after being married five years or more, 70 percent of wives report they are having affairs (Lawson, 1988; Hite, 1994).

These data are not inclusive for a number of reasons. First, many extramarital relationships are more open, with the spouse and other friends aware of the relationship. In this sense, the label of "affair" is an erroneous one with its implication of secrecy. Second, single women and men are involved with married women and men, but figures usually only give the married estimates. Third, depending on how an extramarital relationship is defined, a sexual component may or may not be part of it, although the potential is certainly there. Finally, reporting on these kinds of relationships is threatening to many, which is why the Kinsey data were suspect for what was originally believed to be exceptionally high numbers during a period seen as less promiscuous than today. An affair may be viewed as a spousal alternative. High mobility and an increase of women in the paid labor force lead to an increase in such alternatives. Along with increasing the risk of divorce, it is associated with more married people being open to extramarital relationships (South and Lloyd, 1995). In all, it can be assumed that the reported figures for extramarital relationships are lower than the actual.

Extramarital relationships occur, according to Atwater (1982), because we are unrealistic about love and the ability of our spouse to satisfy all our sexual needs. The emotional need category can be added, although an emotional relationship becomes defined as an affair usually when the sexual component is involved. The myths that contribute to our untenable faith in sexual exclusivity include:

1. One person will supply all of another's emotional, social, and sexual needs. Not only is this impossible, but it raises our expectations for satisfaction in marriage to extremely high levels.
2. People grow to love each other more through the years. Divorce rates and research show otherwise.
3. Sexual exclusivity comes easily and naturally. There is no evidence that this is true for humans. Also, as seen above, the double standard gives males different "rights" than females in this regard.
4. Husbands and wives should be best friends. A best friend is an intimate confidant who can share all subjects openly. Yet in marriage the shared burdens

and responsibilities, and the special kind of intimacy dictate the need for more emotional privacy.

5. Extramarital affairs will destroy a marriage. The need for growth, variety, or an antidote for boredom suggest otherwise. Extramarital sex may enhance some marriages, make no difference to others, but can be destructive to many (Atwater, 1982:18; Lazarus, 1987:75-76). I would also add that emotional rather than purely sexual liaisons have similar potentials for all these occurrences.

Atwater (1982:18) contends that "we have seduced ourselves with myths of monogamy" and retain romantic attachments to these myths despite the pain and disillusion these unexamined beliefs are bound to bring us." On the other hand, Pittman (1995) argues that unfaithfulness is not normal or acceptable. While a crisis of infidelity can reawaken a petrified marriage and therapy can save the adulterous marriage, first-time divorce occurs in the wake of an affair.

As would be expected, men and women differ as to their desires and expectations in extramarital relationships. Although men and women may eventually act on their desire to have an affair, men express a greater willingness to pursue them (Seal et al., 1994). In this sense, there is less of a gap between what men say and actually do compared to what women say and actually do. Sexual excitement is a stronger rationale for men to pursue such relationships than it is for women. Married women report that their affairs are less for sexual fulfillment and more for emotional support and companionship. Men report the reverse. The most frequent reason men give for having sex outside of marriage is the sexual rejection by their wives and at the same time, the boring nature of repeated sex with the same person. Hite (1994:142–3) explains this inconsistency as an alienation built into marriages due to the inequality of women and men. Men who eventually seek reasons for their boredom or lack of sexual closeness with their wives are happier in the long run than those who continue a pattern of interim affairs. This may be tied to financial liabilities. One man reports that the affair has not had an effect on his marriage except that it "costs too much money to support a family and a girlfriend." A study of London men who "keep mistresses" finds that they conceive of their behavior as honorable rather than antisocial, governed by a code of conduct and gentlemanly etiquette (Nelson, 1993).

Who are these girlfriends/women? One of the best studies on extramarital relationships among married women has been done by Atwater (1982), who finds that nearly all the women she interviewed identify the least satisfactory area of their marriage as the expressive area. Half of these women also say that their relationships with their husbands actually improved as a result of the extramarital situation (Atwater, 1982:74). As their needs are being met outside the marriage, their behavior changed in the marriage. As one woman reports:

> Since I have this second relationship on-going, I have been able to draw my husband out more and get him to talk more . . . and to be more open in expressing my feelings with him. . . . I am slowly but surely trying to bring our relationship up to a level that meets more of my needs. (Atwater, 1982:75)

This research may not be generalized to other women involved in extramarital relationships because she specifically chose feminist-oriented women to interview. The sample reflects an interest in exploring the impact of social change, thereby allowing an understanding of women open to personal and social change (Atwater, 1982:28). It is less surprising, then, that even if the expressiveness dimension is emphasized in the involvements with other men, Atwater finds no evidence of a traditional model of female sexuality. These women did not live vicariously through their extramarital partners and evolved their own script of female-centered sexuality (Atwater, 1982:140).

This study is significant because it offers a different view of the extra-marital relationship. Certainly the women in Atwater's study are not immune to the deceit and guilt which accompany many of the relationships. The case of the single woman-married man suggests a different pattern. They are primarily secret relationships that appear to protect both parties. We can see the double standard at work when a woman's reputation is threatened by exposure of the affair, with fewer penalties for married or single men involved in extra-marital relationships. We may have the "other woman" but where is the "other man"?

With the marriage squeeze at work, more single women are opting for relationships with married men. Many of these women have no desire to marry their extramarital partner or anyone else. In thorough interviews with numerous "other women," Richardson (1986) finds that unlike women who became mistresses in the past, this group has a very different agenda. "Today's woman wants to finish her education, build a career, recover from a divorce, raise her children, explore her sexuality. Getting married is not necessarily her primary goal" (Richardson, 1986:24).

She can be vulnerable and express weakness, which her professional role does not allow. The support and listening the married man offers strengthens her emotional attachment to him. In turn he exposes his own insecurities and the bond between them is strengthened. This allows some women to report that they prefer the mistress role (Wolfe, 1993). The life of the second (not "other") woman is more interesting than the life of a wife, and she can gain confidence as a lover in her own right. When he visits her he does so because he wants to. The following examples (Wolfe, 1993:138) show this preference:

> I felt like a teenager exploring womanhood for the first time. We were both virgins exploring this new world together. All directions were possible and no road maps existed.

> I'd felt different than I'd ever felt before—fresh, new and genuine. We were navigating a whole new territory of relationship: something deeply emotional, spiritual, intellectual—and perhaps slightly sensual.

These comments fit with another study by Richardson (1988:368) which suggests that single women in liaisons with married men "experience greater control over their sexuality because they feel freer to repudiate their sexual repressions, to abstain, to have safe sex, and to explore their sexual preferences."

The picture presented here is a rosy one, but many cautions should be noted. Systematic work on the single woman-married man from the woman's perspective is still lacking. However, some patterns are evident. If a woman desires to eventually marry at all, her relationship with the married man will effectively keep her out of the marriage market. By having her needs met by him, she does not avail herself of opportunities to meet other men. This is especially true for younger single women with low-paying, uninteresting jobs who enjoy the material benefits a successful married man can bring to the relationship. Women must also bear the brunt of the infidelity if it is discovered.

Adultery is based on her marital status and not his. As Batten (1992:90) notes, female adulterers are treated more harshly than male adulterers, both socially and legally.

It is likely that there will be more "other women" in the future, some who are satisfied in their relationships but others who invest too much and end up with a great deal of pain that is not easily, if ever, overcome. From a feminist perspective, the *second* woman ultimately contributes to the perpetuation of male power and privilege and female distrust of other women (Richardson, 1986:27). In the long run, women have more to lose than to gain by extra-marital relationships.

CHAPTER 8

GENDER AND FAMILY RELATIONS

> Desire for a feminine destiny—husband, home and children—and the enchantment of love are not always easy to reconcile with the will to succeed.
>
> —Simone DeBeauvoir, *The Second Sex* (1953)

What is a family? Academic debates on the topic have profound consequences when one or another definition is used in determining public policy on family-related issues, such as divorce, child custody, and single parenting. Political rhetoric has focused attention on the undesirable changes in family structure. This is associated with the theme that the family is doomed. Other views celebrate family diversity, flexibility, and the creation of new roles for all family members. Gender-based parental roles are called into question as alternate definitions of the family emerge. Narrow views of gender severely restrict opportunities for exploration and growth for both children and their parents. They also have profound social, psychological, and economic consequences for men and women as subgroups.

THE PARENTHOOD TRANSITION

The transition from the marital dyad to the family triad is a significant one. The addition of the first child brings with it numerous changes which affect the marriage itself and profoundly alter the lifestyle of the couple. To say that parenthood is filled with uncertainty is an understatement. Parenting is based on skills that need to be learned but cannot adequately be mastered, if at all, until after the child is born. Preparation for parenthood is based on one's own family experiences, dealing with others' children, formal classes, folklore, and reading a variety of child-care and parenting manuals. Whatever the degree of advance planning, new parents are likely to discover that the anticipation of what it means to be a parent is far different from the reality. Parenthood has differential experiences and consequences for women in comparison to men.

Because of the element of uncertainty, and even shock, which first-time parents experience, the literature on the transition to parenthood has focused on parenthood as a crisis. Backett (1982:16) finds that new parents retrospectively tend to devalue the objective preparations they made for the parental role, seeing them "as at best irrelevant and occasionally a direct hindrance." The strains of parenthood can be overwhelming and the demands alter the quality as well as quantity of the marital relationship. More energy is spent on children-related issues than on marriage-related ones (Baldwin, 1995). The marital relationship that is taken for granted is the one at most risk for dissolution. Flexibility and efforts to enhance closeness of the couple ease the stress associated with parenting roles. Again, gender roles intrude on this process.

Parenthood as a crisis has gradually been replaced with the view that it is a normal developmental stage to which new parents gradually become accustomed. The major shifts in lifestyle which may add tension and anticipated or undesirable role change must also be viewed in light of the gratification the child brings to the new parents (Neal et al., 1989; Belsky and Kelly, 1995).

Obviously, parenthood will alter marital roles and create new family roles. Whether the parenthood transition is seen as a crisis, a stage in normal development, or something in between depends on how the family structures itself to meet the parenting challenge. This structure will be largely dependent on beliefs regarding gender roles. The labels husband and wife suggest different realities; the same can be said for motherhood and fatherhood.

Motherhood

The belief that a woman's ultimate fulfillment will be in her role as a mother is socialized into girls very early in life. The motherhood mandate issues a command to females of all ages instructing them that motherhood demands selfless devotion to their children and a subordination of one's own life to the needs of children and family. Although this means foregoing any other activities that she may feel personally worthwhile, a woman willingly submits herself first to her child-rearing responsibilities. The power of this mandate instills guilt in women who work outside the home, especially if employment is associated with psychological, social, or personal benefits. Employed women who must work purely for financial reasons are not immune.

Although American culture idealizes the motherhood role, the actual support new mothers may receive varies considerably. If women are socialized into believing that becoming a good mother is easily achieved, they are severely jolted by initial parenting responsibilities. The tension and strain experienced by first-time mothers can be perceived as personal failure, in turn lessening their motivation to seek help. We saw earlier that the notion of a human maternal instinct is not empirically supported, but the view that the mother's role "comes naturally" stubbornly persists. The motherhood mandate combines with a mystique surrounding motherhood which Hoffnung (1995:167) states is made up of certain qualities:

1. Ultimate fulfillment as a woman is achieved by becoming a mother.
2. The body of work assigned to mother's caring for child, home, and husband fits together in a noncontradictory manner.
3. To be a good mother, a woman must like being a mother as well as all the work that goes with motherhood.
4. A woman's intense, exclusive devotion to mothering is good for her children.

From a functionalist viewpoint, motherhood is an institution and the motherhood mandate is essential. The mystique associated with it encourages girls to readily accept the role. Mothers are reproducers biologically and as primary socializers of the children, necessary ingredients for the maintenance, productivity, and continuity of society. If socialization is inadequate, the goals of the broader society may be compromised. There is no argument that the family is the critical institution for socialization. Functionalism assumes that the traditional division of labor within a patriarchal family is the most efficient and least contentious arrangement. Implicit in the view is that if something "goes wrong" with the children, it is the mother's fault. She takes the responsibility, the blame, and ultimately the guilt for all child-rearing functions. Contemporary functionalism recognizes that social benefits accrue when women, including those with school-age children, work outside the home. Women should be allowed, even encouraged, to pursue the same work as men. However, Oakley (1993:199) asserts that equality applies only to the world outside the home. And even this world is dictated by family responsibilities. Inside the home she is different, driven by her biology and own socialization to willingly accept the motherhood mandate. To be equal and different at the same time are thus compatible and justified.

Another consequence of the motherhood mandate/mystique is that children who suffer from any later psychological problems also tend to blame their mothers. This is linked to the trend of the "professionalization" of motherhood and the pressures it puts on women's performance as mothers (Woollet and Phoenix, 1993:216). Women are expected to seek out all available information to gain expertise in fulfilling their roles as mothers. It is a no-win situation for mothers. If she works outside the home using others as caretakers and her children manifest psychological problems, she is at fault as a neglectful parent. If she is the primary caretaker in a traditional housewife role and her children experience problems, she is still at fault. Only this time it is because she was overprotective and dominating. She instilled guilt in her family because she did too much for them. She may take on a martyr role. In either instance she incurs social disapproval, family resentment, and in the most painful circumstances, a diminished sense of self-worth.

Functionalism points to the responsibilities associated with motherhood. But rights accrue as well. The motherhood mandate is in tandem with the motherhood mystique which is a glorification of the role. Child rearing brings joy and pride for a child's accomplishments, for which mothers take a great deal of credit. It is apparent, nonetheless, that mothers are more likely to share the credit for what goes right, but assume the burden of blame for what goes wrong.

An often overlooked fact about the motherhood mandate/mystique is that it is recent in the United States. By the middle of the nineteenth century, a frontier economy based on subsistence farming required women to carry a multitude of productive roles, with child rearing being a lesser one. These roles were deemed more important for the survival of the family. As Hoffnung (1995) states, productive work was placed before reproductive concerns. Even children were viewed for their productive qualities. It is only since the turn of the century that the notion of having children for purely psychological reasons became firmly ingrained on the American consciousness.

Conflict theory argues that the motherhood mandate contributes to the social powerlessness experienced by women in their family and extradomestic roles. Since a woman's earnings from paid employment alter the power relations within the family, men will evoke the motherhood mandate to ensure that women concentrate their energies on domestic roles. Child-rearing responsibilities serve as handicaps to career growth or other personal achievements for women. Women's well-being in the workplace is compromised by their involvement with the family emotion work required in their domestic roles (Wharton and Erickson, 1995:289). Money, status, and power are linked to roles outside the home commanded by men (Polatnick, 1993). The choices wives make regarding child rearing weaken their bargaining power at home and on the job and reinforce economic dependence on their husbands (Gerstel and Gross, 1995). In the workplace this translates to lower salaries and sagging careers. At home it translates to shouldering the bulk of child-care tasks. From a conflict perspective, Mahony (1995) argues that not until as many men as women truly want to stay home with the children can women hope to achieve real economic parity. The motherhood mandate ensures that women will not be serious contenders for extradomestic roles and that the patriarchal power structure of the family and the workplace remains unchallenged.

An acceptance of the motherhood mystique precludes much individual growth for women. By this definition, motherhood is the only worthwhile role. The obvious problems and contradictions emanating from the mystique are conveniently overlooked. Can women feel good about themselves as mothers if they also seek other roles?

One answer lies in the demographics of motherhood, which have changed significantly, especially since the 1950s. As women achieved career and educational goals, marriage and motherhood were delayed. The decline of the fertility rate since World War II is linked to higher levels of education, rising wages, and the opportunity costs of child rearing for women (Whittington et al., 1990; Pampel, 1993). This explains why so many women in their 30s and 40s are now having children for the first time. It also supports the idea of motherhood as a salient goal. Most women are unwilling to give up biological parenthood but opt for smaller families than in their parents' generation. And even with the ambivalence and multiple role conflicts associated with motherhood, in reflecting on their parenting experiences, the vast majority of mothers would do it all over again (Genevie and Margolies, 1987). Since career-oriented women are also unwilling to give up either motherhood *or* professional roles, they are adapting their beliefs about family and parenting accordingly.

Today's young women assume that motherhood, as the mystique suggests, gives them a sense of personal fulfillment. But unlike their own mothers and grandmothers, they are challenging the ideas that childbearing is a requisite for completeness and that motherhood is always desirable (Bartholet and Draper, 1994). This is especially true for younger professional women, who already demonstrate higher rates of childlessness than older professional women (Yogev and Vierra, 1983). This study finding is unusual since we have already seen that the majority of young, professional women expect to pursue motherhood as well as their careers. The authors suggest that the women in their study may not be as confident in the ability to combine conflicting motherhood and career roles. If this is indeed the case, it may indicate a further weakening of the motherhood mandate.

The acceptance of feminist values by a larger proportion of women would also likely affect notions about motherhood. Scott and Morgan (1983) show that women who have traditional gender role orientations desire families, especially larger families, when compared to nontraditional women. College women who subjectively identify with feminism are less interested in having children, which reinforces other studies indicating that there is generally a negative relationship between feminism and motherhood (Gerson 1984:289). But a unique point about these findings is that for feminists who desire motherhood and intend to have the same number of children as other women, they also believe that motherhood offers opportunities for active mastery and assertiveness (Gerson, 1984:395). In interviews with mothers in the labor force, Chira (1992) reports that the old view of motherhood is unacceptable since work has become so important to their identities. They firmly believe that simply being home all day does not automatically qualify one as a good mother. Motherhood can be redefined in terms acceptable to feminists who want to creatively master a number of roles. The motherhood mandate is itself being redefined to fit the newer lifestyles of contemporary women.

It is clear that while traditional definitions of motherhood are being challenged, their lingering effects make newer ones ambivalent at best. Society is at a critical juncture where two paths are available. Consistent with a functionalist framework, one path reflects the commodification of children theme which treats children as commodities produced in the workplace because they are "had," if at all, in response to women's increased labor force participation and as a finished product of mothering (Folbre, 1994; Chesler, 1995). The other path suggests that the qualities we associate with the idea of maternal can be more widely shared by both men and women in a variety of family contexts. This is the contribution of a feminist perspective on fertility. The perspective reflects a linkage between symbolic interaction and conflict approaches by examining gender labels and fluid definitions of family, household, children, and their multiple-lived realities as well as the power relations existing between and among women, men, and their children (McDaniel, 1996).

Fatherhood

When considering nurturing and child-care functions, the American father is viewed as peripheral at best when compared to the mother. Unlike our colonial American ancestors who expected the father to provide for both the economic needs and spiritual education of his children with the less literate mother as his able assistant (Vinovskis, 1986:188), the contemporary father is cast mainly into the breadwinning role.

Public policy and legislation regarding custody of children, child support, welfare, definitions of desertion and child neglect, and so on have served to fortify the emphasis on the primary role of father as the economic provider for the family. However, current efforts directed at unwed fathers to contribute both financially and psychologically in the care and upbringing of their children may alter this somewhat. Economic involvement is seen essentially as a punitive measure. Whether this will mean that fathers then voluntarily take an active role in child rearing remains to be seen.

The fact that most fathers take their breadwinning role very seriously does not diminish other interests they have in their families. Like women, men also see raising a family as an important life goal, although they still believe women should be primarily responsible for child care (Astin, 1985). As will be documented in the next chapter, fathers have been discouraged from involvement with their children by a masculine ethic which deters them from other parenting roles.

As first-time parents, men appear to adapt more easily to the rigors of fatherhood than women do to motherhood, and husbands can predict with more success than their wives what kind of parents they are likely to be (Feldman and Nash, 1984; Harriman, 1986). Traditional fatherhood may not bring the same profound personal and marital changes that mothers experience, but research reveals that fathers can and do form strong bonds with their young children and are actively and successfully taking on child-care tasks more than in the past (Mooney, 1985; LaRossa et al., 1991). From these data, we can presume that it is mainly the emphasis on the provider role and the de-emphasis on the childhood socialization role which keep men from assuming greater responsibility for ordinary nurturing. We have accepted a masculine imperative that denies men the opportunities for more meaningful parent-child relationships.

The prime directive for fathers is to provide for the economic support of their families. Yet in comparison to mothers, the effect of fathers on the development of their children is often overlooked. Chapter 3 demonstrated that parental influence on childhood socialization is critical. Mothers assume the major responsibility in this area. But fathers also send important messages regarding roles to their children that are probably accentuated by the reduced contact and differing quality of interaction. A father's time with their children is spent more on recreational activities than with their ongoing physical upkeep (Snarey, 1993). Research finds that a father's level of engagement, accessibility, and responsibility are a fraction of the mother's. When asked about involvement with their children, fathers respond with answers that they have to "put in some time with the kids." In conducting this research LaRossa and his colleagues (1991:313) state that fathers see themselves as "doing time" with their children, an example of a technically present but functionally absent father. American fathers are not much different than those in other parts of the developed world. Data indicate that fathers in 11 countries are alone in a room with their young children less than 45 minutes a day (Schwartz, 1994).

As children get older, fathers become more involved with their children and spend more time with them, directing more attention to their sons than their daughters (Lamb, 1979). This is the time when gender-typed behavior is particularly encouraged for sons and socialization into masculine-oriented activities such as sports begins in earnest. Compared to mothers, fathers expect their sons to conform to gender roles much more than their daughters (McGuire, 1988). The concern for gender-appropriate behavior carries through to father-child interactions during adolescence. Research indicates a strong positive relationship between fathers and adolescent sons' gender role beliefs and expectations (Emihovich et al., 1984). Fathers who are less traditional in their gender role beliefs, holding less stereotyped expectations, have sons who match their fathers in this regard. Since the father is the critical figure in determining his adolescent son's willingness to accept changes in his own gender role, despite changes in broader society, we cannot expect sons to drastically modify their gender role behavior unless their fathers support them (Emihovich et al., 1984:867).

Traditional gender role expectations, though stronger for sons, carry through to daughters as well. The tendency is for fathers to use strong discipline on sons in order to enhance what they view as masculine behavior, while at the same time allowing their daughters to retain elements of dependence, thereby encouraging a continuation of childhood qualities. The extreme scenario of undue discipline for boys treating girls as sex objects during adolescence revolves around violence, abuse, and incest. Cross-gender play during childhood can result in childhood sexual abuse, particularly for girls (Lamb and Coakley, 1993). For adults, increased parent-child conflict during adolescence is typical, but it is heightened as far as fathers are concerned. Fathers who are inconsistent in their discipline, or who are neglectful or cold are more likely to have adolescent sons who are delinquent or express irresponsible behavior (Martin, 1985:1983). When a father engages in incest with his adolescent daughter, he expresses his right of access to any female. Herman's (1981) study of father-daughter incest indicates that it is the daughter and not the father who stops the sexual involvement, with most girls reporting that fathers would continue the contact if possible. Incest survivors suffer confusion and indelible psychological scars as they face parenting roles (Cole et al., 1992). Roth (1993:2) describes her own sexual abuse as a little girl at the hands if her father:

> I was too afraid to turn my head and look at his face. He didn't speak to me while this happened. After he stopped moving he would gently say, "You're my special girl." So I figured that even though I was uncomfortable, this was something daddies do with their special daughters.

Incest is difficult to document and estimates of its prevalence are questionable. When the media draw attention to the topic, one dysfunctional consequence is a further retreat of fathers from their children, especially their daughters. It is evident that relationships are enhanced when fathers are nurturant rather than aloof, visible rather than invisible, and consistent and fair when administering discipline to both their sons and daughters. As suggested by the socialization literature (see Chapter 2), there are few major differences in the way mothers and fathers treat their children, but the differences that do occur are significant. Fathers who are successful in parenting provide the kind of caring and warmth that may be contradictory to the established patriarchal family role assumed by most past and many contemporary fathers. Notions of fatherhood are gradually changing and fathers are now encouraged to develop those nurturing qualities that will make them not just better fathers but better partners. Converging gender roles may serve to enhance parental role quality (Barnett et al., 1994). The optimism expressed in altering the father's traditional role is tempered with other analyses suggesting that changes have been minimal at best, and have occurred largely within the confines of the middle class (LaRossa, 1992:532).

Although the conduct of fatherhood has been given the mandate to change, continued gender role stereotyping severely limits the options. Young men have not adopted a fatherhood mandate as part of their role requirements (Lawson, 1990). Fathers who move in the direction of androgyny, with its inherent role flexibility, will meet the demands but may also reap the rewards of contemporary society. Research suggests that they will also be better parents.

Voluntary Childlessness

A note on the voluntarily childless couple is necessary. Even if the motherhood mandate is weakening, couples must still contend with a prochild orientation in society. While data suggest that childless marriages are steadily increasing and that more women of childbearing age will not have children (Bloom and Bennett, 1986; U.S. Bureau of the Census, 1995), it is unlikely that this signals a revolution against a pronatalist ideology. The media are replete with stories of women who "successfully" challenge their biological clocks to have children before it is too late. A billion dollar fertility and adoption industry has mushroomed to meet this challenge. The belief that couples should have children is so strong that those who choose not to do so, especially the women, are viewed as misguided, incomplete, selfish, and frigid (May, 1995).

An outsider may view a marriage which is voluntarily child-free with a combination of pity, scorn, or suspicion. This view, however, is fundamentally different than the empirical reality. A literature review by Peterson (1983:322) concludes that the voluntarily childless spouse is "just as adjusted and happy as the spouse who is a parent or plans to be a parent," and that "evidence of a negative view of the childless spouse can be interpreted as a negative bias more than as a statement of reality." While children bring joy to the couple, they also bring increased marital tension. Married couples without children express similar or greater amounts of marital satisfaction as those with children, with voluntarily childless women significantly higher than mothers in this regard (Callan, 1987; Houseknecht, 1987; Rogers and Larson, 1991; Abbey et al., 1994).

Although couples in general and women in particular continue to view parenthood as desirable, the increased number of voluntarily childless couples implies that, along with the weakening of the motherhood mandate, there is also less pressure to conform to traditional family norms regarding parenthood. Nemy (1995) reports that there is now more support for the idea that remaining childless for some couples is a fulfilling and productive alternative to rearing children.

Parents as Dual Earners

With the influx of women into the paid labor force the dual-earner family is now the normative family. As noted in the last chapter, there are now more dual-earning nuclear families with children present than one-earner nuclear families with children present. The largest overall increase is in families with preschoolers. Since women are traditionally responsible for child care, particularly in the preschool years, all eyes turn to them when questions arise as to how children are affected when both parents work outside the home. It is the wives rather than their husbands who reap society's disapproval if it is established that when both parents enter the world of paid labor their children suffer. Disregarding the claim that women should be solely responsible for primary socialization of their children anyway, how legitimate is the "suffering children" theme?

It has already been demonstrated that paid employment benefits women socially and psychologically, especially when they work in positions that they find challenging, rewarding, and personally meaningful. Their marriages appear to be enhanced, and shared decision making makes for a semblance of an egalitarian arrangement. The cost for women involves maintaining responsibilities at home and for the children when husbands do not share on anything near an equal basis household and child-care chores. These women can suffer from an overloaded role which may add strains which the employment per se cannot eradicate. In general, however, the evidence from dual-earner families shows that women are enriched by their labor force activities.

If parents are happy and the family is enhanced by a dual-earning structure, this should logically carry over to the children. Not so, states writer Harry Stein (1987), who maintains that with infant day care as the answer to the needs of the dual-earning couple, the child is not provided with a sustained one-to-one relationship with a primary caregiver that is essential to her or his healthy emotional development. According to Stein (1987:162), surrogate care is more of a luxury when one parent is free not to work but both partners are intensely career oriented. He points his finger at women who choose to work outside the home rather than stay home with the children. He states:

> Now, there's no reason to be coy here. Invariably the parent who is obliged. . . . to grapple with the choice between home and office is the woman; no matter how unfettered by convention any of us purports to be, no matter how vividly we might wish it to be otherwise . . . men simply do not put their careers on hold in the interests of family. (Stein, 1987:162)

Apparently both men and women are condemned by unalterable roles, "no matter how vividly we might wish it to be otherwise."

This case for the mother staying home rests on the argument that the long-term consequences of day care result not just in "mere inconvenience or temporary dislocation but a wounding sense of loss" when the young child is removed from the primary caregiver (Stein, 1987:164). If parents, especially mothers, are not filled with remorse and guilt by this stage, he goes on to say that parents have an obligation to find some other way of coping than day care. Implicit in this is that most other options which do not involve mother staying home are either deemed unrealistic by working parents or dismissed as unacceptable. The contention is that a generation which was denied love as children will soon be upon us unless something is drastically changed. Parents are abandoning their children to day care so they can selfishly pursue their own careers which in later years will damage children and by extension, society. Is the evidence sufficient to warrant such a conclusion?

One major source of information is often overlooked by both sides in debating the issue. When women were desperately needed during World War II to work in defense plants, they were recruited by the thousands in campaigns designed to alleviate their anxiety and guilt about leaving their children with others. Creative approaches to day care became the norm of the day. Day-care centers grew in response to the needs of women who could not rely on relatives or whose other care options were limited. Given the tenor of the time, the potential negative consequences which may have accrued in the long run for these children were dismissed or conveniently ignored. After the war, traditional attitudes prevailed and women were expected to return home and be full-time housewives and mothers. They were not guilty of being neglectful mothers during the war, but if they chose to continue to work outside the home afterward, the guilt returned. The script that employed mothers are "bad" mothers returned with a vengeance.

Almost 30 years of research data on the effects of the dual-earner family on children does not support the "suffering children" theme. Employed mothers are not "bad" mothers and children are not jeopardized by maternal employment. There is near consensus by developmental psychologists that child care per se is not a risk factor in children's lives. The problem comes if it is poor quality care and the child is from a troubled family (Barnett and Rivers, 1995). There are no differences in the home environment or development of children with employed mothers than those who are not (Berg, 1987; Barnett and Rivers, 1995).

Other studies demonstrate that an enriched group child-care experience can enhance and stimulate the development of infants and preschoolers (Belsky, 1991). Dual-earner parents actually spend as much time in direct interaction with their children as single-earner parents (Nock and Kingston, 1988; Scarr and McCartney, 1989). As an added bonus for employed wives, recent research now indicates that at least modest increases in husbands' participation in household labor may result from the growing diversity of work schedules (Presser, 1994).

Though myths and ideology about the effects of a working mother prevail, children of dual-earning couples appear to express high degrees of confidence, resourcefulness, and independence. Evidence suggests that children are neither deprived nor neglected with maternal employment and, in fact, may demonstrate more positive social, psychological, and interpersonal characteristics than do children of mothers who do not work outside the home. Female achievement is encouraged by an employed mother as a role model (St. John-Parsons, 1978; Etaugh, 1980; Joy and Wise, 1983; Scarr, 1984; Margolis, 1984; Kuttner, 1988; Nock and Kingston, 1988).

If maternal employment could be shown to have adverse effects on the child, many of these should logically show up during adolescence, since this is often a time filled with a great deal of stress and family turmoil. Again, research does not warrant this conclusion. Stephan and Corder (1985) find that adolescents from dual-career families actually prefer this kind of family structure, and not surprising, have less traditional gender role attitudes than children from traditional single-earner homes. In general, adolescents in dual-career families view their lifestyle positively and report high degrees of parental closeness, supportiveness, and interest in their personal problems. As would be expected, a problem area adolescents identify is that of time constraints faced by their parents related to a dual-career family lifestyle (Knaub, 1986).

The idea that children are adversely affected by maternal employment is simply not supported, especially with the dual-earner family. In dual-career families where both parents are employed in professional capacities, children may be enriched by the resources two incomes can bring. For poor women who receive inadequate pay and single mothers who must rely on less than adequate child-care arrangements, maternal employment paints a different picture. But for dual-earner couples, a woman's identity and fulfillment are linked to satisfying roles at home and in the labor force. The verdict on how women feel about these roles is a positive one. Despite the rhetoric, women are defining family values in the context of nurturing and supporting their families, with economic activities as vital to this process. When women's work roles are not valued, families are not valued. In citing this research, Mann (1995b:E3) notes

> The study underscores the point that it is time to end the debate about whether women who work outside the home end up undermining their families. We need to replace that debate with a realistic commitment to finding ways in which communities, employers and society in general can help men and women manage all their responsibilities effectively.

FAMILIES IN MULTICULTURAL PERSPECTIVE

Family patterns in the United States have been altered and become more diverse in response to a rapidly changing society. Since the family is our most conservative institution, when we begin to witness modifications in the family, we know that broader social change must be rampant. Dual-earner families have helped pave the way for the emergence of an egalitarian family alternative, at least on the attitudinal level. American families have adapted to changing norms and in turn these norms are being refashioned to accommodate a diversity of families.

African-American Families

Compared to other races, African-American families exhibit a wider variety of family and household structures and a pattern of familial gender relations marked by a greater degree of role sharing. The major factor in the development of these patterns is traced to economic oppression rooted in racial discrimination. Recently available data from the turn of the century (1910) reveal that African-American households were less likely to be nuclear and more likely to be headed by women, a pattern that persists today (Morgan et al., 1993). Other demographics show that, compared to European Americans, African-American family lifecycles are marked by less formal marriages, parenthood earlier in marriage, later and less likelihood of remarriage, and a higher divorce rate (London, 1990; Littlejohn-Blake and Darling, 1993). About 80 percent of African-American children and 36 percent of white children are likely to experience part of their life in a female-headed household, with black children more likely to live with a grandparent than are white and Hispanic children (Teachman and Paasch, 1993; O'Hare et al., 1995). While these statistics may not be normative in terms of the broader culture, they can be viewed as functionally adaptive.

African-American families are characterized by resilience and resourcefulness which are reflected in household structures. While the vast majority of the ten million black households are made up of family members related by blood, marriage, or adoption, about half are headed by married couples (O'Hare et al., 1995). With the other half headed mostly by women who are single mothers and grandparents and who exhibit marked economic need, there is an advantage to changing the household structure to accommodate varying sources of internal and external pressure. African-American families demonstrate a strong willingness to absorb others into kin structures by creating a network of **fictive kin**, where friends "become" family. Fictive kinship brings an array of exchange and support that benefit all members of the household. Although the household may shift in the composition of its members, it indicates structural flexibility that is advantageous in a time of crisis when resources must be mobilized in creative and dynamic ways and offers a diversity of models for childhood socialization and parenting roles. Employed mothers who are the family breadwinners can readily turn to kin network in caring for sick and out-of-school children (Winkler, 1993; Dill, 1994; Jarrett, 1994; Benin and Keith, 1995; Raley, 1995). On the other hand, there are costs associated with the benefits, the most obvious being a "leveling [making it] difficult for any one person or family to move ahead (Rapp, 1991:208-9).

Financial needs have may have dictated the formation of such living arrangements, but they also promote upward social mobility by offering sources of intergenerational support from both the family and community (Billingsley, 1992). Managerial black families may experience stress and social isolation when kin support networks are disrupted due to job relocation (Toliver, 1993). The strengths that come with diversity and spiritual beliefs have helped build a strong sense of self and nurtured an optimistic outlook for the future (Littlejohn-Blake and Darling, 1993). Thus demographics alone do not capture the structural differences between black and white families. African-American family patterns have developed around a series of cultural constraints (Heaton and Jacobson, 1994). They are also sustained and remain viable by cultural traditions which emphasize diversity and role flexibility.

Nowhere is this role flexibility more evident than in the gender patterns of African-American families. With the underemployment of black men, black women have traditionally assumed family provider roles essential to the stability and survival of many families. According to Malson (1983:101), "one of the fundamental differences in the lives of black and white females is the experience of black females as paid workers." Their paid work has been a necessary and constructive adaptation to the reality of economic and social inequality in America. Yet this very strength has been viewed as a weakness inherent in black families. In a report which gained widespread national attention, Moynihan (1965) intimated that in the numerous black families headed by women a "black matriarchy" exists in which decision making and other family powers and responsibilities rest with women rather than men. By this way of thinking black men are emasculated, stripped of authority, and driven from the family under an aura of self-defeat. The family is left with fewer defenses against poverty, delinquency, and illegitimacy. The notion of a black matriarchy gained support with a demographic trend indicating the rapid increase of female-headed households.

The idea of a black matriarchy has done untold damage by creating and reinforcing stereotypes of superhuman women and weak and absent men, who are then blamed for the circumstances in which they find themselves. The myth of the black matriarchy has been challenged on many fronts. Half of all African-American families are headed by married couples and two-thirds of the black population are *not* classified as low-income (Eshleman, 1994:180). And as McAdoo (1990) indicates, married couples are likely to exist in an egalitarian family structure whose roles are complementary yet flexible, with the husband engaged in stable employment. This kind of family pattern is most common in working-class and middle-class families (Smith and Welch, 1986; Eshleman, 1994).

An egalitarian arrangement is supported by black women who work outside the home by choice rather than economic necessity. Using a Boston sample, Malson (1983:111) finds that most married mothers work in spite of having husbands earning over the median income for area families. Dugger (1991) contends that black women exist in a subculture where employment is integral and normative, complementing a tradition which does not view the roles of wife-mother and wage earner as mutually exclusive. Like their white counterparts, African-American employed wives take on the bulk of household and child-care responsibilities. However, African-American husbands appear to be more willing than white husbands to accommodate themselves and the household to the needs of their employed wives, with some data indicating more gender role convergence in African-American families (Ross, 1987; Hossain and Roopnarine, 1995). This is the family structure that tends to be ignored by social science.

Most attention is focused on poverty-ridden or near poor African-American families headed by married couples, unmarried couples, or single-female parents. These are the families where the stereotype of black matriarchy persists. The family is seen as a cause rather than as a consequence of continued poverty. Whether married or not, role sharing by the poorest black couples is a necessary adaptation which enhances their ability to remain together as a family unit (Blackwell, 1985). Even among female-headed families, households are likely to have other male relatives and fictive kin who diverge from traditional gender roles. The dilemma is that the acceptance of rigid gender roles by such families would be potentially harmful, yet by altering them, the family is considered deviant or unstable. Such explanations conveniently dismiss the structural legacy of institutionalized racism. According to Staples and Johnson (1993), the evolution of the fatherless family is a result of the deterioration of the economic opposition of black men. Role flexibility may actually help cement the couple's relationship. This is not to dismiss the tension which arises in periods of economic uncertainty, only to suggest that less rigid gender roles can be indicative of family strength in difficult situations.

When combining race and gender, black women who work outside the home have the lowest earnings of any group. African-American women must carry the double burden of their minority group status. Few would argue with Staples' (1993) conclusion that the black female is exploited by virtue of both race and gender. If she is a single parent, the prospects of decent wages to maintain her family above the poverty level are severely reduced. This is intensified by the kind of jobs black women have. While women earn less than men overall, the likelihood of poverty is significantly higher for women in occupations with a prevalence of black women and lower in occupations dominated by white women (Catanzarite and Ortiz, 1995). This is in spite of a strong commitment to employment and socialization messages to girls emphasizing self-reliance, independence, and resourcefulness (Collins, 1993).

While African-American women are worse off economically and face the double-minority burden, African-American men must contend with a double bind of their own. Men are socialized into instrumental family roles that tie masculinity with being a good provider and father. Black men accept this standard for masculinity but are denied access for opportunities to do so. An Afri-centric view suggests that models are provided for people who cannot obtain them in a "culturally oppressive and race-conscious society" (Langley, 1994:242). Masculinity must then be affirmed in other ways. African-American males take on a variety of masculine roles used as coping behavior that are now referred to as "cool pose" in the research literature (Majors and Billson, 1992). Reflecting a symbolic interaction perspective, cool pose is used by black males to create and manage their self-presentation to others. For the coping styles of inner-city youth living in poverty who grow up on the streets, it is associated with "violent behavior, on the streets and at home, to sexual promiscuity and to problems at school" (Majors et al., 1994:251).

Compulsive masculinity related to cool pose takes its toll on the family. Data indicate that low-income single black mothers who are parenting boys have higher levels of depressive symptoms, more negative perceptions of children, especially boys, and that there is a poorer quality overall home environment (Jackson, 1994b; Mott, 1994). For married couples, the number of teenagers is negatively related to marital happiness (Ball, 1993). If these teenagers are boys, it is likely to increase this tension. Family life inevitably suffers as a result.

In addition, the African-American community is not immune to other stereotypes concerning black male-black female relationships. Some research reports that black men believe that black women have more opportunity than black men, with a large minority feeling that black women are in part responsible for the low status of black men (Cazenave, 1981). The prediction that black women will achieve superiority over black men in terms of education, occupation, and income may serve to heighten tension (Staples and Johnson, 1993). As pointed out earlier, the marriage squeeze is more acute for African-American women searching for same-race men of comparable age and educational levels. Increased joblessness and higher death rates from violent crime, disease, and poor health care deplete the pool of marriageable black males in absolute numbers and render those who are available as less desirable to marry (Tucker and Mitchell-Kernan, 1995). Besides contributing to the increase in interracial marriages, many black women who remain single shoulder a greater share of family responsibilities and are more vulnerable to poverty and all its consequences. It appears that it is the economic position of African-American men that will significantly determine the course of many African-American families and how gender roles will be enacted. Consider these trends in light of answers Collins (1993:171) received when asking her black female students: "What did your mother teach you about men?"

> Go to school first and get a good education—don't get too serious too young.

> Make sure you look around and that you can take care of yourself before you settle down.

> Don't trust them and want more for yourself than just a man.

The Moynihan report (1965) and its bequest of black matriarchy serves as a reminder of the connection between sexism and racism. The report was attacked in a large part because black men were usurped of their rightful place as family head. To untangle the pathology surrounding the black family, the father must be returned as the dominant person in the household. If women remain assertive and independent, "they were ruining the family and ruining the race" (Giddings, 1993:252). Black women apparently do not suffer the same humiliation as black men and "neither feel nor need what other human beings do either emotionally or materially" (Smith, 1995:157). According to Giddings (1993:252)

> The Moynihan Report was not so much racist as it was sexist. Although it can't be held responsible for the intense Black male chauvinism of the period, it certainly didn't discourage it, and the report helped shape Black attitudes.

Such views may suggest a self-fulfilling prophecy. Although the black matriarchy argument has been successfully challenged, many black men have likely internalized its assumptions, which in turn creates tension between the genders. Stereotyping increases during periods of economic uncertainty. The high unemployment rates of black men may herald a trend which counters the legacy of role flexibility and egalitarianism evident in many African-American families.

Hispanic-American Families

Although African-Americans are currently the largest minority group in the United States, Hispanics, or Latinos, will become the largest group by early in the next century. The term "Hispanic" has been used in such as way as to gloss over the significant social, cultural, and historical differences in the subgroups constituting this population, particularly related to their immigrant status and years or generations in the United States (Williams, 1993). The three largest subgroups of the Hispanic population are Mexican-Americans (Chicanos), Puerto Ricans, and Cuban-Americans. While all three groups suffer the economic burdens of minority status, poverty is most acute for Puerto Ricans and least acute for Cuban-Americans. Although Mexican-Americans hover near the poverty line as a group, there are wide variations in overall economic status. Latinos share a heritage of Spanish colonialism and through this, a solid connection to the Catholic church. Fundamental values linking these heterogeneous groups include family relations characterized by respect and honor, the notion of **familism**, the extension of kinship ties to relatives and community members outside the nuclear family, and a strong adherence to patriarchal gender roles (Del Carmen and Virgo, 1993). How these values are translated into behavior differ according to such factors as SES and degree of acculturation.

Patriarchal gender roles are rooted in a well-defined and accepted belief system that categorizes men and women. Men are characterized by **machismo**, a cult of virility associated with courage, aggressiveness, arrogance, and sexual prowess. Women are characterized by **marianismo**, where the ideal woman is seen as morally superior and spiritually strong, with an infinite capacity for humiliation and sacrifice for her role as mother, but submissive to the demands of men in her family (Stevens, 1993). The machismo-marianismo duality is found throughout all social classes in Latino cultures. Along with familism, they exist as stereotypical images but still serve as potent models for childhood socialization. There is no doubt that there is extensive deviation from these models (Del Carmen and Virgo, 1993; Stevens, 1993), but that the behavior can still be justified according to them. Thus they can serve as a backdrop for approaching a variety of gender-related information.

By far most research on gender and the family in Hispanic subcultures has centered on the link between employment and home for employed women and their families. Puerto Ricans have the lowest income level of any Latino group. This is clearly linked to the facts that almost half of all Puerto Rican households are headed by women, only half of Puerto Rican women are high school graduates, and that there has been a declining demand for labor in those industries where these women have historically been employed, such as light manufacturing (Zambrana, 1994). Families are often divided with children being raised by grandparents in Puerto Rico and husbands migrating back and forth between the island and New York in search for employment. Despite the "marianismo mandate" nonmarital cohabitation among Puerto Ricans is high, with just over half of all families demonstrating this pattern. This compares to three-fourths of Mexican- and Cuban-American families consisting of married couples (Landale and Fennelly, 1992). Kin networks offering support and intergenerational exchange are vital to the well-being of these families (Sanchez-Ayendez, 1986; Cantor et al., 1994).

Women are caught in a double bind. They must provide for their families in the context of a powerful island-centered subculture in which sexism and male chauvinism remain entrenched (Acosta-Belen, 1986). Marriages are fragile, cohabitation is high, and abandonment of women and their families is common. Households demonstrate high male dominance and emotional distancing between husbands and wives. This contributes to the "deep psychological investment in their children" (Almquist, 1995:585). Research on working- and middle-class Puerto Rican women who migrated with their husbands to the United States indicates that they provide as much continuity as possible in re-creating family life. Some resisted the move but eventually were compelled to follow their husbands in their roles as wives and mothers. However, better educated women gave more equal values to career and family life (Toro-Morn, 1995). Clearly defined gender roles are common, but some erosion of the double standard is evident, especially as women seek expanded roles outside the family (Chilman, 1995).

Mirroring the marianismo-machismo duality, Cofer (1995:204–5) writes of her experiences growing up in a Puerto Rican community in New Jersey.

> As a girl I was kept under strict surveillance, since virtue and modesty were, by cultural equation, the same as family honor. . . . But it was a conflicting message girls got, since Puerto Rican mothers also encouraged their daughters to look and act like women. . . . The extended family and church structure could provide a young woman with a circle of safety; if a man "wronged" a girl, everyone would close in to save her family honor.

She asserts that her education gave her stronger footing to survive this kind of duality in mainstream culture and saved her from the harsher forms of racial and ethnic prejudice. Familism serves to buffer girls from the "harshness" of the outside world, but it also does not adequately prepare them for the role conflict they will inevitably face when they enter it as wives, mothers, and employed workers.

Mexican-American (Chicana) women also confront gender roles tied to ideology surrounding marianismo-machismo and familism. The nuclear family is embedded in a network of kin who maintain intergenerational ties by passing on cultural traditions and serving as sources of social, and sometimes economic, support (Paz, 1993; Dietz, 1995). Ideology functions to allow men to dominate and control the household as well as the women in their lives. Although men are expected to be discrete, extramarital relations are tolerated outcomes of a belief in male sexual prowess. As to the home, males are taught that household work is "women's work." But male dependence on females to carry out tasks such as cooking and laundry have actually given women a source of power (Horowitz, 1991).

Early writing on gender relations stressed the subordination of women to men but recent work is now questioning the concept of the all-dominant and controlling male. Machismo has been interpreted as a male defense against the adversity of racial discrimination and poverty. The authoritarian and belittling world that the Mexican-American laborer faces every day is reproduced in the home (Mirande, 1979; Almquist, 1995). He is bolstered by keeping "women in their place." Notice how the concepts of machismo and black matriarchy can be used to justify the same conclusion and then used to perpetuate inequality between the genders.

Later data demonstrate that families are not as patriarchal as had been assumed and that there is a real trend toward egalitarianism. While couples reply in more traditional terms about the separation of their spheres, research shows that fathers and mothers share in child rearing and household tasks as needed and that joint decision making is becoming normative, especially when women are employed outside the home (Williams, 1990; Chilman, 1995). Extended family ties are also weakening (Williams, 1993a) so couples may expect less support but also less bolstering of cultural norms emphasizing male dominance. This pattern will accelerate as educational and employment opportunities increase for women. Cultural lag is evident in that attitudes have not changed as fast as behavior. A persistent problem confronting the Chicana is that employment is usually restricted to jobs occupationally segregated by gender and offering little job mobility (Segura, 1994). In summarizing these trends, Eshleman (1994:194) states that husbands still exert more power than wives and wives (like their Anglo sisters) still do the majority of domestic work. But compared to their parents and grandparents, traditional patterns have been altered significantly.

Cuban-Americans have enjoyed the highest standard of living of all Latino groups in the United States. This reflects the fact that the first immigrants were likely to be highly educated and from the professional ranks of Cuban society. Women, too, were well educated but not likely to be employed for pay. Education for women in the middle and upper classes was encouraged to bolster the status of the family but not to interfere in the world of business and politics. The double standard of sexual morality lives on in the Cuban-American subculture. Parents want their daughters to be educated but also to remain virginal, uncorrupted, and sequestered. If the process of acculturation is successful, younger women will not accept such restrictions. Egalitarian family and work roles are in line with their future expectations (Almquist, 1995; Chilman, 1995.)

DIVORCE

The United States has the highest divorce rate in the world (Goode, 1993). The choice to dissolve a marriage has been an alternative throughout most of the history of the United States. The fact that it is now a largely acceptable alternative has contributed to a staggering divorce rate which has shown overall steady increases since as early as the mid-nineteenth century. Though subject to historical anomalies and economic fluctuations such as the Depression and World War II, the rate of divorce appears to have increased rapidly during the 1970s, peaked in 1981, and plateaued or shown modest decreases since. Divorce rates are difficult to calculate but a fair assessment is to say that just under half of all marriages end in divorce. This does suggest some cautious support that the increase in divorce may be leveling off, and that if the divorce trend does continue, it will do so at a slower rate (National Center for Health Statistics, 1993; U.S. Bureau of the Census, 1990–1995). Whatever the future trend, America now has the highest divorce rate in its relatively short history.

Marital dissolution has profound social, psychological, and economic effects for the divorcing couple and their families. Research is accumulating which shows that divorce has differential consequences for women compared to men. While it is difficult to separate out economic from noneconomic factors, the overall conclusion is that women adjust better to divorce than men

(Diedrick, 1991). Men and women who are defined as nontraditional in their gender role orientation adjust better to the divorce trauma. This indicates that those who are less conventional, such as the androgynous man and the assertive, independent woman, are better at reconciling themselves to divorce than passive women and men with very traditional gender role perspectives (Chiriboga and Thurnher, 1980; Hansson et al., 1984). We have already seen that high femininity is associated with lower self-esteem in women and that masculinity is associated with independence for both men and women. Less traditional women are also likely to hold multiple roles, a factor which we have already fully documented as beneficial to self-esteem and good psychological health. Self-esteem is also a factor in duration of marriage. Women with higher self-concepts opt out of unsatisfactory marriages at a faster rate. This suggests that they may view marriage as an optional status compared to women with lower-self esteem (Esterberg et al., 1994:303). Since these are the very characteristics which are essential for coping with the loss and bereavement often concurrent with divorce and its aftermath, the woman who rejects traditional gender roles would be better off should she find herself facing dissolution of her marriage.

Younger women are also better at rebuilding their lives after a divorce. In a ten-year followup of divorced families, Wallerstein (1984) finds that, for both men and women, the ones who first sought the divorce have adjusted more readily. But for younger women, especially those under 40, divorce leads to a wider range of growth options and enhanced psychological changes when they are compared to men and older women. Older women suffer greater psychological trauma in divorce. In a study of mothers with children who are between the ages of 7 and 13, after some early reservations, the women accepted the divorce and were not eager for a reconciliation, though the children remained committed to the parents as couple (Grossman, 1986).

When a divorce involves children, the mother usually gains custody. Although men and women have a statutory equal right to custody in almost all states, approximately 90 percent of the time custody is granted to the mother and is the preferred pattern for most mothers and fathers (Weitzman, 1985:49). Most often fathers give in to the mother's demand for full custody without further legal action (Kelly, 1993). Women must now take on an array of previously shared roles. Even if she is working outside the home, the divorce increases financial obligations, child care, and household responsibilities. Conflicts at work which were previously resolved with less effort can intensify and create a greater sense of insecurity. Older women, housewives, and those reentering the labor force after a long absence are in an extremely precarious position. They are at a distinct disadvantage in the job market at the exact time when they need an adequate income to support the family.

Although women appear to fare better than men in the psychological trauma of divorce, the economic consequences are disastrous for women as a group (Smock, 1994; Starrels et al., 1994; Kurz, 1995). One of the most widespread misconceptions about divorce involves the belief that a divorce settlement "sets up" a woman and her children for life. The newspapers are replete with examples of women who are awarded huge sums of money from their famous and wealthy husbands. The truth is that the economic effects of divorce on women and children are dismal. Alimony is itself a myth, awarded to only a small percentage of women. Weitzman (1985:144-45) reports that only 14 percent of divorced wives in a census survey indicated that they were awarded alimony, and then in amounts so meager that they barely matched welfare or Social Security payments anyway. Such awards certainly do not free these women from "worldly cares or assure them a perpetual state of secured indolence" (Weitzman, 1985:145).

A related issue concerns not simply what is awarded by the courts but if what is awarded can be collected. Less than 50 percent of mothers actually receive child support from nonresidential fathers and only about 25 percent of mothers receive the full amount (Teachman and Paasch, 1993). In almost half of divorced families there is no contact by the nonresidential parent, usually the father, two years after the divorce (Hewlet, 1987; Johnston, 1993). For those few women who are nonresidential parents, they are still more likely to remain in contact with their children (Bray and Berger, 1993). When fathers do pay support, the courts often consider his circumstances rather than the needs of the mother and children (Teachman, 1991). These data must be viewed in light of the continued wage gap between men and women. They are augmented by statistics showing that in the first year after a divorce, women with minor children suffer a 73 percent decline in standard of living while men experience a 42 percent rise in their living standard within the same period (Weitzman, 1985:36).

Alimony is rarely awarded, child support is insufficient, and both are not guaranteed to be collected. Making economic matters worse for women is the trend toward the no-fault divorce. States are increasingly allowing couples to decide for themselves if they want to remain married without the expectation that one must prove that the other is guilty of some transgression, such as mental cruelty or adultery. The no-fault divorce can also allow one spouse to divorce the other without her or his consent. Most important, alimony and/or property settlements are supposedly designed to treat the man and woman on an equal basis in order to amend the gender biases of past laws. The no-fault divorce is seen as an amicable and just solution to a bad marriage.

Although such divorces may be amicable, they are assuredly not just. The idea of equity is a sham when it is assumed that a 40-year-old woman who may have been sporadically employed is on an equal footing with her husband at the time of a divorce. The trend in the no-fault divorce settlement is to divide current property equally, focusing on savings and the family home. Courts have been reluctant to consider assets such as future earnings, medical and life insurance, or pensions in no-fault settlements. This explains why housewives are penalized in later divorces. The prior agreement between a husband and wife which gives priority to his career and assumes career assets will be shared with her has little legal standing (Weitzman, 1985; Weitzman and Dixon, 1988).

When the home is sold and the assets divided, it is unlikely that either partner can purchase another home right away. The loss of the family home makes an already difficult situation worse for the children who must adapt to a new physical environment while simultaneously dealing with the emotional turmoil of the lessened contact with one parent. The financial hardship and lowered living standard of divorced women and their children have literally changed the picture of poverty in the United States. Some women are forced into the morally deplorable situation of marrying simply to escape poverty. We are aware of many secure, financially independent women who choose not to marry. Unfortunately, numerous women who were encouraged to choose other routes become so economically trapped that they succumb to dependent roles to allow a better lifestyle for their children.

For those divorced mothers who recognize that they simply do not have the financial capability to adequately provide for their children, the decision may be to give up custody. The belief that children should stay with their mothers is so strong and pervasive that women who voluntarily give up custody are viewed as unnatural and immoral, a pariah in society's eyes (Markey, 1986). She may relinquish custody out of love, knowing that her ex-husband is financially in a better position to offer them what she cannot. But the anguish and guilt can continue for years, reinforced by negative societal definitions telling her she has abandoned her children. As Markey (1986) states, noncustodial fathers are not made to feel like freaks. That is reserved for the noncustodial mother.

While custody is essentially a woman's domain, there has been a recent trend of fathers gaining full custody in contested divorces. Custody revisionists have begun to challenge the maternal preference argument, citing factors beneficial to children if they remain with the father (Depner, 1993). These factors are imbued with the kinds of gender stereotypical thinking that permeates the entire divorce process. Fathers can be favored over mothers because they are financially better off. The courts do not award alimony to women capable of earning a living, so divorce requires women to capitulate any thought of maintaining the status of homemaker if that was her predivorce existence. Earning a living can jeopardize her chances of gaining custody, especially if she has young children. Not only does the father make more money, but if he remarries, he has the possibility of another full-time caretaker. Although uncontrollable economic factors are the likely reasons for a mother losing a custody battle, she is cast into the socially stigmatized role of unfit parent (West and Kissman, 1991). Crean (1993:514) contends that the case for fathers' rights is more of a case against mothers and that "instead of admitting the systematic discrimination which debilitates their ex-wives and families after divorce, they claim that the reverse is true, that women are the privileged ones in divorce." Gender-neutral standards are supposedly in effect to ensure parity in divorce and child custody decisions, but persistent gender role stereotyping works against this in both principle and practice.

One "solution" to the problems associated with child custody has been the trend toward joint custody arrangements where co-parenting occurs in a variety of contexts, from simply sharing day-to-day decisions about children with their ex-spouses, to actually moving children, and sometimes parents, to different homes on a rotating basis. There are vigorous debates among experts on the effects of such arrangements on children. Research indicates that joint-custody fathers are more involved in their children's lives and increases contact with them, and that they actively participate in shared decision making regarding their children. Complicated scheduling is a downside, but less strain is reported than if one carries the full burden of parental responsibilities (Irving and Benjamin, 1991; Seltzer, 1991a, 1991b). Joint custody may also be agreed on during a divorce mediation process where parents meet with an impartial third party to reach mutually acceptable agreements (Kelly, 1993). For the 10 percent of cases where sole custody is not awarded, joint custody is prevalent. A critical point is degree of parental cooperation. If channels of communication remain open and children are not used as pawns, a joint-custody arrangement is a constructive option for all family members (Folberg, 1991; Depner and Bray, 1993).

While the benefits for children are still being debated, it is already clear that women are under great financial risk with joint custody. Most women do not have the financial resources to co-parent on an equal basis with their ex-husbands. As one attorney puts it:

> Joint custody is a big lie. What's really going on is that the man will ask for joint or sole custody so he can pay less child support, and there's no redress. Let's say he doesn't show up. What are you supposed to do? You have less child support than you should—you can't force visitation. (Webb, 1988:245)

The legal costs of returning to court often prevent single mothers from contesting the joint-custody arrangement. Noncustodial fathers tend to gradually remove themselves from their former families, especially if they remarry. Joint-custody fathers maintain a better record at both maintaining contact with their children and supporting them financially. But as equitable as the arrangements may seem on paper, women are less able to take on the greater economic burden that is now demonstrably associated with joint custody.

The new divorce laws assume that husbands and wives are being fairly treated while in reality it is wives and mothers who are penalized. According to Weitzman (1985:371), if the newer laws would have provisions which gave each spouse "credit" for the roles they had chosen in marriage, such as breadwinner or homemaker, they would more accurately reflect the complex variety of marital options couples are now assuming. As existing now, however, flexibility and individual choice are denied. Given the legal reality and its economic results, it is preposterous to believe equity is being served.

If women with dependent children are perceived as a financial liability, they are also at a disadvantage as far as remarriage. Although most divorced people remarry, the rate for women is lower than for men. Up to 85 percent of men remarry and they do it quicker than women (Bray and Berger, 1993). Many men who may want to marry are reluctant to take on a ready-made family. These women may be caught in the old scripts which tell them that men are the initiators as far as dates. There is the anxiety and insecurity of entering new relationships for romantic purposes soon after a divorce. If she was a full-time homemaker during the marriage, this anxiety is heightened. Finally, divorced women must contend with the marriage squeeze and the limited options that they feel are acceptable.

ALTERNATIVES TO TRADITIONAL FAMILIES

The massive social changes occurring in all segments of society have impacted the family to a great extent. Expanded employment opportunities for women and men, divorce and remarriage, and definitions regarding acceptable parenting behavior have spawned a variety of family alternatives. These alternatives not only exhibit different structures when compared to the traditional nuclear family model, but also almost by necessity the structures have produced variations in gender roles. It is impossible for these families to exist without almost profound deviations from traditional notions concerning female and male, wife and husband.

Househusbands

When out of choice or necessity a husband takes on the tasks tradition-ally assigned to a wife, there is limited social support for these roles. In inves-tigating college students' attitudes toward male and female housespouses, there is still a devaluation of the housespouse role, particularly when it is taken on by men (Rosenwasser et al., 1985). The paths are virtually uncharted for men who give up their breadwinning roles to take on primary responsibilities for household tasks and child care. With few models and guidelines from which to draw, Lutwin and Siperstein (1985:272) say that the passage to the househusband role is an emergent one that is being created, discovered, and shaped as they proceed.

Their research focuses on men, ages 23 to 57, who made the transition to househusband. The majority of these men are white, middle-class managers and professionals who had been at the mid or top level in their careers, most of whom left their jobs because of disability or being fired. Lutwin and Siper-stein (1985:281) find that the degree of adjustment is related to a number of variables. The best adjusted househusband:

1. Has entered the role voluntarily
2. Is committed to an alternative lifestyle
3. Has definite plans for the future
4. Receives support from extended family and friends
5. Does not experience stress from boredom, alienation, and other related fac-tors

They conclude that the role reversal does not alter the perception of their mar-riage or how their wives and children view them. However, they become more appreciative of their family, their former job, and the household work for-merly assigned to their wives (Lutwin and Siperstein, 1985:278).

Beer's (1983) study of New York area househusbands is more inclusive and has similar findings. Though disliking the routine, boredom, and inevitability associated with household tasks, the relaxed pace, feeling of accomplishment, and "artistry" of the job appeals to many househusbands. While it cannot be said that these men have an androgynous orientation to work and family, the househusband role allows for insight into problems housewives face and for more egalitarian attitudes in their marriages.

Though we have seen that husbands in dual-earner families take on some additional household tasks and increase recreational time with their children, wives take on overall child-care responsibilities. But the househusband role requires this traditional division of labor to change. Pruett's (1987) research on families with primary nurturing fathers demonstrates that these men resemble traditional mothers. Though having been raised in traditional fami-lies themselves and coming from all social classes, the fathers form deep reci-procal relationships with their children, are competent in their child-care skills, and help to create thriving, robust children. Pruett (1987:251) believes that joint ownership of the children can create a place where both fathers and mothers can "mother" in a way that does not induce competition for being the "first-place" parent. He thoughtfully suggests that it is not the sharing but the competition which can confuse children. Free from child-care worries, moth-ers report a high degree of satisfaction with their careers, a factor also con-tributing to higher marital satisfaction.

For the househusband role to be accepted as a legitimate choice for men, there must be considerable change in the way both male and female gender roles are viewed. Household tasks and child care need to be valued as much as paid employment. Research has yet to determine the extent of shared housework and child care between partners in a househusband family. It is probable that the wives of full-time househusbands take on more domestic tasks than the husbands of full-time housewives. Perceptions of fairness and marital quality are related to household task sharing (LaFollette, 1992; Deutsch et al., 1993). The household division of labor pattern that ultimately emerges in househusband families may be the key to determining whether the role become viable.

Gay and Lesbian Families and Relationships

Marriage between homosexuals is not legally recognized, although many churches will conduct the religious rites for such unions. Family law works against sanctioning these arrangements not only by prohibiting marriage but also by denying custody to the homosexual parent. Yet a small but growing number of gay men and lesbians have gained custody of their own children or have adopted children and live in permanent households with them and/or their homosexual partners.

These families face a great deal of hostility and suspicion by a society accepting myths about homosexuality in general and idealized notions of the family in particular. We have seen that the concept of "family" is contested both in legal and informal contexts. A family to a gay man or lesbian is a chosen one and may incorporate a network of kin and nonkin relationships including friends, lovers, former lovers, co-parents, children, and adopted children. They are organized through ideologies of love, choice, and creation (Weston, 1993). Many family members are fictive kin and assume the rights and responsibilities associated with them, similar to what we witness in African-American and Hispanic families. Political rhetoric concerning definitions of the family is linked to antigay campaigns focusing on homosexuality as the enemy of the patriarchal family and the American way of life. It is doubtful that this sentiment can be subjected to much evidence, but gay families do exhibit characteristics which are in opposition to the traditional structure and behavior patterns of the patriarchal family. This seems more to the credit of these families than to their detriment.

Gay men and lesbians have been in the vanguard of a movement to redefine family structure in part to receive benefits that have previously been available only to those who are legally married. Recognizing that domestic partners are more than roommates in that they have achieved a different level of emotional intimacy and economic interdependence, a California court ruling defined them as a "family" (Horn, 1992:517). Besides homosexual couples, this ruling also applies to a myriad of nontraditional family forms that have been excluded from benefits ranging from employer-sponsored family health and dental plans, parental leave, day care, and moving expenses. As would be expected, legal and political challenges will keep the issue of the rights of homosexual domestic partners who, unlike POSSLQs, do not have the right to marry, unresolved for some time. As Horn (1992:520) notes, traditional values may rule in the courts, but by taking the issue to the workplace, to the unions, and to the legislatures, progress can be made on assuring rights to couples and families who are "nontraditional" in both family structure and sexual orientation.

Although homosexual relationships exhibit the range of diversity that is found in the structure and intimacy of heterosexual relationships, some patterns can be ascertained. In the now classic literature review by Maccoby and Jacklin (1974), homosexual couples were found to exhibit more equality in their arrangements than did heterosexual couples. The stereotyped image that gay relationships have one partner in the dominant, breadwinning, sexually active "male" role and one in the subservient, housekeeping, sexually passive "female" role is a myth (Caldwell and Peplau, 1984; Harry, 1991; Kitzinger, 1988; Huston and Schwartz, 1996). An overall egalitarian arrangement is more prevalent in homosexual than heterosexual relationships. This pattern appears to hold true for both lesbians and gay men, although lesbians are more successful at maintaining egalitarianism (Kurdek, 1993). Gay men are less influenced by the feminist movement than are lesbians, and as men are more susceptible to cultural norms that equate power with money (Basow, 1992; Huston and Schwartz, 1996).

While homosexual couples tend toward egalitarianism, one of the major differences that separates homosexual men and women mirrors gender roles in the wider society. Monogamy is valued among gay men, but it is more difficult to achieve. Sexual prowess is admired by heterosexual and gay males and is often the most important part of a relationship, mainly in the beginning stages. As one would expect, regardless of sexual orientation, for women, sex is less important than emotional expressiveness and commitment (Garnets and Kimmel, 1993). Research confirms this to be the case for lesbians who maintain that sex grows out of later feelings as the relationship progresses and that sex and physical closeness are less important than friendship (Peplau, 1991; Noeller and Fitzpatrick, 1993). As Garnets (1996:145) notes, "lesbian couples frequently adopt a peer-friendship model of intimate relationships."

Children growing up in households with lesbian mothers would be likely to experience more equitable family arrangements, if custody is indeed granted to the mother. We have already seen that in the vast majority of cases women gain custody of their children. With lesbian women, however, this is less likely. Some women hide their lesbian identity to win custody and then live in constant fear of being exposed by their husbands and having the courts reverse the decision (Harne, 1993). Others who are granted custody after bitter court battles may endure continual harassment from their ex-husbands and even their own relatives and friends. Some mothers fear their children will be traumatized by a publicized custody fight and voluntarily accede to their husbands' demands.

Lesbian mothers themselves can internalize the stigma of their sexual preference to the extent that they fear their children will be harmed if they know their mothers are lesbians or will grow up with severe problems in a household with one or two lesbian parents. To the contrary, research is now reporting that children are more adaptable, understanding, and accepting than society, the courts, or even their lesbian mothers assume. Lesbian parents cite tolerance for diversity from family and friends and growing up in a loving environment as important benefits of raising a child in a lesbian family (Hare, 1994:27). Psychosocial development among children of lesbian versus heterosexual parents is similar. Where differences occur, children of lesbians show more reaction to stress but also a greater sense of well-being (Patterson, 1994). In reviewing the research on the personal and social development of children with gay and lesbian parents, it is concluded that there is no evidence that the child's development "is compromised in any significant respect relative to that among children of heterosexual parents in otherwise comparable circumstances" (Patterson, 1992:1025). These data are used as ammunition for custody and adoption cases. When problems arise with the children of these natural or adoptive parents, it is usually due to outside interference and the degree to which society accepts the negative stereotypes of lesbian mothers.

Just as lesbian mothers can lose the opportunity of raising their children, gay fathers are even more likely to be denied custody. It is estimated that 20 percent of gay men have been married at least once and that between 350,000 and 700,000 are natural fathers (Bozett, 1985:328). Gay fathers can find that visiting their children is so discouraged that they may be reluctant to subject themselves and their children to the turmoil and upset accompanying visits or attempted visits. If their children remain unaware of their father's gay identity, the gay fathers live compartmentalized existences and, like lesbian mothers, fear being exposed and traumatizing their children. Bozett (1985) suggests that when these men make the transition to the gay world after a divorce, they do so without the "fetter of marriage" but maintaining their identity as fathers.

Miller (1992) contends that gayness may not be compatible with traditional marriage but it is compatible with fathering. After resolving the tensions of an undisclosed gay identity in marriage, divorce and movement into the gay world resolve some tension. For publicly gay fathers who do have custody of their children or who adopt through "marginally legitimate channels" and are living with a lover, Miller's study shows positive histories for these families. Problems in rearing children exist, but several studies demonstrate that once men resolve how to deal with their gay identity, gay fathers appear to have no more problems than single heterosexual fathers who have custody of their children (Bozett, 1987; Miller, 1992).

Gay men have limited opportunities for raising children if they proclaim themselves to be gay, despite the fact they may be natural fathers. Another possibility is to maintain a liaison with a heterosexual woman with whom he may have children. Women who desire children without the confines of marriage may choose to have a child with a gay man with whom she may or may not be emotionally attached, who then provides help with parenting and financial support. There is no legal obligation, they do not live together, and the child is "hers." In this way, desires on both sides are met.

Alternative forms of relationships involving gay men and heterosexual women are evolving. Nahas and Turley (1980:11) report on the "new couple" which involves a primary love commitment between a man and woman but one in which the man is gay and the woman is heterosexual but is accepting of his sexual orientation. Sex may not be part of their relationship but the intimacy and time spent together makes for a unique relationship. By this definition, the new couple are lovers, but sex is not the qualifying factor. As Nahas and Turley (1980:12) state, other factors predominate, "such as compatibility, mutual acceptance and need for companionship of a sort which the gay life of the male and the heterosexual experiences of the female have not provided." Success with such an arrangement varies considerably, but its acceptance by a number of couples indicates that relationships and families may be even more nontraditional in the future.

SINGLE-PARENT FAMILIES

High divorce rates and the greater tolerance and acceptance of the children of unwed parents have led to a dramatic increase in the number of single-parent families. Sixty percent of divorcing couples have children (Bray and Berger, 1993). Since 1970 the number of single-parent households has more than doubled. The increase of joint-custody arrangements and fathers gaining sole custody are more than offset by the rapid increase of never-married women with children. The staggering prediction is that for those born in 1980, 70 percent of white children and 94 percent of black children will live in a single-parent household before they reach age 18 (Hofferth, 1985). Most of these children will be living with their mothers.

Mothers and the Single-Parent Household

Not only are female-headed families the fastest growing type of family in the United States, but when a family with children is headed by a woman, the odds that it is in poverty approach one in two. Median family income is almost four times less than in husband-wife families (Costello and Stone, 1994:328-29). In the United States, over half of all poor children live in families headed by women. When race is factored in, the poverty rate for white, black, and Hispanic children is 46 percent, 66 percent, and 71 percent, respectively (Gimenez, 1994:288). Many factors contribute to this situation. We know that child support, alimony, and joint custody are not the financial salvation for these women. Neither are welfare payments in a restrictive system which may contribute to, rather than deter, the cycle of poverty. Since women are more likely than men to be undereducated and engaged in menial or low-paying jobs, if employed at all, the income is far from adequate to meet the needs of the family. The financial burdens of the single-parent family headed by a woman have created a situation known as the **feminization of poverty.** The distinctive character of a woman's poverty is that she has the economic responsibility for children (Pearce, 1993). At this point in time, public policy has been unable to satisfactorily address the issue.

Financial uncertainty is one of a number of problems faced by the single-parent family, particularly for women. The exorbitant demands on the single parent lead to stresses perhaps more easily faced in two-parent homes. Economic uncertainty tied to overloads of both physical demands and psychological responsibility intensify the problem. Single mothers must rely more on their children to get certain household tasks completed yet are also expected to be available to their children for any crisis which comes up at home or in the workplace. These conclusions are corroborated by other studies showing that women who are single parents not only experience more stress than married women but that they have fewer social and psychological supports, experience downward social mobility, have lower income and educational levels, a poorer self-image, and raise children who are more likely to be poor as adults and become single parents themselves (McLanahan and Booth, 1989; Grella, 1990; Gimenez, 1994; Arendell, 1995). Overall, many of these women experience chronic life strain which impacts their physical, social, and psychological well-being.

If there is a positive side to all of this, it comes with the autonomy in decision making that makes it better to be divorced than to stay in a miserable marriage. As would be expected, the key to achieving this autonomy and recognizing it as positive is linked to economic issues. Women who are financially more secure are better able to adjust to the situation and may find themselves much closer to their children after the divorce. Family type is less of a predictor of a child's well-being and achievement than is the quality of relationships in the home. It may be better for some children to be in a well-functioning single-parent home than in a nuclear family marked by high levels of conflict (Chollar, 1995). Problems which arise are more likely attributable to poverty and stigmatizing by the wider society rather than the fact the household is headed by a woman or by the divorce per se.

Fathers and the Single-Parent Household

We have seen that more fathers than in the past are gaining custody of their children or are sharing the responsibility with their ex-wives. Between 1970 and 1982 the number of children living with their single custodial fathers increased by 101 percent (Hanson, 1985:370). About 13 percent of all single-parent households are headed by men, and 3 percent of children live with their fathers only (U.S. Bureau of the Census, 1995). With different standards being adopted by the courts in terms of custody arrangements and adoptions, the rise in numbers of fathers heading single-parent households is likely to continue.

When compared demographically with single-parent mothers, single-parent fathers present a far different picture. The fathers are usually better educated and occupy professional or higher-level employment roles and continue their prior career patterns after becoming single parents, which means a financial situation that contributes to their being awarded custody in the first place (Hanson, 1985:372-73). However, there is a trend where fathers of all socioeconomic categories are starting to gain custody as well.

As for household tasks and child care, single fathers appear to adapt rather well, perceive themselves as capable as the primary parent, share most of the household responsibilities with their children, and do not rely on outside help to a great extent (Chang and Deinard, 1982; Greif, 1985a; Risman, 1986, 1987). They report that the most significant problem they face is balancing the demands of work and single parenting. Successfully coping fathers have more cooperative work situations and support networks (Greif et al., 1993). When they became single fathers, they set out to learn new tasks and domestic skills. Fathers who are more involved with housework before the divorce make a smother transition to their new domestic roles. After divorce, single-parent mothers do less housework; fathers do more (Fassinger, 1993).

For the most part, the children are also resilient and seem to pull together after the divorce (Greif, 1985b:148). As children get older, they participate more in housework, but with gender role differences evident. Fathers who are raising teenage girls receive more help from them than fathers raising teenage boys (Greif, 1985a). These fathers are in nontraditional roles as the custodial single parent but "fall into traditional patterns of handling home-related tasks."

One of the best studies to date is Geoffrey Greif's (1985b) examination of single fathers and the tasks they face in parenting. Like single mothers, they have difficulty in balancing the added demands, dealing with the legal system, and maintaining satisfactory relationships with their ex-spouses (Greif, 1985b). For fathers who adapt well, the following characteristics are present, according to Greif (1985b:151):

1. They have higher incomes.
2. They were involved in housework and child care during the marriage.
3. They attribute the marital breakup to shared reasons; they do not entirely blame themselves or their wives.
4. Their ex-wives are involved with the children on a regular basis.
5. They sought custody or said they wanted sole custody at the time of the breakup.

When these factors are not present, fathers are more likely to have a difficult time adjusting to the rigors of single parenthood. As he notes, "it is not the sex of the parent that makes parenting difficult or easy, but the task with which the parent is confronted." Considering the inordinate responsibilities associated with single parenting, he concludes that it is impossible to weigh whether single fathers or single mothers as a group have an easier time adapting (Greif, 1985b:153).

There is limited research on single-father households. Data are needed to document the realities associated with this family lifestyle. Fathers must deal with gender role stereotyping which assumes that they cannot be as competent parents as women (Gardner, 1995). They must somehow prove their parenting ability to a wider social community who may view them almost suspiciously, something which women as single parents do not have to face.

CHAPTER 9

MEN AND MASCULINITY

A woman can do the same job as I can do—maybe even be my boss. But I'll be *damned* if she can go out on the football field and take a hit. . . .
—(Cited in Messner, 1995:172)

Since men are regarded as the superior gender and imbued with power and privilege, it seems ironic to consider their roles as potentially lethal to themselves. Whereas women wage uphill battles for equity in economic, political, and social spheres, men wield the power which will determine the outcome of the fight. Both men and women perceive the male role as envied and desired.

Although any role is made up of both responsibilities and rights, the latter for men is viewed as outweighing the former. Men have careers; women have jobs. Men are breadwinners; women are breadbakers. Men are sexually aggressive. A man's home is his castle. Father knows best. Is this the true story? The male mystique is based on a rigid set of expectations which, as we shall see, few men can attain. The social and psychological consequences of striving for the impossible plus the impractical can be devastating. We shall see that the role which appears to offer so many rewards also has its deadly side as well. In discovering more about this role, we should come to the realization that a men's liberation movement is not a contradiction in terms.

HISTORICAL NOTES AND MASCULINE MARKERS

Today the images of masculinity appear to be confusing and contradictory. The media heroes are courageous, competent, and always in control, such as Kevin Costner, Arnold Schwartzenegger, Clint Eastwood, and the enduring images of Sylvester Stallone's Rocky and Rambo. Yet these images exist side by side with infallible antiheroes such as Dustin Hoffman, Robin Williams, and Dudley Moore. Women praise the sensitive man who can admit to his vulnerability yet admire the toughness of the man who refuses to bend in the face of overwhelming odds. Most men fall short when attempting to satisfy both standards. History provides some insights into how this situation arose.

Patriarchy is tied to male dominance, a theme in Western, or for that matter, Eastern civilization. It is a theme that remains unquestioned, taken for granted, and accepted. Using a Western civilization perspective, Doyle (1995) categorizes the male role in terms of five historical periods, ranging from the Graeco-Roman era to the eighteenth century. Table 9-1 suggests that the contemporary concept of masculinity which most men strive to meet continues to be based on ancient beliefs. When the basic features of a male ideal persist after two centuries, this attests to the stubborn rigidity of a definition which defies even global social change.

TABLE 9-1   Five Historical Male-Role Ideals

Ideal	Source(s)	Major Features
Epic Male	Epic sagas of Greece and Rome (800–100 B.C.)	Action, physical strength, courage, loyalty, and beginning of patriarcy.
Spiritual Male	Teachings of Jesus Christ, early church fathers, and monastic tradition (400–1000 A.D.)	Self renunciation, restrained sexual activity, antifeminine and anit-homosexual attitudes, and strong partiarchal system.
Chivalric Male	Feudalism and chivalric code of honor (twelfth-century social system)	Self-sacrifice, courage, physical strength, honor and service to the lady, and primogeniture.
Renaissance Male	Sixteenth-century social system	Rationality, intellectual endeavors, and self-exploration.
Bourgeois Male	Eighteeth-century social system	Success in business, status, and worldy manners.

Source: Doyle, 1995:27.

With patriarchy already firmly entrenched, the peculiarities of American history tightened its hold. From the Puritans to the frontier era to the Civil War and World War I, the value of individualism had furiously taken hold of the nation. Americanism and individualism became inseparable and eventually took root in the consciousness of the new nation as masculine markers. Opportunities with few restraints other than initiative beckoned men into farming, politics, business, or whatever the imagination sought. Granted that some (nonwhite) men and most women were to be excluded from these opportunities. The "lone man against the world" theme remained a powerful image throughout the early period of preindustrial expansion (Gerson, 1993). Popular myth supported the notion that nothing could stand in the way of dedicated American males in achieving their objectives. Most objectives related to financial rewards from hard work and physical endurance, with a secondary emphasis put on intellectual cunning. Success based on material wealth and getting ahead were, and are, integral to American notions of masculinity.

War and soldiering provide another validation mechanism. War historically brings with it idealized rhetoric emphasizing its virtue and glory, while ignoring its destruction and sheer horror. Gray (1992:25) asserts that there are secret attractions for war: "the delight in seeing, the delight in comradeship and the delight in destruction." Functionalism views war as integrative for society when disparate elements rally together to face a common enemy. In both World Wars, military training was seen as the way to build the manhood of the nation. Women served men as nurses, clerical help, or during World War II, builders of war equipment. Women were considered helpmates to the men who fought the "real" battles. War and the preparation for war supposedly induces men to their highest levels of masculinity. Several forms of masculinity are interfaced in war—physical violence, subordination to the orders of others, dominance, competition, and organizational competence (Connell, 1992:181). It is as if war becomes the quintessential guideline for defining masculinity.

World War II helped bring the nation out of the Depression, a time which had serious consequences for the American version of masculinity. The loss of jobs and daily economic uncertainty for those fortunate enough to have jobs during the Depression assaulted the self-esteem of men accustomed to their role of breadwinner. The fact that the entire nation faced similar circumstances offered little assurance to these men. Many blamed themselves for their inability to get or retain a steady job. When their wives were able to find work outside the home, their emasculation may have been complete. The effects of this kind of male self-indictment reverberated throughout the nation. Beyond the economic results of a high jobless rate, the psychological toll was also sadly demonstrated. Many men became estranged from their families, others coped by deserting them. Alcoholism, mental illness, and attempted suicide increased. Contrary to the image of the American man as invincible and able to overcome any obstacle, men and women alike recognized how vulnerable they really were.

The Depression provided an opportunity to seriously question an impractical definition of masculinity. This was not to be the case. With war came a revitalization of the old image, and the harshness of the Depression added luster to it. Even considering that Korea and Vietnam were not the victories Americans had learned to expect, beliefs about war as a proving ground for manhood continued. A "cult of toughness" emerged to sway public opinion in favor of escalating the war in Vietnam (Fasteau, 1974). America, like its fighting men, was tough. Although politicians cultivated this image of toughness, the carnage of Vietnam, which was seen on the nightly news, coupled with an untenable political situation abroad, served to fuel protest against the war. The first young men who burned draft cards or sought asylum in Canada or Sweden were viewed as cowards and sissies, afraid to face the test of war. As the protesters grew in number and the war became increasingly unpopular, more potential draftees joined in the antiwar movement. Comments about bravery and cowardice were not wiped out, merely driven underground for a time.

Here was another opportunity to challenge what it means to be a man. War, at least as embodied in Vietnam, was not the answer. But the cult of toughness reasserted itself in the 1980s. The Reagan era was predicated on a show of toughness and not backing down. During his presidential campaign, George Bush was able to successfully demonstrate that deriding labels such as "wimp" did not in any way characterize him. Like Reagan, he was a "man's man." Indeed, the height of both his credibility and popularity during his four years as president came with Operation Desert Storm. Politicians believe that this image must be maintained at all costs. To do otherwise is "unmanly." Masculinity is almost synonymous with toughness. And behind this assumed toughness lurks aggression.

The Depression and Vietnam War did not effectively alter the image of masculinity. In fact, I would argue that after periods when assaults on traditional masculine ideals are at their heights, the old definitions reemerge with a greater tenacity. This was clearly the case during the Gulf War. The Vietnam "syndrome" was "kicked out" in the Gulf War. In analyzing the gendered imagery of the war McBride (1995:45) states that

> the model of character ethics summoned forth by the president, his advisers and the mass media alike. . . . reflected a compelling need to "gender" the moral discourse of war in order to reaffirm the dominant, masculine identity of America as the world's one remaining superpower.

Contemporary masculinity cannot rely on war for validation and sports have unquestionably emerged to fill this need. Whether as player or spectator, sports build character and comradeship, provide heroes and role models, and offer stories of courage and overcoming adversity. It can be argued that even today the intellectual aspects of masculinity have not kept up with the physical aspects where sports are considered. A billion-dollar industry flourishes on contests where winning can literally call for the obliteration of the athlete. Boxing, race car driving, football, hockey, skiing, diving, and even gymnastics often brutalize competitors. Sabo (1992) maintains that sport is an area of our culture where boys learn that pain is more important than pleasure. Bodies and emotions are injured, but they are hidden or ignored for the sake of efficiency and team goals. In-depth interviews with former and current adult male athletes indicate that potential and actual injury are framed as masculinizing experiences and reinforce highly valued notions of masculinity (Young et al., 1994). With sports as such an intense masculine marker, it offers camaraderie and self-esteem for some but crippling insecurity for others (Messner, 1992). Brutalization is the price for winning friends and carving out one's place in the male pecking order (Sabo, 1992:158).

Sports violence occurs on and off the playing field, including violence toward women. Sports heroes have figured so prominently in violence toward women that efforts are being made to provide young athletes with messages that do not equate male strength with dominance over women (Katz, 1995). And scandals involving payoffs and kickbacks to athletes and college programs do not dampen the thirst for sports. The physical and mental stamina required of modern athletes allow men who are not themselves athletes to validate their own masculinity, if only in a vicarious manner.

ON MASCULINITY

As previously mentioned, masculine images have a contradictory quality which may seem confusing to men. Such contradictions are explained with particular reference to the impact of the women's movement and the media. Men are presented with alternative images which challenge the traditional version of a male mystique. In accepting these revised images as legitimate and offering more benefit than liability, it has been assumed that men would soon rally behind a new definition of masculinity. This assumption has proven false for the vast majority of American men.

Definitions of masculinity have remained remarkably consistent over time. Contemporary images flow from the past and history has demonstrated their tenacity. The women's movement helped to raise the consciousness of men concerning definitions of masculinity. At the height of the movement Robert Brannon (1976) characterized masculinity according to the following roles. And over 20 years later these roles have intensified. They will serve as a framework for approaching a variety of issues concerning masculine gender roles.

1. No Sissy Stuff: The stigma of all stereotyped feminine characteristics and qualities, including openness and vulnerability. (antifeminine norm)
2. The Big Wheel: Success, status, and the need to be looked up to. (money makes the man)
3. The Sturdy Oak: A manly air of toughness, confidence, and self-reliance.
4. Give 'Em Hell: The aura of aggression, violence, and daring.

To this list I add a fifth:

5. Macho Man: An emphasis on sexual prowess, sexual conquests, and sexual aggression.

As we will see in this chapter, in the two decades that have passed since they were formulated, these markers of masculinity have intensified.

The first characteristic admonishes males to reject any behavior which has a feminine quality. To be masculine by this standard is also to be antifeminine. Research by Thompson and his colleagues (1985) demonstrates that college males who endorse traditional male role norms are also likely to be intolerant of homosexuals and are supportive of Type A behavior where rationality and tough-mindedness are revered despite the heightened medical risks of stress-related diseases. They also disapprove of equal decision-making power with their partner or spouse.

It is the endorsement of antifemininity that is most significant here. The authors state that this does not necessarily mean misogyny is endorsed as well. It simply recognizes that the "antifeminine norm within the traditional male role is more pervasive and salient than other norms" (Thompson et al., 1985:425). However, it is difficult to separate misogyny from the antifeminine norm. The feminine labels that boys use in name-calling denigrate other boys precisely because the word is associated with a devalued group—females. During high school, Hopkins (1992:111) relates that the most popular insult/name that was used over and over again by male jocks was simply "girl."

> If a male student was annoying, they called him "girl." If he made a mistake during some athletic event, he was called "girl." Sometimes "girl" was used to challenge boys to do their masculine best (don't let us down, girl).

In reflecting on the fact that his school was a conservative Christian institution where profanity was not allowed, Hopkins observes that the blatantly sexist insulting use of "girl" by students and staff alike was an allowable and acceptable non-profane substitute for words ranging from "asshole" to "faggot" to "cocksucker" (Hopkins, 1992:112). He notes that the use of "girl" signifies a failure of masculinity.

Another consequence of the antifeminity norm is that by refusing to identify with anything that is viewed as feminine, males reduce their interpersonal skill level. If intimacy and self-disclosure are seen as feminine qualities which men must disavow, men learn to conceal their emotions. Chodorow (1993) uses a psychoanalytic perspective in explaining this norm. A young boy rejects his mother, his dependence on her, and his deep personal identification with her. He does so by repressing any sense of internal feminine elements he may have appropriated. Externally, he comes to devalue and denigrate all that he sees as feminine in the outside world. Chodorow (1993:60) contends that men may be guaranteed sociocultural superiority over women, but at the enormous expense of remaining psychologically defensive and insecure. The quest for invulnerability has the opposite effect. As documented in Chapter 2, the ultimate consequence of "no sissy stuff" can offer more liabilities than benefits.

The second theme of the "Big Wheel" suggests that men are driven to succeed at all costs. Their manliness is tied to career success and the ability to provide for their families in the breadwinner role. As Bernard (1992:207) points out, the "good provider" is also playing the "male competitive macho game" by providing for his family in a manner that other men are compelled to emulate, with families becoming display cases for his economic success. Prestige is gained from their work outside rather than inside the home. Competency as a parent is less important than competency in the world of paid labor. It is expected that the wives, children, colleagues, and peers of these men judge them accordingly. Self-esteem suffers with the loss of a job and the inability to quickly gain another one, a finding that is consistent for many Western cultures. Research from Australia shows that for males, suicide rates and annual unemployment rates are highly correlated (Morrell et al., 1993). Employment is also highly correlated with social support and physical and mental well-being (Ross and Mirowsky, 1995; Thoits, 1995). Men are told that ensuring the family's financial security is their top priority in life, a message that eclipses every other role. In old age men experience less continuity in values than women, but they express more dissatisfaction as they begin a process of life review (Helterine and Nouri, 1994).

In the occupational sphere, Astrachan (1993) contends that men are threatened by women's competence and their entry into traditional masculine occupations, thereby kindling controversy about what constitutes a "man's" job. Blue-collar men express the most hostility, but the resistance comes from men in the professions as well. These feelings relate to both the antifeminine and success themes. They may believe that their jobs will take on the taint of something feminine, hence unmanly. An influx of women in an occupation decreases its attractiveness to men, but males who work in predominantly female fields have more advantages than females in these fields (Reskin and Roos, 1990; Williams, 1993b). From a symbolic interaction view, a cycle of labeling occurs. The job is "feminized," men desert it, working conditions deteriorate, and pay decreases. The job is resegregated, going from almost all men to almost all women. A self-fulfilling prophecy occurs originating from the "Big Wheel" concept of masculinity. Success at a job where women are doing essentially the same work can be demeaning for men who favor conventional gender roles. Males remain bound by a concept of masculinity which assumes occupational dominance of women and a strong breadwinner role, with their self-esteem tied to both. Females reinforce the label by viewing men as "success objects."

Men also face confusion when they are challenged by the reality of a new economy which has transformed the traditional provider role for men. As discussed earlier, dual-earner couples are not the exception but the norm. Egalitarian attitudes and intellectual companionship are expressed by both men and women, but a retrenchment favoring the conventional norm of male superiority in terms of success and the "Big Wheel" theme remains. When wives work outside the home, both husbands and wives, but particularly husbands, are reluctant to define her role as a co-provider (Potucheck, 1992; Spade, 1994). Conflict theory suggests that the reason married men embrace traditional ideology linked to the breadwinner role is that is gives them privileges in the home to which they perceive the breadwinning role entitles them.

The success orientation is associated with the traditional norm of male intellectual superiority. The feminist movement ushered in the idea of intellectual companionship between the genders, which conflicts with the older norm. The traditional pattern, with few modifications, is still strong. Women are admired for their careers but should take full responsibility for child care and household responsibilities. Careers should be interrupted to do so. More importantly, males expect that the husband should be the superior achiever and are threatened by equal achievement in occupational roles between husband and wife. Pride and self-esteem are lowered in the eyes of young men if they see their future wives as "winning" over them occupationally. In research on gender-related attitudes of college men, Willinger (1993) finds that in the last decade there has been a reemphasis on work roles for men and maternal roles for women. She states that men's attitudes are as strongly influenced by the social and historical period in which they live as they are by personal experiences and structural characteristics. This suggests that cultural mandates for the "Big Wheel" image of masculinity linked to the all pervasive provider role remain entrenched.

The "Sturdy Oak" perspective of masculinity tells men to be tough and independent. He must express confidence in his ability to carry out tasks that appear insurmountable. He must do so with a sense of stoicism which shows he is in command of the situation. Again, the antifeminine element intrudes here by implying that compliance and submissiveness are the negative qualities which the "Sturdy-Oak" male disdains. The henpecked husband of the Dagwood Bumstead variety possesses such qualities. The opposite of the "Sturdy Oak" is the "wimp." It is truly frightening that the rise of the "wimp" is associated with men who relate to their wives and are sensitive and understanding of their children (Cose, 1995:93).

We have seen that manliness as connected to aggression has been central throughout history, and the "Give 'Em Hell" theme endures today. Boys learn early that turning the other cheek is less respected than fighting one's way out of a difficult situation, especially if bullied. The media reinforce these images by directing stories at youngsters that show war comprised of guts and glory on the battlefield of honor. As a nation we readily bestow the title of hero on those who come out on top through the use of physical means. Diplomats who quietly work behind the scenes hammering out vital peace agreements are less likely to command public admiration than frontline soldiers. President Jimmy Carter, who pursued a diplomatic solution to the Iran hostage situation, was seen as soft for his refusal to use military channels. The aborted rescue attempt was a way to escape some of this pressure.

It can be argued that aggression, even war, is necessary at times. By socializing boys into a masculinity with the aura of violence and aggression surrounding it, the soldier role, which they may eventually assume, will be easier to accept. In this view, the aggressive masculinity needed in wartime is latently functional. Such views are again linked to the antifeminity norm. Toughness, the repression of empathy, and less concern for moral issues are deemed essential if the goal is winning. In the name of political realism, the human cost of war is set aside (Gerson, 1993:32). The problem with this view is that aggression and masculinity become inextricably linked and carry over into the nonwar existence of men. A soldiering mentality is maladaptive in a man's daily life, but he hauls its baggage as surely as a battlefield pack.

The final theme is the "Macho Man" image which portrays manliness in terms of sexual ability, an image that is basic to contemporary masculinity. Male sexual identity, according to Stoltenberg (1995:68), is experienced only in "sensation and action, in feeling and doing, in eroticism and ethics." Indeed, the image of men as primarily sexual beings even questions their motives for semen donation. Gamete donation is a medical practice where semen or eggs are donated by third parties to enable infertile couples to become parents. While both are needed and accepted, egg donation is seen as asexual and altruistic, but semen donation is viewed more suspiciously in the context of dubious sexual motives (Haimes, 1993).

The man who is seen as impotent is cast into a stigmatized, demeaned category since the term is used to describe more than just his penis. Sexual performance is used to confirm his masculinity, with success in sex linked to success in life. Making love becomes an achievement endeavor (Keen, 1991). Mostly used as a front, boys develop stories and routines documenting their sexual escapades and describing successful pick-ups ploys. Among white male adolescents, friends are often chosen on the basis of sexual activity rather than sexual activity being influenced by friends' behavior (Miller et al., 1993:61). As boys mature and strive to be "masculine," they soon understand that credibility is achieved with male peers through sexual talk and some sexual behavior, both laced with aggressive overtones and unflattering remarks about girls (Fine, 1992:137).

The kind of script that relies on sexual function to describe masculinity inevitably leaves males vulnerable. Tiefer (1993:597) calls for a transformation of sexuality from a rigid standard defining masculine adequacy to one that does not impose control but instead affirms relating and cooperation. She aptly points out that in pursuing the illusion of masculinity, one set of anxieties will be exchanged for another.

The cultural construction of masculinity encompasses a series of inflexible elements. They stay as defining characteristics in spite of evidence attesting to their negative consequences for men as well as women. For a time it was thought that the older labels were on the decline and that sensitivity and openness could be added to the accepted male role. Gross (1992:429) points out that the characterization of a heterosexual man as an exploitive sexual animal exists alongside a man as competent lover who is striving to create pleasure for his partner. The latter, more "sensitive" view is not particularly progressive or egalitarian if masculinity is still associated with control. The male takes charge of sexual activity and decides the sequence, the pace, the positions, and how best to stimulate his partner. Women may want to lead or communicate other needs. This can be difficult for a goal-oriented male who has not been socialized into thinking he "might also gain pleasure from being receptive to his partner in the sexual sphere" (Rabinowitz and Cochran, 1994:98).

Both genders adhere to quite rigid views of masculinity. Men in particular are threatened by changes in definitions of masculinity regardless of the virtual impossibility of meeting the traditional standards. Social change has influenced the male role, whether it is acknowledged or not. Reflecting cultural lag, changes in attitudes take a longer time. As far as masculinity is concerned, the more things change, the more they remain the same.

HOMOPHOBIA

Men are discouraged from entering the domain of women's work, whether inside or outside the home. The decision to reject the "world of women" is due less to economic than to social and psychological factors. Contemporary American society can be described as **homophobic**, defined as fear, loathing, and/or overall intolerance expressed in both prejudicial attitudes and discriminatory behavior against homosexuals (gay men and lesbians) and homosexuality. Homophobia is such an integral part of heterosexual masculinity, that being a man means not being a homosexual (Badinter, 1995:115).

Males disapprove of homosexuality more than females and are more intolerant of gay men than lesbians (Astin, 1985; Lehne, 1992; Herek, 1994). Homophobia functions to reinforce culturally stereotyped definitions of masculinity, particularly the antifeminine norm. The most devastating label a young boy can receive from his peers is that of *sissy* or *queer*. Homophobia is learned early. The vast majority of teenage males express disgust and intolerance concerning images of homosexual men (Marsiglio, 1993). As adults, men still fear the labels of gay, faggot, or homosexual. "Men devalue homosexuality then use this norm of homophobia to control other men in their male roles" (Lehne, 1992:389). Men thereby distance themselves from any behavior suggestive of these labels.

The traditional male role encourages homophobia for several reasons. First, women and anything perceived as feminine are less valued than men and anything perceived as masculine, so why would a man take on roles offering fewer rewards? Second, men generally accept pervasive myths about gays and homosexuality. As we shall see, although these myths are generally untrue, are uniformly negative and incredibly powerful. Men see little if any need to seek out the facts because, just by doing so, they may be threatened by a homosexual label. Finally, early socialization offers few alternative models for boys other than the rigid standard of masculinity already described. Boys learn quickly that gestures of intimacy with other males are discouraged and that any expression of femininity, verbally or nonverbally, is not tolerated. Culturally inbred homophobia keeps teenage boys in particular from expressing feelings toward other boys on pain of being ridiculed as "queers" (Strikwerda and May, 1992). Male role models—fathers, teachers, and brothers—provide the cues and sanctions to ensure compliance on the part of the young boy.

In school, boys strictly segregate themselves from girls to bolster their formative masculinity. But that very segregation means that intimacy with other boys must be achieved in other culturally acceptable ways. Throughout childhood and into adult life, male camaraderie occurs in male-only secret clubs, fraternal organizations, the military, sports teams, or the neighborhood tavern. Garfinkel (1985:106) suggests that even though men are taught that intimacy among males is taboo, the desire to have at least some opportunity for informal interaction is so strong that men must form separate groups. The gregarious propensities which all people need are acted out in safety from a broader society which would otherwise be suspicious of such close male interaction. Letich (1991:85) contends that men rarely talk about friendship. "Instead we hear about something called male bonding, as if all possible non-sexual connection between men is rooted in some crude instinctual impulse," and even this is viewed as something either "terribly juvenile or possibly dangerous." Homophobia blocks the expression of the deepest feelings of affection between men.

Homophobia also takes its toll on gay men who undergo the same socialization processes as heterosexual men. Gay relationships, sexual and otherwise, demonstrate the impact of socialization into masculinity and its homophobic stance. For example, a machismo element is steadily growing in the gay subculture. Exaggerated masculinity taking the form of dress (leather, motorcycle regalia, military uniforms), rough language, and potentially violent sexual encounters may result. Gay machismo is popular, Humphries (1985) believes, because it allows gays to present an image of masculinity which they have been taught is the proper one. Sexual potency, power, and control are its integral characteristics. But the adoption of a standardized, stereotyped view distorts reality because it is merely an approximation. The man is still gay and is "open to being a scapegoat for the fears of others" (Humphries, 1985:79).

Beyond becoming a scapegoat for others, gay men must contend with their own feelings of self-worth in a society which labels them as deviant. The message gays receive from the heterosexual world is that "I am straight, correct, normal, and good. You are abnormal, wrong, deviant, and bad" (Garfinkel, 1985:167). By internalizing the negative labels of the dominant group, minorities such as gay men may learn to accept the stereotyped, pejorative view of themselves. The other side of homophobia is its counterpart in gay persons: "self-loathing" and the guilt and shame associated with their sexual orientation (Shidlo, 1994). Self-hatred is a common result.

In challenging the notion that heterosexuality is universal, the emergence of a gay rights movement has helped gays to affirm positive identities and the right to sexual self-determination (Kinsman, 1992:491). In this manner, both individual and political agendas are being met. Patterned after the women's movement to some extent, one faction of the movement is working to escape the bonds of a sexist culture where they recognize the common oppression they share with women. Abandoning restrictive role playing with women and casting aside the emotional straightjackets which keep men distant from one another are avenues currently being pursued. In the gay community's longstanding critique of stereotyped masculinity, the men's movement has learned from this group that men need to be more emotionally open to other men as well as to women (Williams and Doyle, 1994). There are increasing numbers of gay men who have recognized that homosexuals and women share a common bond of oppression (Kleinberg, 1992). On the other hand, there is a small but significant segment of gay men who recognize that in a society which sees women and gay men as subordinate, men can use their male advantage to deal with their own oppression regardless of how it undermines women, such as in the workplace. This response can be explained from a conflict-minority perspective with reference to how oppressed classes are stratified. Male remains higher in the stratification system than female. What is recognized is simply the power of socialization. Males are socialized into accepting standards of masculinity to which they continue to adhere, whether they are gay or not.

HUSBANDS AND FATHERS

Can men have it all? We usually connect this phrase with women who want to combine a satisfying career with marriage and children. Ideas of femininity have been flexible enough to accommodate women with such aspirations.

Masculinity norms are more inflexible. They dictate that men take on the responsibilities of parenthood primarily through their breadwinning roles.

Like women, most men want marriage and children. Men envision the American Dream as a successful career, contented children, and a beautiful and understanding wife who is good in bed (Hamill, 1986). Idealism notwithstanding, men willingly abdicate daily family living duties to their wives. They are stunned with the realization that fatherhood means more than a weekly paycheck and picnics with the family. Hamill believes that career priorities for men do not allow for the broader education they really need for other family roles. Males cannot segment their lives into convenient packages which deny them the opportunities to take on parenting chores. Images of success for men do not presently include diapers. Contrary to what many women and men believe, men do not "have it all." Men can be better fathers and husbands, but not if they continue to enter marriage as if they were accepting parts in a movie (Hamill, 1986:82).

Fatherhood means more than paternity. The word *fathering* is associated with sexual and biological connotations. The word *mothering* is associated with nurturance. The biological father who takes his economic responsibilities to his family seriously has met the necessary criterion for masculinity in American culture. This narrow outlook disregards, even belittles, those men who want to expand their parenting and other household duties. This is reinforced by the myth of the maternal instinct which can have devastating effects for fathers. It promotes the idea of an exclusive attachment of mother to child and legitimizes the exclusion of the father (Badinter, 1995:63).

The demeaning stereotypes of bumbling men who do not know the proper way to hold a baby or turn on a washing machine persevere. A column on "laundry-impaired men" implores women to teach men to do the wash properly, "just as soon as the playoffs are over" (Barry, 1992). The antifemininity norm of masculinity serves to bolster such images. Men who freely choose either to take care of their own children as househusbands or take care of others' children in careers like early childhood education are suspect. They must justify their existence to a skeptical society which questions their manhood. The late John Lennon was an exception to this rule. He wanted to project an image that included more than his talent for singing, songwriting, and making tremendous amounts of money. Pride in his parenting skills is shown with the following quotation shortly before his death: "I like it to be known that, yes, I looked after the baby and I made bread and I was a househusband and I am proud of it" (Gerzon, 1982:207). He apparently disdained the sex object, macho rock-and-roll image into which he had been cast.

Although fathers traditionally have had fewer expectations built into their roles as far as socialization of the children is concerned, the child-care roles they do take have been important ones. We have already seen that fathers, especially in the working class, are stricter overall in gender-typed intentions for their children. As indicated earlier, with the notable exception of fathers as single parents, in all socioeconomic classes males are given less latitude than females in experimenting with different role definitions.

A replication study by Intons-Peterson (1985) comparing fathers today with those of 30 years ago in terms of what aspirations they hold for their children shows how these socialization patterns continue. Sons and daughters are still gender-typed by their fathers but with the qualification that both should receive college degrees. The college degree, however, provides a different option for the son rather than the daughter. Fathers continue to pay close attention to the breadwinning role of their sons. In sum, gender stereotyping occurs in an atmosphere of more latitude in roles, but much less so in boys, and much less so in the working class. For the middle and upper classes, socialization of sons extends from a Victorian standard where father is distant, gone much of the time, and sons were sent off to prep school, thus minimizing contact during the formative years. Fathers were mysterious beings who wielded power in the household but who distanced themselves from it. A hundred years later we can see the vestiges of Victorian standards in the father's role.

To make parenthood more of a partnership, fathers and children need to be brought closer together. Recent research suggests this is what is highly desired by fathers. In interviews with new fathers, Cohen (1993) finds that the majority offer role definitions where nurturing was put on an equal or higher footing than breadwinning. Fathers mention repeatedly that they want to be role models, teachers, companions, and playmates to their children. As one 31-year-old retail manager says,

> I think the most important responsibility is that of nurturing the child. . . . it's important for fathers to be with a child as much as mothers . . . . they ought to try to make it possible, even if it means giving up something. (Cohen, 1993:12)

Desire for more nurturant activities by fathers is tempered with reality that makes this difficult to achieve. A father's participation in family life is enhanced when expanded role definitions are accepted on all fronts. Wives, other family members, friends, and co-workers can be supportive of men who take on a variety of not just child rearing but child maintenance responsibilities. Family-supportive workplace policies which allow flextime and paternity leave serve nurturing purposes as well. One problem is that even when such options are available, few fathers avail themselves of these opportunities. Leaves are often unpaid so sometimes they are luxuries new parents cannot afford. But as Pleck (1993:231) notes, a general disincentive to paternity leave is that employers and co-workers have negative attitudes about them. While they look great on paper the "first guy that uses it will have an arrow in his back" (quoted in Pleck, 1993:231). The rigidity of the masculine role repeatedly intrudes.

Another mechanism is the father's inclusion in the childbirth experience—from training to be a labor coach and preparenting classes to the delivery room itself. Brown (1994) describes the Lamaze class he attended with 12 pregnant couples in their thirties. While he jokes about how women control the class and the entire moral discourse of the subject of childbirth, there is an underlying fear in the message he conveys. The fears are associated with motherhood and the physical pain of childbirth, with fatherhood and the isolation men feel during their wives' pregnancy. Compared to the recent past, these classes have at least cracked opened the door for contemporary expectant fathers. Earlier images portrayed them as nervously pacing in the waiting room until the doctor brings him news of the birth. Until the mid-1960s, fathers were kept out of the delivery room, and even now some hospitals discourage fathers from remaining with their wives throughout the whole birth process. The father is viewed as an irrelevant appendage who gets in the way when his wife needs to be calm. Gerzon (1982:203) argues that males are not destined biologically to be remote from their infants and that being present at childbirth offers a bond which will never be erased. After sharing in the birth of the child, the marriage itself is likely to be stronger, particularly if the father is involved in child care, including trips to the pediatrician's office (Mooney, 1985:100).

At childbirth, men are constrained by a double standard built into their role. They are encouraged today to actively participate, but at the same time they are seen as outsiders (Shapiro, 1987). Shapiro states that while we view pregnancy and motherhood as positive, there is no corresponding view for the expectant father. Except for his laughable nervousness, his fears are not addressed. Fear of his wife's death during childbirth and anxiety over new family responsibilities are two concerns most men have but rarely discuss. While fatherhood is a major transition, their feelings are overlooked, with most attention turned toward the mother (Strong and DeVault, 1992:279). When natural fears experienced by expectant fathers are discussed openly and unashamedly with their spouses, relationships are deepened. The therapeutic and medical communities must be aware of their own stereotypes in working with expectant fathers. The evidence is clear that benefits will be realized for the marriage and for later parenting.

Divorced fathers must contend with restrictions on their parenting role when many would like to take on more responsibilities for their children. Many get depressed and anxious when they feel cut off from their children. Masculine gender roles often interfere with responsible parenting. We have documented the bleak statistics concerning child support payments by fathers. When a joint-custody arrangement is determined, child support payments increase (Fox et al., 1995), perhaps because it allows for more self-esteem on the part of the father. In investigating postdivorce father absence, Arendell (1992:565) finds that men engage in a "masculinist discourse of divorce," which is buttressed by a "gendered ideology or masculinist ethic." Using symbolic interactionist imagery, Schwalbe (1992:29) argues that a masculinist self flows from a male supremacist society which causes men to adopt a narrow moral self. Once a narrow moral self is internalized, men lack the impulses to engage in the type of role taking necessary for responsible moral action. For many men, postdivorce absence is a strategy aimed at controlling their ex-spouses. The refusal to pay child support is described as a legitimate response to unfair treatment by the courts and as a way of punishing their former wives. Their children suffer as well. These regrettable practices suggest that fathers may be "locked in" by a system shaped by gendered ideology which discourages "reciprocally nurturant postdivorce relationships" (Arendell, 1992:582).

MEN AT MIDDLE AGE AND IN LATER LIFE

The idea that men at midlife, around the ages of 40 to 55, experience a crisis of sorts has been debated by professionals seeking to explain a series of physical and emotional symptoms which appear unique to this group. Some researchers argue that this stage is a normal and even healthy time of life because it allows all people to have the opportunity to make choices and change their lives. Others view this life stage as an unsettling transition for people who believe their "social clocks" are "off-time" (Hayslip and Panek, 1993:31). Decisions made earlier in life influence the time they have left. The result is a major change in how they view themselves. Research fails to document the existence of a midlife crisis for most people, although women report more uncertainty in their lives when they were in their twenties than at later ages (Cavanaugh, 1993:272). The subject is complex, and there is no consensus about what actually constitutes a midlife crisis. But some men fit the profile that a crisis occurs somewhere during middle age that creates significant psychological turmoil and social difficulties. It is variously referred to as the male climeractic, male menopause, or midlife crisis where many men present symptoms of night fears, drenching sweats and chills, and depression which, upon investigation, have no specific cause.

Male menopause is associated with a sharp decline in testosterone for a few men but most experience a slow but gradual change where there is considerable hormonal variation. Unlike women where there is more noticeable change heralding the cessation of menses, in normal aging for men, the changes are subtle. Older men retain much of their interest in sex, but the performance of their sex organs becomes less predictable. A new testoterone patch recently approved for prescription use may help menopausal men in boosting their mood, libido, and energy (Schieszer, 1996). Gender scripts linking masculinity to sexual performance create a fear of impotence. As Atchley (1994:126) states, ill health can influence sexual arousal, but "fear of impotence can literally make that fear come true." Thus hormonal changes must be considered in light of social and psychological factors. Men at midlife become acutely aware that time is finite. They sense their own mortality and review their accomplishments and their goals, many times focusing on what they have not done rather than what they have done. Unless the man alters his environment to produce a more optimistic mindset, his health can be adversely affected.

Some men turn to family to sustain them when they realize that a career orientation cannot meet all their needs. As we saw in Chapter 2, contrary to the stereotype, women experience an upturn in life satisfaction and psychological well-being when the children are launched. For men, they discover that their children have been launched and may regret the fact that contact with them has been limited due to career priorities. There is some evidence that men may experience more psychological difficulty with the departure of their children than women (Smolak, 1993:286). In an attempt to recapture the lost parenting experience, men may turn to grandchildren. Grandchildren provide a sense of biological continuity and emotional self-fulfillment. Grandparenting for many men is a rewarding, emotional time, and the aloof, stern family patriarch is the stereotypical exception. Grandfathers are frequently the soft spot in man-to-man relationships. As Garfinkel (1985:45) notes, the grandfather "is quite possibly one of the very few men in a man's world with whom you were practically guaranteed to be free of power struggles, competitiveness and ego-class."

The significant personal transition of midlife and elderly men has been associated with both negative and positive consequences. On one hand, satisfying grandparenting roles, a revitalization of the marriage, and more freedom from breadwinning responsibilities are positive outcomes. Given that satisfying marital relationships typify older couples, it is not surprising that at the loss of a spouse, men choose to remarry and do so at faster rates than women. Men who are inexperienced in looking after themselves want to remarry in part because their wives can provide these domestic services (Hayslip and Panek, 1993). Marriage prospects remain bright for widowers, with many embarrassed by all the attention they receive from older women who want to "do" things for them (Atchley, 1994). In addition to the number of women of their own age or younger who are available to widowers as potential dating or mating partners, men are better off financially to actually support a spouse. Men may have a stronger need to be remarried so they move quickly through the dating stage to make that a reality (Hess and Soldo, 1985). Adjustment to widowhood may be different for men and women, but it remains unclear as to which gender fares better.

On the other hand older men are at higher risk for depression and suicide, particularly those who experienced an unresolved midlife crisis. Gender roles are important in interpreting suicide rates occur among older, isolated white males (Canetto and Lester, 1995). Older couples are at higher risk for divorce if they "stayed together for the sake of the children." Older divorced or widowed men are at higher risk for a range of psychological problems. The role of widower is much more vague than that of widow. Adjustment may be more difficult because men lose their most important source of emotional support and probably their major, if not only, confidant. Wives typically take responsibility for maintaining the couple's social calendar and network of friendships. Lacking the strategies for either preserving or reestablishing primary relationships, widowers have reduced social contacts (Norris, 1994). Retirement increases social isolation. Widowhood intensifies it. The net result is a loss of significant personal relationships. Older men are also less likely prepared to take on the everyday domestic responsibilities necessary for taking care of themselves. Combined with a gender role which discourages sharing personal concerns with others, when ongoing relationships and customary responsibilities are shattered, **anomie** or normlessness can follow. This pattern helps explain the high suicide rate of elderly men.

The provider role script for males sharpens an already strong American work ethic from which identity and self-esteem are gained. The transition to retirement requires major adjustments in all phases of life. While most men express a preference for early retirement (Hooyman and Kiyak, 1993), they have a great deal of psychological investment in the world of paid employment. Available data now suggest that retirement satisfaction is based on the same factors for men and women (Calasanti, 1993). A sense of purpose and intrinsic satisfaction are associated with employment. But for those men who have strongly identified with traditional gender roles and overinvested themselves in the world of paid work, retirement can bring depression rather than freedom.

A man's heightened sense of self during midlife can be useful for reintegration of the masculine and feminine traits which our culture mandates as being separate for most of a man's life. His masculine drive is tempered by a more well-rounded personality which takes into account his roles of husband and father as well as breadwinner. Gilligan (1982a; 1982b) suggests that women approach midlife differently than men and that their ethic of caring needs focus on themselves more than others. Men are seeking greater interdependence at old age, whereas women are seeking greater autonomy. At this stage men become more nurturant and women more independent. Her capability of standing apart from him may help relieve him of the burden of responsibility he feels he has carried for the family. It is interesting that the woman who grows in assertiveness and independence provides the best source of support for a man in this phase of life. Each spouse may begin to loosen the bonds of restrictive gender roles as they make the transition from middle to old age.

VIOLENCE AGAINST WOMEN

It is abundantly clear that the acceptance of traditional masculine gender roles in a patriarchal society is closely connected with escalating violence toward women. As noted above, masculine scripts call for antifemininity, status and the need to be revered, toughness, self-reliance, aggression, and sexual conquest. In a society emphasizing individualism and economic achievement through competition, there are functional elements in certain of these scripts. However, the maladaptive dysfunctions are evident in many contexts, such as compromised psychological and physical health in men, and they are most vividly documented in violence against women. In a world that grants permission to men to subordinate women, sexual terrorism is a common result. According to Sheffield (1995:3), "sexual terrorism includes nonviolent sexual intimidation and the threat of violence as well as overt violence."

Rape

The threat of sexual terrorism, especially rape, is so all pervasive that firsthand experience is not needed to instill rape fear in women. Representations of rape in the media serve to legitimize male aggression and reinforce gender stereotypes. According to Freeman (1993), the media lessons from coverage of the Kennedy Smith and Mike Tyson rape trials provided a disciplinary function to women. Rape fear is heightened and women's freedom of movement is restricted even further. But press coverage ignores the fact that women can and do escape rape and that there are four attempted rapes for every one completed. Sensationalist reporting exaggerates a woman's helplessness and instills a lack of confidence in her ability to fight back (Rozee, 1996). Research indicates that women have avoided being raped by a combination of yelling and fighting back (Herzog, 1993). The burden of responsibility falls on women to always protect themselves, to always be on the alert, to always avoid vulnerable places. Pharr (1995:483) states that fear of rape is not so commonplace that it is unacknowledged but shapes women's lives and curtails their freedom.

Until recently, rape had been viewed as a crime committed by a few demented men of lower intelligence who have uncontrollable impulses. These few psychotic men cannot be responsible for the staggering statistics on rape and attempted rape indicating 1 in every 12 women is at risk (Federal Bureau of Investigation, 1993). Considering that rape is differentially defined by legal standards, by both victims and perpetrators, and according to context of occurrence, such as marital or nonmarital, even this figure may be an underestimate. Rapes reported to police are a fraction of all rapes (Koss, 1992). A major problem in using victimization surveys to determine the extent of physical and sexual abuse of women is in underreporting, especially when the abuser is a male intimate (Smith, 1994). Both in the United States and Canada, almost 30 percent of college women report a rape or attempted rape (Barnes et al., 1991; Koss et al., 1994). As for the perpetrators, the reality is that there is no consistent personality type that reliably distinguishes rapists from other groups and that men are not psychotic at the time of the rape (Scully and Marolla, 1990:65). A number of surveys on college males asking them if there was any chance they would rape a woman if they could be assured they would not be punished show that about one-third admit to it as at least a slim possibility (Meyers, 1996:461). Despite substantial empirical evidence to the contrary, rape myths persist (see Box 9-1) and sexual aggression toward women increases.

Rape is behavior learned by men through interaction with others which is consistent in critical ways with socialization into masculinity. Violence and male sexuality are blended. Rape is sexually aggressive behavior and therefore masculine behavior. When sex is viewed as a male entitlement, it suggests that when a woman says "no," rape is a fitting way of conquering the "offending" subject (Scully, 1993:234). Such behavior reestablishes traditional male dominance. Patriarchy expresses the theme of domination, with rape as the end logic of masculine sexuality (Kokopeli and Lakey, 1995:451).

BOX 9–1   Rape Myths

Myth	Reality
1. Rape is a sexual act.	Rape is an act of violence to show dominance of the rapist and achieve submission by the victim.
2. Rapes are committed by strangers.	Rape is more likely to occur between acquaintances. Date rape is an example.
3. Most rapes are spontaneous, with the rapist taking advantage of the opportunity to rape.	Rape is likely to be preplanned. If spontaneity occurs, it may be an added "bonus" to a robbery.
4. Women wear provocative clothing or flirt with men.	This is the classic blaming the victim myth. Since most rapes are preplanned, the rapist will strike regardless of appearance.
5. Women enjoy being raped.	The pain, violence, degradation, and psychological devastation experienced by the victim are overwhelming. Consider, too, that she may be killed while being raped.
6. Most rapists are psychopathic or sexually abnormal.	It is difficult to distinguish the rapist from other men in terms of personality or ideas about sexuality.
7. When she says no to sex she really means yes.	When she says no she really means no.

Because we exist in a culture which still condones relationships between men and women which are aggressive-passive and dominant-submissive, definitions of masculinity are associated with overtones of force and violence (Herman, 1989). Socialization into masculinity is reinforced by stereotypes concerning women. The rape myths mentioned above are imbued with such images. Another example is the belief that women want to be dominated by men. This rationalizes men's violent behavior in rape as an expression of that domination. Blaming the victim justifies the crime. Also, if women are viewed as passive, sex is something that is done "to them." Deckard (1983:431) asserts that the very words *fuck* and *screw* signify both sexual intercourse and "doing someone in." Men not only dominate but sexually conquer passive women. The rape fulfills the prophecy of the stereotypical image.

With so many men admitting that rape is a possibility, the profile of the rapist is difficult to determine. Rape is a crime perpetrated by a wide spectrum of men. Although there are certain characteristics shared by some rapists, these must be viewed with caution since incarcerated men and convicted rapists usually make up the samples. Rape convictions are fewer in comparison to other crimes. It is therefore not surprising that an estimated 2 to 3 percent of men who rape outside of marriage actually go to prison (Beneke, 1992:370). In one case, a judge freed a man who had pleaded guilty to rape because the victim was "such a pitiful woman" and "anyone who could be so stupid to take up with this woman deserves some consideration" (*St. Louis Post-Dispatch*, 1990). Women who do call the police risk being demeaned as a result. It is only recently that some municipalities have incorporated counseling and more humane approaches in questioning victims of rape. And for rape trials, many courts will no longer allow the sexual history of the victim as part of the proceedings. Unfortunately, the victim herself is still often treated like the criminal.

Given the problems of accurate statistics, the following profile of the rapist is at best a tentative one. He appears to have a high need for dominance and a low need for nurturance. He deals with his perceived inadequacies by aggression and the sexual control of women. Socially insecure and interpersonally isolated, his aggression is likely to be followed by expressions of remorse. He sees himself as compelled to rape. He justifies his behavior in terms of rape stereotypes that he has learned as a member of society. In doing so, his victim is made to seem culpable. The rape act is presented in socially acceptable terms. Sexual violence is used as a means of revenge or punishment (Malamuth, 1989; Scully and Marolla, 1990; McElhiney, 1993b; Scully, 1993). The following comments by convicted rapists reported by Scully's (1990; 1993) research serve as examples of these beliefs:

> Rape gave me the power to do what I wanted to do without feeling I had to please a partner . . . I felt in control, dominant.

> I have never felt that much anger before . . .The rape was for revenge. I didn't have an orgasm. She was there to get my hostile feelings off on.

> Rape is a man's right. If a woman doesn't want to give it, the man should take it. Women have no right to say no.

It is not difficult to understand why this profile is a sketchy one. It can fit many men.

This assertion is accurate considering the growing recognition that date or acquaintance rape is a fact of life on college campuses, with data indicating that half of college men have engaged in some form of sexual aggression on a date, with between one-fourth and one-half of college women reporting being sexually victimized (Herman, 1989; Koss et al., 1987, 1994). Despite these high numbers, when victim and offender know one another, it is less likely to be reported and even less likely to gain a criminal conviction. From a legal point of view, the "ideal" rape victim is one who is raped by a stranger, is a virgin, had obvious physical damage, had an eyewitness, and was of a different race than the perpetrator (Holmstrom and Burgess, 1988). Date rape can never satisfy these criteria (Rickel et al., 1993). Date rape is also associated with alcohol use, the belief that men are entitled to sex after initiating and paying the expenses of the date, fraternity parties, and length of time the couple has been dating, with more rapes occurring on the first few dates (Goodchilds et al., 1988; Shotland, 1989; Hirsch, 1990; Richardson and Hammock, 1991; Martin and Hummer, 1993). Dating violence among adolescents and college students is so prevalent because the structure of dating gives men more power (White and Bondurant, 1996). Given that these characteristics are also indicative of a masculinity ethic to which men feel they must adhere, date rape may be considered an outgrowth of socialization into masculinity.

Pornography and sexually explicit material as factors in sexual aggression have come under much scrutiny. Aggressive stimuli, like rape scenes and erotic films, stimulate sexual arousal (Silbert and Pines, 1984; Briere and Malamuth, 1985). Males exposed to pornography which focuses on sexual violence become desensitized and see rape victims as both less injured and less worthy (McManus, 1986). Whether the arousal actually leads to later aggression has not been fully determined. Gray (1990b:217) contends that it is anger that is a greater social problem than pornography and that it is most dangerous in men who cannot effectively distinguish between aggression, control of women, and sexual arousal. While the data remain incomplete on a causal link between exposure to different forms of pornography and sexual violence and rape, it is clear masculinity's antifeminine norm encourages anger toward women that pornography and other cultural components related to gender roles continue to fuel.

The issue of what actually constitutes pornography and once determined, making it illegal, is hotly debated. Much of this side of the debate focuses on pornography as a condoned symbol of a society where the victimization of women is rampant. It argues that violence against women is increasing and we are more desensitized to it and more accepting of rape myths due to exposure to pornography (Taylor et al., 1994:462). The other side contends that pornography may actually reduce sex crimes because it provides for a non-harmful release of sexual tension. This side does not deny that women's degradation is associated with pornography but that campaigns against it obscure more urgent needs of women as well as the fact that censorship historically is more likely to be used to silence feminists rather than pornographers (Rosen, 1994). There is concern in both camps that constitutional issues are involved and that banning sexually explicit material amounts to censorship. Some consensus has been reached on distinguishing pornography according to its degree of violent imagery. Both sides rely on social scientific research to support their contentions. The battle lines are clearly drawn, but to date neither side has been victorious.

Domestic Violence and Battered Women

Domestic violence encompasses a wide array of physical, sexual, and emotional abuse. Marital rape and wife beating have been commonplace throughout history, but until recently a husband's right to a wife's body was considered a personal privilege which amounted to a legal right. Most states now have some kind of legal protection for marital rape, but there is considerable variation, with 33 states allowing for spousal exemptions (Bergen, 1994). A man may be prosecuted if there is obvious and sustained physical injury, the couple had separated or filed for divorce, or if his wife is physically or mentally incapacitated. He may be exempt if she fails to report it to the police within a specified period of time, if the couple is not legally married, or if there is any hint that she consented to intercourse (Russell, 1990; Donat and D'Emilio, 1992; Bergen, 1994). While it has been estimated that 15 percent of women have been raped by their spouses or partners, the vast majority do not report it, especially if no weapon was used or no physical injury was sustained (Michael et al., 1994).

Like marital rape, the law has generally supported a man's right to beat his wife, even for such infringements as talking back to him. The infamous "rule of thumb" can be traced back to feudal times. This allowed a husband to beat his wife with a stick no bigger than his thumb. In the United States, it has only been since the end of the last century that the courts began to decide that wife beating was not a husband's right. Wife beating spans all ages, classes, and racial groups. The murder of Nicole Brown Simpson elevated the issue of domestic violence to the public consciousness with court documents clearly indicating that she had been battered by her former husband, football star O.J. Simpson (Vobejda, 1994).

Domestic abuse is the leading cause of injury to women in the United States and wife battering is the most underreported of all crimes (Brush, 1990; Russell, 1990; Goodman, 1994; Smith, 1994). The privacy of the American family and the reluctance of police to get involved in family disputes worsens the problem of getting accurate statistics on family violence in general and wife battering in particular. Underreporting is linked with the persistent belief that wife beating is either not improper or a part of "normal" marriage. Some research indicates that between 5 and 12 percent of husbands beat their wives (Straus, 1980; 1992) with other estimates ranging from 4 percent to as high as 40 percent (Resick, 1983). While it cuts across all demographic groups, it is more prevalent in families with low income and unemployment and is associated with alcohol use, family isolation, and with a husband under age 30 (Smith, 1990; Straus, 1993; Gelles, 1995). When race is factored in, black women are more than twice as likely than white women to experience more violence and more severe violence, a persistent pattern even when controlling for financial stress and quantity of alcohol use (Hampton and Gelles, 1994; Neff et al., 1995).

Between 2,000 and 4,000 women a year die at the hands of their husbands and lovers, and 30 percent of all women who are murdered are killed by husbands or boyfriends (Reid, 1991; Thomas-Lester, 1995). In a Kansas City study, 96 percent of family homicides were preceded by a call to the police for domestic disturbance (cited in Deckard, 1983:438). When abused women retaliate and kill their attackers, the courts have been reluctant to use self-defense as a justification for acquittal. A number of studies indicate justifiable homicide is accepted as the right to kill in response to a clearly lethal assault, but when applied to women, this right is viewed differently (Browne, 1987; Walker, 1989; Gillespie, 1989). Courts have also been disinclined to use evidence of "battered women's syndrome" as justification for a retaliatory attack on their husbands.

Public education on family violence has found its greatest strength in dealing with child abuse. Wife battering has not gained as much attention because it remains subtly condoned. Both men and women approve of slapping, shoving, and hitting one another under certain conditions (Gelles and Strauss, 1988). Both women and men assault one another in marriage through physical violence. Mutual abuse is more common than either alone, although the effects are more lethal for women with many more women than men needing medical attention due to marital violence (Straus, 1980; Saunders, 1989; Henslin, 1996).

When battering becomes a public issue, many express disbelief as to why women remain in abusive households. Battered women usually have a poor self-image, which contributes to their feelings of powerlessness and dependence. They may believe they are responsible for the violence against them and attempt to alter their behavior to conform to their husbands' expectations. Expressions of remorse by the batterer leads to a short-lived honeymoon period, followed by recurrence of the abuse, with the likelihood of its increasing in severity (Gelles and Cornell, 1985; Walker, 1989; Johann and Osanka, 1989; Stahly, 1996). A pattern of learned helplessness emerges for these women. The beatings are endured, they feel guilty about them, and they are unlikely to speak to others, even close friends and family, about the situation. There are many battered women who seemingly accept their situation because they feel financially trapped, especially if they have small children. Women are also at risk for increased violence if she threatens to leave, files for divorce, or calls the police. To add insult to injury (literally), insurance companies routinely deny coverage to battered women because of their dangerous lifestyle (Shen, 1995). As Erlanger (1987:44) reports, the sense of being trapped alters your thinking and leads to living in terror.

But many women do leave abusing husbands and partners, especially when helped by social and legal means. Antistalking laws have been enacted to protect celebrities from deranged fans, but battered women stalked by former husbands and boyfriends have emerged as the primary beneficiaries of them (Stahly, 1996). The advent of shelters for women and children, crisis hot lines, and self-defense classes have also helped. In St. Louis, ALIVE (Alternatives to Living in Violent Environments) has been instrumental in providing shelter and counseling for abused women and their children. It is estimated that over 100,000 women in this metropolitan area alone will suffer physical abuse. It is a beginning, but the shelter-crisis-counseling concept needs to be supplemented with public education documenting the scope of the problem. The O.J. Simpson trial provides a latent function in this regard. In reflecting on the trial, Staples (1995) reminds us that battering happens not just in Hollywood but everywhere, and that "the country has as many shelters for neglected dogs and cats as for bloodied and fearful wives."

Violence against women in general and wives in particular is an extension of a patriarchal system where men hold power over women. Egalitarian marriages have the lowest rates of violence (Yllo, 1984). The greater the inequality and the more that power resides in one person, the greater the risk of violence. Perceived threat to domination is the underlying issue in almost all acts of family violence (Gelles and Straus, 1995:374). Yet domination and control are the very characteristics which are embodied in accepted notions of masculinity.

MEN'S LIBERATION

Change cannot occur in a vacuum. As women have been taking on new roles, changes inevitably occur for men, some which they eagerly support, others which they find unpalatable. The movement for male liberation originated on college campuses as a reaction, albeit a positive one, to the feminist movement. These men recognized that their support of feminist causes and their involvement with feminist women as husbands, partners, and friends had influenced images of themselves as men. The movement began with informal consciousness-raising groups on college campuses and the formation of men's centers throughout the nation. Since the mid-1970s men interested in altering conceptions of gender roles, particularly in regard to rigid conceptions of masculinity, and who embrace a decidedly feminist stance have met nationally about once a year. The themes around which these conferences are organized vary and include issues related to parenting, sexism, violence against women, sexuality, sexual orientation, and friendship. Unlike the women's movement and the lead taken by the National Organization for Women, these conferences first focused on personal and social rather than political change.

These meetings have been instrumental in forming groups such as RAVEN (Rape And Violence End Now) in St. Louis and MOVE in San Francisco, which are concerned about the objectification of women, its toleration, and how it is violently manifest in American culture. They contend that the support system for oppressive behavior toward women is so pervasive that an individual man's decision to reject such behavior targets him for ridicule and exclusion. The following is an example from a man who tested the waters when he told an office colleague he wasn't interested in seeing pictures of nude women because he did not agree with the objectification of women. The co-worker asked him, "What's the matter, are you getting soft on us?"

> I joked it was not a matter of getting soft. . . . simply a decision I had made due to a "new and improved consciousness. . . . " By the end of the day I was being called every derogatory homosexual slur in the English language. I was no longer "one of the boys. . . ." Since men decide how masculine another man is by how much he is willing to put down women and gays, I was no longer considered masculine. (Hernandez, 1996:399)

Masculine labels serve to undermine men who refuse to go along with the system. RAVEN has since established a counseling resource and support center for men seeking to change a system in which violence against women is institutionalized. Although individual men are aided through counseling services, the organization is expanding with the intention of educating the public on abuse of women. Broader social change is a long-term goal.

The men's movement is becoming more politically oriented, with each conference more activistic in this regard than the previous one. But its lack of unity on basic goals has hampered resolutions. Most men support a liberation movement to free men from culturally restrictive roles. Beyond this, there is broad disagreement on the role of gays in the organization, the support for some feminist causes, such as abortion or male contraception, divorce and child custody laws, and the critical question of power. Some men in the movement believe that power itself creates the conditions for oppressiveness so it is to be avoided. Others see feminism as challenging men's power. Feminist men have been able to support liberal feminism's view that men and women should have equal rights, hence equal power. But in doing so they cannot continue to ignore questions related to inherited forms of masculinity. These are the very questions that will allow for changing conceptions of masculinity and for the liberation of men (Seidler, 1992).

This men's movement with its efforts at male liberation and consciousness raising related to power and the disabling effects of the masculine gender role has attracted a minority of men. Conferences consist mainly of men in the helping professions, social sciences, or from academia. Other professional men, attorneys, corporate executives, and politicians, are rarely seen. Working-class men and men of color, unless they are students, are nonexistent. This supports the contention that few men really identify with a men's movement that not only frees men from masculine stereotypes but also empowers women. Unlike the women's movement which has touched the lives of millions of women, the same cannot be said for the impact of a men's movement on men.

This lack of public awareness of the first men's movement is revealed in how the media have publicized the emergence of a second movement. Just as the women's movement became more heterogeneous and attracted a diverse array of supporters, it was almost inevitable that it would branch into different segments each focusing on a specific area of interest, but with the same overall principles. While both men's movements are concerned about the negative effects of a masculine ethos that is unrealistic, unattainable, and potentially deadly, the second movement did not emerge from the first. In fact, it has been referred to as the dawn of *the* men's movement: the first postmodern social movement stemming from a general malaise of men (Adler, 1991:47). This malaise became apparent on January 8, 1990, when Bill Moyers hosted a documentary on public television titled "A Gathering of Men" in which he introduced poet Robert Bly to a mass audience. The second men's movement was born.

Based on the idea that modern men are caught in a toxic masculinity which insists that men be autonomous, efficient, power-oriented, competitive, uncaring, and disconnected from community, earth, and each other (Bliss, 1990; Kimbrell, 1993), this movement certainly resonates with the first. However, in overcoming this toxicity, it is Bly's (1990) contention that men must first rediscover a more positive masculinity which was lost when the Industrial Revolution created a separate world of work where men were cut off from other aspects of their lives, especially from their families. In particular, it is the growing absence of fathers that is at the root of the male dilemma, since now young boys turn to women to meet their emotional needs (Meacham, 1990). With overtones from Carl Jung and through the use of images from poetry and medieval art, a male's essential, primordial masculinity that has been buried will be unearthed and celebrated (Gurian, 1992; Meade, 1993).

To find this lost masculinity and reclaim its ancient power, Bly has devised an elaborate series of rituals where men come together to open up their emotions and find the hidden "wild man" in them. At his wild men retreats, men chant, scream, and dance through a weekend where they gain communion with other men, a substitute for the missing relationship with their fathers which they erroneously seek from women (Adler, 1991:51). Meacham (1990:31) states that this does not mean that reclaiming power is also reclaiming aggression, but that masculinity is reframed beyond "one dimensional cartoon characters who perform great deeds but feel nothing." While communication is encouraged, the "sensitive" man who is out of touch with his masculinity because he turns to women as authority figures is not. With the implication that women have been partially responsible for the demise of this earlier masculinity, the second men's movement is certainly not supportive of men's "surrendering their natural birthrights of righteous anger and self-assertion" (Adler, 1991:50). It is also strikingly similar to the masculinist response of a century ago which, while indifferent to women in the public sphere, sought to dislodge women's dominance in the home where "boys were distracted from becoming men" (Kimmel, 1995). To counter this concern, all-male organizations such as the Boy Scouts and YMCA emerged. While it is still uncertain as to how this movement will impact men's relationships with one another as well as with women, it has at least focused attention on the dysfunctional aspects of the male role.

It is debatable if there has really been a rupture in the men's movement since they do not intersect on the basic question of equality of rights. The earlier movement was and remains profeminist. The promasculinist stance emerged in part as a reaction against, but not support for, the first group. Doyle (1995:9) notes that profeminists argue against men's privilege and the promasculinists seek to heal men's pain. But it can also be argued that while the profeminists would also like to heal men's pain through gender role change, promasculinists ultimately support patriarchy through continued gender segregation. Feminism is supportive overall for men coming together in exclusive male groups for healing and sharing. But when promasculinists blame women for the problems of men, it serves to undermine constructive dialogue both between men and between men and women.

The recent "Million Man March" in Washington, D.C. provides an instructive instance. Research contends that African-American males have constructed alternative definitions of masculinity in explicit opposition to Euro-American male models as well as being structurally blocked from opportunities to achieve masculine goals offered by mainstream society (Franklin, 1994; Roberts, 1994; Hunter and Earl, 1994). At age 18, African-American males report similar perspectives about masculinity as do Euro-American males, but "as they get older their views of masculinity tend to diverge" (Harris et al., 1994:703). The march on Washington was an effort to bring African-American men together in cooperation and support of one another and their communities. These men offered positive role models for society as a whole and African-American families in particular.

These efforts were met with success. However, the luster of the march was tarnished not necessarily by its promasculinist quality but by its antiwoman thrust. Unlike the United Nations Conference on Women in Beijing, women were explicitly *not* invited to join in the march. And the organizer of the march, Louis Farakhan, later applauded Iran for setting a shining example to the world on behalf of democratic principles. Given the unquestionably brutal record that Iran has regarding women, any existing schism between men and women was intensified. It is difficult to untangle the goodwill that emerged from the march with a blatantly sexist leadership that organized it.

On a more optimistic note, Gerzon (1982) believes that new masculinities are emerging which emphasize the development of a deeper awareness of the mutuality of the two genders. Gender identity is being transformed, which allows us the opportunity to acknowledge and respect its diversity. The range of masculinities and femininities is so wide that they overlap (Gerzon, 1982:236). He calls for an examination of what works and does not work in gender roles, not for a codified set of rules which define men and women, masculine and feminine. In support of this, Thompson (1995:478) calls for a new socialization for boys emphasizing nurturance and nonviolent means of resolving conflict. Accepting attitudes that have been traditionally labeled as feminine is necessary for "full human development."

Men's roles have not kept pace with the changes in women's roles. The evidence is clear that the attitudes toward masculinity have served to hamper those men seeking to free themselves from restrictive male stereotypes. The majority of men, however, are on no such quest. They quietly adhere to images and roles which society tells them are proper but which may be disabling in their effects.

CHAPTER 10

GENDER AND THE WORKPLACE
by Sandra Christie and Linda Lindsey

> From all I am able to gather, the girls make good wives. There is nothing in
> clerical training that detracts from the finest womanly qualities, and men
> have outgrown their admiration for feminine helplessness and have come
> to look upon independence as something worth having.
> —On women clerks in New York, 1891, by Clara Lanza
> (Cited in Norton and Alexander, 1996a:288)

"A woman's place is in the home!" While this may express a nostalgic preference, it is clearly not the norm in American society, nor is it the norm in most
of the world. Theoretically, the interactive affects of home and work are generally recognized. The problem is that there is a tendency to treat these inter-
relations as assumptions upon which theories can be built and supportive evidence is then gathered, rather than treating them as variables for hypothesis
testing. Consequently, the objective determination of causal factors in the
development of women's work roles and the effects of women working on
their families and on society in general are often difficult to disentangle.
Regardless, as this chapter will document, the attitude which places more value
on a woman's home-based life collides with women's work outside the home
and is associated with all levels of economic disparities existing between men
and women.

HISTORICAL OVERVIEW

Throughout both prehistory and history, women have made major economic
contributions to their societies and families through their labor. From the van-
tage of archeological evidence from prehistory through to the documentary
evidence of history, the myths of feminine fragility and the nonworking
woman are easily discounted. Through to the present day, when the activities
of foraging, horticultural, and hunting and gathering societies are examined,
women provide most of the food for their families and villages (Ehrenberg,
1993; Marti, 1993). Women have traditionally engaged in three types of production: producing goods or services at home for sale or exchange elsewhere
(cottage industry), producing goods or services for consumption within the
household itself, and working for wages outside the household. It was only with
the advent of the Industrial Revolution that men, and later women, turned to
work outside the home for wages as their major type of work (Blau and Ferber,
1992).

Women's work roles have traditionally been closely tied to the home.
Farm work required all family resources, including the extradomestic labor of
women and children. Women produced cloth from raw material, soap, shoes,
candles, and most other consumable items required in each household.

Female domestic servants in the seventeenth and eighteenth centuries produced most necessary items for their employers' households as well. Colonial women functioned as innkeepers, shopkeepers, crafts workers, nurses, printers, teachers, and child-care providers. In more remote areas, women also acted as dentists, physicians, and pharmacists. Widows and single women were most likely to work outside the home (Thornborrow and Sheldon, 1995; Norton and Alexander, 1996a).

With the advent of the water-powered textile factory in 1789, the Industrial Revolution was underway in the United States. Women and female children continued to be the producers of cloth, but now in a factory rather than at home. As exemplified by the famous Lowell Mills in Massachusetts, female employment in textile mills also reflected the lack of available surplus male labor which was still needed on the farm (Dublin, 1996). Many of the other products women traditionally produced at home gradually switched to factory manufacturing. The transition of America and Western Europe from agrarian societies to urban industrial societies took about 150 years. When the family was transformed from a unit of production to a unit of consumption, a dramatic shift occurred in both the attitudes and norms surrounding the work roles of women.

By the end of the nineteenth century, Victorian norms ascended to define middle-class women as physically and mentally incapable of working in factory settings. This attitudinal shift also impacted those working for wages in clerical and service jobs. Public disapproval combined with the reluctance of employers to hire women for any positions severely restricted their possibilities for paid work. However, as we have already seen, these patterns were indicative of Eastern urban life and for certain categories of women. Single and widowed white women remained employable in both industrial and service jobs. Farm woman throughout America and those who migrated West were not only valued for their nondomestic work roles but were also expected to engage in them. Also, doors to factories remained open for women of color and immigrant women who were judged by a different set of standards. For others who were literally tied to the home with child-care responsibilities, "homework" was an option, especially among poor immigrants. Mostly consisting of piecework, it was dependent on the whims of bosses and swings of a seasonal market and encouraged the exploitation of its dominantly female workers (Daniels, 1993). The current ideology was that women's place was at home and, as exploitative as it was, "homework" allowed the ideology to be bolstered. However, most of these other groups, through necessity, were working outside the home.

During this same time, women were establishing their control in several occupational categories including nursing and elementary and secondary teaching. Teaching was transformed into a female profession during the Civil War and was continued in part because of the shortage of men and because women could be paid less. Similarly, the two World Wars resulted in major changes in the deployment of women into new industrial areas because men were in short supply as laborers. It was during this period that women replaced men in both factories and offices. Greenwald (1980) points out that World War I mainly reshuffled existing female workers into new areas rather than increasing the overall participation rates. Until the early twentieth century, clerical work was a good-paying, male occupation. However, the invention of the typewriter in 1873 brought with it both an increase in the number of clerical jobs and female employment. Between 1870 and 1900, the number of clerical jobs increased 8 times while female employment increased 340 times, and by the late 1920s, over half of all clerical workers were female (Glenn and Feldberg, 1995). It should also be noted that as women increasingly took over the male clerical positions, there was a marked decrease in the status and wages of these positions.

After World War II, women were again told to go back home, but they did not return to hearth and home in the same proportions as after World War I. They did lose the more lucrative industrial jobs, but a new trend developed—married women began entering the labor force in greater numbers—a trend that heralded major repercussions for all areas of American society.

FACTORS INFLUENCING WOMEN'S CHOICE OF WORK, OCCUPATION, OR CAREER

This section will briefly review the factors that influence a woman's decision to work outside the home, as well as the type of employment chosen. It is difficult to separate out the impact of the various institutions on gender roles as related to work since the interaction effects are both complicated and powerful. Macrosociological theory from all traditions, including functionalism and conflict, recognizes the economic institution, in which labor force activities are placed, as the most rapidly changing social institution and the one which has a profound impact on all the others. In terms of social change, the institution of the family is the most conservative. As already documented in Chapters 7 and 8, the changes in the structure and function of the family which we have witnessed during the last 30 years attest to the powerful influence of interinstitutional linkages. With this in mind, the factors that influence the work roles of women can be divided into two broad categories. One set is more directly influenced by the family and the second set is influenced by broader sociocultural patterns.

Family Factors

Most people have two families which exert differential influences on their lives and activities. The **family of orientation** is the family in which one grows up. The **family of procreation** is the family established when one marries.

Effects of the Family of Orientation. The family of orientation's effects can be broken into three areas: socialization, status and role correlations, and differentiation of opportunity structures. As discussed in Chapter 3, socialization may be broadly defined as the inculcation of attitudes and skills needed for carrying out social roles. "Differentiation of opportunity structure" means those overt behaviors wherein parents allow children to receive necessary training and rewards because most families cannot provide all opportunities and resources for all their children. In terms of gender roles this translates into differential treatment of boys and girls for such things as toy and game selection, educational choices and opportunities, and part-time paid work. These are examples of how the family of orientation is vital to the socialization of children.

However, families do not have sole responsibility for this task, especially after the child enters the educational system. But the power of the family is evident in that by the time the child is ready to enter nursery school or kindergarten, basic gender role identities are formed. Much of this socialization directly affects later work force participation. Boys have learned to be more aggressive, competitive, and demanding, and to be more valued than girls. These traits are considered absolutely necessary for success in many occupations, especially in business and the professions.

Differential gender role identities are also fostered by the media and educational systems. Except for teaching, girls are offered few role models suggestive of work roles outside the home. Since school and home-based socialization can impact cognitive styles and creative interests, the impact on career choice then becomes obvious. Women tend to select occupations that match the creative areas and cognitive skills which they have or can acquire. The conclusion reached about the impact of a women's family orientation on her decision to work is fairly unequivocal: She is socialized to be passive, affectionate, supportive, marriage and family oriented, and noncompetitive. Women receive the message that home and family are of paramount importance and jobs are secondary to these obligations, regardless of occupational preparation.

Two trends related to institutional interdependence are challenging this. First, American ideology regarding education and equality is also operating within the family, and if possible, all children will be equally educated. For example, data now indicate that more females are attending college than males (Eisenhart, 1996). However, in accordance with the differentiation in family opportunity structure, males still benefit from the situations when resources disallow education for all children. Second, most college women assume they will combine career and family roles. The dilemma that women must still reconcile is the degree to which marriage and family responsibilities take precedence over paid work. This decision is more difficult in light of the nearly unanimous research conclusion that despite growing equity in the workplace, women retain the homemaker role and take on a "second shift" after a day of paid employment (Hochschild, 1989; Perkins and DeMeis, 1996).

Effects of the Family of Procreation. This discussion will focus on continuing socialization, the acquisition of new role-playing skills or attitudes necessitated by changes encountered in adulthood, and status and role correlations. When a woman marries, a new set of family contingencies has impact on her decision to work and her choice of occupations. The socialization process continues at this point because the woman now has new roles and statuses to consider, those of wife and eventually, mother. There is little preparation for these roles so the process appears to be one of trial and error, all the time influenced by the gender models of her family of orientation. Family structures have shifted considerably so that the family of procreation must also be considered in light of divorce and single parenting, which have great impact on work choices outside the home.

While the dual-earner family is the American norm, there is research agreement that husbands who are supportive of their wives' employment are significantly more likely to have wives working outside the home (see Chapters 7 and 8). Since women with higher educational attainment are more likely to work outside the home, these same attitudes regarding support for improving the quality and quantity of work preparation through the educational process are crucial. On the other hand, the explanations for lack of husband support are extensive and include the following: Men will no longer have a wife as a refuge from the work world; wives are male success or status symbols, especially a leisured wife; wives need to be available to support the husband's career mobility; he may be threatened by her achievements, especially if she earns more money or requires supportive work from him, or he may be less mobile if his wife also has a career.

But it is the role of mother that clearly has the greatest impact on all areas of work choices for women. Obligations of the maternal role spill over into other roles and consume increasing amounts of time and energy. Women, even those with professional careers, retain responsibility for child care, as well as housework (Wharton, 1995; Perkins and DeMeis, 1996). If a mother decides to continue or start working after the birth of a child, a factor which significantly influences her ability to carry out this decision has to do with adequate child-care arrangements. Increased demands for child care come at a time when the supply of domestic help is shrinking, grandmothers are returning to the labor force, and the necessary government support for increasing day care is not forthcoming. The "Nannygate" scandal not only prevented Zoë Baird from becoming Attorney General in 1993 but highlighted the issue of a child-care crisis that affects all working women, regardless of ability to pay for adequate care. As more women with young children are joining the labor force, both out of desire and need, this crisis must be addressed. This problem looms larger for single parents or women on welfare who are required to work or be in work training programs to retain benefits.

Career achievement is also impacted by a host of other family-related variables including age at marriage, age at childbirth, and professional status when married. Women who marry after they have completed their education and begun their career bring more maturity to their marital relationship, thus reducing the likelihood of a spouse expecting the woman to give up her career. Smaller family size is also correlated with paid employment. The percentage of employed mothers decreases rapidly for families with five children or more (U.S. Bureau of the Census, 1995). A key consequence of family-related factors on career is that a single break in employment has immediate, adverse effects which translates to lower gains in wages and job status (Fermlee, 1995). Married women with children have significantly higher rates of interrupted job mobility.

The main conclusions reached about the impact of the family of procreation on women's decisions and choice of labor force participation are unequivocal: She must perform the household domestic duties, assume primary responsibility for child rearing, and accept her husband's training or career as taking precedence over hers. A woman's age at marriage, age at childbearing, family financial condition, and marital status greatly influence whether or not she will work and the probable level of occupational advancement she will be able to attain. Finally, the availability of child care and family size also have a great deal of impact.

Sociocultural and Political Factors

The important social and cultural factors that influence employment patterns are based on institutional constraints and opportunities mostly flowing from our systems of education and training, politics, and law. Economic trends reinforce these patterns. In addition, a host of cultural values and norms converge with the various social institutions which help explain gender trends in employment. Remember, too, that each of these factors interacts with the family influences outlined above.

The more education a woman has attained, the greater the likelihood that she will engage in paid employment (U.S. Bureau of the Census, 1995:401,416). Conversely, the lower the educational attainment, the more likely a woman is a full-time homemaker. This pattern challenges the myth that those who have the choice would prefer exclusive domestic roles. By virtue of her education, she is the least likely to be financially dependent but the most likely to work outside the home. And as would be expected, there is a strong correlation between years of education and type of occupation.

Economic factors serve to enhance or impede a woman's paid employment. In times of need, such as in war, women are pressed to join the labor pool so function as a reserve labor force to be called upon or discarded as needs change. The effects of industrialization and advanced machine technology, followed by information technology, have facilitated employment for both women and men. However, the family in a consumer-oriented society exerts counterpressures for women in their consumer roles. From classic sociological theory, Veblen's (1899/1953) work on conspicuous consumption and conspicuous leisure first dealt with the phenomenon of middle-class women as consumers. The fact is that America is a consumer society and the majority of consumption is carried out by women in their family roles. Women in paid employment have less time but more money available for consumption and the American economic system has responded to this reality. The retailing sector, in particular, caters to employed women by lengthening times they are open, by locating near homes and new housing developments, through the use of mail catalogs and, increasingly, the computer marketplace.

There are numerous legal and political factors that influence women's work roles and their decisions relating to them. The Equal Pay Act (EPA) was passed in 1963 and is the first federal legislation that addresses the issue of equal pay for men and women. It allows for differences in pay based only on a nondiscriminatory seniority system, a merit-based system, or "piecework" basis. The most important legal prohibition against gender discrimination in employment is Title VII of the 1964 Civil Rights Act. While the language is not gender neutral, the following two key provisions impacting women make discrimination and occupational segregation illegal.

1. To fail or refuse to hire or to discharge any individual, or otherwise discriminate against any individual with respect to his compensation, terms, conditions, or privileges of employment, because of such individual's race, color, religion, sex or national origin; or
2. To limit, segregate, or classify his employees in any way which would deprive or tend to deprive any individual of employment opportunities or otherwise adversely affect his status as an employee, because of such individual's race, color, religion, sex or national origin. (Civil Rights Act of 1964)

The provisions of this bill are enforced by the Equal Employment Opportunity Commission (EEOC), whose powers of enforcement were strengthened in 1972 by Executive Orders 11246 and 11375 which extended the provisions of the Civil Rights Act legislation to all federal contracts. Title IX of the 1972 Educational Amendments further extended them to all educational programs or activities receiving federal funding. EPA and Title VII of the Civil Rights Act have allowed the "equal work for equal pay" doctrine to resound throughout the American economy and it is difficult to circumvent them in any kind of formal way. However, both laws are vulnerable to the gendering of occupations and the informal systems which evolve in the workplace. More important, since they were originally designed to deal with discrimination against minority men, this legislation may have actually reinforced women's dependence on men in families (Blankenship, 1993:204).

Recognizing the realities of a continuing gender wage gap, the legal approach was altered from barring discrimination to providing preferential treatment through Affirmative Action to women and minorities who are underrepresented in a job category or occupation. As documented more fully in Chapter 14, Affirmative Action has had more positive effects for women entering professions (although not for women already there) and management. However, with the decline in skilled trade jobs and the limited number of women in these and other blue-collar categories, the idea that job integration policy has benefited most women is clearly false (Rosenbaum, 1985; Blum, 1987). This is confirmed by Greer (1986), who asserts that the 23 percent increase of women in high-level professional occupations affects only a small proportion of all female workers. The positive effect of Affirmative Action has not reached the bulk of women who work in lower-level jobs and has not redressed continuing wage inequalities that still exist 30 years after the critical legislative efforts of 1963 and 1964.

Comparable worth is another strategy that is attempting to gain legitimacy through legislation and the judicial process, and like Affirmative Action, the evidence is mixed in terms of its success. Comparable worth aims to upgrade the wage scales for jobs that employ large numbers of women (Sorensen, 1994). While Affirmative Action challenges the allocation of *jobs* on the basis of stereotypical gender traits, comparable worth challenges the allocation of *rewards* on the basis of such traits. Because comparable worth arguments were successfully used in Washington and California when it was documented that women received far less pay in comparable jobs, such as police and fire dispatching, most states have taken some legislative action to deal with broadly based pay inequity.

The judicial thrust has been generally the same as the legislative by emphasizing that employers cannot discriminate on the basis of gender if a woman meets the necessary qualifications. The judiciary can be seen as the policers of legal imperatives. Since the 1960s, there have been thousands of gender discrimination cases. A landmark case demonstrates the importance of these actions. The 1971 unanimous Supreme Court decision in *Reed* v. *Reed* ruled that an Idaho law giving males preference over females in selecting administrators of an estate was in violation of the Fourteenth Amendment. This was the first time the Court ruled that an arbitrary discrimination law against women was unconstitutional.

Political and legal mandates have functioned to remove barriers that unfairly limit or circumscribe women's potential choices. They cannot focus on the decision-making process that has been viewed as the personal province of a woman and her family. However, the atmosphere has changed considerably over the years and should be expected to continue changing. The advocacy of the 1970s has given way to the entrenchment of the 1980s and the backlash of the 1990s. A renewed commitment to fairness is needed to take the earlier accomplishments into the twenty-first century.

WOMEN IN THE LABOR FORCE

The most important economic trend in the twentieth century has been the consistent increase in the labor force participation of all categories of women (see Table 10-1). Today, nearly 60 percent of all women 16 years and over are in the labor force. The labor force participation rate of married women in general and married women with children has tripled since 1960. For married women with children, the age of the youngest child greatly influences the probability of participating in the work force. In 1994, almost 60 percent of married women with children under the age of 3 were in the labor force compared to 77.2 percent with children between the ages of 14 and 17. Female single parents (single, divorced, separated, or widowed) participate in even greater proportions: 69.2 percent overall. Women are more likely than men to be working part time (under 35 hours per week). While some find that part-time work allows them needed flexibility to juggle roles, about one-fourth of part-time female workers do so simply because they cannot obtain full-time

Table 10–1 Percent Employment by Sex, Age, Employment Status, Marital Status, and Age of Children, 1970–1995

Status	1970	1975	1980	1985	1990	1995
Total employed women 16+	43.3	46.3	51.5	54.5	57.5	58.9
Employed full time	76.6	75.6	76.4	76.1	77.4	73.0
Employed part time	23.4	24.4	23.6	23.9	22.6	27.0
Total unemployed women 16+	5.9	9.3	7.4	7.4	5.4	5.6
Total employed men 16+	79.7	77.9	77.4	76.3	76.1	76.7
Employed full time	94.6	93.8	93.6	92.7	92.6	89.3
Employed part time	5.4	6.2	6.4	7.3	7.4	10.7
Total unemployed men 16+	4.4	7.9	6.9	7.0	5.6	5.6
Female employment by age						
16 to 19	44.0	49.1	52.9	52.1	51.8	49.4
20 to 24	57.5	64.1	68.9	71.8	71.6	69.2
25 to 34	45.0	54.9	65.5	70.9	73.6	75.4
35 to 44	51.1	55.8	65.5	71.8	76.5	77.6
45 to 54	54.4	54.6	59.9	64.4	71.2	74.8
55 to 64	43.0	40.9	41.3	42.0	45.3	48.9
65+	9.7	8.2	8.1	7.3	8.7	8.5
Female employment by marital status						
Single	56.8	59.8	64.4	66.6	66.9	66.7[a]
Married with spouse	40.5	44.3	49.8	52.8	58.4	60.7[a]
Other	40.3	40.1	43.6	45.1	47.2	47.5[a]
Mother employment by child age						
Child under age 2	NA	31.8	39.1	48.0	52.0	61.7[b]
Child age 2 to 3	NA	39.1	51.0	54.6	61.2	62.9[c]
Child age 4 to 5	NA	48.0	54.8	61.7	65.8	65.5
Child age 6 to 17	NA	52.0	64.4	69.9	74.7	76.4

[a]1994 data
[b]children birth to 2 years
[c]children age 3 years only

Source: U.S. Bureau of the Census, *Statistical Abstract of the United States,* 1991, 1995; *Employment and Earnings,* U.S. Bureau of Labor Statistics, Vol. 43(1), January 1996.

employment (Reskin, 1993). At the same time, men's labor force participation has been consistently declining, from a high of 86.8 percent in 1947 to 75.3 percent in 1994.

Middle-aged women (45-64) almost doubled their participation rate during the same period (36 percent in 1960 to 61.9 percent in 1994), with about 80 percent of the nearly three million women aged 50 to 60 who graduated from college still in the work force (Uchitelle, 1994; U.S. Bureau of the Census, 1995). Data indicate that although middle-aged women lack the material resources and status relative to men in various occupations, they have as high or higher self-esteem (Reitzes et al., 1994). Middle-aged women report general contentment with their jobs and the satisfaction that comes with the belief that their jobs have social value (Uchitelle, 1994). As documented throughout this text, these data also provide support for the consistent finding that for both men and women paid work is a mental health enhancement and for women, multiple roles which combine family and job are beneficial for overall well-being.

Although nearly all women are housekeepers, paid work roles are normative. Marital status, age, number of children, and age of children are factors which produce differential rates of labor force participation for women, but they have not mitigated the overall increase. The Department of Commerce estimates that 62.6 percent of all women will be working in the civilian labor force by the year 2000 and that nearly two-thirds of all labor force growth will be among women. If these trends continue, the proportion of women in the labor force will approach that of men.

Occupational Distribution of Women

As would be expected, women are not equally distributed throughout the occupational structure (Table 10-2). Occupational segregation by gender bolsters gender-typing. Although most occupations have some degree of gender typing which differentially distributes males and females throughout the labor force, when the majority of the occupation are those of one gender, it becomes a normative expectation. While women make up almost half of top-level managerial and professional occupations and require requisite educational credentials even at the entry level, the jobs are occupationally segregated and gender-typed, therefore associated with less prestige and pay. For example, the professional category includes accountants, architects, and engineers, who are mostly male, and teachers, nurses, and social workers, who are mostly female. While all these occupations are associated with advanced degrees, the female occupations are far lower in degree of pay, prestige, authority, and other job-related reward criteria.

It is interesting, too, that gender-typing extends to the way a job is perceived. Nursing, social work, and teaching are "engendered" as feminine professions linked with caring and nurturing. Nursing, in particular, is attempting to increase its professional status by challenging the jurisdictional boundaries that have been determined by physicians (Manley, 1995). As a female-dominated profession, nursing, until recently, has been in virtual servitude to the male-dominated profession of medicine. Upgrading the profession as a whole has challenged both the gender-based and occupationally based hierarchy of medicine and health care.

TABLE 10–2 Occupational Distribution of Labor Force by Percent Female in Selected Occupations for 1983 and 1994

Occupational Category	1983	1994
Executive, administrative, and managerial	32.4	43.0
Officials and public administrators	38.5	46.1
Personnel managers	43.9	61.6
Purchasing managers	23.6	37.0
Professional specialty	48.1	52.8
Engineers	5.8	8.3
Dentists	6.7	13.3
Dietitians	90.8	92.0
Nurses (RNs)	95.8	93.8
Physicians	15.8	22.3
University teachers	36.3	42.5
Elementary school teachers	83.3	85.6
Secondary school teachers	51.8	55.6
Librarians	87.3	84.1
Clergy	5.6	11.1
Lawyers	15.3	24.6
Technicians and related support	64.6	64.3
Health technicians	84.3	81.6
Science technicians	29.1	36.7
Legal assistants	74.0	79.9
Sales occupations	47.5	49.1
Real estate sales	48.9	48.4
Insurance sales	25.1	35.1
Securities/financial services sales	23.6	29.9
Cashiers	84.4	79.8
Administrative support, including clerical	79.9	78.9
Secretaries	99.0	98.9
Computer operators	63.7	60.6
Messengers	26.2	25.7
Service occupations		
Child-care workers	96.9	97.3
Cleaners and servants	95.8	95.8
Police and detectives	9.4	15.6
Firefighting, fire prevention	1.0	2.1
Precision production, craft, and repair	8.1	9.3
Mechanics and repairers	2.8	4.2
Construction trades	1.8	2.2
Carpenters	1.4	1.0
Operators, fabricators, and laborers	26.6	24.3
Textile/furnishing machine operators	82.1	74.4
Truck drivers	3.1	4.5
Freight, stock material handlers	15.4	20.1
Laborers (except construction)	19.4	18.2
Farming, forestry, and fishing	16.0	19.3
Farm operators and managers	12.1	25.4
Farm workers	24.8	16.6
Fishing, hunters, and trappers	4.5	6.2

Source: U.S. Bureau of the Census, *Statistical Abstract of the United States,* 1995. Adapted from Table No. 649:411–13.

These professions provide other illustrative examples of what happens when men enter predominately female occupations. In tracing the trajectories of males in female-dominated occupations, Williams (1993) finds that while men face some disadvantages, they have more advantages than women in these jobs. In such jobs males are likely to hold the higher positions. They differentiate themselves from the devalued female work they do by dominating "that which is female." For males who cross over into nursing, social work, elementary school teaching, and librarianship, they face some prejudice from those outside the professions but have clear advantages inside them. As Williams (1992:263) notes, both men and women who are employed in nontraditional occupations (as defined by gender), face discrimination, but the forms and consequences are different for males in female professions than the reverse. Both men and women perceive men as given fair, even preferential, treatment in hiring and promotion and being accepted by supervisors and colleagues and integrated into the subculture of the workplace. Williams (1992:263) refers to the subtle mechanisms which enhance a man's position in these professions as the "glass escalator effect." Men take their gender privileges with them to female occupations and experience upward mobility as a result. Thus even when the occupation is designated female, most women are subordinate to males who hold the most powerful, high-status, and high-paying positions. This phenomenon is called hierarchical segregation and is seen as a strategy that further prevents women from earning equal pay and/or exercising equal power with males.

Women have significantly increased their numbers in the elite professions such as law, medicine, and university teaching. Today almost one-third of physicians and lawyers and almost half of college professors are women, and it is expected that women will represent half of these professions within the next decade. While these gains are impressive, gender-typing is pervasive. Women are clustered in the overcrowded, less prestigious specialties that are associated not only with less pay, but with more competition and less authority (Bellas, 1993; Fox, 1995; Kaufman, 1995). In medicine, for example, women constitute large proportions of pediatricians, psychiatrists, and public health physicians. Female lawyers are generally restricted in their choices of occupational specialties and are hence more likely to be in domestic law or trust specialties rather than corporate law, and few (less than 10 percent in the top firms) attain the rank of law partner (Pollock and Ramirez, 1995). Within male-dominated professions, these subspecialties are considered more appropriate for women. Vetter and Babco (1988:vii) report that the salaries of women in all science and engineering fields are lower than their male counterparts with similar levels of experience. Although the dramatic increase of women in the professional and managerial ranks cannot be discounted as long as informal mechanisms exclude them from those networks which offer the highest career mobility, they remain not only marginal but invisible (Kaufman, 1995:302).

Within white-collar occupations women are clustered in clerical and retail sales positions. Office jobs in particular exhibit strong patterns of gender typing which are hierarchally arranged. Glenn and Feldberg (1995:264) find that there are three separate groups: the female clerical staff (secretaries and data entry clerks); the male managerial staff (vice-presidents, sales and product managers); and the mixed-gender technical staff (computer programmers and systems analysts). Clerical is a female hierarchy, but where the highest-level female supervisor reports to a male superior. Management is a male hierarchy with some lower-level female supervisors. Technical has lower-ranked jobs filled by both men and women but higher-ranked jobs are almost exclusively men.

Women work throughout all occupational categories but are most under-represented in blue-collar, transportation, and nonfarm labor areas. Barriers have been legally lifted for women to pursue the skilled elite blue-collar trades to become plumbers, electricians, machinists, carpenters, and craftspeople. However, they have not done so to any great degree. For those women who do enter the skilled trades, they remain in the female-dominant ones, such as dressmaker and electronic equipment assemblers. The resistance to women in the blue-collar trades remains strong (Cohn and Vobejda, 1992). Even among lower-level semiskilled operative jobs which can be learned quickly, women are underrepresented in those which are unionized. They have made their greatest strides in public sector operative jobs such as letter carrier and bus driver, where their numbers have doubled since 1980 (Cohn and Vobejda, 1992). The majority of women who hold blue-collar jobs are those which require few skills, have poor working conditions, high fluctuations in employment, and command low pay (Glenn and Feldberg, 1995). In the hierarchy of the lower-level blue-collar jobs (as distinct from the elite trades), men still have received more job-related rewards than women.

Gender-typing of occupations is an integral part of our economic system, though it violates one of capitalism's basic premises—obtaining the best person for the particular job—especially as it acts to limit or channel women's choice of jobs. Gender-typing links occupational roles with gender roles and tends to designate female occupations, such as nursing and social work, as those involving nurturing, helping, and high levels of empathy. Conversely, occupations associated with detachment, leadership, and outspokenness, like medicine and politics, are designated as masculine. While gender-typing is generally universal throughout the occupations, some jobs have changed their gender distribution, such as pharmacy, which is becoming female dominated. And we have already seen that teaching and secretarial work were transformed from male to female. These patterns are important in countering the argument that gender-typing is based on the "naturalness" of one gender or another being suited for a given occupation.

The Wage Gap

Numerous studies on gender differences at work consistently report that women earn less than men, even with comparable levels of educational attainment and work experience. The pattern holds true across racial and ethnic groups and throughout occupations (Jacobs and Steinberg, 1990; England and Browne, 1992; Almquist, 1995; Thornborrow and Sheldon, 1995). The wage gap has been a persistent economic fact in America since records have been available. Contrary to what many believe, the wage gap between men and women has not substantially decreased. Between 1967 and 1974, this gap actually widened from 62 percent to less than 61 percent. For the last three decades it has wavered somewhere between 60 and 70 percent and only in the mid-1990s has it narrowed to any appreciable degree, now hovering at the 75 percent mark (U.S. Bureau of the Census, 1995).

In explaining the slight narrowing of the gap as well as its tenacious persistence, several factors are suggested. First, whereas it reflects some "real" increases, it has changed in part because men's incomes were lower. This also helps clarify the declining labor force participation of men. Second, the "real" increase is linked to women's increased educational attainment. Finally, women now demonstrate less discontinuous work patterns than in the past, a factor that builds on human capital theory (Thornborrow and Sheldon, 1995). Human capital models view individual characteristics such as education and occupational selection as individually motivated, so that any resulting inequality is due to these choices. Women's human capital resources are diminished when they choose to interrupt their labor force activities for child rearing. This is a supply-side explanation which argues that their work experience and productivity are compromised when they return to the job market and lower wages are the result (Blau and Ferber, 1992; Fermlee, 1995). Thus uninterrupted employment will spill over into a decrease in the gender wage gap. Becker (1994) contends that the law of supply and demand has helped women achieve occupational success and that to artificially intervene with counterproductive legislative efforts will create more harm than good. In essence, this explanation has functionalist overtones since it perpetuates a status quo built on the assumption that any adjustments must be made by the women themselves rather than a change in the system overall.

From the conflict perspective, the concept of power is readily applied. **Power** can be viewed as the ability of one person or group to impose their will on another person or group, regardless of what the other desires. Reskin (1988:61) restates the position when she says that

> the basic cause of the income gap is not sexual segregation, but men's desire to preserve their advantaged position and their ability to do so by establishing rules to distribute valued resources in their favor.

In other words, men exercise their power in a manner which will maintain their differential advantage. For example, one major strategy used to maintain power is through a "protégé system" where an already powerful member serves as a sponsor for the entry and upward movement of a novice in a job setting. An effective old "old boy system" operates to keep power in the hands of a few designated men. Kaufman (1995) points out that professional women's networks need to include people of high rank and status who can provide the full range of mentor role functions. This could eventually create an "old girl" system that allows comparable opportunities for the advancement of women in the corporate sphere.

Although these factors are linked to the narrowing of the wage gap, its persistence is explained by three key factors. First, female occupations are devalued because the work women do, regardless of its content, skillbase, or functional necessity, is less valued overall than the work men do. This is also linked to the internal gender segregation of the same occupations. Over one-third of the male-female earnings gap is correlated with such differences (Kemp, 1994:249). Second, the wage gap is due not to people performing the same jobs, but between people in different occupations (Fuchs, 1988). The gendered occupational structure is the mechanism which operates here. Third, gender discrimination in the workplace endures (Hagen, 1993; Wendt and Slonaker, 1994; Ruth, 1995). Women's patterns of employment are different from men's, but for equal work there is not equal pay.

While discrimination is "alive and well in the American labor force" (O'Donnell and O'Neill, 1985; Lewin, 1994), explanations for the male-female gap in earnings cannot be reduced to this simple fact. Perhaps it depends on how discrimination is defined. Legal mandates have all but eradicated the most blatant forms of gender discrimination in the workplace. Subtle ones continue. Women's options for paid work roles are constrained by socialization factors that also constrain men's options for expanded family roles. Men's breadwinning responsibilities take precedence, and women's family responsibilities take precedence. Are these discriminatory? Given the interdependence of our institutions, elimination of the gender wage gap requires a concerted effort at gender role change at all institutional levels. However, gender role socialization at the family level is an important starting point.

Double Jeopardy: Race and Ethnicity

There is a venerable sociological tradition that focuses on questions of racial and ethnic effects in the area of work and occupations. Racial differentiation in occupational prestige, segregation, earnings, and power are well documented, as are gender stratification effects. Furthermore, a general consensus on the existence of an interactive effect between race, ethnicity, and gender is also developing in the United States. However, as Xu and Leffler (1992) point out, most research and theory focus on one of these areas and minimize the importance of the other. Consequently, the actual impact of this double jeopardy is unclear. King (1988) cautions us to avoid thinking about the double jeopardy of gender and race discrimination as either a simple constant or additive.

Occupational distribution of minority women reflects both changes in the American labor force and inequality. African-American women moved into the white-collar clerical areas in large numbers after World War II, but Glenn and Feldberg (1995) point out that they are concentrated in public sector jobs or in the lowest wage level positions of private sector jobs, such as filing or data entry clerks. Jones (1985) notes that African-American middle-class women began moving into the professions earlier than white women because economic success was valued in their communities as early as the 1950s. Yet black women professionals continue to be steered into traditionally female occupations and are at a disadvantage for both race and gender in career attainment. Higginbotham (1994:127) states that in both male- and female-dominated occupations, their professional training and lower levels of discrimination in public sector jobs, such as teaching and social work, keep their numbers in the private sector low. These are also the very jobs associated with higher pay for all categories of professionals.

Such a pattern substantiates Reskin and Hartmann's (1986) finding that much of the increase in gender integration for nonwhites occurs at the lower end of the occupational distribution. Collins (1989) further points out that African-American professionals enter fields, like personnel and public relations, which are particularly vulnerable to changing economic conditions and governmental priorities. Another subhierarchy of race exists within gender. Xu and Leffler (1992:3–82) find more white and Asian-American women in higher prestige occupations than their Hispanic and African-American counterparts.

Wage levels of minority women are also unequal when compared to males of the same groups. African-American women, Asian-American women, and white women earn between two-thirds and four-fifths what men earn in the same categories, with the greatest disparity between white men and women (Almquist, 1987, Marini, 1989; Xu and Leffler, 1992). The range of labor force difficulties minority women experience appears to differ and to be based on racial or ethnic group membership. These figures fit with Almquist's (1995:594) conclusions that first, the actual level of gender inequality reflects the opportunities and achievements of men as much as it does those of women. And second, groups with the greatest economic resources (higher social class) exhibit the greatest disparities between men and women. While the general experience of discrimination remains, as we have seen throughout this text, it is difficult to disentangle gender from the effects of race and class on explaining social and economic trends.

WOMEN IN BUSINESS

An important business trend of the last two decades is the rise of small female-owned businesses. Five times more women were starting small businesses in the first half of the decade compared to men and total employment among women-owned business firms grew nearly 12 percent from 1991 to 1994 compared with 5.5 percent overall (Noble, 1994; Walsh, 1995). Female-owned sole proprietorships are increasing at triple the rate as those owned by men. Women have also been entering the business ranks as sole proprietors one-third more often than as wage or salaried employees (American Demographics, 1985). These entrepreneurial women have found small business formation an alternative to management positions in large organizations which have seen few women enter the ranks of upper management.

Most of this increase has come from traditional areas of female work, such as services and the retail trades. Loscocco and Robinson (1991:527) suggest that small business entrepreneurship in the United States offers women "peripheral economic niches that are unattractive to white men." Female-owned businesses tend to be concentrated in industries with very low-volume sales, that lack access to capital and government contracts, and that are often in need of more management expertise (Hisrich and Brush, 1984; Gregg, 1985; Committee on Small Business, 1988). Women view these small businesses as a way to gain autonomy and flexibility which help in balancing career with family responsibilities. Until a generation of data are produced which judge the financial and psychological successes of these businesses, Moore (1990:279) concludes that the jury is still out on the fate of the female entrepreneur.

Barriers to Advancement of Corporate Women

What is clear, however, is that a critical reason why women are deserting the ranks of larger organizations and seeking alternative employment options is that they continue to be denied access to the ranks of upper management (Rosener, 1995). Fryxell and Lerner (1989:342) conclude that there has been documented improvement in women's participation at lower- and middle-management levels, but that the "social goal of equitable representation at the top is far from realized." The original strategy for many businesses was to increase female participation by adding one woman to their corporate board of directors (Elgart, 1983; Kesner, 1988). But the vast majority of business promotion ladders are gender segregated (Baron et al., 1986). Thus by the early 1990s, corporate officerships, top executive positions, and female senior executive personnel represented between 1 and 4 percent of the most powerful Fortune 500 companies as well as businesses overall (Lott, 1994; Rosener, 1995). And Fryxell and Lerner (1989) point out that the situation has worsened since the mid-1980s. Eighty percent of business promotional ladders are totally gender segregated and 74 percent of the integrated ladders only promoted men (Baron et al., 1986).

A number of studies continue to support the conclusion that barriers to upward mobility by women are almost insurmountable (Kesner, 1988; Morrison et al., 1992). Gregory's (1990:261) literature review suggests that while these barriers are often perceptual, they maintain gender segregation and produce profound negative effects for women. Such effects include career immobility and role conflict as well as differences in feedback, training and development, and power. And in the elite ranks of some of the most powerful companies, regardless of legal prohibitions, "old style" gender bias emerges which effectively thwarts a woman's move up the corporate ladder (Antilla, 1995).

Several popular explanations have emerged to explain the continued barriers faced by women managers. The idea of the **glass ceiling** argues that women fail to rise to senior positions because they encounter invisible and artificial barriers constructed by male management. While lateral movement is possible, women are not able to advance hierarchically. Although it is unintentional, executives hire and promote by the "white male model" and image their recruits in terms of this ideal standard (Stuart, 1992). All women, all men of color, and many men who do not exude the aggressiveness also associated with this model cannot measure up. As Rosener (1991:147) aptly notes, "as long as sameness is valued, women will continue to be disadvantaged merely because they are women."

Given this reality, in conjunction with private enterprise the federal government began a series of glass ceiling initiatives in 1991. These aim at promoting a quality, inclusive, and diverse work force capable of meeting the challenge of global competition and of promoting corrective and cooperative corporate problem solving (U.S. Department of Labor, 1991). With the continued leadership of former Secretary of Labor Lynn Martin, the message is that companies whose rigid policies are throwing out half their talent pool had better change for their own good. Too many promising female employees are being lost because the company refuses to acknowledge the realities of the home and family environments and how they impact on one's work life (Morgan, 1994). Other research confirms this. The loss of female talent is bad for business (Schwartz, 1994b; Rosener, 1995).

The workplace itself is organized, structured, and administered according to models which can be described as male oriented and disadvantageous to women. In the creation of rules on the relationships between the genders in the workplace culture, men and women inevitably "do gender" (Gherardi, 1994). Both the formal and informal structure of the corporate organization reinforce this model. For example, if grasping the intricacies of the power structure is the key to corporate survival, women are routinely excluded from the very communication networks necessary for access to the power base. Encouraged to specialize in a small area of the corporate enterprise, women find themselves in networks which lack diversity and control and removed from understanding the broader workings of the system. With job functions also specialized via gender, a kind of corporate purdah emerges (Lindsey, 1992). This is an example of the pervasive, powerful, and seemingly intractable impact of a lifetime of gender role socialization.

Related to this is the notion that women in management are categorized into two distinct groups: those with a career and family and those with only a career. The former may be "mommy track" women who will not be subject to the same set of demands as other career-only corporate women (Spiller, 1993). Businesses justify this track by arguing that their investment in women managers is lost when careers are interrupted by family concerns. When they return to the corporate world, the dues they pay go beyond catching up on seniority or retooling their skill based. They are treated virtually as beginners. For those who scale back even one day a week, that one day keeps them forever behind in their careers in terms of salary, title, and responsibility (Jacobs, 1994). Schwartz (1989:68) sums up the situation as follows:

> The barriers to women's leadership occur when potentially counterproductive layers of influence on women—maternity, tradition, socialization—meet management strata pervaded by the largely unconscious preconceptions, stereotypes, and expectations of men. Such interfaces do not exist for men and tend to be impermeable for women.

There is a definite trend heralding a strong career comitment for women. The most committed women are those who select their career, obtain the requisite education for that career, and organize their role clusters, generalized self, and construction of reality around being a career woman (Lopata, 1993:257). However, it is difficult to establish all these contingencies in a climate which continues to rank a women's occupational roles as less important than her domestic ones. In summarizing the barriers to women in management, Hill (1993) reports that historical practices of recruitment and promotion, reluctance and fear of change and diversity, lack of a network for women, and lack of mentors are ongoing factors. Overall, the cultural stereotyping of women is the most formidable barrier. In the organizational sense, the term "male corporate America" is redundant.

Gendered Management Styles and the Partnership Alternative

Despite this bleak picture, there are some indications that a woman's socialization may offer an advantage to the corporate world. Helgesen's (1990) qualitative research suggests that successful women managers exhibit qualities which are now viewed as beneficial to the modern corporation. Her female respondents indicate that they have developed a "weblike" structure of leadership style which is in sharp contrast to the traditional corporate hierarchy. Such a structure relies on "skills and attitudes that have value in the workplace" and "where innovation, entrepreneurship and creativity are in demand, and the authoritarian chain of command is increasingly obsolete" (Helgesen, 1990:37). The web extends to roles outside the corporation, so that these women find that they can positively integrate their various worlds. Male executives give up significant parts of their private life to be successful in the traditional hierarchical structure of business and as a result become "quietly desperate" (Halper, 1988), a situation which is emotionally detrimental for the man both as an individual and as an employee.

Research is documenting the differences in male and female systems of management which emerge in companies which are more receptive to alternative visions of corporate life. Helgeseen (1990) and Rosener (1990) suggest that men and women possess distinct management styles and leadership qualities that are culturally and institutionally conditioned. Women managers adopt styles compatible with whom they are as women, such as encouraging participation, sharing power and information, interacting with all levels of employees, and identifying themselves as multifaceted persons whose on-job identities are connected to who they are off the job. Loden (1985) summarizes the different leadership styles of men and women:

> The key characteristics of the male model are high control, strategic, unemotional and analytical; of the female model, low control, empathetic, collaborative and high performance.

Companies can embrace alternative models emphasizing the female characteristics more, not because it is good for their female managers, but because it is good for business. For example, these are the very characteristics which are hallmarks of Japanese-style management (JSM). Given the success of Japanese capitalism, many American businesses have begun to adopt certain of these management strategies and modify them according to their own workplace needs. JSM is compatible with traditional gender role socialization among women which emphasize sharing, mutual trust, and socioemotional bonding with colleagues. If adapted to the American workplace, such a model may be easier for female managers to embrace. American corporations can capitalize on already existing female talent by celebrating rather than devaluing those characteristics which have previously been defined as disadvantageous for the corporate world (Lindsey, 1990).

This also fits with the new partnership models that are emerging in innovative corporations. JSM may also be viewed as a "partnership model" with its emphasis on linking rather than ranking and a consensus style of decision making. Rosener (1991) points out that dictatorial styles of leadership are preferred by men with women preferring interactive, participative, and conciliatory styles. It can be argued that gender role socialization would be a strong predictor of the corporate success of men and women managers depending on the management approach adopted by their firms. According to Eisler and Loye (1990), partnership is related to an egalitarian social structure, trust, teamwork, creativity, openness, nurturing, and sharing. When adapted to an appropriate, compatible workplace, such characteristics are indicative of employee satisfaction and corporate productivity.

The "unnerving state of turbulence" that exists in corporate America due to company reorganization, downsizing, and permanent workforce reductions have taken its toll on American employees. Research indicates that employees are now willing to trade compensation for quality of work life. Workers also do not perceive men and women managers as all that different. However, managers with child-care responsibilities themselves are viewed as more sympathetic and understanding of employees who also have such concerns, whether they are male or female. Conflicts between work and family are usually resolved in favor of the job, but usually to the detriment of the worker and his or her family (Noble, 1993). Clearly companies which adopt a partnership approach can benefit by recognizing that employee job satisfaction is critically linked to quality of life—both on and off the job.

Partnership models are largely based on those characteristics which are traditionally associated with the feminine gender role. The problem arises when the "celebration" of the female advantage may lead to increased stereotyping and a reaffirmation of the differences between men and women. Faludi (1991) believes that even if the workplace needs to be humanized, an emphasis on women being the ones to do it may further the chasm between men and women. The nurturing women who soothe over problems is as stereotypical as the corporate men who create the problems. The "fiercest polarity on this issue is marked by those who wish to celebrate gender differences and those who are wary of such a move" (Billard, 1992:107). On the positive side, virtually everyone in the business world today recognizes that individuals have different interpersonal styles and that difference does not imply better or worse or stronger or weaker (Segal, 1991:117).

As there are a diversity of companies, there are also a diversity of leadership styles. When organizations accept nontraditional styles which may favor women, they are also encouraging the high performance associated with the style. Rosener (1991:125) suggests that when larger, established companies expand their definitions of effective leadership, the glass ceiling may be shattered and wider opportunities for both men and women executives will be available.

WOMEN AND WORK: A GLOBAL OVERVIEW

Global patterns related to gender and work mirror those found in the United States except that the effect is more devastating for women and their families in much of the world. Women represent half the world's population yet they perform two-thirds of the world's work, receive one-tenth of its income, and own less than one-hundredth of its property (United Nations, 1985:3). Women in rural Africa, for example, produce, process, and store up to 80 percent of the food supply for the continent, yet they receive only a small fraction of the technical assistance and credit provided by farmers. On average, only 55 percent of the women in developing nations are literate, but a study of 88 nations shows that a 20-30 percent literacy gain can bolster a nation's gross domestic product (GDP) by 8 to 16 percent (*Connections*, 1995a). As documented in Chapter 6, in 31 countries if you take into account women's uncompensated work plus the wage discrimination against women for their compensated work, the economic value of what they do is estimated at $11 trillion (United Nations Development Program, 1995).

Women in the developed world fare much better on all economic indicators than their sisters in the developing world. The United States is given the world's second highest overall human development after Canada and before Japan, which ranks third, but falls to fifth place behind Sweden, Finland, Denmark, and Norway when income and health disparities are factored in (United Nations Development Program, 1995). Hong Kong, Cyprus, and Barbados rank first in GDP among the developing countries, but their unique political and economic situation as well as their small size explains much of this. Three continents—Africa, Asia, and South America—are virtually excluded from the higher ranks on all economic measures which would serve as markers to an enhanced economic role for women in their societies. What is a telling fact is that while the United Nations has been at the vanguard of a drive to document global gender inequity, women who work for the United Nations say that discrimination against them is pervasive in hiring, promotion, and job assignments (Crossette, 1995b). How do UN officials respond to this charge? Like other officials and executives throughout the world, they simply state: "There aren't enough qualified women for jobs." While the answer is the expected one, we have seen that it is an empirically invalid one.

Although most women's labor throughout the world is unpaid, movement of women into the paid labor force has increased in almost all nations at all levels of development, especially in the industrialized world. The global gender earnings gap in the industrialized world is lowest in the Scandinavian countries, with Iceland at a remarkable 94 percent, but others are in the range of 77 to 90 percent. Canada and the United States have the most disparate male-female wage gap in the developed world.

Only part of the wage gap can be explained by occupational gender segregation, since it is highest in Scandinavia and Canada, followed by the United States, and lowest in Australia (Blau and Ferber, 1990). According to Charles' (1992:483) explanation for similar findings in the cross-national data, this discrepancy is because "women's greater integregation in the labor force also contributes to a deepening insitutionalization of gender within the occupational structure." Benefit packages do not keep pace with men either. Widening gender differences in public pensions in most countries in North America and Europe cannot be solely explained by labor marker differences. As Hill and Tiges (1995) assert in their cross-national study of the quality of women's pensions, the gap is explained by a system designed by men with men in mind. Using the U.S. Social Security system as a case example, they find gender bias and not gender neutrality.

These patterns mirror the gender-related attitudes of men and women in general and, according to Baxter and Kane (1995), have a probable reciprocal effect. In support of other conclusions from cross-cultural research (Chapter 6), they find the greatest level of egalitarianism in Scandinavia, especially Sweden, and the lowest levels in the United States. This supports the view that levels of egalitarianism are highest in nation's where a woman's dependence is lowest. Both men and women are more consistent in their gender role attitudes in countries where women are the most dependent on men (Baxter and Kane, 1995:210–11).

While cross-cultural studies on women in management are limited, it can be concluded that women are few in numbers, their salaries are lower, the conflict between home and work is universal and employed women cannot count on men to take their share of domestic tasks and child care (Ross, 1987; Gregory, 1990). Japan provides an illustrative example that can be applied to much of the world: "It would seem the topic of women managers in Japan could be handled in one sentence: there are none" (Maital, 1989:7).

The technologically advanced countries of the world share basic demographic trends which have made a huge impact on the lifestyles and attitudes of their populations. The increase in the female labor force is associated with declining fertility, higher divorce and the rise of single-parent households,

(Jacobsen, 1994). While all of these countries have initiatives related to equal pay and enhanced economic opportunities for women, they have yet to be translated in a way that has markedly decreased either the male-female earning gap or the degree of occupational segregation that continues to devalue women's work. Until the adage that "women's place is in the home" is seriously challenged on all institutional fronts, these disparities are likely to persist both globally and in the United States.

CHAPTER 11

THE IMPACT OF EDUCATION ON GENDER ROLE PERSISTENCE AND CHANGE

Why should girls be learn'd and wise?
Books only serve to spoil their eyes.
The studious eye but faintly twinkles
And reading paves the way to wrinkles
—John Trumbull, 1890s
(Cited in Kerber, 1993)

At the turn of the twentieth century the pervasive image was that the emotion associated with a woman's mind doomed her to failure in all but the minimal educational enterprises. As satirical as it is, this poem demonstrates the turn of the century notion, that beauty is a more important asset to a woman than her brain. Yet one of the hallmarks of the twentieth century has been the stellar educational achievement of women.

Compared to society's other institutions, education is probably the most equitable. As children face the educational odyssey with eager anticipation, parents approach it with the conviction that the success of their children will be directly tied to how well they do in school. Increasingly, we are becoming a credential-oriented society and formal schooling provides us with those pieces of paper that allow access to the most prestigious and financially rewarding positions. Faced with the prospect of at least 12 years of education for their children, parents are likely to be concerned with the quality of teaching and extent of curricular offerings. For them, the issue of equity may focus on the amount of federal and state monies reserved for their district. Certainly, they want the best education possible for their children. Many of these concerned parents would indeed be shocked if they discovered that their sons are experiencing a very different educational process than their daughters. In the most equitable of our institutions, the gender of the child becomes a key determinant of his or her educational experience.

GLOBAL FOCUS: THE EDUCATIONAL GENDER GAP IN THE DEVELOPING WORLD

In measuring the quality of life, educational opportunities for all people must be included. Despite international progress in access to schooling, girls lag significantly behind boys in such opportunities in 50 countries. As judged by enrollment statistics, 76 million fewer girls in these countries are in primary and secondary schools (Conley, 1994). Two-thirds of the illiterate people in the world are women and in 17 countries, 90 percent or more of the female population is illiterate (Jacobsen, 1994:449). In the developing world, the highest female illiteracy rates among adults are in South Asia (72 percent compared to 46 percent of men) and in Africa (62 percent compared to 44 percent

percent of men). Chad, Mali, and Niger in Africa and Afghanistan, Pakistan, and Bangladesh in South Asia have the lowest overall rankings on an index measuring female education (Snyder, 1990; Conley, 1994). Whereas the illiteracy rate in China has been cut by 64 percent since 1949, about 180 million people, comprising 16 percent of the total population, are illiterate. Seventy percent of the illiterate in China are females and less than half of all girls complete primary school (Bartels and Eppley, 1995; *People and Development Challenges*, 1995). Although rates of illiteracy and lower educational attainment for women in the developing world are staggering, they are worse for rural, refugee, displaced, and migrant women.

Explanations for these trends are ultimately traced to traditional gender-based practices. School attendance is considered optional or unnecessary for girls who are needed to take care of younger siblings and take on domestic responsibilities, especially when their mothers are engaged in subsistence farming. Girls help in nondomestic areas as well, including gathering firewood and carrying water. This also explains the high dropout rates of girls in rural areas throughout the developing world. In this sense, education is less important than the valuable but unpaid resources female children bring to the family. Marriage customs often require women to leave their villages and live with their husbands' family. So the return investment for a girl's education is seen as negligible, particularly in a poverty ridden family. Expectations for early marriage and early pregnancy discourage girls from any kind of literacy training, much less years of formal education. The grim cumulative effect for such practices is that women themselves have lowered expectations and desires. Women may end up affirming the status quo when they themselves believe they have no need for literacy. It is "difficult to desire what one cannot imagine as a possibility" (Nussbaum and Sen, 1993). This again reflects the incredible power of a gender-specific nonconscious ideology.

While lack of educational opportunities for females are unequivocally related to justice and gender equity, closing the global educational gender gap has immediate practical benefits for women, their families, and their communities—in other words, for everyone. What is the best way to aid people in the developing world? The answer from many sources of data is to educate their daughters. A consistent correlation exists between female literacy and fertility. The United Nations estimates that for every year beyond the fourth grade that girls go to school, family size shrinks 10 percent, child death rates drop 10 percent, and wages rise 20 percent (*Connections*, 1995b:1). In India, at current rates, women with at least a high school education will have an average of two children, whereas illiterate women will have four (U.S. Agency for International Development, 1994). More educated children marry later, want fewer children, and have only the number of children they want. Birth rates and child death rates decline fastest where there is access to family planning, health services, *and* educational opportunities for girls (Conley, 1994). South Korea, Taiwan, Singapore, Thailand, and Sri Lanka all represent family planning success stories, with most reporting that they have reached the goal of replacement fertility. These countries also have high levels of female education and literacy, at least to the sixth grade level (*Asia-Pacific Population and Policy*, 1994; Conley, 1994).

High infant mortality and low life expectancy are two of the most important indicators of overall well-being of a society. The World Bank suggests that the best way to reduce the former and increase the latter is to teach girls to read. The children of a literate mother have a better chance of survival than the children living in the same place at the same level of income of a mother who is illiterate (Bernard, 1987:7). Investing in women's education will bring high returns globally.

A BRIEF LESSON IN HISTORY

The history of Western civilization demonstrates that education in general, and literacy in particular, was reserved for the elite of society, with the vast majority of the population excluded from even the rudiments of formal learning. It must be recognized that until the eighteenth century both men and women remained unschooled. During the classical Greek and Roman eras, certain upper-class women were educated in the arts, with a focus on poetry and music, in order to entertain household guests. This tradition continued into the Middle Ages and served to reinforce the image of women as sources of diversion from a tedious world. As already documented, it was during the Middle Ages that Christianity enveloped Europe and established a stronghold on most institutions. Convent schools arose to meet the need for some women to learn reading and writing, although even here it was essentially for religious purposes, especially as preparation for entering the convent to become nuns. The few other select women who attended these institutions became part of a system where schooling was designed to produce socially proper behavior and ensure sexual purity. Functionalism would view even the mediocre education during this era as paralleling family and broader societal values, with the religious institution dominating the entire system. By the seventeenth century even the few educational opportunities in convents deteriorated, fueled by the suspicion that communities of educated, semiindependent women might prove dangerous. As Weitz (1995) points out, whereas some convents worked to preserve their intellectual traditions, Latin ceased to be taught. Nuns were thus rendered powerless in church decisions. Overall, then, in spite of the rise of universities in the twelfth and thirteenth centuries and the profound impact of the Renaissance, education was aimed at the sons of nobility and the emerging bourgeoisie, who would enter scholarly professions, law, medicine, or become clerics.

The first real rumblings of equality of education for both genders and all classes came with the Enlightenment. It was during this period when Jean-Jacques Rousseau published *Emile* (1762), a book that was destined to become one of the most influential works in the history of education. In describing a man, Emile, and a woman, Sophie, who would be Emile's wife, Rousseau provides educational principles consistent with his broader philosophy of naturalism. Whereas a man would be schooled or trained according to his natural talents and encouraged to cultivate his mind and spirit without restraint or coercion, a woman should be passive, weak, and humbly submissive, accepting a man's judgment in all matters. Rousseau would not deny literacy to women, but even this should be "practically" oriented, since intellectual pursuits could wreak havoc on their naturally weak temperament. Also, education for women should be in accordance with their family roles as wife and mother—roles which are freely chosen by women. Women have power over men because they have power over men's hearts. Men have power over women because they contribute to their economic upkeep in the home. Women gain more from their dependence on men (Green, 1995:79). Ultimately Rousseau justifies the inequality between men and women because the patriarchal family is a structural precondition for modern society founded on a woman's *acceptance* of her subservience to a man (Fermon, 1994). Sustained education for women, therefore, is impractical, unwise, and detrimental to social stability.

Considered radical at that time, Rousseau's discourses on boys' education laid the foundation for the twentieth-century movement known as Progressive Education. Certainly his views on women caused little room for debate as they reflected accepted thought on her "nature" anyway. His theory of civic egalitarianism was used to justify continued gender inequality. The so-called leveling effects of the Enlightenment were directed mainly at glaring class differences, with little thought given to equalizing educational opportunities for women. Given the roles men and women were expected to play, men's education was regarded as definitely unsuitable for women. This discussion also demonstrates how the concepts of gender and class can be discussed together yet remain analytically distinct. Unlike Marx, Rousseau's defense of civic egalitarianism is weakened because he did not account for the intersecting, interdependent relationship of gender and class which perpetuates women's subordinate position. In terms of sociological theory, an interesting contradiction results. Sounding like Marx and a conflict perspective, Rousseau advocates social change that would bolster class equality. But the final outcome is decidedly functionalist, in support of the patriarchal family that is viewed as the moral structure at the foundation of the social order.

Other dissonant voices were heard during the eighteenth century. The Marquis de Condorcet declared that society should not only be responsible for education in general but that it also had a duty to instruct both genders in common. Equality and justice demanded it. Madame de Lambert advised women to study Latin, philosophy, and science to bolster their resources in a world where the usual roads to success were closed to women. She bitterly lamented that women have but "coquetry and the miserable function of pleasing" as their wealth (Greard, 1893). In essence, the true spirit of the Enlightenment emerged in the late nineteenth century in both Europe and the United States as policies advocating free and compulsory education for all children were adopted. These principles were strengthened during the civil rights turmoil of the 1960s when the issue of equality of opportunity, especially in education, was seriously debated.

Today Americans wholeheartedly subscribe to the belief that education is the key to success and is the vehicle for upward mobility. Children may begin their formal education as early as three years of age, with preschool, and spend the next 12 to 20 years of their lives in educational institutions. As mentioned above, equality in education is assumed during these years. Yet when the female kindergarten teacher first removes Dick's mittens and helps Jane off with her coat, by virtue of gender alone, their long educational journey will contain essential differences.

THE PROCESS OF EDUCATION

Preschool and Kindergarten

Preschool is rapidly becoming normative throughout society and introduces children to rudimentary educational expectations. Research clearly documents that gender segregation occurs swiftly in the preschool environment and that it is reinforced by teacher expectations, play and game activities, types of toys available, and desires of the children themselves (Maccoby, 1994; Serbin et al., 1994; Ramsey, 1995). Children have strong preferences for same-gender contacts in all preschool activities. Whether intentional or not, gender segregation produces more active and disruptive behavior in boys and more passivity and social sensitivity in girls. When compared to race, gender becomes the first and more salient feature of segregation in the early school years. In classroom interaction, children are more likely to cross racial lines than gender lines (Sadker and Sadker, 1990:178). Segregated play groups during preschool have powerful socialization outcomes because children are acquiring distinctive interaction skills that hamper cross-gender relationships throughout their lifetimes.

The transition to the formal learning process begins with kindergarten. For those without a preschool experience, the trepidation that is often associated with this new environment is tempered with the excitement of being with others of the same age and realizing that the kindergarten classroom is to some degree an extension of familiar household surroundings. Kindergarten allows for the gradual structuring of the child's day so that ample time is set aside for play activities. Both boys and girls eagerly anticipate the time reserved for playing with the myriad of toys and games available in most kindergarten classrooms, toys which they have probably already played with at home.

When play period begins, the girls rush off to the minikitchen reserved for them. Here they can pretend to cook, set the table, and clean with miniature household artifacts that are specially constructed for their small hands. This miniature house comes complete with dolls on which Jane can practice her domestic artistry. Since the doll corner is not designed for vibrant, rough-and-tumble play, Jane is less restricted by her clothing. Girls are princesses, brides, and mothers in this part of the kindergarten world, fantasies which are easily accomplished by the way the classroom is structured (Davies, 1989). But Jane is now accustomed to wearing "boy clothes" as well. This allows her to run with the other children and play on the schoolyard equipment unencumbered by clothing that inhibits such activities. Lest she be labeled a tomboy, however, both teacher and parents reinforce these kinds of play activities to only a limited extent. The logic is simple. Her adult roles will not be substantially in line with this kind of behavior; thus socialization within the school should reflect this idea. While the four-year-old girl may occasionally exchange the domestic roles of the doll corner for Wonderwoman and Supergirl, it is "mother and baby which reign supreme and will continue to do so throughout the kindergarten year" (Paley, 1984:xi).

In the kindergarten year Jane gains approval from peers, parents, and teacher for her quiet demeanor as she pours tea for her dolls and her studiousness as she intently pages through her first schoolbooks. She may secretly envy the boys as they display both power and freedom in their play, but that admiration is tempered in light of the teacher's obvious disapproval of their boisterous behavior in the classroom. Jane rarely plays with the boys anymore and would prefer to play house or jump rope with her best friends. This also indicates that kindergarten continues a pattern of self-selected gender segregation that increases throughout the school years. As Paley (1984:ix) poignantly notes, "kindergarten is a triumph of sexual self-stereotyping," with adult subterfuge or propaganda doing little to deflect the child's passion for segregation by gender.

Meanwhile, Dick enters kindergarten more psychologically unprepared for the experience than Jane. His higher level of physical activity is incompatible with the sedate atmosphere of even the kindergarten classroom. He begins to realize that his teacher approves of the girls but is more stern with him. Rather than gaining her attention through emulating the girls and being threatened with the devastating label of sissy, he plays games which are physically vibrant and selects toys which reinforce these activities (Thorne, 1993). Dick discovers that the teacher pays attention to him, listens to him, and even scolds him for his disruptive behavior, but he may also believe it is better to be reprimanded than ignored. While many preschool teachers maintain that they do not treat girls and boys differently, it is clear that aggressive boys and dependent girls gain their attention (Lips, 1993:286).

When boys venture into the doll corner, accommodation and resistance occur depending on the activities. Domestic play is accepted and tolerated if it is not disruptive. On the other hand, when the boys use the area for nondomestic games, particularly based on fighting and destruction, conflict erupts. In a study of an Australian kindergarten, Jordan and Cowan (1995) find that when boys use the doll corner, they invent "warrior narratives" to structure their play—games involving good and bad, pirates and sword play, police and bad guys—and alter the domestic artifacts to fit their needs. New adaptations require new accommodations, which the teacher, who encourages free and imaginative play otherwise, will not allow. Such activities belong on the playground but not in the classroom. However, the boys do not abandon their warrior narratives in the classroom entirely. They are driven underground, to become part of a subterranean masculine subculture full of secret identity and hidden meaning (Jordan and Cowan, 1995).

Dick and his friends regard trucks and building blocks as acceptable alternatives in toys. Occasionally, a girl may wander over and attempt to join in the louder and seemingly more interesting activities of the boys. She is likely to be discouraged from long-term participation, however, by their rough-and-tumble play and the very spiritedness by which she was originally attracted. Such activities are merely extensions of preschool environments which reward boys for being independent, active, and assertive, in sharp contrast to school norms, which call for docility and passivity, a realm where girls feel more at ease. It is understandable that boys find their first school experience disconcerting, coping with a system of what they see as incongruous rewards and punishments. And more importantly, these patterns established in kindergarten set the stage for the next crucial socialization level, the elementary years.

Elementary School

For girls, elementary school provides a vehicle for achievement. They exceed boys in most areas of verbal ability, reading, and mathematics, which is reflected in the higher grades they receive. Their teachers also put a premium on being good and being tidy, which may account for the more sparing use of negative comments given. It would appear that high achievement coupled with low criticism would provide an ideal environment for girls. Yet simultaneous processes are occurring which send different messages and which can have damaging consequences. The message that is communicated to girls very early in their elementary school lives is that they are less important than boys. Compared to boys, girls are called on less, have less overall interaction with teachers, and get less criticism but also less instruction (Boudreau, 1986; Acker, 1994; Mincer, 1994). When teachers criticize boys for inadequate academic work, they suggest that lack of effort rather than intellectual flaw is the root cause. Since teachers are less likely to suggest to girls that more effort will remedy academic problems, girls begin to internalize the notion that they have less intellectual ability (Boudreau, 1986; Sadker and Sadker, 1990). When such evaluative feedback is linked to research indicating that teachers encourage boys to remedy their mistakes through greater effort, girls are told not to worry about mistakes and are frequently passed over in talking about the quality of their work (Sadker and Sadker, 1994). Elementary school teaches boys that problems are challenges to overcome. Girls get the message that failure is beyond their control.

Another powerful indicator of the greater importance attached to boys than girls involves the curricular material upon which most time in elementary school is spent. Over 30 years of research demonstrates that girls are virtually invisible or, at best, play insignificant roles in a variety of such material. Current curriculum materials are more egalitarian today than in the 1970s, but stereotyped portrayals are still prevalent (Cooper, 1989; Grossman and Grossman, 1994). Studies of textbooks which teach reading, social studies, and even mathematics consistently demonstrate that less importance is attached to females by the number of female characters represented and the roles they play. When female characters are depicted, they are described as timid, uncreative, unambitious, and inactive. Females are rarely mentioned as making any meaningful contributions to history, science, or government. Girls help their mothers. Women do not usually work outside the home, but if they do it is in a gender stereotyped job. Boys do interesting and exciting things. Girls do not (Best, 1983; Heintz, 1987; Purcell and Stewart, 1990; American Association of University Women, 1992; Grossman and Grossman, 1994). For example, while girls in children's books are shown as brave, they still need to be rescued; while boys are shown babysitting, they are still forced to deny their full range of emotions lest it compromise their manhood; and girls and women are still underrepresented in both numbers and diversity of activities and occupations (Purcell and Stewart, 1990).

A pioneering study of these patterns of female invisibility was conducted by Lenore Weitzman and her associates (1972) with their thorough examination of children's picture books. How are gender roles treated in those books which are considered the very best that are offered to children during these formative years? Weitzman defines "the best" as books chosen for the coveted Caldecott Medal given by the Children's Service Committee of the American Library Association for excellence in books geared to school-age children, mainly in the third through sixth grades. She also examined bestsellers among the popular *Little Golden Book* series. The findings are consistent with other research:

> We found that females were underrepresented in the titles, central roles, pictures, and stories of every sample of books we examined. Most children's books are about boys, men, and male animals, and deal exclusively with male adventures. Most pictures show men singly or in groups. Even when women can be found in the books, they often play insignificant roles, remaining both inconspicuous and nameless. (Weitzman et al., 1972:1128)

The few female characters who can be described as independent or adventurous are successful only through their unobtrusiveness or ability to toil quietly behind the scenes. And since not one of the women in the Caldecott sample had a job or profession outside the home, it is realistic to assess socialization in these books as training girls for service activities and limited, more dependent roles. What is perhaps more revealing is that the Caldecott sample is in fact less stereotyped in portrayals than the other book series she examined and are not indicative of the "most blatant examples of sexism" (Weitzman et al., 1972:1127).

Considering the fact that Weitzman's study is now almost three decades old and that the consciousness of a nation has been raised regarding the extent of gender role stereotyping in education, it would be expected that instructional materials are today more reflective of the expanded roles of many women and some men. The research evidence is mixed in this regard. In replicating and extending the Weitzman study, Williams and associates (1987) do not find this to be true. The books children read today continue to present characters in line with traditional gender roles. Women and girls are portrayed as being dependent, cooperative, passive, submissive, and nurturing, whereas men and boys are seen as independent, creative, explorative, aggressive, and active. The Williams study does find, however, that the visibility of female characters increased significantly by the early 1980s with only 12.5 percent of the Caldecotts having no female characters.

More recent research on gendered images in children's books has compared Caldecott winners and runners-up in the Coretta Scott King competition, which specifically honors black authors and illustrators (Clark et al., 1993). This study reveals that by the late 1980s, the percentage of Caldecotts with no female characters was at 25 percent but that *all* of the King award books included them. When gender of the central character is examined, Caldecotts of the late 1980s had 44 percent but Kings of the same period had 63.6 percent. The authors conclude that less stereotyped portrayals are evident in both samples with male and female characters depicted in more egalitarian roles. And consistent with the aims of black feminist theorists, "black illustrators are more apt than others to highlight women's involvement in an ethic of caring and an ethic of personal accountability" (Clark et al., 1993:227). While gender parity has not been reached, strides toward more realistic portrayals are being made.

Schau and Scott's (1984) review of research on the impact of gender-typed curricular materials concludes that gender role attitudes of students at all grade levels, from elementary school through college, are compromised. Instructional materials that perpetuate gender role stereotyping in turn reinforce gender-typed beliefs, with children in the younger grades being the most susceptible. On the other hand, it is clearly demonstrated that when textbooks in particular portray girls and boys and women and men in nontraditional roles and in situations where gender equity rather than gender stratification is evident, less gender-typed attitudes result. In educational institutions in general and in curricular materials in particular, Sadker and Sadker (1994) have determined it is boys who are the central figures, while girls are assigned a second-class status.

The following historical example illustrates what today would be considered gender stereotyping and sexism in the extreme. Published in 1970, the book in which this poem appeared has long since been removed from stores. The theme is not indicative of the current editorial policies of the company that published the poem or of most other publishers of children's books. While it reflects the blatant sexism of the past, we have seen from research that gendered images still flourish in reading material for children.

A girl can be:

a nurse, with white uniforms to wear, or
a stewardess, who flies everywhere.
a ballerina, who dances and twirls around, or
a candy shop owner, the best in town.
a model, who wears lots of pretty clothes or
a big star in the movies and on special TV shows.
a secretary who'll type without mistakes, or
an artist, painting trees and clouds and lakes.
a teacher in nursery school some day, or
a singer and makes records people play.
a designer of dresses in the very latest style, or
a bride, who comes walking down the aisle.
a housewife, someday when I am grown, and
a mother, with some children of my own.

Jane learns that her intellectual achievement is going to be less important than her physical attractiveness, and that options outside motherhood are seen as less desirable. As we shall see, this becomes more crystallized in high school.

Boys, on the other hand, are experiencing elementary school quite differently. We saw that they do not easily adjust to a classroom environment which emphasizes quietness and physical inactivity. Teachers reprimand them more and give them lower grades. Lipmen-Blumen (1984) reports that, even though boys possess the same intellectual capabilities as girls, they receive lower grades on report cards. Yet when boys learn that more effort and less disruptive classroom behavior will remedy this, their self-esteem is protected. Teachers talk to them more about the subject matter, listen more to their complaints and questions, and praise them most for their intellectual competence (Dweck et al., 1978; Eccles and Blumenfeld, 1985; Sadker and Sadker, 1990). Despite classroom protocol, boys shout out answers to questions, whether right or wrong, and get attention. Girls raise their hands and get ignored (Halberstam, 1994).

The textbooks boys read in elementary school are replete with male characters doing interesting and exciting things, both in occupational and recreational activities, such as sports. They see active and resourceful adult males who are jobholders and boys their own age who build, create and discover, as well as protect and rescue girls (Weitzman, 1984; Cooper, 1989; Purcell and Stewart, 1990). It is true that males are also cast into father roles, but in contrast to mothers, they have a separate life and identity outside the home. They are fathers as well as scientists, firefighters, and police officers. For recreation, males are involved in a variety of sports activities. When females are depicted in sports, they are primarily in traditional female sports, such as gymnastics and ice skating (Grossman and Grossman, 1994). Although research consistently reveals a gender bias that is more detrimental to girls, what is now historical research on first-grade readers lamented that girls were more catered to than boys in that outdoor activities which interest boys, such as fishing and bike riding, were seldom shown. It also indicated that joint father-son activities were rarely depicted (Byers, 1964). While there is less information on the father-son depiction issue, it is apparent from the next 30 years of research that boys' activities have received a great deal of curriculum coverage. For boys, if a bias existed, it has been corrected, but the same cannot be said of girls.

Although Dick may find some aspects of elementary school frustrating and confusing, curricular materials confirm his masculine role and serve to strengthen his male identity. His primary role in life will be as a wage earner and, as reflected in the poem from a 1970 book for boys, Dick can aspire to heights not available to Jane.

> A boy can be:
>
> a fireman who squirts water on the flames, and
> a baseball player who wins lots of games.
> a bus driver who helps people travel far, and
> a policeman with a siren in his car,
> a cowboy who goes on cattle drives, and
> a doctor who helps to save people's lives.
> a sailor on a ship that takes you everywhere, and
> a pilot who goes flying through the air.
> a clown with silly tricks to do, and
> a pet tiger owner who runs the zoo.
> a farmer who drives a big red tractor, and
> on a TV show if I become an actor.
> an astronaut who lives in a space station, and
> someday grow up to be President of the nation.

The parallel poems for girls and boys show the ultimate aspirations associated with traditional gender roles in American society—wife and mother versus president. They also reveal the continued rigidity associated with the male role. Even if Jane chooses a stereotyped occupational role (ballerina and secretary), it still assumes that at least a minimal identity beyond the home is possible, if only until marriage. Dick is completely bound to expectations of high achievement in a nondomestic environment. The fact that he will also be a husband and father is ignored.

High School

Based on Jane's intellectual achievement and superior grades in elementary school, it would appear that academic success in high school could be easily predicted. But the process begins to reverse. While gender differences continue to narrow, academic achievement as measured by standardized tests decreases for girls (Dauber, 1986; Burton et al., 1988; Sadker and Sadker, 1994). While girls in elementary school are confident and assertive, they leave adolescence with a poor self-image. Girls experience a precipitous drop in self-esteem, the sharpest occurring between elementary and middle school (American Association of University Women (AAUW), 1992; Orenstein, 1994). While this is the case for white girls, it is even more pronounced for Hispanic girls who start out with the highest levels of self-esteem. However, this pattern is altered and academic achievement rises when Hispanic girls perceive liberal attitudes toward women. This suggests that they modify their achievement according to their perceptions of compatibility between liberal attitudes and academic success (Valenzuela, 1993). For African-American girls, the AAUW report presents an interesting finding. Unlike whites, although they retain a high level of self-esteem throughout high school, they drop significantly in positive feelings about their teachers and their academic work. Scholastic achievement for all girls begins to decline in areas such as reading and writing, but especially in mathematics, where boys are beginning to excel.

Gender and Mathematics. This finding has been seized as demonstrating that girls have lower analytic ability than boys and furthermore that it is biologically based. The biology argument in explaining gender differences in math and science posits everything from chromosomes, hormones, brain hemisphere, brain organization, and/or genetic codes as responsible for the male edge in mathematics (Cresswell et al., 1988; Christen, 1991; Peters, 1991; Rosser, 1992; Casey et al., 1992). On the biology side, no gene has been identified that traces enhanced spatial ability from mother to son and researchers are skeptical that such a "complex ability as spatial reasoning could possibly rest in a single gene" (McLoughlin, 1988:55). Yet since mathematics and spatial tests are related, those math items which males perform better than females have a spatial component and there may be biological underpinnings to this. Gender differences in rate of development play an important role. In summarizing this research Hoyenga and Hoyenga (1993:400) conclude

> not only do very-late maturing females score higher on spatial tasks, the magnitude of the sex difference in spatial scores matches the sex difference in the age at which hormone levels begin increasing. However, development rate itself is completely determined by genes, prenatal hormones, and the postnatal environment. The major importance is that sex differences can be manipulated— magnified, minimized, or even reversed—by . . . relevant environmental factors and developmental experiences.

This conclusion is compatible with what we have already seen in Chapter 2 in terms of explaining of gender differences overall: Both biology and environment (sociocultural influences) are factors.

However, the fact that gender differences in mathematics have been steadily decreasing gives more weight to the counterargument that powerful sociocultural factors are responsible for propelling boys and deterring girls in mathematical pursuits. While male scores on tests involving mathematical reasoning exceed scores for females, they are influenced by the content of the item (Rosser, 1989). When the content was changed to include "feminine" subjects such as cooking and sewing, while retaining the same logical reasoning process, female scores increased (Weitzman, 1984). When verbal processes are used in mathematical questions, girls outperform boys. When spatial-visual abilities are used, boys outperform girls (Doyle and Paludi, 1995:13).

There is disagreement about what constitutes mathematical ability, which indicates that such definitional problems make comparisons difficult (Linn and Petersen, 1985; Caplan et al., 1985). It may be deceptive to label spatial perception, or the capacity to see things out of context, which is lower in girls, as comprising analytic ability. Verbal perception, in which girls score higher, should also be included. Several studies have concluded that when the number of math-oriented courses is controlled, there are no real differences in spatial perception or overall mathematical capability (Fennema and Sherman, 1977; Fox, 1981; Chipman and Thomas, 1985; Chipman et al., 1985). Boys begin to outperform girls in math only in high school, when girls take fewer math courses. As Weitzman (1984:84) poignantly states, "One might speculate that if women had higher scores on spatial perception and men had higher scores on verbal perception, the latter would have been called analytic ability, for what the researchers have done is to seize upon one of the few traits in which men score higher and label it analytic ability."

Although the media have been responsible for highlighting a gender divergence in math performance and in spatial and quantitative ability, it is now clear that not only are these gender differences declining, they may not have been as great as previously believed, with only between 1 to 5 percent of the variance which does exist explained by gender (Hyde, 1981; Linn and Petersen, 1985; Friedman, 1989; Tartre, 1990). Studies also find that while gender differences in verbal performance are consistent, these, too, are small (Plomin and Foch, 1981; Linn and Hyde, 1989). What is perhaps even more important, is that a recent research review indicates that females now have an *advantage* in computational problems and understanding mathematical concepts. Boys retain an advantage in complex problem solving. But as in other research, these gender differences are quite small and reflect more selected, less representative samples (Hyde at al., 1990). In reviewing all these data, Caplan and Caplan (1994:43) conclude that the claim that male superiority in mathematics is innate is unjustified.

While the reality is that gender differences in mathematical and verbal ability are declining, the downturn of overall academic performance and self-esteem in high school girls must still be explained. From a gender role viewpoint several answers can be suggested. Many girls equate scholastic success with a loss of femininity. Popularity with boys is the key to fulfillment in high school, so girls choose to hide their intellectual abilities so as not to appear competitive to the boys they would like to attract. The peer pressure of high school may force some bright young women to view themselves as inadequate or unfeminine if they succeed academically or are interested in supposedly masculine subjects, like mathematics, an image which is often subtly reinforced by teachers (Koehler, 1990; Leung, 1990; Andersen, 1993). And since teachers of math and science are more likely to be male, high school girls are limited in finding role models to whom they would likely turn for help in pursuing advanced quantitative coursework. It is understandable, then, that not only do grades decline, but upon graduation many girls do not have the prerequisites for majoring in science, engineering, or other subjects where a strong math-based competency is required.

Finally, academic success in math and science has one of the strongest relationships to high levels of self-esteem among high school girls. When a high school girl enjoys math, she also feels good about herself and her school work, sees herself as important, and feels better about her family relationships. While boys at all grade levels maintain confidence in math ability, for girls there is a major decline as they move through adolescence (American Association of University Women, 1992; Orenstein, 1994). Girls who do poorly in math are less likely than boys to believe that more effort will produce success (Stipek and Gralinski, 1991). The link between mathematics and computer literacy is also a strong one psychologically for girls. Computer literacy is no longer an optional life skill; it is a necessary one. The male-computer connection is a strong one which discourages girls (Kramer and Lehman, 1990; Mark, 1992). While there is no sign on the computer room door saying "no girls allowed," females internalize it mentally (cited in Sadker and Sadker, 1994:123). In addressing this issue, work is being done on college campuses to "establish a community of support and a culture of success for women in science" (Rayman, 1993). While high schools lag behind, public awareness is growing that the "glass ceiling" starts in schools and support for such programs is growing (Hegger, 1993). Both girls and boys need to be educated and encouraged to understand that math and science are important and relevant to their lives.

Gendered Tracking and Vocational Education.   High school girls are more often tracked into academic courses like English and vocational courses like word processing and home economics, where they can succeed and, at the same time, pose no threat to boys. Contrary to popular belief, more girls graduate from high school than boys and more girls are enrolled in vocational education courses than boys. Girls are likely to need proof of competency for even rudimentary clerical work, and this proof usually comes in the form of a high school diploma. Also, the higher female enrollment in vocational education courses reflects the fact that more men intend to pursue college. Women take courses where they can be employed immediately upon graduation. The overwhelming majority of students in courses geared to retail sales, health assistance, and secretarial and other office occupations are female. Yet most vocational programs for girls are still dominated by the teaching of household skills, which mirrors the cultural assumption that working outside the home is optional for women. The myth of female dependence on males for their income is not a benign one. When young women graduate from high school with severely restricted career options, it often translates to poor economic outcomes which are worsened by divorce and single parenthood. Overall, high school vocational education for girls is geared to the noncollege bound who either marry or wind up in low-paying, dead-end jobs.

Whereas more and more middle-class girls are going to college, working-class girls may not see this as a realistic option. This means that marriage looms as the proper alternative and obtaining a marketable vocational skill is important until they marry. In addressing this issue, feminist thinking is now being introduced on the federal level to improve gender equity in vocational education and, concomitantly, empower its students. As Burge and Culver (1990:161) suggest, vocational education has historically been committed to the less powerful of society, whether they are women, the working poor, or other skilled laborers. When supported by federal legislation, vocational education can provide training in nontraditional areas which can freely be chosen by both high school boys and girls.

For Dick, the confusion of elementary school begins to dissipate as his independence is now rewarded more often. His grades have improved considerably, and he is able to demonstrate his talents in courses specifically designed for boys. Compared to Jane, Dick experiences consistent gains in status and believes he is "good at a lot of things" (American Association of University Women, 1992; Eder and Kinney, 1995). Although intent on pursuing a college education, he also finds industrial and graphic arts and woodworking and metallurgy open to him. For his friends who are not going to college, high school vocational education courses will help prepare them for jobs in printing, carpentry, engineering technology, and computer science. Unlike courses for girls, vocational education for boys will have potentially higher economic returns after high school graduation.

Although enrollment by girls in what have been traditionally labeled as "male" courses is exploding, boys are less likely to take courses associated with "feminine" activities. When course titles are not as reflective of feminine content, boys will enroll more freely. For instance, "Bachelor Living" and "Home Mechanics" will allow boys to gain at least basic household skills without the stigma of taking a "girl's" course. Changing the title of a course to entice males to enroll may appear to be pandering, and again, it serves to devalue courses that females have taken all along, but it at least provides a mechanism to expose boys to needed content and helps to increase their skills in very practical domestic tasks.

Differential vocational education tracking is reinforced by other school mechanisms which help perpetuate the system. Both genders are exposed to the same history and social studies courses. As with elementary school, these courses demonstrate that "boys do" and "girls don't." In history books, when women are mentioned, it is usually in the context of a traditional role, Betsy Ross for sewing and Florence Nightingale for nursing, or of becoming notable because they marry famous men. Thus not only are few women portrayed, but those who are conform to a definite stereotypical image of what women are supposed to be. The content of history courses in college is beginning to reflect newer ideas about diversity in general and women in particular (see Chapter 5), but this trend is lagging in high schools. Controversial men are portrayed. Potentially controversial women are omitted.

Even the standardized achievement and career interest tests taken by high school students represent a consistent male bias, from the content to the pronouns used. While standardized tests continue to be evaluated in terms of gender bias, to date, they are not balanced in this regard (Berger, 1989; Parelius, 1991; Sadker and Sadker, 1994). These tests are then administered by counselors who themselves may not be objective in helping with vocational and college planning. Gender bias in counseling is a problem that can affect students' attitudes to career selection, choice of major, or even willingness to pursue a college education. Recognizing the insidious nature of this trend, there is now a call for developing intervention strategies that will help raise the gender role consciousness of counselors and also help them understand how their own cultural beliefs influence their work with students (American Association of University Women, 1992).

High school provides another instance of staffing patterns that demonstrate to students and the community alike that males are the leaders. The male high school principal reports to the male school superintendent who regularly meets with primarily male school board members. The community bestows laurels on the coaches who steer their basketball and football teams to victorious heights. Male achievement on the playing fields of high schools across America is invariably associated with community and school pride and respectability. How does this affect the boys who strive to become members of the coveted team?

Athletics.   Whereas popularity with boys is linked to prestige for girls, athletic success provides the same function for boys. At early ages, boys are told that athletic accomplishments will aid in success in life. They also realize that their prestige with both genders rests on it (Coleman, 1961). This report is now a historical document, but the situation has not changed. In fact, it has accelerated as the public is more aware of the millions of dollars spent on professional sports and sees the personal glory of the athletes themselves. Their image is not tarnished but made more lustrous by the injuries, fights, and general mayhem that occur in football and hockey games.

As documented in Chapter 9, team sports demonstrate the importance of competition and allow for participants to gain in confidence, concentration, and courage, which are traits associated with successful American males. If boys cannot withstand the physical or emotional strains of athletics, they may feel inadequate and unpopular. If a boy gauges himself by his athletic prowess or physical deeds, and by his estimation cannot measure up to his peers, his self-esteem will suffer. A boy may experience a sense of failure when he does not reach the top of the athletic hierarchy (Messner, 1995). By his values, academic achievement is no real substitute for athletic rewards. In more extreme cases, he may begin to doubt his masculinity and harbor resentment toward women. A male gender identity can be formed and polished by sports. More important, this identity could be tarnished if a boy engages in coeducational sports, especially if a girl can outperform a boy in the same athletic competition. This kind of argument not only discourages coed teams but again provides ammunition that implicitly deprecates those activities where girls can succeed at an equal or better level than boys.

The importance attached to high school athletics can be measured by the financial and organizational support given to male as opposed to female sports. Boys' teams have better equipment and facilities and higher paid coaches than comparable girls' teams, if the latter are represented in team sports at all (Weitzman, 1984). With these kinds of statistics, it is understandable that athletics are still viewed as a road to success for high school males. This is a gilded road for those boys who intend to pursue college through an athletic scholarship.

Higher Education

If high school tracking mechanisms have been successful, the best and the brightest students will pursue a college education. Since World War II, there has been a steady increase of both men and women attending college; women now exceed men, and these women are increasingly older (over 35), part-time students. This pattern is likely to accelerate in the next decade as women who have not previously worked outside the home, especially on a full-time basis, realize they are no longer limited to domestic roles. It is augmented by single parents who know that a college degree will provide at least a modicum of financial security for themselves and their children. Others see education as enhancing career choices later in life. Ideally, college should be the one educational institution which objectively evaluates students on criteria related to academic achievement and the potential for success. But the lessons of elementary school and high school are not easily forgotten.

Sexual Harassment.   Although many barriers have fallen as doors in higher education increasingly open to women, the classroom climate still offers subtle, as well as not so subtle, cues for women. Sandler (1987:115) reports that even overt discriminatory comments are frequently heard in the college classroom, as the following research example illustrates.

> In . . . classes they hear women described as fat housewives, dumb blondes, as physically dirty, as broads, chicks or dames, depending upon the age of the speaker. Class time is taken up by some professors with dirty jokes which . . . often happen to be derogatory to women (i.e., referring to a woman by a part of her anatomy, portraying women in jokes as simple-minded or teases, showing women as part of the "decoration" on a slide).

Such comments are indicative of research suggesting that even with explicit policies condemning it, sexual harassment on college campuses continues to be widespread. Just what constitutes sexual harassment varies by definition, but it is generally seen to encompass physical or verbal behavior that is sexual in nature, is unwanted, and is experienced as a threat to job or ability to perform work or educational activities (Martin, 1995:23). A recent survey of high school students shows that about one-third either observed or experienced sexual harassment (Sauerwein, 1996). Examples from these students included: "talking about people with large chests," "pinching butts on the bus," and "half of everything said in the Commons." On college campuses, research indicates that between 30 and 70 percent of female faculty and female students have experienced it in some form (Paludi and Barickman, 1991; Martin and Hummer, 1993; Dziech and Weiner, 1993). While sexual harassment of males is infrequent, cases are growing. Although fear of reprisal makes women reluctant to report it, the assault on gender identity makes it even less likely for males to do so (American Association of University Women, 1993; Paludi, 1996).

Shannon Faulkner received notoriety by being the first female cadet admitted to The Citadel in 1993, a military college in South Carolina and the (then) only female to drop out. The hatred expressed with her admittance and the joy expressed by her classmates when she dropped out are issues related both to sexual harassment and the rigidity of gender roles. In 1996, and now in line with the Supreme Court, The Citadel officially ended its 153 year old men-only policy. Shannon Faulkner was subjected to death threats, ugly jeers, and her car and home were vandalized. Yet she inspired other women who have already taken her place (*St. Louis Post-Dispatch*, 1995a, 1995b, 1996b).

Gendered College Classrooms. Women discover early in their college years that they will receive less faculty encouragement for their work and will be listened to less and interrupted more than their male classmates, thereby promoting lower expectations of achievement (Lee and Bryk, 1986; Sandler, 1987, Kramarae and Treichler, 1990; Chilly Collective, 1995; Fox, 1995). Women shun aggressiveness throughout their lives and the intellectual battles in the college classroom require difficult adjustment. Even highly motivated women will likely experience a moderate degree of anxiety as such values collide. As in high school, self-esteem drops for women and increases for men during college (American Association of University Women, 1992). Traditional values intrude again as the inevitable confrontation resurfaces for the college woman. There is pressure to find a partner and simultaneously work toward career goals. If the future is uncertain because of role conflicts, the present becomes more anxiety ridden.

It is interesting that many of these patterns are altered when women outnumber men in the classroom or when female faculty represent a larger proportion of overall faculty, especially in math and the physical sciences. When academic experiences in single-gender and coeducational institutions are measured by scholarship, degree aspirations, attitudes toward studies, leadership, and self-confidence, the research is favorable for single-sex education (Miller-Bernal, 1991:124-25). While men may also benefit from single-gender education, data suggest that the benefits to women are greater, leading to success for women both during and beyond their college years. Women from single-gender colleges outperform women who have not attended single-gender schools, and they are more likely to attend graduate or professional school (Fox-Genovese, 1995). Research also indicates that women's colleges offer particularly hospitable environments for minority and returning, nontraditional age students (Association of American Colleges and Universities, 1995). Among high school students, African-American and Hispanic females have higher leadership scores and a higher perception of environmental control (e.g., a student's belief that she can overcome external obstacles) than their counterparts in coed schools (Riordan, 1994). When females make a transition from a single-gender to coeducational educational environment, they may experience a "clash of cultures" and report discomfort and dissatisfaction with the coed format. For example, in a study of a college that changed to a coeducational system, women express concern that friends will become competitors when men are a regular part of campus life (Association of American Colleges and Universities, 1994).

Critics of single-gender education point to the negative effects of an already pervasive gender-segregated society. We have documented that while within-gender solidarity is enhanced through gender segregation, between-gender understanding is diminished. Educational institutions at all levels are microcosms of the real world, so they should model that world. Coeducation can certainly provide a major mechanism for reducing gender segregation and its associated gender stereotyping. In addition, if there is a problem of male dominance in the classroom that is detrimental to girls, a convincing argument can be made that it is also detrimental to boys. Rather than retreating into gender-segregated schools, the classroom atmosphere can be altered to reflect not only a more gender-sensitive campus or school culture, but one which is beneficial to both females and males. Feminist pedagogy places a high value on cooperative learning techniques in a supportive environment that can reduce competition and the fear of failure (Maher and Tetreault, 1994). While consensus is valued, skill building for success in a competitive society is also learned. Regardless of which side of the debate one is on, classroom environments can be modified to capitalize on the successful learning strategies provided by single-gender education.

In tracing the collegiate experiences of 23 women, Holland and Eisenhart (1990) find it is difficult for even high-achieving women on campus to resist the "culture of romance" where a high-pressure peer system urges women to seek out the most attractive men. The authors conclude that the ultimate effect is lowered ambitions and a subversion of academic achievement. Propelled by gendered expectations, the notorious peer pressure of high school transfers with relative ease to the college campus. In studying achievement-related conflicts in women, Horner's classic work (1969, 1972) suggests that success in college may be seen as unfeminine. It is not that failure is the desirable outcome, but that anxiety is produced by success. She proposed a "fear of success" concept to explain the anxiety women feel when they see their femininity threatened and may explain women's drop in grades in high school and lowered self-esteem in college. It also became a convenient explanation for the failure of women to gain the top positions in industry and academia, thus reinforcing a blame-the-victim ideological stance. Partly because of the media publicity the original studies received and the debate they generated in academic circles, already more than 200 studies have been conducted on the topic (Walsh, 1987). Since much of this research has been inconclusive or produced inconsistent results, the fear of success concept itself has been criticized on both methodological and theoretical grounds (Sadd et al., 1978; Paludi, 1984, 1992), and Horner's notion that it is a consistent personality trait connected with certain expectations for behavior has been questioned.

Basow (1992) points out that a more satisfactory explanation is to consider fear of success as a situational variable where women can realistically evaluate the negative results from success in a given situation. Women do not fear success but are aware that men and women are evaluated differently when they do achieve. Other research suggests that for both women and men, higher scores on scales measuring fear of success are correlated with lower levels of instrumentality, a trait considered to be more masculine (Gerber, 1984; Cano et al., 1984; Wong et al., 1985). Finally, if the drop in self-esteem is associated with lack of confidence to successfully compete in male-oriented environments where females also have high achievement aspirations, it is not the fear of success which is potentially disabling, but the fear of failure.

In an extensive review of the literature, Paludi (1992:244) concludes that while there does seem to be a relationship between fear of success and gender role identity, the data are inconsistent and that whether fear of success taps a motive or a cultural stereotype is also not clear. What is clear, however, is that both genders are sensitive to the results of their achievement, whether they are successes or otherwise. And regardless of which dimension the concept may or may not be tapping, recent studies demonstrate that there is much less fear of success among women but that it represents a continued, stabilized pattern among men (Marini and Brinton, 1984). To say that socialization into the female role motivates girls and women to avoid success is simply not empirically verifiable and does not do justice to the immense change that has taken place since Horner's original work. Without a doubt, an academic environment that does not reinforce the invisibility of women would be beneficial.

Clear-visioned college women may choose the well-traveled road of majoring in the arts and humanities and continue to reserve science and mathematics for men. Forty percent of women who enter college wanting to be scientists switch to other majors (Masters, 1994). Both precollege preparation and lack of peers in the field are key factors in explaining this. When coupled with the psychological barriers women face in college, for those who opt for graduate education, the routes on the academic map are already indelibly marked. Today women receive just over half of all undergraduate and master's degrees, but only one-third of doctorates. However, women earn slightly more than half of all doctorates in fields other than science and engineering (*Feminist Teacher*, 1991:9). Gains in professional degrees have been steady, especially in law, where women now receive close to half of all degrees, and medicine, where they receive just over one-third of all degrees (Fox, 1995). Considering that the opportunity for any higher education for women is a relatively recent phenomenon, these numbers are impressive.

However, at both the undergraduate and graduate level, gender-specific patterns emerge. As would be expected, women are concentrated in nursing, literature, home economics, certain of the social sciences, education, and library science with men dominating areas such as mathematics, the physical sciences, and architecture. The disparity is greatest in doctoral level studies, which find women in traditionally "female" areas and those disciplines already glutted with Ph.D.s. Not only are men distributed in a wider variety of studies, but they are also in the expanding, more lucrative technical fields, such as engineering and the physical sciences. Psychological roadblocks are accentuated in graduate and professional education for both genders as competition for grades and grants also increases. Besides dealing with pressures involving career, marriage, having children, and femininity, women must also cope with restrictive admission policies and the subtle discrimination existing in many, if not most, graduate departments. Academic careers blossom through a protégé system which matches a talented graduate student with a recognized, established faculty member. Women graduate students spend less time with faculty, are less relaxed when they do, and find they are not suitable as protégés. Although not overtly discriminatory, these pervasive patterns keep both faculty and graduate student males in control of the powerful subculture of graduate school. Fox (1995:229) demonstrates how this operates on the professional level by quoting a Berkeley student.

> Have I been overtly discriminated against? Probably no. Have I been encouraged, congratulated, received recognition, gotten a friendly hello, a solicitous "can I help you out?" The answer is no. Being a woman here just makes you tougher, work harder, and hope that if you get a 4.0 GPA someone will say "You're good."

Female faculty are important for undergraduate and graduate women as both role models and mentors. Where does the academic path lead for women Ph.D.s? Most are in two- and four-year state colleges, usually satellite campuses, with heavy teaching loads and administrative responsibilities. They are clustered in less prestigious schools and the less powerful fields. They are likely to be instructors and assistant professors. Women constitute about 15 percent of full professors but just under half of all assistant professors (American Association of University Professors, 1990; Fox, 1995). The pattern repeats itself throughout academia—the higher the rank, the fewer the women.

When tenure decisions are made, the years of subtle discrimination become manifest. The majority of men on the faculties of four-year colleges and universities have tenure and the majority of their female counterparts do not, a pattern which has remained steady for at least a decade (National Center for Education Statistics, 1994). Women are denied often because they have fewer publications in lesser-known journals, devote a greater amount of their time to teaching, and engage in more unpaid professional service than their male colleagues (Association of American Colleges and Universities, 1995:3). Research by Statham and her colleagues (1991) find that in the classroom women are evaluated differently than men by students, colleagues, and administrators alike. They are expected to be "nice" as well as competent, to maintain a pleasant classroom atmosphere, be overly accessible to students outside class, and to engage students in a variety of learning modes. Women are judged more harshly when they deviate from the gender-imposed model of a "caring" professor. Other data show that both men and women university faculty members adopt stereotyped gender role images, a pattern which intrudes on peer evaluation and the informal network in which female faculty are first assessed (Gallant and Cross, 1993; Street et al., 1995). Besides the clear inequity of such patterns, it is a sad comment on college education in general that good teaching, where women excel, is not usually rewarded with tenure.

And even at the most prestigious colleges, women faculty often find themselves pulled away from career goals by the same challenges faced by other bright, ambitious women—gender bias and the multiple demands of family and the university. Jane may then be caught with the agonizing decision of uprooting her life to seek employment elsewhere or finding part-time work at other local colleges. The latter course will be her likely choice, especially if she has children and an employed spouse. She will remain in academia but in a marginal position with little hope of advancement, influence, or tenure.

Although both well-qualified women and men are likely to be admitted to college, once admitted, men find that American academic life exemplifies a male mode of performance. Dick, too, is caught in the pressure to perform at a high scholastic level and still be socially adept. Yet the classroom atmosphere is probably easier for males to handle, with rewards coming for vigorous discussion and winning in classroom debate. Male faculty as role models and mentors reinforce this pattern. Compared to female law students, for example, males report a greater degree of comfort with both formal and informal interaction with faculty members (Association of American Colleges and Universities, 1995).

College men are not immune to the gender role changes which are occurring on campuses, which means some are now caught in a double bind. Komarovsky (1987) states that many men are now coming to value originality and intelligence in their female classmates and associates, yet they have been unable to relinquish the cherished belief and internalized norm that men should be superior. Some of the following attitudes are typically expressed:

> I am looking for an intelligent girl who has opinions on politics, social problems—someone I could talk to about things guys talk about.

> If I were a woman I would want a career. It must be boring sitting around the house doing the same thing day in and day out.

> I would not want to marry a woman whose only goal is a housewife. (Komarovsky, 1987:124, 127)

Such remarks indicate several things. First, men may be more sympathetic to women who are in housewife roles. Second, they demonstrate the continued negative values associated with being a housewife. Finally, tantalizing egalitarian ideals are held out to the college men who want to accept them. But as Komarovsky (1987:129) points out, they represent both "the lure and the threat" of the articulate, educated woman. A lifetime of socialization into gender roles is difficult to negate.

Men dominate the most influential fields where graduate work is required, such as engineering, medicine, and law. They also remain concentrated at the top of the prestige hierarchy within such fields. Men are overrepresented as surgeons, and women are overrepresented as pediatricians. Although pharmacy colleges now enroll well over 60 percent women, men are more likely to be retail store owners, chain store managers, and directors of hospital pharmacies. Women hold positions in pharmacy of considerably less power and prestige (Lindsey, 1984). The attorneys who represent international corporations are most often men. Women attorneys practice family law and work for the Legal Aid Society. In private firms, men are law partners; women are associates. The culmination of college or graduate school, whether as a holder of B.A., M.D., or Ph.D., is also the culmination of a lifetime of socialization into attitudes and behavior regarding gender roles.

The Lessons of Title IX

The educational patterns described here should become obsolete if gender discrimination in education becomes legally banned. At least, this was the intent behind the passage of Title IX of the Educational Amendment Act of 1972 (see Chapter 14 for more details). This act prohibited sex (gender) discrimination in any school receiving federal assistance, which meant that the majority of educational institutions fell under its mandate. At the overt and formal level it can be said that gender discrimination has decreased, especially in the areas of college admissions, athletics, and scholarships.

We have seen, however, that at all educational levels noticeable discriminatory policies and practices still exist. As overviewed by McMillen (1985:27), women academics still say they "suffer extensively from stereotypes and sexist attitudes." They are still being called "girls" by male colleagues and are often ignored when serving on committees. Sympathetic women who can serve as role models for aspiring female faculty and administrators are cited as a key to help change such attitudes. Title IX has done little to alter gender segregation of academic fields, at either the student or faculty level. This pattern continues to show up throughout all levels of educational institutions. Girls take home economics in junior high school. Boys major in mathematics in college. Women Ph.D.s teach French. Even the more liberal world of the university remains gender role oriented and gender separated.

It may be possible to reduce, even eliminate, blatant gender discrimination through legal means. This assumes the existence of a favorable political climate that actively initiates and enforces such change. Certainly, this is not a priority in these fiscally harsh times. Title IX can serve as a catalyst of change only if it is coupled with a major modification in those socialization practices that restrict the educational opportunities for girls and boys, women and men. Gender discrimination may disappear by the time Jane reaches college, yet it is conceivable that her children and grandchildren will be influenced by lingering prejudices throughout their own school years.

Reflecting on education a century ago, M. Carey Thomas (1857-1935), former president of Bryn Mawr College, stated

> that women, like men, are quickened and inspired by the same love of learning, the same love of science, [and] the same love of abstract truth; that women, like men, are immeasurably benefited, physically, mentally and morally, and are made vastly better mothers, as men made vastly better fathers, by subordinating the distracting instincts of sex to the simple human fellowship of similar education and similar intellectual and social needs. (Thomas, 1991:338)

While prejudices may linger for generations to come, this chapter has documented some encouraging signs that perhaps Thomas's call for the "simple human fellowship of similar education" is within our grasp.

CHAPTER 12

RELIGION AND PATRIARCHY

Something went terribly wrong with Christianity's original gospel of love.
—Riane Eisler, *The Chalice and the Blade* (1988:131)

This is why one of the most important creative challenges of our time is to disentangle love from all the cruel meanings it has acquired over these last millennia . . . And the exciting fact is that this too is already underway.
—Riane Eisler, *Sacred Pleasure* (1995:382)

The transformation of ancient spirituality into modern institutionalized religion has come with a heavy price. Religious myths have been used to maintain injustice, suffering, and oppression—of men against men and men against women. Institutionalized religion, whether it is pagan, Hebrew, or Christian, has helped to maintain hierarchies of domination as well as alleviate part of the suffering caused by these very hierarchies (Eisler, 1995:203). It is paradoxical that in the one institution which theoretically offers the most freedom of expression through liberating spirituality, religion still finds itself encumbered by undeniably sexist interpretations and practices. As with the other institutions, it is difficult to separate religion from the cultural framework in which it is embedded; hence religious principles and experiences are interpreted accordingly. The impact of science and technology, universal education, and the almost daily exposure to worldwide violence are often associated with the decline of religious significance in our lives. Yet surveys indicate that fully 90 percent of Americans at least identify with a particular religion, with almost two-thirds stating that they have a formal affiliation (Macionis, 1995:503).

Religion is a powerful agent of socialization, especially in its influences on our gender role identity. Degree of religious involvement has been correlated with a number of gender-related issues including attitudes to abortion, ERA, family decision making and female submission within marriage, homosexuality, nonmarital sex, and use of contraceptives (Luker, 1984; Himmelstein, 1986; Morgan, 1988; Melton, 1991; Elizondo, 1994; Balmer, 1994). Although measures of religiosity vary, it is safe to conclude that a strong religious commitment in traditionally oriented religions, especially fundamentalist Protestantism, is also predictive of a preference for traditional gender roles.

As will be demonstrated, in some of the ancient religions and the societies in which they functioned, women exercised a great deal of influence. Evidence from the earliest spiritual traditions suggests that men and women were more likely to be partners without domination by either gender, but that this was lost as religions became more institutionalized. In this sense, partnership declined when spirituality was eclipsed by formal religion. It is clear that the progress of civilization is associated with universal education, technological advancement, and net gains in overall equality. Yet in most postindustrial societies organized religion has lagged behind in the amount of religious authority granted to women in relation to men.

REDISCOVERING THE GODDESS

The last decade has witnessed an explosion in scholarly research on the role and status of women in the world's religions as well as investigations into the interdependence of the feminine and masculine principles on which many religions are based. Based on archaeological religious evidence found in both prehistoric and historic societies, such explorations now suggest that the first civilizations were likely to be gynocentric, with goddess-based religions and an emphasis on female and feminine interests (Eisler, 1988; Gimbutas, 1989, 1991; Sered, 1994). We also now know that the most ancient human image of the divine was female (Ruether, 1983:47). A gynocentric society is not necessarily a matriarchal one. As Eisler (1988) points out, the terms patriarchy and matriarchy refer to a ranking of one part of humanity over the other. She prefers to use a model indicative of partnership, based on the principle of linking, where males and females may be different but these differences are not associated with either inferiority or superiority (Eisler, 1988:xvii).

Perhaps more revealing is the notion shared by some feminist religious scholars that when gynocentrism was replaced by androcentrism, the millennia of goddess prehistory and history were relegated to academic oblivion or dismissed by scholars as incidental to the span of human history. Arguing from a conflict perspective, Christ (1987:111) takes this a step further by stating that goddess images in Western religion were suppressed because their power was so threatening to the male-dominated religious status quo. Yet she also believes that even if the goddess heritage is rooted in women's experiences and women need to rediscover this heritage to affirm their own sense of power and well-being, it is not intended to exclude men. From Eisler's partnership viewpoint, both men and women can share in and celebrate the principles rooted in the goddess heritage.

The emerging picture, then, demonstrates a religious portrait of ancient civilizations where women played a central role, where female deities were often worshipped, and where religious life was essentially a partnership between men and women, much more than modern institutionalized religion would have us believe. The intent here is to provide a brief chronicle of some images of women as they appear in the mythology and religious heritage of people in the ancient world. Such an account is important for grasping the significance of attitudes toward women in modern religion, which is the focus of the latter part of this chapter.

Because of the heightened interest, there has been a proliferation of thorough accounts of the archaeological and anthropological evidence for the goddess heritage and the significance of women's ancient religious roles (Ruether, 1983; Christ, 1987; Eisler, 1988; Carmody, 1989; Gimbutas, 1989, 1991; Goodrich, 1991). In an earlier work, James (1959, cited in Ruether, 1983) argues that one of the oldest and longest surviving religions was the cult of the mother-goddess, whose image has been found throughout the Paleolithic to Neolithic periods in sites from Western Europe, through the

Mediterranean world, and into India. A decade later Davis (1971) set out to document woman's dominance of prehistoric civilization. In her then-controversial book, *The First Sex*, she states that not only is there massive evidence of the matriarchal origins of human society but that the "further back one traces *man's* history, the larger loomed the figure of woman" (Davis, 1971:16, emphasis added). Whereas Eisler (1988) refrains from the use of the term *matriarchy* to describe this period, Davis (1971:39) maintains that in all myth the goddess is synonymous with gynocracy, and this means that where the goddess reigned, women ruled. Though scholars continue to debate the amount of power women held in goddess-dominated societies, the abundant archaeological evidence on goddess worship suggests the gynocentric origins of civilization.

For example, some of the best preserved and oldest villages of civilization have been uncovered in Catal Huyuk in what is now Turkey. This largest and most significant Neolithic site in the Near East has produced compelling evidence attesting to a gynocentric religious and artistic tradition. As documented by Eisler (1988:11) this tradition spans 800 years, from 6500 to 5700 B.C.E. and is vividly represented by numerous goddess figurines, all emphasizing worship of a female deity. The artifacts of the prehistoric European peoples demonstrate representations of the goddess as a symbol of fertility, creativity, regeneration, and also death (Gimbutas, 1989). Although the most numerous artifacts are associated with life-giving qualities, all of these symbols indicate the veneration and powerful sacredness of women.

The goddess image is carried through to the idea of the creator when examining accounts from different parts of the world, including ancient Sumer, Babylon, Assyria, Greece, Egypt, and China. Nammu is the Summerian goddess who gives birth to heaven and earth, Tiamet is the Babylonian Creator of All, the mother of gods, and in Greek mythology, Metis, loosely translated as the creative power of female intelligence, brings the world into being without a male partner. In the *Tao te ching*, creation is the reproduction of all matter from the womb of the Mother. Paleolithic peoples saw the original source of life on earth not as a divine Father but a divine Mother, and the creative sexual power of women as a miracle of nature, to be revered and blessed. In Chinese Buddhism the goddess of compassion is Kuan Yin, in Hinduism the goddess of destruction is Kali, the consort of Siva who is revered both as a giver and destroyer of life. The 21 representations of the Tibetan deity Tara symbolize compassion, the easing of human suffering, and the guidance to wisdom and salvation. The goddess as the first creator is associated with mythology and religious principles in all corners of the world. It is only in later myth where she is replaced by a god (Reed, 1987; Engelsman, 1994; Carmody, 1992; O'Brien and Palmer, 1993; Eisler, 1995).

With the emergence of Babylonia as an empire in the developing urban-agricultural world, the warrior-champion Marduk arises as the god of the new city-state. The Marduk-Tiamet story tells of the defeat of Tiamet and her consort, who represent the power of chaos, by the new god Marduk and his followers, who represent the power of order (Ruether, 1983:50). Yet even with the emergence of the new gods, female names and reminiscences remained. Marduk fashions the cosmos out of Tiamet's body, so she maintains her place as the first creator. Siva in India, Atea in Polynesia, and Ea in Syria are also names of goddesses carried over to the male gods who replaced them. Gimbutas (1989) also indicates that goddess worship was never completely eradicated but many practices were driven underground by religious persecution. Perhaps the female names given to male gods were, and are, the vestiges of such practices.

Anthropologists recognize Africa as the continent that has the oldest record of human habitation, and it is here where perhaps the best examples of the goddess as the Mother of All are found. On this continent with an incredible diversity of peoples, customs, and religious symbolism, the images of the goddess vary as well, from Mawu, creator of the world among the Dahomey, to Goddess as the Moon to several Zimbabwe tribes, to the goddess as She Who Sends Rain among the Zulu of Natal and the Woyo of Zaire (Stone, 1979:131–33). In Ghana, Nigeria, and other parts of west and central Africa, particularly among the Asante and Brong, tribal religions often recognize a divinity that may be male or female, with a number of cults having primarily female spirit beings. The spirit world makes no direct link between gender and divinity. When much of this region was Christianized, Oduyoye (1988:44) speaks of her grandmother who had no problem with an all-male Christian clergy since she saw them simply as functionaries who served God. Even given such diversity, the symbolism that emerges most consistently among African indigenous religions involves the concerns for honesty, courage, sympathy, hope, and humanitarianism, which the goddesses represented and the peoples who worshipped them revered. The roots of this heritage are expressed in the many female-dominated religious cults and secret societies which continue to function throughout contemporary Africa and give meaning and power to women (Sered, 1994).

The ancient texts of China also speak clearly to the goddess image. Taoism, the native religious tradition of China, is illustrated by the *Chuang Tzu*, written in the third century B.C.E. Part of this account is a description of the Era of the Great Purity, a utopian matrilineal society, where life was characterized by happiness, harmony, innocence and spontaneity. Most of the symbols in this and other Taoist works are explicitly female and focus on female reproduction and the unqualified nature of motherly love (Reed, 1987:164). It is interesting that Taoism, where women served as models, developed within the highly patriarchal, hierarchical, and aggressive society dominated by Confucian principles, where women were viewed as inferior by nature. Although Confucianism remained the dominant religion, Taoist elements could be discovered within other parts of ancient Chinese culture. And contemporary Taoism yet maintains that the "creative principle is symbolically female because the Tao, like an empty womb, is the origin of all things" (Reed, 1987:181).

Beyond the goddess images that dominated many ancient practices and beliefs, some religious systems also incorporated principles of balance where, in principle, neither gender was superior. Most notable among these is the ancient Chinese concept of Yin and Yang. Although Western interpretation often misrepresents the female principal of Yin as being completely passive and dominated by the more active and aggressive male principal of Yang, this is a distortion of the ancient belief, which emphasized equilibrium and complementarity. The Yin-Yang ideal of harmonious balance is yet part of the Chinese value system. However, much of the original intent was lost with the advent of the patriarchy that influenced all cultural elements, including religion. Tantric Buddhism in medieval India and Tibet was amenable to both male and female *siddhas,* or accomplished ones, whose gender was considered irrelevant to the goal of enlightenment. In support of this was the belief that since the same teachings were given by Buddha to his female and male disciples and the same spiritual path was opened to both, men and women have the same potential for enlightenment (Barnes, 1987; Kloppenborg, 1995). Even among some American Indian cultures, the complementarity of men and women may be discovered, with each gender sharing in the religious practices of the tribe. The matrilineal Iroquois tribes of eastern North America participated in religious ceremonies where both the male and female dimensions were considered necessary, such as rites to encourage the male activity of hunting or the female activity of agriculture (Shimony, 1985). Although it is difficult to generalize about American Indians since their cultures are incredibly diverse, we know that virtually all of them tended to be holistic, with a belief that nature and humans were inextricably linked and that over half of them organized their worldviews in terms of a dimorphic, male-female set of correspondences, with male and female powers balancing each other (Carmody, 1989:21).

Though such religious systems incorporated aspects of male and female complementarity and equilibrium, this is not to suggest that this kind of balance inevitably carried over into other realms. If Tantric Buddhism was a path open to both genders, the Indian and Tibetan cultures made it very difficult for women to pursue such a path, given their restrictions in other institutional settings. Women who wished to follow the path as nuns had to submit to the standards of male control established by the monks (Kloppenborg, 1995). The Iroquois also denied public expression of women in a variety of settings. Gender complementarity is not necessarily associated with gender equity. Complementarity assumes males and females are "designed to make up for one another's deficiencies, rather than inspiring one another to overcome them" (Webster, 1995:194).

Regardless of the inequality that doubtlessly existed in other parts of the society, these accounts of goddess images and male-female complementarity in religious systems provide us with an alternative view of the heritage of religion. Such a perspective should help offset the more accepted interpretations offered by contemporary organized religions. Though the world is dominated by a relatively small number of "principal" religions, over two and a half billion people can be said to at least minimally subscribe to their beliefs. The vast majority of these numbers are made up of Muslim, Hindu, Jewish, and Christian adherents. Unlike many ancient beliefs, within these religions, misogynous interpretations are the rule rather than the exception.

ISLAM AND PURDAH: SEXUAL APARTHEID

As the mists of time veiled the ancient goddess images, the emergence of organized religion produced another veil for millions of women who adhere to Islam. Although Muslim women are more likely to fall under the shroud of purdah, numerous Hindu women also observe this practice. **Purdah**, a Persian word loosely translated to mean "curtain," has come to refer to the separate world of males and females along with the virtual concealment of most women in Islamic cultures. The specific practices of purdah may vary considerably, but the fact remains that in these cultures, there is an overall separation of the genders that is continually reinforced by daily activities in virtually all of their social institutions. Jeffery (1979) labels such customs as "sexual apartheid" not only because of the physical separation of men and women but also due to the complexity of arrangements that sustain social distance. Certainly the most recognized form of concealment of women is found in their distinctive clothing which symbolizes their separation. Whether the clothing takes the form of the *burqa*, consisting of a skull cap attached to mounds of material that drop around the face and all the way to the ground, or a *chaddar*, an immense shawl used to hide their faces and bodily features, women are, in essence, made invisible. As Jeffery (1979:4) poignantly notes,

> The effect of all these garments is the same, though, for the woman is rendered anonymous, a non-person, unapproachable, just a silent being skulking along, looking neither to the right nor left. To those who do not know her personally, she is nameless and faceless.

Purdah is seen by many as primarily a characteristic of Islam as a religion rather than as resulting from broader, non-Islamic sociocultural forces. But it is also extremely difficult and probably impractical to disentangle religion from other elements of the culture, so to unravel the chain of causation meets with many obstacles. Smith (1987:236) cites research which suggests that some pre-Islamic women, such as soothsayers, priestesses, and queens, had powerful and esteemed social roles. It is clear, however, Islam arose in response to unique Arab needs and circumstances, including Muhammad's desire to aid the poor and provide economic resources for those who were not under the care and protection of others, including widows, orphans, and unmarried women. The Koran introduced changes that were advantageous for women in the areas of marriage, divorce, and inheritance (Smith, 1987; Minai, 1991). Much of what is expected of women is based on short narratives about the sayings and deeds of Muhammad's many wives which were passed down in oral form. These stories are part of the commentaries on the Koran which have since become authoritative sources for Islamic teaching. The accuracy of these thousands of narratives is questionable and each period interprets them according to prevailing cultural standards. They have been used to justify a wide range of contradictory attitudes and practices concerning Islamic women. As Ascha (1995:107) suggests, women are ideal, obedient, gentle, affectionate, and veiled, yet they are also jealous, angry, conspiratorial, and endowed with an imperfect mind. At the same time they are described as erudite, intelligent, politically active, and even as capable fighters and leaders in war. Undoubtedly those characteristics which were valued are linked to the extent of women's power in broader society. In the early centuries of Islam, patriarchal culture was certainly maintained and in many respects strengthened through the institutionalization of Islam, but once the Koran was codified, at least some recourse was available for women to seek help beyond their immediate families or kinship structures.

Pre-Islamic Arabian women may have benefited from such changes, but what about the impact of Koranic interpretations for contemporary women? Ahmed (1986) maintains that by the third century of Islam, women were more secluded and degraded than anything known in the early Islamic decades. Smith (1987:235-36) indicates that the Koran is still viewed as the literal and unmitigated word of God, untainted by any interpretations. It is adhered to with such strictness that changes in Muslim law affecting women, especially in regard to the family, are extremely slow.

Contemporary Islam defines the roles of men and women in terms of their complementarity rather than their equality per se. The Koran explicitly states that men are a step above women and that men are the protectors of women; thereby God gives preference to men over women, including authority over the females in their families (Smith, 1987:236). Mernissi (1987) points out that women's inferiority is the result of institutions developed to subordinate her legally and socially to the male in the family structure. Islamic law is nurtured by a code of ethics which sees woman's role as providing legitimate male heirs. This role may be compromised if women are not restricted in their activities, especially during childbearing years. Muhammad himself was awed by woman's power and what he saw as a mysterious, unlimited sexual drive that, if left unfettered, could wreak social havoc by casting doubt on the legitimacy of the husband's heirs. From a functionalist perspective, the practices involving purdah arose as a response to these attitudes. Therefore, Islam assumes that woman is both potentially powerful and dangerous. Among other institutions, the custom of purdah may be viewed as a strategy for restraining her passion and potential power. Though Islam recognizes the "democratic glorification of the individual," Muslim ideology socializes men and women to perceive each other as enemies, keeps them as separate as possible, and creates institutions that are repressive to women (Mernissi, 1987). Badawi (1995) takes exception to both using religiously based cultural arguments to justify oppression of Muslim women as well as painting a stereotypical portrait of these women as submissive and enslaved by "women-hating chauvinist men." He argues that a gap does exist between the ideal of equality which he finds inherent in Islam and the reality of the cultural practices and understanding which serve to undermine the truth of the revelatory sources.

The emergence of a new scholarship on the role of women in Islam written by Muslim women is providing alternative interpretations of the Koran and transforming the women of the Koran into feminist role models. Sufism, the mystical school of Islam, is replete with women saints. Their shrines exist throughout North Africa, India, and the Middle East and are visited by women in search of special needs connected with their family life. Studies of the female Sufi saints suggest that while most were virgins and/or unmarried, all kinds of women could become saints, especially in the Indian cultural context (Bonouvrié, 1995). As Muslim women have gained in education, they have also gained insight into the holy texts. In regard to the wives of Muhammad, for example, these "Mothers of Believers" can be used in the present debate concerning women's place in society.

> When we listen here to these women who surrounded the Prophet and whose words and actions held his attention. . . . then it is not only a faraway echo that we hear, but rather a very present-day message. . . . Do not these wives, Mothers of Believers, remind us . . . that a society of progress and justice takes place through the restoration of women, to all women, of the dignity and the position which the religion award them? (Morsy, 1989, cited in Ascha, 1995:107)

HINDUISM

For Hindu women the customs and clothing surrounding purdah are extremely varied, with some regions exhibiting more exclusionary and separatist tactics than others. It is also difficult to assess and generalize about Hindu doctrine as it affects women since Hinduism is as incredibly diverse as the Indian subcontinent on which it is primarily practiced. As Islam is to Arab cultures, Hinduism is ancient and incorporated into the cultural milieu in so many ways that it is impossible to visualize what India would be like without it.

As we have seen with other preinstitutionalized religious eras, the oldest scriptural texts (1500 to 500 B.C.E.) which became the basis for later Hinduism, the Vedas, demonstrated an esteem for femininity and the complementarily between marital partners, even within a patrilineal and patrilocal family structure. The Vedic view of women saw them as "auspicious, vital to the well-being of the family and necessary for the presence of the gods" (Young, 1987:71). The Vedas also celebrate a number of prominent female deities who continue to be worshipped in contemporary India, such as Usas, called variously the Daughter of Heaven, the Goddess of Hope, and the Mother of Gods (Carmody, 1989). Unlike Muslims in India where males control religious practice and where virtually all significant religious figures are male, Hindu Indians have an ancient goddess heritage and allow women to serve in temples and lead religious rituals (Williams and Best, 1990).

The Hindu ideal is that male and female are meant to be complementary, with man as the creator and woman as the lover, and with woman's sexual tendencies being no less variational than man's. However, Hindu women are severely criticized for being too ambitious, energetic, and masculine and for forsaking the most important roles they can ever assume, those of wife and mother. In an influential work written half a century ago Radhakrishnan (1947:142) describes them. Such women

> take pride in proving that they never developed a talent for domesticity . . .(and) society will have to allow for them. Such "masculine" women do not reach the highest of which womanhood is capable.

Such beliefs are fostered by interpretations of the *Ramayana* and *Mahabharata* epics which describe many Hindu ideals, especially in terms of marriage and family roles, and which are powerful determinants of gender role socialization.

Despite this diversity of both Hinduism and India, it is safe to conclude that Hindu women practice rituals and ceremonies that are congruent with their roles as mothers, wives, and homemakers. These customs exemplify the domestic sphere of life, the only one known to most Hindu women. For example, childbirth practices in some central Indian villages involve an elaborate series of rituals lasting from pregnancy until the child is introduced to a life outside of the home (Jacobson, 1980). Again, from a functionalist interpretation, these customs help increase cohesiveness among women who are required to live and work together in an extended family structure reigned over by their husbands or fathers. Many North Indian Hindu women also practice rituals which express their concerns for family and household. Observed only by women, these particular ceremonies do not require the services of male priests. Although these are not shared with men, they reflect a strong patriarchal society. Some practices involve the direct worship of husbands and brothers for the purpose of obtaining their protection while others offer prayers and supplications for the happy marriages of daughters and for the joys of being blessed with male offspring. The extent of regard for males may be demonstrated through a letter written by an Indian judge to a friend in England which told of the death of his small daughter. His own grief is somewhat abated by the thought that it "would have been more disastrous had it been the death of a son" (Nehra, 1934).

It is appropriate to end this section on Hindu women with a look at the ritual that has gained the most attention and infamy throughout Indian history, that of **suttee**, or widow burning. It is evident that the practice originated during the ancient Vedic period where the widow performed a symbolic self-immolation upon her husband's death, although in later centuries, the symbol became the reality. This ritual meant that the widow would be buried alive with her dead husband or, more commonly, self-immolated on his funeral pyre. More than anything else, the practice of suttee and the veneration of the ritual itself speak to the inferior status of women.

Suttee, literally translated to mean "virtuous woman," was mainly confined to the aristocracy and courts. There are instances, however, of its occurring on a massive scale such as among widows of soldiers who were spared the humiliation of surrendering to the victors. As late as the mid-nineteenth century the accepted options for Hindu widows involved either suttee or the more common rite of passage into widowhood. Becoming a suttee was considered the most auspicious moment of her existence where she is given the "supreme opportunity for self-sacrifice that consummates her life of dedication to her dead husband." She has brought dignity and honor to her family and her community. A living widow, however, was seen as "not only unfortunate but positively inauspicious, an ogress who ate her husband with karmic jaws" (Young, 1987:83). With her social status so completely transformed, she would lead a dismal life, especially if no sons were present to support her. As a widow she would feel guilty the rest of her life that her husband died before her. This sense of guilt was even heightened by the classical Hindu belief that a sin in her previous life was responsible for his earlier death.

In principle, this was a voluntary rite on the part of the widow. As indicated before, her husband was often given deity status, and here was her chance to rejoin him through the purification of the flames on his funeral pyre. In practice, her grief was often used by relatives who desired the honor associated with a suttee ceremony. Only faithful wives could have the honor of becoming a suttee, so a widow's refusal could be construed as an admission of infidelity (Weitz, 1995). Brought up in a culture where widow remarriages were discouraged, where women were considered primarily in terms of their husbands, and where widows were even more likely to be dependent, subservient, and perhaps sexually exploited and abandoned, the grief-stricken woman, if she could think rationally at this point in time, might consider that becoming a suttee would be the only feasible alternative. When India was ruled by Muslim Mughals, attempts were made to abolish the practice, and the British outlawed it as early as 1829. Yet the British lack of success in eliminating it altogether speaks to the intransigence of religious beliefs tied to personal law and their intimate connection to the Hindu social order.

India is rapidly modernizing, though many villages and rural areas remain virtually untouched by this trend. It speaks to the extraordinary power of socialization that suttee is still much associated with the image of virtue for numerous Hindu women. In 1903 over 275 women immolated themselves around Calcutta alone and as late as 1980 there were still six. A column appearing in an Indian publication noted that there is continuing, perhaps resurgent, enthusiasm for the practice of suttee since it stems from society's conviction that the woman is the property of man to dispose of at his discretion. No longer do dying husbands extract oaths for suttee from grieving wives. But, as noted by this same columnist,

In a village of Rajasthan, the seventh of a series of recent suttees burnt herself to death on the funeral pyre of her husband. Astrologers had predicted nine, so the village is breathlessly waiting for the remaining two. (*India Today*, 1981:92)

JUDAISM

In the almost four thousand year span of what can be considered Jewish heritage, Jewish women have lived within the confines of patriarchal institutions. Carmody (1989:133) notes that "biblical, talmudic, medieval and modern Judaism all assumed that men were to read, teach, and legislate while women were to follow." As with earlier religions, there were exceptions to this rule, but throughout Jewish history a woman's preeminent role was domestic. With religious persecution so much a part of Jewish heritage, survival of Judaism itself was dependent on growth in numbers; hence motherhood not only meant individual sacrifice for children and family but sacrificing for religious identity as well.

This concern for stability in family life resulted in excessive control over women's sexuality. The ancient Hebrews severely punished infidelity on the part of a wife, but a husband was punished for infidelity only if he violated another man's rights by consorting with his wife (Daly, 1991:139). A woman's sexuality was thus controlled in part because she was also treated as a piece of property. Another example of this control can be found in the following verse:

> I took this woman and when I came near her I did not find the tokens of virginity. . . . The father of the young woman shall say to the elders . . . "he has made shameful charges against her . . . these are the tokens of my daughter's virginity" . . . then the elders . . . shall take the man and whip him . . . But if the thing is true, that the tokens of virginity were not found in the young woman, then . . . the men of the city shall stone her to death. (Deuteronomy 22:14-21)

Women were denied access to the goddess religions which coexisted with Judaism during early biblical times. These religions stressed female sexuality and were seen as threatening not only to Jewish monotheism but also to "the male dominance that patriarchal Israel assumed was necessary for social order" (Carmody, 1987:184). As we shall see, any assault on this social order was dealt with harshly.

The two most important documents which continue to be used as governing laws for the conduct of Jewish women and men are the Torah, the whole of God's teaching as revealed to the Jewish people as found in the first five books of what is the Old Testament of the Christian Bible, and the Talmud, the main collection of rabbinic interpretations of scripture promulgated around the middle of the first century (Carmody, 1989:237). Since the Hebrew and Christian Bibles contain the Old Testament, it becomes the shared heritage of both peoples. Taken together these documents provide guidance on all aspects of life. Although interpretations have been fairly flexible to account for the varying circumstances and environmental challenges Jewish people have encountered, views of women and their accepted roles have remained remarkably stable. Overall, Jewish tradition prescribed daily, rigorous religious duties for men from which women were exempt, since they could interfere with her domestic functioning. If a wife was fulfilling her household responsibilities, including those religious functions centered in the household, then her husband was able to concentrate on his religious obligations. A study by Sered (1991:10) on contemporary Jewish women in Jerusalem supports the continued dichotomy between women's family and religious lives. Women who conduct their religious lives in the public sphere tend to face conflict with their families over issues of allegiance and time devoted to the various activities of both realms. However, Sered contends that women who have more control in both systems are more successful at coping with these conflicts, but only if patriarchal authorities do not view this control as too threatening. As would be expected, women who "suffer the most from the opposition between religion and family are those who choose a religious path very different from the traditional women's way" (Sered, 1991:25). Early religious ideology viewed a woman in terms of her domestic life, as the property of fathers and husbands, praised her for bearing sons, pitied her when she was a childless widow, scorned her as a prostitute, stoned her for adultery, and distrusted her simply for being a woman.

In an extreme example of biblical ideology impacting Israelite women, Trible (1984) comments on the terrifying brutality of what she calls "the texts of terror." These texts (Genesis 16:1–16 and 21:9–21; II Samuel 13:1–22; Judges 19:1–30, and Judges 11:29–40) testify to rape, murder, human sacrifice, and the widespread abuse of women and girls. In Judges 19:1–30, a concubine flees from her Levite master back to her father's house, where he is entertained by her father, and then prepares to return with her to his own home. Along the way he is invited into the home of a man from Ephraim when the home is besieged. In pleading for the safety of the Levite, the Ephraimite host says, as the text continues:

> Behold, here are my virgin daughter and his concubine; . . . Ravish them and do with them what seems good to you; but against this man do not do such a vile thing. So the man seized his concubine, and put her out to them; and they knew her and abused her all night . . . And as the dawn began to break they let her go . . . And her master rose up in the morning . . . there was his concubine lying at the door of the house . . . He said to her, "Get up, let us be going." But there was no answer. Then he put her upon the ass . . . and went away to his home. And when he entered his house, he took a knife, and laying hold of his concubine he divided her, limb by limb, into twelve pieces, and sent her throughout all the territory of Israel.

Virgin daughters and concubines are treated as property to be used at will by fathers or masters to entertain male guests.

Fischer (1994) identifies a number of other references that should be included in these texts of terror. They serve as testimony to justify rape of virgins, abandonment of wives, and sexual violence against slave girls and women taken as prisoners of war. Through the use of biblical texts, androcentric law is reinforced by legitimizing the overall oppression of women. Even when revisions of these narratives blunt the approval of the terror, the rewritten documents attest to an androcentric theology protecting its interest by setting up social structures in the name of God. This extends to the image of the widow. On the one hand she is a "monument of devotion, wisdom and charity," but also seen as vulnerable to religious fanatics, a gossip and of questionable morals, and loose sexual habits. Van Der Torn (1995:13) notes that the ancient Israelite texts are more prescriptive than descriptive. Once a respectful daughter and obedient wife, she is now free. Female independence is checked by the emphasis on poverty and virtue that keeps a widow fettered to others. From biblical times to the present day it is predominantly women and children who become victims of such a (pseudo-)theological terror (Fischer, 1994:82).

Today, all branches of Judaism are engaged in making its religious heritage more palatable to contemporary women. Much of this effort is focused on reinterpreting Talmudic legislation and demonstrating the variety of roles Jewish women assumed throughout their religious history. For instance, Van Der Horst (1995) demonstrates that positive counter-voices exist throughout scripture which confirm God's high regard for women. In first century documents Eve is visioned as a woman who may have been naive but certainly not wicked— an unselfish woman whose good character Satan abused. Throughout the diaspora women had opportunities to climb to prestigious positions and to assume leadership roles in Jewish communities (Van Der Horst, 1995). The negative and hostile images of women coincide with positive ones that are being rediscovered. As will be discussed, the feminist movement provides a major impetus for dealing with the injustices faced by Jewish women and others of many religions as they confront the misogyny of their own religious traditions.

CHRISTIANITY

The roots of Christianity are found in the heritage of Judaism, with the oppressive situation of women, compared to men, reflected throughout the Hebrew and Christian Bible. As with Jews, it is the Bible to which Christians turn to discover their origins and the basis of their beliefs and laws. Religious socialization of the young is apt to proceed from the teaching of Bible stories replete with colorful pictures of David confronting Goliath or Moses parting the sea. These childhood images are nurtured and strengthened by interpretations that perpetuate gender role stereotypes. Religion lends to socialization a pervasive credibility that is rarely questioned. The Bible is often evoked as the final authority in settling disputes in many areas but in particular those involving women and men. This results in a divinely sanctioned patriarchy that is again reinforced.

The Bible and Patriarchy

Since the Bible expresses the basic attitudes of the patriarchal cultures in which it was written, it is logical that its most popular texts would be representative of those cultures. Alternative images do exist, but those that are congruent with prevailing sentiments are favored. Hence, biblical interpretations provide another illustration of Bem and Bem's (1970) concept of "non-conscious ideology," which results in a lack of awareness concerning alternative beliefs about women. Certainly alternative beliefs would remain unimagined by the male leadership and writers of what would become the most sacred documents of the Judeo-Christian tradition. As will be documented later, this does not mean that the Bible is devoid of other, more positive views of women and the relationships between men and women, but that scripture which points to the subordination of women is more favored in part because it is more known. When such references are congruent with prevailing sentiment, they continue to both legitimize and work against altering the existing patriarchal power structure.

The following examples, which are oft-repeated from the pulpit, demonstrate how androcentric ideology permeates the Bible. It is appropriate to begin with the version of the creation story that is most accepted as representing the traditional view of the Christian as well as Jewish faiths.

> And the rib which the Lord God had taken from man, made he woman and brought her unto the man. And Adam said, This is now bone of my bones, and flesh of my flesh; she shall be called Woman, because she was taken out of Man. (Genesis 2:20–23)

Contrary to all subsequent natural law, woman is made from man. Her status as helpmate and server to man (read "males") is confirmed. The idea that Eve was not only created out of Adam's rib, but also that she was created second, has been used to justify the domination of man-husband over woman-wife. Yet the order of creation is not an issue in supremacy when we consider that animals were created before humans.

In supporting this perspective Paul has the dubious honor of formulating views, or having writings attributed to him, that continue to serve as bulwarks for contemporary Christian images of women. Although he is associated with advocating a "Christianity of female subordination," recent studies indicate that he accepted most assumptions and practices of the earlier charismatic, more inclusive Christianity. These included women functioning as local leaders, evangelists, and prophets (Ruether, 1987:212). It may be that his acceptance of the theology of equivalence of women with men was tempered by his concern for order in society, fear of creating scandal or ridicule of the fledgling Christian sect, and his ambivalence in the theological basis for women in ministry (Ruether, 1987; Daly, 1991). Schussler-Fiorenza (1983) argues that Paul acknowledges the idea of equality but insists on the divinely given quality of sexual differences. Paul's contradictory beliefs about women are evident in the Pauline texts, which consist of those biblical passages attributed to Paul that contain both striking misogynies as well as more egalitarian material. However, as illustrated by the following passages, it is the former that are the most well known and used to justify the subordinate roles of Christian women.

> But I want you to understand that the head of every man is Christ, the head of every woman is her husband, and the head of Christ is God. (I Corinthians 11:3)

> For a man ought not to cover his head since he is the image and glory of God; but woman is the glory of man. For man was not made from woman, but woman from man. Neither was man created for woman but woman for man. (I Corinthians 11:7-11)

> Let a woman learn in silence with all submissiveness. I permit no woman to teach or have authority over men; she is to keep silent. (I Timothy 2:11-12)

> Wives be subject to your husbands, as to the Lord. For the husband is the head of the wife as Christ is the head of the Church. As the Church is subject to Christ, so let wives also be subject in everything to their husbands. (Ephesians 5:22-24)

Taken a step further, women are repeatedly viewed in terms of their status as possessions of men. The Ten Commandments lists a neighbor's wife, along with his house, fields, manservant, ox, and ass as property not to be coveted (Exodus 20:17). Lot offers his daughters to the male guests in his house.

> Behold, I have two daughters who have not known man. Let me bring them out to you and do to them as you please. (Genesis 19:8)

Pervasive views such as these continue today through compilations of stories about biblical women. On the surface it would seem that works like Edith Deen's *Wisdom from Women in the Bible* (1978) are focusing on women's accomplishments at a period in history where a liberating consciousness raising in terms of religious interpretation is simultaneously occurring. Yet Deen presents narratives of women which provide ammunition for reinforcing stereotypes about women. For example, Jochebed, the mother of Moses, is praised for her role, as are modern mothers who recognize exceptional promise in their children. Selfish and possessive women, like the wife of Potiphar who was responsible for the unfair imprisonment of Joseph, are admonished for their wickedness and deceit. Though Deen asserts that women are different than, but not inferior to men, the images that emerge from this book are consistently in line with women's traditional or "acceptable" roles. Those women who either refuse or challenge such roles are chastised, negatively portrayed, or cast into historical oblivion (Lindsey, 1979:793).

Overall, these views explicitly support the notions that women should be admired for their unselfish, nurturing roles as wives and mothers and scorned, or at best dismissed as insignificant, for all else. Although the Christian tradition portrays men as both rational in leadership roles but irrational in their ability to resist women, they are still multifaceted beings who adapt to a variety of roles. In contrast, women are dualistically cast with no room for deviation. Eve may be the mother of humanity, but it is her fault that paradise is lost and people are forever cursed with original sin. Eve's pride and her lack of self-assertiveness in confronting the serpent are used to justify the incapability of women for assuming critical leadership roles (Diehl, 1990:56). As the temptress, Adam apparently succumbs to her feminine wiles and loses responsibility for his actions. On the other hand, Mary as the mother of Christ, is the idealized image of the perfect woman—humble, submissive, and a virgin. It is obvious that with such women as powerful symbols, contemporary views are likely to be congruent. The fact that they are contradictory is deemed unimportant.

As discussed in Chapter 4, language is a potent force in socialization, and nowhere is this more apparent than in the language of religion. This language can be subdivided into broader religious language, which uses imagery and symbols appealing to emotion and imagination, and theological language, which uses abstractions and systematic ordering evolving out of formal, critical appraisals of religious experience (cited in King, 1989:44). Considering this distinction, religious language would be more open to female imagery in that it is spontaneous. According to King (1989:44-45), theological language uniformly is "the creation of a male specialist group, whether Brahmans, priests, rabbis, monks or whoever."

That God and God-language have taken on masculine traits is due to linguistic accident (Stendahl, 1974). We evoke male imagery when conceptualizing God and in turn such images are used to support the subordination of women. The supposed equality of the genders cannot easily be dismissed when the spiritual nature of human beings is related in male terms with sexuality viewed in female terms. Miller and Swift (1991a) suggest that women are portrayed as distracting men from godliness, as Eve did with her temptation of Adam. The language is clear in this regard; we have "Sons of God" but "Daughters of Eve" (Miller and Swift, 1991a:80). Sociologists, linguists, and even theologians would not argue with the notion that the use of the generic *man* impedes the understanding of God's view of the genders. Yet when congregations begin the arduous task of altering liturgy, hymns, and prayers to conform to nonsexist language standards, resistance runs very high. The argument reappears that one is not only tampering with tradition but, more importantly, the "language of God."

Alternative Views of Biblical Women

Biblical alternatives to traditional viewpoints do exist but are for the most part overlooked. Many have been resurrected by reformists eager to demonstrate that the Bible is abundant with stories, images, and metaphors that offer interpretive options as far as women's role. Even Paul presents a forceful alternative with the statement that

> there is neither Jew nor Greek, there is neither slave nor free, there is neither male nor female, for you are all one in Jesus Christ. (Galatians 3:28)

Such a passage from the Pauline texts directly relates to the idea that the equality of the genders under God is yet possible.

On the heels of the equality issue is the rediscovery of the nontraditional roles women played in biblical times. Mary Magdalene and the women who went to Jesus's tomb may be said to hold the credibility of Christianity since Jesus first appeared to them and were instructed to gather the disciples. Hollander (1994:115) asserts that this makes Mary Magdalen the "first prophet of the new religion, the first of Christ's disciples to see and hear, to believe and to speak: the first Christian." Deborah, in the book of Judges, is seen as an arbitrator, queen, and commander of the army that she led in the defeat of the Canaanites. In Exodus it is the women who first disobeyed Pharoah, with his own daughter adopting Moses as her child. Women are seen as wives and mothers as well as leaders, prophetesses, teachers, and tillers of the soil. Even Mary's supposed humility and submissiveness are being taken to task by feminists who argue that Mary submitted to God alone and not to Joseph or other male authority figures. She was an independent actor when she affirmed the course of her life (Ostling, 1991:64). Such stories and alternative viewpoints often remain hidden or have purposely been ignored in favor of those representing traditional patriarchal viewpoints.

Perhaps more than anything else it is a rereading of the Gospels with an examination of the life and teachings of Jesus which is providing the best message to those interested in recasting biblical imagery concerning women. Jesus' very open attitude toward women is found throughout the Gospels. McClelland (1990:61) notes that his acceptance of women was so uncharacteristic of the times that it could not be seen as anything short of scandalous. Women were prominent in Jesus' ministry from the beginning and served vital functions. They were involved in the recognition of him as the Messiah, they witnessed his death and resurrection, they conversed with him on theological topics, and they were the most faithful and persistent in following him through even the lethal portions of his ministry (McClelland, 1990:62). Women of biblical times would have been the major beneficiaries of Jesus' ministry. Examples are numerous: He preached that divorce should be forbidden at a time when only men had the right of divorce, which often meant abandoning their wives; he rejected the double standard of sexual morality, which helped to absolve women of their temptress image that previously made them solely responsible for sexual misdeeds; and he legitimated a monastic life for both men and women, which provided options for women other than marriage and childbearing (Carmody, 1989:163-64). Through his actions he demonstrated not only that women would be unencumbered in their spiritual quest but also that men and women would be relating in ways radically different than the patriarchy of the times (McClelland, 1990:62).

THE CLERGY ISSUE

Alternative explanations in terms of the Bible become more important for how they have been applied to women seeking equal footing with men as leaders of the contemporary church. Three major Christian faiths have not ordained women: Missouri Synod Lutheran, Eastern Orthodox, and Roman Catholic. In 1972, Reform Judaism made possible rabbinical ordination, with Sally Priesand becoming the first female rabbi. In 1973, ordination was open to women in the Conservative branch. In the Orthodox branch new religious roles outside the home are being embraced by women, but ordination is still forbidden. To date, however, there are fewer than 200 female rabbis, and of these only a handful are Conservative. After a long and bitter struggle which culminated in a controversial ceremony in Philadelphia in 1974 where 11 women were ordained Episcopal priests, the legal right for female priesthood was finally given in 1976. Twelve years later, by a margin of two votes, that right was extended to women in the Church of England (Ostling, 1992). This came about despite an earlier warning by the Archbishop of Canterbury for limiting ordination of women because he feared it would hurt dialogue with the Roman Catholic Church (Apple, 1984). A pastoral letter which took nine years to formulate and which addresses Catholic women's concerns in a number of areas, including their place in the church, was rejected by U.S. bishops in 1992. This was the first time in history that a pastoral letter which was proposed for a final vote was defeated (Filteau, 1992). In addressing the concerns over women's ordination by both Catholics and Episcopalians, Heyward (1984) suggests that they need to go their separate ways. She asserts that the time is past for convincing "our own denomination that God is with us" and that we have better things to do, vocations to live, and ministries to fulfill. "We must let the dead bury the dead and do what we can among the living" (Heyward, 1984:4). And even with the right to be ordained, Christian women clergy remain underrepresented in most denominations. Considering that the number of female theology students has increased exponentially and that in many seminaries the majority of students are women, it is difficult to dismiss these numbers (King, 1989:43).

Although women are gradually assuming new roles within the religious hierarchy, the battle is far from won. Some parishes still refuse to accept female ministers, rabbis, or priests, whether legally ordained or not, which propels many of these women to seek leadership roles in more peripheral positions. It is probable that such women would be found on university campuses as heads of religious coalitions or leaders of campus churches or temples. The crux of the clergy issue can be traced back to interpretations of the theological language and doctrine of biblical and Talmudic law. Overall, it is the exclusivity of the male image of God that makes it difficult for many to see women as representing this image. While theologians uniformly reject the notion that God is a "male being," centuries of patriarchy, institutional sexism, and linguistic convention provide barriers to those women who strongly desire more authoritative religious roles.

Jewish and Lutheran women have at least the option of shifting synods or branches without changing their religion per se, but for those Catholic women who seek the priesthood, their choices are limited. They can assume leadership roles as lay members of the church, or they can become nuns. This is not to minimize the leadership roles nuns assume or the other vital services they provide, but to suggest that, compared to priests, these roles are both confining and secondary (Weaver, 1985). In any case, they remain excluded from the position that allows the greatest authority on both doctrinal and parish matters—that of priest. The tradition of nuns as humble helpmates is also impacting their very livelihood. Unlike priests of a diocese, they are not employees of the local bishop; hence they receive no pension. There are 78,000 fewer nuns than twenty-five years ago and 85 percent fewer candidates entering the convent. Although nuns are better educated than most women and seldom retire from work unless their health fails, they are facing grim financial prospects in old age because there will be far fewer younger nuns to support them. Ironically, their current financial plight is a result of the very generosity, idealism, and service that their roles entail (Woodward et al., 1990).

The Second Vatican Council (1963 to 1965) brought monumental changes within the Catholic Church, but when the question of women's ordination was nominally debated, it was obvious that the church was unwilling to take this additional step. Hoping to put the women-as-priests issue at rest, early in 1996 the Catholic Church issued a strong statement that women can never be candidates for ordination. The storm of protest that erupted clearly demonstrated that the issue is *not* at rest. Expanded roles for lay people, including women, have been forthcoming, but ordination not one of them. Since Vatican II, there has been a swing back to more conservative stances, and Vatican opposition was reiterated with the 1976 Declaration on the Question of the Admission of the Women to the Ministerial Priesthood. Although there is some recognition that ordained women would be able to alleviate the serious shortage of priests in many parts of the world, the Catholic Church has chosen to deal with the issue by encouraging married men to become priests under certain conditions. Thus it appears that the ordination of women will not be given serious consideration by the church hierarchy again soon.

American Protestantism has fared better in terms of women in positions of authority, with many women preachers emerging as early as the colonial era from the ranks of Quakers. America's first successful religious commune, the Shakers, was founded by Ann Lee who preached that God is both male and female. Although the Shakers had no formal ordination process, all adherents, regardless of gender, were permitted complete freedom in teaching and preaching. This is also generally true of other religious sects and churches where women are credited as founders or proved to be the dominant influence in their establishment. Included here would be the Seventh Day Adventists, the Spiritualist Church, and the Christian Science Church. By the middle of the twentieth century most of the mainstream Protestant denominations such as the Methodist and Presbyterian Churches, the United Church of Christ, and the merged Evangelical Lutheran Church in America (ELCA) granted full ordination rights to women. Ordination also allows for women to begin the climb to significant positions of administrative leadership within their religious groups. "First ever" women include Maria Jepson, Lutheran

Bishop of Hamburg; Barbara Harris of Boston, Anglican Bishop; and Joan Campbell, General Secretary of the National Council of Churches (Goldman, 1990a; Fuehrmann, 1992; Ostling, 1992). Again, this must be tempered with the fact that ordination does not mean that the call to a church is readily forthcoming. The vast majority of ordained women in all religious groups serve as associate pastors, youth ministers, educational directors, or in some other institutional capacity. Many female African-American Baptist ministers find themselves as assistant pastors in dead-end job tracks. In response to this, they have started their own churches or are leading struggling congregations passed over by men (Goldman, 1990a).

The issue of women assuming more viable roles within their respective religions, especially as clergy, becomes all the more significant when put in context of sociological research which demonstrates that women have a greater degree of religious orientation than men. This orientation is suggested by women's higher rates of church and synagogue attendance, expression of the need for a religious dimension in their daily lives, and the belief that religion is an answer to contemporary problems (Gallup and Castelli, 1989). Given these data, it is not surprising that when women do assume leadership positions they usually fall within social and domestic realms with men dominating major administrative functions, such as overseeing the legal and financial matters of the church. Once they become clergy, do women differ in their approach to the pastoral ministry compared to men? According to Lehman (1993) the answer depends on aspect of ministry style, type of minister one has in mind, and type of ministry. In general, male and female ministers differ in their willingness to use power over congregations, with women more willing to give the congregation the power over its own affairs. On the other hand, men and women do not systematically differ in desire for positions of formal authority, approach to preaching, and involvement in social issues beyond the congregation (Lehman, 1993). Throughout the text it has been demonstrated that gender role socialization encourages females to adopt interactional styles that can be described as relational, open, nonconfrontive, and consensual. These are characteristics which can serve congregations well when adopted by both male and female clergy.

Church and family roles are also consistent. Women are more likely to be held responsible for the religious socialization of the children, with the patriarchal family structure carrying over to a similar one existing in the church. Finally, from a conflict theory viewpoint, and as exemplified by a Marxian perspective, women are more apt to accept an "other worldly" ideology. Women would share this orientation with other oppressed minorities. Biblical interpretation that adopts such a model is referred to as "liberation theology" and issues a challenge to the supposed objectivity of academic theology. It recognizes that all theologies are ultimately engaged for or against the oppressed (Schussler-Fiorenza, 1983:6). Overall then, with women having limited access to the leadership structure, the church may be viewed as an institution controlled by men for the purpose of serving women and children.

TOWARD AN INCLUSIVE THEOLOGY

From this account of religious misogyny, it might seem that feminism and the patriarchal vision of the church cannot be reconciled. Granted that harmony on both fronts may be exceedingly difficult, many feminists are unwilling to equate religion with oppression. They believe it is not real liberation to sever ties with an important element of their heritage and belief system. Instead they choose to work at reform in a number of areas, with a focus on providing a historical account of women's roles in ancient religions as well, such as reevaluating scripture, whether it be in the Koran, Talmud, Vedas, or Bible. Carmody (1989) argues that even if religious experience is filtered through misogynous cultural traditions, religion can transcend gender and be based on the willingness of the individual person to participate in what she refers to as the "Mystery." Only when women become aware of the root causes of their contemporary status and the sociopolitical nature of religious doctrine can they truly experience their religion. Historical reanalysis of world religions provides a consciousness-raising means for women coming to grips with their religious identity.

Doctrinal reinterpretation of scripture is also viewed as a mode of reform, especially if coupled with changes in linguistic reference. By pointing out alternative translations of key words, introducing nonsexist, inclusive language that minimizes the powerful aspects of male imagery, and discovering lesser known biblical texts and other significant religious works that demonstrate both gender equity and nontraditional images of women, a gradual shift in religious awareness regarding gender roles and relationships will occur. In Christianity, for example, because theology and preaching are so strongly oriented to masculine images of God, such as king, father, and shepherd, the feminine corollary of God goes unrecognized. In Matthew 13:31, while it is acknowledged that the man who sowed the mustard seed is God, most miss the parallel image that immediately follows in Matthew 13:33 where God is presented as a woman hiding leaven in meal. Maternal images of God abound, for instance, when Christians hear Jesus say people must be born spiritually to enter God's realm, as they were born physically from their mother's wombs (Schneiders, 1995).

We have already demonstrated that the world's institutionalized religions emerged out of an egalitarian heritage concerning gender. It is mainly with the esoteric and mystical schools of Christian Gnosticism, Islamic Sufism, and the Kabbalah movement of Judaism that women emerge as equal partners with men. This is pointed out by Pagels (1979) in her recounting of the archaeological discovery in Upper Egypt of what are now referred to as the Gnostic Gospels, which offer astonishing evidence that the early Christians viewed women in very different terms than those implied by the practices of the contemporary church. The texts on which these views are based are critical for providing alternative perspectives concerning women.

Many biblical writings can be reevaluated with these standards of reform in mind. Consider the lesser quoted of the creation stories:

> So God created man in his own image, in the image of God he created him; male and female he created them. (Genesis 1:27)

This version clearly does not have the implication that the image of God is different depending on one's gender. Quoting Paul Jewett (1975), McClelland (1990:55) states that in such a patriarchal culture this passage must have been "the first great surprise of the Bible." Surely the second one would be Paul's annihilation of differences as reflected in Galatians 3:28 (see page 302). Snodgrass (1986:177) maintains that the diverse sexual distinctiveness remains, but "valuation or status based on these differences is rejected." Even Paul's most restrictive passages may be reevaluated with the idea that the Gospel liberates people to stand equally before God. Reread Ephesians 5:22-24 with the idea that the words "be subject" were not in the original biblical text. Religious scholars suggest that Paul is calling for mutual submission of the genders within marriage and not the superiority of the husband (Gundry, 1979; Ruether, 1983, 1987; Schussler-Fiorenza, 1983, 1984; Carmody, 1989). Paul's writings must be scrutinized carefully with an eye toward context, taking into account the historical setting, as well as in light of the gospel of Jesus (Megill-Cobbler, 1993). Given these new directions, the misogyny of Paul, hence its impact on all women since, continues to fade. The life of Jesus is also being scrutinized by reformists intent on altering misconceptions about his teachings as they relate to women. New Testament statements by Jesus do not reflect the antifeminism of the times. In fact, Daly (1975:79) asserts that because Jesus related to women as *persons*, which was in such contrast to the prevailing customs, many were astonished by his actions.

The question of inclusive language has already had an impact on liturgy by suggesting significant changes which incorporate a neutral or inclusive position. This is proceeding in congruence with the ecumenical trends some religions are emphasizing. The Lutheran Book of Worship, issued in 1978, contains substantial changes from the 1958 Service Book and Hymnal and has allowed for more inclusive imagery. Hymns, prayers, and elements of the service in use by the Evangelical Lutheran Church in America (ELCA) shifted to a less sexist posture in language. Reprinted here is a portion of the Nicene Creed which demonstrates that a one-word change suggests a meaningful difference in imagery.

> Who for us men, and for our salvation, came down from heaven. . . . (1958 version)

> For us and for our salvation he came down from heaven. . . . (1978 version)

Though it is inappropriate to remove the word "he" from the second version since it refers directly to Jesus, the word "men" is now deleted. And a hymn was titled "Good Christian *Men*, Rejoice and Sing" in the older hymnal; the newer version is "Good Christian *Friends*, Rejoice and Sing." Seemingly subtle changes can have a profound impact on views regarding men and women. It is expected that the gradual introduction of inclusive language will be followed by shifts in imagery that, at a minimum, will be less male oriented.

Religious reform related to the genders is perhaps best expressed by a rapidly growing and evolving feminist theology, which draws on women's experience as a basic source of content and which has been shut out of past theological reflection. As Ruether (1983:12-13) states, it "makes the sociology of theological knowledge visible, no longer hidden behind mystifications of objectified divine and universal authority." It may also be viewed as one example of a liberation theology which interprets the Bible from the perspective of an oppressed group. In this sense female experience is an appropriate metaphor for the divine. Feminist theology is necessary when the female experience is excluded from traditional theology and when women are excluded from institutionalized religious structures. Although she speaks from a Christian heritage, Thurston's (1995:4) passionate call for feminist theology articulates with the female experience in any of the world's major religions.

> The fathers of the church and academy controlled the discourse; when I tried to speak my language they would not hear me. I wanted to talk at gut level where the mercy of God comes from—the bowels of the earth—the language of the Hebrew Bible and not of the Greek philosophers.

Feminist theology is ecumenical from its origins and borrows models from a wide range of disciplines (Carr, 1993). While it accepts the idea that a major critique of God symbolism is called for, there is much disagreement on the solutions to the problems resulting from such a critique, and many theologians have been unwilling to work out the ambiguities of their respective positions (Hogan, 1995). Christ (1987:144) states that the views of religious tradition advocated by feminist theologians are in three categories:

Type 1: Tradition is essentially nonsexist in vision that becomes clear through proper interpretation.

Type 2: Tradition contains both sexist and nonsexist elements; the nonsexist must be affirmed as revelation and the sexist repudiated using both the nonsexist vision as a basis along with the contemporary experience of the full humanity of women.

Type 3: Tradition is essentially sexist and must be repudiated with new traditions created on the basis of both past experience and/or nonbiblical religion.

God symbolism would be altered depending on which viewpoint one subscribes to. For example, those subscribing to the third position would likely advocate female symbolism for God found both inside and outside of biblical tradition since the Bible often excludes women's religious experience in general, as well as non-Western religion in particular. They would also introduce Goddess symbolism, since God is best symbolized by dual imagery (Christ, 1987:144; Pui-Lan, 1988:29).

Thus like feminists in general, feminist theologians hold varying positions on religious tradition and its interpretation. Diehl (1990:38-39) has developed a typology of theological positions on feminism that allows us to review the major issues of theology and feminism. Although designed to accommodate Christian theology, its outline can be readily applied to other religions.

1. *Strict hierarchalist (traditionalist).* The Bible is the infallible word of God and teaches that man is the leader and woman is subordinate. The feminist crusade for egalitarianism is unbiblical and a product of modern secular humanism. Patriarchal language in the Bible and in church liturgy should be maintained.

2. *Modern hierarchalist (liberated traditionalist).* The Bible is the infallible word of God and teaches the hierarchical structure of woman being subordinate to man. However, this hierarchy is more moderate and less authoritarian than the patriarchy in Judaism. Christ's attitudes to women, for example, were different than the culture in which he preached.

3. *Biblical feminist (evangelical feminist).* The Bible is the infallible word of God but does not teach patriarchalism as God's ideal. Paul, for example, applied his principles in relation to existing customs. With changed customs, contemporary women should not be subordinate to any kind of male church authority.

4. *Mainstream feminist (reformist feminist).* The Bible contains the word of God but is not itself the infallible word of God. When the Bible supports patriarchy, it should not be considered divine revelation. The word of God is found in its redemptive themes or prophetic tradition that criticizes oppression. Christians should work for the full liberation of women in all areas of life.

5. *Radical feminist (revolutionary feminist).* The radical Christian position is that since patriarchy and androcentrism pervade the Bible, revelation cannot be found in it. Revelation is in the experience of a community of women-affirming Christians seeking liberation from patriarchal oppression. The radical *post-Christian* position is that both biblical authority *and* Christianity as a whole be rejected. Women must engage in spiritual revolution and rename God based on their own religious experience that is totally free of men.

Both of these outlines clearly demonstrate that what is now commonly referred to as feminist theology takes on a myriad of forms and generalizations. For example, Stortz (1984) acknowledges the power of church patriarchy to the extent that she suspects this very patriarchy of actually creating feminist theology. The rationale would be to direct feminist energy into areas viewed by the church as "safe," such as on matters involving suggestions for inclusive language (words), rather than deeds. The church, then protects itself from meaningful change. According to this logic,

> Only a patriarchy would suggest that feminist theology exists, hire women to teach it and segregate it from other classical theological disciplines, so that it might not tarnish the patriarchal grandeur of the disciplines of Bible, systematic theology, and church history. (Stortz, 1984:21)

Although Stortz presents a plausible argument, it is likely that through processes such as scriptural reinterpretation and the elimination of sexist language, attitude shift will ultimately result in behavior change. This view is congruent with the sociological perspective that words do influence deeds. And regardless of the position held by any one person, feminist theology has been the major source of new research, scholarship, and critiques on gender as related to religious tradition. Perhaps feminist theology will serve to infuse institutionalized religion with the inclusive spirituality of its heritage.

CHAPTER 13

THE MEDIA

> On Marilyn Monroe: The restriction on her spirit in the airtight prison of her beauty was so complete that she literally feared aging more than death itself.
>
> —Gloria Steinem, *Marilyn* (1986:157)

The mass media impact us on a daily basis. This impact is all the more significant because most of it occurs without our conscious awareness. We are bombarded by visual and auditory stimuli from the media throughout the day. We hear music, news, and advertising at our office desks, in elevators, while jogging or driving to and from school or work. Advertisements on billboards and in buses and subways shout out the newest, best, modern, and most efficient products and services available. Cinema and television offerings allow for almost every conceivable programming taste. With the advent of video recorders and cable television, we can choose our entertainment specialties without ever leaving home.

As documented in Chapter 3, the process of socialization into gender roles occurs on multiple fronts. Although parents provide the earliest source, television soon becomes a potent socializer as well, even in the preschool years. And as we increasingly rely on the mass media, especially television, to filter the massive amount of information we receive from other social institutions, there is a profound impact on our ideas about gender. Indeed, one of the most documented, consistent findings in this regard is that among all age groups and with both genders, heavy television viewing is strongly associated with adherence to traditional and stereotyped gender views (Ross et al., 1982; Eron et al., 1983; Bryant, 1990; Signorielli, 1989, 1991). Eisenstock (1984) finds that this relationship also holds for young adults. Children are especially vulnerable in believing that the images they encounter on television represent reality and truth.

Television is strengthened by advertisements, books, magazines, and other media items which present the genders in stereotyped ways. It is easy to see why, even at an early age, we form relatively rigid beliefs about what is considered "appropriate" behavior for boys and girls, women and men. Though media representatives may argue that what is presented merely reflects the reality of gendered beliefs, the question of reinforcing an already sexist society cannot be dismissed as easily. After reviewing the media's record on how the genders are portrayed, we will return to this question.

MAGAZINES

With the publication of the *Feminine Mystique* in 1963, Betty Friedan challenged the notion that the American woman was completely content in her traditional homebound role. Freidan was one of the first to look at the role of the print media, in this case popular women's magazines, in the formation of attitudes about women. Concentrating on fiction, she traced the images of women from the emancipated views in the 1930s and 1940s to the "happy housewife" and glorified mother of the 1950s and early 1960s, whose aspirations went only as far as her own front door. From this beginning, there has been a great deal of research documenting gender role stereotypes in magazines and popular fiction. Data collected over the next two decades confirmed the earlier patterns, but with some new twists: The home oriented mother represented the ideal of magazine womanhood; women had more children but also experienced more psychological problems because of their wife and mother roles; women working outside the home were viewed as unfeminine and posed threats to otherwise happy marriages; and since women were content in their homemaker roles, they were also experiencing less romantic upheaval.

As the baby boom accelerated in the 1950s, the birth rate also climbed into magazines. Having a baby was a good bet for saving a floundering marriage. Married women who remained childless and spinsters who remained childless and husbandless were pitied for their wasteful, unhappy lives. Fiction of this period cheered heroines, who, through virtue and passivity, won husbands for themselves. Even widows and divorcees were portrayed as unable to cope without a man. The overall conclusion: The happy housewife was even happier (Lefkowitz, 1972; Franzwa, 1974a, 1974b; Ehrenreich, 1983; Ferguson, 1983; Radway, 1984; Cantor, 1987).

But other changes were occurring for women in a number of realms. The birthrate was leveling off, thousands of women moved into the paid labor force, and the feminist movement made headlines nationwide. Magazines focusing on the challenges of working outside the home emerged, some with editorial policies explicitly feminist oriented. Periodicals such as *MS* continue to uphold nonsexist standards and favor articles geared to economic productivity, social awareness, and political engagement. Even the older, more traditional magazines, like *Ladies Home Journal* and *McCall's*, began to reflect some changes. Articles on educational opportunities, employment options, and women's rights appeared with greater frequency. Magazines geared to single women or women who combine employment with marriage also appeared, like *Savvy, New Woman,* and *Working Woman.* These magazines offer advice and tactics to women who are coping with expanded role responsibilities. And compared to the more established magazines which may depict women in traditional occupations, these newer ones profile women who have greater responsibility and influence in their jobs (Ruggiero and Weston, 1985). Topics related to single parenting, adoption, health, self-development, and financial security are increasingly profiled in magazines geared to women.

Nonetheless, considering the social upheaval which has occurred, magazines have been minimally affected. In studying women's magazines over a 30-year cycle, Ferguson (1983) finds that while the first-ranked theme of attracting and keeping a man has been displaced by the theme of establishing one's own identity, few other changes have occurred. A study of *Seventeen* magazine demonstrates that teenage girls are primarily concerned with appearance, romance, and dating, and while the 1970s promoted coverage of topics related to self-development, the 1980s witnessed a decrease back to the levels found in the early 1960s (Peirce, 1990). With four decades of magazines promoting a standard of femininity associated with an almost narcissistic self-absorption (Ferguson, 1983), it is not surprising that the dominant theme of the 1990s in such magazines as *Cosmopolitan, Glamour,* and *Essence* is on relationships with men (getting and keeping them) followed by becoming more beautiful (Renzetti and Curran, 1995:160). With emphases on beauty, hairstyles, dieting, and fashion, "makeover" articles featuring before-after photographs which transform homely girls into alluring women abound. The bottom line is that physical appearance is necessary to attract and ultimately snare a man. While career achievement is also a goal, it is dependent on physical appearance. Magazines for women persevere in this message.

Magazines continue to reward self-sacrificing wives whose identity revolves around the home and who are encouraged in self-expression as long as it does not interfere with traditional roles. Magazines can be held partly accountable for the stereotyped beliefs full-time homemakers hold concerning their own roles as well as those of women who work outside the home. The often repeated but empirically unverified assertion is that homemakers are made to feel guilty about *not* working outside the home, and "feminists" are blamed for the overall deprecation of housewives. It is clear that 25 years ago the women's movement thrust was on paid work roles with a neglect (but not deprecation) of homemakers. It is also abundantly clear today that the same movement is doing everything to bolster women in whatever roles they choose and to counter whatever damage the earlier movement may have inadvertently created. Yet the media in general, and magazines in particular, continue to fuel this homemaker-paid worker competition between women with articles that instill guilt and jealousy for all women—whether they work outside the home or not.

ADVERTISING

Print Advertising

The images of women in magazines are reinforced through advertisements testifying to the glories of shining kitchen floors, soft toilet tissue, and antiseptic children. Whether we view ads on television or through the print media, they are likely to present the genders in stereotyped modes. Extensive research has documented the fact that even with some improvement over time, advertising images of women are based on traditional gender role norms (Courtney and Whipple, 1983; Barthel, 1987; Kilbourne, 1995).

One of the first major studies on gender stereotyping in advertising was done by analyzing magazines in terms of the number and genders of adults, the occupations and activities in which they were presented, and the kinds of products being promoted (Courtney and Lockeretz, 1971). The data showed that women's place is in the home, they do not make important decisions, and are dependent on men, who in turn regard women as sex objects. Women are only interested in buying cosmetics and cleaning aids. Given the fact that by the early 1970s over 30 percent of women were in the work force and represented a critical portion of consumer buying, these ads clearly did not portray reality.

A number of studies quickly followed. A replication of Courtney and Lockeretz (1971) two years later showed that ads were beginning to depict women in more occupational roles, but the vast majority of women were still pictured exclusively in the home (Wagner and Banos, 1973). In viewing ads which span 20 years, Venkatesan and Losco (1975) found that there was a decline in the "most obnoxious" ads, but advertisers continued to be insensitive to the real world. Again, women are viewed as sex objects, interested in physical beauty, and dependent on men. A woman is concerned with appearance and domestic life, rather than with complex decision making (Culley and Bennett, 1976). Advertisements rarely showed them in nontraditional situations, even in magazines oriented to a wider audience such as *Newsweek, Look,* and *Sports Illustrated* (Sexton and Haberman, 1974).

The advertisements of the 1980s and 1990s not only maintain these stereotyped images but in important ways stereotypical portrayals of women as sex objects have increased (Lazier-Smith, 1989; Furnham and Bitar, 1993). With nudity and near-nudity now found in even the more established magazines, it is common to see undressed or scantily dressed women selling a myriad of products. Car and boat ads typically show women in bathing suits provocatively draped over fenders and on cabin decks. Products sold primarily to men, such as machine tools and industrial equipment, use a similar format. In gun magazines we routinely see women in lingerie or evening gowns clutching men who are holding handguns and rifles. Advertising campaigns for a popular jeans label now show near nude women—but no jeans—only the logo of the company. Sporting events are sponsored by products represented by men in commercials, who are given more speaking roles than women (Riffe et al., 1993). Beer campaigns cater to men in both general interest and specialty magazines and show males more often than females. Males represent "face-isms," in that their faces are photographed more often than their bodies. Females in these campaigns represent "body-isms" or "partial-isms" in that their bodies or parts of their bodies are more often shown and appear much more in swimwear than do males (Hall and Crum, 1994). Remember the "Swedish Bikini Team" a few years ago? This campaign showed blonde women with large chests who frolic on the beach while the men drink beer. Although this campaign received much negative publicity for its blatantly sexist overtones, the beer manufacturer ran the ads in magazines and on television for several months before they were dropped. Overall, magazines' advertisers consistently portray women in decorative roles (Wiles, 1991). According to Belknap and Leonard (1991:105), there is some equivocal research arguing that women are now portrayed in a "progressive and less stereotyped fashion." But because commercial advertising "appears most successful by selling products that depict more traditional cultural patterns, [it] has been slow to change."

To be effective, advertising must be aware of trends affecting products and services. The moment an "improvement" is made on a particular product, campaigns begin to sell the public on its virtues. The old is quickly forgotten as the new makes its appearance. To sell means to change. Yet advertising is stubbornly persistent in the manner in which this is done. What is ironic is that ad agencies ignore the research documenting the fact that consumers react negatively to advertising which is sexist and desire campaigns which portray both men and women in nonstereotyped ways (Whipple and Courtney, 1985). Considering this research and the numerous instances of public outrage over certain advertisements, the adage that "sex (and sexism) sells" must be questioned.

We know that in selling products opinions about men and women are being shaped as well. For example, drug advertising carries messages about women which are powerful and potentially harmful. Medical journals are a major source of information on drug products for physicians. Men receive drugs for angina and related heart disease. Advertisers depict these men in board rooms, in the stock market and forever dealing with financial crises. For women, ads promote the idea that women do not have the psychological strength to solve their problems so they turn to the physician who is ready and willing to prescribe psychotropic drugs. The answer to the problems of house-wives who cannot cope with the responsibilities of husband and children or to the women who cannot cope with demanding employers is to give an antide-pressant.

In these ads, women are the sicker gender and especially prone to emo-tional trauma. We have already documented in Chapter 2 that women are the primary users of psychoactive drugs and are the target market for drug manu-facturers. While multiple roles are beneficial to women, they are stereotyped in ads which endorse both psychological and sexual insecurity from these roles. They are shown in patronizing ways which endorse both psychological and sexual insecurity. Older women are virtually invisible in product ads except for medical journals showing them as heavy consumers of anti-depres-sants and psychotropic drugs (Jamieson, 1995). Drugs, rather than a change of lifestyle, are encouraged to solve problems. Most important, these ads rein-force the physician's expectation that female patients presenting symptoms which cannot be readily correlated with a specific physical illness are in need of psychotropics and may contribute to physicians being less likely to take their complaints seriously compared to males (Leppard et al., 1993). The deluge of new psychoactive drugs occurred in the late 1960s when research on the bio-chemical processes in mental illness was at its peak. Physicians who graduated from medical school before 1960 are especially vulnerable to such ads.

It is relatively easy to analyze ads according to general themes and images. But in order to assess the overall impact, we must recognize that ads also sell products and reinforce attitudes in ways that often go unrecognized by the casual reader. Goffman's early work (1979) concentrated on the sub-tleties of posture and relative size and positioning of hands, eyes, knees, and other parts of the body in ads. A man is pictured taller than a woman unless he is socially inferior to her. Men and boys are shown instructing women and girls. A woman's eye is averted to the man in the picture with her, but a man's eye is averted only to a superior. Women's hands caress or barely touch. They are rarely shown grasping, manipulating, or creatively shaping. Women have far-away looks in their eyes, especially in the presence of men. Women act like chil-dren and are often depicted with children.

More recent data indicate that women continue to be depicted in terms of Goffman's categories in ways which bolster gender stereotyping (Akert and Chen, 1984; Nigro et al., 1988; Belknap and Leonard, 1991). In visual repre-sentations of men and women, Archer et al. (1983) find that the face-ism ads still dominate for men as does body-ism for women. They suggest that the face is associated with qualities such as character and intellect while the body is associated with qualities such as weight and emotion, thus contributing to our beliefs about what is deemed important for men and women. According to Kil-bourne (1995), women make desperate efforts to conform to a beauty ideal manipulating their faces and bodies to achieve an impossible standard. Adolescents are particularly vulnerable to such advertising and are its prime targets.

Age stereotyping of older women by advertisers can increase their insecurity about beauty and physical attractiveness as well, only this time the desperate clinging to youthfulness is induced. Young women advertise products to older ones. The fear-of-aging theme has increased cosmetics sales dramatically for the over-40 baby boomers. But there are almost no older models who sell these products. Whereas younger women sell lipstick and hair color to older women, when older women are used in ads at all, it is to tout products signaling body decline, such as for dentures and adult diapers (Jamieson, 1995:153).

Besides beauty products, clothing represents another method to attain the beauty standard by manipulating the body. The most successful models are paid millions to reinforce unnatural images of womanhood, which keeps women chained to seasonal, changing, and expensive fashion trends. There is a growing market for seductive clothing designs aimed at little girls. As indicated by Evans (1993:117),

> When a slinky ensemble for young children, identical to one worn by Madonna on "Saturday Night Live," received rave reviews . . . buyers and parents instantly snapped them up . . . People went nuts for those little Madonna outfits . . . women who buy Escada and Chanel for herself flips when she sees something like that for her daughter.

Considering the avalanche of physical appearance messages women receive in advertising, symbolic interaction correctly predicts that self-fulfilling prophecies follow. We have seen that these are demonstrated in everything from self-esteem, cigarette smoking, eating disorders, and mental health, as well as a host of attitudes regarding gender. Another ominous trend is that males exposed to ads where females are portrayed as sex objects are more accepting of rape-supportive attitudes and predictive of subjective levels of exploitation (Rudman and Verdi, 1993; Lanis and Covell, 1995). Advertising artificially creates images that become the reality. In a recent study of fourth graders, half of the girls said they were dieting and three-quarters said they were overweight. As reported by one student: "We don't expect boys to be that handsome. We take them as they are." Another added, "But boys expect girls to be perfect and beautiful. And skinny" (Kilbourne, 1995:395).

As already mentioned, what is remarkable about such findings is that women themselves are very critical of the images. Feminists and even antifeminists do not disagree about the way women are portrayed in advertising (Duker and Tucker, 1977). If the people to whom the ads are directed find them distasteful and irritating, how can a double standard continue? Pearson (1989) quotes the president of a large-circulation women's magazine, who suggests that an influential minority of advertisers dominate the industry. These few people would continue to sanction the idea that some products are beyond the comprehension of women and should not be advertised to them at all.

From a pure business viewpoint, this type of sexism is disadvantageous in that the true market potential for products is not realized. Another problem is that advertisers are the lifeblood of magazines and they must make concessions to receive their business. Advertisers demand that a "supportive editorial atmosphere" or "complementary copy" appear with their ads. This means that an article about beauty to support or complement an ad about a beauty product must be included on the same page. In this way advertisers literally control the editorial content of the entire magazine (Steinem, 1995:316). In resisting such interference and in an effort to create a more egalitarian organization, *MS* magazine ran into obstacles when advertising dollars dwindled. It also split the editorial staff between those who identified with the women's movement and those with women's magazines (Farrell, 1994). The magazine ceased publication temporarily and reorganized to become a subscription journal-type publication with no advertising. Such problems hamper the broader changes that are occurring in other societal institutions.

Eventually, the newer status of women must be recognized by advertisers if they are to succeed with their sales pitches. Although minimal, some changes have occurred, primarily with regard to depicting women in more diverse occupational roles and in more general interest magazines (Sullivan and O'Connor, 1988; Busby and Leichty, 1993). Older women are recognized as a potential market if the proper marketing mix is discovered. While proclaiming that older women are (still) beautiful, advertisers are beginning to use themes suggesting that fitness, vitality, and blazing new trails are associated with aging (Darling, 1994; Krasnow, 1995). These suggest that advertisers may create a new kind of woman. Regardless of age, she is active, involved in an array of projects, and enjoys her home but is not monopolized by it. Some advertisers are only beginning to recognize that women are diverse, lead successful lives, and can balance home and career. The impact of this remains to be seen. The caution here is that another artificial creation emerges along with another set of standards to which women are expected to adhere.

Television Advertising

Advertising carries over the images initiated by the print media into television. But the images are even more powerful and affect a larger audience. While nonverbals in print ads can be used effectively, their use is limited compared to what can be done with commercials appearing on television. Television uses hundreds of techniques to create a particular view of a product. Lighting, camera angle, tone of voice, body movement, animation, and color, to name a few, can be infinitely manipulated to provide the "ideal" sales mix.

Thousands of commercials have been studied to determine the gender roles in television advertising. The results are similar to print advertisements. The single largest occupation for a female is housewife. She is usually shown in the home testifying to the merits of bathroom and kitchen products. Though she is selling products to other women, a man's voice in the background tells her what to do. Ninety percent of voice-overs are male. She is portrayed in dependent, subordinate, and helping roles to her husband, her children, and her male employer if she works outside the home (Courtney and Whipple, 1983; Bretl and Cantor, 1988; Lovdal, 1989; Silvas et al., 1993). And consistent with print ads, television commercials emphasize that women must first and foremost be attractive in order to be acceptable. In a study of 4,294 commercials, Downs and Harrison (1985) find that in one out of every 3.8 commercials a statement about attractiveness occurs, particularly addressed to women and using a male voice-over. While women now appear with about equal frequency to men in prime-time commercials, they are shown in domestic situations as wife or mother, and as more foolish, less mature, and less successful than male characters (Bretl and Cantor, 1988; Metzger, 1992). Consider the portrayal of the Mr. Whipple contingent at the toilet tissue shelf in the supermarket as an example of this.

Advertisements geared to children are even more gender role oriented. Given the fact that it is estimated that every year a child typically views about 20,000 commercials, the potential impact on gender attitudes is enormous (Condry et al., 1988). Girls are shown in more passive activities and dependent upon another person or a doll for entertainment. They learn how to help their mothers, assist in household tasks, serve men and boys—especially where food is concerned—and see how to become beautiful or stay cute. The ads focus on softness and quiet play and use dreamy content, soft music, and fades or dissolves for sequencing and ending (Cattin and Jain, 1979; Welch et al., 1979; Courtney and Whipple, 1983; Schneider, 1989; Kahan and Norris, 1994). Commercials do not teach independence or autonomy for young girls. Consider the following excerpts from commercials for a boy and girl:

For Nerf Bow and Arrow™

Man's voice:	Nerf Bow and Arrow is coming your way, and it means business.
Male singer:	The power is pumping, an arrow's in your hand.
	Now your heart is pumping, fire as quick as you can. . . .
	The enemy's coming, now they're in your sights. . . .

For Starlight Sparkles™

Female chorus:	What girls do:
Starlight Sparkles	
Shiny, how you love me	
Sparkle when I hug you	
Light my world above. . . .	Girl in ad: "Oooooh!"
See the colored stars go round	Girl: "Wow"
You fill my world with love	Friend: "Beautiful"
	(Cited in Kahan and Norris, 1994:281-82)

A lifetime of viewing these commercials may actually inhibit achievement aspirations for women (Geis et al., 1984).

Changes in patterns of how women are portrayed in commercials are not encouraging. They still need men to tell them what to do or buy, even for products like window cleaner, deodorant, or hair color. When a voice is heard in the background but no person is shown, that voice is from a male. Since the 1970s, male voice-overs increased to 92 percent of daytime commercials and 90 percent of prime-time commercials (Pesch et al., 1981). In both the United States and England gender role stereotyping in television advertisements has remained constant over time (Furnham and Bitar, 1993). Gender stereotypes in children's commercials have actually increased. Only a tiny portion of gender possibilities are imaged in children's advertisements. As Gottfreid (1994:256) declares

> In keeping with advertising's nostalgic, yet wishful, imaging, advertisements which picture children nostalgically reproduce a world in which girls are girls and boys are boys, and gender works as a simple binary opposition.

FILM

Unlike the other media, women have played a more central position in the film industry. Although director and producer remain the province of men, women have succeeded as screenwriters, editors, costume designers, critics, and actors. In the early days of film when the studio system was at its height, women dominated the star spotlight. This was reflected in popularity polls and the billings female leads received. Although the contract system allowed studios to virtually own actors, women had influence in determining their careers and the parts they received. It has only been since the 1940s that female stars have been overshadowed by male ones. With a few exceptions, this decline has continued to the present. In contrast to the reality of women's diverse contemporary roles, current film portrayals are sorely lacking in depth and authenticity.

World War II encouraged the independence and initiative of women, which were reflected in screen images. Women were shown as efficient homemakers who could make the transition from kitchen to the war industry smoothly, without severely disrupting family life. Or they were shown as nurses serving overseas and even as combatants who at times, like men, could die for their country. Movies were a critical part of the war effort and emphasized the need for self-sacrifice if victory was to be won. Women on the home front were necessary components for this effort. The double-duty woman who worked in a defense plant was symbolized by Rosie the Riveter, who became the heroine of the home front.

Although women on the World War II screen had self-confidence and strength, a certain ambiguity was also evident. The taken-for-granted functional balance of home and workplace was upset. Both men and women left home to engage in the unlikely occupations of soldier and defense worker. They were fighting to save the American home, and films reassured audiences that after the war women would be as eager as men to return to the natural order of things. True to this message, by the 1950s films reaffirmed the domestic subservience of women.

Whereas the war years presented women as multifaceted, after the war they were portrayed as unidimensional, as either good or bad. The "good" woman embodied the feminine mystique. She was virtuous throughout her courtship. She might have a successful career, but Mr. Right would change her priorities and definitions of success. After marriage she became the perfect wife and mother. Doris Day and Debbie Reynolds represented this image. The "bad" woman, on the other hand, was the sexpot, who could entice a man away from his faithful wife and loving family. Marilyn Monroe and Ava Gardner symbolized this view of sexuality which hinted broadly of immorality in the innocent fifties.

Although the films of the fifties appear to display a concern for domestic righteousness, French (1978) asserts that they reflect a period which also shows women struggling with narrowly defined roles. A number of movies combined progressive and reactionary elements with women involved in the transition between domestic roles and newer alternatives.

> The transitional woman is often torn between her desire for a conventional, secure lifestyle and her longing for an unconventional, adventurous, largely uncharted course of action. (French, 1978:xxiii)

The conflicts and contradictions of the transitional women helped set the stage for the changes of the next two decades.

If the early days of film romanticized women and put them on a pedestal, the 1960s and 1970s compensated by adding a more blatant sexual dimension. The new women of this era were loosened from the constraints of family life, but with the breaking of the bonds, an attitude of "they deserve what they get" arose. Women who ventured outside the home were negatively portrayed and eventually punished. The favorable images of the war years disintegrated and women were accorded fewer roles than ever before. Male speaking roles outdistanced female by twelve to one (Klemesrud, 1974). Haskell (1987:323) calls this period the "most disheartening in screen history." She believes that as the women's liberation movement gained momentum and women were asserting themselves in new realms, a backlash occurred in commercial film.

Film romance was replaced by sexuality and violence, and this continues to the present. Romantic couples of the Fred Astaire-Ginger Rogers variety are gone, with prostitutes and girlfriends of questionable morals filling the void. Themes of love and adultery are infused with violence and murder. Movies such as *Basic Instinct, Fatal Attraction,* and *What's Love Got to Do with It?* exemplify this trend. The focus of love is narrowed so that it now coincides with violence. "Romantic films are now mining for conflict in smaller veins or in arteries designed to spurt blood and shock the audience" (Jones, 1996). Females are victims in movies of horror, murder, and especially rape, in which film directors seem to have a macabre interest. During the past 20 years movies with a rape theme increased dramatically. While women as rape victims are more sympathetically depicted than in the past, it is likely that moviegoers are also becoming more desensitized to the issue, reinforcing the notion that rape is an inescapable burden women must face.

By the 1970s sex and sexual violence became explicit enough to create a rating system which determined the degree of suitability for audiences below a certain age. This system emphasizes sex more than violence so that love scenes are more apt to get the film a restricted rating than rape scenes. The rating system also helps perpetuate the ideas that rape is inconsequential and that rapists are heroic. In three decades of the James Bond films women are depicted enjoying rape, especially since Bond is the "good guy" and the supposed fantasy of every woman. But James Bond gets to play out men's fantasies—he drives fast cars, fights ruthless villains, wears a nice suit, and has sex with any "girl" he desires, and they always eventully say "yes" to him (Corbett, 1995). Once raped they are then ignored by the male star, sometimes murdered by him and often murdered by someone else. Bond must always be free of women. If he inadvertently falls in love with her, she is doomed to die before the end of the picture. Rapes and murders are especially likely alternatives to women in token roles. A "now you see them, now you don't" pattern occurs. And, as Bond ages, his "girls" do not. The two most enduring Bonds, Sean Connery and Roger Moore, were often 30 years older than their leading ladies. The women are as sleek and young as ever, picture after picture. As Hanna (1995) notes, the "007 films must hold the record for past political incorrectness." As throughout the Bond movie decades, the fashion world continues to be "stalked by the ghosts of Bond Girls":

> "Killer Babes" shrieks *Cosmopolitan* over eight pages of thigh, breast, and buttock revealing outfits from current designer catwalks. (Hanna, 1995)

Perhaps the flagrant abuse of women in past Bond films has been at least minimally acknowledged by producers. The newest Bond, Pierce Brosnan, has been paired with a strong, intelligent, but always beautiful leading lady, Femke Jennsen, in a film (*Goldeneye*) which does highlight *their* partnership rather than *her* submission. In an effort at emancipation from Bond, she is publicized as the Bond "woman" rather than the Bond "girl" (Hanna, 1995; Lister, 1995). While perhaps not as blatantly misogynous, the James Bond mystique, which overshadows any of his "girls," endures. In a recent article publicizing the release of *Goldeneye* and profiling all the Bonds and Bond "Golden Girls" of the past (Lipton, 1995), Femke Jennsen was not even mentioned.

Unlike men, women must have youth to be seriously considered for romantic leads, which means their careers suffer in terms of longevity. Clint Eastwood gets more distinguished as he ages. Meryl Streep gets old. After a certain age, women are consigned to play shrews and jealous housewives as their movie husbands are turned by pretty faces and slim figures. New, younger female faces are sought to replace the "aging" 40-year-old star.

The film industry offers a number of excuses for not focusing on female stars or for portraying women in limited, stereotyped roles. They maintain that the public does not like "macho" women and that television offers a diverse range of female roles for free (Rosen, 1974). Another explanation is that men dominate the industry and are in the position of determining the image of women in it. Although the numbers are increasing, male studio executives outnumber females by about three to one (Silvas et al., 1993). This may suggest that men create inappropriate images for female roles simply because their feedback from women is limited. Roles emerge out of male fantasies or the fear of dealing with women in positions of power. This is a reasonable assessment considering that the average moviegoer is a male between the ages of 14 and 24 and it is his fantasies that are being catered to (Basow, 1992). According to Silvas and her colleagues (1993), the limited range of female characters continuously puts them in the same roles: as madonnas, whores, bimbos, psychotics, and bitches. Filmmakers are only beginning to deal with the struggles facing contemporary women, and few directors are willing to confront the issues. So movies retreat into an unrealistic stereotyped world.

There are a few positive signs which suggest a return of women to movies offering greater role latitude and chances to display a wider range of talent. Critically acclaimed as well as popular films that do not rest on a male lead and highlight sensitive issues related to friendship and loyalty among women include *Joy Luck Club, Turning Point, Steel Magnolias, Waiting to Exhale, Fried Green Tomatoes, Sense and Sensibility,* and *Thelma and Louise.* However, the success for some of these was bittersweet. *Fried Green Tomatoes* and *Silkwood* were criticized for lesbian overtones. While successfully countering masculinist bias in some movies which portray lesbians, other stereotypes persist to make the films more palatable to a wider audience (Kabir, 1994). Again, filmmakers believe an injection of violence satisfies this criterion. Sharon Stone's portrayal of the bisexual murderer in *Basic Instinct* drew storms of protest from gay men and lesbians. But screen writer and actress Guinevere Turner, who has done other movies with similar themes, was not bothered. She states, "I'd much rather have killer lesbians than lesbians who kiss once in the beginning and then use a man to get to each other" (Smith, 1994). *Thelma and Louise* was criticized for violence directed toward men. It is apparent that film critics, too, subscribe to a gender-stereotyped world which is suspicious of loving and cooperative relationships between women. It reveals much about the tenacity of our gendered society when for decades females in movies are routinely mutilated, maimed, murdered, and raped film after film, but when a "good" movie reverses the scenario, a charge of "man-bashing" is leveled against it. The issue society must address is not so much that turnabout is fair play but that violence is viewed as an acceptable mode of conflict resolution.

While such movies offer female actors multidimensional portrayals, they are certainly the exception. With the greater number of successful film releases in the late 1970s and 1980s, which countered the stock Hollywood formula related to gender, there was some hope that more female superstars were on the horizon. Barbara Striesand was the bankable female lead for a decade, but actresses like Meryl Streep, Jessica Lange, Diane Keaton, Julia Roberts, Susan Sarandon, and Sally Field assumed more starring roles. It now appears that these gains have been short-lived, with even fewer diverse and starring roles offered to females in the 1990s. Over 70 percent of feature-film roles go to men (Silvas et al., 1993). Offering a "wholesome" role to a female signals doom in Hollywood. It is a sign she is an aging-bygone. So she remains marketable by "shedding her clothes and her dignity" (Anderson, 1994). A rather cynical comment on the paucity of either featured or supporting parts for mature, skilled actresses came in 1993 when the theme for the Academy Awards was "Oscar Celebrates Women in the Movies." Six of the ten nominees for Best Actress and Best Supporting Actress came from Australia, England, and France because Hollywood simply did not offer enough meaningful roles for women to even get nominated for the award. In 1996, the public was told that screen actresses had their "meatiest choice of roles in ages" making it difficult to predict Oscar winners (Ciabattari, 1996b). This was the "Year of the Backlash" where Hollywood blockbusters were replaced by family friendly and small art films. But most of the "meaty" roles to women in this backlash year were for their portrayals as prostitutes or ex-prostitutes.

In 1990, the Screen Actors' Guild held its first National Women's Conference where Meryl Streep addressed the group to express concern about the declining number of strong female characters. Even a cursory look at the current film offerings in the local paper will testify to the scarcity of female stars, strong or otherwise. Demi Moore, Michelle Pfeiffer, Julia Roberts, Sharon Stone, and Susan Sarandon have managed to endure the Hollywood roller coaster for women. There is also less tolerance for films that are box office bombs starring women. Jack Nicholson, Mel Gibson, Tom Hanks, or Kevin Costner may emerge relatively unscathed from bad reviews and bad movies, but studios are reluctant to offer parts to women who have fallen victim to the critics' ax. Women are almost hidden among the faces of numerous male actors who endure as superstars.

While complaints abound that women are held hostage by Hollywood, "the marketing studies, the box office, the bottom line all dictate male domination of movie marquees" (Anderson, 1994). As noted by British actor Emma Thompson, Oscar winner for *Howards End* (1993) in the Best Actress category and for Best Adapted Screenplay with *Sense and Sensibility* (1996), "My agenda is to always represent women as positively as I can." If a role is offered where she may have to play a neurotic women suffering under stress, she may turn it down. She states that rather than seeing another woman tearing her hair out, she wants to "see a woman succeeding, triumphing," and as a three-dimensional being (Italie, 1993).

The dilemma faced by that part of the film industry concerned with the image of women is how to successfully combine the elements of fantasy and realism which are what attract the public to the movies in the first place. Mainstream cinema represent women as either "idealized objects of desire or as threatening objects to be tamed" (Pribram, 1993). On the other hand, should women be portrayed as victims of a patriarchal society, or as "vanquishers of mighty odds"? (Haskell, 1983). Will romance be forever crushed by realism? Haskell (1983) maintains that the movies can still have the requisite fantasy and magic without accepting a narrow range of behavior from female actors. In Emma Thompson's view, women have to debrief themselves to resist the messages that they have no history or no heroines and to unlearn the stereotypes that chip away at their sense of self-esteem (Italie, 1993). Movies are creations of male fantasies. Women need to invent their own fantasies and portray these as well. While movies do not have to provide answers for questions concerning gender role change, they can at least offer challenges.

MUSIC

The media are change oriented, geared to an often fickle public that demands new sights and sounds to satisfy an unending thirst for entertainment variety. Nowhere is this more apparent than in the world of popular music. Whether it is defined as country, rock, pop, new wave, alternative, or heavy metal, the quest for musical notoriety, as evidenced by the volume of CD and tape sales, continues unabated. Although the music industry is diverse, it recognizes that a significant portion of the record market is controlled by teens and young adults. With the advent of the rock video, the competition for the "teen dollar" becomes even stronger. Considering the money and time spent on records, especially by teens, contemporary music is an important source of socialization.

Experiments in musical patterns are responsible for trends being set and altered so rapidly. Music is always at the vanguard of change. Protest movements are fired by songs which unify members against a common foe. Rock musicians take conventional morality to the limits. Such music challenges the traditional and creates the conditions for further change. Since contemporary music in particular challenges social norms, it would appear to be the one medium where traditional gender roles are minimized. But the evidence counters this reasonable assumption. In the realm of popular music, rock music now claims artistic supremacy and has emerged as a "major creative force and structuring principle" (Regev, 1994:97). This claim as a recognized art form of artistic value thus legitimizes its representations of society, including the portrayal of the genders.

Popular music of the last four decades sings to the beauty and sex appeal of women, who use them to control men. Through passivity and submissiveness, a woman can manipulate even a possessive man so that she is in control of him and the relationship (Talkington, 1976; Wilkinson, 1976). Control, however, may be difficult to determine since she remains dependent on him. Unlike rock music, while country music is not generally misogynistic, it is definitely stereotyped. Country music stereotypes women in two categories: They are temptresses to men as well as wives who wait patiently for their two-timing husbands to return (Sims, 1974). No matter what the consequences, "stand by your man" is the appropriate response for even the long-suffering woman.

Since the 1950s, views of women in rock music have become increasingly associated with sexual violence. The virginal girl-next-door, teen-angel, and California girl have been replaced by whores, bitches, and fantasy figures on whom violence is perpetrated. The misogyny in "cock rock" lyrics is unconcealed, with little attempt to be subtle. Considering that lyrics are reflective of a chauvinistic rock culture, it is interesting that more images of "predatory females" as aggressors toward male victims are emerging (Sherman and Dominick, 1986; Seidman, 1992).

Overall, music is perhaps the most stereotypical of all the media in its portrayal of women. Again, while images of women in song contain elements of positive regard side by side with blatant misogyny, they are cast into rigid categories determined by their perceived gender role characteristics. As summed up by Pavletich (1980:4):

> Wife, lover, mother. She is the fallen angel of country, the glamorous fatale of pop, the sassy fox of R&B, the sister of folk. She's tramp, bitch and goddess, funky mama, sweetheart, the woman left lonely, the hapless victim of her man. (Cited in Groce and Cooper, 1990:221)

These images are expanded by CD covers depicting women being brutalized by men and animals. The love-hate dichotomy is featured on covers where men are kissing and killing women at the same time. Although more stylized in form, rock videos present similar views. Boycotts of records showing violent themes against women on their covers have generally failed. But as rock lyrics have become more sexually explicit, some record companies have agreed to put a "warning label" on their album covers indicating that the words may be unsuitable for audiences below a certain age. It is a significant comment on our society that sexual themes per se are considered more offensive than violence against women.

Before the advent of rock and roll music in the 1950s, female singers occupied one-third of the positions on singles charts, but by 1985 that figure had decreased dramatically to 8 percent (Groce and Cooper, 1990:221). A number of female entertainers, such as Patti Page, Rosemary Clooney, and Doris Day, were popular before World War II and were commercially successful for two decades by combining music and film careers. With the emergence of rock music and its appeal to teenagers, younger male entertainers moved into the spotlight. It is only with the "girl groups" such as the Supremes of the 1960s and 1970s, that a number of women charted success in rock music.

In the 1960s Janis Joplin broke into the rock culture and emerged as a unique, controversial, and often contradictory symbol for young women caught in the middle of a confusing period of history. She was viewed as a floozy as well as one who sang of the pains of womanhood. Rodnitzky (1976) states that she was a "victim of sexism within a sexual revolution she fueled," but she was also a feminist symbol who paved the way for other women destined to enter the sacred realm of the male rock kingdom. Rock musician Melissa Etheridge's supports this:

> In 1967, Janis was strange and freakish. Today she would be hip and alternative. Because of her drive to be true to her soul, girls like me in 1976 didn't feel so strange wanting to sing rock 'n' roll. Because she wrote, "either take the love I

offer or let me be," I didn't feel so different for wanting power in my life. We did-n't have to be secretaries or housewives; we could be rock stars. (Cited in Levins, 1995)

A number of rock bands either led by women or with female and male lead singers and musicians, have emerged drawing large crowds at concerts. The names of Madonna, Gloria Estefan, Paula Abdul, Mariah Carey, and even Cher are recognizable as leading women in the rock charts. Their talent is being recognized by the music industry's most prestigious awards (Sicoli, 1988). It cannot be said, however, that their songs are feminist in orientation. They, too, sing of love and pain, but with an abundance of masochistic reflec-tions. With gyrating cleavages and tight costumes, female artists chant songs of vulnerable women being abandoned by men. Revenge for a woman is to taunt the man she loves.

Female rock artists do not produce many popular songs that show other women in a sympathetic light. Although some music is considered to be "women-identified" (Petersen, 1987) and reflective of a feminist orientation in content and style, performers of this genre are not as commercially successful. Madonna may be the exception in this regard, but she is also an enigma. Some view her music as countering traditional feminine ideals of dependency and reserve, representing a postmodern feminist image that combines elements of the "new woman" (Kaplan, 1987). Others suggest that her songs and videos are sending a "potent message to teenagers about the glamour of sex, pregnancy and childbearing" through a fantasy world (cited in Brown and Schulze, 1990:92). But as she has transitioned successfully into film, her multidimen-sional talents are receiving high marks. Janis Joplin died early in her career. It will be interesting to see if Madonna becomes the feminist role model that may have been Joplin's destiny.

In a study of women in local rock groups, Groce and Cooper (1990) find the women would like to change the sexist material of their bands but are com-pelled to dress and sing in a sexually provocative way. They are not taken seri-ously as musicians for these very kinds of actions and are often paid less. They are attempting to break out of the mold in which they are embedded by the rock culture but find themselves in a no-win situation. Indeed, few can act as role models and challenge rock's misogynous lyrics. Madonna may be chal-lenging dependency in women, but her sexual image serves to reinforce the women-as-sex-object orientation already ingrained in rock culture. With possi-ble exceptions of people such as Tina Turner, who reemerged in rock and has been catapulted to the superstar category, alternative views of women, demon-strated by female artists themselves, are rarer today than in the 1960s.

Rock Videos

In 1981, MTV (music television) was introduced to cable subscribers, and by 1984, it was considered to be a major financial success, as evidenced by the increasing number of commercials. For adolescents, it is one of the most widely consumed forms of popular culture (Kalof, 1993). Such commercials are especially targeted to high school youth whose daily video diet averages two hours (Sun and Lull, 1986). Though adolescents may be the primary audi-ence, third and fourth graders represent an important segment of music video viewers (Signorielli, 1991:8-9). The three- to five-minute vignettes may include concert footage or what are called concept videos, which tell a story in an often dreamlike or impressionistic way. Signorielli, (1991:8) refers to these as "manufactured fantasies."

Music videos provide a visual extension of the cock rock and other lyrics described above. Rock videos reproduce and support a gender ideology of male power and dominance and continue to reinforce negative attitudes toward women (Lewis, 1990; Sommers-Flanagan et al., 1993). On MTV males appear on the videos twice as often as females. When race is factored in, whites outnumber nonwhites by four to one, with nonwhite females being the least represented (only 1 percent as featured singers during a typical MTV ratings period). However, when they are portrayed, African-American women tend to have more active roles, such as dancing or playing an instrument, while white women are used more for decoration or having no clear purpose in the video (Brown and Campbell, 1986; Sherman and Dominick, 1986). It may be speculated, however, that with the increased popularity of rap music and the virtual domination of the market by black males, black females may be relegated to more background, passive roles. In general, rock videos depict females as emotional, illogical, deceitful, fearful, dependent, and passive while men are seen as adventuresome, domineering, aggressive, and violent (Hansen and Hansen, 1988; Seidman, 1992). Research also suggests that the ideological message of traditional gender arrangement and sexual interaction is received differently by men and women. From a symbolic interaction perspective, Kalof (1993:646) finds that women read female images in certain rock videos as either powerful and in control or vulnerable and weak. Men read the same images as teasing and hard-to-get or submissive and indecisive. Yet for male images, there are no major gender differences in interpretations. This demonstrates how gender is a social construction shaped by patriarchal social myths as articulated in popular culture (Denzin 1992; Kalof, 1993).

Perhaps the most disheartening statistic with regard to rock videos is that most videos combine sexual images with acts of violence (Sherman and Dominick, 1986). Heavy metal and rap songs display the most violent lyrics and videos. Women are routinely depicted as sex objects on whom violence is perpetrated, with videos increasingly enacting rape scenes (Vincent et al., 1987). According to research by Binder (1993:764),

> While heavy metal songs use more double entendres and symbolic allusions to refer to sexual acts and male domination of women, rap makes these acts more graphic and explicit.

The publicity that surrounds the graphic violence, particularly sexual violence, is exactly what some performers desire. In addition to sales of records, cable subscribers will pay extra for premium channels that show controversial videos which other networks refuse to air.

Since most research on rock videos has been descriptive to date, their impact on views of gender is yet to be documented. However, it can be argued that since they routinely depict sexual and violent imagery together, they reflect other research which suggests that exposure to such images not only desensitizes viewers to erotica but increases callousness toward women (Comstock and Paik, 1991; Donnerstein and Linz, 1992). Indirectly, they may create an environment in which males become indifferent to or mildly supportive of violence, especially sexual violence directed against women (Malamuth, 1989).

TELEVISION

Though magazines, songs, and films are important mass media socializers, television is by far the most pervasive. Statistics indicate that 98 percent of American households have at least one television, and 40 percent have two or more. The average person watches almost thirty hours of television each week, almost five hours a day. While people over age 55 are the heaviest viewers, children between the ages of 2 and 11 watch over three hours each day (Nielsen Media Research, 1994). Unlike films, we see the same television characters come directly into our home, week after week, year after year. We learn about their joys and sorrows, how they raise their children, what their children like, and how they relate to one another as parents, spouses, siblings, employees, employers, and in the infinite variety of other roles that emerge from television series.

Television takes on a certain reality in the minds of many viewers, with some even finding it difficult to separate an actor from the character the actor is playing. Actors portraying TV doctors and lawyers receive mail from viewers asking for medical and legal advice. Soap opera actors are berated or praised for how they conduct their television lives. Viewers distinguish certain characters as personally meaningful for them. Women are more likely to identify with less-than-perfect or demeaning rather than glamorous images. Compared to middle-class women, working-class women view television through the lens of class rather than gender (Press, 1991). The women of Melrose Place are less likely to be role models than are Roseanne Barr and Ellen DeGeneris. Because television exerts such a powerful influence on how we view and understand our culture, fact and fiction become entangled. Talk shows exemplify this and bolster misogyny. Judge this from a typical week of talk show topics (cited in *Parade Magazine*, 1995:12).

1. Maury Povich—Mothers who dislike their daughters.
2. Ricki Lake—Women who are dependent on men.
3. Gordon Elliott—Women who spy on their husbands.
4. Richard Bey—Criminals who blame their mothers.
5. Jenny Jones—Women who stick with cheating men.

When women and men are depicted stereotypically, whether in a documentary, talk show, or a fictional situation comedy, these images come together as being correct, appropriate, and realistic.

Violence and Women

More disturbing is the research which reveals that television may actually encourage behavior that would be defined as antisocial. The National Institute of Mental Health concludes that there is now overwhelming scientific evidence that among teenagers, viewing excessive television violence leads to aggression and violent behavior (Kornblum and Julian, 1995:205). When dehumanization and physical abuse are glamorized throughout all the media, "it is hard to imagine how that message could fail to be internalized and sometimes acted on" (Burk and Shaw, 1995:437).

Much of this violence is directed toward females. Television has a penchant for showing women as victims. Research invariably concludes that both prime-time and daytime weekend television for children portray a man's world of crime and violence—ten times as frequent as in the real world (Signorielli,

1990). White adult males are most likely to be involved with violence and more likely to get away with it. For every 10 male perpetrators of violence there are 11 who are victimized by it; for every 10 female perpetrators, there are 16 victims, with women of color, older women, and foreign women the most likely targets. Men in general kill more than twice as often as they are killed. Overall, men kill and women get killed (Signorielli, 1991:89,94; Gerbner, 1993a:7). In order to find the killer, women police officers dress up as prostitutes and put themselves in vulnerable situations, or they use their sex appeal to gain information. As the heroines of the series, and against all advice, they attempt to take the killers on their own. Of course, they become emotionally involved in the justice of it all, find themselves surrounded by the bad guys, and need their male companions to rescue them. The message of this standard plot is clear: Women are vulnerable, cannot fend for themselves, and rely on men to be saved from adversity.

Prime Time

As indicated above, television prime time revolves around men, with male characters outnumbering female over two to one, a consistent trend since the early days of television (Signorielli, 1989; Davis, 1990). Besides numerical underrepresentation of women, since the 1960s a great deal of research has focused on the unrealistic, stereotyped portrayals of both television men and women. Men dominate dramatic shows, especially those involving action, adventure, and crime. They play tough and emotionally reserved characters who remain unmarried but have beautiful female companions (Greenberg, 1980; Signorielli, 1989). In many of these shows, female characters are simply bystanders who may add sex appeal. Consider *Baywatch* and *Beverly Hills: 90210* in this regard. In comedies, women appear in about equal frequency with men. Added to the typical dependent housewife role in early comedy series like *Leave It to Beaver*, *I Love Lucy*, and *Father Knows Best* were the "liberated" women of the 1970s, such as *Maude* and *That Girl*. The immense popularity of the long-running *Mary Tyler Moore Show* is linked to the fact that this was the only show where a single woman with a challenging career was depicted without a steady boyfriend, or any major storyline revolving around the fact that she remained unmarried and seemingly unconcerned about childbearing. This show, however, was the exception and the 1990s version of Mary Richards is not to be found on prime-time television.

Television exists because of advertising dollars, and it is females in the 18-to-49-age group who are most sought by advertisers (Pennington, 1995). In the rush to create new settings for women, by 1989 three-quarters of prime-time female characters were employed for pay, 20 percent more than women in real life (Walters and Huck, 1989). However, their roles are still centered on marital and family relationships and if seen occupationally, they are subordinate to men even if they are in high prestige positions, such as law and medicine (Greenberg, 1980; Cantor, 1987; Brown 1990). When powerful women are shown, they are ruthless and will use any means to maintain their positions, like *Dynasty's* Alexis Carrington, *Falcon Crest's* Angela Channing, and the newest entry, Zoe of *Good Company*. Unlike a man, a woman cannot "have it all"—beauty, power, position, loving family—and still be viewed favorably on television.

The low quality of women's roles is reflected in a comprehensive study of 555 television characters which concludes that "the vast majority conformed to male fantasies of scantily clad half-wits who need to be rescued" (cited in Atkin et al., 1991:679). These images continue despite the increase in the number of shows featuring female leads. Teenage girls are particularly vulnerable to stereotyping and are almost invariably depicted as obsessed with beauty, clothes, shopping, and dating (Steenland, 1988). The character of Kelly in *Married With Children* is the teenage caricature of this, but numerous shows have portrayed young women in this light, such as in *Fresh Prince, Full House, Living Single,* and *Beverly Hills: 90210.*

Yet there are indications that such trends may be challenged. The prime-time police series *Cagney and Lacey* is a case in point. This series deviated from the prime-time television norm and did so successfully for many years. It featured women in lead roles as crime fighters, bringing them together as partners. The show was an anomaly as well because the vast majority of prime-time television portrays women as younger, more attractive, and single or on constant surveillance for a man (Stabiner, 1985; Condry, 1989). The series dealt with issues rarely seen on police shows, such as breast cancer, abortion, and child neglect. Clearly the television audience appreciates these themes and how they are portrayed. The Cagney and Lacey roles have been reprised by the original stars in a series of immensely popular made-for-television movies. Dealing with issues women face in terms of career and ambition and disappointment and hope at mid-life in a realistic, compassionate, yet entertaining way appeals to a large segment of viewers (Pennington, 1995).

It is now common to see more social issues being introduced on entertainment-focused dramas and increasingly even on comedy series. In an excellent student paper of an analysis of gender roles in the top-25 rated prime-time television shows from 1951 to 1991, only during the 1990–1991 season did nontraditional gender portrayals outweigh traditional ones (Schanche, 1992). Women and men are seen pursuing a diversity of occupational roles and maintain living arrangements which are far removed from the *Leave It to Beaver* variety of family. These shows include *Roseanne, Ellen, Cybill, Grace Under Fire, Medicine Woman, Roc,* and *Murder She Wrote* and demonstrate that diversity in terms of class, race, age, and gender can be successfully portrayed. In 1992, the *Murphy Brown* series became a political football when former Vice-President Dan Quayle argued that it glorified motherhood for unmarried women. The producers countered by using the controversy in the series itself and brought in examples of many "nontraditional" families, a tactic that enhanced its popularity.

Yet these changes in prime-time television must be considered in light of overall programming, including cable TV and the market for reruns dating back four decades. As mentioned above, even with the increase of women in lead roles in a few popular series, they still do not typically include major roles, especially for minority women (Greenberg et al., 1983; Atkin, 1987; Condry, 1989). Some research suggests that when African-American women are shown, they have more favorable and positive role portrayals than their white counterparts (Hill and Hill, 1985). However, this higher number of characters is still not represented in terms of variety. According to Goodwin (1996:185), the dominant characterizations of African-American women are narrow and excessive—she is either an asexual mother figure or a sexpot.

Gender role diversity overall has had minimal impact on the stereotypes embedded within the very programs that are often promoted as representing more realistic gender images. Consider the implication of the title *Who's the Boss?* where the male domestic determines the household functioning and his female employer, whom he eventually will marry, is portrayed as an insecure and sometimes neurotic woman. The *Golden Girls* represented stereotypical images of an aging woman obsessed with beauty and sexuality and another portrayed as "dumb, but nice." And when older women are referred to as "girls," the title itself is stereotypical. As shows enter the rerun market, *Roseanne* must compete with *Charlie's Angels* (whose angels are they?) and *Cheers*, the bar owned by womanizer Sam Malone. Regardless of any intent to make programming more gender realistic, reruns may counter these efforts. Finally, alongside the fewer "nontraditional" television series are top-rated shows such as *Home Improvement*, where male superiority, as judged by the number of times a girl or woman is "put down" per episode, is a pervasive theme, and *Friends*, where the interpersonal relationships are gender stereotypical.

Soap Operas

Directed at a female audience, soap operas have about a 50-50 split in terms of male and female characters. The soaps are ludicrous in their distortion of reality but are popular because of it. Soaps provide the daytime opportunity for women to escape into a fantasy world of romance and adventure. Soap opera women come to one another for advice on family and sexual matters (Fine, 1981). They are schemers, victims, and starry-eyed romantics. The importance of family relationships equate women with motherhood, but lust and adultery lurk forever in the background (Benokraitis and Feagin, 1995). Thus the soap opera family becomes a dominant concern of the women. The family suffers because sexual partners are not married and usually affairs are revealed. The forgiving wife holds the family together until her errant husband returns and temporarily makes amends.

Afternoon TV is replete with sexual content which bolsters this storyline. Explicit petting and references made to sex and sexual activities are in abundance (Greenberg et al., 1981; Hayes, 1987). Teenage girls, who are heavy viewers of soap operas, have unrealistically high estimates of the extent of extramarital affairs and frequency of intercourse in the general population (Cantor, 1987). The most popular soap opera, *General Hospital*, has the largest teen audience and the highest rate of sexual acts per hour (Lowry et al., 1981). The double standard in terms of gender role is alive and well on daytime television.

More than in prime-time TV, however, women are portrayed as intelligent, self-reliant, and articulate beings who may not fear getting old and can do so gracefully. Nochimson (1992) contends that soap operas should be taken seriously as gendered screen fiction where women predominate and where male power is buffered. Geraghty (1993:496) asks: Are soaps a space where women can enjoy their superiority or a place where women are corralled even if they know they want something better? She answers this by suggesting that soaps have the capacity to do both—engage and distance the viewers at the same time and keep them entertained. The strength of soap opera women and their questioning of patriarchy may hint at progressive change regarding gender roles on television.

Children's Programming

Children's programs parallel adult shows but in many ways are even more gender stereotyped. Male characters outnumber females four to one, and in cartoons, females are rarely seen or in support roles, even as animals or make-believe characters, and those who are shown are often rescued by males (Lott, 1988; Gerbner, 1993b). The *Star Wars* movies have helped create a number of cartoon shows where a female princess who has been ousted from her planet by a villainous robotlike (male) creature needs help to restore her to her rightful place. She is kidnapped and rescued by her stalwart, heroic, male companions, who usually kill, at least in the cartoon sense, the villains. The rate of violence in children's programs has reached an all-time high and continues to be more violent than even in prime-time television (Gerbner, 1993a).

An analysis of the most popular television shows for children reveals that the overwhelming majority of characters are males, who are portrayed as aggressive and rewarded for their behavior. Females are deferential and, if shown in high activity levels, are either ignored or punished (Sternglanz and Serbin, 1974). Even twenty years later the subservience of female to male is not simply a reflection of the taken-for-granted gender structure. In 1991, a policy statement was issued by television executives indicating that dominant male characters will be in all Saturday morning children's shows (Carter, 1991). Those parents who scrupulously guard the television habits of their children may find much programming directed at children unsuitable.

They do applaud public television's efforts to both educate and entertain. *Sesame Street* has been recognized for its excellence in content which does exactly that. Moreover, this program has made every effort to minimize racial stereotypes. Its record on the portrayal of the genders is not so distinguished. As with other children's programs, male characters outnumber female characters. Some of the most popular characters, like Big Bird, Bert, Ernie, Oscar the Grouch, and the Cookie Monster are all male. And in the *Sesame Street* prime-time spinoff *Muppet Show* of the 1970s and now again in the 1990s, Miss Piggy is the only female puppet most children, and adults who watched the program as children, recall. And she is vain, demanding, obsessed with her beauty, and out to trap Kermit the Frog into matrimony. The introduction of more female characters in more diverse roles has lessened gender stereotyping somewhat. This show has been on over two decades, is aired in certain cities two or three times a day, and represents a major source of preschool television. It is a program of unquestionably superior educational value, especially in terms of preparation for reading and writing, but the gender role implications leave much to be desired.

Television News

Compared to overall television programming, women appear to be making the greatest strides in the news and documentary areas, at least gaining more on-screen visibility. Barbara Walters, Diane Sawyer, and Connie Chung, for example, demonstrate the professionalism and integrity of women broadcasters. Using her popular daytime talk show as a springboard, Oprah Winfrey is moving into more "serious" broadcast journalism with prime-time specials on topics such as drugs and child abuse. Until recently the few women who were seen during news programs were billed as "weather-girls" and held third-rate positions on the news teams. Today, many female meteorologists are responsible for preparing and broadcasting the weather. Metropolitan areas have male-female news teams that vie with one another for ratings. Gradually, inroads have been made by women in the news and weather departments, but the sports anchor is invariably a man.

But does increased visibility in news and information programs mean that barriers are finally eroding? The answer is both yes and no, and a look at early morning television helps explain why. Each of the three networks has produced morning shows which can be described as combining news with entertainment. Currently, each of these shows is hosted by a male and female team, with commercial ratings indicating that this kind of format is necessary for success. No longer can a man or completely male news team expect to carry the show. Yet the networks insist that the audience favors the male over the female, which justifies more money, more air time, and better stories being given to the male. Joan Lunden, cohost of "Good Morning America" with Charles Gibson, receives substantially less than his salary. Jane Pauley, formerly of the "Today" show, lost in her battle to gain equal status with relative new-comer Bryant Gumbel, a former sportscaster (Bachrach, 1985). And even if women are on the morning news shows, there is no permanent female anchor on any network evening news. During the last two decades, the number of female correspondents has increased only slightly, and even if they are employed by the major networks, the likelihood of on-air reporting is slim (Nash, 1989). The scarcity of women in the news media can also be associated with the way feminism is portrayed in television news coverage. While there is overwhelming support for feminist goals, the news media consistently repre-sent feminism as an unpopular fringe movement (Douglas, 1995).

Joan Lunden suggests that audience research and the political climate combine to hurt the advances gained by women in the news department. She adds that male network executives are the ones who

> can really put you under their thumbs. It's a boy's club, and if you're a male on the show you belong to the club. If you're a woman on the show, men barely say hello to you in the morning. (Bachrach, 1985:48)

This sentiment is shared by Christine Craft, a former Kansas City anchor, who gained national attention in her sex discrimination suit against Metromedia, which she initially won but which was later overturned on appeal. She was told that people of Kansas City did not like her.

> I was too old, too unattractive, and didn't defer to men . . . The people who make the hiring decisions (for the networks) are aging, white males. . . . They're the ones who say, "Adios, señorita," after they see the first crow's foot on a woman anchor. And the thing is, the terrible thing is, that decision creates a model for the rest of society. (Bachrach, 1985:48)

GENDER AND MASS MEDIA INDUSTRIES

All the media discussed have produced images of women which are based on stereotypes. When we consider the lack of women in creative and decision-making positions in media industries, this pattern may be at least partly explained. Except as secretarial staff, women are numerically underrepre-sented in all phases of advertising. Since advertising is the medium with the most pervasive and consistent stereotyping, an influx of women into manage-rial positions may provide the industry with more realistic images of women.

The same can be said for television. In 1980 about 30 percent of the employees at network headquarters and network-owned stations were women, but only 10 percent were at the managerial level (UNESCO, 1980). Ten years later almost 20 percent of new directors of commercial television stations were women, but this declined to about 17 percent by the early 1990s (Women's Institute for Freedom of the Press, 1989; *Media Report to Women*, 1993). Although women participate as actors in commercials, soap operas, and prime-time television, their representation in production, management, and news is limited. Since World War II the status of women in the film and television industry has deteriorated (Muir, 1993). The notable exception is the successful production and writing team, led by CBS's Linda Bloodworth, who is responsible for shows such as "Murphy Brown" and "Designing Women."

The major qualifications for entry into these positions are educational background and experience. Although women have very similar educational profiles, their experience is less favorable when compared to male counterparts. Most women managers in television have entered the industry within the last decade. Until they move up the hierarchy, hopefully creating opportunities for those women who follow, occupational segregation of the genders in the television industry will be the norm.

In film, the golden days of Hollywood occurred before and during the Depression. Ironically, this period was also the golden age for women in the industry. Women participated in every phase of production except camera operation. The position of director is considered the apex of the film industry. In the silent screen and prewar era, there were over 20 female directors (UNESCO, 1980). Today there are only a handful and these are products only of the last decade. Ida Lupino is one of these few, and she established herself even before World War II. Barbara Streisand directed the acclaimed film *Prince of Tides*, which was a multiple Oscar winner. She was notably passed over for receiving what many thought was a certain Oscar nomination for her directorial efforts. The Directors' Guild in 1980 listed 3,000 members, of which a mere 23 were women (UNESCO, 1980) and in the 1990s the numbers increase mainly in for women making "alternative" movies. These figures are similar for Britain and Australia, but continental Europe has produced a number of internationally renowned women film directors in the commercial industry.

In 1981 a Women's Steering Committee was formed by the Directors' Guild of America in order to address the continued low numbers of films directed by women. Between 1939 and 1979, of the 7,332 Hollywood feature films, only 14 were directed by women. In 1990, women directed 5 percent (23 of 406) of such films, representing only a slight rise from the 4.2 percent average maintained for the previous seven years (Schickel, 1991:78). There are probably about 15 or 20 women directors working steadily in Hollywood, but several dozen are coming along (Barnes, 1993). While Schickel maintains that women in film may be a product of diminished expectations, there are other female directors who are clearly challenging such notions. When access to contracts is allowed, directors such as Penny Marshall, Martha Coolidge, and Jodie Foster have made outstanding and highly acclaimed films. And as actor-director Jodie Foster poignantly notes, "This is not a business that is kind to women, but it needs them" (Corliss, 1991:72).

Whereas the position of director remains a male bastion, the number of women producers, editors, and screenwriters is increasing. Although less likely to be established with major studios which produce box office blockbusters, they are responding to opportunities which offer creative work in newer cinematic forms and techniques. Art, documentary, educational, experimental, and the emerging "alternative" cinema are areas where women are demonstrating their talents. Because women film critics do hold influential positions in the industry, efforts outside of so-called mainstream filmmaking are not ignored. This has helped the field of feminist film theory to emerge. In addition, prominent women critics have reviewed films in terms of newer perspectives, such as an evaluation of how women are portrayed, the quality of the roles women are being offered, and the degree to which films reflect social reality.

These achievements are impressive, but for the most part, they account for films outside the mainstream of well-known studios. These are the studios producing the movies for which people will line up outside on a cold Saturday night to see. Significant monetary reward and public recognition of one's creative work are reserved for commercially successful films. Although alternative cinema may provide creative, though not lucrative, outlets for women filmmakers, a male monopoly in the established film industry makes the switch from one system to the other difficult.

We have seen that the media are prime socializers and that women hold a minimum of influential positions within the industry. It would seem logical to assume that as women gain positions of power and prestige, stereotyped images will be altered. But the media are entrenched in a broader social system that supports the notion of female subordination. Thus, when advertisers are singled out for their blatant sexist portrayals, they defend themselves by saying they are trend followers, not trend setters. Although this ignores the impact of reinforcing stereotypes, it is a defensible argument in that other social institutions engage in similar, but perhaps more subtle, practices. For women in media industries to make truly significant impact, social change must also continue in other institutions as well.

MALE IMAGES IN THE MEDIA

When considering their multidimensional roles in the real world, women have not fared well in the media. Men star more in television series, sell more records, make more movies, and get greater financial rewards. But the price of this popularity is that men, too, must succumb to images which are less than realistic. From the media's standpoint, a man is a breadwinner who cheats on his wife, has no idea how to use a vacuum cleaner or an oven, is manipulated by his children, and uses brute force to solve problems. Men are also becoming more identified as sex objects in the media. How have the media contributed to these images?

Advertisers believe products can be divided according to their emotional appeal; hence, some are seen as masculine and some as feminine. Cars, life insurance, and beer are masculine, so men do the selling to other men. Men also sell women's products, such as cosmetics and pantyhose. In fact, men do most of the selling on television, as evidenced by the increased use of male voice-overs in both daytime and prime-time television. Advertising puts men in positions where they direct what women buy, which subtly states to both genders that men are in control and are literally the voice of authority.

Beer commercials, shown on television especially during sports events, are almost exclusively male oriented. Themes surrounding these commercials are camping, cowboys, competition, and camaraderie. The "good old boys" who drink beer are adventuresome, play hard at sports, and have a country spirit. More than any other type of advertising geared to men, beer commercials instill the importance of a macho image.

Overall, men are positively portrayed in TV commercials, especially on prime time. When compared to women, men are viewed as more mature, less foolish, and more successful, particularly since men are primarily shown in prestigious, higher-income positions (Condry, 1989). Although women have increased their activities outside the home, advertising has assumed men have not taken on additional family roles. They are still inept in the kitchen and cannot fathom the habits of a newborn infant. There is a trend toward showing more males in other than wage-earning positions, but rather than put them in the home, advertisers prefer to associate them with entertainment and sports. The ironic result of this is that, like women, men are increasingly filling a sex-object role in advertising (Sharits and Lammers, 1982; White and Gillett, 1994).

Whereas films also contribute to men being viewed as sex objects, they are at least shown as more multifaceted than women. The hard living, tough guy portrayals of actors like John Wayne and Gary Cooper of the past and Mel Gibson and Jean Claude Van Dame of the present, are contrasted with "anti-heroes and soulful ethnics" like Al Pacino, Dustin Hoffman, and Robert DeNiro (Haskell, 1983). Popular, too, are the "buddy" movies where two males are linked together in one or a series of films. The plot invariably calls for them to be competitive on the surface and then gradually move toward genuine, if begrudging, respect and camaraderie. They learn to admire one another for traits they see lacking in their own personalities. This formula has been successful in movies pairing Robert Redford and Paul Newman (*The Sting* and *Butch Cassidy and the Sundance Kid*), Dan Aykroyd and the late John Belushi (*Blues Brothers, Neighbors*, and *1941*), Gene Wilder and Richard Pryor (*Stir Crazy*), and Eddie Murphy and Judge Reinhold in the *Beverly Hills Cop* movies.

These films may be the contemporary versions of the comedian buddy teams of the past. Laurel and Hardy, Abbot and Costello, the Marx Brothers, Martin and Lewis, and even the Three Stooges starred in numerous movies combining adventure and comedy. If romance entered in, it was short-lived. Women may be necessary diversions, but not permanent enough to keep the men from coming back together and continuing their carefree escapades. Through movies like these, men learn that family ties are tenuous, not particularly desirable, and keep them from adventuresome good times with their buddies.

Crime movies, war movies, and Westerns are also film avenues to demonstrate male courage and accomplishment. Recently, two other genres have emerged, possibly reemerged, which speak to men about characteristics they should admire. Pure fantasy exists in adventure movies where the hero escapes unscathed from the very jaws of death. The twist for some of these movies is that the hero starts out insisting he is not brave, but really cowardly at heart. Circumstances prove otherwise as he rescues the maiden, finds the gold, or saves the world, all in reckless abandon, not seeming to care for his own life. The *Star Wars* epics, *Indiana Jones*, and *Braveheart* follow this pattern. Second, we have those films which seem to be released solely for the sake of violence. Both heroes and villains are violent, and more violence is needed to end the violence. The kill and maim plots of films like *Death Wish*, and the gruesome and plentiful *Halloween* or *Friday the Thirteenth* movies attest to the belief that revenge and violence in a "good" cause are acceptable. Males who do not agree with this formula are viewed as unfit and are often labeled as wimps or nerds.

Violence is a recurrent theme in popular songs as well. Successful male rock bands combine sexual imagery with violent overtones. Men are to use women for their own needs and then cast them aside. The lyrics to the song "Squealer" by AC/DC provide an example: "she'd never been, never been balled before/'n I don't think she'll ever ball no more (fixed 'er good) . . . /made her understand/ . . . made it hard to stop." "Squealer" affirms the notion that women cannot resist certain men. The song is in praise of sexual exploitation and implicitly condones sexual acts regardless of the woman's intent.

These are standard rather than exceptional lyrics. Heavy metal and rap music abound with such images. Groups such as Guns 'n Roses, Van Halen, Judas Priest, 2 Live Crew, Ice-T, and Geto Boys, have best selling records that continue this sexploitation tradition. Consider the lyrics from Van Halen's "OU812": "Slip'n slide, push it in/Bitch sure got the rhythm . . . don't draw the line/honey I ain't through with you." Or 2 Live Crew's "The Fuck Shop": "Now spread your wings open for the flight/let me fill you with something milky and white/'cause I'm gonna slay you rough and painful/you innocent bitch, don't be shameful." These represent blatant sexual violence. Millions of CDs are sold to teens who learn that rape, violence, sexual victories, and crime are male prerogatives.

The argument that these groups are not representative of the recording industry is somewhat valid, but popular music geared to a mainstream and older audience provides similar, though less overt impressions. Kenny Rogers, who has successfully combined country and "Top 40" music for two decades, has produced a string of hit records portraying men as violent or potentially violent in their thoughts or behavior. The violence is seen as acceptable and usually involves a woman. In "Ruby, Don't Take Your Love to Town," the singer is a man who is paralyzed from war and whose wife is seeing another man. He loves her dearly, but if he could move "he'd get a gun and put her in the ground." His own wretched condition and her apparent lack of sympathy justify it. In "Coward of the County," we learn of a man who is told "you don't have to fight to be a man." He continually turns the other cheek until his wife, Becky, is "assaulted." He avenges Becky's honor, actually his own, by fighting it out. These songs support a sexual double standard and legitimize physical force in the way men handle problems. They do have to fight to be men.

Finally, we turn to television, which generally portrays men as being in control of most situations. They also recognize that power may bring adversity as well as rewards, but are willing to accept whatever the consequences. Men are active, less tied to relationships, and can solve their own problems (Downs, 1981). Although television depicts men positively overall, as we would expect, the less favorable portrayal compared to women is the common use of violence, danger, and force for problem solving or dealing with ongoing relationships. In addition, television equates male strength with lack of emotion and self-reliance as well as the ability to fight out of a difficult spot.

The major exception to this image is the situation comedy where men take on a childlike dependence to their wives in terms of domestic functioning. There are a multitude of television images where the man is outwitted by his wife, his children, or the washing machine. His good intentions are bungled when he foolishly attempts to carry out household responsibilities without the direction of a more skilled female. While we are beginning to witness shows depicting men in loving and nurturing relationships with their children, such as *Evening Shade*, television historically has refused to allow men to be shown as competent fathers who are capable of raising young children on their own. In the *Andy Griffith Show*, there was Aunt Bea; in the *Courtship of Eddie's Father*, there was Mrs. Livingston; and in *Family Affair* there was Mr. French. From the early days of television, only the *Rifleman* was shown as a parent who essentially was raising his son Mark alone. Contemporary shows like *Full House, My Two Dads*, or *Who's the Boss?* have the fathers in amazingly nontraditional living arrangements where there are other adults always present. Unlike series' featuring women as single parents, almost ludicrous circumstances must be invented to accommodate single fathers. The media allow men to display a greater range of roles than women, but stereotypes still account for the majority of this imagery. Like the women the media have created, men cannot be all that they are meant to be, or all that they are. There is some evidence that men now want to be identified as "regular Joes" and are attaching less importance to money and status. Michael Jordan, Tom Hanks, and Robert Redford exemplify this; Howard Stern and Donald Trump do not. In presenting this trend, Kanne (1995) states that marketers docked the bumbling klutz image of men, so that "guy stuff is back." The problem is that they have also docked the "sensitive man cradling a newborn." Until we see men consistently portrayed as loving fathers, compassionate husbands, and household experts, our attitudes about masculinity will not be significantly altered.

MEDIA AND SOCIAL CHANGE

We have seen that the media present views of women and men which are not in line with reality. Although men are portrayed as more multidimensional than women, the additional characteristics are stereotyped as well. Media producers, especially advertisers, argue that categorical images are what the public wants to see and that even if somewhat inaccurate, these portrayals generally reflect society. If a sexist society exists, the media reinforce it. From their viewpoint, to do otherwise would risk public acceptance and monetary returns. The question of moral responsibility is rarely an issue in deliberations over media images of the genders.

To some extent, the media are powerful because of their ability to take the mundane and create fantasy and excitement. Is it possible to retain fantasy and public acceptance while simultaneously providing alternative, more realistic images of the sexes? Since it has been demonstrated that many people are uncomfortable with what they see and that financial success can occur when media formulas do change, the answer to this question is affirmative. One of the ironies of the media is that they thrive on change, yet seem unwilling to deviate from rigid, traditional patterns. When convinced that success can be packaged differently, media change will likely excel.

Finally, there is the question of moral responsibility, which usually becomes an issue when sexual and violent content of the media are examined. Publicity is directed at effects of programming on children, with little explicit concern for gender role portrayals. Yet this does provide a latent function.

Since gender roles are inextricably bound to this content anyway, change in one will effect change in the other.

The media are formidable socializers and provide images that both reflect and reinforce gender roles. They have this responsibility whether they acknowledge it or not. The media also have the power to alter stereotypes, which they do whenever more genuine views of the sexes are presented. As the public demands entertainment, news, and advertising that are more indicative of social reality, the media will respond with realistic images.

CHAPTER 14

POWER, POLITICS, AND THE LAW

> We, men and women who hereby constitute ourselves as the National Organization of Women (NOW), believe that the time has come for a new movement toward true equality for all women in America, and toward a fully equal partnership of the sexes, as part of the world-wide revolution of human rights now taking place within and beyond our national borders.
> —From NOW's Statement of Purpose (1966)

The political institution and its legal foundation provide the critical lens through which all gender relations are viewed. In the United States while we accept the belief that "equal justice for all" is the principle around which our legal system operates, most people also recognize that this principle can be compromised. For example, cultural definitions related to gender, race, social class, region, age, and sexual orientation often determine *how* justice will be served. Power is a basic element of the fabric of society and is possessed in varying degrees by different social actors in different social categories. Max Weber (1946) defined power in terms of the likelihood a person may achieve personal ends despite possible resistance from others. Since this definition views power as potentially coercive, Weber also considered ways in which power can be achieved through justice. Authority, he contended, is power which people determine to be legitimate rather than coercive. When power becomes encoded into law, it is legitimized and translated into the formal structure of society. In Weberian terms, this is known as *rational-legal authority*. As will be demonstrated, women as a group are at a distinct disadvantage when both power and authority are considered.

We have already seen how this holds true economically through a hierarchy of occupations in which women are rewarded less than men in terms of money and prestige. Interpersonal power is also compromised, even in the family where women are assumed to carry more weight in terms of decision making. To this list can be added the limited political and legal power which women wield. Social stratification is based on differential power which in turn underlies all inequality. Thus, inequality between the genders persists because the power base women possess is more circumscribed than that of men. Restrictions in terms of political power and legal authority are at the core of inequality.

THE LAW

According to Richardson (1988:104) certain assumptions about the genders permeate the law and these provide the bases for how the law is then differentially applied.

1. Women are incompetent, childlike, and in need of protection.

2. Men are the protectors and financial caretakers of women.
3. Husband and wife are treated as "one" under the law. The "one" is the husband.
4. Males and females are biologically different which gives them differing capabilities and differing standards on which to judge their actions. Richardson calls this a double standard of morality based on biological deterministic thought.

Because these are assumptions, they are taken for granted and are rarely questioned. When formally developed into law, they become sacrosanct.

Throughout this text, reference has been made to legislation which has served to perpetuate yet also alter traditional gender roles. At all governmental levels, laws have been enacted which may be viewed as giving one gender certain advantages or disadvantages. There is considerable variation on how laws are interpreted and how they are enforced. This means that even federal legislation is inconsistently applied depending on the specifics of the situation. What will become clear is that, regardless of the notions of equality and justice which are supposedly inherent in the legal process, the law cannot realistically be defined as gender-neutral, much less gender-equal. Although efforts to remedy this continue, the following discussion will demonstrate the difficulty of the task ahead. Note that to date all legal statutes use the word "sex" rather than "gender" in both the law itself as well as most discussions concerning it. For consistency, this designation will generally be retained when considering the differential impact of politics and the law on females and males.

Employment

One of the most important pieces of legislation to prohibit discrimination in employment based on sex is the 1964 Civil Rights Act. The story of how this act was eventually passed at all is both instructive in regard to our legal process and ironic as well. The original bill called for the elimination of job discrimination based on race, color, religion, or national origin. Despite conservative opposition in Congress, Howard W. Smith (D., Va.), chair of the House Rules Committee at the time, introduced the word sex to these provisions. The story has since been circulated that Smith was an ultraconservative who did not want to see the bill passed at all and felt that even liberals would consider the elimination of job discrimination based on sex as too radical a step. If this was his strategy, it backfired, and the bill was passed with the word sex included in the amendment. The obvious irony is that someone who would have otherwise taken an extremely conservative position by the standards of the day was responsible for a major advance of a "liberal" cause. However, as Stetson (1991:166) points out, if people came to accept the idea that the Smith Amendment was added only as a joke or a ploy by Southerners who did not want to see any civil rights bill passed, enforcement of its provisions would be more difficult. Regardless, Title VII of the 1964 Civil Rights Act makes it unlawful for an employer to refuse to hire an applicant, to discharge an employee, or to discriminate against any individual with respect to "compensation, terms, conditions, or privileges of employment, because of such individual's race, color, religion, sex, or national origin."

The only way that Title VII can be legally circumvented is through the "bonafide occupational qualification" (BFOQ), which allows for hiring an employee on the basis of one sex, thereby "discriminating" against the other, if it is deemed as critical for carrying out the job. For example, a woman can be hired over a man as an actor for a specific part in a movie to establish "authenticity or genuineness" of the role. Also, if characteristics of one sex are necessary for the job, a person of that sex is hired, such as for the job of wet nurse. The courts have also rejected "customer preference" arguments to hire women over men as flight attendants or "job preference" beliefs that exclude women from positions where they may be required to work night shifts, such as in law enforcement. With few exceptions, the BFOQ rule is very narrowly interpreted by the courts and is seldom used as a defense for charges of sex discrimination.

Another accomplishment of Title VII has been the elimination of many policies used by employers which may appear to be neutral but can have a "disparate impact" on women. When an employer states that all employees have to be within certain height or weight limits, it often means that a large proportion of one gender or the other is excluded from that particular job option. Women have been systematically denied employment opportunities in areas such as law enforcement, security, paramedical fields, mining, and construction through setting such limits. In defending these qualifications, the employer must now demonstrate that the policy is a "business necessity" without which the job could not be safely or efficiently carried out. Height and weight designations are often used to assess strength levels, so a direct strength test would be more beneficial to the company and could be accomplished with less disparate impact on women, as well as some men.

If Title VII mandates the elimination of sex as a basis for hiring, the corollary should be an end to wage discrimination on the same basis. In 1963 the Equal Pay Act (EPA) which requires that females and males receive the same pay for the same job became federal law. However, we have already seen that, even when controlling for educational level and occupational classification, women earn less on the average than men, an earnings gap that has only slightly improved during the last two decades. How can this obvious disparity in pay continue with the definite provision of the EPA? The answer is found in the fact that women and men typically hold different jobs, and women's jobs remain undervalued and, hence, underpaid, in comparison to those held by men. Occupations are gender-segregated and become gender stratified. The question then becomes how to assess jobs on the basis of skill level, effort, and responsibility. By this argument, equal pay should be judged in terms of "equal worth."

Comparable Worth   This has been translated into the issue of "comparable worth" and interpreted through the provisions of Title VII. In a suit against the state of Washington, Helen Castelli charged that as a hospital secretary she was being paid much less than men employed by the state even though her job was "worth" much more. The same case brought evidence showing that laundry workers who are mostly female earned $150 less per month than truck drivers who are mostly male. In 1983, a federal court ordered the state of Washington to raise the wages of 15,500 employees in predominantly female occupations, which amounted to almost $1 billion in back pay. Two years later a higher court overturned the decision with the argument that market forces created the inequity and the government has no responsibility to correct them.

Thus, even if objective measurements for comparable worth can be established, some interpretations suggest that the government should not interfere if the assumption is that "supply and demand" in a free-market economy determines wages. If the pay differential between males and females is a true reflection of impersonal market forces, then there must be other reasons which bolster this wage gap. According to Rhoads (1993), the market-driven pay system is so neutral that if women get paid less, they must either prefer less demanding jobs or are less productive in the jobs they do get. This justifies the wage gap and offers no room for the possibility that gender discrimination occurs. In this context, comparable worth is seen as a radical departure from traditional economic beliefs and one which would create unnecessary bias in an already fair and neutral system.

On the other hand, the notion of comparable worth issues a challenge to reevaluate all the work that women do, and it can ultimately call into question the gender-based hierarchy in American society, particularly as it systematically denies comparable earnings to women. Sorensen (1994) uses economic modeling techniques to measure the disparate effect on pay associated with work in female-dominated occupations in both the public and private sectors. Employers typically use gender to assign people to jobs, which in turn results in wage discrimination. In the public sector, women are assigned to jobs with less pay and shorter career ladders. In the private sector, women are assigned to already overcrowded female-dominated jobs, which in turn creates an over-supply of labor. Again, wage discrimination results. This trend is confirmed by Canadian data on computer professionals indicating that women make less money and have lower job status than men in the same company. Organizations hiring more women professionals hire those who are less well educated and with less work experience than male employees, thus justify paying them less. Recruitment strategies are aimed at limiting a woman's success to positions of authority (Ranson and Reeves, 1996).

Unlike Rhoads (1993) who adamantly defends the neutrality of the marketplace, Sorensen (1994) contends that systematic discrimination occurs and workers are not paid according to measurable productivity. This also suggests that comparable worth can be used to redress not only the gender wage gap, but the damage done to overall market productivity. Although it is a departure from the traditional model, functionalism would applaud comparable worth if the system becomes more efficient, productive, and, ultimately, functional. In discussing Sorensen's work Figart (1995:780) mentions that comparable worth has had significant and positive effects on women's wages but negligible effects on employment or employment growth rates. It is a reaction against "an economics discipline that is attached to textbook models of how the world ought to work." As such, a powerful economic argument is used to support an institutional theory of wage discrimination. To date, the courts have been inconsistent in decisions regarding comparable worth. Title VII and EPA notwithstanding, the courts subscribe to rigid textbook standards and are reluctant to seriously confront comparable worth if it means "interfering" in economic principles which allow employers to determine salary structures.

Sexual Harassment Until recently, the sexual harassment issue has been another area where a noteworthy lack of interference in business is evident. Sexual harassment is a form of sex discrimination that is prohibited under Title VII of the 1964 Civil Rights Act. The Equal Employment Opportunity Commission (EEOC) adopted the following definition of sexual harassment:

> Unwelcome sexual advances, requests for sexual favors, and other verbal or physical conduct of a sexual nature constitute sexual harassment when:

1. submission to such conduct is made either explicitly or implicitly a term of condition of an individual's employment;
2. submission to or rejection of such conduct by an individual is used as a basis for employment decisions affecting such individuals; or
3. such conduct has the purpose or effect of unreasonably interfering with an individual's work performance or creating an intimidating, hostile, or offensive working environment.

Although sexual harassment is a pervasive problem existing throughout all levels of education, business, and government (Rubin and Rogers, 1990; Martin, 1995), the 1991 Senate Judiciary hearings on the confirmation of Clarence Thomas for Supreme Court Justice dramatically brought the issue to the attention of the public. For three days the nation was riveted to the television during Anita Hill's testimony that Clarence Thomas had engaged in numerous instances of sexual harassment. Hill's testimony centered on Thomas's comments to her regarding sex and sexual matters, her personal appearance, and pressure for dates when she worked as his assistant at the Department of Education and later with the Equal Employment Opportunity Commission (EEOC). The intensity of this testimony transformed the hearing into a trial where, "regardless of the confirmation, the public decided who was telling the truth." As Hill stated:

> It would have been more comfortable to remain silent . . . I took no initiative to inform anyone. But when I was asked by a representative of this committee to report my experience I felt I had to tell the truth. I could not keep silent. (Cited in Norton and Alexander, 1996b:502)

The nation got a firsthand view of what sexual harassment can encompass. A poll conducted by *Parade Magazine* (1991) immediately after the hearings found 70 percent of the women who serve in the military, 50 percent who work in congressional offices, and 40 percent who work for federal agencies had experienced sexual harassment. Many men who were polled said they were sympathetic but also bewildered, suggesting that a communications gap between the genders may be as wide as the political one.

As a result, sexual harassment lawsuits mushroomed, prompting companies to adopt more rigorous policies to protect the rights of their employees and specifically to help female employees deal with the issue more effectively (Solomon, 1991; Powers, 1992). With the Supreme Court ruling that employers may be responsible for harassment even if they are unaware of it, adopting such policies also protected companies. The Thomas-Hill confrontation allowed attention to be focused on what had previously been regarded as an uncomfortable but routine component of the subculture of the workplace. Sexual harassment is associated with emotional problems, compromised work productivity, and a deterioration in morale (Gehry et al., 1994). It has serious impact on one's personal and professional lives. Yet sexual harassment is hard to identify in part because accepted cultural definitions of sexuality disguise and ignore a great amount of sexual domination and exploitation in the workplace (Giuffre and Williams, 1994:397). In addition, few women actually file sexual harassment grievances because they believe it can amount to "career suicide" and that they will be dealt with in an unjust manner (Riger, 1993:227).

Nonetheless, whereas the EEOC adopted regulations defining sexual harassment in 1980, the Thomas-Hill hearings 11 years later made the issue one which could no longer be ignored. As Martin (1995) reports, the turn-about of the courts has been dramatic. Earlier instances of even blatant abuses of power by supervisors were likely to be disregarded, with the belief that "natural" attraction by supervisor to employee or personal circumstances unrelated to the job situation were operating. Times have changed. In a straightforward, unreserved, and unanimous opinion, in speaking for a recent Supreme Court ruling, Sandra Day O'Connor said that the targets of sexual harassment do not need to show that they suffered psychological damage to win their suits. The court wanted to trumpet the message that sexual harassment violates workplace equality (Freivogel, 1993). With research documenting that sexual harassment is widespread and culturally patterned,

> the law now acknowledges the socially defined character of sexual harassment by recognizing that the unwanted sexual advances are "based on sex" and that women are sexually harassed because they are women. (Martin, 1995:41–42)

Affirmative Action Another bulwark of federal policy impacting women is Affirmative Action, the generic term for an employment policy which takes some kind of voluntary or involuntary (under the compulsion of the law) initiative to increase, maintain, or alter the number or position of certain members, usually defined by race or gender (Johnson, 1993b:236). It was devised primarily to promote the economic status of African-Americans although women and other ethnic minorities now come under its mandate. In the involuntary situation, the Civil Rights Act allows courts to order an employer found guilty of discrimination to devise and implement an Affirmative Action plan. Although it is viewed as a program that is directly beneficial to women, Johnson finds mixed results in this regard. In compliance reviews, African-American males and other minority males have been advanced more than African-American females and significantly more than white females. In a study of hiring patterns of new Ph.D.s, despite Affirmative Action, neither race nor gender affected the prestige of the department where first jobs are obtained (Baldi, 1995). In terms of Affirmative Action, how can this research be interpreted? Using Census Bureau and Department of Labor statistics as well as other secondary sources, Johnson (1993b:248) concludes that nonwhite women have clearly benefited directly, but all women may be benefiting indirectly. She also counters criticism that Affirmative Action is the "opposite" of a merit system. Affirmative Action calls for a fairer distribution of social benefits, a principle that has been constitutionally accepted and applied throughout our history.

Prompted both by partisan politics using it as a "wedge issue" in upcoming elections as well as polls showing "big government" controls too much of our lives (Horner, 1996), media attention to Affirmative Action has increased dramatically. The Clinton administration has strongly supported Affirmative Action and new initiatives concerning it, and even with a Republican-controlled Congress, the program will survive in some fashion. The more the public knows about Affirmative Action, the more support it receives. A recent nationwide poll indicates that 79 percent agree there should be programs that set up objectives, but not rigid quotas, to allow opportunities for women and minorities to get hired. Opposition declines significantly when the possible consequences of ending Affirmative Action initiatives are made clear, such as discouraging women and minority businesses from competing and discouraging programs to help them achieve equal opportunity (Jackman, 1995:12). However, it is also apparent that public opposition increases when Affirmative Action is associated with specific quotas and preferential hiring, whether to do with race or gender (Puddington, 1996). The courts are mandating tough new standards for federal Affirmative Action programs, are suggesting that programs which give equal opportunities are no different from programs that discriminate, and that social benefits of a diverse work force cannot be used to justify the program's existence. According to Eleanor Smeal, president of the Feminist Majority, the courts cannot see the difference between equal opportunity and discrimination so the case must be made in the political arena. While preferential treatment and Affirmative Action are not the same, the media have created a full-fledged deception by perpetuating this belief (Jackman, 1995:13). Given these confusing messages, politicians will likely reconstruct, but not dismantle, Affirmative Action.

Opponents argue that when women receive special assistance, it actually reinforces assumptions about gender roles that society is attempting to eliminate and stigmatizes those women who gain a job on the grounds of Affirmative Action. They are put in a double bind. They may be in a work environment where suspicion and adversity abound because of the belief they got the job over others who were better qualified or that they could not get it through conventional means. When they do succeed in the job, the preferential treatment they received at the outset will tend to devalue their performance (Rhode, 1993). Self-esteem can also be endangered when everyone, including the recipient, believes that being awarded a privilege overrides being given an opportunity to achieve. Cruz (1996) recounts her psychological pain at being called a "twofer" after being accepted to a prestigious graduate program in science—a woman of color in a male-dominated field. Despite her outstanding credentials, her status was defined by race and gender. But stigma is a double-edged sword. When former Assistant Attorney General Barbara Babcock was asked how she felt about gaining the position because she was a woman, she answered, "It feels better than being *denied* the position because you're a woman" (emphasis added) (Rhode, 1993:263).

Equal Opportunity Employment Commission (EEOC)   The viability of a law is demonstrated by how earnestly it is enforced. Although the Equal Employment Opportunity Commission (EEOC) was created to ensure that Title VII mandates are carried out, enforcement is primarily aimed at protecting minorities, particularly black men, rather than women. Freeman (1995b) points out that EEOC essentially ignores the sex provision since there is fear it would dilute enforcement efforts for minorities. Fortunately, as Freeman notes, the National Organization for Women was formed in part to protect women's rights and directed its initial efforts at changing EEOC guidelines. These efforts were seriously hampered during the Reagan years where cases of sex discrimination filed by EEOC dropped by over 70 percent (Kennelly, 1984). This figure would not have changed significantly during the Bush presidency if Anita Hill had not presented a major challenge to the Clarence Thomas confirmation hearings for his Supreme Court post. EEOC has been revived and strengthened with the Clinton presidency since his administration is more supportive of civil rights legislation for minorities in general and women in particular.

Education

As mentioned in Chapter 11, Title IX of the Educational Amendments Act of 1972 was enacted to prohibit sex discrimination in any school receiving federal assistance. Specifically, the key provision of Title IX states that

> No person in the United States, shall, on the basis of sex, be excluded from participation in, be denied the benefits of, or be subjected to discrimination under any educational program or activity receiving federal financial assistance.

Overall, this law is very comprehensive and has at least helped to alter, and in some instances eliminate, blatant discriminatory practices involving the genders in relation to admissions, promotion, and tenure of faculty, health care, dress codes, counseling, housing, formerly sex-segregated programs, financial aid, and organizational membership. In each of these cases, policies must be made in regard to equitable treatment of both genders.

The courts have allowed for a number of exceptions to the law. Fraternities and sororities may still be gender segregated, as can sex education classes. Housing and living arrangements can also be restricted by gender as long as comparable facilities are available for both men and women. However, the most notable exception concerns the number of educational institutions which remain exempt from Title IX provisions—those that do not receive federal funds as well as public institutions that have historically always been gender segregated. When considering *all* schools, those that fall under the Title IX mandate include previously integrated public schools and universities and most vocational, professional, and graduate schools (Thorkelson, 1985:485). A number of private, religious, and military institutions remain excluded. If by choice or legal mandate any single-gender school does begin to admit the other gender, equal admissions requirements must be followed. Whereas issues involving equity for women are at the forefront, in *Mississippi University* v. *Hogan*, the case related to a violation of men's rights. In this case the United States Supreme Court narrowed the scope of gender-based classifications by holding that an all-female state institution which excluded qualified males from its nursing program was in violation of the equal protection clause of the Fourteenth Amendment. It is often overlooked that both men and women have benefited from gender equity legislation originally formulated for women.

Beyond the elimination of flagrant sex discrimination policies in schools, Title IX has had a large impact on athletic programs. Traditionally, budget allocations to female athletic activities have been minimal in comparison to monies provided for male sports. Fearing that an equal redistribution of financial resources would hamper men's programs, the National Collegiate Athletic Association (NCAA) strongly opposed any federal interference which could fall under Title IX mandates. In a compromise to the storm of controversy generated by potential "interference" in sacrosanct men's sports, the final regulations did not insist on equal spending but instead called for "reasonable opportunities" for financial assistance for each sex in proportion to the numbers who participated in intercollegiate sports (cited in Stetson, 1991:11-12). As Stetson notes, big-ticket men's sports were protected by "pesky demands for sex equity," but improvements were made to support women's athletics and opportunities for women to receive athletic scholarships.

Before Title IX, few colleges offered female athletes adequate facilities or training, and no institution of higher education offered females athletic scholarships. Budgetary allotments for female athletics in schools have steadily increased as well, which may account for the incredible 600 percent increase in the number of girls in interscholastic athletics in secondary schools between 1971 and 1978 (Basow, 1992). Before Title IX there were few female athletes on campus and those who participated in athletics at all did so with poor facilities, funding, and rewards. Today 40 percent of women students participate in college sports (Fox, 1995; Gavora, 1995). Women have also increased their visibility in athletic programs by assuming leadership positions, and by 1992, 11 Division I schools had appointed women as their athletic directors (Dorr, 1992). Impressive as these figures are, indicative of the uphill climb is the fact that in 1972 women's athletic programs at 90 percent of all colleges were administered by females, but in 1992 the figure had dramatically dropped to 16.8 percent.

The power behind Title IX lies in the potential to cut off federal funding to schools not in compliance with its dictates. The conservative political climate of the Reagan-Bush years and inconsistent court rulings hampered Title IX enforcement. A major setback occurred with the *Grove City College* v. *Bell* Supreme Court ruling which states that if an educational institution is proven to be in violation of Title IX, only the specific program involved would have federal funding eliminated, and not the institution as a whole. Many programs which practice some form of gender discrimination, intentional or not, are allowed to continue in schools although they may directly violate the intent of Title IX. This is particularly true of athletic programs which can exist independent of school budgets since they are often supported by revenue from sports events and contributions from parents of team members and alumni.

In overriding a veto by President Reagan, the 1988 Civil Rights Restoration Bill was passed, which in effect nullified the *Grove City College* v. *Bell* decision and reestablished the earlier broad interpretation of Title IX. In 1992, the Supreme Court also ruled that plaintiffs in Title IX lawsuits now have the right to seek monetary damages. Until this precedent was set, women were only able to use Title IX suits to gain back pay and "injunctive help," but now million-dollar lawsuits are a possibility (Gordon, 1992). Financial recourse has put teeth back into Title IX and has opened the door for equity in all of college athletics.

While Title IX is over two decades old, until the Clinton administration, efforts at enforcement have been severely curtailed. Any institution receiving federal monies over $50,000 must undergo a self-evaluation on how it measures up to gender equality. If found to be discriminatory, a formal plan must be submitted to rectify the problem. Until recently, most schools ignored this provision. In a more favorable federal climate, the number of compliance reviews increased fourfold in 1993, with Title IX complaints doubling.

But like Affirmative Action, Title IX also has some charges that preferences for one group can hurt another group. In this case, however, gender equity is seen as robbing racial equity in sports programs such as when men's opportunities are cut in basketball and football—those programs which have high concentrations of minority participation. Also, while some schools are adding women's teams, such as soccer and tennis, they are eliminating men's teams, such as gymnastics and swimming (Gavora, 1995).

Admittedly, Title IX is a major effort in dealing with gender inequity in education. But political maneuvering and charges of reverse sexism are damaging to consensus building. And Title IX is a formal, legal approach which must be assessed in light of the informal biases in education, particularly higher education. Men and women are segregated into different areas of study. High school females are discouraged from taking science and math courses which are required for certain majors in college, such as engineering or medicine. If discouraged from pursuing athletics in high school, even limited scholarship opportunities for college athletics are unavailable. There are far fewer women than men in the higher ranks in academic institutions. As such, they have limited exposure and influence in serving as role models for aspiring students or for impacting social change. As Fox (1995:234) points out, "the presence and availability of female faculty members would serve to broaden women's aspirations, to increase their opportunities for interaction with faculty, and most important, to reduce the male dominance of educational practices and processes." Informal processes that continue gender discrimination are powerful. Any legal approach needs to take into account the sources of bias emanating from informal sources as well.

Domestic Relations

Perhaps more than any other area, it is in domestic law where gender inequity is most evident. Legal statutes regarding expected wife-husband marital roles are based on three theories (Stetson, 1991:132):

1. Unity—husband is dominant, and the wife has few rights and responsibilities
2. Separate but equal—husband is breadwinner and wife is companion and nurturer of children, but they share similar legal rights. This is the traditional functionalist model that assumes nonoverlapping, complementary responsibilities.
3. Shared partnership—husband and wife have equal rights and overlapping responsibilities.

Historical circumstances dictate whether one theory dominates at any point in time. As Stetson (1991:132) notes, contemporary law is a mixture of elements of each theory, with each state having its own pattern. The "development of a new theory did not abolish remnants of previous theories"; thus any reform in family law is an exceedingly complicated task.

We have already documented the impact of divorce on women and the failure of the law to do much about collecting child support or alimony when it is awarded. The fact that women gain custody of children who are minimally or not supported by their fathers propels many divorced women into poverty. The sharp increase in the number of all families in poverty is largely due to the number of female-headed families in this category, the fastest growing family type in the United States.

Property division at the dissolution of the marriage has been partly responsible for this as well. Although the trend is to have individual attorneys work out the details of the divorce, these details must be considered in the light of overriding state laws. In a *community property* state, all property acquired during the marriage is jointly owned by the spouses, so in the event of divorce, each partner is entitled to half of the said property. Community property at least implicitly recognizes the value of the housewife role. Residing in a community property state, however, is not a panacea. Weitzman (1985) states that equal division of property, which originally was intended to help women, can actually hurt them. A woman is forced to sell her home, often the couple's only "real" property, and she and her children find themselves in less than desirable rental property, often in a new location.They are dislocated from home, friends, schools, and other primary relationships at the very time these are psychologically most needed.

The other states are referred to as "common law" states with property belonging to the spouse in whose name it is held. Any property acquired during the marriage belongs to each spouse individually. Unless a house or car is also in the wife's name, the husband can lay claim to it in a divorce. Since the common law system has severely restricted and penalized women economically, most states (all but 3 of the 42 that do not have community property laws) have also passed "equitable distribution" laws. Rather than viewing property solely on the basis of whose name it is in, courts are now considering a number of factors, such as length of the marriage, the contributions of both parties to child care and domestic functions, earning ability, age, health, and other resources (Thorkelson, 1985:489). Most important, this kind of arrangement takes into account the fact that marriage is an economic partnership where both wage earning and homemaking should be considered as contributions, even though the latter is unpaid. This is at least an attempt to redress past abuses where the legal system puts women at a major disadvantage in divorce. But this must be tempered with the fact that regardless of the more recent equitable distribution laws, women still get much less than half of marital property in divorce. Many divorced women who are also single parents were not covered by such laws when their divorces were finalized, and community property is the exception rather than the rule.

Confusion reigns in divorce law. As Buehler (1995:99) notes, the emergence of punitive and sexually biased legislation means that confusion remains over such issues as disposition of the family home, rights to the ex-spouse's future income, and updating child-support orders to reflect inflation and shifts in family income. As a result, the number of conflicting interpretations in family law have increased. More important, gender bias becomes entrenched as a major influence in decisions, in turn contributing to an adversarial relationship to men's and women's positions (Erickson and Babcock, 1995). While rapid changes in family form and functioning will worsen this confusion, a positive sign is that there has been at least a shift from lethal patriarchy to partnership. As Erickson and Babcock (1995) suggest, a change in legal rhetoric will not remedy the situation, but a change in the culture itself will. In reviewing Supreme Court decisions regarding men's rights and responsibilities, they offer a promising vision of gender equity.

With regard to Social Security, the housewife role is an economic liability. Women are unpaid for this role and do not contribute to disability or retirement funds for ensuring their future. If a woman is married less than ten years before divorce from or the death of her husband, she is not eligible for his benefits. All the years she put into child rearing and domestic duties are ignored. Social Security policies were originally based on a division of labor and family life that do not exist today (Gilbert, 1994). In 1984, the Retirement Equity Act (REA) was passed to deal with some of these issues and to make pension benefits fairer to women. Under the REA, an employer is now required to get the spouse's approval before an employee is permitted to waive any spousal benefits offered through the employer, such as pensions or health insurance. More important, REA allows for pensions to be included as part of property settlements in divorces.

Statistics are dismal in indicating how poverty has become "feminized," particularly for elderly and black women. Inequities related to Social Security can be seen as partly responsible for this trend. The "separate but equal" theory of the marital relationship which establishes that husbands and wives have reciprocal but not equal rights is still strongly evident in domestic law. A husband is required to support his wife and children and in return a wife must provide services as companion, housewife, and mother. It is left up to the individual couple to determine how these requirements are actualized. In some families the wife controls all household expenses and decides on how one or both salaries are apportioned. In others, husbands provide their wives with allowances and "pin money" to take care of household or personal needs. She may file for divorce if there is evidence of gross financial neglect, or he may do so for unkempt children, a dirty house, or if she refuses to have intercourse. As discussed in Chapter 9, until recently spouses have been excluded from charges of rape since sexual intercourse has traditionally been viewed as "his right and her duty." This exemption had also included separated, divorced, and cohabiting couples. Today, there are more provisions for prosecution if the couple is legally divorced or separated, but because of questions concerning consent, most states allow for spousal exemptions.

Given the doctrine of reciprocity, it is understandable that the courts have been inconsistent in efforts to prosecute cases of wife abuse. It is ironic that perhaps the most disheartening evidence that the courts continue to be gender biased is in the area of "domestic relations," which is also the most life threatening. We have seen how Western history reflects the belief that wives are expected to be controlled by their husbands with the use of physical force as an often acceptable means of control. The women's liberation movement has been helpful in publicizing the issue of wife abuse to the extent that there is at least a growing awareness of its incidence. This awareness has led to police training programs in family violence and the establishment of hot lines to provide emergency help and counseling. Judges are now handling cases of wife abuse with greater frequency, with all indications suggesting this trend will continue. The problem is that while societal disapproval of wife abuse has grown, judges have not rejected the traditional viewpoint that wives are to be controlled by husbands. While more judges are assuring that the rights of abused wives are enforced, a significant number remain unwilling to implement the newer legislation protecting battered women.

Justification is tied to historical beliefs concerning women and the family as well as which laws are viewed as the more important ones to enforce. Temporarily barring a husband from his home means the due process rights of the husband may be violated and is more important than his wife's right to be protected from assault. The abusive husband is protected over the wishes of the victim. Many judges also accept the stereotype that it is the wife's behavior which caused the battering anyway, the classic "blaming the victim" ideology. Crites (1987:50) cites the case of an Ohio judge's comments to a woman who appeared in court to testify against her husband regarding his attacks on her. He told her to study the Bible and "try harder to be a good wife." The law is gradually changing to allow for more protection of battered wives. But enforcement will be hampered as long as judges maintain a stereotyped, traditional image of the husband-wife relationship.

Reproductive Rights

From the colonial era to the nineteenth century, a woman's right to an abortion could be legally challenged only if there was "quickening"—when she felt the first movements of the fetus. In 1800, not only were there no known statutes concerning abortion, but drugs to induce abortion were widely advertised in virtually every newspaper. By 1900, abortion was banned in every state except to save the life of the mother. This changed on January 22, 1973, with two landmark decisions by the Supreme Court. In *Roe* v. *Wade* and *Doe* v. *Bolton*, the Supreme Court voted seven to two in support of the right to privacy of the women involved in the cases. The states in question, Texas and Georgia, had failed to establish "any compelling interest" that would restrict abortions to the first trimester of pregnancy. Abortion in this instance would be between a woman and her physician. In the second trimester, when an abortion is deemed more dangerous, the state could exert control to protect the health of the mother. While these cases concluded that a pregnant woman does not have an absolute constitutional right to an abortion on demand, a broadening of the legal right to an abortion was established.

In 1995, support for abortion rights and identification as pro-choice hit an all-time high of 74 percent, representing about a 15 percent increase since 1991 (Lake and Breglio, 1992; Women's Equality Poll, 1995). While the majority of both men and women describe themselves as pro-choice, especially among adolescent males (Marsiglio and Shehand, 1993), men are higher than women. When comparing male and female state legislators, the trend reverses, with 74 percent of females and 61 percent of males considered to be pro-choice (Mandel and Dodson, 1992). However, these numbers mask the complexity of the reproductive rights issue, a fact that attitudes to abortion are related to a host of other variables and that seeming contradictory data exist. For example, whites are more supportive of abortion rights than are African-Americans, but there are no significant differences between black and white females of childbearing age (Lynxwiler and Gay, 1994). Those who describe themselves as religious or affiliated with a fundamentalist church have a low rate of approval for abortion rights. And even among those who profess a religious affiliation, approval ratings are highest when the mother's life is endangered or when the pregnancy resulted from rape (Jorgensen, 1993; Muraskin, 1993; Walzer, 1994; Welch et al., 1995). Other polls show that only 14 percent would want abortion completely outlawed (U.S. Department of Justice, 1993).

Yet since the 1973 decisions to legalize abortion, persistent campaigns have been waged to limit or eliminate this reproductive right of women. Tactics range from providing antiabortion films, commercials, and brochures to picketing or boycotting hospitals where abortions are performed, and in the extreme, death threats to physicians and staff who perform abortions and bombing clinics where women go as outpatients for abortions. It is difficult to judge the success of these campaigns. For example, the nation was horrified when a Florida physician who had performed abortions was murdered by an antiabortion activist outside a clinic. Given the public outcry, the majority of those lobbying against abortion rights were quick to point out that this was an isolated incident and not at all reflective of either the strategies they advocated or the training their supporters received. They even agreed for the first time to allow the press into what had formerly been their secretive training sessions. Similar to any advocacy group drawing support from a wide variety of people, they must also contend with the small number of extremists in their ranks who condoned the killing and publicly stated that this physician would no longer be able to "commit further murders." Concern has been expressed that the "justifiable homicide" antiabortion contingent has removed itself from the larger group and is recruiting supporters for clandestine terrorist activities. Public opinion is against any tactic that promotes violence to achieve a goal.

Legally the evidence is mixed. In 1983 the Supreme Court reaffirmed the 1973 decisions by ruling that second trimester abortions may be performed in other sites than hospitals since data clearly showed that outpatient clinics and other surgical facilities provide safe conditions. Also, a city ordinance requiring a physician to inform the woman that "the unborn child is a human life from the moment of conception" was struck down because the *Roe* v. *Wade* decision held that a "state may not adopt one theory of when life begins to justify its regulation of abortion" (Bishop, 1984:44). The same ordinance was also unacceptable because it intruded on the discretion of the woman's physician. The fact that such an ordinance was put on the books after the right to seek a legal abortion was granted demonstrates the tenacity of organized attempts to work around the law.

While this can be seen as a victory for reproductive rights, a major setback occurred in 1977 with the enactment of the Hyde Amendment which restricts funding for abortions for women who also receive Medicaid (unless the pregnancy is considered life threatening). Because Medicaid is the health insurance program for the very poor which is paid out of public monies, some supporters of the Hyde Amendment argue that the government should not be in the business of funding abortions. In 1980, a federal judge in New York ruled that a denial of Medicaid funds for medically necessary abortions was unconstitutional. If funds for therapeutic abortions were denied, a woman's religious freedom and right to privacy were impinged upon (Bishop 1984:45). Although he ordered the state government to resume funding, two weeks later the Supreme Court overturned this ruling, thereby upholding the constitutionality of the Hyde Amendment.

With the Supreme Court reducing the availability of legal abortions to poor women, it may ultimately have an effect on access to abortions in general. The major test of *Roe* v. *Wade* came in 1989 with *Webster* v. *Reproductive Health*, in which the Supreme Court allowed for additional controls on abortion through upholding a Missouri law that said life begins at conception and requires physicians to conduct viability tests on fetuses of 20 weeks or more before an abortion could be performed. But *Roe* v. *Wade* was not overturned. A Reagan Supreme Court appointee, the first woman on the Supreme Court, Sandra Day O'Connor, voted with the majority to retain the constitutionality of legal abortions. The impact of the Hyde Amendment is stated in Justice Thurgood Marshall's dissenting opinion.

> The enactments challenged here brutally coerce poor women to bear children society will scorn for every day of their lives . . . I am appalled at the ethical bankruptcy of those who preach a "right to life" that means under present social policies, a bare existence in utter misery for so many poor women and their children.

... The effect will be to regulate millions of people to lives of poverty and despair. (Cited in Bishop, 1984:45)

Although the economy was the key issue of the 1992 election, President Clinton was elected to office on a platform that included a pro-choice plank. On the twentieth anniversary of *Roe* v. *Wade,* less than two weeks after his inauguration and only days before the death of Thurgood Marshall, President Clinton issued an executive order rescinding the so-called gag rule that had prohibited the discussion of abortion as an alternative in clinics receiving public funds. The Republican agenda is to reinstate the gag rule. While reproductive rights will not be a defining issue which squarely divides the public into two opposing camps, it will remain on the political burner in the foreseeable future.

POLITICS

The ability to change the law to reflect equality and justice regarding gender is linked to the presence of women in legislative bodies at all governmental levels. In addition, once the law is changed, interpretation and enforcement must be consistent with gender equality. This also assumes that the women who serve the nation in their political roles view issues related to gender differently than men. Thus, voting behavior should mirror such differences. As we shall see, this assumption has been confirmed. However, women represent only a small minority of the political elites who wield power in the United States.

Women are increasingly being elected to public office but not in the numbers necessary for achieving parity with men. In the decade between 1974 and 1984, women elected to the fifty state legislatures increased by 100 percent, with six states (California, Florida, Hawaii, Kansas, Maryland, and Rhode Island) averaging 300 percent increases (Rule, 1993). It is important for long-term impact that women increase their numbers in state legislatures. In 1994 women held 71 out of 324 elective state offices in the executive branch, a total of 21.9 percent. In 1993 there were four women governors, 11 lieutenant governors, and eight attorneys general. In the 547 federally recognized American Indian tribes, 20 percent of all elected tribal chairpersons are women (*Who Are the Women of the U.S?,* 1995). In reflecting on such gains a decade ago, Poole and Zeigler (1985) suggested that a 50 percent male-female ratio in state elected officials would occur by the year 2000. Considering how close we are to that date, this forecast appears overly optimistic.

For congressional seats, some major changes have occurred. Except for a decline in the years 1961 through 1969, women have been slowly increasing their numbers in Congress, specifically with expansion in the House of Representatives. As Table 14-1 indicates, the number of women in the House has gradually increased, with those in the Senate holding at two for 14 years, until 1992, when six women held Senate seats. The 1992 election was heralded as the Year of the Woman, with sharp increases in women being elected officials throughout the United States. Although increases have occurred, no clear consistent growth pattern is evident. Two years later the 104th Congress shows an addition of one Senator and no change in House of Representatives (Table 14-1). Thus it is uncertain whether the 1992 election represents the beginning of a viable growth trend for women in Congress. Note, too, that women who filled Congressional seats in the past were likely to have completed the unex-

TABLE 14–1   Women in Congress, 1947–1997

Congress		Senate	House
80th	(1947–49)	1	7
81st	(1949–51)	1	9
82nd	(1951–53)	1	10
83rd	(1953–55)	1	12
84th	(1955–57)	1	17
85th	(1957–59)	1	15
86th	(1959–61)	1	17
87th	(1961–63)	2	18
88th	(1963–65)	2	12
89th	(1965–67)	2	11
90th	(1967–69)	1	10
91st	(1969–71)	1	10
92nd	(1971–73)	1	13
93rd	(1973–75)	1	16
94th	(1975–77)	0	17
95th	(1977–79)	2	18
96th	(1979–81)	1	16
97th	(1981–83)	2	19
98th	(1983–85)	2	22
99th	(1985–87)	2	22
100th	(1987–89)	2	23
101st	(1989–91)	2	28
102nd	(1991–93)	2	28
103rd	(1993–95)	6	48
104th	(1995–97)	8	48

*Excludes nonvoting House delegates.
Sources: Congressional Quarterly's Guide to Congress (4th ed.), 1991; *Special Supplement to Congressional Quarterly*, vol. 50 (November 7, 1992); *Vital Statistics on Congress*, 1995–1996, Washington, DC: Congressional Quarterly, Inc.

pired terms of their late husbands. Recently elected Senators and Representatives are definitely a new breed of Congressional women who have carved out stellar professional and political careers in their own right. But because of such traditions as the seniority system in Congress, it will be some time before this small group gains prominence on important committees and exerts the influence necessary to see goals realized. In examining measures of congressional success by gender as related to when the member first entered Congress, total years served, and reason for leaving, women are less successful than men (Whicker et al., 1993:146). As this study points out, even when women began to be represented in Congress in significant ways, their role in shaping law and public policy has still been extremely limited. The current cohort of women in Congress may significantly alter this pattern.

Women have been appointed to high administrative positions, but again the growth pattern is inconsistent and unclear, indicating both gains and losses. Reagan was criticized for being the first president in a decade who failed to appoint more women to high-level federal posts than his immediate predecessor. Reagan can be credited with being the first president to appoint a woman, Sandra Day O'Connor, as a justice to the Supreme Court. But as Lynn (1984:419) notes, this appointment lagged far behind public opinion. A Gallup Poll showed that 86 percent of those surveyed approved of a woman serving on the Supreme Court. Justice O'Connor's appointment came long after the public was willing to accept a female in this position. According to a 1991 National Women's Political Caucus Factsheet, Bush did appoint more women to Senate-confirmed positions in his first two and a half years in office (20 percent of all appointees) than Reagan did during his eight years as president (12 percent). Even though this percentage decreased as other appointments were made during the Bush administration, it still represents an overall gain for women in higher-level public offices. However, these figures must be viewed in light of the fact that many women who *did* receive political appointments during this period were from the New Right, and usually held positions with inflated titles and no authority (Schroeder, 1993:34).

Yet when considering the previous 12 years, Clinton has made an auspicious move in countering the tokenism that has been the hallmark of presidential top-level appointees for women. He immediately appointed four women to cabinet-level positions, including Attorney General Janet Reno. Of the 21 members of the Clinton cabinet, 6 (29 percent) are women including department heads of Justice, Energy, and Health and Human Services as well as the Ambassadorship to the United Nations. Perhaps more significant is that he soon appointed Ruth Bader Ginsberg, a long time advocate for women's rights, to the Supreme Court. As part of an unprecedented rate of gender and race diversification of the federal judiciary, by 1994 59 percent of judgeships (74 of 126) went to women (38) or minority men (36). Jimmy Carter was the first president to stress diversity on the federal branch, with 34 percent of judicial appointees being women and minority males. Reflecting the belief that the federal judiciary in particular should mirror the life experiences of a wide spectrum of society, Clinton has surpassed Carter in such appointments (McGonigle, 1994; *Who Are the Women of the U.S?*, 1995). As would be expected, conservative legal organizations contend that Clinton is using a quota system to reward liberal allies. And as already indicated, the "q-word" is politically inflammatory.

Barriers to the Female Candidate

While these women have been pioneers in terms of their achievement and leadership in areas traditionally assigned to men, they faced, and will continue to face, a myriad of different obstacles encountered by men in the political arena. Women must do politics differently, according to former Democratic Governor of Vermont Madeleine Kunin, and endure the experience of intimidation, being demeaned and being ignored. Using symbolic interactionist language, Kunin (1994) suggests that women officeholders must "invent" themselves continuously. Since political structure are not their creations women must adjust to a male-defined space. This would imply that the space can also be redefined to accommodate a political partnership between the genders.

Public opinion has changed to the extent that there is now a willingness to elect qualified women to public office at all levels. Female elected and appointed officials have proven themselves in competence, decisiveness, and fairness as they confront the issues of the day. Although the Democratic loss to the Republican Reagan-Bush ticket was overwhelming, the fact that the Democrats chose a woman, Geraldine Ferraro, as a vice-presidential candidate was significant. The Mondale-Ferraro ticket made it clear that women would no longer be relegated to behind-the-scenes positions. It cannot be said that prejudice against female candidates has been eliminated but only that there is growing public support for them (Bennett and Bennett, 1993). Yet women still find themselves hindered from entering the political arena in large numbers.

Socialization into gender roles may impede political participation for women. If politics demands a self-serving style and a high degree of competitiveness to be effective, men have the advantage. Women in public office appear to be more public-spirited and oriented to principles rather than narrower issues. Although politicians are expected to have higher moral standards than those who elected them to public office, women are expected to be higher than men in this regard. Both men and women must run a gauntlet to counter the rumors and smear campaigns now routinely associated with political life, but women have a more difficult time overcoming the hurdles. Female politicians are viewed as interlopers in a political realm dominated by men in accepted occupational roles. Schroeder (1993) points out that some believe that women will gain in public office because of the antiincumbent mentality and disillusionment with politics in general. While in the long run it works more to women's political disadvantage, the stereotype of the trustworthy woman who is a political outsider may actually be used to gain political office. It is ironic that to be successful in "masculine" politics, strategies are called for which are less likely to serve broader public interest.

Beyond the impact of socialization, a major situational barrier to women in politics is the constraint imposed by being a mother and a wife. Women must contend with the potential for social disapproval if the public believes their children and husbands are being neglected in the quest for public office. As Senator Dianne Feinstein of California notes, every career woman with a family keeps house, does the wash and cleans the bathrooms; men generally do not—it comes with the gender (Burros, 1993). This is consistent with the weighty research (see Chapter 7) showing that gender equity in the workplace does not translate into domestic tasksharing. Male candidates can begin their ascent in politics sooner in their careers than women. Even activist women who have a high degree of political saliency must often wait until their children are grown to reduce the risk of being labeled a neglectful mother. By earnestly starting their political careers later in life, women as a group have a difficult time catching up to men and seeking the higher public offices. A woman must also be mindful of the relationship with her husband who may be unwilling or unprepared to deal with his wife's candidacy. Some husbands play vital, supportive roles in promoting their wives' campaigns, but cultural proscriptions are likely to prevent men from enthusiastically carrying out such activities (Romer, 1990; Whicker and Areson, 1993).

Irrespective of political party, women must face questions about their appearance, marital status, and traditional responsibilities rarely asked men. Reporters reinforce the notion that women are exceptions. The persistent place of "woman" in headlines indicates that gender is a category of evaluation for women but not for men. Jamieson (1995:167) uses the example from a headline reading "It was a big night for Bay Area women" when Barbara Boxer and Diane Feinstein won Senate seats. Was it not also a big night for Bay Area men who favored these candidates? As one consultant on women's political issues notes, "if a woman is single, she is either a lesbian or whore; if she's married, she's ignoring her husband and children." Women candidates have been accused of practicing Satanism, being "femi-Nazis," and having abortions, illegitimate children, and affairs with men and women (cited in Schneider, 1992). When newly elected Bill Clinton was attempting to gain support for his first two female candidates for Attorney General, the defining qualification for these women became the manner in which child-care and household help was arranged and paid for (Woo, 1993). It is unlikely that male nominees would have been subjected to such questions.

It is ironic that it attests to the growing strength of female candidates that opponents must resort to such tactics. Harriet Woods, recent past president of the National Women's Political Caucus, points out that people may deplore what men do, but they often excuse it. She believes that voters are choosing women since they do represent integrity and reform of a scandal-ridden system (Schneider, 1992). Morris (1992:101) states that nobody is yet quite sure about what kinds of women can be elected to public office. She asks: "Must they be sexless? Must they be ladies? Must they be proper, blameless, and old?" The following questions can also be added: Must they be attractive or unattractive? Must they be single or married? Must they have young children? Must they have supportive husbands? In other words, must they be traditional women pursuing a nontraditional path? While this question is contradictory in its implications, to date the answer is still yes.

Countries that are more traditional and socially conservative in attitudes and behavior regarding women have elected women to the highest public office. Women have served as prime ministers and presidents in countries as diverse as Ireland, Norway, Britain, the Philippines, Pakistan, Israel, Sri Lanka, and Argentina. Yet American women have been unable to overcome obstacles that prevent them from becoming serious contenders for the presidency. The electorate must be convinced that domestic roles will not hamper them for political officeholding. This is a key factor in maintaining the image of the "U.S. presidency as a bastion of maleness" (Whicker and Areson, 1993:165).

Whether differential socialization patterns restrict the supply of female candidates remains debatable. The generation of women who is now seeking office have pioneers behind them who helped pave the way. Marginality can be psychologically debilitating but activist women have honed their psychological skills in confronting their own professional careers so the jump into the political arena may be less stressful. Socialization into the female gender role may initially be an inhibiting factor for women entering politics, but one which can be adequately dealt with to achieve political success.

Hillary Rodham Clinton may be the first First Lady to break the mold of the expected and accepted roles of women in public life. While it has long been known that presidential wives exert a great deal of behind-the-scenes influence, she has assumed an unprecedented leadership role in the Clinton administration. Her confidence and ability to carry out this role have won her much praise, but beliefs about the "proper place" of the First Lady have also brought harsh, relentless criticism. As exemplified by the label "Billary," the administration has been accused of her having undue influence on presidential policy. She has been criticized for everything from her investments to her wardrobe (Quindlen, 1994). An eloquent public speaker and writer, especially on issues related to children, she states she is surprised by how she is perceived.

Regardless of the fairness of the criticisms, she admits her lack of political savvy and is making inroads to soften her image (Burros, 1995).

Overall, public reaction to Hillary Clinton's position has been much more positive than what would have been predicted by gender role research. As honorary head of the U.S. delegation to the United Nations Conference on Women, she received high marks for criticizing China's record on human rights on its own turf in Beijing. While on the one hand she is accommodating gender role norms by the "softer image" approach, she is at the same time challenging gender stereotypes and creating new definitions of what is acceptable for women in the political sphere. As she states, "if you're going to ask people to support your direction and vision, you have to give them good information" (Romano, 1995). Again, whether just or not, the acceptance of that information will be contingent on gendered perceptions related to the role of the First Lady. A generation of Americans is witnessing a presidential couple who appear to exemplify a nontraditional, partnership style marriage. Bill Clinton values Hillary Rodham Clinton's opinions and political judgments, a respect which is a good thing for men (in particular) to see (McGrory, 1992). It is also significant that, according to Ehrenreich (1992:63), "Clinton and Gore represent the first generation of presidential candidates to have shared their law school classes with women or their homes with actual feminists." As role models, an egalitarian "First Couple" will have a great deal of influence in altering gender role stereotypes on a variety of fronts, especially in the family and political institutions.

Finally, structural barriers limit women in their political pursuits. To be viewed as realistic and eligible candidates for public office, both women and men must fall within a range of acceptability in terms of educational and occupational background. There are certain professions such as private law practice, journalism, and university teaching which are compatible with a political career. Celebrities in the fields of sports and acting have been drawn into the political arena. Such occupations offer visibility, flexibility, opportunities for developing communication skills, and substantial financial rewards, thus serving as significant training grounds for future politicians. We have already witnessed the financial and social effects of occupational segregation on women. Politically, such segregation hampers women from being recruited as candidates. On the positive side, women have made great inroads into a major source of political eligibility, the legal profession, if only at the lower levels. It is likely that the next decade will witness a rise in women seeking public office who are drawn from these ranks.

The Gender Gap

When women gained the right to vote in 1920 it was widely believed that women's opinions regarding social and political issues differed considerably from those held by men and that such differences would be evident in voting behavior. For over half a century this belief remained unfounded; women, like men, tended to vote along class, ethnic, and regional lines. By the early 1980s, however, a new political trend emerged, first showing up in the shift in party identification of women. By May 1982, 55 percent of women and 49 percent of men identified themselves as Democrats. Only 34 percent of women identified themselves as Republican compared to 37 percent of men (Lynn, 1984:404).

Women have shifted to the Democratic side at a faster rate than men. The political "gender gap" was born.

The gender gap phenomenon was so named after the 1980 presidential election which demonstrated a higher percentage of males voting for Ronald Reagan than females. In this election, Reagan won with eight percentage points less support from women than from men (Abzug and Kelber, 1984:1). Abzug and Kelber also point out that within two years of his election, the gap had widened. Women were increasingly more opposed to Reagan's policies regarding the economy, foreign relations, environmental protection, and the treatment of the genders. In 1988, Bush received 50 percent of women's votes compared to 57 percent of those cast by men, with 8 percent more women than men supporting Dukakis (Lake and Heidepriem, 1988). During the Dukakis-Bush campaign the gender gap narrowed considerably from the beginning to the end of the campaign, and Dukakis was overwhelmingly defeated. In order to diffuse the gender gap it was necessary for the Republican Party to seriously address issues such as parental leave, child care, education, and women's employment. The military bravado that highlighted the Reagan years was substituted for rhetoric that focused on a domestic agenda in a "kinder, gentler" nation. As reflected in George Bush's acceptance speech, "the presidency provides an incomparable opportunity for gentle persuasion . . . Prosperity with a purpose means taking your idealism and making it concrete by certain acts of goodness" (cited in Mueller, 1993:462-63).

It may be that the Republican response to the gender gap actually narrowed what was perceived as a chasm between the two major parties and set the stage for the election of Clinton. In the 1992 election, the gender gap was formidable with exit polls showing 47 percent of women voting for Clinton and 36 percent for Bush. For men, the comparable figures were 41 percent and 37 percent (Barrett, 1992). Overall, women cast 7 percent more votes than men (Fineman, 1992), a statistic that both parties carefully considered in the 1996 election. Both Democrats and Republicans acknowledge that today the gender split encompasses virtually all politics. Married, middle-aged white men are a critical force for the Republicans and single women, both white and African-American are a key constituency of the Democrats (Edsall, 1995).

If women and men are viewed in terms of those issues which have a differential impact on women, the gap may be wider. Until the 1970s, it would have been difficult to separate the way men and women viewed social and political issues, with the major exception that women are more opposed to military involvement and capital punishment (Abzug and Kelber, 1984). If there was a gender gap before 1980, it could be summed up with the phrase that men were more likely to be hawks and women more likely to be doves on issues dealing with violence. Whereas this statement still holds true today, the gender gap has broadened. Research on political attitudes suggests that a significant gap exists in a number of areas, including women's rights, such as the Equal Rights Amendment and abortion; defense spending; human compassion, such as help for the needy and support for minority rights; child care and welfare aid for the poor; moral issues, such as substance abuse and alternative lifestyles; and political corruption, such as opposition to graft and influence peddling. While women are more likely to take a liberal position on most of these, they are more conservative on moral issues and "antiestablishment" on the political corruption issue (Clark and Clark, 1993:35).

Whether this indicates that women will vote as a block on any one issue is still debatable. Some research suggests that age, SES, and education may be as important as gender in some areas (Lynn, 1984; Mandel and Dodson, 1992). Although political analysts believe that concerns such as reproductive rights and the Equal Rights Amendment may be more salient for women, younger men and women are equally supportive of them. Women are much more likely to support social programs which can impact on them, such as funding for day care, and are sympathetic to programs involved with helping the poor and disadvantaged. As suggested before, this support may be related to the economically disadvantageous position in which women find themselves.

In addition, men and women are closing ranks on a number of issues that clearly favor feminist attitudes. Among legislators, for example, "The percentage of feminist men who gave top priority to a woman's distinctive concern equaled that of the nonfeminist women and was much closer to the comparable percentage of the feminist women legislators than to that of the nonfeminist men" (Mandel and Dodson, 1992:167). While the gender gap is smallest at the municipal level and largest at the state level, women and men in public office and at all levels differ in attitudes both within their own political parties and across ideologies. Research indicates that Republican women, for example, express "more liberal and feminist views than Republican men, and women who call themselves conservative appear to be somewhat more liberal about policy issues and more feminist about 'women's' issues than men labeling themselves conservative" (Mandel, 1995:423). This may suggest that issues which have previously been considered feminist oriented or relevant only to women are becoming more mainstream in scope, interest, and priority. It may also be speculated that politically conservative women who are officeholders become more sympathetic to feminist issues as they, too, confront the male stronghold of politics. They may recognize that by virtue of their gender alone, they find themselves hindered in political effectiveness.

If more coalition building occurs, the gender gap may begin to close. Both political parties understand that women have the potential for voting as a bloc if the right mix of issues and circumstances are present. Women are not a homogeneous group, but mobilization around issues of gender may occur. Whether that gap continues to increase will depend on how party leaders respond to the political power women are beginning to demonstrate and even take for granted. They cannot afford to ignore existing gender differences and will attempt to use them to the realization of their political goals.

THE EQUAL RIGHTS AMENDMENT

Although the Equal Rights Amendment (ERA) to the United States Constitution was first introduced in Congress in 1923 and proposed yearly after that, Congress did not pass it until almost half a century later. The House of Representatives passed it with a vote of 354 to 23; the Senate approved it with a vote of 84 to 8. After passage by the Senate on March 22, 1972, the Ninety-Second Congress submitted it to the state legislatures for the three-fourths vote needed for ratification. The original deadline for ratification was in 1979, but ERA proponents managed to muster the support to get this extended until 1982. Despite ratification by 38 states, three additional votes were needed by 1982 when the deadline ran out. Since then, the ERA has been reintroduced yearly into Congress, and Congress has not passed it again. Whereas in this regard history seems to be repeating itself, ERA proponents remain optimistic. The battle for ratification has enhanced their political sophistication and provided a basis of understanding for dealing with the forces that challenge them.

The complexity of issues surrounding the ERA is shrouded by its deceptively simple language. The complete text of the ERA is as follows:

> **Section 1.** Equality of rights under the law shall not be denied or abridged by the United States or by any State on account of sex.

> **Section 2.** The Congress shall have the power to enforce, by appropriate legislation, the provisions of this article.

> **Section 3.** This Amendment shall take effect two years after the date of ratification.

When again passed by Congress, the state legislatures will have another seven years to ratify it. Once ratified, it will become the Twenty-Seventh Amendment to the Constitution.

Support for the ERA is wide, and its passage is favored by a majority of both genders. It has been part of the platform of both political parties and supported by presidents as diverse as Eisenhower, Kennedy, Johnson, and Nixon. Almost 500 major organizations (with well over 50 million members), representing men and women with different interests and philosophies support it. This broad base of support is seen with organizations which include the National Education Association, the International Union of Electrical Radio and Machine Workers, the American Public Health Association, and the United Presbyterian Church. Yet even with this kind of public affirmation, the ERA has yet to be ratified.

During the ten-year ratification process, a number of factors combined to defeat the ERA. It is not simply a matter of saying who is in favor of equality and who is not. Few would argue against the principle of equality, but many are suspicious of how equality is to be implemented. According to Mansbridge (1986:4), the death of the ERA was related to other changes which were occurring in American political attitudes. One had to do with the increased "legislative skepticism" concerning the U.S. Supreme Court's authority to review legislation. States feared that the Supreme Court would be harsh in reviewing efforts at implementation and balked at what they assumed would be undue interference in state proceedings.

The second change had to do with the growing power and organization of the New Right. Where once national defense and communism were targeted issues of the "old" Radical Right, the ERA became a focus for new attacks. Mansbridge (1986:5) states that "for many conservative Americans, the personal became political for the first time when questions of family, children, sexual behavior and women's roles became subjects of political debate." Aligned with fundamentalist churches and interpretations which made traditional homemakers sympathetic to the anti-ERA cause and anxious to retrieve what they believed was a lost status, the New Right mounted a massive effort against ratification. With opponents like Phyllis Schlafly fueling "nonissues" like unisex bathrooms and an end to alimony, enough fear and innuendo were generated which minimized viable debate on substantive issues such as the increasing economic disparity between men and women. Marshall

(1995:548) contends that the anti-ERA literature also embodied an ideology of antifeminism and the reaffirmation of divinely ordained gender differences that were necessary for the continuation of society. "The women's rights issue is thus cast as a moral battle over the basic institutions and values of American society." Scare tactics were not only used against ERA ratification but also served to heighten and reinforce conventional suspicion between the genders.

During the ratification process, much confusion was generated over what ERA would actually change, augment, or accomplish. Whereas anti-ERA groups capitalized on this lack of understanding to help sow the seeds for its defeat, even interpretations among its supporters were somewhat inconsistent. Some help in this regard comes from the 17 states which already have equal rights amendments in their constitutions. Feinberg (1986:4) provides the following information from several states which illustrate what a fully enacted ERA could mean. For example, although both parents are required in Texas to provide child support, the services of a housewife are counted in kind. In this way Texas recognizes the value of a mother's services not just in terms of financial contributions. Pennsylvania has a similar specification under its own equal rights amendment which has been interpreted to mean that a divorced mother is not required to work outside the home because her value as a homemaker is recognized. When Medicaid money for abortion was curtailed, Massachusetts and Connecticut ordered funding on privacy and other grounds. And state equal rights amendments do not protect males for committing sex crimes. These examples give some indication of how equal rights have been carried out in the various states and can serve as a basis for considering the impact of a federal ERA. Organizations such as Common Cause, the National Organization for Women, and the American Civil Liberties Union have provided partial answers to the unsettling questions which many have raised regarding ERA. The summary outlined below is indicative of some probable interpretations of ERA:

1. Women will not be deprived of alimony, child custody, or child support. However, men will be eligible for alimony under the same conditions as women, as they are already in one-third of the states.
2. Individual circumstances and need will determine domestic relations and community property. ERA does not require both spouses to contribute equal financial support to the marriage. But the law will recognize the homemaker's contribution to the support of the family. Social custom and interpersonal relations in a marriage remain a matter of individual choice.
3. ERA will fit into existing constitutional structures regarding privacy. The sexes will continue to be segregated with regard to public restrooms, sleeping quarters at coeducational colleges, prison dormitories, and military barracks.
4. It will be illegal to enact "protective" labor regulations. Such laws have been shown to restrict employment opportunities by keeping women out of those jobs offering higher pay and advancement.
5. ERA will allow meaningful choices to women in terms of family, careers, or both, as well as any alternatives to these roles. Those who choose to be housewives will not be deprived in any way.
6. Since ERA applies to government practices only, it cannot have a direct effect on the private sector's credit practices. However, it will have a long-range effect on lessening discrimination; and it will abolish sex discrimination in government credit programs such as loans from the Federal Housing Administration and the Veterans Administration.

7. ERA will nullify state laws which have greater penalties for one sex or the other when committing the same crime. But it will not invalidate laws which punish rape, since the Senate has already stated that such laws are designed to protect women which suggests that they (women) are uniformly distinct from men.

8. The ERA will require that all the benefits of publicly supported education be available to women and men on an equal basis. Enforcement of Title IX has been uneven. ERA will ensure against discrimination in admissions, curriculum, facilities, counseling, and placement. (Adapted from Common Cause, n.d.)

A critical issue related to the defeat of ERA had to do with military service and the draft at a time when America was barely recovering from the psychological wounds of the Vietnam war. Congress already has the power to draft women and were prepared to do so, such as drafting nurses during World War II, but the tide turned in favor of the Allies before it occurred. While it could be assumed that ERA would subject women to the draft, the facts that there now is no draft, that military service is now more difficult to enter even voluntarily, and that young men are no longer required to register for Selective Service at age 18 will make a major difference in the next ratification campaign.

For women who do choose military roles, there is no evidence that they are incapable of performing in combat. In both Operation Desert Storm and Operation Just Cause (the Panama invasion), women served in all military occupational specialties except those relating to direct combat. When inadvertently drawn into combat areas, women responded appropriately and in many instances, with distinction. Given these recent experiences, Congress has repealed the law barring women from flying combat aircraft, though it is up to the individual armed services to determine how this option is carried out. ERA would eliminate the barriers to women's full participation in the armed services. This means that they will no longer be discriminated against in terms of assignment or promotion and would be entitled the same benefits as men, such as in education and health care, when they leave active duty. This is unlikely to mean, however, that a gender-neutral armed forces will exist. As Hooker (1993:262) notes, gender differences between men and women in the armed forced can be muted, compensated for, and even exploited to enhance military performance, but they cannot be ignored.

FEMINISM IN THE TWENTY-FIRST CENTURY

The New Right hailed the defeat of the ERA as a defeat for feminism in general and a harbinger of returning women to the pedestal. The inability to garner enough support in the last three states pointed out not only the power of the New Right but the internal problems which were seen as hampering the feminist movement. The movement of the 1960s and 1970s focused on the root causes of gender inequality, yet in doing so, issues surrounding motherhood and family were given less priority. Minority women in particular felt overlooked in the quest for economic parity with men and the inclusion of women in higher level positions. The movement itself was spawned by women who wanted to escape the shackles of the feminine mystique and gain a new sense of independence. To a great extent, this has been accomplished. The challenge ahead is to integrate this new-found independence with continuing concerns related to marriage, motherhood, and parenting.

According to Friedan (1994) the confrontational tactics which worked 20 years ago may be less effective today. Recognizing that the early movement was most vulnerable on the family issue, she suggests that a postfeminist generation needs to address the fact that the family is the "new frontier." An economic agenda focusing on the family which allows for flexibility in the workplace to enhance family life is part of such an approach. The "enemy now is not sexism . . . but a business structure that pits everyone against one another" in the pursuit of profit (Cited in Rosenfeld, 1995:D1). She is promoting a new paradigm which seeks to transcend polarized gender roles. She would use such a paradigm to help move "from the politics of self-interest to the politics of generativity, integrity and the common good" (Friedan, 1994:1141).

These are the politics of accommodation, which are starkly different from the old politics of separatism. While it provides an alternative view, many women do not accept accommodation as a goal (Wickenden, 1986). In the 1970s Chafe (1974:515) argued that a major obstacle faced by the women's movement is that of internal dissension that existed despite the advantages of a decentralized structure. This dissension mainly concerned visions of the family. Chafe's words may be haunting the movement today.

On the positive side, however, the movement is reconciled to the fact that women do not have to be in full agreement with one another to work for feminist goals. Chavez (1987) notes that the basic questions which inspired the movement over 20 years ago have been resolved, but as has been documented throughout this book, this has resulted in women now being confronted with new issues surrounding home, children, mates, and careers. It has also produced an atmosphere where discrimination is subtler and less easy to document. The decentralized structure may provide the very catalyst for the feminist movement to work on the myriad of issues confronting women today. Local feminist groups can target specific concerns which they deem most critical, such as delivering the message to area corporations that maternity leave or adequate day care are necessities. They may lobby for safe homes for abused women or work with other organizations to deal with the problem of violence within families. The National Organization for Women will continue to work for broader political goals and will spearhead the next ERA campaign.

Although tactics like these are hallmarks of the earlier movement, they are approached today with a more sophisticated understanding of the political intricacies involved and greater knowledge and skill in how to deal with opponents. The 1980s witnessed a rise in antifeminism coupled with the advance of a New Right allied with the conservative politics of the nation. A backlash occurred which tried

> to make real problems of work and family go away by pushing us back to traditional solutions we know won't work. It attempts to redirect our energies away from equalizing and humanizing our world, by dismissing feminism's accomplishments and making our goals seem impossible. Its cruelest side is that it plays on things some women value most—their legitimate desire to have families . . . It implies that for women there must be a choice between equality and humanity, between work and family. (Chodorow et al., 1984:102)

But as we approach the next century, there are already signs that the winds of political change have shifted toward a more favorable outlook for a feminist agenda. It is perhaps indicative of the success of the women's movement that this agenda has widespread support. People no longer question the right of women to achieve their fullest individual potential, whether inside or outside the home or through a combination of both. As Freeman (1995:528) suggests, the next revolution is a social one—in personal and family relationships. If the earlier movement was characterized by mass mobilization and confrontation, the current one is less visible, with protest taking many forms on many fronts. Feminism at the turn of the twenty-first century will be diverse in programs, tactics, and goals. The United Nations Conference on Women in Beijing was a watershed for women, both globally and in America. By encouraging open dialogue, inclusiveness, and consensus building, it attested to the ability of women to work toward goals of sisterhood, female empowerment, and partnering with men. With a heightened degree of political sophistication, that very diversity will contribute to the strength of the movement.

REFERENCES

Abbey, Antonia, Frank M. Andres, and L. Jill Halman. 1994. "Psychosocial predictors of life quality: How are they affected by infertility, gender and parenthood." *Journal of Family Issues* 15(2):253-71.

Abramovitz, M. 1988. *Regulating the Lives of Women: Social Welfare Policy from Colonial Times to the Present.* Boston: South End.

Abzug, Bella, and Mim Kelber. 1984. *Gender Gap: Bella Abzug's Guide to Political Power for American Women.* Boston: Houghton-Mifflin.

Acker, Joan. 1989. "Making gender visible." In Ruth A. Wallace (ed.), *Feminism and Sociological Theory.* Newbury Park, CA: Sage.

Acker, Sandra. 1994. *Gendered Education: Sociological Reflections on Women, Teaching and Feminism.* Buckingham, UK: Open University Press.

Acosta-Belen, Edna. 1986. "Puerto Rican women in culture, history and society." In Edna Acosta-Belen (ed.), *The Puerto Rican Woman.* New York: Praeger.

Adams, Abigail. 1776/1996. "Remember the ladies letters." In Mary Beth Norton and Ruth M. Alexander (eds.), *Major Problems in American Women's History.* Lexington, MA: D. C. Heath.

Adams, David. 1992. "Biology does not make men more aggressive than women." In Kaj Björkqvist and Pirkko Niemelä (eds.), *Of Mice and Women: Aspects of Female Aggression.* San Diego: Academic Press.

Adams, Karen L., and Norma C. Ware. 1995. "Sexism and the English language: The linguistic implications of being a woman." In Jo Freeman (ed.), *Women: A Feminist Perspective.* Mountain View, CA: Mayfield.

Adams, Kathryn. 1980. "Who has the final word? Sex, race, and dominance behavior." *Journal of Personality and Social Psychology* 38:1-8.

Adamsky, C. 1981. "Changes in pronominal usage in a classroom situation." *Psychology of Women's Quarterly* 5:773-79.

Adelmann, Pamela. 1994. "Multiple roles and physical health among older adults." *Research on Aging* 16(2):142-66.

Adler, Jerry. 1991. "Drums, sweat and tears." *Newsweek* (June 24):48-51.

Afshar, Haleh. 1991. "Women and development: Myths and realities—Some introductory notes." In Haleh Afshar (ed.), *Women, Development and Survival in the Third World.* Essex, UK: Longman Group.

Agassi, Judith Buber. 1989. "Theories of gender equality: Lessons from the Israeli kibbutz." *Gender & Society* 3(2):160-86.

Ahmad, Zubeida, and Martha Loutfi. 1985. *Women Workers in Rural Development.* Geneva: International Labour Office.

Ahmed, Leila. 1986. "Women and the advent of Islam." *Signs* 11:665-91. 1992. *Women and Gender in Islam: Roots of a Modern Debate.* New Haven, CT: Yale University.

Akert, R. M., and J. Chen. 1984. "Gender display: The incidence of facial prominence in print and television media." Paper presented at the Eastern Psychological Association Meeting, Baltimore, MD.

Alcock, B., and J. Robson. 1990. "Cagney and Lacey revisited." *Feminist Review* 35 (Summer):42-53.

Aldridge, Delores P. 1978. "Interracial marriages: Empirical and theoretical considerations." *Journal of Black Studies* 8(March):355-68.

Allen, Paula Gunn. 1986. *The Sacred Hoop.* Boston: Beacon. 1995. "When women throw down bundles: Strong women make strong nations." In Sheila Ruth, *Issues in Feminism: An Introduction to Women's Studies.* Mountain View, CA: Mayfield.

Allott, Susan. 1985. "Soviet rural women: Employment and family life." In Barbara Holland (ed.), *Soviet Sisterhood.* Bloomington, IN: Indiana University.

Almquist, Elizabeth M. 1987. "Labor market gender inequality in minority groups." *Gender & Society* 1:400-14. 1995. "The experiences of minority women in the United States: Intersections of race, gender, and class." In Jo Freeman (ed.), *Women: A Feminist Perspective.* Mountain View, CA: Mayfield.

Alsbrook, Larry. 1976. "Marital communication and sexism." *Social Casework* 57(October):517-22.

Amato, Paul R. 1994. "The impact of divorce on men and women in India and the United States." *Journal of Comparative Family Studies* 25(2):207-21.

Amato, Paul R., and Alan Booth. 1995. "Changes in gender role attitudes and perceived marital quality." *American Sociological Review* 60(1):58-66.

Ambah, Faiza S. 1995. "Saudi girls show pen is mightier than their lords." *Christian Science Monitor* March 24:1,6.

Ambrose, S.F. 1989. "Men and women can be friends." In N. Bernards and T. O'Neill (eds.), *Male/Female Roles: Opposing Viewpoints.* San Diego, CA: Greenhaven.

American Association of University Professors. 1990. "Some dynamic aspects of academic careers: The urgent need to match aspirations to compensation." *Academe* (March-April):3-29.

American Association of University Women. 1992. *The AAUW Report: How Schools Shortchange Girls.* Prepared by the Wellesley College Center for Research on Women. Washington, DC: AAUW Educational Foundation 1993. *Hostile Pathways: The AAUW Survey on Sexual Harassment in America's Schools.* Washington, DC: American Association of University Women.

American Demographics. 1985. "Entrepreneurial eighties." 7:11.

American Psychological Association. 1985. *Developing a National Agenda to Address Women's Mental Health Needs.* Washington, DC: American Psychological Association.

Andersen, Margaret L., 1993. *Thinking About Women: Sociological Perspectives on Sex and Gender.* New York: Macmillan.

Andersen, Margaret L. and Patricia Hill Collins. 1995. "Shifting the center and reconstructing knowledge." In Margaret L. Andersen and Patricia Hill Collins (eds.), *Race, Class and Gender: An Anthology.* Belmont, CA: Wadsworth.

Anderson, John, 1994b. "Held hostage in Hollywood: Female stars buy into bad roles, big time." *St. Louis Post-Dispatch* December 4:3C.

Anderson, Karen Tucker. 1996. "Persistent discrimination against black women during World War II." In Mary Beth Norton and Ruth M. Alexander (eds.), *Major Problems in American Women's History.* Lexington, MA: D.C. Heath.

Anderson, Michael. 1994a. "What is new about the modern family?" In Michael Drake (ed.), *Time, Family and Community: Perspectives on Family and Community History.* Oxford, UK: The Open University.

Anson, Ofra, Arieh Levenson, and Dan Y. Bonneh. 1990. "Gender and health on the kibbutz." *Sex Roles* 22(3-4):213-236.

Anson, Ofra, Esther Paran, Lily Neumann, and Dov Chernichovsky. 1993. "Gender differences in health perceptions and their predictors." *Social Science and Medicine* 36(4):419-27.

Antilla, Susan. 1995. "Young white men only, please: Women accuse a broker of blatant discrimination." *New York Times* April 26:C1,D7

Anzaldua, Gloria E. 1995. "The strength of my rebellion." In Sheila Ruth, *Issues in Feminism: An Introduction to Women's Studies.* Mountain View, CA: Mayfield.

Apple, R. 1984. "Church of England moves toward letting women be priests." *New York Times* (November 6):7.

Araujo, Maria, Jose Oliveira, and C. Simone Griilo Diniz. 1995. "Women, sexuality and AIDS in Brazil." *World Health.* Special Issue on Women and Health (September):29-30.

Archer, D., B. Iritani, D. D. Kimes, and M. Barrios. 1983. "Faceisms: Five studies of sex differences in facial prominence." *Journal of Personality and Social Psychology* 45:725-35.

Archer, J., 1989. "The relationship between gender-role measures: A review." *British Journal of Social Psychology* 28:173-84.

Archer, J., and K. Westeman. 1981. "Sex differences in the aggressive behaviour of schoolchildren." *British Journal of Sociology* 20:31-36.

Arendell, Terry. 1992. "After divorce: Investigations into father absence." *Gender & Society* 6(4):562-86. 1995. "Downward mobility." In Mark Robert Rank and Edward L. Kain (eds.), *Diversity and Change in Families: Patterns, Prospects, and Policies*. Englewood Cliffs, NJ: Prentice Hall.

Arliss, Laurie P. 1991. *Gender Communication*. Englewood Cliffs, NJ: Prentice Hall.

Aron, A., and E.N. Aron. 1991. "Love and sexuality." In K. McKinney and S. Sprecher (eds.), *Sexuality in Close Relationships*. Hillsdale, NJ: Lawrence Erlbaum.

Arthur, Marilyn B. 1984. "Early Greece: The origins of the Western attitude toward women." In John Peradotto and J. P. Sullivan (eds.), *Women in the Ancient World: The Arethusa Papers*. Albany: SUNY.

Ascha, Ghassan. 1995. "The 'Mothers of the Believers': Stereotypes of the Prophet Muhammad's wives." In Ria Kloppenborg and Wouter J. Hanegraaff (eds.), *Female Stereotypes in Religious Traditions*. Leiden, Netherlands: Brill.

Ashton-Jones, Evelyn, and Gary A. Olson (Eds.). 1991. *The Gender Reader*. Boston: Allyn & Bacon.

Asia-Pacific Population and Policy. 1994. "After the demographic transition: Policy responses to low fertility in four Asian countries." East-West Center Program on Population No. 30:1-4. 1995a. "Evidence mounts for sex-selective abortion in Asia." East-West Center Program on Population No. 34 (May-June). 1995b. "New survey finds fertility decline in India." East-West Center Program on Population No. 32 (January-February). 1995c. "India's National Family Health Survey provides new information on maternal and child health and AIDS awareness." East-West Center Program on Population No. 33 (March-April).

Association of American Colleges. 1982. *The Classroom Climate: A Chilly One for Women?* Project on the Status and Education of Women. Washington, DC: Association of American Colleges.

Association of American Colleges and Universities. 1994. "Going coed: What difference does it make?" *On Campus with Women* 23(3):1-2. 1995. "Valuable lessons from women's colleges." *On Campus with Women* 24(5):3.

Astin, A. W. 1985. "Freshman characteristics and attitudes." *Chronicle of Higher Education* 16(January):15-16.

Astrachan, Anthony. 1993. "Dividing lines." In Virginia Cyrus (ed.), *Experiencing Race, Class, and Gender in the United States*. Mountain View, CA: Mayfield.

Astron, E. 1983. "Measures of play behavior: The influence of sex-role stereotyped children's books." *Sex Roles* 9:43-47.

Atchley, Robert C. 1994. *Social Forces and Aging*. Belmont, CA: Wadsworth.

Atkin, David J. 1987. "Looks like you'll make it after all." Paper presented to the Television Drama Conference, Lansing, MI (May).

Atkin, David J., Jay Moorman, and Carolyn A. Lin. 1991. "Ready for prime time: Network series devoted to working women in the 1980s." *Sex Roles* 25(11-12):677-85.

AtKisson, Alan. 1995. "What makes love last." In Kathleen R. Gilbert (ed.), *Marriage and the Family 95/96* (Annual Editions). Guilford, CT: Dushkin/Brown & Benchmark.

Atoh, Makoto. 1994. "An era of later marriages, fewer kids." *Economic Eye: A Quarterly Digest of Views from Japan* 15(2):19-22.

Atwater, Lynn. 1982. *The Extramarital Connection: Sex, Intimacy, Identity*. New York: Irvington.

Babb, Florence E. 1990. "Women and work in Latin America." *Latin American Research Review* 25(2):236-47.

Bachrach, Judy. 1985. "What goes with scrambled eggs and toast? The professional problems of Pauley, Shriver and Lunden." *SAVVY* (November):46-50.

Backett, Kathryn C. 1982. *Mothers and Fathers*. New York: St. Martin's.

Badawi, Jamal. 1995. *Gender Equity in Islam: Basic Principles*. Plainfield, IN: American Trust.

Badinter, Elisabeth. 1995. *XY: On Masculine Identity*. New York: Columbia University.

Baker, Robert. 1993. "'Pricks' and 'chicks': A plea for 'persons.'" In Anne Minas (ed.), *Gender Basics: Feminist Perspectives on Women and Men*. Belmont, CA: Wadsworth.

Balanoff, Elizabeth. 1990. "The American woman and the labor movement: Bitter fruit in the economy of profit." In Frances Richardson Keller (ed.), *Views of Women's Lives in Western Tradition.* Lewiston, NY: Edwin Mellen.

Baldi, Stephane. 1995. "Prestige determinants of first academic job for new sociology Ph.D.s, 1985-1992." *Sociological Quarterly* 36(4):777-89.

Baldwin, Bruce A. 1995. "The family circle." In Kathleen R. Gilbert (ed.), *Marriage and Family 95/96.* (Annual Editions). Guilford, CT: Dushkin/Brown & Benchmark.

Ball, Richard E. 1993. "Children and marital happiness of black Americans." *Journal of Comparative Family Studies* 24(2):203-18.

Balmer, Randall. 1994. "American fundamentalism: The ideal of femininity." In John Stratton Hawley (ed.), *Fundamentalism and Gender.* New York: Oxford University.

Bandura, Albert. 1986. *The Social Foundations of Thought and Action: A Social Cognitive Theory.* Englewood Cliffs, NJ: Prentice Hall.

Bandura, Albert, and Richard H. Walters. 1963. *Social Learning and Personality Development.* New York: Holt, Rinehart & Winston.

Banner, Lois W. 1984. *Women in Modern America: A Brief History.* San Diego: Harcourt Brace Jovanovich.

Baraka, Iqbal. 1986. "The influence of contemporary Arab thought on the women's movement." In Nahid Toubia (ed.), *Women of the Arab World: The Coming Challenge.* London: Zed.

Barash, David P. 1982. *Sociobiology and Behavior.* New York: Elsevier.

Barcus, F. Earle, 1983. *Images of Life on Children's Television: Sex Roles, Minorities and Families.* New York: Praeger.

Bardwell, J. R., S. W. Cochran, and S. Walker. 1986. "Relationship of parental education, race and gender to sex-role stereotyping in five-year-old kindergartners." *Sex Roles* 15:275-81.

Barnard, Judith, and Michael Fain. 1988. "Why living together was not enough." In J. Gipson Wells (ed.), *Current Issues in Marriage and the Family.* New York: Macmillan.

Barnes, Gordon E., Leonard Greenwood, and Reena Sommer. 1991. "Courtship violence in a Canadian sample of male college students." *Family Relations* 40:37-44.

Barnes, Harper. 1993. "Women in the director's chair." *St. Louis Post-Dispatch* November 21:3C,14C.

Barnes, Nancy Schuster. 1987. "Buddhism." In Arvind Sharma (ed.), *Women in World Religions.* Albany, NY: State University of New York.

Barnett, Rosalind C., Robert I. Brennan, and Nancy L. Marshall. 1994. "Gender and the relationship between parent role quality and psychological distress: A study of men and women in dual-earner couples." *Journal of Family Issues* 15(2): 229-52.

Barnett, Rosalind C., and Caryl Rivers. 1995. "The myth of the miserable working women." In Kathleen R. Gilbert (ed.), *Marriage and the Family 95/96* (Annual Editions). Guilford, CT: Dushkin/Brown & Benchmark.

Baron, J. N., A. Davis-Blake, and W. T. Beilby. 1986. "The structure of opportunity: How promotion ladders vary within and among organizations." *Administrative Science Quarterly* 31:248-73.

Barrett, Laurence I. 1992. "A new coalition for the 1990s." *Time* November 16:47-48.

Barry, Dave. 1992. "Dealing with the laundry-impaired." *St. Louis Post-Dispatch* (February 2):2C.

Barstow, Anne Llewellyn. 1994. *Witchcraze: A New History of the European Witch Hunts.* London: Pandora.

Bartels, Deanna T., and Felecia C. Eppley. 1995. "Education in Mainland China." *Social Education* 59(1):31-37.

Barthel, Diane. 1987. *Putting on Appearances: Gender and Advertising.* Philadelphia: Temple University.

Bartholet, Elizabeth, and Elaine Draper. 1994. "Rethinking the choice to have children." *American Behavioral Scientist* 37(8):1058-73.

Basow, Susan A. 1984. "Ethnic group differences in educational achievement in Fiji." *Journal of Cross-Cultural Psychology* 15:435-51. 1992. *Gender Stereotypes: Traditions and Alternatives.* Belmont, CA: Wadsworth. 1996. "Gender stereotypes and roles." In Karen E. Rosenblum and Toni-Michelle C. Travis (eds.), *The Meaning of Difference: American Constructions of Race, Sex and Gender, Social Class and Sexual Orientation.* New York: McGraw-Hill.

Batten, Mary. 1992. *Sexual Strategies.* New York: Jeremy P. Tarcher/Putnam.

Baxter, Janeen, and Emily W. Kane. 1995. "Dependence and independence: A cross-national analysis of gender inequality and gender attitudes." *Gender & Society* 9(2):193-215.

Beach, S.R.H., and A. Tesser. 1988. "Love in marriage: A cognitive account." In Robert J. Sternberg and M.L. Barnes (eds.), *The Psychology of Love*. New Haven, CT: Yale University.

Beal, Carole R. 1994. *Boys and Girls: The Development of Gender Roles*. New York: McGraw-Hill.

Beck, Aaron T. 1993. "Static in communication." In Virginia Cyrus (ed.), *Experiencing Race, Class and Gender in the United States*. Mountain View, CA: Mayfield.

Becker, Gary S. 1994. "Working women's staunchest allies: Supply and demand." In Susan F. Feiner (ed.), *Race & Gender in the American Economy: Views from across the Spectrum*. Englewood Cliffs, NJ: Prentice Hall.

Beddoe, Deirdre. 1989. *Back to Home and Duty: Women Between the Wars, 1918-1939*. London: Pandora.

Beer, William R. 1983. *Househusbands: Men and Housework in American Families*. New York: Praeger.

Beijing Review. 1995. "Historic liberation of Chinese women." 38(36):6-9.

Belknap, Penny, and Wilbert M. Leonard II. 1991. "A conceptual replication of Erving Goffman's study of gender advertisements." *Sex Roles* 25(3-4):103-18.

Bellas, Marcia L. 1993. "Faculty salaries: Still a cost of being female." *Social Science Quarterly* 74(1)62-75.

Belle, Deborah. 1990. *Lives in Stress: Women and Depression*. Ann Arbor, MI: Books on Demand.

Bellinger, David C., and Jean Berko Gleason. 1982. "Sex differences in parental directives to young children." *Sex Roles* 8:1123-39.

Belsky, Jay. 1990. "Parental and nonparental child care and children's socioemotional development: A decade in review." *Journal of Marriage and the Family* 52:885-903. 1991. "Patterns of marital change and parent-child interaction." *Journal of Marriage and the Family* 53:487-98.

Belsky, Jay, and John Kelly. 1995. "His and hers transition." In Mark Robert Rank and Edward L. Kain (eds.), *Diversity and Change in Families: Patterns, Prospects and Policies*. Englewood Cliffs, NJ: Prentice Hall.

Bem, Sandra Lipsitz. 1974. "The measurement of psychological androgyny." *Journal of Consulting and Clinical Psychology* 42:155-62. 1975. "Sex role adaptability: One consequence of psychological androgyny." *Journal of Personality and Social Psychology* 31:634-43. 1981. "Gender schema theory: A cognitive account of sex-typing." *Psychological Review* 88:354-64. 1983. "Gender schema theory and its implications for child development: Raising gender-aschematic children in a gender-schematic society." *Signs* 8:598-616. 1985. "Androgyny and gender-schema theory: A conceptual and empirical integration." In T.B. Sonderegger (ed.), *Nebraska Symposium on Motivation 1984: Psychology and Gender* 32:179-226. Lincoln, NB: University of Nebraska. 1993. *The Lenses of Gender: Transforming the Debate on Sexual Inequality*. New Haven, CT: Yale University. 1996. "Transforming the debate on sexual inequality: From biological difference to institutionalized androcentrism." In Joan C. Chrisler, Carla Golden, and Patricia D. Rozee (eds.), *Lectures on the Psychology of Women*. New York: McGraw-Hill.

Bem, Sandra Lipsitz, and Daryl J. Bem. 1970. "Case study of a nonconscious ideology: Training the woman to know her place." In Daryl J. Bem (ed.), *Beliefs, Attitudes and Human Affairs*. Belmont, CA: Brooks and Cole.

Beneke, Tim. 1992. "Men on rape." In Michael S. Kimmel and Michael A. Messner (eds.), *Men's Lives*. New York: Macmillan.

Beneria, Lourdes, and Martha Roldan. 1987. *The Crossroads of Class and Gender: Industrial Homework, Subcontracting and Household Dynamics in Mexico City*. Chicago: University of Chicago.

Benin, Mary Holland, and Joan Agostinelli. 1988. "Husbands' and wives' satisfaction with the division of labor." *Journal of Marriage and the Family* 50:349-61.

Benin, Mary Holland, and Verna M. Keith. 1995. "The social support of employed African American and Anglo mothers." *Journal of Family Issues* 16(3):275-97.

Benjamin, Jessica. 1988. *The Bonds of Love: Psychoanalysis, Feminism and the Problem of Domination*. New York: Pantheon.

Bennett, Linda L. M., and Stephen E. Bennett. 1993. "Changing views about gender equality in politics: Gradual change and lingering doubts." In Lois Lovelace Duke (ed.), *Women in Politics: Outsiders or Insiders?* Englewood Cliffs, NJ: Prentice Hall.

Benokraitis, Nijole V. 1996. *Marriages and Families*. Upper Saddle River, NJ: Prentice Hall.

Benokraitis, Nijole, and Joe Feagin. 1995. *Modern Sexism: Blatant, Subtle, and Covert Discrimination.* Englewood Cliffs, NJ: Prentice Hall.

Berg, Barbara J. 1987. "Good news for mothers who work." In Ollie Pocs and Robert H. Walsh (eds.), *Marriage and Family* (Annual Editions). Guilford, CT: Duskin.

Bergen, Raquel Kennedy. 1994. "Violence in the family: A focus on marital rape." In Daniel J. Curran and Claire M. Renzetti (eds.), *Contemporary Societies: Problems and Prospects.* Englewood Cliffs NJ: Prentice Hall.

Berger, Joseph. 1989. "All in the game." *New York Times Education Supplement* August 6:23-24.

Bergkvist, L., H.O. Adami, I. Persson, R. Hoover, and C. Schairer. 1989. "The risk of breast cancer after estrogen and estrogen-progestin replacement." *New England Journal of Medicine* 321:293-97.

Berk, Richard A., and Sarah F. Berk. 1979. *Labor and Leisure at Home: Content and Organization of the Household Day.* Beverly Hills, CA: Sage.

Berkin, Carol. 1989. "Clio in search of her daughters/Women in search of their past." In Mary Beth Norton (ed.), *Major Problems in American Women's History.* Lexington, MA: D.C. Heath.

Bernard, Jessie. 1972. *The Future of Marriage.* New York: World. 1975. "The future of motherhood." *Penguinews* (August). 1981. *The Female World.* New York: The Free Press. 1982. "The two marriages." In Jeffrey P. Rosenfeld (ed.), *Relationships: The Marriage and Family Reader.* Glenview, IL: Scott, Foresman. 1987. *The Female World from a Global Perspective.* Bloomington, IN: Indiana University. 1992. "The good-provider role: Its rise and fall." In Michael S. Kimmel and Michael A. Messner (eds.), *Men's Lives.* New York: Macmillan.

Best, Raphaela. 1983. *We've Got All the Scars: What Boys and Girls Learn in Elementary School.* Bloomington, IN: Indiana University.

Betz, N. 1993. "Career development." In Florence L. Denmark and Michele A. Paludi (eds.), *Handbook on the Psychology of Women: Future Directions for Research.* Westport, CT: Greenwood.

Beyani, Chaloka. 1995. "The needs of refugee women: A human-rights perspective." *Gender and Development* 3(2):1-7.

Billard, Mary. 1992. "Do women make better managers?" *Working Women* March:68-71,106-7.

Billingsley, Andrew. 1970. "Black families and white social science." *Journal of Social Issues* 26:132-33. 1992. *Climbing Jacob's Ladder: The Enduring Legacy of African-American Families.* New York: Simon & Schuster.

Billson, Janet. 1994. "Bringing new knowledge into the development program." American Sociological Association, *Footnotes* 22(Dec.):6-7.

Binder, Amy. 1993. "Constructing racial rhetoric: Media depictions of harm in heavy metal and rap music." *American Sociological Review* 58(6):753-67.

Binion, V.J. 1990. "Psychological androgyny: A Black female perspective." *Sex Roles* 22:487-507.

Bird, Caroline, 1975. "The case against marriage." In Kenneth C.W. Kammeyer (ed.) *Confronting the Issues: Sex Roles, Marriage and the Family.* Boston: Allyn & Bacon.

Bischoping, Katherine. 1993. "Gender differences in conversation topics." *Sex Roles.* 28(1-2):1-18.

Bishop, Nadean. 1984. "Abortion: The controversial choice." In Jo Freeman (ed.), *Women: A Feminist Perspective.* Palo Alto, CA: Mayfield.

Björkqvist, Kaj. 1994. "Sex differences in physical, verbal and indirect aggression: A review of recent research." *Sex Roles* 30:177-88.

Björkqvist, Kaj, and Pirkko Niemelä. 1992. "New trends in the study of female aggression." In Kaj Björkqvist and Pirkko Niemela (eds.), *Of Mice and Women: Aspects of Female Aggression.* San Diego: Academic Press.

Black, Jan Knippers. 1991. "Dowry abuse: No happily ever after for Indian brides." *Contemporary Review* 258:237-39.

Blackwell, James E. 1985. *The Black Community.* New York: Harper & Row.

Blackwood, Evelyn. 1984. "Sexuality and gender in certain Native American tribes: The case of cross-gender females." *Signs* 10(2):27-42.

Blair, Sampson Lee. 1993. "Employment, family, and perceptions of marital quality among husbands and wives." *Journal of Family Issues* 14(2):189-212.

Blake, Judith. 1989. *Family Size and Achievement.* Berkeley, CA: University of California Press.

Blankenship, Kim M. 1993. "Bringing gender and race in: U.S. Employment Discrimination Policy. *Gender & Society* 7(2):204-26.

Blau, Francine D., and Marianne A. Ferber. 1990. "Women's work, women's lives: A comparative economic perspective." Working Paper, National Bureau of Economic Research, Cambridge, MA. 1992. *The Economics of Women, Men and Work.* Englewood Cliffs, NJ: Prentice Hall.

Bliss, Sheperd. 1990. "Overcoming toxic masculinity." *Changes* (September-October): 36-39.

Block, Jeanne H. 1984. *Sex Role Identity and Ego Development.* San Francisco: Jossey-Bass.

Blood, Robert O., Jr., and Donald M. Wolfe. 1960. *Husbands and Wives: The Dynamics of Married Living.* New York: Free Press.

Bloom, David E., and Neil Bennett. 1986. "Childless couples." *American Demographics* 8 (August):23-25, 54-55.

Blotnick, Srully. 1986. "Dangerous times for middle managers." *SAVVY* (May):33-37.

Blum, L. 1987. "Possibilities and limits of the comparable worth movement." *Gender & Society* 1(4):380-99.

Blumstein, Philip and Pepper Schwartz. 1983. *American Couples.* New York: Pocket Books.

Bly, Robert. 1990. *Iron John.* Reading, MA: Addison-Wesley.

Bock, Gisela. 1996. "Challenging dichotomies in women's history." In Mary Beth Norton and Ruth M. Alexander (eds.), *Major Problems in American Women's History.* Lexington, MA: D.C. Heath.

Bolsa de Mujeres. 1995. "Nicaragua in Beijing." A publication of Emigdio Suarez Ediciones. Managua, Nicaragua.

Bolt, Christine. 1993. *The Women's Movements in the United States and Britain from the 1790s to the 1920s.* Amherst, MA: University of Massachusetts.

Boneparth, Ellen. 1986. "In the land of the patriarchs: Public policy on women in Israel." In Lynn B. Iglitzen and Ruth Ross (eds.), *Women in the World, 1975–1985, The Women's Decade.* Santa Barbara, CA: ABC-Clio.

Bonouvrie, Netty. 1995. "Female Sufi saints on the Indian subcontinent." In Ria Kloppenborg and Wouter J. Hanegraaff (eds.), *Female Stereotypes in Religious Traditions.* Leiden, Netherlands: Brill.

Boserup, Ester. 1970. *Women's Role in Economic Development.* London: Allen and Unwin.

Bosmajian, Haig. 1995. "The language of sexism." In Paula S. Rothenberg (ed.), *Race, Class and Gender in the United States: An Integrated Study.* New York: St. Martin's.

Boudreau, F.A. 1986. "Education." In F.A. Boudreau, R.S. Sennott, and M. Wilson (eds.), *Sex Roles and Social Patterns.* New York: Praeger.

Boustany, Nora. 1994. "Saudi women try new ways to overcome bars to advancement." *Washington Post* August 31:31.

Bowen, Gary Lee, and Dennis K. Orthner. 1983. "Sex role congruency and marital quality." *Journal of Marriage and the Family* 45:223-30.

Bozett, Frederick W. 1985. "Gay men as fathers." In Shirley M. H. Hanson and Frederick W. Bozett (eds.), *Dimensions of Fatherhood.* Beverly Hills, CA: Sage. 1987. *Gay and Lesbian Parents.* New York: Praeger.

Brannon, Robert. 1976. "The male sex role: Our culture's blueprint of manhood and what it's done for us lately." In D. David and Robert Brannon (eds.), *The 49% Majority.* Reading, MA: Addison-Wesley.

Bray, James H., and Sandra H. Berger. 1993. "Nonresidential parent-child relationships following divorce and remarriage." In Charlene E. Depner and James H. Bray (eds.) *Nonresidential Parenting: New Vistas in Family Living.* Newbury Park, CA: Sage.

Breakaway. 1995. "Mass wedding in India aims to evade dowry tradition." *St. Louis Post-Dispatch* April 9:12D.

Brehm, S.S. 1992. *Intimate Relationships.* New York McGraw-Hill.

Brems, Christine, and Robert S. Schlottmann. 1988. *Journal of Psychology* 122(1):5-14.

Bretl, D. J., and J. Cantor. 1988. "The portrayal of men and women in U.S. television commercials: A recent content analysis and trends over 15 years." *Sex Roles* 18:595-609.

Bridger, Susan. 1992. "Soviet rural women: Employment and family life." In Beatrice Farnsworth and Lynne Viola (eds.), *Russian Peasant Women.* New York: Oxford University.

Briere, J., and N. Malamuth. 1983. "Self-reported likelihood of sexually aggressive behavior: Attitudinal versus sexual explanations." *Journal of Research in Personality* 17:315-23.

Brinn, Janet, Kathey Kraemer, and Joel S. Warm. 1984. "Sex-role preferences in four age levels." *Sex Roles* 11:90–9.

Bronstein, P. 1988. "Father-child interaction." In P. Bronstein and C. P. Cowan (eds.), *Fatherhood Today: Men's Changing Role in the Family*. New York: John Wiley.

Brooke, James. 1994. "Women in Colombia move to job forefront: Aggressively pursuing new freedom." *New York Times* July 15:A6.

Brooks, Virginia R. 1982. "Sex differences in student dominance behavior in female and male professor's classrooms." *Sex Roles* 8:683–90.

Brooks-Gunn, Jeanne. 1986. "The relationship of maternal beliefs about sex typing to maternal and young children's behavior." *Sex Roles* 14:21–35.

Broverman, I., D. M. Broverman, F. E. Clarkson, P. S. Rosenkranz, and S. R. Vogel. 1970. "Sex-role stereotypes and clinical judgments of mental health." *Journal of Consulting and Clinical Psychology* 34:1-7.

Broverman, I., S. R. Vogel, D. M. Broverman, F. E. Clarkson, and P. S. Rosenkranz. 1972. "Sex-role stereotypes: A current appraisal." *Journal of Social Issues* 28:59-78.

Brown, Dorothy M. 1987. *Setting a Course: American Women in the 1920s*. Boston: Twayne.

Brown, Ian. 1994. *Man Medium Rare: Sex, Guns and Other Perversions of Masculinity*. New York: Dutton.

Brown, Jane D., and Kenneth Campbell. 1986. "Race and gender in music videos: The same beat but a different drummer." *Journal of Communication* 36:94-106.

Brown, Jane D., and Laurie Schulze. 1990. "The effects of race, gender and fandom on audience interpretations of Madonna's music videos." *Journal of Communication* 40(2):88-102.

Brown, M. E. 1990. *Television and Women's Culture*. Newbury Park, CA: Sage.

Brown, P., and R. Manela. 1978. "Changing family roles: Women and divorce." *Journal of Divorce* 1:315-28.

Browne, Angela. 1987. *When Battered Women Kill*. New York: Free Press.

Browning, Genia. 1985. "Soviet politics: Where are the women?" In Barbara Holland (ed.), *Soviet Sisterhood*. Bloomington, IN: Indiana University.

Bruess, Carol J., and Judy C. Pearson. 1996. "Gendered patterns in family communication." In Julia T. Wood (ed.), *Gendered Relationships*. Mountain View, CA: Mayfield.

Brumberg, J.J. 1988. *Fasting Girls*. Cambridge, MA: Harvard University.

Brush, Lisa D. 1990. "Violent acts and injurious outcomes in married couples: Methodological issues in the National Survey of Families and Households." *Gender & Society* 4(1):56-67.

Bryant, Jennings (Ed.). 1990. *Television and the American Family*. Hillsdale, NJ: Lawrence Erlbaum.

Brydon, Lynn, and Sylvia Chant. 1989. *Women in the Third World: Gender Issues in Rural and Urban Areas*. Hants, UK: Edward Elgar.

Buckley, Mary. 1992. "Glasnost and the woman question." In Linda Edmondson (ed.), *Women and Society in Russia and the Soviet Union*. Cambridge, UK: Cambridge University.

Buehler, Cheryl. 1995. "Divorce law in the United States." *Marriage and Family Review* 21(3-4):99-120.

Buhrke, R., and D. Fuqua. 1987. "Sex differences in same- and cross-sex supportive relationships." *Sex Roles* 17:339-52.

Bullers, Susan. 1994. "Women's roles and health: The mediating effect of perceived control." *Women and Health* 22(2):11-30.

Bumiller, Elisabeth. 1995a. "The jewel in the town: What Hillary Clinton can learn from a heroine of modern India." *Washington Post* March 26: 1995b. *The Secrets of Mariko*. New York: Times Books.

Bumpess, Larry L., James A. Sweet, and Andrew Cherlin. 1991. "The role of cohabitation in declining rates of marriage." *Journal of Marriage and the Family* 53:913-27.

Bunch, Charlotte. 1993. "Women's subordination worldwide: Global feminism." In Alison M. Jaggar and Paula S. Rothenberg (eds.), *Feminist Frameworks: Alternative Theoretical Accounts of the Relations between Women and Men*. New York: McGraw-Hill. 1995. "An equal voice." In United Nations High Commissioner for Refugees (ed.), *Human Rights: The New Consensus*. London: Regency Press.

Bunker, Barbara B., Josephine M. Zubek, Virginia J. Vanderslice, and Robert W. Rice. 1992. "Quality of life in dual-career families: Commuting versus single-residence couples." *Journal of Marriage and the Family* 54:399-407.

Bunster-Bunalto, Ximena. 1993. "Surviving beyond fear: Women and torture in Latin America." In Alison M. Jaggar and Paula S. Rothenberg (eds.), *Feminist Frameworks: Alternative Theoretical Accounts of the Relations between Women and Men.* New York: McGraw-Hill.

Bureau of National Affairs, 1989. *Working Women's Health Concerns: A Gender at Risk?* Washington, DC: Bureau of National Affairs.

Burge, Penny L., and Steven M. Culver. 1990. "Sexism, legislative power and vocational education." In Susan L. Gabriel and Isaiah Smithson (eds.), *Gender in the Classroom: Power and Pedagogy.* Urbana, IL: University of Illinois.

Burk, Martha, and Kirsten Shaw. 1995. "How the entertainment industry demeans, degrades and dehumanizes women." In Sheila Ruth, *Issues in Feminism: An Introduction to Women's Studies.* Mountain View, CA: Mayfield.

Burn, Shawn Meghan. 1996. *The Social Psychology of Gender.* New York: McGraw-Hill.

Burros, Marian. 1993. "Even women at top still have floors to do." *New York Times* May 31:1,11. 1995. "Hillary Clinton seeks to soften a harsh image." *New York Times* January 10:A1, A15.

Burstyn, Linda. 1996. "Asylum in America: Does fear of female mutilation qualify?" *Washington Post* March 17:C5.

Burton, N.W., C. Lewis, and N. Robertson. 1988. "Sex differences in SAT scores." *College Board Report* No. 88-9.

Busby, Linda J., and Greg Leichty. 1993. "Feminism and advertising in traditional and nontraditional women's magazines." *Journalism Quarterly* 70(3):247-64.

Buss, David M. 1985. "Human mate selection." *American Scientist, Journal of Sigma Xi* 73:47-51.

Buss, David M., and Michael Barnes. 1986. "Preferences in human mate selection." *Journal of Personality and Social Psychology* 50:559-70.

Bussey, K. and Albert Bandura. 1992. "Self-regulatory mechanisms governing gender development." *Child Development* 63:1236-50.

Byers, L. 1964. "Pupils' interests and the content of primary reading texts." *The Reading Teacher,* pp. 227–33.

Cafferata, G.L., and S.M. Meyers. 1990. "Pathways to psychotropic drugs: Understanding the basis of gender differences." *Medical Care* 28(4):285-300.

Cagatay, Nilufer, Caren Grown, and Aida Santiago. 1989. "The Nairobi Women's Conference: Toward a global feminism." In Laurel Richardson and Verta Taylor (eds.), *Feminist Frontiers II: Rethinking Sex, Gender and Society.* New York: Random House.

Calasanti, T.M. 1993. "Bringing in diversity: Toward an inclusive theory of retirement." *Journal of Aging Studies* 7:133-50.

Caldera, Y. M., A. C. Huston, and M. O'Brien. 1989. "Social interactions and play patterns of parents and toddlers with feminine, masculine and neutral toys." *Child Development* 60:70-76.

Caldwell, M. A., and L. Anne Peplau. 1984. "The balance of power in lesbian relationships." *Sex Roles* 10:587-99.

Callan, Victor J. 1987. "The personal and marital adjustment of mothers and of voluntarily and involuntarily childless wives." *Journal of Marriage and the Family* 49:847-56.

Campbell, A., S. Muncer, and E. Coyle. 1992. "Social representation of aggression as an explanation for gender differences: A preliminary study." *Aggressive Behavior* 18:95-108.

Campbell, Carole A. 1995. "Male gender roles and sexuality: Implications for women's AIDS risk and prevention." *Social Science and Medicine* 41 (2):197-210.

Campbell, D'Ann. 1984. *Women at War with America: Private Lives in a Patriotic Era.* Cambridge, MA: Harvard University.

Cancian, Francesca M. 1986. "The feminization of love." *Signs* 11:692-709. 1987. *Love in America: Gender and Self Development.* New York: Cambridge University.

Canetto, Silvia Sara. 1994. "Gender issues in the treatment of suicidal individuals." *Death Studies* 18(5):513-27.

Canetto, Silvia Sara and David Lester. 1995. "Gender and the primary prevention of suicide mortality." *Suicide and Life-Threatening Behavior* 25(1):58-69.

Cann, A., and S. Palmer. 1986. "Children's assumptions about the generalizability of sex-typed abilities." *Sex Roles* 15:551-57.

Cano, L., S. Solomon, and D. S. Holmes. 1984. "Fear of success: The influence of sex, sex-role identity, and components of masculinity." *Sex Roles* 10:341-46.

Cantor, Marjorie H., Mark Brennan, and Anthony Sainz. 1994. "The importance of ethnicity in the social support systems of older New Yorkers: A longitudinal perspective (1970-1990)." *Journal of Gerontological Social Work* 22(3-4):95-128.

Cantor, Muriel G. 1987. "Popular culture and the portrayal of women: Content and control." In Beth B. Hess and Myra Marx Ferree (eds.), *Analyzing Gender: A Handbook of Social Science Research.* Newbury Park, CA: Sage. 1993. Book review of *Women and Print Culture: The Construction of Femininity in the Early Periodical,* by Kathryn Shevelow. *Gender & Society* 7(2):301-2.

Caplan, Paula J., and Jeremy B. Caplan. 1994. *Thinking Critically about Research on Sex and Gender.* New York: HarperCollins College Publications.

Caplan, Paula J., G. MacPherson, and P. Tobin. 1985. "Do sex-related differences in spatial ability exist? A multilevel critique with new data." *American Psychologist* 40(7):786-99.

Carllson, Ingvar. 1995. "Why?" Foreward to *Men on Men: Eight Swedish Men's Personal Views on Equality, Masculinity and Parenthood.* Stockholm, Sweden: Equality Affairs Division of the Ministry of Health and Social Affairs.

Carlson, Allan. 1995. "The family: Where do we go from here?" *Society* 32(5):63-71.

Carlson, Douglas W. 1990. "Discovering their heritage: Women and the American past." In June Steffensen Hagen (ed.), *Gender Matters: Women's Studies in the Christian Community.* Grand Rapids, MI: Zondervan.

Carlson, Mary. 1994. "A Trojan horse of worldliness? Maidservants in the burgher household in Rotterdam at the end of the seventeenth century." In Els Kloek, Nicole Teeuwen, and Marijke Huisman (eds.), *Women of the Golden Age: An International Debate on Women in Seventeenth-Century Holland, England and Italy.* Amsterdam: Hilversum Verloren.

Carmody, Denise Lardner. 1987. "Judaism." In Arvind Sharma (ed.), *Women in World Religions.* Albany: State University of New York. 1989. *Women and World Religions.* Englewood Cliffs, NJ: Prentice Hall. 1992. *Mythological Women: Contemporary Reflections on Ancient Religious Stories.* New York: Crossroad.

Carovano, Kathryn. 1994. "More than mothers and whores: Redefining AIDS prevention needs of women." In Elizabeth Fee and Nancy Krieger (eds.), *Women, Health, Politics and Power: Essays on Sex/Gender, Medicine and Public Health.* Amityville. NY: Baywood.

Carr, Anne E. 1993. "The new vision of feminist theology." In Catherine Mowry LaCugna (ed.), *Freeing Theology: The Essentials of Theology in Feminist Perspective.* San Francisco: HarperSan Francisco.

Carr, Lois Green, and Lorena S. Walsh. 1989. "The advantageous position of women in New England." In Mary Beth Norton (ed.), *Major Problems in American Women's History.* Lexington, MA: D. C. Heath.

Carr, Peggy G., and Martha T. Mednick. 1988. "Sex role socialization and the development of achievement motivation in black preschool children. *Sex Roles* 18(34):169–80.

Carson, R., J. Butcher, and J. Coleman. 1988. *Abnormal Psychology and Modern Life.* Glenview, IL: Scott, Foresman.

Carter, D. Bruce, and Laura A. McCloskey. 1983. "Peers and the maintenance of sex-typed behavior: The development of children's conceptions of cross-gender behavior in their peers." *Social Cognition* 2(4):294–314.

Carter, R. 1991. "Children's TV, where boys are king." *New York Times* May 1:A1,C18.

Casas, J. Manuel, Burl R. Wagenheim, Roberto Banchero, and Juan Mendoza-Romero. 1994. "Hispanic masculinity: Myth or psychological schema meriting clinical consideration." *Hispanic Journal of Behavioral Sciences* 16(3):315-31.

Casey, M.B., E. Pezaris, and R.L. Nuttall. 1992. "Spatial ability as a predictor of math achievement: The importance of sex and handedness patterns." *Neuropsycholgia* 30:35-45.

Castro, Ginette. 1990. *American Feminism: A Contemporary History.* New York: New York University.

Catanzarite, Lisa, and Vilma Ortiz. 1995. "Racial/ethnic differences in the impact of work and family on women's poverty." *Research in Politics and Society* 5:217-37.

Cattin, Philippe, and Subhash C. Jain. 1979. "Content analysis of children's commercials." In N. Beckwith, M. Houston, R. Mittelstaedt, K. B. Monroe, and S. Ward (eds.), *Educators' Conference Proceedings.* Chicago: American Marketing Association.

Cavanaugh, John C. 1993. *Adult Development and Aging.* Pacific Grove, CA: Brooks/Cole.

Cazenave, Noel A. 1981. "Black men in America: The quest for 'Manhood.'" In Harriet Pipes McAdoo (ed.), *Black Families*. Beverly Hills, CA: Sage. 1983. "Black male-black female relationships: The perceptions of 155 middle class black men." *Family Relations* 32:341-50.

CBS. 1993. "The year of the woman." A *60 Minutes* Television Report. January 24.

Chafe, William. 1974. "Feminism in the 1970's." *Dissent* 21 (Fall):508–17. 1977. *Women and Equality: Changing Patterns in American Culture*. New York: Oxford University.

Chafetz, Janet Saltzman. 1988. *Feminist Sociology: An Overview of Contemporary Theories*. Itasca, IL: F.E. Peacock.

Chang, P., and A. Deinard. 1982. "Single father caretakers: Demographic characteristics and adjustment process." *American Journal of Orthopsychiatry* 52:236-43.

Chang, Yvonne. 1990. "Groom school polishes bachelors to shine in prospective brides' eyes." *Japan Times* June 28:16.

Chant, Sylvia. 1987. "Family structure and female labor in Queretaro, Mexico." In Janet Momsen and Janet Townhend (eds.), *Geography of Gender in the Third World*. London: Hutchinson.

Charles, Maria. 1992. "Cross-national variation in occupational sex segregation." *American Sociological Review* 57(4)483-502.

Charlton, Sue Ellen M. 1984. *Women in Third World Development*. Boulder, CO: Westview. 1993. "Debating the impact of development on women." In Caroline B. Brettell and Carolyn F. Sargent (eds.), *Gender in Cross-Cultural Perspective*. Englewood Cliffs, NJ: Prentice Hall.

Chavez, Lydia. 1987. "Women's movement, its ideals accepted, faces subtler issues." *New York Times* (July 17):A10.

Chesler, Ellen. 1995. "Imperfectly rational, somewhat economic." *Women's Review of Books* (Feburary):15-16.

Chesler, Phyllis. 1972. *Women and Madness*. Garden City, NY: Anchor/ Doubleday.

Chesser, Barbara. 1991. "Building family strengths in dual-career marriages." In Leonard Cargan (ed.), *Marriages and Families: Coping with Change*. Englewood Cliffs, NJ: Prentice Hall.

Chilly Collective (Eds.). 1995. *Breaking Anonymity: The Chilly Climate for Women Faculty*. Waterloo, Ontario: Wilfrid Laurier University.

Chilman, Catherine Street. 1995. "Hispanic families in the United States: Research perspectives." In Mark Robert Rank and Edward T. Kain (eds.)., *Diversity and Change in Families: Patterns, Prospects, and Policies*. Englewood Cliffs, NJ: Prentice Hall.

Chino, A., and D. Funabiki. 1984. "A cross-validation of sex differences in the expression of depression." *Sex Roles* 11:175-87.

Chipman, S. F., L. R. Brush, and D. M. Wilson (Eds.). 1985. *Women and Mathematics: Balancing the Equation*. Hillsdale, NJ: Lawrence Erlbaum.

Chipman, S. F., and V. G. Thomas. 1985. "Women's participation in mathematics: Outlining the problem." In S. F. Chipman, L. R. Brush, and D. M. Wilson (eds.), *Women and Mathematics: Balancing the Equation*. Hillsdale, NJ: Lawrence Erlbaum.

Chira, Susan. 1992. "New realities fight old images of mother." *New York Times* October 4:1, 32.

Chiriboga, D. A., and M. Thurnher. 1980. "Marital lifestyles and adjustments to separation." *Journal of Divorce* 3:379-90.

Chodorow, Nancy. 1978. *The Reproduction of Mothering: Psychoanalysis and the Sociology of Gender*. Berkeley: University of California. 1993. "Family structure and feminine personality." In Stevi Jackson et al. (eds.), *Women's Studies Essential Readings*. New York: New York University.

Chodorow, Nancy, Deidre Englis, Arlie Hochschild, Karen Paige, Ann Swidler, and Norma Winkler. 1984. "Feminism 1984: Taking stock of an uncertain future." *MS* January:102.

Chollar, Susan. 1995. "Happy families: Who says they all have to be alike?" In Kathleen R. Gilbert (ed.), *Marriage and the Family 95/96* (Annual Editions). Guilford, CT: Dushkin/Brown & Benchmark.

Chow, Esther Ngan-Ling. 1993. "The feminist movement: Where are all the Asian American women?" In Alison M. Jaggar and Paula S. Rothenberg (eds.), *Feminist Frameworks: Alternative Theoretical Accounts of the Relations between Women and Men*. New York: McGraw-Hill.

Christ, Carol. 1987. *Laughter of Aphrodite: Reflections on a Journey to the Goddess*. San Francisco: Harper & Row.

Christen, Yves. 1991. *Sex Differences: Modern Biology and the Unisex Fallacy*. Nicholas Davidson (tr.). New Brunswick, NJ: Transaction.

Christensen, Kathleen E. 1987. "Women and home-based work." *Social Policy* 15:54-57.

Ciabattari, Jane. 1996a. "Where women are still outsiders." *Parade Magazine* March 24:24. 1996b. "Oscar picks in the year of the backlash." *Parade Magazine* March 17:26.

Ciernia, James R. 1985. "Myths about male midlife crises." *Psychological Reports* 56:1003-7.

Clark, Cal, and Janet Clark. 1993. "The gender gap 1988: Compassion, pacifism and indirect feminism." In Lois Lovelace Duke (ed.), *Women in Politics: Outsiders or Insiders.* Englewood Cliffs, NJ: Prentice Hall.

Clark, Roger, Rachel Lennon, and Leana Morris. 1993. "Of Caldecotts and Kings: Gendered images in recent American children's books by black and non-black illustrators." *Gender & Society* 7(2):227-45.

Clements, Barbara Evans. 1994. *Daughters of Revolution: A History of Women in the USSR.* Arlington Hts., IL: Harlan Davidson.

Cleveland, William. 1994. *A History of the Modern Middle East.* Boulder, CO: Westview.

Clive, Alan. 1989. "Women's conservative choices during and after the war." In Mary Beth Norton (ed.), *Major Problems in American Women's History.* Lexington, MA: D. C. Heath.

Coates, Jannifer. 1988. "Gossip revisited: Language in all-female groups." In Jennifer Coates and Deborah Cameron (eds.), *Women in Their Speech Communities: New Perspectives on Language and Sex.* Harlow, Essex, UK: Longman. 1993. *Women, Men and Language: A Sociolinguistic Account of Gender Differences in Language.* London: Longman.

Cockerham, William C. 1995. *Medical Sociology.* Englewood Cliffs, NJ: Prentice Hall.

Cofer, Judith Ortiz. 1995. "The myth of the Latin woman: I just met a girl named Maria." In Paula S. Rothenberg (ed.), *Race, Class, and Gender in the United States: An Integrated Study.* New York: St. Martin's.

Cohen, Theodore F. 1993. "What do fathers provide? Reconsidering the economic and nurturant dimensions of men as parents." In Jane C. Hood (ed.), *Men, Work, and Family.* Newbury Park, CA: Sage.

Cohn, D'Vera, and Barbara Vobejda. 1992. "For women, uneven strides in the workplace: Census data reflect decade of white-collar progress, blue-collar resistance." *Washington Post* December 21:A1,A12.

Coker, Dana Rosenbert. 1984. "The relationships among gender concepts and cognitive maturity in preschool children." *Sex Roles* 10:19-31.

Cole, Pamela M., Christie Woolger, Thomas G. Power, and K. Danielle Smith. 1992. "Parenting difficulties among adult survivors of father-daughter incest." *Child Abuse and Neglect* 16:239-49.

Coleman, James S. 1961. *The Adolescent Society: The Social Life of the Teenager and Its Impact on Education.* Glencoe, IL: Free Press.

Coleman, Marilyn, and Lawrence H. Ganong. 1985. "Love and sex role stereotypes: Do macho men and feminine women make better lovers?" *Journal of Personality and Social Psychology* 49:170-76.

Colison, Michele N-K. 1993. "Many students press colleges to substitute 'first-year student' for the term 'freshman.'" In Virginia Cyrus (ed.), *Experiencing Race, Class, and Gender in the United States.* Mountain View, CA: Mayfield.

Collins, Patricia Hill. 1989. "A comparison of two works on black family life." *Signs* 14:875-84. 1993. "The meaning of motherhood in black culture and black mother/daughter relationships." In Jodi Wetzel, Maro Linn Espenlaub, Monys A. Hagen, Annette Bennington McElhiney, and Carmen Braun Williams (eds.), *Women's Studies: Thinking Women.* Dubuque, IA: Kendall/Hunt. 1995. "Symposium: On West and Fenstermaker's 'doing difference.'" *Gender & Society* 9(4):491-513. 1996. "Toward a new vision: Race, class and gender as categories of analysis and connection." In Karen E. Rosenblum and Toni-Michelle Travis (eds.), *The Meaning of Difference: American Constructions of Race, Sex and Gender, Social Class and Sexual Orientation.* New York: McGraw-Hill.

Collins, Randall. 1975. *Conflict Sociology.* New York: Academic Press. 1979. *The Credential Society: An Historical Sociology of Education and Stratification.* New York: Academic Press.

Coltrane, Scott, and Masako Ishii-Kuntz. 1992. "Men's housework: A life course perspective." *Journal of Marriage and the Family* 54:43-47.

Committee on Small Business. 1988. *New Economic Realities: The Rise of Women Entrepreneurs.* Washington, DC: U.S. Government Printing Office.

Common Cause. No date. *Questions and Answers to the Proposed ERA.* (Pamphlet).

Comstock, George, and Haejung Paik. 1991. *Television and the American Child*. San Diego, CA: Academic Press.

Condry, J. C. 1989. *The Psychology of Television*. Hillsdale, NJ: Lawrence Erlbaum.

Condry, J. C., P. Bence, and C. Scheibe. 1988. "Nonprogram content of children's television." *Journal of Broadcasting and Electronic Media* 32(3):255-70.

Conley, Shanti (Ed.). 1994. *Closing the Gender Gap: Educating Girls*. Washington, DC: Population Action International.

Connections. 1995a. "Women at work around the world: Why Americans should care." 1(6):1. Published by Alliance for a Global Community. 1995b. "Girls = gains." 1(8):1. Published by Alliance for a Global Community.

Connell, Bob. 1992. "Masculinity, violence and war." In Michael S. Kimmel and Michael A. Messner (eds.), *Men's Lives*. New York: Macmillan.

Connelly, Maureen, and Patricia Rhoton. 1988. "Women in direct sales: A comparison of Mary Kay and Amway sales workers." In A. Statham, E. Miller, and H. Mauksch (eds.), *The Worth of Women's Work: A Qualitative Synthesis*. Albany: State University of New York.

Connor, Jane, Fiona Byrne, Jodi Mindell, Donna Cohen, and Elizabeth Nixon. 1986. "Use of the titles Ms., Miss, or Mrs.: Does it make a difference?" *Sex Roles* 14(9/10):545-49.

Conrad, Peter, and Joseph W. Schneider. 1990. "Professionalization, monopoly and the structure of medical practice." In Peter Conrad and Rochelle Kern (eds.), *The Sociology of Health and Illness: Critical Perspectives*. New York: St. Martin's.

Cook, Alice. 1980. "Collective bargaining as a strategy for achieving equal opportunity and equal pay: Sweden and West Germany." In Ronnie S. Ratner (ed.), *Equal Employment Policy for Women*. Philadelphia: Temple University.

Cook, Ellen Piel. 1985. *Psychological Androgyny*. New York: Pergamon.

Coontz, Stephanie. 1992. *The Way We Never Were: American Families and the Nostalgia Trap*. New York: Basic Books.

Cooper, P. 1989. "Children's literature: The extent of sexism." In C. Lont and S. Friedly (eds.), *Beyond Boundaries: Sex and Gender Diversity in Education*. Fairfax, VA: George Mason University.

Copeland, Rebecca L. 1992. "Motherhood as institution." *Japan Quarterly* 39:101-10.

Corbett, Colleen. 1995. "Bond babes: Leaner, meaner, dumber." *U.S. Women*. December.

Corliss, Richard. 1991. "A screen gem turns director." *Time* 138(October 14):68-72.

Corsaro, W. A., and D. Eder. 1990. "Children's peer cultures." In W. R. Scott (ed.), *Annual Review of Sociology*. Palo Alto, CA: Annual Reviews.

Cose, Ellis. 1995. *A Man's World: How Real is Male Privilege and How High Is Its Price?* New York: HarperCollins.

Costello, Cynthia, and Anne J. Stone (Eds.). 1994. *The American Woman 1994-95: Where We Stand*. New York: W.W. Norton.

Courtney, Alice E., and Sarah Wernick Lockeretz. 1971. "A woman's place: An analysis of the roles portrayed by women in magazine advertisements." *Journal of Marketing Research* 8:92.

Courtney, Alice E., and Thomas W. Whipple. 1983. *Sex Stereotyping in Advertising*. Lexington, MA: Lexington Books.

Coverman, Shelley W. 1989. "Women's work is never done: The division of household labor." In Jo Freeman (ed.), *Women: A Feminist Perspective*. Mountain View, CA: Mayfield.

Crane, M., and Hazel Rose Markus. 1982. "Gender identity: The benefits of a self-schema approach." *Journal of Personality and Social Psychology* 43:1195-97.

Crawford, Alan. 1980. *Thunder on the Right*. New York: Pantheon.

Crawford, Mary. 1995. *Talking Difference: On Gender and Language*. London: Sage.

Crawford, Mary, and M. MacLeod. 1990. "Gender in the college classroom: An assessment of the 'chilly climate' for women." *Sex Roles* 23:101-22.

Crean, Susan. 1993. "Anna Karenina, Scarlett O'Hara, and Gail Bezaire: Child custody and family law reform." In Anne Minas (ed.), *Gender Basics: Feminist Perspectives on Women and Men*. Belmont, CA: Wadsworth.

Cresswell, J.L., C. Gifford, and D. Huffman. 1988. "Implications of right/left brain research for mathematics educators." *School Science and Mathematics* 88(2):119-31.

Crites, Laura L. 1987. "Wife abuse: The judicial record." In Laura L. Crites and Winifred L. Hepperle (eds.), *Women, the Courts and Equality.* Beverly Hills, CA: Sage.

Croll, Elisabeth. 1995. *Changing Identities of Chinese Women: Rhetoric, Experience and Self-perception in Twentieth-century China.* Hong Kong: Hong Kong University.

Cromie, Stanley. 1987. "Motivations of aspiring male and female entrepreneurs." *Journal of Occupational Behavior* 8:251-61.

Crosby, Faye J. 1982. *Relative Depression and Working Women.* Oxford, UK: Oxford University. 1987. *Spouse, Parent, Worker.* New Haven, CT: Yale University.

Cross, Susan E., and Hazel Rose Markus. 1993. "Gender in thought, belief and action: A cognitive approach." In Anne E. Beall and Robert J. Sternberg (eds.), *The Psychology of Gender.* New York: Guilford.

Crossette, Barbara. 1995a. "U.N. documents inequities for women as world forum nears." *New York Times* August 18. 1995b. "Does the U.N. offer fair employment? The women say no." *New York Times International* April 10:A1,A6.

Crouter, Ann C., Beth A. Manke, and Susan M. McHale. 1995. "The family context of gender intensification in early adolescence." *Child Development* 66(2):317-29.

Cruz, Yolanda. 1996. "A twofer's lament." In Harold A. Widdison (ed.), *Social Problems 96/97* (Annual Editions). Guilford, CT: Dushkin/Brown & Benchmark.

Crystal, David. 1985. *A Dictionary of Linguistics and Phonetics.* Oxford, UK: Basil Blackwell.

Cubitt, Tessa. 1988. *Latin American Society.* London: Longman.

Culley, James D., and Rex Bennett. 1976. "Selling women, selling blacks." *Journal of Communication* 26:160-74.

Culp, R. E., A. S. Cook, and P. C. Housley. 1983. "A comparison of observed and reported adult-infant interactions: Effects of perceived sex." *Sex Roles* 9:475-79.

Dahrendorf, Ralf. 1959. *Class and Class Conflict in Industrial Society.* Stanford, CA: Stanford University.

Daly, Frederica Y. 1994. "Perspectives of Native American women on race and gender." In Ethel Tobach and Betty Rosoff (eds.), *Challenging Racism and Sexism: Alternatives to Genetic Explanations.* New York: The Feminist Press.

Daly, Kathleen. 1993. "Class-race-gender: Sloganeering in search of meaning." *Social Justice* 20(51-52):56-71.

Daly, Mary. 1975. *The Church and the Second Sex.* New York: Harper & Row. 1990. *Gyn/Ecology: The Metaethics of Radical Feminism.* Boston: Beacon. 1991. "I thank thee, Lord, that thou has not created me a woman." In Evelyn Ashton-Jones and Gary Olson (eds.), *The Gender Reader.* Boston, MA: Allyn & Bacon.

Dames, Joan. 1996. "In deed: Young volunteers give new meanings to meetings." *St. Louis Post-Dispatch* February 18:1S.

Dan, Alice J. (Ed.). 1994. *Reframing Women's Health: Multidisciplinary Research and Practice.* Thousand Oaks, CA: Sage.

Daniel, Robert L. 1987. *American Women in the Twentieth Century: The Festival of Life.* San Diego: Harcourt Brace Jovanovich.

Daniels, Cynthia. 1993. "There's no place like home." In Alison M. Jaggar and Paula S. Rothenberg (eds.), *Feminist Frameworks: Alternative Theoretical Accounts of the Relations between Women and Men.* New York: McGraw-Hill.

Darling, Lynn. 1994. "Age, beauty and truth." *New York Times* January 23 (Section 9): 1,5.

Darnton, Nina. 1985. "Women and stress on job and at home." *New York Times* August 8:C1.

Dauber, S. 1986. "Sex differences on the SAT-M, SAT-V, TWSE and ACT among college-bound high school students." Paper presented at the American Education Research Association, Washington, DC.

Daugherty, Cynthia, and Marty Lees. 1988. "Feminist psychodynamic therapies." In Mary Ann Dutton-Douglas and Leonore E. A. Walker (eds.), *Feminist Psychotherapies: Integration of Therapeutic and Feminist Systems.* Norwood, NJ: Ablex.

Davidman, Lynn. 1995. "Gender play." *Qualitative Sociology* 18(1):105-7.

Davidson, E. S., A. Yasuna, and A. Tower. 1979. "The effects of television cartoons on sex-role stereotyping in young girls." *Child Development* 50:597-600.

Davidson, J. Kenneth, Sr., Carol Anderson Darling, and Michael R. Penland. 1994. "Multiple sex partners among college women and men: Sexual behaviors and sexual satisfaction revisited." *Sociological Spectrum* 14(4):313-26.

Davidson, Sara. 1988. "Having it all." In J. Gipson Wells (ed.), *Current Issues in Marriage and the Family.* New York: Macmillan.

Davidson, T. Kenneth, and Nelwyn B. Moore. 1994. "Masturbation and premarital sexual intercourse among college women: Making choice for sexual fulfillment." *Journal of Sex and Marital Therapy* 20(3):178-99.

Davies, Bronwyn. 1989. *Frogs and Snails and Feminist Tales: Preschool Children and Gender.* Sydney: Allen & Unwin.

Davis, D. M. 1990. "Portrayals of women in prime-time network television: Some demographic characteristics." *Sex Roles* 23(5-6):325-32.

Davis, Elizabeth Gould. 1971. *The First Sex.* New York: Penguin.

Davis, Keith E. 1985. "Near and dear: Friendship and love compared." *Psychology Today* 19(February):22-30.

Davis-Friedmann, D. 1985. "Old age security and the one-child campaign." In E. Croll, D. David, and P. Kane (eds.), *China's One-Child Policy.* London: Macmillan.

De Baar, Mirjam. 1994. "Transgressing gender codes: Anna Maria van Schurman and Antoinette Bourignon as examples." In Els Kloek, Nicole Teeuwen, and Marijke Huisman (eds.), *Women of the Golden Age: An International Debate on Women in Holland, England and Italy.* Amsterdam: Hilversum Verloren.

De Lange, Janice. 1995. "Gender and communication in social work education: A cross-cultural perspective." *Journal of Social Work Education* 31(1):75-81.

De St. Croix, Geoffrey. 1993. "The class struggle in the ancient Greek world." In Stevi Jackson et al. (eds.), *Women's Studies Essential Readings.* New York: New York University.

Deaux, Kay, and Brenda Major. 1987. "Putting gender into context: An interactive model of gender-related behavior." *Psychological Review* 94(3):369-89.

DeBeauvoir, Simone. 1953. *The Second Sex.* H. M. Parshey (tr.). New York: Knoft.

DeBuono, Barbara A., Stephen H. Zinner, Maxim Daamen, and William M. McCormack. 1990. "Sexual behavior of college women in 1975, 1986, and 1989." *New England Journal of Medicine* 322:821-25.

Deckard, Barbara Sinclair. 1983. *The Women's Movement: Political, Socioeconomic and Psychological Issues.* New York: Harper & Row.

Deen, Edith. 1978. *Wisdom from Women in the Bible.* San Francisco: Harper & Row.

Del Carmen, Rebecca, and Gabrielle N. Virgo. 1993. "Marital disruption and nonresidential parenting: A multicultural perspective." In Charlene E. Depner and James H. Bray (eds.), *Nonresidential Parenting: New Vistas in Family Living.* Newbury Park, CA: Sage.

Delaney, Janice, Mary Jane Lupton, and Emily Toth. 1988. *The Curse: A Cultural History of Menstruation.* Urbana, IL: University of Illinois.

Deleon, B. 1993. "Sex role identity among college students: A cross-cultural analysis. *Hispanic Journal of Behavioral Sciences* 15:476-89.

DeMaris, Alfred, and K. Vaninadha Rao. 1992. "Premarital cohabitation and subsequent marital stability in the United States: A reassessment." *Journal of Marriage and the Family* 54:178-90.

Demos, John Putnam. 1996. "The poor and powerless witch." In Mary Beth Norton and Ruth M. Alexander (eds.), *Major Problems in American Women's History.* Lexington, MA: D.C. Heath.

Denzin, Norman. 1992. *Symbolic Interactionism and Cultural Studies: The Politics of Interpretation.* Cambridge, MA: Blackwell. 1993. "Sexuality and gender: An interactionist/poststructural reading." In Paula England (ed.), *Theory on Gender/Feminism on Theory.* New York: Aldine De Gruyter.

Depner, Charlene E. 1993. "Parental role reversal: Mothers as nonresidential parents." In Charlene E. Depner and James H. Bray (eds.), *Nonresidential Parenting: New Vistas in Family Living.* Newbury Park, CA: Sage.

Depner, Charlene E., and James H. Bray (Eds.). 1993. *Nonresidential Parenting: New Vistas in Family Living,* Newbury Park, CA: Sage.

Desrochers, Stephan. 1995. "What types of men are most attractive and most repulsive to women?" *Sex Roles* 28:1-19.

Deutsch, Francine M., Jennifer L. Lozy, and Susan Saxon. 1993. "Taking credit: Couples' reports of contributions to child care." *Journal of Family Issues* 14(3):421-37.

Devens, Carol. 1996. "Resistance to Christianity by the native women of New France." In Mary Beth Norton and Ruth M. Alexander (eds.), *Major Problems in American Women's History*. Lexington, MA: D.C. Heath.

Diamond, Milton. 1982. "Sexual identity, monozygotic twins reared in discordant sex roles and a BBC follow-up." *Archives of Sexual Behavior* 11:181-86.

Dickson, G.L. 1990. "The metalanguage of menopause research." *Image: The Journal of Nursing Scholarship* 22(3):169–73.

Diedrick, P. 1991. "Gender differences in adjustment to divorce." In S.S. Volgy (ed.), *Women and Divorce, Men and Divorce*. New York: Hayworth.

Diehl, David. 1990. "Theology and feminism." In June S. Hagen (ed.), *Gender Matters: Women's Studies for the Christian Community*. Grand Rapids, MI: Zondervan.

Dietz, Tracy L. 1995. "Patterns of intergenerational assistance within the Mexican American family: Is the family taking care of the older generation's needs?" *Journal of Family Issues* 16(3):344-56.

Dill, Bonnie Thornton. 1994. "Fictive kin, paper sons, and compadrazgo: Women of color and the struggle for family survival." In Maxine Baca Zinn and Bonnie Thornton Dill (eds.), *Women of Color in U.S. Society*. Philadelphia: Temple University.

Dino, Geri A., Mark A. Barnett, and Jeffrey A. Howard. 1984. "Children's expectations of sex differences in parent's responses to sons and daughters encountering interpersonal problems." *Sex Roles* 11:709-15.

Dixon-Mueller, Ruth. 1985. *Women's Work in Third World Agriculture*. Geneva: International Labour Organization.

Dodge, Norton D., and Murray Feshbach. 1992. "The role of women in Soviet agriculture." In Beatrice Farnsworth and Lynnes Viola (eds.), *Russian Peasant Women*. New York: Oxford University.

Dodson, B. 1987. *Sex for One: The Joy of Self-Loving*. New York: Crown.

Dolgin, Kim G., Leslie Meyer, and Janet Schwartz. 1991. "Effects of gender, target's gender, topic and self-esteem to best and middling friends." *Sex Roles* 25(5-6):311-29.

Donat, Patricia L.N., and John D'Emilio. 1992. "A feminist redefinition of rape and sexual assault: Historical foundations and change." *Journal of Social Issues* 48:9-22.

Donnerstein, Edward, and Daniel Linz, 1992. "Mass media, sexual violence and male viewers: Current theory and research." In Michael S. Kimmel and Michael A. Messner (eds.), *Men's Lives*. New York: Macmillan.

Donovan, Josephine. 1985. *Feminist Theory: The Intellectual Traditions of American Feminism*. New York: Frederick Ungar.

Dorr, Dave. 1992. "Breaking barriers: Women athletic directors prove leadership isn't a gender issue." *St. Louis Post-Dispatch* (November 8):1,14.

Douglas, Emily Taft. 1966. *Remember the Ladies: The Story of Great Women Who Helped Shape America*. New York: G. P. Putnam.

Douglas, Susan J. 1995. "Missing voices: Women and the U.S. news media." In Sheila Ruth, *Issues in Feminism: An Introduction to Women's Studies*. Mountain View, CA: Mayfield.

Dovidio, J.F., J.A. Piliavin, S.L. Gaertner, D.A. Schroeder, and R.D. Clark. 1991. "The arousal: Cost-reward model and the process of intervention: A review of the evidence." In M.S. Clark (ed.), *Prosocial Behavior*. Newbury Park, CA: Sage.

Downs, A. C., and S. K. Harrison. 1985. "Embarrassing age spots or just plain ugly? Physical attractiveness stereotyping as an instrument of sexism on American television commercials." *Sex Roles* 13(1-2):9-19.

Downs, Chris A. 1981. "Sex-role stereotyping on prime-time television." *Journal of Genetic Psychology* 138:253-58.

Downs, Chris A., and Darryl C. Gowan. 1980. "Sex differences in reinforcement and punishment on prime time television." *Sex Roles* 6:683-94.

Doyal, Lesley. 1995. *What Makes Women Sick: Gender and the Political Economy of Health*. Basingstoke, UK: Macmillan.

Doyle, James A. 1995. *The Male Experience*. Dubuque, IA: Brown & Benchmark.

Doyle, James A., and Michele A. Paludi. 1995. *Sex and Gender: The Human Experience.* Dubuque, IA: Brown & Benchmark.

Dressel, Paula L. 1994. "Gender, race and class: Beyond the feminization of poverty in later life." In Eleanor Palo Stoller and Rose Campbell Gibson (eds.), *Worlds of Difference: Inequality in the Aging Experience.* Thousand Oaks, CA: Pine Forge.

Driscoll, Mary, Marge Cohen, Patricia Kelly, Deane Taylor, Mildred Williamson, and Gigi Nicks. 1994. "Women and HIV." In Alice J. Dan (ed.), *Reframing Women's Health: Multidisciplinary Research and Practice.* Thousand Oaks, CA: Sage.

Drummond, Hugh. 1979. "Diagnosing marriage: *Mother Jones* 4(July):14-21.

D'Souza, Neila, and Ramini Natarajan. 1986. "Women in India: The reality." In Lynn B. Iglitzin and Ruth Ross (eds.), *Women in the World, 1975-1985: The Women's Decade.* Santa Barbara, CA: ABC-Clio.

Dublin, Thomas. 1996. "Women workers in the Lowell mills." In Mary Beth Norton and Ruth M. Alexander (eds.), *Major Problems in American Women's History.* Lexington, MA: D.C. Heath.

Duck, Steve, and P. H. Wright. 1993. "Re-examining gender differences in same-gender friendships." *Sex Roles* 32(5-6):375-91.

Dugger, Karen. 1991. "Social location and gender-role attitudes: A comparison of black and white women." In Judith Lorber and S.A. Farrell (eds.), *The Social Construction of Gender Gap.* Newbury Park, CA: Sage.

Duker, Jacob M., and Lewis R. Tucker. 1977. "'Women libbers' versus independent women: A study of preferences for women's roles in advertisements." *Journal of Marketing Research* 14:469–75.

Duley, Margot I. 1986. "Women in India." In Margot I. Duley and Mary I. Edwards (eds.), *The Cross-Cultural Study of Women: A Comprehensive Guide.* New York: Feminist Press.

Dunn, Angela. 1986. "Why women are the superior sex." An interview with Ashley Montagu. *St. Louis Post-Dispatch* January 12:C1,C13.

Duxbury, Linda, and Christopher Higgins. 1994. "Interference between work and family: A status report on dual-career and dual-earner mothers and fathers." *Employee Assistance Quarterly* 9(3-4):55-80.

Dweck, C. S., W. Davidson, S. Nelson, and B. Enna. 1978. "Sex differences in learned helplessness. II. The contingencies of evaluative feedback in the classroom. III. An experimental analysis." *Developmental Psychology* 14:268-76.

Dziech, Billie Wright, and Linda Weiner. 1993. "The lecherous professor: A portrait of the artist." In Laurel Richardson and Verta Taylor (eds.), *Feminist Frontiers III.* New York: McGraw-Hill.

Eagly, A.H., R.D. Ashmore, M.G. Makhijani, and L.C. Longo. 1991. "What is beautiful is good, but....: A meta-analytic review of research on the physical attractiveness stereotype." *Psychological Bulletin* 110:109-28.

Eagly, A. H., and V. J. Steffen. 1986. "Gender and aggressive behavior: A meta-analytic review of the social psychological literature." *Psychological Bulletin* 100:309-30.

Eakins, Barbara Westbrook, and R. Gene Eakins. 1978. *Sex Differences in Human Communication.* Boston: Houghton Mifflin.

Eccles, Jacquelynne S., and P. Blumenfeld. 1985. "Classroom experiences and student gender: Are there differences and do they matter?" In L.C. Wilkinson and C.B. Marrett (eds.), *Gender Influences in Classroom Interaction.* New York: Academic Press.

Eccles, Jacquelynne S., Janis E. Jacobs, and Rena D. Harold. 1990. "Gender role stereotypes, expectancy effects and parents' socialization of gender differences." *Journal of Social Issues* 46(2):183-201.

Eckert, Penelope, and Sally McConnell-Ginet. 1994. "Think practically and look locally: Language and gender in community-based practice." In Camille Roman, Suzanne Juhasz, and Cristanne Miller (eds.), *The Women and Language Debate: A Sourcebook.* New Brunswick, NJ: Rutgers University.

Eder, Donna, and David A. Kinney. 1995. "The effect of middle school extracurricular activities on adolescent's popularity and peer status." *Youth and Society* 26(3):298-324.

Edsall, Thomas B. 1995. "Gender gap: It's here, huge, permanent." *St. Louis Post-Dispatch* August 16:5B.

Ehlers, Tracy Bachrach. 1993. "Debunking marianismo: Economic vulnerability and survival struggles among Guatemalan wives." In Mari Womack and Judith Marti (eds.) *The Other Fifty Percent: Multicultural Perspectives on Gender Relations.* Prospect Heights, IL: Waveland.

Ehrenberg, Margaret. 1993. "The role of women in human evolution." In Caroline B. Brettell and Carolyn F. Sargent (eds.), *Gender in Cross-Cultural Perspective.* Englewood Cliffs, NJ: Prentice Hall.

Ehrenreich, Barbara. 1983. *The Hearts of Men: American Dreams and the Flight from Commitment.* Garden City, NY: Doubleday (Anchor). 1992. "What do women have to celebrate?" *Time* (November 16):61-62.

Ehrlich, Susan, and Ruth King. 1993. "Gender-based language reform and the social construction of meaning." In Stevi Jackson et al. (eds.), *Women's Studies Essential Readings.* New York: New York University.

Eisenhart, Margaret. 1996. "Contemporary college women's career plans." In Paula Dubeck and Kathryn Borman (eds.), *Women and Work: A Handbook.* New York: Garland.

Eisenstock, B. 1984. "Sex role differences in children's identification with counterstereotypical televised portrayals." *Sex Roles* 10:417-30.

Eisler, Riane. 1988. *The Chalice and the Blade: Our History, Our Future.* San Francisco: HarperSanFrancisco. 1995. *Sacred Pleasure: Sex, Myth, and the Politics of the Body.* San Francisco: Harper SanFrancisco.

Eisler, Riane, and David Loye. 1990. *The Partnership Way.* New York: HarperSanFrancisco.

Eisler, Riane, David Loye, and Kari Norgaard. 1995. *Women, Men and the Quality of Life.* Pacific Grove, CA: Center for Partnership Studies.

Ekman, Paul, Wallace V. Friesen, and S. Ancoli. 1980. "Facial signs of emotional experience." *Journal of Personality and Social Psychology* 39:1125–34.

Elgart, L. D. 1983. "Women on Fortune 500 boards." *California Management Review* 24:121–27.

Elizondo, Felisa. 1994. "Violence against women: Strategies of resistance and sources of healing in Christianity." In Elisabeth Schüssler-Fiorenza and Mary Shawn Copeland (eds.), *Violence Against Women.* London: Stichting Concilium/SCM Press.

Elliot, D.S., and B.J. Morse. 1989. "Delinquency and drug use as risk factors in teenage sexual activity." *Youth and Society* 21:32-60.

Elliot, Patricia. 1991. *From Mastery to Analysis: Theories of Gender in Psychoanalytic Feminism.* Ithaca, NY: Cornell University.

Elliott, Brian, 1994. "Biography, family history and the analysis of social change." In Michael Drake (ed.), *Time, Family and Community: Perspectives on Family and Community History.* Oxford, UK: Open University.

el Saadawi, Nawal. 1980. *The Hidden Faces of Eve: Women in the Arab World.* London: Zed. 1986. "The political changes facing Arab women at the end of the twentieth century." In Nahid Toubia (ed.), *Women of the Arab World.* London: Zed.

Emihovich, Catherine A., Eugene L. Gaier, and Noreen C. Cronin. 1984. "Sex-role expectations changes by fathers for their sons." *Sex Roles* 11:861-67.

Engel, John W. 1995. "Marriage in the People's Republic of China: Analysis of a new law." In Mark Robert Rank and Edward L. Kain (eds.), *Diversity and Change in Families: Patterns, Prospects and Policies.* Englewood Cliffs, NJ: Prentice Hall.

Engels, Friedrich. 1942 (original 1884). *The Origin of the Family, Private Property, and the State.* New York: International.

Engelsman, Joan Chamberlain. 1994. *The Feminine Dimension of the Divine.* Wilmette, IL: Chiron.

England, Paula, and Irene Browne. 1992. "Trends in women's economic status." *Sociological Perspectives* 35(1):17-51.

Epstein, Cynthia Fuchs. 1991. "It's all in the mind: Personality and social structure." In Laura Kramer (ed.), *The Sociology of Gender: A Text-Reader.* New York: St. Martin's.

Erben, Rosemarie. 1995. "Special AIDS threat to women." *World Health.* Special Issue on Women and Health (September):26-28.

Erickson, B., E. A. Lind, B. C. Johnson, and W. M. O'Barr. 1977. *Speech Style and Impression Formation in a Court Setting: The Effects of "Power" and "Powerless" Speech.* Law and Language Project Report No. 13. Durham, NC: Duke University.

Erickson, Rebecca J., and Ginna M. Babcock. 1995. "Men and family law: From patriarchy to partnership." *Marriage and Family Review* 21(3-4):31-54.

Erlanger, Howard S. 1987. "A widening pattern of abuse as exemplified in the Steinberg case." *New York Times* (November 8):1.

Eron, Leonard D. 1992. "Gender differences in violence: Biology and/or socialization?" In Kaj Björkqvist and Pirkko Niemelä (eds.), *Of Mice and Women: Aspects of Female Aggression.* San Diego: Academic Press.

Eron, Leonard D., L. R. Brice, P. Fischer, and R. Mermelstein. 1983. "Age trends in the development of aggression, sex typing, and related television habits." *Developmental Psychology* 19(1):71-77.

Erwin, Phil. 1993. *Friendship and Peer Relations in Children.* Chichester, UK: John Wiley.

Escobar, Gabriel. 1994. "Peruvians move into congress, cabinet, courts." *Washington Post* November 13:A31.

Eshleman, J. Ross. 1994. *The Family: An Introduction.* Boston: Allyn & Bacon.

Esterberg, Kristin, Phyllis Moen, and Donna Demster McClain. 1994. "Transition to divorce: A life course approach to women's marital duration and dissolution." *Sociological Quarterly* 35(2):289-307.

Esu-Williams, Eka. 1995. "AIDS in the 1990s: Individual and collective responsibility." In Beth E. Schneider and Nancy E. Stoller (eds.), *Women Resisting AIDS: Feminist Strategies of Empowerment.* Philadephia: Temple University.

Etaugh, Claire. 1980. "Effects of nonmaterial care on children." *American Psychologist* 35:309-19.

Etaugh, Claire, and T. Duits. 1990. "Development of gender discrimination: Role of stereotypic and counterstereotypic gender cues." *Sex Roles* 23(5-6):215-22.

Etaugh, Claire, and Marsha B. Liss. 1992. "Home, school, and playroom: Training grounds for adult gender roles." *Sex Roles* 26:129-47.

Ettorre, E. 1992. *Women and Substance Abuse.* New Brunswick, NJ: Rutgers University.

Evans, Debra. 1993. *Beauty and the Best.* Colorado Springs, CO: Focus on the Family Publishing.

Evans, Sara. 1991. "The first American women." In Linda K. Kerber and Jane Sherron De Hart (eds.), *Women's America: Refocusing the Past.* New York: Oxford University.

Fagot, Beverly I. 1984. "The child's expectancies of differences in adult male and female interactions." *Sex Roles* 11:593-600. 1985. "Beyond the reinforcement principle: Another step toward understanding sex role development." *Developmental Psychology* 21:1097-104. 1994. "Peer relations and the development of competence in boys and girls." In Campbell Leaper (ed.), *Childhood Gender Segregation: Causes and Consequences.* San Francisco: Jossey-Bass.

Fagot, Beverly I., and Mary D. Leinbach. 1989. "The young child's gender schema: Environmental input, internal organization." *Child Development* 60:663-72. 1995. "Gender knowledge in egalitarian and traditional families." *Sex Roles* 32(7-8):513-26.

Faludi, Susan. 1991. *Backlash: The Undeclared War Against American Women.* New York: Crown. 1996. "Backlash." In Karen E. Rosenblum and Toni-Michelle Travis (eds.), *The Meaning of Difference: American Constructions of Race, Sex and Gender, Social Class and Sexual Orientation.* New York: McGraw-Hill.

Faragher, John Mack. 1996. "The separate worlds of men and women on the Overland Trail." In Mary Beth Norton and Ruth M. Alexander (eds.), *Major Problems in American Women's History.* Lexington, MA: D.C. Heath.

Faragher, Johnny, and Christine Stansell. 1980. "Women and their families on the Overland Trail, 1842-1867." In Esther Katz and Anita Rapone (eds.), *Women's Experience in America: An Historical Anthology.* New Brunswick, NJ: Transaction.

Farber, Stephan. 1974. "The vanishing heroine." *Hudson Review* 27:570-76.

Farrell, Amy Erdman. 1994. "A social experiment in publishing: *MS Magazine,* 1972-1989." *Human Relations* 47(6):707-30.

Fassinger, Polly A. 1993. "Meanings of housework for single fathers and mothers." In Jane C. Hood (ed.), *Men, Work, and Family.* Newbury Park, CA: Sage.

Fasteau, Marc F. 1974. *The Male Machine.* New York: McGraw Hill.

Fausto-Sterling, Anne. 1985. *Myths of Gender.* New York: Basic Books. 1993. "Hormonal hurricanes: Menstruation, menopause and female behavior." In Laurel Richardson and Verta Taylor (eds.), *Feminist Frontiers III: Rethinking Sex, Gender and Society.* New York: McGraw Hill. 1996.

"The five sexes: Why male and female are not enough." In Karen E. Rosenblum and Toni-Michelle C. Travis (eds.), *The Meaning of Difference: American Constructions of Sex and Gender. Social Class and Sexual Orientation*. New York: McGraw-Hill.

Federal Bureau of Investigation. 1993. *Uniform Crime Reports of the United States* 1992. Washington, DC: U.S. Government Printing Office.

Feinberg, Renee. 1986. *The Equal Rights Amendment: An Annotated Bibliography of the Issues, 1976-1985*. Westport, CT: Greenwood.

Feingold, A. 1992. "Good-looking people are not what we think." *Psychological Bulletin* 10(3):202-214.

Feinman, S. 1981. "Why is cross-sex behavior approved more for girls than for boys? A status characteristic approach." *Sex Roles* 7:289-99.

Feldman, S. Shirley, and Sharon Churrin Nash. 1984. "The transition from expectancy to parenthood: Impact of the firstborn child on men and women." *Sex Roles* 11:61-69.

Feminist Teacher. 1991. "Women increase share of doctorates." 6(1):9.

Fengler, Alfred P. 1974. "Romantic love in courtship: Divergent paths of male and female students." *Journal of Comparative Family Studies* 5:134-39.

Fennema, Elizabeth, and Julia Sherman. 1977. "Sex related differences in mathematics achievement: Spatial visualization and affective factors." *American Educational Research Journal* 14:51-71.

Ferber, Reginald. 1995. "Is speaker's gender discernible in transcribed speech?" *Sex Roles* 32(3-4):209-23.

Ferguson, M. 1983. *Forever Feminine: Women's Magazines and the Cult of Femininity*. Exeter, NH: Heinemann Educational Books.

Fermlee, Diana H. 1995. "Causes and consequences of women's employment discontinuity, 1967-1973." *Work and Occupations* 22(2):167-87.

Fermon, Nicole. 1994. "Domesticating women, civilizing men: Rousseau's political program." *Sociological Quarterly* 35(3):298-324.

Fidell, L., D. Hoffman, and P. Keith-Speigal. 1979. "Some social implications of social choice technology." *Psychology of Women Quarterly* 4:32-42.

Figart, Deborah M. 1995. Book review of Elaine Sorensen's *Comparable Worth: Is It a Worthy Policy? Gender & Society* 9(6):779-81.

Figert, Anne E. 1995. "The three faces of PMS: The professional, gendered and scientific astructuring of a psychiatric disorder." *Social Problems* 42(1):56-73.

Filteau, Jerry. 1992. "Bishops reject proposed pastoral on women." *St. Louis Review* 51(November 20): 1, 10.

Fine, Gary Alan. 1992. "The dirty play of little boys." In Michael S. Kimmel and Michael A. Messner (eds.), *Men's Lives*. New York: Macmillan.

Fine, Marlene G. 1981. "Soap opera conversations: The talk that binds." *Journal of Communication* 31(Spring):97-107.

Fineman, Howard. 1992. "The torch passes." *Newsweek*, Special Election Issue (November-December):5-10.

Fischer, Irmgard. 1994. "'Go and suffer oppression' said God's messenger to Hagar." In Elisabeth Schüssler Fiorenza and M. Shawn Copeland (eds.), *Violence Against Women*. London: Stichtin Concillium/SCM Press.

Fisher, B., and J. Berdie. 1978. "Adolescent abuse and neglect: Issues of incidence, intervention and service delivery." *Child Abuse and Neglect* 8:173-92.

Fisher, Jo. 1993. *Out of the Shadows: Women, Resistance and Politics in South America*. London: Latin American Bureau.

Fishman, Waldo K. 1982. *The New Right: Unraveling the Opposition to Women's Equality*. New York: Praeger.

Fiske, A.P., N. Haslam, and S.T. Fiske. 1991. "Confusing one person with another: What errors reveal about the elementary forms of social relations." *Journal of Personality and Social Psychology* 60:656-74.

Flannagan, Dorothy, Lynne Baker-Ward, and Loranel Graham. 1995. "Talk about preschool: Patterns of topic discussion and elaboration related to gender and ethnicity." *Sex Roles* 32(1-2):1-15.

Flannagan, Dorothy, and Susan D. Hardee. 1994. "Talk about preschoolers' interpersonal relationships: Patterns related to culture, SES, and gender of the child." *Merrill-Palmer Quarterly* 40(4):523-37.

Fleming, Anne Taylor. 1986. "The American wife." *New York Times Magazine* (October 26):29-39.

Folberg, J. 1991. (ed.), *Joint Custody and Shared Parenting*. New York: Guilford.

Folbre, Nancy. 1994. *Who Pays for the Kids? Gender and the Structure of Constraint*. London: Routledge.

Forden, Carie. 1981. "The influence of sex-role expectations on the perception of touch." *Sex Roles* 7:889-94.

Fortnightly Review. 1995. "Chronicle of women's major events in new China." Special Issue to the Fourth World Conference on Women: 4-8.

Fowers, Blaine J. 1991. "His and her marriage: A multivariate study of gender and marital satisfaction." *Sex Roles* 24(3-4):209-21.

Fox, Greer Litton, and Priscilla White Blanton. 1995. "Non-custodial fathers following divorce." *Marriage and Family Review* 20(1-2):257-82.

Fox, Lynn H. 1981. *The Problem of Women and Mathematics*. New York: Ford Foundation.

Fox, M., M. Gibbs, and D. Auerbach. 1985. "Age and gender dimensions of friendship." *Psychology of Women Quarterly* 9:489-502.

Fox, Mary F. 1995. "Women and higher education: Gender differences in the status of students and scholars." In Jo Freeman (ed.), *Women: A Feminist Perspective*. Mountain View, CA: Mayfield.

Fox-Genovese, Elizabeth. 1995. "For women only." *Washington Post* March 26.

Fraczek, Adam. 1992. "Patterns of aggressive-hostile behavior orientation among adolescent boys and girls." In Kaj Björkqvist and Pirkko Niemelä (eds.), *Of Mice and Women: Aspects of Female Aggression*. San Diego: Academic Press.

Franklin, Clyde W. 1994. "Men's studies, the men's movement, and the study of black masculinities: Further demystification of masculinities in America." In Richard G. Majors and Jacob U. Gordon (eds.), *The American Black Male: His Present Status and His Future*. Chicago: Nelson-Hall.

Franzwa, Helen H. 1974a. "Pronatalism in women's magazine fiction." In Ellen Peck and Judith Senderowitz (eds.), *Pronatalism: The Myth of Mom and Apple Pie*. New York: T. Y. Crowell. 1974b. "Working women in fact and fiction." *Journal of Communication* 24(2):104-09. 1975. "Female roles in women's magazine fiction, 1940-1970." In Rhoda Unger and Florence Denmark (eds.), *Women: Dependent or Independent Variable*. New York: Psychological Dimensions.

Freedman, Rita. 1995. "Myth America grows up." In Sheila Ruth, *Issues in Feminism: An Introduction to Women's Studies*. Mountain View, CA: Mayfield.

Freeman, Jo. 1995a. "From suffrage to women's liberation: Feminism in twentieth-century America." In Jo Freeman (ed.), *Women: A Feminist Perspective*. Mountain View, CA: Mayfield. 1995b. "The revolution for women in law and public policy." In Jo Freeman (ed.), *Women: A Feminist Perspective*.

Freeman, Jody. 1993. "The disciplinary function of rape's representation: Lessons from the Kennedy-Smith trial and Tyson trials." *Law and Social Inquiry* 18(3):517-46.

Freeman, Rebecca, and Bonnie McElhinny. 1996. "Language and gender." In Sandra Lee McKay and Nancy H. Hornberger (eds.), *Sociolinguistics and Language Teaching*. Cambridge, UK: Cambridge University.

Freivogel, William H. 1993. "Acceptable behavior: Sexual harrassment message swift and clear—Don't do it." *St. Louis Post-Dispatch* November 14:1B, 7B.

French, Brandon. 1978. *On the Verge of Revolt: Women in American Film of the Fifties*. New York: Frederick Ungar.

Freud, Sigmund. 1962. *Three Contributions to the Theory of Sex*. A. A. Brill (trans.). New York: E. P. Dutton.

Freudiger, Patricia. 1983. "Life satisfaction among three categories of married women." *Journal of Marriage and the Family* 45:213-19.

Frey, Sylvia R., and Marion J. Morton. 1986. *New World, New Roles: A Documentary History of Women in Pre-Industrial America*. Westport, CT: Greenwood.

Friedan, Betty. 1963. *The Feminine Mystique*. New York: W. W. Norton. 1981. *The Second Stage*. New York: Summit Books. 1983. "Twenty years after the Feminine Mystique." *New York Times Mag-*

azine (February 27):35-36,42,54-57. 1994. "Afterward: Feminism as a step in human evolution: A paradigm shift in values for women, men, and society." *American Behavioral Scientist* 37(8):1138-141.

Friedman, Ariella, and Ayala Pines. 1991. "Sex differences in gender-related childhood memories." *Sex Roles* 25(1-2):25-32.

Friedman, L. 1989. "Mathematics and the gender gap: A meta-analysis of recent studies on sex differences in mathematical tasks." *Review of Educational Research* 59:185–213.

Frodi, Ann, Jacqueline Macaulay, and Pauline Ropert Thome. 1977. "Are women always less aggressive than men? A review of the experimental literature." *Psychological Bulletin* 84(4):634-60.

Fryxell, Gerald E., and Linda D. Lerner. 1989. "Contrasting corporate profiles: Women and minority representation in top management positions." *Journal of Business Ethics* 8:341-52.

Fuchs, Victor R. 1988. *Women's Quest for Economic Equality.* Cambridge, MA: Harvard University.

Fuehrmann, Dina Morello. 1992. "German bishop is symbol of hope." *The Lutheran* (June):36.

Fugita, B. N., R. G. Harper, and A. N. Weins. 1980. "Encoding-decoding of nonverbal emotional messages: Sex differences in spontaneous and enacted expressions." *Journal of Nonverbal Behavior* 4:131-45.

Fujita, Mariko. 1989. "It's all mother's fault: Childcare and the socialization of working mothers in Japan." *Journal of Japanese Studies* 15(1):67-91.

Fujiwara, Mariko. 1994. "Roads without signposts: Women must make most of their opportunities." *Japan Update* 35(August):8-9.

Furnham, Adrian, and Nadine Bitar. 1993. "The stereotyped portrayal of men and women in British television advertisements." *Sex Roles* 29(3-4):297-310.

Gabin, Nancy. 1989. "Women's protests after the war." In Mary Beth Norton (ed.), *Major Problems in American Women's History.* Lexington, MA: D. C. Heath.

Gadberry, James H., and Richard A. Dodder. 1993. "Educational homogamy in interracial marriage: An update." *Journal of Social Behavior and Personality.* 8(6) (special issue) 155-63.

Gallagher, Bernard J.III. 1987b. *The Sociology of Mental Illness.* Englewood Cliffs, NJ: Prentice Hall.

Gallagher, Winifred. 1987a. "Rx for mental menopause: Estrogen." *American Health* (November):49-51.

Gallant, Mary J., and Jay E. Cross. 1993. "Wayward Puritans in the ivory tower: Collective aspects of gender discrimination in academia." *Sociological Quarterly* 34(2):237-56.

Gallup, G., and J. Castelli. 1989. *The People's Religion.* New York: Macmillan.

Gallup, George. 1980. "Most women want marriage and babies." *St. Louis Post-Dispatch* June 15:3F.

Ganley, Anne L. 1988. "Feminist therapy with male clients." In Mary Ann Dutton-Douglas and Leonore E. A. Walker (eds)., *Feminist Psychotherapies: Integration of Therapeutic and Feminist Systems.* Norwood, NJ: Ablex.

Garcia, A.M. 1991. "The development of Chicana feminist discourse." In Judith Lorber and S.A. Farrell (eds.), *The Social Construction of Gender Gap.* Newbury Park, CA: Sage.

Gardner, Marilyn. 1995. "Of super dads, and absent ones." In Kathleen R. Gilbert (ed.), *Marriage and the Family 95/96* (Annual Editions). Guilford, CT: Dushkin/Brown & Benchmark.

Garfinkel, Perry. 1985. *In a Man's World: Father, Son, Brother, Friend and Other Roles Men Play.* New York: New American Library. 1991. "Mentors we never meet: Reflections of men in the media's eye." In Laura Kramer (ed.), *The Sociology of Gender: A Text-Reader.* New York: St. Martin's.

Gargan, Edward A. 1991. "A back seat to nobody in fight against sexism." *New York Times International* December 30:A2.

Garnets, Linda D. 1996. "Life as a lesbian: What does gender have to do with it?" In Joan C. Chrisler, Carla Golden, and Patricia D. Rozce (eds.), *Lectures on the Psychology of Women.* New York: McGraw-Hill.

Garnets, Linda D., and D. Kimmel. 1993. *Psychological Perspectives on Lesbian and Gay Male Experiences.* New York: Columbia University.

Garon, Sheldon. 1993. "Women's groups and the Japanese state: Contending approaches to political integration, 1890-1945." *Journal of Japanese Studies* 19(1):5-41.

Gavora, Jessica. 1995. "Winners and losers in gender equity game." *St. Louis Post-Dispatch,* December 10:3B.

Geer, Claudia G., and Stephanie A. Shields. 1996. "Women and emotion: Stereotypes and the double bind." In Joan C. Chrisler, Carla Golden, and Patricia D. Rozee (eds.), *Lectures on the Psychology of Women*. New York: McGraw-Hill.

Geerkin, Michael, and Walter Gove. 1983. *At Home and at Work: The Family's Allocation of Labor.* Beverly Hills, CA: Sage.

Gehry, Frank, B.J. Hateley, and Susan Rose. 1994. "The politics of empowerment: A paradigm shift in thought and action for feminists." *American Behavioral Scientist* 37(8):1122-1137.

Geis, Florence L. 1993. "Self-fulfilling prophecies: A social psychological view of gender." In Anne E. Beall and Robert J. Sternberg (eds.), *The Psychology of Gender*. New York: Guilford.

Geis, Florence L., Virginia Brown, J. Jennings, and N. Porter. 1984. "TV commercials as achievement scripts for women." *Sex Roles* 10(7-8):513-25.

Gelles, Richard J. 1995. *Contemporary Families: A Sociological View*. Thousand Oaks, CA: Sage.

Gelles, Richard J., and Claire P. Cornell. 1985. *Intimate Violence in Families*. Beverly Hills, CA: Sage.

Gelles, Richard J., and Murray A. Straus. 1979. "Determinants of violence in the family: Toward a theoretical integration." In Wesley R. Burr, Reuben Hill, F. Ivan Nye, and Ira L. Reiss (eds.), *Contemporary Theories about the Family*, Vol. 1. New York: Free Press. 1988. *Intimate Violence*. New York: Simon & Schuster. 1995. "Profiling violent families." In Mark Robert Rank and Edward L. Kain (eds.), *Diversity and Change in Families: Patterns, Prospects, and Policies*. Englewood Cliffs, NJ: Prentice Hall.

Gender Equality in Norway. 1994. *The National Report to the Fourth UN Conference on women in Beijing, 1995*. Oslo: Royal Ministry of Foreign Affairs.

Genevie, Lou, and Eva Margolies. 1987. *The Motherhood Report: How Women Feel about Being Mothers*. New York: Macmillan.

Geraghty, Christine. 1993. "Women and soap opera." In Stevi Jackson et al. (eds.), *Women's Studies Essential Readings*. New York: New York University.

Gerber, G. L. 1984. "Attribution of feminine and masculine traits to opposite-sex dyads." *Psychological Reports* 55(3):907-18.

Gerbner, George. 1993a. "Violence on television." *Challenging Media Images of Women* 5(2):1,4,7-9. 1993b. *Women and Minorities on Television: A Study of Casting and Fate*. A Report to the Screen Actors Guild and the American Federation of Radio and Television Artists. June. Philadelphia: University of Pennsylvania.

Gerson, Kathleen. 1993. *No Man's Land: Men's Changing Commitments to Family and Work*. New York: Basic Books.

Gerson, Mary Joan. 1984. "Feminism and the wish for a child." *Sex Roles* 11(5–6): 389–97.

Gerstel, Naomi, and Harriet Engel Gross. 1984. *Commuter Marriage: A Study of Work and Family*. New York: Guilford. 1995. "Gender and families in the United States: The reality of economic dependence." In Jo Freeman (ed.), *Women: A Feminist Perspective*. Mountain View, CA: Mayfield.

Gerzon, Mark. 1982. *A Choice of Heroes: The Changing Faces of American Manhood*. Boston: Houghton Mifflin.

Gherardi, Silvia. 1994. "The gender we think, the gender we do in our everyday organizational lives." *Human Relations* 47(6):591-610.

Giddings, Paula. 1993. "Strong women and strutting men: The Moynihan Report." In Virginia Cyrus (ed.), *Experiencing Race, Class, and Gender in the United States*. Mountain View, CA: Mayfield.

Giele, Janet Zollinger. 1988. "Changing sex roles and changing families." In J. Gipson Wells (ed.), *Current Issues in Marriage and the Family*. New York: Macmillan.

Gilbert, Neil. 1994. "Gender equality and Social Security." *Society* 31(4):27-33.

Gilder, George. 1974. "In defense of monogamy." *Commentary* 58 (November):31-36.

Gillespie, Cynthia K. 1989. *Justifiable Homicide*. Columbus, OH: Ohio State University.

Gilligan, Carol. 1982a. *In a Different Voice*. Cambridge, MA: Harvard University. 1982b. "Adult development and women's development: Arrangements for a marriage." In J. Giele (ed.), *Women in the Middle Years*. New York: Wiley.

Gilroy, F. D., and R. Steinbacher. 1983. "Pre-selection of child's sex: Technological utilization and feminism." *Psychological Reports* 53:671-76.

Gimbutas, Marija. 1989. *The Language of the Goddess: Unearthing the Hidden Symbols of Western Civilization.* San Francisco: Harper & Row. 1991. *The Civilization of the Goddess: The World of Old Europe.* San Francisco: HarperSanFrancisco.

Gimenez, Martha E. 1994. "The feminization of poverty: Myth or reality." In Elizabeth Fee and Nancy Krieger (eds.), *Women's Health, Politics, and Power: Essays on Sex/Gender, Medicine, and Public Health.* Amityville, NY: Baywood.

Giudice, Lucia. 1991. *Women's Health Research: Prescription for Change.* Annual Report, Society for the Advancement of Women's Health Research. Washington, DC: Bass and Howes.

Giuffre, Patti A., and Christine L. Williams. 1994. "Boundary lines: Labeling sexual harassment in restaurants." *Gender & Society* 8(3):378–401.

Glass, Becky L. 1988. "A rational choice model of wives' employment decisions." *Sociological Spectrum* 8:35-48. 1992. "Housewives and employed wives: Demographic and attitudinal change, 1972–1986." *Journal of Marriage and the Family* 54:559–69.

Glass, Jennifer, and Tetsushi Fujimoto. 1994. "Housework, paid work and depression among husbands and wives." *Journal of Health and Social Behavior* 35(2):179–191.

Glenn, Evelyn N., and Roslyn L. Feldberg. 1995. "Clerical work: The female occupation." In Jo Freeman (ed.), *Women: A Feminist Perspective.* Mountain View, CA: Mayfield.

Glenn, Norval D., and Charles N. Weaver. 1988. "The changing relationship of marital status to reported happiness." *Journal of Marriage and the Family* 50(May):317–24.

Glick, Paul C., and Arthur J. Norton. 1977. "Marrying, divorcing and living together in the U.S. today." *Population Bulletin.* Washington, DC: Population Reference Bureau.

Glickman, Rose L. 1992. "Peasant women and their work." In Beatrice Farnsworth and Lynnes Viola (eds.), *Russian Peasant Women.* New York: Oxford University.

Goffman, Erving. 1959. *The Presentation of Self in Everyday Life.* Garden City, NY: Doubleday (Anchor). 1963. *Behavior in Public Places.* New York: Free Press. 1971. *Relations in Public.* New York: Basic Books. 1979. *Gender Advertisements.* New York: Harper & Row.

Goldman, Ari L. 1990a. "Ecumenist in charge: Joan B. Campbell." *New York Times* (November 18):32. 1990b. "Black women's bumpy path to church leadership." *New York Times* July 29:1,28.

Goldman, Emma. 1910/1995. "Marriage and love." In Sheila Ruth, *Issues in Feminism: An Introduction to Women's Studies.* Mountain View, CA: Mayfield.

Goldman, N., C. Westoff, and C. Hammerslough. 1984. "Demography of the marriage market in the United States." *Population Index* 50(Spring):5-25.

Goodchilds, J. D., G. L. Zellman, P. B. Johnson, and R. Giarrusso. 1988. "Adolescents and their perceptions of sexual interactions." In A. W. Burgess (ed.), *Rape and Sexual Assault,* Vol. 2. New York: Garland.

Goode, Erich. 1989. *Drugs in American Society.* New York: Alfred A. Knopf.

Goode, William J. 1993. *World Changes in Divorce Patterns.* New Haven, CT: Yale University.

Goodman, Ellen. 1994. "Women's tales of torture..." *Washington Post* March 19.

Goodrich, Norma Lorre. 1991. *Priestesses.* New York: HarperCollins.

Goodwin, Beverly J. 1996. "The impact of popular culture on images of African American women." In Joan C. Chrisler, Carla Golden, and Patricia D. Rozee (eds.), *Lectures on the Psychology of Women.* New York: McGraw-Hill.

Goodwin, Robin, and Tatiana Emelyanova. 1995. "The perestroika of the family: Gender and occupational differences in family values in modern day Russia." *Sex Roles* 32(5-6):337-51.

Gordon, Jeff. 1992. "Gender agenda: Women's basketball flourishes, but needs marketing to keep growing." *St. Louis Post-Dispatch* (July 12):1, 11.

Gottfried, Barbara. 1994. "The reproduction of gendering: Imaging kids in ads for adults." In Harry Eiss (ed.), *Images of the Child.* Bowling Green, OH: Bowling Green State University Popular Press.

Gould, Stephen J. 1981. *The Mismeasure of Man.* New York: W.W. Norton.

Gove, Walter R. 1972. "Relationships between sex roles, marital status and mental illness." *Social Forces* 51(1):34-44.

Gove, Walter R., and Jeanette F. Tudor. 1973. "Adult sex roles and mental illness." *American Journal of Sociology* 78(4).

Grambs, Jean Dresden. 1991. "Mom, apple pie and the American dream." In Leonard Cargan (ed.), *Marriages and Families: Coping with Change*. Englewood Cliffs, NJ: Prentice Hall.

Grant, Linda, and Layne A. Simpson. 1994. "Marriage and relationship satisfaction of physicians." *Sociological Focus* 27(4):327-42.

Gray, Alastair. 1993. *World Health and Disease*. Ballmoor, UK: Open University Press.

Gray, Francine du Plessix. 1990a. *Soviet Women: Walking the Tightrope*. New York: Doubleday. 1991. "Sex roles in the Soviet Union." In Carol J. Verburg (ed.), *Ourselves Among Others: Cross-Cultural Readings for Writers*. Boston: Bedford.

Gray, J. Glenn. 1992. "The enduring appeals of battle." In Larry May and Robert Strikwerda (eds.), *Rethinking Masculinity: Philosophical Explorations in Light of Feminism*. Lanham, MD: Rowman & Littlefield.

Gray, Susan H. 1990b. "Exposure to pornography and aggression toward women: The case of the angry male." In William Feigelman (ed.), *Readings on Social Problems: Probing the Extent, Causes, and Remedies of America's Social Problems*. Fort Worth, TX: Holt, Rinehart and Winston.

Greard, Octavia. 1893. *L'Education des Femmes par les Femmes*. Paris: Librairie Hachette.

Green, Karen. 1995. *The Woman of Reason: Feminism, Humanism and Political Thought*. New York: Continuum.

Greenberg, Bradley S. 1980. *Life on Television: Content Analysis of U.S. TV Drama*. Norwood, NJ: Ablex.

Greenberg, Bradley S., Robert Abelman, and Kimberly Neuendorf. 1981. "Sex on the soap operas: Afternoon delight." *Journal of Communication* 31(Spring):83–89.

Greenberg, Bradley S., B. Burgoon, M. Burgoon, and F. Korzenny. 1983. *Mexican Americans and the Mass Media*. Norwood, NJ: Ablex.

Greenwald, Maurine W. 1980. *Women, War, and Work: The Impact of World War I on Women Workers in the United States*. Westport, CT: Greenwood.

Greer, W. 1986. "Women gain a majority in jobs." *New York Times* March 19: C1.

Gregg, G. 1985. "Women entrepreneurs: The second generation." *Across The Board* 22:10–18.

Gregory, Ann. 1990. "Are women different and why are women thought to be different? Theoretical and methodological perspectives." *Journal of Business Ethics* 9:257-66.

Greif, Geoffrey L. 1985a. "Children and housework in the single father family." *Family Relations* 34:353-57. 1985b. *Single Fathers*. Lexington, MA: D. C. Heath.

Greif, Geoffrey L., Alfred Demaris, and Jane C. Hood. 1993. "Balancing work and single fatherhood." In Jane C. Hood (ed.), *Men, Work, and Family*. Newbury Park, CA: Sage.

Grella, Christine E. 1990. "Irreconcilable differences: Women defining class after divorce and downward mobility." *Gender & Society* 4(1):41-55.

Grob, Gerald N., and George Athan Billias (Eds). 1992. *Interpretations of American History, Patterns and Perspectives, Volume II: Since 1877*. New York: The Free Press.

Groce, Stephen B., and Margaret Cooper. 1990. "Just me and the boys? Women in local-level rock and roll." *Gender & Society* 2(4):220-28.

Gross, Alan F. 1992. "The male role and heterosexual behavior." In Michael S. Kimmel and Michael A. Messner (eds.), *Men's Lives*. New York: Macmillan.

Gross, Harriet Engel. 1980. "Dual career couples who live apart: Two types." *Journal of Marriage and the Family* 42:567-76.

Gross, L., and S. Jeffries-Fox. 1978. "What do you want to be when you grow up, little girl?" In G. Tuchman, A. Daniels, and J. Benet (eds.), *Hearth and Home*. New York: Oxford University.

Grosskopf, D. 1983. *Sex and the Married Woman*. New York: Simon & Schuster.

Grossman, Herbert, and Suzanne H. Grossman. 1994. *Gender Issues in Education*. Boston: Allyn & Bacon.

Grossman, Tracy Barr. 1986. *Mothers and Children Facing Divorce*. Ann Arbor, MI: UMI Research.

Gruenbaum, Ellen. 1993. "The movement against clitorectomy and infibulation in Sudan: Public health policy and the women's movement." In Caroline B. Brettell and Carolyn F. Sargent (eds.), *Gender in Cross-Cultural Perspective*. Englewood Cliffs, NJ: Prentice Hall.

Guisso, Richard. 1981. "Thunder over the lake: The five classics and the perception of women in early China." In R. Guisso and Johannesen (eds.), *Women in China*. New York: Philo.

Gundry, Patricia. 1979. *Woman Be Free.* Grand Rapids, MI: Zondervan.

Gurian, M. 1992. *The Prince and the King.* Los Angeles: Tarcher/Putnam.

Gwartney-Gibbs, Patricia A. 1990. "The institutionalization of premarital cohabitation: Estimates from marriage license applications, 1970 and 1980." In Christopher Carlson (ed.), *Perspectives on the Family: History, Class and Feminism.* Belmont, CA: Wadsworth.

Haas, Linda. 1993. "Nurturing fathers and working mothers: Changing gender roles in Sweden." In Jane C. Hood (ed.), *Men, Work, and Family.* Newbury Park, CA: Sage.

Haber, Barbara. 1983. *The Women's Annual.* Boston: G. K. Hall.

Hagen, Monys A. 1993. "Women and economics." In Jodi Wetzel, Margo Linn Espenlaub, Monys A. Hagen, Annette Bennington McElhiney, and Carmen Braun Williams (eds.), *Women's Studies Thinking Women.* Dubuque, IA: Kendall/Hunt.

Haimes, Erica. 1993. "Issues of gender in gamete donation." *Social Science and Medicine* 36(1):85-93.

Halberstadt, A.G., and M.B. Saitta. 1987. "Gender, nonverbal behavior, and perceived dominance: A test of the theory." *Journal of Personality and Social Psychology* 53:257-72.

Halberstam, David. 1994. "Popular, pretty, polite, not too smart." *New York Times Book Review* September 11:15-17.

Hall, Christine C., and Matthew J. Crum. 1994. "Women and 'bodyisms' in television beer commercials." *Sex Roles* 31(5-6):329-37.

Hall, Edward T. 1966. *The Hidden Dimension.* Garden City, NY: Doubleday.

Halper, Jan. 1988. *Quiet Desperation: The Truth about Successful Men.* New York: Warner.

Hamill, Pete. 1986. "Great expectations: The American imperative for perfection meets a new generation." *MS* 15(3):34-37.

Hamilton, Mykol C. 1988. "Using masculine generics: Does generic 'he' increase male bias in the user's imagery?" *Sex Roles* 19 (11/12):785-99.

Hamilton, Mykol C., Barbara Hunter, and Shannon Stuart-Smith. 1994. "Jury instructions worded in the masculine generic: Can a woman claim self-defence when 'he' is threatened?" In Camille Roman, Suzanne Juhasz, and Cristanne Miller (eds.), *The Women and Language Debate: A Sourcebook.* New Brunswick, NJ: Rutgers University.

Hampton, Robert L., and Richard J. Gelles. 1994. "Violence toward black women in a nationally representative sample of black families." *Journal of Comparative Family Studies* 25(1):105-19.

Hanna, Lynn. 1995. "Escape from Bondage? Yesterday's 007 girl is set to become today's empowered woman." *Guardian* February 13:T6.

Hansen, Christine H., and Ranald D. Hansen. 1988. "How rock music videos can change what is seen when boy meets girl: Priming stereotypic appraisal of social interaction." *Sex Roles* 19:287-316.

Hanson, Shirley M. H. 1985. "Single custodial fathers." In Shirley M. H. Hanson and Frederick W. Bozett (eds.), *Dimensions of Fatherhood.* Beverly Hills, CA: Sage. 1988. "Divorced fathers with custody." In P. Bronstein and C. P. Cowan (eds.), *Fatherhood Today: Men's Changing Roles in the Family.* New York: John Wiley.

Hansson, Robert O., Marieta F. Knoft, Anna E. Downs, Paula R. Monroe, Susan E. Stegman, and Donna S. Wadley. 1984. "Femininity, masculinity and adjustment of divorce among women." *Psychology of Women Quarterly* 8(3):248-49.

Hardesty, Constance, Deeann Wenk, and Carolyn Stout Morgan. 1995. "Paternal involvement and the development of gender expectations in sons and daughters." *Youth and Society* 267(3):283-97.

Hardt, Ulrich H. 1982. *A Critical Edition of Mary Wollstonecraft's A Vindication of the Rights of Women: With Strictures on Political and Moral Subjects.* Troy, NY: Whitston.

Hare, Jan. 1994. "Concerns and issues faced by families headed by a lesbian couple." *Families in Society* 75(1):27-35.

Harne, Lynne. 1993. "Lesbian custody and the myth of the father." In Stevi Jackson et al. (eds.), *Women's Studies Essential Readings.* New York: New York University.

Harragan, Betty Lehan. 1977. *Games Mother Never Taught You.* New York: Rawson.

Harrigan, Jinni A., and Karen S. Lucic. 1988. "Attitudes about gender bias in language: A reevaluation." *Sex Roles* 19(3-4):129-40.

Harriman, Lynda Cooper. 1986. "Marital adjustment as related to personal and marital changes accompanying parenthood." *Family Relations* 34:233-39.

Harris, Ian, Jose B. Torres, and Dale Allender. 1994. "The responses of African American men to dominant norms of masculinity within the United States." *Sex Roles* 31(11-12):703-19.

Harris, Shanette M. 1994. "Racial differences in predictors of college women's body image attitudes." *Women and Health* 21 (4):89-104.

Harry, Joseph. 1984. *Gay Couples.* New York: Praeger. 1991. "Gay male and lesbian relationships." In Leonard Carrgan (ed.), *Marriages and Families: Coping with Change.* Englewood Cliffs, NJ: Prentice Hall.

Hartmann, Heidi. 1993. "The unhappy marriage of Marxism and feminism." In Stevi Jackson et al. (eds.), *Women's Studies Essential Readings.* New York: New York University.

Hartmann, Susan M. 1982. *The Home Front and Beyond: American Women in the 1940's.* Boston: Twayne.

Haskell, Molly. 1974. "Women in films: A decade of going nowhere." *Human Behavior* 3(3):64-69. 1983. "Women in the movies grow up." *Psychology Today* 17(January):18-27. 1987. *From Reverence to Rape: The Treatment of Women in the Movies.* New York: Holt, Rinehart and Winston.

Hatfield, Elaine. 1983. "What do women and men want from love and sex?" In E. R. Allegeier and N. B. McCormick (ed.), *Changing Boundaries: Gender Roles and Sexual Behavior.* Mountain View, CA: Mayfield. 1988. "Passionate and companionate love." In Robert J. Sternberg and M.L. Barnes (eds.), *The Psychology of Love.* New Haven, CT: Yale University.

Hatfield, Elaine, and Susan Sprecher, 1986. "Measuring passionate love in intimate relationships." *Journal of Adolescence* 9:383-410.

Haugen, Marit S., and Berit Branth. 1994. "Gender differences in modern agriculture: The case of female farmers in Norway." *Gender & Society* 8(2):206-29.

Hayes, C. D. (Ed.). 1987. *Risking the Future: Adolescent Sexuality, Pregnancy and Childbearing.* Washington, DC: National Academy.

Hayslip, Bert, Jr., and Paul E. Panek. 1993. *Adult Development and Aging.* New York: HarperCollins.

Healy, B. 1991. "The Yentl syndrome." *New England Journal of Medicine* 325(4):274-76.

Heaton, Tim B., and Cardell K. Jacobson. 1994. "Race differences in changing family demographics in the 1980s." *Journal of Family Issues* 15(2)290-308.

Hegger, Susan C. 1993. "Lawmakers pushing gender equity say 'glass ceilings' start in schools." *St. Louis Post-Dispatch* September 16.

Heintz, K. 1987. "An examination of sex occupational role presentations of female characters in children's picture books." *Women's Studies in Communication* 11:67-78.

Heiss, Jerold. 1991. "Gender and romantic-love roles." *Sociological Quarterly* 32(4):575-91.

Helgesen, Sally. 1990. *The Female Advantage: Women's Ways of Leadership.* New York: Doubleday.

Helson, Ravenna, and James Picano. 1990. "Is the traditional role bad for women?" *Journal of Personality and Social Psychology* 59(2):311-20.

Helterine, Marilyn, and Marilyn Nouri. 1994. "Aging and gender: Values and continuity." *Journal of Women and Aging* 6(3):19-37.

Hendrick, Susan S., and Clyde Hendrick. 1992a. *Romantic Love.* Newbury Park, CA: Sage. 1992b. *Liking, Loving and Relating.* Monterey, CA: Brooks-Cole. 1995. "Gender similarities and differences in sex and love." *Personal Relationships* 2: 55—65.

Hendrick, Susan S., Clyde Hendrick, and N.L. Adler. 1988. "Romantic relationships: Love, satisfaction and staying together." *Journal of Personality and Social Psychology* 54:980—88.

Hendry, Joy. 1993. "The role of the professional housewife." In Janice Hunter (ed.), *Japanese Women Working.* London: Routledge.

Henley, Nancy M. 1975. "Power, sex and nonverbal communication." In Barrie Thorne and Nancy Henley (eds.), *Language and Sex: Difference and Dominance.* Rowley, MA: Newbury. 1977. *Body Politics: Power, Sex and Nonverbal Communication.* Englewood Cliffs, NJ: Prentice Hall. 1989. "Molehill or mountain: What we know and don't know about sex bias in language." In Mary Crawford and Margaret Gentry (eds.), *Gender and Thought: Psychological Perspectives.* New York: Springer-Verlag.

Henley, Nancy M., B. Gruber, and L. Lerner. 1985. "Studies on the detrimental effects of 'generic' masculine usage." Paper presented at the Eastern Psychological Association, Boston (March).

Henley, Nancy M., and Cheris Kramarae. 1994. "Gender, power and miscommunication." In Camille Roman, Suzanne Juhasz, and Cristanne Miller (eds.), *The Women in Language Debate: A Sourcebook.* New Brunswick, NJ: Rutgers University.

Henneberger, Melinda. 1994. "In the young, signs that feminism lives." *New York Times* April 27:B1,B2.

Herman, Dianne F. 1989. "The rape culture." In Jo Freeman (ed.), *Women: A Feminist Perspective.* Mountain View, CA: Mayfield.

Herman, Judith. 1981. *Father-Daughter Incest.* Cambridge, MA: Harvard University.

Henslin, James M. 1996. *Social Problems.* Upper Saddle River, NJ: Prentice Hall.

Herek, Gregory M. 1994. "Assessing heterosexuals' attitudes toward lesbians and gay men: A review of empirical research with the ATLG Scale." In Beverly Greene and Gregory M. Herek (eds.), *Lesbian and Gay Psychology: Theory, Research and Clinical Applications.* Thousand Oaks, CA: Sage.

Hernandez, Francisco. 1996. "Just something you did as a man." In Karen E. Rosenblum and Toni-Michelle C. Travis (eds.), *The Meaning of Difference: American Constructions of Race, Sex and Gender, Social Class and Sexual Orientation.* New York: McGraw-Hill.

Herrera, Ruth S., and Robert L. DelCampo. 1995. "Beyond the superwoman syndrome: Work satisfaction and family functioning among working-class, Mexican American women." *Hispanic Journal of Behavioral Sciences* 17(1):49-60.

Herzog, Sandra. 1993. "Sex without consent: The hidden story of date rape." In Jodi Wetzel, Margo Linn Espenlaub, Monys A. Hagen, Annette Benington McElhiney, and Carmen Braun Williams (eds.), *Women's Studies Thinking Women.* Dubuque, IA: Kendall/Hunt.

Hess, Beth B., Elizabeth W. Markson, and Peter J. Stein. 1988. *Sociology.* New York: Macmillan.

Hess, Beth B., and Beth J. Soldo. 1985. "Husband and wife networks." In W.J. Sauer and R.T. Coward (eds.), *Social Support Networks and the Care of the Elderly: Theory, Research and Practice.* New York: Springer.

Hewlett, Sylvia Ann. 1987. "When a husband walks out." *Parade Magazine* June 7:4-5.

Heymann, David L. 1995. "AIDS: Mother to child." *World Health* Special Issue on Women and Health (September):31-32.

Heyward, Carter. 1976. *A Priest Forever: The Formation of a Woman and a Priest.* New York: Harper & Row. 1984. *Our Passion for Justice: Images of Power, Sexuality and Liberation.* New York: Pilgrim.

Higginbotham, Evelyn Brooks. 1985. *Blacks on Television.* Metuchen, NJ: Scarecrow. 1992. "African-American women's history and the metalanguage of race." *Signs* 17(21):251-74. 1994. "Black professional women: Job ceilings and employment sectors." In Maxine Baca Zinn and Bonnie Thornton Dill (eds.), *Women of Color in U.S. Society.* Philadelphia: Temple University. 1996. "Afro-American women in history." In Mary Beth Norton and Ruth M. Alexander (eds.), *Major Problems in American Women's History.* Lexington, MA: D.C. Heath.

Hill, Dana, Carol Davis, and Leann M. Tigges. 1995. "Gendering welfare state theory: A cross-national study of women's public pension quality." *Gender & Society* 9(1):99-119.

Hill, G.H., and Hill, S.S. 1985. *Blacks on Television.* Metuchen, NJ.: Scarecrow.

Hill, R. Jane. 1993. "Women and work." *Risk Management* 40(7):26.

Hiller, Dana V., and William W. Philliber. 1991. "The division of labor in contemporary marriage: Expectations, perceptions and performance." In John N. Edwards and David H. Demo (eds.), *Marriage and Family in Transition.* Boston: Allyn & Bacon.

Himmelstein, Jerome L. 1986. "The social basis of antifeminism: Religious networks and culture." *Journal for the Scientific Study of Religion* 25(1):1-15.

Hirsch, K. 1990. "Fraternities of fear." *MS* 1(2):52-56.

Hisae, Sawachi. 1989. "The political awakening of women." *Japan Quarterly* 36:381-85.

Hisrich, Robert D., and Candida G. Brush. 1984. "The woman entrepreneur: Management skills and business problems." *Journal of Small Business Management* 22:30-37.

Hite, Shere. 1994. "Women as Revolutionary Agents of Change: The Hite Reports and Beyond." Madison, WI: University of Wisconsin. 1995. "Women and love." In Sheila Ruth, *Issues in Feminism: An Introduction to Women's Studies.* Mountain View, CA: Mayfield.

Hochschild, Arlie. 1989. *The Second Shift: Working Parents and the Revolution at Home.* New York: Viking.

Hockstader, Lee. 1995. "For women, new Russia is far from liberating." *Washington Post* September 1: A25,A31.

Hofferth, Sandra L. 1985. "Updating children's life course." *Journal of Marriage and the Family* 47:93-115.

Hoffman, Charles D., and Edward C. Teyber. 1985. "Naturalistic observations of sex differences in adult involvement with girls and boys of different ages." *Merrill-Palmer Quarterly* 31(1):93–97.

Hoffman, L. W. 1977. "Changes in family roles, socialization, and sex differences." *American Psychologist* 32:644–57.

Hoffnung, Michele. 1995. "Motherhood: Contemporary conflict for women." In Jo Freeman (ed.), *Women: A Feminist Perspective*. Mountain View, CA: Mayfield.

Hogan, Linda. 1995. *From Women's Experience to Feminist Theology*. Sheffield, UK: Sheffield Academic Press.

Hole, Judith, and Ellen Levine. 1995. "Historical precedent: Nineteenth-century feminists." In Sheila Ruth, *Issues in Feminism: An Introduction to Women's Studies*. Mountain View, CA: Mayfield.

Holland, Dorothy, and Margaret A. Eisenhart. 1990. *Educated in Romance: Women, Achievement and College Culture*. Chicago: University of Chicago.

Hollander, Anne. 1994. "A woman of extremes." Book review of Susan Haskins' *Mary Magdalen: Myth and Metaphor*. *New Yorker* (October) 3:112-17.

Holmstrom, Lynda, and Ann Burgess. 1988. *The Victim of Rape: Institutions' Reactions*. New York: John Wiley.

Hong, Jinkuk, and Marsha Mailick Seltzer. 1995. "The psychological consequences of multiple roles: The nonnormative case." *Journal of Health and Social Behavior* 36(4):386–98.

Hong, Lawrence K. 1987. "Potential effects of the one-child policy on gender equality in the People's Republic of China." *Gender & Society* 1(3):317–26.

Honig, Emily, and Gail Hershatter. 1988. *Personal Voices: Chinese Women in the 1980's*. Stanford, CA: Stanford University.

Hooker, Richard D., Jr. 1993. "Affirmative Action and combat exclusion: Gender roles in the U.S. Army." In Lois Lovelace Duke (ed.), *Women in Politics: Outsiders or Insiders?* Englewood Cliffs, NJ: Prentice Hall.

hooks, bell. 1992. "Feminism: A transformational politic." In Paula S. Rothenberg (ed.), *Race, Class and Gender in the United States: An Integrated Study*. New York: St. Martin's.

Hooyman, Nancy, and H. Asuman Kiyak. 1993. *Social Gerontology*. Boston: Allyn & Bacon.

Hopkins, Patrick D. 1992. "Gender treachery: Homophobia, masculinity, and threatened identities." In Larry May and Robert Strikwerda (eds.), *Rethinking Masculinity: Philosophical Explorations in Light of Feminism*. Lantham, MD: Rowan & Littlefield.

Horn, Patricia. 1992. "To love and to cherish: Gays and lesbians lead the way in redefining the family." In Michael S. Kimmel and Michael A. Messner (eds.), *Men's Lives*. New York: Macmillan.

Horner, Constance. 1996. "Reclaiming the vision: What should we do after affirmative action?" In Harold A. Widdison (ed.), *Social Problems 96/97*. Guilford, CT: Dushkin/Brown & Benchmark.

Horner, Martina S. 1969. "Fail: Bright women." *Psychology Today* 3(6):36-38. 1972. "Toward an understanding of achievement related conflicts in women." *Journal of Social Issues* 28:157-76.

Horowitz, Ruth. 1991. "The expanded family and family honor." In Mark Hutter (ed.), *The Family Experience: A Reader in Cultural Diversity*. New York: Macmillan.

Hossain, Hameeda. 1995. "Introduction." In Hameeda Hossain and Salma Sobhan (eds.), *Sanglap: Attack on Fundamentals*. Dhaka, Bangladesh: Ain O Salish Kendra.

Hossain, Ziarat, and Jaipaul L. Roopnarine. 1993. "Division of household labor and child care in dual-earner African-American families with infants." *Sex Roles* 39:571-83.

Houseknecht, Sharon K. 1987. "Voluntary childlessness." In Marvin B. Sussman and Suzanne K. Steinmetz (ed.), *Handbook of Marriage and the Family*. New York: Plenum.

Houston, Marsha, and Julia T. Wood. 1996. "Difficult dialogues, expanded horizons: Communicating across race and culture." In Julia T. Wood (ed.), *Gendered Relationships*. Mountain View, CA: Mayfield.

Hoyenga, Katharine Blick, and Kermit T. Hoyenga. 1993. *Gender-Related Differences: Origins and Outcomes.* Boston: Allyn & Bacon.

Hrdy, Sarah Blaffer. 1986. "Empathy, polyandry and the myth of the coy female." In Ruth Bleier (ed.), *Feminist Approaches to Science.* New York: Pergamon.

Hubbard, Ruth. 1994. "Race and sex as biological categories." In Ethel Tobach and Betty Rosoff (eds.), *Challenging Racism and Sexism: Alternatives to Genetic Explanations.* New York: Feminist Press at City University of New York.

Huesmann, L. Rowell (ed). 1994. *Aggressive Behavior: Current Perspectives.* New York: Plenum.

Hughes, Fergus P. 1991. *Children, Play, and Development.* Boston: Allyn & Bacon.

Humphries, Martin. 1985. "Gay machismo." In Andy Metcalf and Martin Humphries (eds.), *The Sexuality of Men.* London: Pluto.

Hunt, Janet. 1990. *Understanding Human Sexuality.* New York: McGraw-Hill.

Hunt, K., M. Vessey, and K. McPherson. 1990. "Mortality in a cohort of long-term users of hormone replacement therapy: An updated analysis." *Journal of Obstetrics and Gynaecology* 97:1080-86.

Hunt, M. 1974. *Sexual Behavior in the 1970's.* Chicago: Playboy.

Hunter, Andrea G., and James Earl Davis. 1994. "Hidden voices of black men: The meaning, structure and complexity of manhood." *Journal of Black Studies* 25(1):20-40.

Huston, Michelle and Pepper Schwartz. 1996. "Gendered dynamics in the romantic relationships of lesbians and gay men." In Julie T. Wood (ed.), *Gendered Relationships.* Mountain View, CA: Mayfield.

Hyde, Janet Shibley. 1981. "How large are cognitive gender differences? A meta-analysis using w and d." *American Psychologist* 36:892-901. 1984. "Children's understanding of sexist language." *Developmental Psychology* 20:697-706. 1991. *Half the Human Experience: The Psychology of Women.* Lexington, MA: D. C. Heath.

Hyde, Janet Shibley, Elizabeth Fennema, and S.J. Lamon. 1990. "Gender differences in mathematics performance: A meta-analysis." *Psychological Bulletin* 107:139-55.

Ide, Sachiko. 1986. "Sex differences and politeness in Japanese." *International Journal of the Sociology of Language* 58:25-36.

Ide, Sachiko, and Naomi Hanaoka McGloin (Eds). 1990. *Aspects of Japanese Women's Language.* Tokyo: Kurosio.

Ignico, Arlene A., and Barbara J. Mead. 1990. "Children's perceptions of the gender-appropriateness of physical activities." *Perceptual and Motor Skills* 71:1275-81.

India Today. 1981. "Ladies are for burning." February 1-15:92.

Inman, Chris. 1996. "Friendships among men: Closeness in the doing." In Julia T. Wood (ed.), *Gendered Relationships.* Mountain View, CA: Mayfield.

Institute of Medicine. 1994. Anna C. Mastroianni, Ruth Faden, and Daniel Federman (eds.). *Women and Health Research: Ethical and Legal Issues of Including Women in Clinical Studies, Volume I.* Washington, DC: National Academy Press.

Intons-Peterson, Margaret Jean. 1985. "Fathers' expectations and aspirations for their children." *Sex Roles* 12(7-8):877-95. 1988. *Children's Concepts of Gender.* Norwood, NJ: Ablex.

Intons-Peterson, Margaret Jean, and J. Crawford. 1985. "The meanings of marital surnames." *Sex Roles* 12:1163-71.

Iranian Resistance. 1994. "Iranian resistance movement is waiting for its time." *St. Louis Post-Dispatch* October 23:10A.

Irving, H.H., and M. Benjamin. 1991. "Shared and sole-custody parents: A comparative analysis." In J. Folberg (ed.), *Joint Custody and Shared Parenting.* New York: Guilford.

Italie, Hillel. 1993. "Emma Thompson: Fame, feminist, Forster." *St. Louis Post-Dispatch* (January 3):6C.

Iwao, Sumiko. 1993. *The Japanese Woman: Traditional Image and Changing Reality.* Cambridge, MA: Harvard University.

Izraeli, Dafna N. 1994. "Money matters: Spousal incomes and family/work relations among physician couples in India." *Sociological Quarterly* 35(1):69-84.

Jacklin, Carol N. 1989. "Female and male: Issues of gender." *American Psychologist* 44:127-33.

Jackman, Jennifer. 1995. "1995 women's equality poll released." *Feminist Majority Report* 7(2):1, 12-13.

Jackson, Aurora P. 1994b. "Psychological distress among single, employed, black mothers and their perceptions of their young children." *Journal of Social Service Research* 19(3-4):87-101.

Jackson, Kathy Merlock. 1994a. "Targeting baby-boom children as consumers: Mattel uses television to sell talking dolls." In Harry Eiss (ed.), *Images of the Child.* Bowling Green, OH: Bowling Green State University Popular Press.

Jackson, L. 1983. "On living together unmarried." *Journal of Social Issues.* 4(1):35-59.

Jacobs, Deborah L. 1994. "Back from the mommy track." *New York Times* October 9(Section 3):1,6.

Jacobs, Jerry A., and Ronnie J. Steinberg. 1990. "Compensating differentials and the male-female wage gap: Evidence from the New York State Comparable Worth Study." *Social Forces* 69:439-68.

Jacobsen, Cardell K., Tim B. Heaton, and Karen M. Taylor. 1988. "Childlessness among American women." *Social Biology* 35:186-97.

Jacobsen, Joyce. P. 1994. *The Economics of Gender.* Cambridge, MA: Blackwell.

Jacobson, Doranne. 1980. "Golden handprints and the red-painted feet: Hindu childbirth rituals in central India." In Nancy Auer Falk and Rita Gross (eds.), *Unspoken Worlds: Women's Religious Lives in Nonwestern Cultures.* New York: Harper & Row.

Jacquette, Jane. 1986. "Female political participation in Latin America: Raising feminist issues." In Lynn B. Iglitzin and Ruth Ross (eds.), *Women in the World, 1975-1985: The Women's Decade.* Santa Barbara, CA: ABC-Clio.

James, E. O. 1959. *The Cult of the Mother Goddess: An Anthropological and Documentary Study.* New York: Barnes and Noble.

Jamieson, Kathleen Hall. 1995. *Beyond the Double Bind: Women and Leadership.* New York: Oxford University.

Jamieson, Lynn. 1994. "Theories of family development and the experience of being brought up." In Michael Drake (ed.), *Time, Family and Community: Perspectives on Family and Community History.* Oxford, UK: Open University Press.

Japan. 1996. *Japan: An International Comparison.* Tokyo: Keizai Koho Center (Japan Institute for Social and Economic Affairs).

Jarrett, Robin L. 1994. "Living poor: Family life among single parent, African-American women." *Social Problems* 41(1):30-49.

Jayakar, Pupul. 1987. "Hinduism: Rural traditions." In *The Encyclopedia of Religion* 7:176-77. New York: Macmillan.

Jeffery, Patricia. 1979. *Frogs in a Well: India Women in Purdah.* London: Zed.

Jelin, Elizabeth. 1977. "Migration and labor force participation of Latin American women: The domestic servants in cities." In Wellesley Editorial Committee (eds.), *Women and National Development.* Chicago: University of Chicago. 1991. *Family, Household and Gender Relations in Latin America* (edited volume). London: Kegan Paul.

Jensen, Joan M. 1994. "Native American women and agriculture: A Seneca case study." In Vicki L. Ruiz and Ellen Carol DuBois (eds.), *Unequal Sisters: A Multicultural Reader in U.S. Women's History.* New York: Routledge.

Jewett, Paul. 1975. *Man as Male and Female.* Grand Rapids, MI: Eerdmans.

Joe, Jennie R., and Dorothy Lonewolf Miller. 1994. "Cultural survival and contemporary American Indian women in the city." In Maxine Baca Zinn and Bonnie Thornton Dill (eds.), *Women of Color in U.S. Society.* Philadelphia: Temple University.

Johann, Sara Lee, and Frank Osanka. 1989. *Representing Battered Women Who Kill.* Springfield, IL: Charles C. Thomas.

Johansson, Sten, and Ola Nygren. 1991. "The missing girls of China: A new demographic account." *Population and Development Review* 17:35-51.

John, Daphne, Beth Anne Shelton, and Kristen Luschen. 1995. "Race, ethnicity, gender, and perceptions of fairness." *Journal of Family Issues* 16(3):357-79.

Johnson, Fern L. 1996. "Friendships among women: Closeness in dialogue." In Julia T. Wood (ed.), *Gendered Relationships.* Mountain View, CA: Mayfield.

Johnson, Hortense. 1943/1996. "Hortense Johnson on black women and the war effort, 1943." In Mary Beth Norton and Ruth M. Alexander (eds.), *Major Problems in American Women's History.* Lexington, MA: D.C. Heath.

Johnson, Kay. 1986. "Women's rights, family reform and population control in the People's Republic of China." In Lynn B. Iglitzin and Ruth Ross (eds.), *Women in the World, 1975–1985: The Women's Decade.* Santa Barbara, CA: ABC-Clio.

Johnson, Miriam M. 1989. "Feminism and the theories of Talcott Parsons." In Ruth A. Wallace (ed.), *Feminism and Sociological Theory.* Newbury Park, CA: Sage. 1993a. "Functionalism and feminism: Is estrangement necessary?" In Paula England (ed.), *Theory on Gender/Feminism on Theory.* New York: Aldine de Gruyter.

Johnson, Roberta Ann. 1993b. "Affirmative Action as a woman's issue." In Lois Lovelace Duke (ed.), *Women in Politics: Outsiders or Insiders?* Englewood Cliffs, NJ: Prentice Hall.

Johnson, Warren R. 1968. *Human Sexual Behavior and Sex Education.* Philadelphia: Lea and Febiger.

Johnson, Winston A. 1990. "Gender, society, and church." In June S. Hagen (ed.), *Gender Matters: Women's Studies for the Christian Community.* Grand Rapids, MI: Zondervan, Jones.

Johnston, Janet. 1993. "Children of divorces who refuse visitation." In Charlene E. Depner and James H. Bray (eds.), *Nonresidential Parenting: New Vistas in Family Living.* Newbury Park, CA: Sage.

Jones, Bill. 1996. "Make war, not love: Romantic movies latch on to violence." *St. Louis Post-Dispatch* March 3:3C, 7C.

Jones, Jacqueline. 1985. *Labor of Love, Labor of Sorrow: Black Women, Work, and the Family from Slavery to the Present.* New York: Basic Books.

Jordan, Ellen, and Angela Cowan. 1995. "Warrior narratives in the kindergarten classroom: Renegotiating the social contract?" *Gender & Society* 9(6):727-43.

Jordan Issues and Perspectives. 1993. "Toujan Feisal, Jordan's first elected female MP: My convictions are based on beliefs in human rights and democracy." No.16(November–December):9.

Jorgensen, Stephen R. 1993. "Adolescent pregnancy and parenting." In Thomas P. Gullota, Gerald R. Adams, and Raymond Montemayor (eds.), *Adolescent Sexuality.* Newbury Park, CA: Sage.

Jorgensen, Stephen R., and J. C. Gaudy. 1980. "Self-disclosure and satisfaction in marriage." *Family Relations* 29(3):281-87.

Josephs, Robert A., Hazel Rose Markus, and Romin W. Tafarodi. 1992. "Gender and self-esteem." *Journal of Personality and Social Psychology* 63(3):391-402.

Joslyn, W. O. 1973. "Androgen-induced social dominance in infant female Rhesus monkeys." *Journal of Child Psychology and Psychiatry* 14:137-45.

Joy, S. S., and P. S. Wise. 1983. "Maternal employment, anxiety, and sex differences in college students' self descriptions." *Sex Roles* 9:519-25.

Judd, Elizabeth. 1990. "The myths of the Golden Age and the Fall: From matriarchy to patriarchy." In Frances Richardson Keller (ed.), *Views of Women's Lives in Western Tradition.* Lewiston NY: Edwin Mellen.

Kabir, Shameem. 1994. "Lesbian desire on the screen: The hunger." In Liz Gibbs (ed.), *Daring to Dissent: Lesbian Culture from Margin to Mainstream.* London: Cassell.

Kahan, Nancie, and Nanette Norris. 1994. "Creating gender expectations through children's advertising." In Harry Eiss (ed.), *Images of the Child.* Bowling Green, OH: Bowling Green State University Popular Press.

Kaledin, Eugenia. 1984. *Mothers and More: American Women in the 1950s.* Boston: Twayne.

Kalleberg, Arne L., and Rachel A. Rosenfeld. 1990. "Work in the familiy and in the labor market: A cross-national, reciprocal analysis." *Journal of Marriage and the Family* 52:331-46.

Kalmijn, Matthijs. 1993. "Trends in black-white intermarriage." *Social Forces* 72(1):119-46.

Kalof, Linda. 1993. "Dilemmas of femininity: Gender and the social construction of sexual imagery." *Sociological Quarterly* 34(4):639-51.

Kamal, Sultana. 1995. "Undermining women's rights." In Hameeda Hossain and Salma Sobhan (eds.), *Sanglap: Attack on Fundamentals.* Dhaka, Bangladesh: Ain O Salish Nendra.

Kaminer, Wendy. 1993. "Feminism's identity crisis." *Atlantic Monthly* (October):51-68.

Kamm, Henry. 1988. "Afghan refugee women suffering under Islamic custom." *New York Times International* March 27:8.

Kandiyoti, Deniz. 1985. *Women in Rural Production Systems: Problems and Policies.* Paris: UNESCO. 1991. *Women, Islam and the State* (Edited volume). Philadelphia: Temple University.

Kanne, Bernice. 1995. "Guy stuff: A new man is regular Joe." *St. Louis Post-Dispatch* October 29:7E.

Kaplan, E. Ann. 1987. *Rocking Around the Clock: Music Television, Postmodernism and Consumer Culture*. New York: Methuen.

Karlsen, Carol F. 1991. "The devil in the shape of a woman: The economic basis of witchcraft." In Linda K. Kerber and Jane Sherron De Hart (eds.), *Women's America: Refocusing the Past*. New York: Oxford University.

Katz, Jackson. 1995. "Reconstructing masculinity in the locker room: The mentors in violence prevention project." *Harvard Educational Review* 65(2):163-74.

Katz, Phyllis A. 1986. "Modification of children's gender-stereotyped behavior: General issues and research considerations." *Sex Roles* 14(11/12):591-603.

Katz, Phyllis A., and Vincent Walsh. 1991. "Modification of children's gender-stereotyped behavior." *Child Development* 62:338-51.

Kaufman, Debra R. 1995. "Professional women: How real are the recent gains?" In Jo Freeman (ed.) *Women: A Feminist Perspective*. Mountain View, CA: Mayfield.

Kawashima, Yoko. 1987. "The place and role of female workers in the Japanese labor market." *Women's Studies International Forum* 10(6):599-611.

Keen, Sam. 1991. *Fire in the Belly: On Being a Man*. New York: Bantam.

Keller, Frances Richardson (ed.). 1990. *Views of Women's Lives in Western Tradition*. Lewiston, NY: Edwin Mellen.

Kelley, Karol. 1994. "A modern Cinderella." *Journal of American Culture* 17(1):87-92.

Kelley, R. M., and M. Boutilier. 1978. *The Making of Political Women: A Study of Socialization and Role Conflict*. Chicago: Nelson Hall.

Kelly, J. 1983. "Sex role stereotypes and mental health: Conceptual models in the 1970's and issues for the 1980's." In V. Franks and E. Rothblum (eds.), *The Stereotyping of Women*. New York: Springer.

Kelly, Joan B. 1993. "Developing and implementing post-divorce parenting plans: Does the forum make a difference?" In Charlene E. Depner and James H. Bray (eds.), *Nonresidential Parenting: New Vistas in Family Living*. Newbury Park, CA: Sage.

Kemp, Alice Abel. 1994. *Women's Work: Degraded and Devalued*. Englewood Cliffs, NJ: Prentice Hall.

Kemper, Susan. 1984. "When to speak like a lady." *Sex Roles* 10(5-6):435-43.

Kennelly, E. 1984. "Republicans in fear of a gender gap, feature women at convention." *National NOW Times* (September-October):3.

Kephart, William M., and Davor Jedlicka. 1991. *The Family, Society and the Individual*. New York: Harper Collins.

Kerber, Linda, K. 1988. "Why should girls be learn'd and wise?: Two centuries of higher education for women as seen through the unfinished work of Mary Baldwin." In John Mack Faragher and Florence Howe (eds.), *Women and Higher Education in American History*. New York: W.W. Norton.

Kerber, Linda K., and Jane Sherron De Hart (Eds). 1991. *Women's America: Refocusing the Past*. New York: Oxford University.

Kesner, I. F. 1988. "Director's characteristics and committee membership: An investigation of type, occupation, tenures, and gender." *Academy of Management Journal* 31:66-84.

Kessler, Suzanne J., and Wendy McKenna. 1978. *Gender: An Ethnomethodological Approach*. New York: John Wiley.

Kessler-Harris, Alice. 1991. "Where are the organized women workers?" In Linda K. Kerber and Jane Sherron De Hart (eds.), *Women's America: Refocusing the Past*. New York: Oxford University.

Keuls, Eva. 1993. *The Reign of the Phallus: Sexual Politics in Ancient Athens*. Berkeley: University of California.

Keville, Terri D. 1993. "The invisible woman: Gender bias in medical research." *Women's Rights Law Reporter* 15(2-3):123-42.

Khanga, Yelena. 1991. "No matryoshkas need apply." *New York Times* November 25:A19.

Khosroshahi, Fatemeh. 1989. "Penguins don't care, but women do: A social identity analysis of a Whorfian problem." *Language in Society* 18:505.

Khotkina, Zoya. 1994. "Women in the labour market: Yesterday, today and tomorrow." In Anastasia Posadskaya and the Moscow Gender Centre (eds.), *Women in Russia: A New Era in Russian Feminism*. London: Verso.

Kilbourne, Jean. 1995. "Beauty and the beast of advertising." In Paula S. Rothenberg (ed.), *Race, Class, and Gender in the United States: An Integrated Study.* New York: St. Martin's.

Kimble, Charles E. 1990. *Social Psychology: Studying Human Interaction.* New York: William C. Brown.

Kimble, Charles E., and J. I. Musgrove. 1988. "Dominance in arguing in mixed-sex dyads: Visual dominance patterns, talking time and speech loudness." *Journal of Research in Personality* 22:1-16.

Kimble, Charles E., J. C. Yoshikawa, and H. D. Zehr. 1981. "Vocal and verbal assertiveness in same-sex and mixed-sex groups." *Journal of Personality and Social Psychology* 40:1047-54.

Kimbrell, Andrew. 1993. "A manifesto for men." In Virginia Cyrus (ed.), *Experiencing Race, Class, and Gender in the United States.* Mountain View, CA: Mayfield. 1995. *The Masculine Mystique.* New York: Ballantine.

Kimmel, Michael S. 1992. "Issues for men in the 90s." *University of Miami Law Review* 46:671-83. 1994. "Masculinity as homophobia: Fear, shame and silence in the construction of gender identity." In H. Brod and M. Kaufman (eds.), *Theorizing Masculinities.* Thousand Oaks, CA: Sage. 1995. "From pedestals to partners: Men's responses to feminism." In Jo Freeman (ed.), *Women: A Feminist Perspective.* Mountain View, CA: Mayfield.

King, Deborah. 1988. "Multiple jeopardy, multiple consciousness: The context of a black feminist ideology." *Signs: Journal of Women in Culture and Society* 14:42-72.

King, Ursula. 1989. *Women and Spirituality.* New York: New Amsterdam.

King, Wesley C., Jr., Edward W. Miles, and Jane Kniska. 1991. "Boys will be boys (and girls will be girls): The attribution of gender role stereotypes in a gaming situation." *Sex Roles* 25(11-12):607-23.

Kinsey, Alfred E., Wardell B. Pomeroy, and Clyde E. Martin. 1948. *Sexual Behavior in the Human Male.* Philadelphia: Saunders.

Kinsey, Alfred E., Wardell B. Pomeroy, Clyde E. Martin, and H. Gephard. 1953. *Sexual Behavior in the Human Female.* Philadelphia: Saunders.

Kinsman, Gary. 1992. "Men loving men: The challenge of gay liberation." In Michael S. Kimmel and Michael A. Messner (eds.), *Men's Lives.* New York: Macmillan.

Kishor, Sunita. 1993. "May god give sons to all: Gender and child mortality in India." *American Sociological Review* 58(2):247-65.

Kittridge, Cherry. 1987. *Womansword: What Japanese Words Say About Women.* New York: Kodansha International.

Kitzinger, Celia. 1988. *The Social Construction of Lesbianism.* Newbury Park, CA: Sage.

Klaiber, E.L., D.M. Broverman, W. Vogel, J.A., Kennedy, and C.J.L. Nadeau. 1982. "Estrogens and central nervous system fluctuations: Electroencephalography, cognition and depression." In R.C. Friedman (ed.), *Behavior and the menstrual cycle.* New York: Marcel Dekker.

Klaus, Marshall H., and J.H. Kennell. 1983. *Bonding: The Beginnings of Parent-Infant Attachment.* New York: Mosby.

Klein, Patricia Vawter. 1991. "For the good of the race: Reproductive hazards from lead and the persistence of exclusionary policies toward women." In Laura Kramer (ed.), *The Sociology of Gender: A Text-Reader.* New York: St. Martin's.

Kleinbaum, Abby Wettan. 1990. "Amazon legends and misogynists: The women and civilization question." In Frances Richardson Keller (ed.), *Views of Women's Lives in Western Tradition.* Lewiston, NY: Edwin Mellen.

Kleinberg, Seymour. 1992. "The new masculinity of gay men and beyond." In Michael S. Kimmel and Michael A. Messner (eds.), *Men's Lives.* New York: Macmillan.

Klemesrud, Judy. 1974. "Feminist goal: Better image at the movies." *New York Times* (October 13):L82.

Klimenkova, Tatiana. 1994. "What does our new democracy offer society?" In Anastasia Posadskaya and the Moscow Gender Centre (eds.), *Women in Russia: A New Era in Russian Feminism.* London: Verso.

Kloek, Els. 1994. "Introduction." In Els Kloek, Nicole Teeuwen, and Marijke Huisman (eds.), *Women of the Golden Age: An International Debate on Women in Seventeenth-Century Holland, England and Italy.* Amsterdam: Hilversum Verloren.

Kloek, Els, Nicole Teeuwen, and Marijke Huisman (Eds). 1994. *Women of the Golden Age: An International Debate on Women in Seventeenth-Century Holland, England and Italy.* Amsterdam: Hilversum Verloren.

Kloppenborg, Ria. 1995. "Female stereotypes in early Buddhism: The women of the Therī gāthā In Ria Kloppenborg and Wouter J. Hanegraaff (eds.), *Female Stereotypes in Religious Traditions.* Leiden, Netherlands: Brill.

Knaub, Patricia Kain. 1986. "Growing up in a dual-career family: The children's perceptions." *Family Relations* 35:431-37.

Knaub, Patricia Kain, Deanna Baxter Eversoll, and Jaqueline Voss. 1983. "Is parenthood a desirable adult role? An assessment of attitudes held by contemporary women." *Sex Roles* 9(3):355-62.

Knox, David, and Caroline Schacht. 1991. *Choices in Relationships: An Introduction to Marriage and the Family.* St. Paul, MN: West.

Knudson, Barbara, and Connie Weil. 1988. "Women in Latin America." In Connie Weil (ed.), *Lucha: The Struggles of Latin American Women.* Minneapolis, MN: Prisma Institute.

Koehler, Lyle. 1989. "The oppression of women in New England." In Mary Beth Norton (ed.), *Major Problems in American Women's History.* Lexington, MA: D. C. Heath. 1991. "The weaker sex as religious rebel." In Kathryn Kish Sklar and Thomas Dublin (eds.), *Women and Power in American History: A Reader, Volume I to 1880.* Englewood Cliffs, NJ: Prentice Hall.

Koehler, M. S. 1990. "Classrooms, teachers and gender differences in mathematics." In Elizabeth Fennema and G. C. Leder (eds.), *Mathematics and Gender.* New York: Teachers College Press.

Kohlberg, Lawrence. 1966. "A cognitive-developmental analysis of children's sex role concepts and attitudes." In Eleanor Maccoby (ed.), *The Development of Sex Differences.* Stanford, CA: Stanford University.

Kokopeli, Bruce, and George Lakey. 1995. "More power than we want: Masculine sexuality and violence." In Margaret L. Andersen and Patricia Hill Collins (eds.), *Race, Class, and Gender: An Anthology.* Belmont, CA: Wadsworth.

Kolaric, Giselle C., and Nancy L. Galambos. 1995. "Face-to-face interactions in unacquainted female-male adolescent dyads: How do girls and boys behave?" *Journal of Early Adolescence* 15(3):363-82.

Komarovsky, Mirra. 1976. *Dilemmas of Masculinity.* New York: W. W. Norton. 1987. "College men: Gender roles in transition." In Carol Lasser (ed.), *Educating Men and Women Together: Coeducation in a Changing World.* Englewood Cliffs, NJ: Prentice Hall.

Kornblum, William, and Joseph Julian. 1995. *Social Problems.* Englewood Cliffs, NJ: Prentice Hall.

Kornblum, William, and Carolyn D. Smith (Eds.), 1994. *The Healing Experience: Readings on the Social Context of Health Care.* Englewood Cliffs, NJ: Prentice Hall.

Koss, Mary P. 1992. "The underdetection of rape: Methodological choices influence incidence estimates." *Journal of Social Issues* 48:61-75.

Koss, Mary P., C. Gidyez, and N. Wisniewski. 1987. "The scope of rape: Incidents and prevalence of sexual aggression in a sample of higher education students." *Journal of Consulting and Clinical Psychology* 55:162-70.

Koss, Mary P., L. Goodman, L. Fitzgerald, N. Russo, G. Keita, and A. Browne. 1994. *No Safe Haven: Male Violence against Women at Home, at Work and in the Community.* Washington, DC: American Psychological Association.

Kotkin, Mark. 1983. "Sex roles among married and unmarried couples." *Sex Roles* 9(9):975-85. 1985. "To marry or live together?" *Lifestyles: A Journal of Changing Patterns* (Spring):160.

Kouba, Leonard, and Judith Muasher. 1985. "Female circumcision in Africa: An overview." *African Studies Review* 28(1):95-110.

Kramarae, Cheris, and Paula A. Treichler. 1990. "Power relationships in the classroom." In Susan L. Gabriel and Isaiah Smithson (eds.), *Gender in the Classroom: Power and Pedagogy.* Urbana, IL: University of Illinois.

Kramer, Pamela, and Sheila Lehman. 1990. "Mismeasuring women: A critique of research on computer ability and avoidance." *Signs* 16(1):158-72.

Krasnow, Iris. 1995. "Women at 50: Fit, fulfilled and blazing." *Washington Post* July 10:D5.

Krause, Neal, A. Regula Herzog, and Elizabeth Baker. 1992. "Providing support to others and well-being in later life." *Journal of Gerontology: Psychological Sciences* 47:300-11.

Kreutz, L., and R. Rose. 1972. "Assessment of aggressive behavior and plasma testosterone in a young criminal population." *Psychosomatic Medicine* 34:321-32.

Kristof, Nicholas D. 1993. "China's crackdown on births: A stunning, and harsh success." *New York Times International* April 25:1, 6. 1995. "Yokohama Journal: Japan invests in a growth stock: Good day care." *New York Times International* February 1.

Kuebli, Janet, and Robyn Fivish. 1992. "Gender differences in parent-child conversations about past emotions." *Sex Roles* 27(11-12):683-98.

Kuhhlman, Annette. 1996. "Indian country in the 1990s: Changing roles of American Indian women." Paper presented at the Midwest Sociological Society, Chicago, April.

Kunin, Madeleine. 1994. *Living a Political Life: One of America's First Governors Tells Her Story*. New York: Alfred A. Knopf.

Kurdek, L.A. 1993. "The allocation of household labor in gay, lesbian, and heterosexual married couples." *Journal of Social Issues* 49:127-39.

Kurtz, Demie. 1995. *For Richer, For Poorer: Mothers Confront Divorce*. New York: Routledge.

Kuttner, Lawrence. 1988. "Children need help forming self-image." *New York Times* February 25:F21.

Lackey, P. N. 1989. "Adults' attitudes about assignments of household chores to male and female children." *Sex Roles* 20:271-81.

LaCroix, Andrea Z., and S. G. Haynes. 1987. "Gender differences in the health effects of work-place roles." In R. C. Barnett, L. Biener, and G. K. Baruch (eds.), *Gender and Stress*. New York: Free Press.

LaFollette, Hugh. 1992. "Real men." In Larry May and Robert Strikwerda (eds.), *Rethinking Masculinity: Philosophical Explorations in Light of Feminism*. Lanham, MD: Rowman & Littlefield.

LaFromboise, Teresa D., Anneliese M. Heyle, and Emily J. Ozer. 1990. "Changing and diverse roles of women in American Indian culture." *Sex Roles* 22(7/8):455-76.

Lake, Celinda C., and Vincent J. Breglio. 1992. "Different voices, different views: The politics of gender." In Paula Ries and Anne J. Stone (eds.), *The American Woman, 1992-93: A Status Report*. New York: W. W. Norton.

Lake, Celinda C., and Nikki Heidepriem. 1988. "The gender gap and the 1988 elections." *The Polling Report* (November 21):2-3.

Lakoff, Robin. 1975. *Language and Woman's Place*. New York: Colsphon. 1991. "You are what you say." In Evelyn Ashton-Jones and Gary A. Olson (eds.), *The Gender Reader*. Boston, MA: Allyn & Bacon.

Lam, Alice. 1993. "Equal employment opportunities for Japanese women: Changing company practice." In Janice Hunter (ed.), *Japanese Women Working*. London: Routledge.

Lamb, Michael F. 1979. "Paternal influences and the father's role." *American Psychologist* 32:938-43.

Lamb, Sharon, and Mary Coakley. 1993. "Normal childhood sexual play and games: Differentiating play from abuse." *Child Abuse and Neglect* 17(4):515-26.

Lamm, M. 1980. *The Jewish Way in Love and Marriage*. San Francisco: Harper & Row.

Landale, Nancy S., and Katherine Fennelly. 1992. "Informal unions among mainland Puerto Ricans: Cohabitation or an alternative to legal marriage?" *Journal of Marriage and the Family* 54:269-80.

Lang, T. 1971. *The Difference Between a Man and a Woman*. New York: John Day.

Langley, Merlin R. 1994. "The cool pose: An Africentric analysis." In Richard G. Majors and Jacob U. Gordon (eds.), *The American Black Male: His Present Status and His Future*. Chicago: Nelson-Hall.

Langlois, Judith H., and Chris A. Downs. 1980. "Mothers, fathers and peers as socialization agents of sex-typed behaviors in young children." *Child Development* 51:1237-47.

Langton, Phyllis A. 1994. "Obstetrician's resistance to independent private practice by nurse-midwives in Washington, D.C. hospitals." *Women and Health* 22(1):27-48.

Lanis, Kyra, and Katherine Covell. 1995. "Images of women in advertisements: Effects on attitudes related to sexual aggression." *Sex Roles* 22(9-10):639-49.

Larned, Deborah. 1975. "The selling of valium." *MS* 4(5):32-33.

LaRossa, Ralph, 1992. "Fatherhood and social change." In Michael S. Kimmel and Michael A. Messner (eds.), *Men's Lives*. New York: Macmillan.

LaRossa, Ralph, Betty Anne Gordon, Ronald Jay Wilson, Annette Bairan, and Charles Jaret. 1991. "The fluctuating image of the 20th century American father." *Journal of Marriage and the Family* 53:531-44.

Lauer, Jeanette, and Robert Lauer. 1991. "Marriages made to last." In Leonard Cargan (ed.), *Marriages and Families: Coping with Change.* Englewood Cliffs, NJ: Prentice Hall.

Lawson, A. 1988. *Adultery: An Analysis of Love and Betrayal.* New York: Basic Books.

Lawson, Carol. 1990. "Class of '90 on the family: Who will mind the family?" *New York Times* June 7:C1,C6.

Lazarus, Arnold. 1987. "The five most dangerous myths about marriage." In Ollie Pocs and Robert H. Walsh (eds.), *Marriage and Family* (Annual Editions). Guilford, CT: Dushkin.

Lazier-Smith, L. 1989. "A new genderation of images of women." In P. J. Creedon (ed.), *Women in Mass Communication.* Newbury Park, CA: Sage.

Leahy, Robert L., and Stephen R. Shirk. 1984. "The development of classificatory skills and sex-trait stereotypes in children." *Sex Roles* 10(3-4):281-92.

Leaper, Campbell. 1994. "Exploring the consequences of gender segregation on social relationships." In Campbell Leaper (ed.), *Childhood Gender Segregation: Causes and Consequences.* San Francisco: Jossey-Bass.

Lebra, Takie Sugiyama. 1984. *Japanese Women: Constraint and Fulfillment.* Honolulu: University of Hawaii.

Lebsock, Suzanne. 1990. "'No obey': Indian, European, and African women in seventeenth-century Virginia." In Nancy A. Hewitt (ed.), *Women, Families, and Communities: Readings in American History, Volume One: to 1877.* Glenview, IL: Scott, Foresman.

Lee, Valerie E., and Anthony S. Bryk. 1986. "Effects of single-sex secondary schools on student achievement and attitudes." *Journal of Educational Psychology* 78:381-95.

Leeft-Pellegrini, Helena M. 1980. "Conversational dominance as function of gender and expertise." In Howard Giles, W. Peter Robinson, and Philip M. Smith (eds.), *Language: Social Psychological Perspectives.* New York: Pergamon.

Lefkowitz, Margaret B. 1972. "The women's magazine short story heroine in 1957 and 1967." In Constantine Safilios-Rothschild (ed.), *Toward a Sociology of Women.* Lexington, MA: Xerox.

Lehman, Edward D., Jr. 1993. *Gender and Work: The Case of the Clergy.* Albany, New York: State University of New York.

Lehne, Gregory K. 1992. "Homophobia among men: Supporting and defining the male role." In Michael S. Kimmel and Michael A. Messner (eds.), *Men's Lives.* New York: Macmillan.

Lemoyne, James. 1990. "Some Saudi women push changes." *New York Times* December 8.

Lennon, Mary Clare, and Sarah Rosenfield. 1994. "Relative fairness and the division of housework: The importance of options." *American Journal of Sociology* 100(2):506-31.

Leppard, Wanda, Shirley Matile Ogletree, and Emily Wallen. 1993. "Gender stereotyping in medical advertising: Much ado about something?" *Sex Roles* 29(11-12):829-38.

Lerner, Gerda. 1995a. "Men's power to define and the formation of female consciousness." In Sheila Ruth, *Issues in Feminism: An Introduction to Women's Studies.* Mountain View, CA: Mayfield. 1995b. "A new angle of vision." In Sheila Ruth, *Issues in Feminism: An Introduction to Women's Studies.* Mountain View, CA: Mayfield. 1996. "Placing women in history." In Mary Beth Norton and Ruth M. Alexander (eds.), *Major Problems in American Women's History.* Lexington, MA: D.C. Heath.

Lester, David. 1985. "Romantic attitudes toward love in men and women." *Psychological Reports* 56:662.

Lester, David, Nancy Brazill, Constance Ellis, and Thomas Guerin. 1984. "Correlates of romantic attitudes toward love: Androgyny and self disclosure." *Psychological Reports* 54(April):554.

Letich, Larry. 1991. "Do you know who your friends are?: Why most men over 30 don't have friends and what they can do about it." *Utne Reader* (May-June): 85-87.

Leung, J. J. 1990. "Aspiring parents and teachers' academic beliefs about young children." *Sex Roles* 23:83-90.

Lever, Janet. 1978. "Sex differences in the complexity of children's play and games." *American Sociological Review* 43:471-83.

Levin, Jack, and Arnold Arluke. 1985. "An exploratory analysis of sex differences in gossip." *Sex Roles* 12(3-4):281-86.

LeVine, Robert A. 1990. "Gender differences: Interpreting anthropological data." In Malkah T. Notman and Carol C. Nadelson (eds.), *Women and Men: New Perspectives on Gender Differences.* Washington, DC: American Psychiatric Press.

Levins, Harry. 1995. "People" column. *St. Louis Post-Dispatch* March 19:2A. 1996. Excerpt from the "People" column. *St. Louis Post-Dispatch* February 18:2A.

Levy, Marion J., Jr. 1989. *Our Mother-Tempers.* Berkeley, CA: University of California.

Lewin, Tamar. 1994. "Working women say bias persists." *New York Times* October 15.

Lewis, Diane K. 1995. "African-American women at risk: Notes on the sociocultural context of HIV infection." In Beth E. Schneider and Nancy E. Stoller (eds.), *Women Resisting AIDS: Feminist Strategies of Empowerment.* Philadelphia: Temple University.

Lewis, Lisa A. 1990. *Gender Politics and MTV: Voicing the Difference.* Philadelphia: Temple University.

Lewis, Sasha Gregory. 1979. *Sunday's Women: A Report on Lesbian Life Today.* Boston: Beacon.

Lewontin, R.C. 1994. "Women versus the biologists." *New York Review* April 7:31-35.

Lichter, Daniel T., Robert N. Anderson, and Mark D. Hayward. 1995. "Marriage markets and marital choice." *Journal of Family Issues* 16(4):412-31.

Liddle, Joanna, and Rama Joshi. 1986. *Daughters of Independence: Gender, Caste and Class in India.* London: Zed.

Linder, Marc. 1983. "Self-employment as a cyclical escape from unemployment: A case study of the construction industry in the United States during the postwar period." *Research in the Sociology of Work* 2:261-74.

Lindsey, Linda L. 1974. "Speech Behavior, Communicative Interference and Interracial Contact." Ph.D. Dissertation. Case Western Reserve University, Cleveland, OH. 1979. Book review of *Wisdom from Women in the Bible* by Edith Deen. *Review for Religious* 38(5):792–93. 1982. "Pharmacy and health care in India." *American Pharmacy* NS22(9):474–77. 1983. "Health care in India: An analysis of existing models." In John H. Morgan (ed.), *Third World Medicine and Social Change.* Lanham, MD: University Press of America. 1984. "Career paths in pharmacy: An exploration of male and female differences." Paper presented at the Midwest Sociological Society, Chicago. 1988. "The health status of women in Pakistan: The impact of Islamization." Paper presented at the Midwest Sociological Society, Minneapolis. 1990. "The health status of Afghan refugees: Focus on women." *Women in Development Forum.* Women in Development Publication Series, Michigan State University (August). 1992. "Gender and the workplace: Some lessons from Japan." Paper presented at the Midwest Sociological Society, Kansas City. 1994. "Women and development." Paper presented at the Midwest Sociological Society, St. Louis. 1995. "Toward a model of women in development." Paper presented at the Midwest Sociological Society, Chicago. 1996a. "Women and agriculture in the developing world." In Paula J. Dubeck and Kathryn Borman (eds.), *Women and Work: A Handbook.* New York: Garland. 1996b. "Gender equity and development: A perspective on the U.N. Conference on Women." Paper presented at the Midwest Sociological Society, Chicago. 1996c. "Full-time homemaker as unpaid laborer." In Paula J. Dubeck and Kathryn Borman (eds.), *Women and Work: A Handbook.* New York: Garland.

Linn, Marcia C., and Janet Shibley Hyde. 1989. "Gender, mathematics and science." *Educational Researcher* 18(8):17-27.

Linn, Marcia C., and Anne C. Petersen. 1985. "Emergence and characterization of gender differences in spatial ability." *Child Development* 56:1479-98.

Lipmen-Blumen, Jean. 1984. *Gender Roles and Power.* Englewood Cliffs, NJ: Prentice Hall.

Lipovskaya, Olga. 1994. "The mythology of womanhood in contemporary 'Soviet' culture." In Anastasia Posadskaya and the Moscow Gender Centre (eds.), *Women in Russia: A New Era in Russian Feminism.* London: Verso.

Lips, Hilary M. 1993. *Sex and Gender: An Introduction.* Mountain View, CA: Mayfield. 1995. "Gender-role socialization: Lessons in femininity." In Jo Freeman (ed.), *Women: A Feminist Perspective.* Mountain View, CA: Mayfield.

Lipton, Michael A. 1995. "The golden girls." *People Magazine* December 4:40-47.

Lister, David. 1995. "Bond's new girls edge slowly toward maturity." *Independent* January 23:3.

Little, E. 1848-1849. "What are the rights of women?" *Ladies Wreath* E2:133.

Little, Marilyn. 1982. "Conflict and negotiation in a new role: The family nurse practitioner." *Research in the Sociology of Health* 2:31-59.

Littlejohn-Blake, Sheila M., and Carol Anderson Darling. 1993. "Understanding the strengths of African American families." *Journal of Black Studies* 23(4):460-71.

Litwak, Eugene, and Stephen Kulis. 1987. "Technology, proximity and measures of kin support." *Journal of Marriage and the Family* 49:649-61.

Lloyd, Cynthia B. 1994. "Investing in the next generation: The implications of high fertility at the level of the family." In Robert Cassen (ed.), *Population and Development: Old Debates, New Conclusions.* Washington, DC: Overseas Development Council.

Lo, Jeannie. 1990. *Office Ladies, Factory Women.* New York: M.E. Sharpe.

Lobel, S.A. 1991. "Allocation of investment in work and family roles: Alternative theories and implications for research." *Academy of Management Review* 16:507-21.

Locksley, A., and M. E. Colten. 1979. "Psychological androgyny: A case of mistaken identity?" *Journal of Personality and Social Psychology* 39:821-31.

Loden, Marilyn. 1985. *Feminine Leadership or How to Succeed in Business Without Being One of the Boys.* New York: New York Times Books.

London, K. A. 1990. "Cohabitation, marriage, marital dissolution and remarriage: United States, 1988." *Advance Data from Vital and Health Statistics,* No. 194. Hyattsville, MD: National Center for Health Statistics.

London, K. A., and B. F. Wilson. 1988. "D-i-v-o-r-c-e." *American Demographics* 10(10):22-26.

Longstreth, M., K. Stafford, and T. Mauldin. 1987. "Self-employed women and their family: Time use and socioeconomic characteristics." *Journal of Small Business Management* 25:30-37.

Lopata, Helen Znaniecka. 1993. "Career commitments of American women: The issue of side bets." *Sociological Quarterly* 34(2):257-77.

LoPiccolo, J., and W. E. Stock. 1986. "Treatment of sexual dysfunction." *Journal of Consulting and Clinical Psychology* 54:158-67.

Lorber, Judith. 1986. "Dismantling Noah's Ark." *Sex Roles* 14(11-12):567-79. 1993. "From the chair." *Sex and Gender : Newsletter of the American Sociological Association Section on Sex and Gender* (Spring):1-4. 1996. "Believing is seeing: Biology as ideology." In Mary F. Rogers (ed.), *Multicultural Experiences, Multicultural Theories.* New York: McGraw-Hill.

Lorde, Audre. 1992. "Age, race, class and sex: Women redefining difference." In Paula S. Rothenberg (ed.), *Race, Class, and Gender in the United States: An Integrated Study.* New York: St. Martin's.

Loring, Marti, and Brian Powell. 1988. "Gender, race and DSM-III: A study of the objectivity of psychiatric diagnostic behavior." *Journal of Health and Social Behavior* 29:1-22.

Loscocco, Karyn A., and Joyce Robinson. 1991. "Barriers to women's small-business success in the United States." *Gender & Society* 6:511-32.

Lott, Bernice. 1988. "Sexist discrimination as distancing behavior, II: Primetime television." *Psychology of Women Quarterly* 13(3):341-55. 1994. *Women's Lives: Themes and Variations in Gender Learning.* Pacific Grove, CA: Brooks/Cole.

Lott, Bernice, and Diane Maluso. 1993. "The social learning of gender." In Anne E. Beall and Robert J. Sternberg (eds.), *The Psychology of Gender.* New York: Guilford.

Lottes, Ilsa L. 1993. "Nontraditional gender roles and the sexual experiences of heterosexual college students." *Sex Roles* 29(9-10):645-69.

Lovdal, L.T. 1989. "Sex role messages in television commercials: An update." *Sex Roles* 21:715-24.

Love, Marsha. 1978. "Health hazards of office work." *Women and Health* 3(3):18-22.

Lowry, Dennis T., Gail Love, and Malcolm Kirby. 1981. "Sex on the soap operas: Patterns of intimacy." *Journal of Communication* 31(Spring):90-96.

Luby, V., and A. Aron. 1990. "Prototype analysis of the constructs of like, love and in love." *Proceedings of the Fifth International Conference on Personal Relationships,* Oxford, UK.

Lucas, Angela M. 1983. *Women in the Middle Ages: Religion, Marriage and Letters.* New York: St. Martin's.

Luker, Kristin. 1984. *Abortion and the Politics of Motherhood.* Berkeley: University of California.

Lutheran Book of Worship. 1978. Minneapolis, MN: Augsburg.

Lutwin, David R., and Gary N. Siperstein. 1985. "Househusband fathers." In Shirley M. H. Hanson and Frederick W. Bozett (eds.), *Dimensions of Fatherhood.* Beverly Hills, CA: Sage.

Lye, Diane N., and Timothy J. Biblarz. 1993. "The effects of attitudes toward family life and gender roles on marital satisfaction." *Journal of Family Issues* 14(2):157-88.

Lynn, David B. 1959. "A note on sex differences in the development of masculine and feminine identification." *Psychological Review* 66:126-35. 1969. *Parental and Sex Role Identification: A Theoretical Formulation.* Berkeley, CA: McCutchan.

Lynn, Naomi B. 1984. "Women and politics: The real majority." In Jo Freeman (ed.), *Women: A Feminist Perspective.* Palo Alto, CA: Mayfield.

Lynxwiler, John, and David Gay. 1994. "Reconsidering race differences in abortion attitudes." *Social Science Quarterly* 75(1):67-84.

Lystra, Karen. 1989. *Searching the Heart: Women, Men and Romantic Love in Nineteenth Century America.* New York: Oxford University.

Maccoby, Eleanor Emmons. 1987. "The varied meanings of 'masculine' and 'feminine.'" In June Machover Reinisch, Leonard A. Rosenblum, and Stephanie A. Sanders (eds.), *Masculinity/Femininity: Basic Perspectives.* New York: Oxford University. 1994. "Commentary: Gender segregation in childhood." In Campbell Leaper (ed.), *Childhood Gender Segregation: Causes and Consequences.* San Francisco: Jossey-Bass.

Maccoby, Eleanor Emmons, and Carol Nagy Jacklin. 1974. *The Psychology of Sex Differences.* Stanford, CA: Stanford University.

MacDonald, Kevin, and Ross D. Parke. 1986. "Parent-child physical play: The effects of sex and age on children and parents." *Sex Roles* 15:367-78.

Macintyre, Sally. 1993. "Gender differences in the perceptions of common cold symptoms." *Social Science and Medicine* 36(1):15–20.

Macionis, John J. 1995. *Sociology.* Englewood Cliffs, NJ: Prentice Hall.

MacKay, D. G. 1983. "Psychology, prescriptive grammar and the pronoun problem." In Barrie Thorne, Cheris Kramarae, and Nancy Henley (eds.), *Language, Gender and Society.* Rowley, MA: Newbury House.

Mackie, Vera. 1988. "Feminist politics in Japan." *New Left Review* 167:53-76.

MacKinnon, Catharine A. 1982. "Feminism, Marxism, method and the state: An agenda for theory." *Signs* 7(3):515-44. 1993. "Sex equality: Difference and dominance." In Alison M. Jaggar and Paula S. Rothenberg (eds.), *Feminist Frameworks: Alternative Theoretical Accounts of the Relations between Women and Men.* New York: McGraw-Hill.

Macklin, Eleanor D. 1980. "Nontraditional family forms: A decade of research." *Journal of Marriage and the Family* 42:905-22. 1983. "Nonmarital heterosexual cohabitation: An overview." In Eleanor D. Macklin and Roger H. Rubin (eds.), *Contemporary Families and Alternative Lifestyles.* Beverly Hills, CA: Sage. 1988. "Cohabitation in the United States." In J. Gipson Wells (ed.), *Current Issues in Marriage and the Family.* New York: Macmillan.

Maclean, Ian. 1980. *The Renaissance Notion of Woman: A Study in the Fortunes of Scholasticism and Medical Science in European Intellectual Life.* Cambridge, UK: Cambridge University.

MacLean, William. 1993. "Woman heads Kuwait University." *Arab News* November 23.

Maher, Frances A., and Mary Kay Thompson Tetreault. 1994. *The Feminist Classroom: An Inside Look at How Professors and Students Are Transforming Higher Education for a Diverse Society.* New York: Basic Books.

Mahony, Rhonda. 1995. *Kidding Ourselves: Breadwinning, Babies, and Bargaining Power.* New York: Basic Books.

Mainstreaming. 1995. *Mainstreaming of Gender Equality in Norway: Introducing the Gender Perspective into Norwegian Public Administration.* Oslo: Royal Ministry of Children and Family Affairs.

Maital, Shlomo. 1989. "A long way to the top." *Across The Board* 26(December):6-7.

Majors, Richard G., and J. Billson. 1992. *Cool Pose: The Dilemmas of Black Manhood in America.* New York: Lexington.

Majors, Richard G., Richard Tyler, Blaine Peden, and Ron Hall. 1994. "Cool pose: A symbolic mechanism for masculine role enactment and coping by black males." In Richard G. Majors and Jacob U. Gordon (eds.), *The American Black Male: His Present Status and His Future.* Chicago: Nelson-Hall.

Malamuth, N. M. 1981. "Rape proclivity among males." *Journal of Social Issues* 37:138-57. 1989. "Sexually violent media, thought patterns and antisocial behavior." In George Comstock (ed.), *Public Communication and Behavior,* Vol. 2. New York: Academic Press.

Malson, Michelene Ridley. 1983. "Black women's sex roles: The social context for a new ideology." *Journal of School Issues* 39(3):101-13.

Mamonova, Tatyana (ed.). 1984. *Women and Russia: Feminist Writings from the Soviet Union.* Boston: Beacon. 1994. *Women's Glasnost vs. Naglost: Stopping Russian Backlash.* Westport, CT: Bergin & Garvey.

Mandel, Ruth B. 1986. "The image campaign." In James David Barber and Barbara Kellerman (eds.), *Women Leaders in American Politics.* Englewood Cliffs, NJ: Prentice Hall. 1995. "A generation of change for women in politics." In Jo Freeman (ed.), *Women: A Feminist Perspective.* Mountain View, CA: Mayfield.

Mandel, Ruth B., and Debra L. Dodson. 1992. "Do women officeholders make a difference?" In Paula Ries and Anne J. Stone (eds.), *The American Woman, 1992-93: A Status Report.* New York: W. W. Norton.

Manley, Joan E. 1995. "Sex-segregated work in the system of professions: The development and stratification of nursing." *Sociological Quarterly* 36(2):297-314.

Mann, Judy. 1995a. "What the House could learn from Peru." *Washington Post* November 3:E3. 1995b. "Moving on to the bigger issues." *Washington Post* May 12:E3. 1996. "Beijing comes home." *Washington Post* March 8:E3.

Mansbridge, Jane J. 1986. *Why We Lost the ERA.* Chicago: University of Chicago.

Maret, Elizabeth, and Barbara Finlay. 1984. "The distribution of household labor among women in dual-earner families." *Journal of Marriage and the Family* 46:357-64.

Margolis, Maxine E. 1984. *Mothers and Such: View of American Women and Why They Changed.* Berkeley, CA: University of California.

Mariko, Fujita. 1989. "It's all mother's fault: Childcare and the socialization of working mothers in Japan." *Journal of Japanese Studies* 15(1):67-91.

Marini, Margaret Mooney. 1989. "Sex differences in earnings in the United States." In W. R. Scott and J. Blake (eds.), *Annual Review of Sociology,* vol. 15. Palo Alto, CA: Annual Reviews.

Marini, Margaret Mooney, and M. Brinton. 1984. "Sex typing in occupational socialization." In Barbara F. Reskin (ed.), *Sex Segregation in the Workplace: Trends, Explanations, and Remedies.* Washington, DC: National Academic Press.

Mark, June. 1992. "Beyond equal access: Gender equity in learning with computers." *Women's Educational Act Publishing Center* (June):1–8.

Markey, Judith. 1986. "When he gets custody." In Ollie Pocs and Robert H. Walsh (eds.), *Marriage and Family* (Annual Editions) Guilford, CT: Dushkin.

Markus, Hazel Rose, M. Crane, S. Bernstein, and M. Siladi. 1982. "Self schemas and gender." *Journal of Personality and Social Psychology* 42:38-50.

Marshall, Susan E. 1995. "Keep us on the pedestal: Women against feminism in twentieth-century America." In Jo Freeman (ed.), *Women: A Feminist Perspective.* Palo Alto, CA: Mayfield.

Marsiglio, William, 1992. "Paternal engagement activities with minor children." *Journal of Marriage and the Family* 53:973-86. 1993. "Attitudes toward homosexual activity and gays as friends: A national survey of 15- to 19-year old males." *Journal of Sex Research* 30(1):12-17.

Marsiglio, William, and Constance L. Shehand. 1993. "Adolescent males' abortion attitudes: Data from a national survey." *Family Planning Perspectives* 25(4):162-69.

Marti, Judith. 1993. "Introduction: Economics, power and gender." In Mari Womack and Judith Marti (eds.), *The Other Fifty Percent: Multicultural Perspectives on Gender Relations.* Prospect Heights, IL: Waveland.

Martin, Carol Lynn. 1994b. "Cognitive influences on the development and maintenance of gender segregation." In Campbell Leaper (ed.), *Childhood Gender Segregation: Causes and Consequences.* San Francisco: Jossey-Bass.

Martin, Carol Lynn, and C. F. Halverson. 1981. "A schematic processing model of sex typing and stereotyping in children." *Child Development* 52:1119-34. 1983. "Gender constancy: A methodological and theoretical analysis." *Sex Roles* 9:775-90.

Martin, Carol Lynn, and Jane K. Little. 1990. "The relation of gender understanding to children's sex-typed preferences and gender stereotypes." *Child Development* 61:1427-39.

Martin, Dorothy H. 1985. "Fathers and adolescents." In Shirley M. H. Hanson and Frederick W. Bozett (eds.), *Dimensions of Fatherhood.* Beverly Hills, CA: Sage.

Martin, Emily. 1994a. "Medical metaphors of women's bodies: Menstruation and menopause." In Elizabeth Fee and Nancy Krieger (eds.), *Women's Health, Politics and Power: Essays on Sex/Gender, Medicine, and Public Health*. Amityville, NY: Baywood.

Martin, George T. 1991. "Family, gender and social policy." In Laura Kramer (ed.), *The Sociology of Gender: A Text-Reader*. New York: St. Martin's.

Martin, Patricia Yancey, and Robert A. Hummer. 1993. "Fraternities and rape on campus." In Laurel Richardson and Verta Taylor (eds.), *Feminist Frontiers III*. New York: McGraw-Hill.

Martin, Susan Erlich. 1995. "Sexual harassment: The link joining gender stratification, sexuality and women's economic status." In Jo Freeman (ed.), *Women: A Feminist Perspective*. Mountain View, CA: Mayfield.

Martyna, W. 1983. "Beyond the he/man approach: The case for nonsexist language." In Barrie Thorne, Cheris Kramarae, and Nancy Henley (eds.), *Language, Gender and Society*. Rowley, MA: Newbury House.

Marx, Karl. 1964 (original, 1848). T. B. Bottomore and Maxilien Rubel (eds.), *Selected Writings in Sociology and Social Philosophy*. Baltimore, MD: Penguin. 1967 (original, 1867-95). *Das Capital*. New York: International.

Masters, Brooke. 1994. "Staying the science course." *Washington Post Education Review* April 3:8,10.

Masters, William H., and Virginia Johnson. 1966. *Human Sexual Response*. Boston: Little, Brown. 1970. *Human Sexual Inadequacy*. Boston: Little, Brown.

Mathis, Susan. 1994. "Propaganda to mobilize women for World War II." *Social Education* 58(2):94-96.

May, Elaine Tyler. 1995. *Barren in the Promised Lane: Childless America and the Pursuit of Happiness*. New York: Basic Books.

Maynard, Mary. 1990. "The re-shaping of sociology: Trends in the study of gender." *Sociology* 24(2):269-90.

McAdoo, Harriette Pipes. 1990. "A portrait of African-American families in the United States." In S. E. Rix (ed.), *The American Woman, 1990-91: A Status Report*. New York: W. W. Norton.

McBride, James. 1995. *War, Battering, and Other Sports: The Gulf Between American Men and Women*. Atlantic Highlands, NJ: Humanities Press.

McBroom, William H. 1981. "Parental relationships, socioeconomic status and sex role expectations." *Sex Roles* 7:1027-33.

McClelland, Scott E. 1990. "The new reality in Christ: Perspectives from biblical studies." In June S. Hagen (ed.), *Gender Matters: Women's Studies for the Christian Community*. Grand Rapids, MI: Zondervan.

McConnell-Ginet, Sally. 1989. "The sexual (re)production of meaning: A discourse-based theory." In F.W. Frank and P.A. Treichler (eds.), *Language, Gender, and Professional Writing: Theoretical Approaches and Guidelines for Nonsexist Usage*. New York: Modern Language Association of America.

McCreery, John L. 1993. "Women's property rights and dowry in China and South Asia." In Caroline B. Brettell and Carolyn F. Sargent (eds.), *Gender in Cross-Cultural Perspective*. Englewood Cliffs, NJ: Prentice Hall.

McDaniel, Susan A. 1996. "Toward a synthesis of feminist and demographic perspectives on fertility." *Sociological Quarterly* 37(1):83-104.

McDonnell, Nancy S., Tsitsi V. Himunyanga-Phiri, and Annie Tembo. 1993. "Widening economic opportunities for women: Removing barriers one brick at a time." In Gay Young, Vidyamali Samarasinghe, and Ken Kusterer (eds.), *Women at the Center: Development Practices for the 1990s*. West Hartford, CT: Kumarian.

McElhiney, Annette Bennington. 1993a. "Redefining women's health." In Jodi Wetzel, Margo Linn Espenlaub, Monys A. Hagen, Annette Bennington McElhiney, and Carmen Braun Williams (eds.), *Women's Studies Thinking Women*. Dubuque, IA: Kendall/Hunt. 1993b. "Violence against women." In Jodi Wetzel, Margo Linn Espenlaub, Monys A. Hagen, Annette Bennington McElhiney, and Carmen Braun Williams (eds.), *Women's Studies Thinking Women*. Dubuque, IA: Kendall/Hunt.

McEwen, Bruce S. 1990. "Sex differences in the brain: What they are and how they arise." In Malkah T. Notman and Carol C. Nadelson (eds.), *Women and Men: New Perspectives on Gender Differences*. Washington, DC: American Psychiatric Press.

McFarlane, Alice. 1996. "The language of menopause." Unpublished manuscript from the School of Health Professions, Maryville University-St. Louis.

McGonigle, Steve. 1994. "Clinton stressing diversity in judicial nominations." *Dallas Morning News* September 2:1A, 32A.

McGrory, Mary. 1992. "A worthy mission for Hillary." *Washington Post* November 26.

McGuire, J. 1988. "Gender stereotypes of parents with two-year-olds and beliefs about gender differences in behavior." *Sex Roles* 19:233-40.

McLanahan, Sara, and Karen Booth. 1989. "Mother-only families: Problems, prospects and politics." *Journal of Marriage and the Family* 51:557-80.

McLoughlin, Merrill. 1988. "Men versus women: The new debate over sex differences." *U.S. News and World Report* August 8:48,51-56.

McManus, Michael J. 1986. "Introduction." In *Final Report of the Attorney General's Commission on Pornography*. Nashville, TN: Rutledge Hill.

McMillan, Julie R., A. Kay Clifton, Diane McGrath, and Wanda S. Gale. 1977. "Women's language: Uncertainty or interpersonal sensitivity and emotionality?" *Sex Roles* 3:545-59.

McMillen, Liz. 1985. "Despite new laws and college policies, women say sexism lingers on campuses." *Chronicle of Higher Education* 29(February 6):27-28.

McMinn, Mark R., Shannan F. Lindsay, Laurel E. Hannum, and Pamela K. Troyer. 1990. "Does sexist language reflect personal characteristics?" *Sex Roles* 23(7-8):389-96.

Meacham, Andrew. 1990. "Masculinity redefined." *Changes* September-October:29-35.

Mead, George Herbert. 1934. *Mind, Self and Society*. Chicago: University of Chicago.

Mead, Margaret. 1935. *Sex and Temperament in Three Primitive Societies*. New York: William Morrow.

Meade, M. 1993. *Men and the Water of Life: Initiation and the Tempering of Men*. San Francisco: HarperSanFrancisco

Mechanic, David. 1989. *Mental Health and Social Policy*. Englewood Cliffs, NJ: Prentice Hall.

Media Report to Women. 1993. "Scoring the news media: Underrepresentation of women continues." (Spring):2-3.

Megill-Cobbler, Thelma. 1993. "Reading Paul on women." *Lutheran Women Today* 6(January):12-15.

Melton, J. Gordon. 1991. *The Church Speaks On: Sex and Family Life*. Detroit, MI: Gale Research.

Melton, Willie, and Linda L. Lindsey. 1987. "Instrumental and expressive values in mate selection among college students revisited: Feminism, love and economic necessity." Paper presented at the Midwest Sociological Society, Chicago, April.

Melton, Willie, and Darwin L. Thomas. 1976. "Instrumental and expressive values in mate selection of black and white college students." *Journal of Marriage and Family* 38:509-17.

Mernissi, Fatima. 1987. *Beyond the Veil: Male-Female Dynamics in Modern Muslim Society*. Bloomington, IN: Indiana University.

Messner, Michael A. 1992. *Power at Play: Sports and the Problem of Masculinity*. Boston: Beacon. 1995. "Masculinities and athletic careers." In Margaret L. Andersen and Patricia Hill Collins (ed.), *Race, Class, and Gender: An Anthology*. Belmont, CA: Wadsworth.

Metzger, G. 1992. "T.V. is a blonde, blonde world." *American Demographics* (November):51.

Meyerowitz, Joanne. 1990. "The roaring teens and twenties reexamined: Sexuality in the furnished room districts of Chicago." In Nancy A. Hewitt (ed.), *Women, Families and Communities: Readings in American History, Volume Two: From 1865*. Glenview, IL: Scott, Foresman.

Meyers, David G. 1996. *Social Psychology*. New York: McGraw-Hill.

Michael, Robert T., John H. Gagnon, Edward O. Laumann, and Gina Kolata. 1994. *Sex in America: A Definitive Study*. Boston: Little, Brown.

Miedzian, Myriam. 1991. *Boys Will Be Boys: Breaking the Link Between Masculinity and Violence*. New York: Doubleday.

Miles, Rosalind. 1989. *The Women's History of the World*. Topsfield, MA: Salem House.

Milkman, Ruth. 1991. "Women work: The sexual division of labor in the auto industry during World War II." In Kathryn Kish Sklar and Thomas Dublin (eds.), *Women and Power in American History: A Reader, Volume II from 1870*. Englewood Cliffs, NJ: Prentice Hall.

Miller, Barbara D. 1981. *The Endangered Sex: Neglect of Female Children in Rural North India*. Ithaca, NY: Cornell University. 1993. "Female infanticide and child neglect in rural north India."

In Caroline B. Brettell and Carolyn F. Sargent (eds.), *Gender in Cross-Cultural Perspective.* Englewood Cliffs, NJ: Prentice Hall.

Miller, Brent C., Cynthia R. Christopherson, and Pamela K. King. 1993. "Sexual behavior in adolescence." In Thomas P. Gullota, Gerald R. Adams, and Raymond Montemayor (eds.), *Adolescent Sexuality.* Newbury Park, CA: Sage.

Miller, Brian. 1992. "Life-styles of gay husbands and fathers." In Michael S. Kimmel and Michael A. Messner (eds.), *Men's Lives.* New York: Macmillan.

Miller, Casey, and Kate Swift. 1991a. *Words and Women Updated: New Language in New Times.* New York: HarperCollins. 1991b. "One small step for genkind." In Evelyn Ashton-Jones and Gary A. Olson (eds.), *The Gender Reader.* Boston: Allyn & Bacon. 1993. "Who is man?" In Anne Minas (ed.), *Gender Basics: Feminist Perspectives on Women and Men.* Belmont, CA: Wadsworth.

Miller, Cristanne. 1994. "Who says what to whom." In Camille Roman, Suzanne Juhasz, and Cristanne Miller (eds.), *The Women and Language Debate: A Sourcebook.* New Brunswick, NJ: Rutgers University.

Miller, Cynthia L. 1987. "Qualitative differences among gender stereotyped toys: Implications for cognitive and social development in girls and boys." *Sex Roles* 16(9-10):473-87.

Miller, Francesca. 1991. *Latin American Women and the Search for Social Justice.* Hanover, NH: University Press of New England.

Miller-Bernal, Leslie. 1991. "Single-sex education: An anachronism or a beneficial structure?" In Laura Kramer (ed.), *The Sociology of Gender: A Text-Reader.* New York: St. Martin's.

Millett, Kate. 1995. "Sexual politics." In Stevi Jackson et al. (eds.), *Women's Studies Essential Readings.* New York: New York University.

Mills, Sara. 1995. *Feminist Stylistics.* London: Routledge.

Minai, Naila. 1991. "Women in early Islam." In Carol J. Verburg (ed.), *Ourselves among Others: Cross-Cultural Readings for Writers.* Boston: Bedford Books.

Mincer, Jillian. 1994. "Boys get called on." *New York Times Education Life* January 9:27–29.

Minces, Juliette. 1982. *The House of Obedience: Women in Arab Society.* London: Zed.

Mintz, Steven, and Susan M. Kellogg. 1988. *Domestic Revolution: A Social History of American Family Life.* New York: Free Press.

Mirande, A. 1979. "Machismo: A reinterpretation of male dominance in the Chicano family." *Family Coordinator* 28:473-79.

Mischel, W. A. 1966. "A social learning view of sex differences in behavior." In E. E. Maccoby (ed.), *The Development of Sex Differences.* Stanford, CA: Stanford University.

Mitchell, Juliet. 1971. *Women's Estate.* Baltimore: Penguin. 1974. *Psychoanalysis and Feminism.* New York: Pantheon.

Mitter, Sara S. 1991. *Dharma's Daughters: Contemporary Indian Women and Hindu Culture.* New Brunswick, NJ: Rutgers University.

Moen, Elizabeth. 1991. "Sex selective eugenic abortion: Prospects in China and India." *Issues in Reproductive and Genetic Engineering* 4:231-49.

Moen, Phyllis, Julie Robison, and Donna Dempster-McClain. 1995. "Caregiving and women's well-being: A life course approach." *Journal of Health and Social Behavior* 36(3):213-301.

Moffatt, Michael. 1989. *Coming of Age in New Jersey: College and American Culture.* New Brunswick, NJ: Rutgers University.

Moghadam, Valentine M. 1995. "Gender and revolutionary transformation: Iran 1979 and East Central Europe 1989." *Gender & Society* 9(3):328-58.

Money, John, and Anke A. Ehrhardt. 1972. *Man and Woman, Boy and Girl.* Baltimore, MD: Johns Hopkins University.

Mongeau, Paul A., Melody Yeazell, and Jerold L. Hale. 1994. "Sex differences in relational message interpretations on male- and female-initiated first dates: A research note." *Journal of Social Behavior and Personality* 9(4): 731-42.

Montagu, Ashley. 1974. *The Natural Superiority of Women.* London: Collier MacMillan.

Mooney, Elizabeth C. 1985. *Men and Marriage: The Changing Roles of Husbands.* New York: Franklin Watts.

Moore, Dorothy P. 1990. "An examination of present research on the female entrepreneur: Suggested research strategies for the 1990's." *Journal of Business Ethics* 9:275-81.

Moore, Molly, and John Anderson. 1993. "Women, fed up and fighting back." *Washington Post* February 18: A1,A34.

Moore, Susan, and Jennifer Boldero. 1991. "Psychosocial development and friendship functions in adolescence." *Sex Roles* 25(9-10):521-36.

Moraga, Cherríe. 1995. "La Guera." In Margaret L. Andersen and Patricia Hill Collins (eds.), *Race, Class, and Gender: An Anthology*. Belmont, CA: Wadsworth.

Morgan, Babette. 1994. "To Lynn Martin, breaking glass ceilings is good business." *St. Louis Post-Dispatch* December 4:E1,E8.

Morgan, Marabel. 1973. *The Total Woman*. New York: Pocket Books.

Morgan, Mary. 1988. "The impact of religion on gender-role attitudes." *Psychology of Women Quarterly* 11:301-10.

Morgan, S. Philip, Antonio McDaniel, Andrew T. Miller, and Samuel H. Preston. 1993. "Racial differences in household and family structure at the turn of the century." *American Journal of Sociology* 98(4):799-828.

Morrell, Stephen, Richard Taylor, Susan Quine, and Charles Kerr. 1993. "Suicide and unemployment in Australia, 1907-1990. *Social Science and Medicine* 36(6):749-56.

Morris, Celia. 1992. "Changing the rules and the roles: Five women in public office." In Paula Ries and Anne J. Stone (eds.), *The American Woman, 1992-93: A Status Report*. New York: W. W. Norton.

Morrison, A. M., R. P. White, F. Van Velsor, and the Center for Creative Change. 1992. *Breaking the Glass Ceiling: Can Women Reach the Top of America's Largest Corporations?* Reading, MA: Addison-Wesley.

Moses, Joel C. 1986. "The Soviet Union in the women's decade." In Lynn B. Iglitzin and Ruth Ross (eds.), *Women in the World: 1975-1985, The Women's Decade*. Santa Barbara, CA:ABC-Clio.

Mott, Frank, L. 1994. "Sons, daughters and fathers' absence: Differentials in father-leaving probabilities and in home environments." *Journal of Family Issues* 15(1):97-128.

Moynihan, Daniel P. 1965. *The Negro Family: The Case for National Action*. Office of Policy Planning and Research, U.S. Department of Labor. Washington, DC: U.S. Government Printing Office.

Moynihan, Ruth B., Susan Armitage, and Christine Fisher Dichamp (eds). 1990. *So Much to Be Done: Women Settlers on the Mining and Ranching Frontier*. Lincoln, NE: University of Nebraska.

Mueller, Carol M. 1993. "The gender gap and women's political influence." In Laurel Richardson and Verta Taylor (eds.), *Feminist Frontiers III*. New York: McGraw-Hill.

Mueller, Eric. 1985. "Revitalizing old ideas: Developments in Middle Eastern family law." In Elizabeth Warnock Fernea (ed.), *Women and the Family in the Middle East*. Austin, TX: University of Texas.

Muir, Anne Ross. 1993. "The status of women working in film and television." In Stevi Jackson et al. (eds.), *Women's Studies Essential Readings*. New York: New York University.

Mulac, A., J.M. Wiemann, S.J. Widenmann, and T.W. Gibson. 1988. "Male/female language differences and effects in same-sex and mixed-sex dyads: The gender-linked language effect." *Communication Monographs* 55:315-35.

Mullan, Bob. 1984. *The Mating Trade*. London: Routledge.

Mullen, Mary K. 1990. "Children's classifications of nature and artifact pictures into female and male categories." *Sex Roles* 23:577-87.

Mumford, Emily. 1983. *Medical Sociology: Patients, Providers and Policies*. New York: Random House.

Muraskin, Roslyn. 1993. "Abortion: Is it abortion or compulsory childbearing?" In Roslyn Muraskin and Ted Alleman (eds.), *It's a Crime: Women and Justice*. Englewood Cliffs, NJ: Prentice Hall.

Murphy, Caryle. 1993. "Lowering the veil: Muslim women struggle for careers in a society ruled by men and religion." *Washington Post* February 17:A1,A24-25.

Murstein, Bernard I. 1980. "Mate selection in the 1970's." *Journal of Marriage and the Family* (November):777-92. 1986. *Paths to Marriage*. Beverly Hills, CA: Sage. 1991. "Dating: Attracting and meeting." In John N. Edwards and David H. Demo (eds.), *Marriage and Family in Transition*. Boston: Allyn & Bacon.

Myers, David G. 1996. *Social Psychology*. New York: McGraw-Hill.

Myers, George C. 1992. "Demographic aging and family support for older persons." In Hal L. Kendig, Akiko Hashimodo, and Larry C. Coppard (eds.), *Family Support for the Elderly: The International Experience.* New York: Oxford University (World Health Organization).

Myres, Sandra L. 1988. "Victoria's daughters: English-speaking women on the nineteenth century frontiers." In Lillian Schlissel, Vicki I. Ruiz, and Janice Monk (eds.), *Western Women: Their Land, Their Lives.* Albuquerque, NM: University of New Mexico.

Nagao, Noriko. 1993. "Marriage partner selection in Japan." Paper presented to Gender Roles class, Maryville University, December 16.

Nahas, Rebecca, and Myra Turley. 1980. *The New Couple: Women and Gay Men.* New York: Seaview.

Najmabadi, Afsaneh. 1993. "Veiled discourse-unveiled bodies." *Feminist Studies* 19(3):487-518.

Nash, A. 1989. "Will women change prime-time TV news?" *Glamour* (October):242, 245, 312-15.

Nash, June. 1990. "Latin American women in the world capitalist crisis." *Gender & Society* 4(3):338-53.

Nathanson, Constance A. 1991. *Dangerous Passage: The Social Control of Sexuality in Women's Adolescence.* Philadelphia: Temple University.

National Center for Education Statistics. 1994. *Digest of Education Statistics, 1993.* Washington, DC: U.S. Department of Education.

National Center for Health Statistics. 1993. *Health, United States, 1992.* Washington, DC: U.S. Government Printing Office.

Neal, Arthur G., H. Theodore Groat, and Jerry W. Wicks. 1989. "Attitudes about having children: A study of 600 couples in the early years of marriage." *Journal of Marriage and the Family* 51:313-27.

Neff, James Alan, Bruce Holamon, and Tracy Davis Schluter. 1995. "Spousal violence among Anglos, blacks and Mexican Americans: The role of demographic variables, psycho-social predictors, and alcohol consumption." *Journal of Family Violence* 10(1):1-21.

Nehra, Arvind. 1934. *Letters of an Indian Judge to an English Gentlewoman.* London: Peter Davies.

Nelson, Debra L., and Michael A. Hitt. 1992. "Employed women and stress: Implications for enhancing women's mental health in the workplace." In James Campbell Quick, Lawrence R. Murphy, and Joseph J. Hurrell, Jr. (eds.), *Stress and Well-Being at Work: Assessments and Interventions for Occupational Mental Health.* Washington, DC: American Psychological Association.

Nelson, E.D. 1993. "Sugar daddies: 'Keeping' a mistress and the gentleman's code." *Qualitative Sociology* 16(1):43-68.

Nelton, Sharon, and Karen Berney. 1987. "Women: The second wave." *National Business* (May):18-27.

Nemy, Enid. 1995. "No children, no apologies." *New York Times* April 6.

Neuman, Shoshana. 1991. "Occupational sex segregation in the kibbutz: Principles and practice." *Kyklos* 44:203-19.

Newcomb, Paul C. 1982. "Cohabiting in America: An assessment of consequences." In Jeffrey P. Rosenfeld (ed.), *Relationships: The Marriage and Family Reader.* Glenview, IL: Scott, Foresman.

Nielsen, Francois. 1994. "Sociobiology and sociology." *Annual Review of Sociology* 20:267-303.

Nielsen Media Research. 1994. *Report on Television.* New York: A. G. Nielsen.

Nigro, Georgia W., Dina E. Hill, and Martha E. Gelbein. 1988. "Changes in the facial prominence of women and men over the last decade." *Psychology of Women Quarterly* 12:225-35.

Nikkei Weekly. 1993. "Couples marry later, date longer: Survey." September 27:26.

Nilsen, Alice Pace. 1993. "Sexism is English: A 1990s update." In Virginia Cyrus (ed.), *Experiencing Race, Class, and Gender in the United States.* Mountain View, CA: Mayfield.

Noble, Barbara Presley. 1993. "Dissecting the 90's workplace." *New York Times* September 19:21. 1994. "Putting women on the agenda." *New York Times* May 1:21.

Nochimson, Martha. 1992. *No End to Her: Soap Opera and the Female Subject.* Berkeley, CA: University of California.

Nock, Steven L. 1995. "Spousal preferences of never-married, divorced and cohabiting Americans." *Journal of Divorce and Remarriage* 23(3-4):91-108.

Nock, Steven L., and Paul W. Kingston. 1988. "Time with children: The impact of couples' work-time commitments." *Social Forces* 67:59-85.

Noeller, Patricia. 1980. "Marital misunderstanding: A study of couples' nonverbal communication." *Journal of Personality and Social Psychology* 39:1135-48.

Noeller, Patricia, and Mary Anne Fitzpatrick. 1993. *Communication in Family Relationships*. Englewood Cliffs, NJ: Prentice Hall.

Nolen-Hoeksema, Susan. 1990. *Sex Differences in Depression*. Stanford, CA: Stanford University.

Norris, J.E. 1994. "Effects of marital disruption on older adults: Widowhood." In L. Ploufe (ed.), *Writings in Gerontology: Late Life Marital Disruptions*. Ottawa: National Advisory Board on Aging.

Norris, Mary E. 1992. "The impact of development on women: A specific-factors analysis." *Journal of Development Economics* 38(1):183-201.

Norton, Arthur J., and Paul C. Glick. 1986. "One-parent families: A social and economic profile." *Family Relations* 35:9-17.

Norton, Arthur J., and L. F. Miller. 1991. "Marriage, divorce and remarriage in the 1990s." Paper presented at the American Public Health Association, Atlanta.

Norton, Mary Beth. 1984. "The evolution of white women's experience in early America." *American Historical Review* 89:593-619.

Norton, Mary Beth, and Ruth M. Alexander (Eds.). 1996a. *Major Problems in American Women's History*. Lexington, MA: D.C. Heath. 1996b. "Anita Hill's testimony before the Senate Judiciary Committee, 1991." In *Major Problems in American Women's History*. Lexington, MA: D.C. Heath.

Norwood, Vera. 1988. "Women's place: Continuity and change in response to Western landscapes." In Lillian Schlissel, Vicki L. Ruiz, and Janice Monk (eds.), *Western Women: Their Land, Their Lives*. Albuquerque, NM: University of New Mexico.

Nowacki, C. M., and C. A. Poe. 1973. "The concept of mental health as related to the sex of the person." *Journal of Consulting and Clinical Psychology* 40:160.

Nussbaum, Martha C., and Amartya Sen. 1993. "Introduction." In Martha Nussbaum and Amartya Sen (eds.), *The Quality of Life: A Study Prepared for the World Institute for Development Economics Research (WIDER) of the United Nations University*. Oxford, UK: Clarendon (Oxford University).

O'Brien, Joanne, and Martin Palmer. 1993. *The State of Religion Atlas*. New York: Simon & Schuster.

O'Connell, Mary. 1984. "Why don't Catholics have women priests?" *U.S. Catholic* (January):6-12.

O'Connor, Pat. 1992. *Friendships between Women: A Critical Review*. New York: Guilford.

O'Donnell, William J., and Karen J. O'Neill. 1985. "The trend in the male-female wage gap in the United States." *Journal of Labor Economics* 3(1):91-116.

O'Farrell, Brigid. 1995. "Women in blue-collar occupations: Traditional and nontraditional." In Jo Freeman (ed.), *Women: A Feminist Perspective*. Mountain View, CA: Mayfield.

O'Hare, William P., Kevin M. Pollard, Taynia L. Mann, and Mary M. Kent. 1995. "African-Americans in the 1990s." In Mark Robert Rank and Edward L. Kain (eds.), *Diversity and Change in Families: Patterns, Prospects, and Policies*. Englewood Cliffs, NJ: Prentice Hall.

O'Neill, June. 1985. "The trend in the male-female wage gap in the United States." *Journal of Labor Economics* 3(1):91-116.

O'Neill, Nena. 1977. *The Marriage Premise*. New York: M. Evans.

O'Neill, Nena, and George O'Neill. 1972. *Open Marriage: A New Life Style for Couples*. New York: M. Evans.

O'Neill, William L. 1989. *Feminism in American History*. New Brunswick, NJ: Transaction.

Oakley, Ann. 1974. *The Sociology of Housework*. New York: Pantheon. 1985. *Sex, Gender and Society*. New York: Harper & Row. 1993. "Becoming a mother." In Stevi Jackson et al. (eds.), *Women's Studies Essential Readings*. New York: New York University.

Obermeyer, Carla Makhlouf. 1994. "Reproductive choice in Islam: Gender and state in Iran and Tunisia." *Studies in Family Planning* 25(1):41-51.

Oduyoye, Mercy Amba. 1988. "Be a woman and Africa will be strong." In Letty M. Russell et al. (eds.), *Inheriting Our Mother's Garden: Feminist Theology in Third World Perspective*. Philadelphia: Westminster.

Ogden, Annegret S. 1986. *The Great American Housewife: From Helpmate to Wage Earner, 1776-1986.* Westport, CT: Greenwood.

Ollenburger, Jane C., and Helen A. Moore. 1992. *A Sociology of Women: The Intersection of Patriarchy, Capitalism and Colonization.* Englewood Cliffs, NJ: Prentice Hall.

Omvedt, Gail. 1980. *We Will Smash This Prison.* London: Zed.

Orenstein, Peggy. 1994. *School Girls: Young Women, Self-Esteem, and the Confidence Gap.* New York: Doubleday.

Ortiz, Vilma. 1994. "Women of Color: A Demographic Overview." In Maxine Baca Zinn and Bonnie Thornton Dill (eds.), *Women of Color in U.S. Society.* Philadelphia: Temple University.

Osawa, Machiko. 1988. "Working mothers: Changing patterns of employment and fertility in Japan." *Economic Development and Social Change* 36(4):623-50.

Osmond, Marie Withers, K.G. Wambach, Dianne F. Harrison, Joseph Byers, Philippa Levine, Allen Imershein, and David M. Quadagno. 1993. "The multiple jeopardy of race, class and gender for AIDS risk among women." *Gender & Society* 7(1):99-120.

Ostling, Richard N. 1991. "The search for Mary: Handmaid or feminist?" *Time* (December 30):62-66. 1992. "The second Reformation." *Time* (November 23):53-58.

Overholt, Catherine A., Kathleen Cloud, Mary B. Anderson, and James E. Austin. 1991. "Gender analysis framework." In Aruna Rao, Mary B. Anderson, and Catherine A. Overholt (eds.), *Gender Analysis in Development Planning.* West Hartford, CT: Kumarian.

Pagels, Elaine. 1979. *The Gnostic Gospels.* New York: Random House.

Paley, Vivian Gussin. 1984. *Boys and Girls: Superheroes in the Doll Corner.* Chicago: University of Chicago.

Paludi, Michele A. 1984. "Psychometric properties and underlying assumptions of four objective measures of fear and success." *Sex Roles* 10:765-81. 1992. *The Psychology of Women.* Dubuque, IA: Brown & Benchmark. 1996. *Sexual Harassment on College Campuses: Abusing the Ivory Power.* Albany, NY: State University of New York.

Paludi, Michele A., and Richard B. Barickman. 1991. *Academic and Workplace Sexual Harassment: A Resource Manual.* Albany, NY: State University of New York.

Pampel, Fred C. 1993. "Relative cohort size and fertility: The Easterlin Effect in context." *American Sociological Review* 58(4):496-514.

Parade Magazine. 1991. "Sexual harassment: Gender gap on Capitol Hill." November 17:10. 1993. "Will Oscar make his day?" March 28:11-12. 1995. "Worst news about family values." December 31:12.

Parelius, Ann P. 1991. "Mathematics and science majors: Gender differences in selection and persistence." In Laura Kramer (ed.), *The Sociology of Gender: A Text-Reader.* New York: St. Martin's.

Park, Chai Bin, and Nam-Hoon Cho. 1995. "Consequences of son preference in a low-fertility society: Imbalance of the sex ratio at birth in Korea." *Population and Development Review* 21(1):59-84.

Parke, Ross D., and S. E. O'Leary. 1976. "Father-mother-infant interaction in the newborn period." In K. Riegel and J. Meacham (eds.), *The Developing Individual in a Changing World,* Vol. 2. The Hague: Mouton.

Parlee, Mary Brown. 1982. "The psychology of the menstrual cycle: Biological and psychological perspectives." In R.C. Friedman (ed.), *Behavior and the Menstrual Cycle.* New York: Marcel Dekker. 1989. "Conversational politics." In Laurel Richardson and Verta Taylor (eds.), *Feminist Frontiers II: Rethinking Sex, Gender and Society.* New York: Random House.

Parry, H. L., M. Balter, G. Mellinger, I. H. Cisin, and D. I. Manheimer. 1973. "National patterns of therapeutic drug use." *Archives of General Psychiatry* 28:769-83.

Parsons, Talcott. 1951. *The Social System.* Glencoe, IL: Free Press. 1964. *Social Structure and Personality.* Glencoe, IL: Free Press. 1966. *Societies: Evolutionary and Comparative Perspectives.* Englewood Cliffs, NJ: Prentice Hall.

Parsons, Talcott, and Robert F. Bales (eds.). 1955. *Family, Socialization, and Interaction Process.* Glencoe, IL: Free Press.

Patterson, Charlotte J. 1992. "Children of lesbian and gay parents." *Child Development* 63(5):1025-42. 1994. "Children of the lesbian baby boom: Behavioral adjustment, self-concepts and sex role identity." In Beverly Green and Gregory M. Herek (eds.), *Lesbian and Gay Psychology: Theory, Research and Clinical Applications.* Thousand Oaks, CA: Sage.

Paul, M., C. Daniels, and R. Rosofsky. 1989. "Corporate response to reproductive hazards in the workplace: Results of the family, work and health survey." *American Journal of Industrial Medicine* 16:267-80.

Pavalko, Eliza K., and Glen H. Elder, Jr. 1993. "Women behind the men: Variations in wives' support of husbands' careers. *Gender & Society* 7(4):548-67.

Pavletich, Aida. 1980. *Sirens of Song: The Popular Female Vocalist in America.* New York: De Capo.

Paz, J.J. 1993. "Support of Hispanic elderly." In Harriet Pipes McAdoo (ed.), *Family Ethnicity: Strength in Diversity.* Newbury Park, CA: Sage.

Pearce, Diana M. 1993. "Something old, something new: Women's poverty in the 1990s." In Sherri Matteo (ed.), *American Women in the Nineties: Today's Critical Issues.* Boston: Northeastern University.

Pearson, Judy Cornelia. 1989. *Gender and Communication.* Dubuque, IA: William C. Brown.

Pederson, F. A., B. Anderson, and R. Cain. 1980. "Parent-infant and husband-wife interactions observed at age 5 months." In F. A. Pederson (ed.), *The Father-Infant Relationship: Observational Studies in a Family Setting.* New York: Praeger.

Peers, Jo. 1985. "Workers by hand and womb: Soviet women and the demographic crisis." In Barbara Holland (ed.), *Soviet Sisterhood.* Bloomington, IN: Indiana University.

Peirce, Kate. 1990. "A feminist theoretical perspective on the socialization of teenage girls through *Seventeen* magazine." *Sex Roles* 23(9-10):491-500.

Pennington, Gail. 1995. "Cagney and Lacey battle World Series: Police duo on whirlwind tour for movie." *St. Louis Post-Dispatch* October 22:4C.

People and Development Challenges. 1995. "Special report: China." (International Planned Parenthood Federation) 2(3):5-18.

Peplau, L. Anne. 1991. "Lesbian and gay relationships." In J.C. Gonsiorek and J.D. Wwinrich (eds.), *Homosexuality: Research Findings for Public Policy.* Newbury Park, CA: Sage.

Peradotto, John, and J. P. Sullivan (eds.). 1984. *Women in the Ancient World: The Arethusa Papers.* Albany: SUNY.

Perdue, Theda. 1994. "Cherokee women and the trail of tears." In Vicki L. Ruiz and Ellen Carol DuBois (eds.), *Unequal Sisters: A Multicultural Reader in U.S. Women's History.* New York: Routledge.

Peretti, P. O., and T. M. Sydney. 1985. "Parental toy stereotyping and its effect on child toy preference." *Social Behavior and Personality* 12:213-16.

Perkins, Daniel F., and Richard M. Lerner. 1995. "Single and multiple indicators of physical attractiveness and psychosocial behavior among young adolescents." *Journal of Early Adolescence* 15(3):269-98.

Perkins, H. Wesley, and Debra K. DeMeis. 1996. "Gender and family effects on the 'second shift' domestic activity of college-educated young adults." *Gender & Society* 10(1):78-93.

Perutz, Kathrin. 1972. *Marriage Is Hell.* New York: William Morrow. 1975. "The anachronism of marriage." In Kenneth C. W. Kammeyer (ed.), *Confronting the Issues: Sex Roles, Marriage and the Family.* Boston: Allyn & Bacon.

Pesch, Marina, et al. 1981. "Sex role stereotypes on the airwaves of the eighties." Paper presented at the Eastern Communication Association, Pittsburgh, April.

Peters, Michael. 1991. "Sex, handedness, mathematical ability and biological causation." *Canadian Journal of Psychology* 45(3):415-19.

Petersen, Anne C. 1980. "Biopsychosocial processes in the development of sex-related differences." In Jacquelynne E. Parsons (ed.), *The Psychobiology of Sex Differences and Sex Roles.* Washington, DC: Hemisphere.

Petersen, Karen E. 1987. "An investigation into women-identified music in the United States." In Ellen Koskoff (ed.), *Women and Music in Cross-Cultural Perspective.* New York: Greenwood.

Peterson, John Brian, and Peter G. Christenson. 1987. "Gender and sexuality in the structure of musical preference." Paper presented at the Women's Studies Conference, Western Kentucky University, Bowling Green.

Peterson, Rolf A. 1983. "Attitudes toward the childless spouse." *Sex Roles* 9(3):321-31.

Petty, R., and H. Mirels. 1981. "Intimacy and scarcity of self-disclosure: Effects on interpersonal attraction for males and females." *Personality and Social Psychology Bulletin* 7:490-503.

Pharr, Susan. 1981. *Political Women in Japan.* Berkeley, CA: University of California.

Pharr, Suzanne J. 1995. "Homophobia as a weapon of sexism." In Paula S. Rothenberg (ed.), *Race, Class, and Gender in the United States: An Integrated Study.* New York: St. Martin's.

Phillips, Roger D., and Faith D. Gilroy. 1985. "Sex-role stereotypes and clinical judgments of mental health: The Brovermans' findings reexamined." *Sex Roles* 12(1-2):179-93.

Piaget, Jean. 1950. *The Psychology of Intelligence.* London: Routledge. 1954. *The Construction of Reality in the Child.* New York: Basic Books.

Pirie, Phyllis L., David M. Murray, and Russell V. Luepker. 1991. "Gender differences in cigarette smoking and quitting in a cohort of young adults." *American Journal of Public Health* 81(3):324-25.

Pittman, Frank. 1995. "Beyond betrayal: Life after infidelity." In Kathleen R. Gilbert (ed.), *Marriage and the Family 95/96* (Annual editions). Guilford, CT: Dushkin/Brown & Benchmark.

Plato. 1991. "The role of women in the ideal society." In Evelyn Ashton-Jones and Gary A. Olson (eds.), *The Gender Reader.* Boston: Allyn & Bacon.

Pleck, Joseph H. 1983. "Husbands' paid work and family roles: Current research issues." In Helen Lopata (ed.), *Research in the Interweave of Social Roles, Jobs and Families.* 1985. *Working Wives, Working Husbands.* Beverly Hills, CA: Sage. 1993. "Are 'family supportive' employer policies relevant to men?" In Jane C. Hood (ed.), *Men, Work, and Family.* Newbury Park, CA: Sage.

Plomin, R., and T. Foch. 1981. "Sex differences and individual differences." *Child Development* 52:383-85.

Podrouzek, W., and D. Furrow. 1988. "Preschoolers' use of eye contact while speaking: The influence of sex, age and conversation pattern." *Psycholinguistic Research* 17:89-98.

Poire, B.A., J.K. Burgoon, and R. Parrott. 1992. "Status and privacy restoring communication in the workplace." *Journal of Applied Communication Research* 4:419-36.

Polatnick, M. Rivka. 1993. "Why men don't rear children." In Anne Minas (ed.), *Gender Basics: Feminist Perspective on Women and Men.* Belmont, CA: Wadsworth.

Pollitt, Katha. 1991. "The smurfette principle." *New York Times Magazine* April 7:22–23.

Pollock, Joycelyn M., and Barbara Ramirez. 1995. "Women in the legal profession." In Alida V. Merlo and Joycelyn M. Pollack (eds.), *Women, Law, and Social Control.* Boston: Allyn & Bacon.

Pomerleau, Andree, Daniel Bolduc, Gerard Malcuit, and Louise Cossette. 1990. "Pink or blue: Gender stereotypes in the first two years of life." *Sex Roles* 22(5-6):359-67.

Poole, Debra A., and Anne E. Tapley. 1988. "Sex roles, social roles and clinical judgments of mental health." *Sex Roles* 19(5-6):265-72.

Poole, Keith T., and L. Harmon Zeigler. 1985. *Women, Public Opinion and Politics: The Changing Political Attitudes of American Women.* New York: Longman.

Pooler, William S. 1991. "Sex of child preferences among college students." *Sex Roles* 25(9-10):569-576.

Posadskaya, Anastasia. 1994. "A feminist critique of policy, legislation and social consciousness in post-socialist Russia." In Anastasia Posadskaya and the Moscow Gender Centre (eds.), *Women in Russia: A New Era in Russian Feminism.* London: Verso.

Potuchek, J.L. 1992. "Employed wives' orientations to breadwinning: A gender theory analysis." *Journal of Marriage and the Family* 54:548-58.

Powers, Susan. 1992. "Sexual harassment: Civil Rights Act increases liability." *HR Focus* 2:12.

Prather, Jane, and Linda S. Fidell. 1975. "Sex differences in the content and style of medical advertisements." *Social Science and Medicine* 9:23-26.

Press, Andrea L. 1991. *Women Watching Television: Gender, Class, and Generation in the American Television Experience.* Philadelphia: University of Pennsylvania.

Presser, Harriet. 1994. "Employment schedules among dual-earner spouses and the division of household labor by gender." *American Sociological Review* 59(3):348-64.

Pribram, E. Deidre. 1993. "Female spectators." In Stevi Jackson et al. (eds.), *Women's Studies Essential Readings.* New York: New York University.

Price-Bonham, S., and P. Skeen. 1982. "Black and white fathers' attitudes toward children's sex roles." *Psychological Bulletin* 50:1187-90.

Prior, Mary. 1994. "Freedom and autonomy in England and the Netherlands: Women's lives and experience in the seventeenth century." In Els Kloek, Nicole Teeuwen, and Marijke Huisman (eds.), *Women of the Golden Age: An International Debate on Women in Seventeenth-Century Holland, England and Italy.* Amsterdam: Hilversum Verloren.

Pruett, Kyle D. 1987. *The Nurturing Father: Journey Toward the Complete Man.* New York: Warner.

Puddington, Arch. 1996. "What to do about affirmative action." In Harold A. Widdison (ed.), *Social Problems 96/97* (Annual Editions). Guilford, CT: Dushkin/Brown & Benchmark.

Pugliesi, Karen. 1995. "Work and well-being: Gender differences in the psychological consequences of employment." *Journal of Health and Social Behavior* 36(1):57-71.

Pui-Lan, Kwok. 1988. "Mothers and daughters, writers and fighters." In Letty M. Russell et al. (eds.), *Inheriting Our Mother's Garden: Feminist Theology in Third World Perspective.* Philadelphia: Westminster.

Purcell, Piper, and Lara Stewart. 1990. "Dick and Jane in 1989." *Sex Roles* 22(3-4):177-85.

Qian, Zhenchao, and Samuel H. Preston. 1993. "Changes in American marriage, 1972 to 1987: Availability and forces of attraction by age and education." *American Sociological Review* 58(4):482-95.

Quick, James Campbell, Lawrence R. Murphy, and Joseph J. Hurrell, Jr. (Eds.). 1992. *Stress and Well-Being at Work: Assessments and Interventions for Occupational Mental Health.* Washington, DC: American Psychological Association.

Quindlen, Anna. 1994. "Hillary at midterm." *New York Times* October 12: 1.

Rabbie, Jacob M., Charles Goldenbeld, and Hein F.M. Lodewijkx. 1992. "Sex differences in conflict and aggression in individual and group settings." In Kaj Björkqvist and Pirkko Niemelä (eds.), *Of Mice and Women: Aspects of Female Aggression.* San Diego: Academic Press.

Rabine, L. W. 1985. "Romance in the age of electronics: Harlequin enterprises." *Feminist Studies* 11:39-60.

Rabinowitz, Frederic E., and Sam V. Cochran. 1994. *Man Alive: A Primer of Men's Issues.* Pacific Grove, CA: Brooks/Cole.

Radcliffe, Sarah A., and Sallie Westwood (Eds). 1993. *Viva: Women and Popular Protest in Latin America.* London: Routledge.

Radhakrishnan, Sarvepalli. 1947. *Religion and Society.* London: Allen and Unwin.

Radosh, Polly F. 1986. "Midwives in the United States: Past and present." *Population Research and Policy Review* 5:129-45.

Radway, J. R. 1984. *Reading and Romance: Women, Patriarchy and Popular Literature.* Chapel Hill, NC: University of North Carolina.

Raley, R. Kelly. 1995. "Black-white differences in kin contact and exchange among never married adults." *Journal of Family Issues* 16(1)77-103.

Ramey, James. 1978. "Experimental family forms: The family of the future." *Marriage and Family Review* 1:1-9.

Ramsey, Patricia G. 1995. "Changing social dynamics in early childhood classrooms." *Child Development* 66(3):764-73.

Ranson, Gillian, and William Joseph Reeves. 1996. "Gender earnings, and proportions of women: Lessons from a high-tech occupation." *Gender & Society* 10(2):168-84.

Rao, V., V. Prakasa, and V. Nandini Rao. 1980. "Instrumental and expressive values in mate selection among black students." *Western Journal of Black Studies* 4(Spring):50-56.

Rapoport, Tamar, Yoni Garb, and Anat Penso. 1995. "Religious socialization and female subjectivity: Religious-Zionist adolescent girls in Israel." *Sociology of Education* 68(1):48-61.

Rapp, Rayna. 1991. "Family and class in contemporary America." In Elizabeth Jelin (ed.), *Family, Household and Gender Relations in Latin America.* London: Kegan Paul.

Raskin, P.A., and A.C. Israel. 1981. "Sex-role imitation in children: Effects of sex of child, sex of model, and sex-role appropriateness of modeled behavior." *Sex Roles* 7:1067-77.

Rawlins, W.K. 1993. "Communication in cross-sex friendships." In Laurie Arliss and D. Borisoff (eds.), *Women and Men Communicating.* Fort Worth, TX: Harcourt Brace Jovanovich.

Rayman, Paula. 1993. *Pathways for Women in the Sciences.* Wellesley, MA: Wellesley College Center for Research on Women.

Rediscovering American Women. 1995. "A chronology highlighting women's history in the United States *and* update—the process continues." In Sheila Ruth, *Issues in Feminism: An Introduction to Women's Studies*. Mountain View, CA: Mayfield.

Reed, Barbara. 1987. "Taoism." In Arvind Sharma (ed.), *Women in World Religions*. Albany: State University of New York.

Reeves, B., and M. M. Miller. 1978. "A multidimensional measure of children's identification with television characters." *Journal of Broadcasting* 22(1):71-86.

Regev, Motti. 1994. "Producing artistic value: The case of rock music." *Sociological Quarterly* 35(1):85-102.

Reid, S. T. 1991. *Crime and Criminology*. Fort Worth, TX: Holt, Rinehart & Winston.

Reineke, Martha J. 1995. "Out of order: A critical perspective on women in religion." In Jo Freeman (ed.), *Women: A Feminist Perspective*. Mountain View, CA: Mayfield.

Reinisch, June, Leonard A. Rosenblum, and Stephanie A. Sanders. 1987. "Masculinity/femininity: An introduction." In June Machover Reinisch, Leonard A. Rosenblum, and Stephanie A. Sanders (eds.), *Masculinity/Femininity: Basic Perspectives*. New York: Oxford University.

Reisine, Susan, and Judith Fifield. 1995. "Family work demands and depressive symptoms in women with rheuymatoid arthritis." *Women and Health* 22(3):25-45.

Reitzes, Donald C., Elizabeth J. Mutran, and Maria E. Fernandez. 1994. "Middle-aged working women: Similar and different paths to self-esteem." *Research on Aging* 16(4):355-74.

Rendely, Judith G., Robert M. Holmstrom, and Stephan A. Karp. 1984. "The relationship of sex-role identity life style, and mental health in suburban American homemakers: 1. Sex role, employment and adjustment." *Sex Roles* 11(9-10):839-48.

Renzetti, Claire M., and Daniel J. Curran. 1992. *Women, Men and Society*. Boston: Allyn & Bacon.

Repetti, Rena L., and Faye J. Crosby. 1984. "Women and depression: Exploring the adult role explanation." *Journal of Social and Clinical Psychology* 2(1):57-70.

Repetti, Rena L., Karen A. Matthews, and Indrid Waldron. 1989. "Employment and women's health: Effects of paid employment on women's mental and physical health." *American Psychologist* 44:1394–401.

Resick, P. A. 1983. "Sex role stereotypes and violence against women." In V. Franks and E. Rothblum (eds.), *The Stereotyping of Women: Its Effects on Mental Health*. New York: Springer.

Reskin, Barbara F. 1988. "Bringing the man back in: Sex differentiation and the devaluation of woman's work." *Gender & Society* 2(1):58-81. 1993. "Sex segregation in the workplace." *Annual Review of Sociology* 19:241-70.

Reskin, Barbara F., and Heidi I. Hartmann (Eds.). 1986. *Women's Work, Men's Work: Sex Segregation on the Job*. Washington, DC: National Academy Press.

Reskin, Barbara F., and Patricia A. Roos. 1990. *Job Queues, Gender Queues: Explaining Women's Inroads into Male Occupations*. Philadelphia: Temple University.

Reynolds, Katsue Akiba. 1985. "Female speakers of Japanese." *Feminist Issues* 5(Fall): 13-46. 1990. "Female speakers of Japanese in transition." In Sachiko Ide and Naomi Hanaoka McGloin (eds.), *Aspects of Japanese Women's Language*. Tokyo: Kurosio.

Rheingold, H., and K. Cook. 1975. "The content of boys' and girls' rooms as an index of parent behavior." *Child Development* 46:459-63.

Rhoads, Steven E. 1993. *Incomparable Worth: Pay Equity Meets the Market*. New York: Cambridge University.

Rhode, Deborah L. 1993. "Gender equality and employment policy." In Sherri Matteo (ed.), *American Women in the Nineties: Today's Critical Issues*. Boston: Northeastern University.

Rhodes, Jewell Parker, and Edward Lao Rhodes. 1984. "Commuter marriage: The toughest alternative." *MS* (June):44-48.

Rhonda, James P. 1996. "The attractions of Christianity for the native women of Martha's Vineyard." In Mary Beth Norton and Ruth M. Alexander (eds.), *Major Problems in American Women's History*. Lexington, MA: D.C. Heath.

Richardson, D. C., and G. Hammock. 1991. "The role of alcohol in acquaintance rape." In A. Parrot and L. Bechhofer (eds.), *Acquaintance Rape: The Hidden Crime*. New York: John Wiley.

Richardson, Laurel. 1986. "Another world." *Psychology Today* (February):23-27. 1988. *The Dynamics of Sex and Gender: A Sociological Perspective*. New York: Harper & Row. 1996. "Gender stereotyping in the English language." In Karen E. Rosenblum and ToniMichelle C. Travis (eds.),

The Meaning of Difference: American Constructions of Race, Sex and Gender and Sexual Orientation." New York: McGraw-Hill.

Rickel, Annette U., and Marie C. Hendren. 1993. "Aberrant sexual experiences in adolescence." In Thomas P. Gullotta, Gerald R. Adams, and Raymond Montemayor (eds.), *Adolescent Sexuality.* Newbury Park, CA: Sage.

Ries, Paula, and Anne J. Stone (eds.). 1992. *The American Woman, 1992-93: A Status Report.* New York: W. W. Norton.

Riffe, Daniel, Patricia C. Place, and Charles M. Mayo. 1993. "Game time, soap time and prime time TV ads: Treatment of women in Sunday football and rest-of-week advertising." *Journalism Quarterly* 70(2):437-46.

Riger, Stephanie. 1993. "Gender dilemmas in sexual harassment: Policies and procedures." In Sherri Matteo (ed.), *American Women in the Nineties: Today's Critical Issues.* Boston: Northeastern University.

Riley, Glenda. 1986. *Inventing the American Woman: A Perspective on Women's History, 1607-1877.* Arlington Heights, IL: Harlan Davidson. 1988. *The Female Frontier: A Comparative View of Women on the Prairie and the Plains.* Lawrence, KS: University of Kansas. 1991. "Women and Indians on the frontier." In Kathryn Kish Sklar and Thomas Dublin (eds.), *Women and Power in American History: A Reader, Volume I to 1880.* Englewood Cliffs, NJ: Prentice Hall.

Rindfuss, R. R., and E. H. Stephen. 1990. "Marital noncohabitation: Absence does not make the heart grow fonder." *Journal of Marriage and the Family* 52:259-70.

Riordan, Cornelius. 1994. "Single-gender schools: Outcomes for African and Hispanic Americans." *Research in Sociology of Education and Socialization* 10:177-205.

Rishmawi, Mona. 1986. "The legal status of Palestinian women in the Occupied Territories." In Nahid Toubia (ed.), *Women in the Arab World: The Coming Challenge.* London: Zed.

Risman, Barbara J. 1986. "Can men mother? Life as a single father." *Family Relations* 35:95-102. 1987. "Intimate relationships from a microstructural perspective: Men who mother." *Gender & Society* 1(1):6-32. 1991. "Gender and perestroika: A personal account." *SWS Network: The Newsletter of Sociologists for Women in Society* 8(4):3, 13.

Risman, Barbara J., Charles T. Hill, Letitia Anne Peplau, and Zick Rubin. 1981. "Living together in college: Implications for courtship." *Journal of Marriage and the Family.* 77:77-83.

Roberts, George W. 1994. "Brother to brother: African American modes of relating among men." *Journal of Black Studies* 24(4):379-90.

Roberts, R. E., and S. J. O'Keefe. 1981. "Sex differences in depression re-examined." *Journal of Health and Social Behavior* 22:394-400.

Roberts, Robert E.T. 1994. "Black-white intermariage in the United States." In Walton R. Johnson and D. Michael Warren (eds.), *Inside the Mixed Marriage: Accounts of Changing Attitudes, Patterns, and Perceptions of Cross-Cultural and Interracial Marriages.* Lanham, MD: University Press of America.

Robson, K., and R. Kumar. 1980. "Delayed onset of maternal affection after childbirth." *British Journal of Psychiatry* 136:347-53.

Rodnitzky, Jerome L. 1976. "The southwest unbound: Janis Joplin and the new feminism." *Feminist Art Journal* 5(4):22-25.

Rogers, Lisa Kay, and Jeffry H. Larson. 1991. "Voluntary childlessness." In Leonard Cargan (ed.), *Marriages and Families: Coping with Change.* Englewood Cliffs, NJ: Prentice Hall.

Romano, Lois. 1995. "First lady, eye to eye with herself." *Washington Post,* January 10.

Romer, Nancy. 1990. "Is political activism still a masculine endeavor?" *Psychology of Women Quarterly* 14(2):229-43.

Roopnarine, Jaipaul L. 1986. "Mothers' and fathers' behaviors toward the toy play of their infant sons and daughters." *Sex Roles* 14:59-68.

Roopnarine, Jaipaul L., and Mohammad Ahmeduzzaman. 1993. "Puerto Rican father involvement with their preschool-age children." *Hispanic Journal of Behavioral Sciences* 15(1):96-107.

Roos, Patricia A. 1985. *Gender and Work: A Comparative Analysis of Industrial Societies.* Albany: SUNY.

Roscoe, Will. 1992. *The Zuni Man-Woman.* Albuquerque, NM: University of New Mexico.

Rose, Jacqueline. 1983. "Femininity and its discontents." *Feminist Review* 14:7-21.

Rose, Kenneth D. 1996. *American Women and the Repeal of Prohibition.* New York: New York University.

Rose, Mary Beth (Ed.). 1986. *Women in the Middle Ages and the Renaissance: Literary/Historical Perspectives.* Syracuse: Syracuse University.

Rosen, Marjorie. 1974. "Isn't it about time to bring on the girls?" *New York Times* December 15:D19.

Rosen, Ruth. 1994. "Not pornography." *Dissent* (Summer) 343-45.

Rosenbaum, J. E. 1985. "Persistence and change in pay inequalities: Implications for job evaluation and comparable worth." In Laurie Larwood, A. Stromberg, and B. Gutek (eds.), *Women and Work: An Annual Review, Vol. 1.* Beverly Hills, CA: Sage.

Rosener, Judy B. 1990. "Ways women lead." *Harvard Business Review* 68:119-25. 1991. "The valued ways men and women lead." *Human Resources* 36(6):147,149. 1995. *America's Competitive Secret: Utilizing Women as a Management Strategy.* New York: Oxford University.

Rosenfeld, Megan. 1995. "A woman's work: Forget sexual politics, Betty Friedan says: Economic empowerment is the real issue." *Washington Post* June 21:D1,D10.

Rosenfield, Sarah. 1989. "The effects of women's employment: Personal control and sex differences in mental health." *Journal of Health and Social Behavior* 30:77-91.

Rosenwasser, Shirley M., M. Hope Gonzales, and Vikki Adams. 1985. "Perceptions of a housespouse: The effects of sex, economic productivity and subject background variables." *Psychology of Women Quarterly* 9:258-64.

Ross, Catherine E. 1987. "The division of labor at home." *Social Forces* 65:816-33.

Ross, Catherine E., and John Mirowsky, 1995. "Does employment affect health?" *Journal of Health and Social Behavior* 36(3):23–43.

Ross, Hildy, and Heather Taylor. 1989. "Do boys prefer daddy or his physical style of play?" *Sex Roles* 20(1-2):23-31.

Ross, L., D. R. Anderson, and P. A. Wisocki. 1982. "Television viewing and adult sex-role attitudes." *Sex Roles* 8(6):589-92.

Rosser, Sue V. 1989. *The SAT Gender Gap: Identifying the Causes.* Washington, DC: Center for Women Policy Studies. 1992. *Biology and Feminism: A Dynamic Interaction.* New York: Twayne. 1994. "Gender bias in clinical research: The difference it makes." In Alice J. Dan (ed.), *Reframing Women's Health: Multidisciplinary Research and Practice.* Thousand Oaks, CA: Sage.

Rossi, Alice. 1968. "Transition to parenthood." *Journal of Marriage and the Family* 30:26-39. 1977. "Biosocial aspects of parenting." *Daedalus* 106:1-32. 1984. "Gender and parenthood: An evolutionary perspective." *American Sociological Review* 49:1-19.

Rossi, J. D. 1983. "Ratios exaggerate gender differences in mathematical ability." *American Psychologist* 38:348.

Rotenberg, Ken J. 1984. "Sex differences in children's trust in peers." *Sex Roles* 11(9-10):953-57.

Roth, Nicki. 1993. *Integrating the Shattered Self: Psychotherapy with Adult Incest Survivors.* Northvale, NJ: Jason Aronson.

Rothman, Barbara Katz. 1989. *Recreating Motherhood: Ideology and Technology in a Patriarchal Society.* New York: W. W. Norton. 1991. "Reproduction." In Laura Kramer (ed.), *The Sociology of Gender: A Text-Reader.* New York: St. Martin's. 1994. "Midwifery as feminist praxis." In William Kornblum and Carolyn D. Smith (eds.), *The Healing Experience: Readings on the Social Context of Health Care.* Englewood Cliffs, NJ: Prentice Hall.

Rothman, Barbara Katz, and Mary Beth Caschetta. 1995. "Treating health: Women and medicine." In Jo Freeman (ed.), *Women: A Feminist Perspective.* Mountain View, CA: Mayfield.

Roy, Debal Kumar Singha. 1993. "Peasant movements and women's responses." *International Journal of Contemporary Sociology* 30(2):185–98.

Roy, Ranjan. 1994. "AIDS explosion feared in India's prostitute towns." *St. Louis Post-Dispatch.* March 27:67G.

Rozee, Patricia D. 1996. "Freedom from fear of rape: The missing link in women's freedom." In Joan C. Chrisler, Carla Golden, and Patricia D. Rozee (eds.), *Lectures on the Psychology of Women.* New York: McGraw-Hill.

Rubenstein, Carin. 1983. "The modern art of courtly love." *Psychology Today* 19:40-49. 1986. "About love." In Carol Travis (ed.), *Everywoman's Emotional Well-Being.* Garden City, NY: Doubleday.

Rubenstein, Carin, and P. Shaver. 1982. *In Search of Intimacy.* New York: Delacorte.

Rubin, Jeffrey Z., Frank J. Provenzano, and Zella Luria. 1974. "The eye of the beholder: Parents' views on sex of newborns." *American Journal of Orthopsychiatry.* 44(4):512–19.

Rubin, Linda J., and Sherry B. Rogers. 1990. "Sexual harassment in universities during the 1980s." *Sex Roles* 23(7-8):397–411.

Rubin, Zick. 1973. *Liking and Loving: An Invitation to Social Psychology.* New York: Holt, Rinehart and Winston. 1983. "Are working wives hazardous to their husband's mental health?" *Psychology Today* 17:70–72.

Rubin, Zick, Letitia Anne Peplau, and Charles T. Hill. 1991. "Loving and leaving: Sex differences in romantic attachments." In John N. Edwards and David H. Demo (eds.), *Marriage and Family in Transition.* Boston: Allyn & Bacon.

Rudman, William J., and Patty Verdi. 1993. "Exploitation: Comparing sexual and violent imagery of females and males in advertising." *Women and Health.* 20(4):1–20.

Ruether, Rosemary. 1983. *Sexism and God-Talk: Toward a Feminist Theology.* Boston: Beacon. 1987. "Christianity." In Arvind Sharma (ed.), *Women in World Religions.* Albany: State University of New York.

Rufus, Anneli S., and Kristan Lawson. 1991. *Goddess Sites: Europe.* San Francisco: HarperCollins.

Ruggiero, J. A., and L. C. Weston. 1985. "Work options for women in women's magazines: The medium is the message." *Sex Roles* 12:535-47.

Ruiz, Vicki L., and Ellen Carol DuBois (Eds). 1994. *Unequal Sisters: A Multicultural Reader in U.S. Woman's History.* New York: Routledge.

Rule, Wilma. 1993. "Why are more women state legislators?" In Lois Lovelace Duke (ed.), *Women in Politics: Outsiders or Insiders?* Englewood Cliffs, NJ: Prentice Hall.

Rushwan, Hamid. 1995. "Female circumcision." *World Health* Special Issue on Women and Health (September):16-17.

Russel, D., and N. Vande Ven. 1976. "International crimes against women." Proceedings Les Femmes: Conference Publication.

Russell, Denise. 1995b. *Women, Madness and Medicine.* Cambridge, UK: Polity.

Russell, Diana E.H. 1990. *Rape in Marriage.* Bloomington, IN: Indiana University.

Russell, Gerald F.M. 1995a. "Anorexia Nervosa through time." In George Szmukler, Chris Dare, and Janet Treasure (eds.), *Handbook of Eating Disorders: Theory, Treatment and Research.* Chichester, UK: John Wiley.

Russo, Vito. 1986. "Whoopi Goldberg: Steven Spielberg chose the Broadway phenom to help him paint the color purple." *Moviegoer* 5(1).

Ruth, Sheila. 1995. *Issues in Feminism: An Introduction to Women's Studies.* Mountain View, CA: Mayfield.

Sabo, Don. 1992. "Pigskin, patriarchy and pain." In Michael S. Kimmel and Michael A. Messner (eds.), *Men's Lives.* New York: Macmillan.

Sadd, S., M. Lenauer, P. Shaver, and N. Dunivant. 1978. "Objective measurement of fear of success and fear of failure." *Journal of Consulting and Clinical Psychology* 46:405-16.

Sadker, Myra, and David Sadker. 1990. "Confronting sexism in the college classroom." In Susan L. Gabriel and Isaiah Smithson (eds.), *Gender in the Classroom: Power and Pedagogy.* Urbana, IL: University of Illinois. 1994. *Failing at Fairness: How America's Schools Cheat Girls.* New York: Charles Scribner's.

Sakol, Jeannie, and Lucianne Goldberg. 1975. "Married is better." In Kenneth C. W. Kammeyer (ed.), *Confronting the Issues: Sex Roles, Marriage and the Family.* Boston: Allyn & Bacon.

Salman, Magida. 1987. "The Arab woman." In Khamsin Series (6) *Women in the Middle East.* London: Zed.

Sanasarian, Eliz. (ed). 1982. *The Women's Rights Movement in Iran: Mutiny, Appeasement and Repression from 1900 to Khomeni.* Westport, CT: Greenwood. 1986. "Political activism and Islamic identity in Iran." In Lynn B. Iglitzin and Ruth Ross (eds.), *Women in the World, 1975-1985: The Women's Decade.* Santa Barbara, CA:ABC-Clio.

Sanborn, Charlotte J. 1990. "Gender socialization and suicide: American Association of Suicidology presidential address." *Suicide and Life-Threatening Behavior* 20(2):148-55.

Sanchez-Ayendez, Melba. 1986. "Puerto Rican elderly women: Shared meanings and informal supportive networks." In Johnnetta Cole (ed.), *All-American Women: Lines that Divide, Ties that Bind.* New York: Free Press.

Sandelowski, Margarete. 1994. "Separate but less unequal: Fetal ultrasonography and the transformation of expectant mother/fatherhood." *Gender & Society* 8(2): 230-45.

Sandler, Bernice R. 1987. "The classroom climate: A chilly one for women." In Carol Lasser (ed.), *Educating Men and Women Together: Coeducation in a Changing World.* Chicago: University of Illinois.

Sandqvist, K. 1987. *Fathers and Family Work in Two Cultures.* Stockholm: Almqvist and Wiksell.

Sapiro, Virginia. 1994. *Women in American Society: An Introduction to Women's Studies.* Mountain View, CA: Mayfield.

Saso, Mary. 1990. *Women in the Japanese Workplace.* London: Hilary Shipman.

Sauerwein, Kristina. 1996. "Survey of students: Sexual harassment an issue for many." *St. Louis Post-Dispatch Metro Post,* January 17:2W.

Saunders, D. G. 1989. "Who hits first and who hurts most? Evidence for the greater victimization of women in intimate relationships." Paper presented at the American Society of Criminology meetings, Reno, NV.

Scanzoni, Letha, D., and John Scanzoni. 1988. *Men, Women and Change: A Sociology of Marriage and Family.* New York: McGraw-Hill.

Scarr, S. 1984. *Mother Care/Other Care.* New York: Basic Books.

Scarr, S., D. Phillips, and K. McCartney. 1989. "Working mothers and their families." *American Psychologist* 44:1402-9.

Schanche, Sheri. 1992. "Gender roles in prime-time network television." Presented to Gender Roles class, Maryville University, St. Louis, November 22.

Schau, C. G., and K. P. Scott. 1984. "Impact of gender characteristics of instructional materials: An integration of research literature." *Journal of Advertising Research* 19:23-27.

Schickel, Richard. 1991. "Hollywood's new directions." *Time* October 14:75-78.

Schieszer, John. 1996. "A new treatment for male menopause." *St. Louis Post-Dispatch Magazine* January 21:16.

Schlafly, Phyllis. 1981. *Testimony: Sex Discrimination in the Workplace.* Washington, DC: U.S. Government Printing Office.

Schmidt, Peter, Lynette K. Nieman et al. 1991. "Lack of effect of induced menses on symptoms in women with Premenstrual Syndrome." *The Journal of the American Medical Association.* 324(17):1174-79.

Schneider, C. 1989. *Children's Television: How It Works and Its Influence on Children.* Lincolnwood, IL: NTC Business Books.

Schneider, Carl J., and Dorothy Schneider. 1994. "American women in World War I." *Social Education* 58(2):83–85.

Schneider, J., and M. Schneider-Duker. 1984. "Sex roles and nonverbal sensitivity." *Journal of Social Psychology* 122:281-82.

Schneider, Karen. 1992. "Women run political gauntlet: Candidates struggle to counteract rumors, while boys will be boys." *St. Louis Post-Dispatch* September 19:B1.

Schneiders, Sandra. 1995. "God is more than two men and a bird." *Call to Action Spirituality/Justice Reprint* (October):1-5.

Schoen, Robert. 1990. "First unions and the stability of first marriages." *Journal of Marriage and the Family* 54:281-84.

Schoenberg, B. Mark. 1993. *Growing Up Male: The Psychology of Masculinity.* Westport, CT: Bergin & Garvey.

Schreiber, C. T. 1979. *Changing Places.* Boston: MIT Press.

Schroeder, Patricia. 1993. "Women and politics." In Jodi Wetzel, Margo Linn Espenlaub, Monys A. Hagen, Annette Bennington McElhiney, and Carmen Braun Williams (eds.), *Women's Studies Thinking Women.* Dubuque, IA: Kendall/Hunt.

Schüssler-Fiorenza, Elizabeth. 1983. *In Memory of Her: A Feminist Theological Reconstruction of Christian Origins.* New York: Crossroads. 1984. *The Challenge of Feminist Biblical Interpretation.* Boston: Beacon.

Schwalbe, Michael. 1992. "Male supremacy and the narrowing moral self." *Berkeley Journal of Sociology* 37:29–54.

Schwartz, A. 1979. "Androgyny and the art of loving." *Psychotherapy: Theory, Research and Practice.* 16:405–8.

Schwartz, Felice N. 1989. "Management women and the new facts of life." *Harvard Business Review* 67:65-76. 1994b. "Women as a business imperative." In Susan E. Feiner (ed.), *Race & Gender in the American Economy: Views from Across the Spectrum*. Englewood Cliffs, NJ: Prentice Hall.

Schwartz, Pepper. 1994a. *Peer Marriage: How Love Between Equals Really Works*. New York: Free Press.

Sciolino, Elaine. 1992. "From the back seat in Iran, murmurs of unrest." *New York Times International* April 23:A4.

Scott, Alison MacEwen. 1986. "Industrialization, gender segregation and stratification theory." In Rosemary Crompton and Michael Mann (eds.), *Gender and Stratification*. Cambridge, UK: Polity.

Scott, Ronald L. 1982. "Analysis of the need systems of twenty male rapists." *Psychological Reports* 51:1119-25.

Scott, W. J., and C. S. Morgan. 1983. "An analysis of factors affecting traditional family expectations and perceptions of ideal fertility." *Sex Roles* 9:901-14.

Scully, Diana. 1993. "Understanding sexual violence." In Stevi Jackson et al. (eds.), *Women's Studies Essential Readings*. New York:New York University.

Scully, Diana, and Joseph Marolla. 1984. "Convicted rapists' vocabulary of motive: Excuses and justifications." *Social Problems* 31(5):530-44. 1990. "'Riding the bull at Gilley's': Convicted rapists describe the rewards of rape." In James M. Henslin (ed.), *Social Problems Today: Coping with the Challenges of a Changing Society*. Englewood Cliffs, NJ: Prentice Hall.

Seal, David Wyatt, Gina Agostinbelli, and Charlotte A. Hannett. 1994. "Extradyadic romantic involvement: Moderating effects of sociosexuality and gender." *Sex Roles* 31(1-2):1-22.

Sears, Robert. 1990. "Relation of early socialization experiences to self-concepts and gender role in middle childhood." *Child Development* 41:253-62.

Segal, Jonathan A. 1991. "Women on the verge . . . of equality." *Human Resources* 36(6):117-18,120,123.

Segura, Denise A. 1994. "Inside the work worlds of Chicana and Mexican immigrant women." In Maxine Baca Zinn and Bonnie Thornton Dill (eds.), *Women of Color in U.S. Society*. Philadelphia: Temple University.

Seidler, Victor J. 1992. "Men, feminism, and power." In Larry May and Robert Strikwerda (eds.), *Rethinking Masculinity: Philosophical Explorations in Light of Feminism*. Lanham, MD: Rowman & Littlefield.

Seidman, Steven. 1992. "An investigation of sex-role stereotyping in music videos." *Journal of Broadcasting and Electronic Media* 36:209-16.

Selnow, Gary W. 1985. "Sex differences in uses and perceptions of profanity." *Sex Roles* 12(3-4):303-12.

Seltzer, Judith A. 1991a. "Legal custody arrangements and children's economic welfare." *American Journal of Sociology* 96:895-929. 1991b. "Relationships between fathers and children who live apart: The father's role after separation." *Journal of Marriage and the Family* 53:79-101.

Serbin, Lisa A., Lora C. Moller, Judith Gulko, Kimberly K. Powlishta, and Karen A. Colburne. 1994. "The emergence of gender segregation in toddler playgroups." In Campbell Leaper (ed.), *Childhood Gender Segregation: Causes and Consequences*. San Francisco: Jossey-Bass.

Serbin, Lisa A., Kimberly K. Powlishta, and Judith Gulko. 1993. "The development of sex typing in middle childhood." *Monographs of the Society for Research in Child Development* 58(2, Serial No. 232):1-74.

Sered, Susan Starr. 1991. "Conflict, complement and control: Family and religion among Middle Eastern Jewish women in Jerusalem." *Gender & Society* 5(1):10-29. 1994. *Priestess, Mother, Sacred Sister: Religions Dominated by Women*. New York: Oxford University.

Service Book and Hymnal. 1958. Lutheran Church in America. Minneapolis, MN: Augsburg.

Sexton, Donald E., and Phyllis Haberman. 1974. "Women in magazine advertisements." *Journal of Advertising Research* 14:41-46.

Shakin, M., D. Shakin, and S. H. Sternglanz. 1985. "Infant clothing: Sex labeling for strangers." *Sex Roles* 12:955-64.

Shami, Seteney, Lucine Taminian, Soheir A. Morsy, Zeinab B. El Bakri, and El-Wathig M. Kameir. 1990. *Women in Arab Society: Work Patterns and Gender Relations in Egypt, Jordan and Sudan*. Paris: UNESCO.

Shapiro, Jerrold Lee. 1987. "The expectant father." *Psychology Today* 21 (January): 36-39.

Shapiro, Judith. 1992. "The industrial labour force." In Mary Buckley (ed.), *Perestroika and Soviet Women.* Cambridge: Cambridge University.

Sharits, Dean, and H. Bruce Lammers. 1982. "Men fill more TV sex roles." *Market Roles* (September):3.

Shearer, Lloyd. 1986. "Money, money, money." *Parade Magazine,* January 12:18-19.

Sheffield, Carole E. 1995. "Sexual terrorism." In Jo Freeman (ed.), *Women: A Feminist Perspective.* Mountain View, CA: Mayfield.

Shehan, Constance L., Mary Ann Burg, and Cynthia A. Rexroat. 1986. "Depression and the social dimensions of the full-time housewife role." *Sociological Quarterly* 27(1):403-21.

Shelton, Beth Anne. 1992. *Women, Men and Time: Gender Differences in Paid Work, Housework and Leisure.* Westport, CT: Greenwood.

Shelton, Beth Anne, and Ben Agger. 1993. "Shotgun wedding, unhappy marriage, non-fault divorce? Rethinking the feminism-marxism relationship." In Paula England (ed.), *Theory on Gender/Feminism on Theory.* New York: Aldine De Gruyter.

Shelton, Beth Anne, and Juanita Firestone. 1989. "Household labor time and the gender gap in earnings." *Gender & Society* 3(1):105-12.

Shelton, Beth Anne, and Daphne John. 1993. "Does marital status make a difference? Housework among married and cohabiting men and women." *Journal of Family Issues* 14(3):401-20. 1993. "Ethnicity, race and difference: A comparison of white, black and Hispanic men's household labor time." In Jane C. Hood (ed.), *Men, Work and Family.* Newbury Park, CA: Sage.

Shen, Fern. 1995. "For the battered spouse, insurers' bias worsens pain." *Washington Post* March 9:A1,A16.

Sherman, B. L., and J. R. Dominick. 1986. "Violence and sex in music videos: TV and rock 'n' roll." *Journal of Communication* 36:94-106.

Sherr, Lynn. 1995. *Failure Is Impossible: Susan B. Anthony in Her Own Words.* New York: Times Books.

Shibamoto, Janet S. 1985. *Japanese Women's Language.* Orlando, FL: Academic Press.

Shidlo, Ariel. 1994. "Internalized homophobia: Conceptual and empirical issues in measurement." In Beverly Greene and Gregory M. Herek (eds.), *Lesbian and Gay Psychology: Theory, Research, and Clinical Applications.* Thousand Oaks, CA: Sage.

Shields, Stephanie A. 1984. "To pet, coddle and 'do for': Caretaking and the concept of maternal instinct." In Miriam Lewin (ed.), *"In the Shadow of the Past": Psychology Portrays the Sexes.* New York: Columbia University.

Shimony, Annemarie. 1985. "Iroquois religion and women in historical perspective." In Y. Y. Haddad and E. B. Findly (eds.), *Women, Religion and Social Change.* Albany: SUNY.

Shortridge, Kathleen. 1989. "Poverty is a woman's problem." In Jo Freeman (ed.), *Women: A Feminist Perspective.* Palo Alto, CA: Mayfield.

Shotland, R. L. 1989. "A model of the causes of date rape in developing and close relationships." In C. Hendrick (ed.), *Close Relationships.* Newbury Park, CA: Sage.

Sicoli, M. L. 1988. "Women winners: Major popular music awards." Paper presented at the Popular Culture Association, New Orleans.

SIDA. 1995. *Gender Equality in Development Cooperation: Taking the Next Step.* Stockholm: Swedish International Development Cooperation Agency.

Siddiqi, Anis. 1993. "Women banking fulfills dual purpose." *Arab News* May 23.

Sidorowicz, Laura S., and G. Sparks Lunney. 1980. "Baby X revisited." *Sex Roles* 6:67-73.

Signorielli, Nancy. 1984. "The demography of the television world." In G. Melischek, K. E. Rosengren, and J. Stappers (eds.), *Cultural Indicators: An International Symposium.* Vienna: Oester–reichischen Akademie der Wissenschaften. 1989. "Television and conceptions about sex-roles: Maintaining conventionality and the status quo." *Sex Roles* 21(5-6):337-56. 1990. "Television's mean and dangerous world: A continuation of the cultural indicators perspective." In Nancy Signorielli and M. Morgan (eds.), *Cultivation Analysis: New Directions in Media Effects Research.* Newbury Park, CA: Sage. 1991. *A Sourcebook on Children and Television.* New York: Greenwood.

Silbert, M. H., and A. M. Pines. 1984. "Pornography and sexual abuse of women." *Sex Roles* 10:857-68.

Silvas, Sharon, Barbara Jenkins, and Polly Grant. 1993. "The overvoice: Images of women in the media." In Jodi Wetzel, Margo Linn Espenlaub, Monys A. Hagen, Annette Bennington McElhiney, and Carmen Braun Williams (eds.), *Women's Studies Thinking Women*. Dubuque, IA: Kendall/Hunt.

Silver, Harry. 1993. "Homework and domestic work." *Sociological Forum* 8(2):181-204.

Silver, Harry, and Frances Goldscheider. 1994. "Flexible work and housework: Work and family constraints on women's domestic labor." *Social Forces* 72(4):1103-9.

Silverman, Joseph A. 1995. "Something new under the sun: Comments on Gerard Russell's 'Anorexia Nervosa through time.'" In George Szmukler, Chris Dare and Janet Treasure (eds.), *Handbook of Eating Disorders: Theory, Treatment and Research*. Chichester, UK: John Wiley.

Silvern, L. E. 1977. "Children's sex-role preferences: Stronger among girls than boys." *Sex Roles* 3:159-71.

Silverstein, Brett, L. Perdue, E. Peterson, and E. Kelly. 1986. "The role of the mass media in promoting a thin standard of body attractiveness for women." *Sex Roles* 14: 519-23.

Silverstein, Brett, and Deborah Perlick. 1995. *The Cost of Competence: Why Inequality Causes Depression, Eating Disorders, and Illness in Women*. New York: Oxford University.

Simenauer, J., and D. Carroll. 1982. *Singles: The New Americans*. New York: Simon & Schuster.

Simon, Robin W. 1995. "Gender, multiple roles, role meaning and mental health." *Journal of Health and Social Behavior* 36(2):182-94.

Simons, R.C., and C.C. Hughes (Eds.). 1985. *The Culture-Bound Syndromes: Folk Illnesses of Psychiatric and Anthropological Interest*. Boston: D. Reidel.

Simpson, J. A., B. Campbell, and E. Berscheid. 1986. "The association between romantic love and marriage." *Personality and Social Psychology Bulletin*. 12(3):363-72.

Sims, Barbara, B. 1974. "She's got to be a saint, lord knows, I ain't: Feminine masochism in American country music." *Journal of Country Music* 5:24-30.

Situation of Chinese Women. 1994. Beijing: Information Office of the State Council of the People's Republic of China.

Sjöö, Monica, and Barbara Mör. 1991. *The Great Cosmic Mother: Rediscovering the Religion of the Earth*. San Francisco: HarperSanFrancisco.

Skinner, Denise A. 1984. "Duel-career family stress and coping." In Patricia Voydanoff (ed.), *Work and Families*. Palo Alto, CA: Mayfield.

Sklar, Kathryn Kish. 1991. "Victorian women and domestic life: Mary Todd Lincoln, Elizabeth Cady Stanton and Harriet Beecher Stowe." In Kathryn Kish Sklar and Thomas Dublin (eds.), *Women and Power in American History: A Reader, Volume I to 1880*. Englewood Cliffs, NJ: Prentice Hall.

Skolnick, Arlene, and Stacey Rosencrantz. 1995. "The new crusade for the old family." In Kathleen R. Gilbert (ed.), *Marriage and the Family 95/96* (Annual editions). Guilford, CT: Dushkin/Brown & Benchmark.

Slipp, Samuel. 1995. *The Freudian Mystique: Freud, Women and Feminism*. New York: New York University.

Sloan, Don, and Lillian Africano. 1988. "Marriage: The traditional alternative." In J. Gipson Wells (ed.), *Current Issues in Marriage and the Family*. New York: Macmillan.

Sloan, Ethel. 1985. *Biology of Women*. New York: Delmar.

Smelser, Neil J. 1981. *Sociology*. Englewood Cliffs, NJ: Prentice Hall.

Smith, Barbara. 1995. "Myths to divert black women from freedom." In Sheila Ruth, *Issues in Feminism: An Introduction to Women's Studies*. Mountain View, CA: Mayfield.

Smith, J. P., and F. R. Welch. 1986. *Closing the Gap: Forty Years of Economic Progress for Blacks*. Santa Monica, CA: Rand.

Smith, Jane E., V. Ann Waldorf, and David L. Trembath. 1990. "Single white male looking for thin, very attractive . . ." *Sex Roles* 23(11-12):675-85.

Smith, Jane I. 1987. "Islam." In Arvind Sharma (ed.), *Women in World Religions*. Albany: State University of New York.

Smith, Janet S. 1992. "Women in charge: Politeness and directives in the speech of Japanese women." *Language in Society* 21:59-82.

Smith, Michael D. 1990. "Sociodemographic risk factors in wife abuse: Results from a survey on Toronto women." *Canadian Journal of Sociology* 15:39-58. 1994. "Enhancing the quality of survey data on violence against women: A feminist approach." *Gender & Society* 8(1):109-27.

Smith, P. M. 1985. *Language, Society and the Sexes*. New York: Basil Blackwell.

Smith, Russell. 1994. "Invisible women: Hollywood puts on blinders when it comes to lesbians." *St. Louis Post-Dispatch.* July 17:3C,6C.

Smith-Lovin, Lynn, and Charles Brody. 1989. "Interruptions in group discussions: The effects of gender and group composition." *American Sociological Review* 54:424-35.

Smith-Rosenberg, Carroll. 1985. *Disorderly Conduct: Visions of Gender in Victorian America*. New York: Oxford University. 1996. "The female world of love and ritual." In Mary Beth Norton and Ruth M. Alexander (eds.), *Major Problems in American Women's History*. Lexington, MA: D.C. Heath.

Smock, Pamela J. 1994. "Gender and the short-run economic consequences of marital disruption." *Social Forces* 73(1):243-62.

Smolak, Linda. 1993. *Adult Development*. Englewood Cliffs, NJ: Prentice Hall.

Snarey, J. 1993. *How Fathers Care for the Next Generation*. Cambridge, MA: Harvard University.

Snodgrass, Klyne, 1986. "Galatians 3:28: Conundrum or solution?" In Alvera Mickelson (ed.), *Women, Authority and the Bible*. Downers Grove, IL: Intervarsity.

Snow, Margaret Ellis, Carol N. Jacklin, and Eleanor Emmons Maccoby. 1983. "Sex-of-child differences in father-child interaction at one year of age." *Child Development* 54:227-32.

Snyder, Margaret. 1990. "Women: The key to ending hunger." *The Hunger Project Papers* 8(August):1-32.

Sokoloff, N. J. 1988. "Evaluating gains and losses by black and white women and men in the professions." *Social Problems* 35:36-55.

Solomon, Charlene. 1991. "Sexual harassment after the Thomas hearings." *Personnel Journal* 70:32-37.

Sommers-Flanagan, R., J. Sommers-Flanagan, and B. Davis. 1993. "What's happening on music television? A gender role content analysis." *Sex Roles* 28(11-12):745-53.

Sorensen, Elaine. 1994. *Comparable Worth: Is it a Worthy Policy?* Princeton, NJ: Princeton University.

South, Scott J., and Kim M. Lloyd. 1995. "Spousal alternatives and marital dissolution." *American Sociological Review* 60(1):21-25.

South, Scott J., and Glenna D. Spitze. 1994. "Housework in marital and nonmarital households." *American Sociological Review* 59(3):327-47.

Spade, Joan Z. 1994. "Wives and husbands' perceptions of why wives work." *Gender & Society* 8(2):170-88.

Spain, Daphne. 1992. *Gendered Spaces*. Chapel Hill, NC: University of North Carolina.

Spanier, Graham B. 1991. "Cohabitation: Recent changes in the United States." In John N. Edwards and David H. Demo (eds.), *Marriage and Family in Transition*. Boston, MA: Allyn & Bacon.

Spender, Dale. 1989. *The Writing or the Sex: Or Why You Don't Have to Read Women's Writing to Know It's No Good*. New York: Teacher's College Press. 1993. "Language and reality: Who made the world?" In Stevi Jackson et al. (eds.), *Women's Studies Essential Readings*. New York: New York University.

Spiller, Katherine. 1993. "The Feminist Majority Report: Corporate women and the mommy track." In Alison M. Jaggar and Paula S. Rothenberg (eds.), *Feminist Frameworks: Alternative Theoretical Accounts of the Relations between Women and Men*. New York: McGraw-Hill.

Spitze, Glenna. 1986. "The division of task responsibility in U.S. households: Longitudinal adjustments to change." *Social Forces* 64(March):689-701.

Sprecher, Susan, and Diane Felmlee. 1993. "Conflict, love and other relationship dimensions for individuals in dissolving, stable and growing premarital relationships." *Free Inquiry in Creative Sociology* 21(2):115-25.

St. John-Parsons, D. 1978. "Continuous dual-career families: A case study." In J. B. Bryson and R. Bryson (eds.), *Dual-Career Couples*. New York: Human Sciences.

St. Louis Post-Dispatch. 1990. "Judge calls victim 'pitiful,' Lets rapist off with probation." September 23. 1995a. "Cadet's ordeal familiar: Military's female 'pioneers' have followed a rough road." August 20:3A. 1995b. "Shannon Faulkner washes out." August 22:14B. 1996a "Why so grumpy? Men's brains shrink as they age, study concludes." April 21:5D 1996b. "4 women cadets complete first week at Citadel." September 1:9D.

Stabiner, Karen. 1985. "Cagney and Lacey: Lacey's pregnancy is a natural for TV social comment." *St. Louis Post-Dispatch* September 29:3F-10F.

Stacey, Judith, and Barrie Thorne. 1985. "The missing feminist revolution in sociology." *Social Problems* 32:301-16.

Stack, Carol. 1994. "Different voices, different visions: Gender, culture and moral reasoning." In Maxine Baca Zinn and Bonnie Thornton Dill (eds.), *Women of Color in U.S. Society*. Philadelphia: Temple University.

Stafford, Rebecca, Elaine Barkman, and Pamela Dibona. 1977. "The division of labor among cohabitating and married couples." *Journal of Marriage and the Family* 39(February):43-57.

Stahly, Geraldine Butts. 1996. "Battered women: Why don't they just leave?" In Joan C. Chrisler, Carla Golden, and Patricia D. Rozee (eds.), *Lectures on the Psychology of Women*. New York: McGraw-Hill.

Staples, Brent. 1995. "Learning to batter women: Wife-beating as inherited behavior." (Editorial-Notebook). *New York Times* February 12.

Staples, Robert. 1973. *The Black Woman in America*. Chicago: Nelson-Hall. 1993. "Black men/black women: Changing roles and relationships." In Anne Minas (ed.), *Gender Basics: Feminist Perspectives on Women and Men*. Belmont, CA: Wadsworth.

Staples, Robert, and Leanor Boulin Johnson. 1993. *Black Families at the Crossroads: Challenges and Prospects*. San Francisco: Jossey-Bass.

Starreis, Marjorie E. 1994. "Gender differences in parent-child relations." *Journal of Family Issues* 15(1):148-85.

Starrels, Marjorie E., Sally Bould, and Leon J. Nicholas. 1994. "The feminization of poverty in the United States: Gender, race, ethnicity and family factors." *Journal of Family Issues* 15(4):590-607.

Statham, Anne, Laurel Richardson, and Judith A. Cook. 1991. *Gender and University Teaching: A Negotiated Difference*. Albany, NY: State University of New York.

Stayton, William R. 1984. "Lifestyle Spectrum 1984." (Sex Information and Educational Council of the U.S.) *SIECUS Reports* 12(3):1-4.

Steedman, Mercedes. 1993. "Who's on top? Heterosexual practices and male dominance during the sex act." In Anne Minas (ed.), *Gender Basics: Feminist Perspectives on Women and Men*. Belmont, CA: Wadsworth.

Steenland, S. 1988. *Growing Up in Prime Time: An Analysis of Adolescent Girls on Television*. Washington, DC: National Commission on Working Women.

Steering Committee of the Physicians Health Study Research Group. 1989. "Final report of the aspirin component of the ongoing physician's health study." *New England Journal of Medicine* 321(3):129-35.

Steil, Janice. 1995. "Supermoms and second shifts: Marital inequality in the 1990s." In Jo Freeman (ed.), *Women: A Feminist Perspective*. Mountain View, CA: Mayfield.

Steil, Janice, and Beth Turetsky. 1987. "Is equal better? The relationship between marital equality and psychological symptomology." In S. Oskamp (ed.), *Family Processes and Problems: Social Psychological Aspects*. Beverly Hills, CA: Sage.

Stein, Harry. 1987. "The case for staying home." In Ollie Pocs and Robert H. Walsh (eds.), *Marriage and Family* (Annual Editions). Guilford, CT: Dushkin.

Steinem, Gloria. 1986. *Marilyn*. New York: Holt, Rinehart and Winston. 1993. "If men could menstruate." In Anne Minas (ed.), *Gender Basics: Feminist Perspectives on Women and Men*. Belmont, CA: Wadsworth. 1995. "Sex, lies and advertising." In Jo Freeman (ed.), *Women: A Feminist Perspective*. Mountain View, CA: Mayfield.

Stendahl, Kristen. 1974. "Enrichment or threat: When the Eves come marching in." In Alice L. Hageman (ed.), *Sexist Religion and Women in the Church*. New York: Association Press.

Stephan, Cookie White, and Judy Corder. 1985. "The effects of dual-career families on adolescent's sex roles, attitudes, work and family plans, and choices of important others." *Journal of Marriage and the Family* 47:921-30.

Stern, M., and K. H. Karraker. 1989. "Sex stereotyping of infants: A review of gender labeling studies." *Sex Roles* 20(3):501-22.

Sternberg, Robert J. 1988. *The Triangle of Love*. New York: Basic Books.

Sternglanz, Sarah H., and Lisa A. Serbin. 1974. "Sex role stereotyping in children's television programs." *Developmental Psychology* 10(5):710-15.

Stets, Jan. 1993. "The link between past and present intimate relationships." *Journal of Family Issues* 14(2):236-60.

Stetson, Dorothy McBride. 1991. *Women's Rights in the U.S.A.: Policy Debates and Gender Roles*. Pacific Grove, CA: Brooks/Cole.

Stevens, Evelyn P. 1993. "Marianismo: The other face of machismo in Latin America." In Anne Minas (ed.), *Gender Basics: Feminist Perspectives on Women and Men*. Belmont, CA: Wadsworth.

Stewart, L.P., A.D. Stewart, S.A. Friedley, and P.J. Cooper. 1990. *Communication Between the Sexes: Sex Differences and Sex Role Stereotypes*. Scottsdale, AZ: Gorsuch Scarisbrick.

Stier, Deborah S., and Judith A. Hall. 1984. "Gender differences in touch: An empirical and theoretical review." *Journal of Personality and Social Psychology* 47:440-59.

Stillion, Judith M. 1985. *Death and the Sexes: An Examination of Differential Longevity, Attitudes, Behaviors and Coping Skills*. Washington, DC: Hemisphere.

Stipek, Deborah J., and J. Heidi Gralinski. 1991. "Gender differences in children's achievement-related beliefs and emotional responses to success and failure in mathematics." *Journal of Educational Psychology* 83:361-71.

Stockard, Jean, and Miriam M. Johnson. 1992. *Sex and Gender in Society*. Englewood Cliffs, NJ: Prentice Hall.

Stohs, Joanne Hoven. 1994. "Alternative ethics in employed women's household labor." *Journal of Family Issues* 15(4):550- 61.

Stoltenberg, John. 1995. "How men have (a) sex." In Sheila Ruth, *Issues in Feminism: An Introduction to Women's Studies*. Mountain View, CA: Mayfield.

Stone, Merlin. 1979. *When God Was a Woman*. San Diego: Harcourt Brace Jovanovich.

Stoneman, Z., G. H. Brody, and C. MacKinnon. 1986. "Same-sex and cross-sex siblings: Activity choices, roles, behavior and gender stereotypes." *Sex Roles* 15:495-511.

Stortz, Martha E. 1984. "The mother, the son and the bullrushes." *Dialog: A Journal of Theology* 23(1):21-26.

Stout, Harry S. (Ed.). 1986. "Benjamin Wadsworth: Rulers feeding and guiding their people." In *The New England Soul: Preaching and Religious Culture in Colonial New England*. New York: Oxford University.

Stratham, Anne, Suzanne Vaughn, and Sharon K. Houseknecht. 1987. "The professional involvement of higher educated women: The impact of the family." *Sociological Quarterly* 28(1):119-33.

Stratton, Jo Anna L. 1981. *Pioneer Women: Voices from the Kansas Frontier*. New York: Simon & Schuster.

Straus, Murray A. 1980. "A sociological perspective on the causes of family violence." In M. Green (ed.), *Violence in the Family*. Boulder, CO: Westview. 1992. "Explaining family violence." In James M. Henslin (ed.), *Marriage and Family in a Changing Society*. New York: Free Press. 1993. "Identifying offenders in criminal justice research on domestic assault." *American Behavioral Scientist* 36(5):587-600.

Street, Sue, Jeffrey Kromrey, and Ellen Kimmel. 1995. "University faculty gender roles perceptions." *Sex Roles* 32(5-6):407-22).

Strickland, B. 1989. "Sex-related differences in health and illness." *Psychology of Women's Quarterly* 12:382-99.

Strikwerda, Robert A., and Larry May. 1992. "Male friendship and intimacy." In Larry May and Robert Strickwerda (eds.), *Rethinking Masculinity: Philosophical Explorations in Light of Feminism*. Lanham, MD: Rowman and Littlefield.

Strong, Bryan, and Christine DeVault. 1992. *The Marriage and Family Experience*. St. Paul, MN: West.

Stuart, Peggy. 1992. "What does the glass ceiling cost you?" *Personnel Journal* 71(11):70-9.

Sugisaki, Kazuko. 1986. "From the moon to the sun: Women's liberation in Japan." In Lynn B. Iglitzin and Ruth Ross (eds.), *Women in the World: 1975-1985, The Women's Decade*. Santa Barbara, CA: ABC-Clio.

Sullivan, Gary L., and P. J. O'Connor. 1988. "Women's role portrayal in magazine advertising: 1958-83." *Sex Roles* 13(3-4):181-88.

Sun, S. W., and J. Lull. 1986. "The adolescent audience for music videos and why they watch." *Journal of Communication* 29(1):116-24.

Surra, C. A. 1991. "Research and theory on mate selection and pre-marital relationships in the 1980's." In Alan Booth (ed.), *Contemporary Families: Looking Forward, Looking Back*. Minneapolis, MN: National Council on Family Relations.

Sutton-Smith, Brian. 1979. "The play of girls." In Claire B. Kopp (ed.), *Becoming Female*. New York: Plenum.

Suzuki, Atusko. 1991. "Egalitarian sex role attitudes: Scale development and comparison of American and Japanese women." *Sex Roles* 24(5-6):245-59.

Swedin, Goran. 1995. "Modern Swedish fatherhood: Challenges which offer great opportunities." In *Men on Men: Eight Swedish Men's Personal Views on Equality, Masculinity and Parenthood*. Stockholm: Equality Affairs Division of the Ministry of Health and Social Affairs.

Sweeting, Helen. 1995. "Reversals of fortune? Sex differences in health in childhood and adolescence." *Social Science and Medicine* 40(1):77-90.

Swirski, Barbara, and Marilyn P. Safir (Eds.). 1991. *Calling the Equality Bluff: Women in Israel*. New York: New York Teacher's College, Columbia University Teacher's College.

Switzer, Jo Young. 1990. "The impact of generic word choices: An empirical investigation of age- and sex-related differences." *Sex Roles* 22(1-2):69-82.

Sylvester, Christine. 1995. "African and Western feminisms: World-traveling the tendencies and possibilities." *Signs* 20(4):941-69.

Tabari, Azar. 1982. "Islam and the struggle for emancipation of Iranian women." In Azar Tabari and Nahid Yeganeh (eds.), *The Shadow of Islam: The Women's Movement in Iran*. London: Zed.

Taeuber, Cynthia M., and Ira Rosenwaike. 1992. "A demographic portrait of America's oldest old." In Ricard M. Suzman, David P. Willis, and Kenneth G. Manton (eds.), *The Oldest Old*. New York: Oxford University.

Takahara, Kumiko. 1986. "Politeness in English, Japanese and Spanish. In John H. Koo and Robert St. Clair (eds.), *Cross-Cultural Communication*. Seoul: Samji. 1991. "Female speech patterns in Japanese." *International Journal of the Sociology of Language* 92:61-85.

Talkington, Tracy F. 1976. "An analysis of sex role stereotypes in popular songs, 1955-1976." Unpublished master's thesis, University of Oregon.

Tanifuji, Etsushi. 1995. "Feminism." *Japan Update* (March) 42.

Tannahill, Reay. 1980. *Sex in History*. New York: Stein and Day.

Tannen, Deborah. 1990. *You Just Don't Understand: Women and Men in Conversation*. New York: William Morrow. 1994. *Gender and Discourse*. New York: Oxford University.

Tartakov, Carlie, and Gary Tartakov. 1994. "Interracial or crosscultural?" In Walton R. Johnson and D. Michael Warren (eds.), *Inside the Mixed Marriage: Accounts of Changing Attitudes, Patterns, and Perceptions of Cross-Cultural and Interracial Marriages*. Lanham, MD: University Press of America.

Tartre, L. A. 1990. "Spatial skills, gender and mathematics." In Elizabeth Fennema and G. C. Leder (eds.), *Mathematics and Gender*. New York: Teachers College Press.

Tavris, Carol. 1996. "The mismeasure of woman." In Karen E. Rosenblum and Toni-Michelle C. Travis (eds.), *The Meaning of Difference: American Constructions of Race, Sex and Gender, Social Class, and Sexual Orientation*. New York: McGraw-Hill.

Tavris, Carol, and Carole Wade. 1984. *The Longest War: Sex Differences in Perspective*. New York: Harcourt Brace Jovanovich.

Taylor, Shelley E., Letitia Anne Peplau, and David O. Sears. 1994. *Social Psychology*. Englewood Cliffs, NJ: Prentice Hall.

Teachman, Jay, D. 1991. "Receipt of child support in the United States." *Journal of Marriage and the Family* 53(August):759-72.

Teachman, Jay D., and Kathleen Paasch. 1993. "The economics of parenting apart." In Charlene E. Depner and James H. Bray (eds.), *Nonresidential Parenting: New Vistas in Family Living*. Newbury Park, CA: Sage.

Teays, Wendy. 1991. "The burning bride: The dowry problem in India." *Journal of Feminist Studies in Religion* 7(Fall):29-52.

Terborg-Penn, Rosalyn. 1991. "Discontented black feminists: Prelude and postscript to the passage of the Nineteenth Amendment." In Kathryn Kish Sklar and Thomas Dublin (eds.), *Women and Power in American History: A Reader, Volume II from 1870.* Englewood Cliffs, NJ: Prentice Hall.

Terrelonge, Pauline. 1995. "Feminist consciousness and black women." In Jo Freeman (ed.), *Women: A Feminist Perspective.* Mountain View, CA: Mayfield.

Thoits, Peggy A. 1986. "Multiple identities: Examining gender and marital status differences in distress." *American Sociological Review* 51:259-72. 1992. "Identity structure and psychological well-being: Gender and marital status comparisons." *Social Psychology Quarterly* 55:246-56. 1995. "Stress, coping and social support processes: Where are we? What next?" *Journal of Health and Social Behavior* (Extra Issue):53-79.

Thomas, M. Carey. 1991. "Educated woman." In Evelyn Ashton-Jones and Gary A. Olson (eds.), *The Gender Reader.* Boston: Allyn & Bacon.

Thomas, William I. 1966 (original, 1931). "The relation of research to the social process." In Morris Janowitz (ed.), *W. I. Thomas on Social Organization and Social Personality.* Chicago: University of Chicago.

Thomas-Lester, Avis. 1995. "Domestic violence." *Washington Post* January 17:C5.

Thompson, Becky W. 1992. "A way outa no way: Eating problems among African-American, Latina and white women." *Gender & Society* 6:546-61. 1994. *A Hunger So Wide and So Deep: American Women Speak Out on Eating Disorders.* Minneapolis: University of Minnesota.

Thompson, Cooper. 1995. "A new vision of masculinity." In Paula S. Rothenberg (ed.), *Race, Class, and Gender in the United States: An Integrated Study.* New York: St. Martin's.

Thompson, Edward H., Christopher Grissanti, and Joseph H. Pleck. 1985. "Attitudes toward the male role and their correlates." *Sex Roles* 13(7-8):413-27.

Thompson, Elizabeth, and Ugom Colella. 1992. "Cohabitation and marital stability: Quality or commitment." *Journal of Marriage and the Family* 54:259-67.

Thompson, Linda and Alexis J. Walker. 1989. "Women and men in marriage, work and parenthood." *Journal of Marriage and the Family* 51:845-72.

Thorkelson, Anne E. 1985. "Women under the law: Has equity been achieved?" In Alice G. Sargent (ed.), *Beyond Sex Roles.* St. Paul, MN: West.

Thornborrow, Nancy M., and Marianne B. Sheldon. 1995. "Women in the labor force." In Jo Freeman (ed.), *Women: A Feminist Perspective.* Mountain View, CA: Mayfield.

Thorne, Barrie. 1993. *Gender Play: Girls and Boys in School.* New Brunswick, NJ: Rutgers University.

Thornton, Arland. 1988. "Cohabitation and marriage in the 1980s." *Demography* 25:497-508.

Thornton, Arland, and Deborah Freedman. 1986. "Changing attitudes toward marriage and single life." In Ollie Pocs and Robert H. Walsh (eds.), *Marriage and Family* (Annual Editions). Guilford, CT: Dushkin.

Thornton, Russell. 1987. *American Indian Holocaust and Survival: A Population History Since 1492.* Norman, OK: University of Oklahoma.

Thurston, Anne. 1995. *Because of Her Testimony: The Word in Female Experience.* Dublin: Gill and MacMillan.

Tiefer, Lenore, 1993. "In pursuit of the perfect penis: The medicalization of male sexuality." In Anne Minas (ed.), *Gender Basics: Feminist Perspectives on Women and Men.* Belmont, CA: Wadsworth.

Tiger, Lionel, and Robin Fox. 1971. *The Imperial Animal.* New York: Dell.

Tohidi, Nayereh. 1991. "Gender and Islamic fundamentalism: Feminist politics in Iran." In Chandra Talpade Mohanty, Ann Russo, and Lourdes Torress (eds.), *Third World Women and the Politics of Feminism.* Bloomington, IN: Indiana University.

Toliver, Susan. 1993. "Movers and shakers: Black families and corporate relocation." *Marriage and Family Review* 19(1-2):113-30.

Toro-Morn, Maura I. 1995. "Gender, class, family, and migration: Puerto Rican women in Chicago." *Gender & Society* 9(6):712-26.

Toubia, Nahid. 1986. "Women and health in Sudan." In Nahid Toubia (ed.), *Women of the Arab World: The Coming Challenge.* London: Zed.

Travis, C. 1993. "Women and health." In Florence L. Denmark and Michele A. Paludi (eds.), *Handbook on the Psychology of Women.* Westport, CT: Greenwood.

Trebilcot, Joyce. 1977. "Two forms of androgynism." *Journal of Social Philosophy* 8(1).

Trecker, Janice. 1974. "Room at the bottom: Girls' access to vocational training." *Social Education* 38(October):533-37.

Trible, Phyllis. 1984. *The Texts of Terror*. Philadelphia: Fortress.

Tuck, Bryan, Jan Rolfe, and Vivienne Adair. 1994. "Adolescents' attitudes toward gender roles within work and its relationship to gender, personality type and parental occupation." *Sex Roles* 31(9-10):547-58.

Tucker, M. Belinda, and Claudia Mitchell-Kernan (Eds.). 1995. *The Decline in Marriage among African Americans: Causes, Consequences, and Policy Implications*. New York: Russell Sage Foundation.

Turner, Heather A. 1994. "Gender and social support: Taking the bad with the good?" *Sex Roles* 30(7–8):521–41.

Turner, Wallace. 1986. "Drive seen as gaining pay equity for women." *New York Times* January 27:22A.

U.S. Agency for International Development. 1994. *National Family Health Survey, India 1992-93*. Government of India and USAID. Washington, DC: U.S. Government Printing Office.

U.S. Bureau of the Census. 1989. "Marital status and living arrangements, March 1988." *Current Population Reports*, Series P-20(433):3-5. Washington, DC: U.S. Government Printing Office. 1990–1995. *Statistical Abstract of the United States*, U.S. Department of Commerce. Washington, DC: U.S. Government Printing Office. 1996. *Employment and Earnings* 43(1): January. Bureau of Labor Statistics. Washington, DC: U.S. Government Printing Office.

U.S. Department of Justice. 1993. *Sourcebook of Criminal Justice Statistics*. Washington, DC: U.S. Government Printing Office.

U.S. Department of Labor. 1991a. *Working Women: A Chartbook*, Bulletin 2385. Washington, DC: U.S. Government Printing Office. 1991b. *A Report on the Glass Ceiling Initiative*. Washington, DC: U.S. Government Printing Office.

U.S. Public Health Service. 1985. *Women's Health: Report of the Public Health Service Task Force on Women's Health Issues, Vol. 1*. 100(1):73-106. 1989. *Monthly Vital Statistics Report* 338(3). Hyattsville, MD: National Center for Health Statistics.

Uchitelle, Louis. 1994. "Women in their 50's follow many paths into workplace." *New York Times* November 28:A1,B8.

Udyogini. 1995. "Enhancing women's empowerment: Women's micro-enterprise management training." Women's Enterprise Management Training Outreach Program (WEMTOP). New Delhi: Udyogini.

UNESCO. 1980. *Women in the Media*. Paris: UNESCO.

Unger, Rhoda, and Mary Crawford. 1992. *Women and Gender: A Feminist Psychology*. New York: McGraw-Hill.

UNHCR. 1995. United Nations High Commissioner for Refugees. "Focus: Refugee women." *Refugees* II (100):1-30.

United Nations. 1985. *The State of the World's Women, 1985*. Report of the World Conference to Review and Appraise the Achievements of the United Nations Decade for Women: Equality, Development and Peace. Nairobi, Kenya (July 15-26). Oxford, UK: New Internationalist Publications.

United Nations Development Program. 1995. *Human Development Report*, 1995. Geneva: UNESCO.

Upham, Frank K. 1987. *Law and Social Change in Postwar Japan*. Cambridge, MA: Harvard University.

Usui, Naoaki. 1991. "Between war cry of career and whisper of sweet home." *Japan Update* 18:12-18.

Valcarcel, Carmen Luz. 1994. "Growing up black in Puerto Rico." In Ethel Tobach and Betty Rosoff (eds.), *Challenging Racism and Sexism: Alternatives to Genetic Explanations*. New York: The Feminist Press at the City University of New York.

Valenzuela, Angela. 1993. "Liberal gender role attitudes and academic achievement among Mexican-origin adolescents in two Houston inner-city Catholic schools." *Hispanic Journal of Behavioral Sciences* 15(3):310-23.

Van De Pol, Lotte C. 1994. "The lure of the big city: Female migration to Amsterdam." In Els Kloek, Nicole Teeuwen, and Marijke Huisman (eds.), *Women of the Golden Age: An International Debate on Women in Seventeenth-Century Holland, England and Italy*. Amsterdam: Hilversum Verloren.

Van Der Horst, Pieter W. 1995. "Images of women in ancient Judaism." In Ria Kloppenborg and Wouter J. Hanegraaff (eds.), *Female Stereotypes in Religious Traditions*. Leiden, Netherlands: Brill.

Van Der Torn, Karel. 1995. "Torn between vice and virtue: Stereotypes of the widow in Israel and Mesopotamia." In Ria Kloppenborg and Wouter J. Hanegraaff (eds.), *Female Stereotypes in Religious Traditions*. Leiden, Netherlands: Brill.

VandeBerg, L.R., and D. Streckfuss. 1992. "Prime-time television's portrayal of women and the world of work: A demographic profile." *Psychology of Women Quarterly* 11:409-25.

Vanek, Joann. 1974. "Time spent in housework." *Scientific American* (November):116-20.

VanEvery, Joan. 1995. *Heterosexual Women Changing the Family: Refusing to be a "Wife."* London: Taylor & Francis.

Vannoy-Hiller, Dana, and William W. Philliber. 1989. *Equal Partners: Successful Women in Marriage.* Newbury Park, CA: Sage.

Veblen, Thorsten. 1953 (original, 1899). *The Theory of the Leisure Class.* New York: Mentor Books.

Veevers, J. E., and E. M. Gee. 1986. "Playing it safe: Accident mortality and gender roles." *Sociological Focus* 19:349-59.

Venkatesan, M., and Jean Losco. 1975. "Women in magazine ads: 1959-71." *Journal of Advertising Research* 15:49-54.

Verbrugge, Lois M. 1984. "Physical health of clerical workers in the U.S., Framingham and Detroit." *Women and Health* 9(1):17-41. 1985. "Gender and health: An update on hypotheses and evidence." *Journal of Health and Social Behavior* 26:156-82. 1989. "The twain meet: Empirical explanations of sex differences in health and mortality." *Journal of Health and Social Behavior* 30(3):282-304.

Verbrugge, Lois M., and Jennifer H. Madans. 1985. "Women's roles and health." *American Demographics* 8:35-39.

Verbrugge, Lois M., and Deborah Wingard. 1991. "Sex differentials in health and mortality." In Laura Kramer (ed.) *The Sociology of Gender: A Text-Reader.* New York: St. Martin's.

Vetter, B., and E. Babco. 1988. *Professional Women and Minorities.* Washington, DC: Commission on Professions in Science and Technology.

Vickers, Jeanne. 1991. *Women and the World Economic Crisis.* London: Zed.

Vilhjalmsson, Runar. 1993. "Life stress, social support and clinical depression: A reanalysis of the literature." *Social Science and Medicine* 37(3):331-42.

Vincent, R. C., D. K. Davis, and L. A. Boruszkowski. 1987. "Sexism on MTV: The portrayal of women in rock videos." *Journalism Quarterly* 64(4):750-55.

Vinovskis, Maris A. 1986. "Young fathers and their children: Some historical and policy perspectives." In Arthur B. Elster and Michael E. Lamb (eds.), *Adolescent Fatherhood.* Hillsdale, NJ: Lawrence Erlbaum.

Vobejda, Barbara. 1994. "Battered women's cry relayed up from grass roots." *Washington Post* July 6:A1,A16.

Von Hassell, Malve. 1993. "Issei women: Silences and fields of power." *Feminist Studies* 19(3):549-69.

Wagner, Louis C., and Janis D. Banos. 1973. "A woman's place: A follow-up analysis of the roles portrayed by women in magazine advertisements." *Journal of Marketing Research* May:213-14.

Waldron, Ingrid. 1982. "An analysis of causes in sex differences in mortality and morbidity." In W. R. Gove and G. R. Carpenter (eds.), *The Fundamental Connection Between Nature and Nurture.* Lexington, MA: Lexington Books. 1988. "Gender and health related behavior." In D. S. Gochman (ed.), *Health Behavior: Emerging Research Perspectives.* New York: Plenum.

Walker, E., B. A. Bettes, E. L. Kain, and P. Harvey. 1985. "Relationship of gender and marital status with symptomatology in psychiatric patients." *Journal of Abnormal Psychology* 94:42–50.

Walker, Karen. 1994. "Men, women and friendship: What they say, what they do." *Gender & Society* 8(2):246–65.

Walker, Kathryn, and Margaret Woods. 1976. *Time Use: A Measure of Household Production of Family Goods and Services.* Washington, DC: American Home Economics Association.

Walker, Lenore E. 1989. *Terrifying Love: Why Battered Women Kill and How Society Responds.* New York: Harper & Row.

Wallace, Ruth A. (Ed.). 1989. *Feminism and Sociological Theory.* Newbury Park, CA: Sage.

Wallerstein, J. 1984. "Children of divorce: Preliminary report of a ten-year follow-up of young children." *American Journal of Orthopsychiatry* 54:444–58.

Walsh, M. R. 1987. *The Psychology of Women: Ongoing Debates.* New Haven, CT: Yale University.

Walsh, Sharon. 1995. "Still looking for a path to the top." *Washington Post* May 28:H6.

Walshok, M. L. 1981. *Blue-Collar Women: Pioneers on the Male Frontier.* Garden City: Anchor.

Walters, H. F., and J. Huck. 1989. "Networking women." *Newsweek* March 13:48-55.

Walters, Vivienne. 1993. "Stress, anxiety and depression: Women's accounts of their health problems." *Social Science and Medicine* 36(4):393-402.

Walzer, Susan. 1994. "The role of gender in determining abortion attitudes." *Social Science Quarterly* 75(3):687-93.

Waring, Marilyn. 1988. *If Women Counted: A New Feminist Economics.* San Francisco: HarperSanFrancisco.

Watkins, Jean, and David Watkins. 1983. "The female entrepreneur: Background and determinants of business choice–some British data." *International Small Business Journal* 2:21-31.

Watson, Roy E. L. 1986. "Premarital cohabitation vs. traditional courtship: Their effects on subsequent marital adjustment." In Ollie Pocs and Robert H. Walsh, *Marriage and Family, 86—87* (Annual Editions). Guilford, CT: Dushkin.

Watson, Rubie S. 1985. *Inequalities among Brothers: Class and Kinship in South China.* Cambridge, UK: Cambridge University Press. 1993. "The named and the nameless: Gender and person in Chinese society." In Caroline B. Brettell and Carolyn F. Sargent (eds.), *Gender in Cross-Cultural Perspective.* Englewood Cliffs, NJ: Prentice Hall.

Weaver, Charles N., and Sandra L. Holmes. 1975. "A comparative study of the work satisfaction of females with full-time employment and full-time housekeeping." *Journal of Applied Psychology* 60(1):117-18.

Weaver, Mary Jo. 1985. *New Catholic Women.* San Francisco: Harper & Row.

Webb, Marilyn. 1988. "The debate over joint custody." In J. Gipson Wells (ed.), *Current Issues in Marriage and the Family.* New York: Macmillan.

Weber, Max. 1946. *From Max Weber: Essays in Sociology.* H. H. Gerth and C. W. Mills (eds. & trs.). New York: Oxford University Press.

Webster, Alison R. 1995. *Found Wanting: Women, Christianity and Sexuality.* London: Cassell.

Weitz, Rose. 1995. "What price independence? Social reactions to lesbians, spinsters, widows and nuns." In Jo Freeman (ed.), *Women: A Feminist Perspective.* Mountain View, CA: Mayfield.

Weitzman, Lenore J. 1979. *Sex Role Socialization: A Focus on Women.* Palo Alto, CA: Mayfield. 1984. "Sex-role socialization: A focus on women" In Jo Freeman (ed.), *Women: A Feminist Perspective.* Palo Alto, CA: Mayfield. 1985. *The Divorce Revolution: The Unexpected Social and Economic Consequences for Women and Children in America.* New York:Free Press.

Weitzman, Leonore J., and Ruth B. Dixon. 1988. "The transformation of legal marriage through no-fault divorce." In J. Gipson Wells (ed.), *Current Issues in Marriage and the Family.* New York: Macmillan.

Weitzman, Lenore J., Deborah Eifler, Elizabeth Hokada, and Catherine Ross. 1972. "Sex-role socialization in picture books for preschool children." *American Journal of Sociology* 77(May):1125-50.

Welch, Michael R., David C. Leege, and James C. Cavendish. 1995. "Attitudes toward abortion among U.S. Catholics: Another case of symbolic politics?" *Social Science Quarterly* 76(1):142-97.

Welch, R. L., A. Huston-Stein, J. C. Wright, and R. Plehal. 1979. "Subtle sex-role cues in children's commercials." *Journal of Communication* 29(3):202-9.

Welter, Barbara. 1996. "The cult of true womanhood, 1820-1860." In Mary Beth Norton and Ruth M. Alexander (eds.), *Major Problems in American Women's History.* Lexington, MA: D.C. Heath.

Wender, Dorothea. 1984. "Plato: Misogynist, phaedophile, and feminist." In John Peradotta and J. P. Sullivan (eds.), *Women in the Ancient World: The Arethusa Papers.* Albany: State University of New York.

Wendt, Ann C., and William M. Slonaker. 1994. "Discrimination reflects on you." In Susan F. Feiner (ed.), *Race & Gender in the American Economy: Views from Across the Spectrum.* Englewood Cliffs, NJ: Prentice Hall.

Werthheimer, Barbara M., and Anne H. Nelson. 1989. "Union is power: Sketches from women's labor history." In Jo Freeman (ed.), *Women: A Feminist Perspective*. Mountain View, CA: Mayfield.

Wertz, Richard W., and Dorothy C. Wertz. 1990. "Notes on the decline of midwives and the rise of medical obstetricians." In Peter Conrad and Rochelle Kern (eds.), *The Sociology of Health and Illness: Critical Perspectives*. New York: St. Martin's.

West, B., and K. Kissman. 1991. "Mothers without custody: Treatment issues." In C.A. Everett (ed.), *The Consequences of Divorce: Economic and Custodial Impact on Children and Adults*. New York: Haworth.

West, Candace. 1994. "Rethinking 'sex differences' in conversational topics." In Camille Roman, Suzanne Juhasz, and Cristanne Miller (eds.), *The Women and Language Debate: A Sourcebook*. New Brunswick, NJ: Rutgers University.

West, Candace, and Sarah Fenstermaker. 1995. "Doing difference." *Gender & Society* 9 (1):8-27.

West, Candace, and Don H. Zimmerman. 1977. "Women's place in everyday talk: Reflections on parent-child interaction." *Social Problems* 24:521-29. 1983. "Small insults: A study of interruptions in cross-sex conversations between unacquainted persons." In Barrie Thorne, Cheris Kramarae, and Nancy Henley (eds.), *Language, Gender & Society*. Rowley, MA: Newbury House. 1985. "Gender, language and discourse." In Tuen A. van Dijk (ed.), *Handbook of Discourse Analysis, Volume 4: Discourse Analysis in Society*. London: Academic Press. 1987. "Doing gender." *Gender & Society* 1(2):125-51.

West, Lee, Jennifer Anderson, and Steve Duck. 1996. "Crossing the barriers to friendships between men and women." In Julia T. Wood (ed.), *Gendered Relationships*. Mountain View, CA: Mayfield.

Westerberg, Bengt. 1995. "Visions of an equal society-with a focus on men." In *Men on Men: Eight Swedish Men's Personal Views on Equality, Masculinity and Parenthood*. Equality Affairs Division of the Ministry of Health and Social Affairs. [Stockholm.]

Weston, Kath. 1993. "Is 'straight' to 'gay' as 'family' is to 'no family'?" In Anne Minas (ed.), *Gender Basics: Feminist Perspectives on Women and Men*. Belmont, CA: Wadsworth.

Wharton, Amy S., and Rebecca J. Erickson. 1995. "The consequences of caring: Exploring the links between women's job and family emotion work." *Sociological Quarterly* 36(2):273-96.

Wharton, Carol S. 1994. "Finding time for the 'second shift': The impact of flexible work schedules on women's double days." *Gender & Society* 8(2):189–205.

Whicker, Marcia Lynn, and Todd W. Areson. 1993. "The maleness of the American presidency." In Lois Lovelace Duke (ed.), *Women in Politics: Outsiders or Insiders?* Englewood Cliffs, NJ: Prentice Hall.

Whicker, Marcia Lynn, Malcolm Jewell, and Lois Lovelace Duke. 1993. "Women in Congress." In Lois Lovelace Duke (ed.), *Women in Politics: Outsiders or Insiders?* Englewood Cliffs, NJ: Prentice Hall.

Whipple, T. W., and A. E. Courtney 1985. "Female role portrayals in advertising and communication effectiveness: A review." *Journal of Advertising* 14:17.

Whitbourne, Susan Krauss, and Joyce B. Ebmeyer. 1990. *Identity and Intimacy in Marriage: A Study of Couples*. New York: Springer-Verlag.

White, Jacquelyn W., and Barrie Bondurant. 1996. "Gendered violence in intimate relationships." In Julia T. Wood (ed.), *Gendered Relationships*. Mountain View, CA: Mayfield.

White, Merry. 1991. *Challenging Tradition: Women in Japan*. New York: Japan Society.

White, Philip G., and James Gillett. 1994. "Reading the muscular body: A critical decoding of advertising in *Flex* magazine." *Sociology of Sport Journal* 11(1):18-39.

Whittington, Leslie A., James Alm, and H. Elizabeth Peters. 1990. "Fertility and the personal exemption: Implicit pronatalist policy in the United States." *American Economic Review* 80:545-56.

Who Are the Women of the U.S.? 1995. Publication for United Nations Fourth World Conference on Women. U.S. Department of State.

Wickenden, Dorothy. 1986. "The women's movement looks beyond equality: What now?" *New Republic* May 5:19-25.

Wiles, Charles. 1991. "A comparison of role portrayal of men and women in magazine advertising in the USA and Sweden." *International Journal of Advertising* 10:259-67.

Wilkie, Jane Riblett. 1993. "Changes in U.S. men's attitudes toward the family provider role, 1972-1989." *Gender & Society* 7(2):261-79.

Wilkinson, Melvin. 1976. "Romantic love: The great equalizer? Sexism in popular music." *Family Coordinator* 25:161-66.

Williams, Carmen Braun. 1993a. "The psychology of women." In Jodi Wetzel, Margo Linn Espenlaub, Monys A. Hagen, Annette Bennington McElhiney, and Carmen Braun Williams (eds.), *Women's Studies Thinking Women*. Dubuque, IA: Kendall/Hunt.

Williams, Christine L. 1992. "The glass escalator: Hidden advantages for men in the 'female' professions." *Social Problems* 39(3):253-67. 1993b. *Doing "Women's Work": Men in Nontraditional Occupations* (Edited volume). Newbury Park, CA: Sage.

Williams, J. Allen, Joetta Vernon, Martha Williams, and Karen Malecha. 1987. "Sex role socialization in picture books: An update." *Social Science Quarterly.* 68(1):148–56.

Williams, J.E., and D.L. Best. 1990. *Measuring Sex Stereotypes: A Thirty Nation Study.* Beverly Hills, CA: Sage.

Williams, Juanita H. 1987. *Psychology of Women: Behavior in a Biosocial Context.* New York: W. W. Norton.

Williams, Juanita H., and Arthur Jacoby. 1989. "The effects of premarital heterosexual and homosexual experience on dating and marriage desirability." *Journal of Marriage and the Family* 51:489-97.

Williams, Norma. 1990. *The Mexican American Family: Tradition and Change.* Dix Hills, NY: General Hall. 1993. "Elderly Mexican American men: Work and family patterns." In Jane C. Hood (ed.), *Men, Work, and Family.* Newbury Park, CA: Sage.

Williams, Walter L. 1996. "The berdache tradition." In Karen E. Rosenblum and Toni-Michelle C. Travis (eds.), *The Meaning of Difference: American Constructions of Race, Sex and Gender, Social Class and Sexual Orientation.* New York: McGraw-Hill.

Williams, Walter L., and John Doyle. 1994. "Rethinking choice for men and polarization among women." *American Behavioral Scientist* 37(8):1104–21.

Williamson, N. E. 1976. *Sons or Daughters: A Cross-Cultural Survey of Parental Preferences.* Beverly Hills, CA: Sage.

Willinger, Beth. 1993. "Resistance and change: College men's attitudes toward family and work in the 1980s." In Jane C. Hood (ed.), *Men, Work and Family.* Newbury Park, CA: Sage.

Wilson, Edward O. 1975. *Sociobiology: The New Synthesis.* Princeton, NJ: Princeton University. 1978. *On Human Nature.* Cambridge, MA: Harvard University.

Wilson, Robert A. 1966. *Feminine Forever.* New York: M. Evans.

Wingard, Deborah L. 1984. "The sex differential in morbidity, mortality and life cycle." In L. Breslow, J. E. Fielding, and L. B. Lave (eds.), *Annual Review of Public Health, Vol. 5.* Palo Alto, CA: Annual Reviews.

Winkler, Ann E. 1993. "The living arrangements of single mothers with dependent children: An added perspective." *The American Journal of Economics and Sociology* 52(1):1-18.

Woldow, Norman. 1996. "Explaining male/female biological differences: Social science, culture and sociobiology." Unpublished manuscript from the Biology Department, Maryville University, St. Louis.

Wolf, Margery. 1975. "Women and suicide in China." In Margery Wolf and Roxanne Wilke (eds.), *Women in Chinese Society.* Stanford, CA: Stanford University. 1985. *Revolution Postponed: Women in Contemporary China.* Stanford, CA: Stanford University. 1993. "The birth limitation program: Family versus state." In Stevi Jackson et al. (eds.), *Women's Studies Essential Readings.* New York: New York University.

Wolfe, B., and G. E. Haverman. 1983. "Time allocation, market work, and changes in female health." *American Economic Review* 73(2):134-39.

Wolfe, Leanna. 1993b. *Women Who May Never Marry.* Atlanta, GA: Longstreet.

Wolfe, Naomi. 1993a. *Fire with Fire: The New Female Power and How It Will Change the Twenty-First Century.* New York: Random House.

Woloch, Nancy. 1992. *Early American Women: A Documentary History, 1600–1900.* Belmont, CA: Wadsworth. 1994. *Women and the American Experience.* New York: McGraw-Hill.

Women and Men in China. 1995. *Facts and Figures.* Beijing: State Statistical Bureau of PRC.

Women's Equality Poll. 1995. *Feminist Majority Report* 7(2):1, 12-13.

Women's Institute for Freedom of the Press. 1989. "Women gain as broadcast news directors in new RTNDA study." *Media Report to Women* September-October: 6-7.

Wong, P. T. P., G. Kettlewell, and C. F. Sproule. 1985. "On the importance of being masculine: Sex role, attribution and women's career achievement." *Sex Roles* 12:757-69.

Woo, William F. 1993. "What we say, what we mean, what we do." *St. Louis Post-Dispatch*, February 14:B1.

Wood, D. B. 1990. "How TV treats women." *Christian Science Monitor* December 12:4.

Wood, Julia T. 1993. "Engendered relationships: Interaction, caring, power and responsibility in close relationships." In Steve Duck (ed.), *Processes in Close Relationships: Contexts of Close Relationships*, Vol. 3. Beverly Hills, CA: Sage. 1994. *Gendered Lives: Communication, Gender and Culture*. Belmont, CA: Wadsworth.

Wood, Wendy, F.Y. Wong, and J.G. Cachere. 1991. "Effects of media violence on viewers' aggression in unconstrained social interaction." *Psychological Bulletin* 109:371-83.

Woodward, Kenneth, Eleanor Clift, and Vicki Quade. 1990. "The graying of the convent." *Newsweek* April 2:50-51.

Woollet, Anne, and Ann Phoenix. 1993. "Issues related to motherhood." In Stevi Jackson et al. (eds.), *Women's Studies Essential Readings*. New York: New York University.

Worell, Judith. 1996. "Feminist identity in a gendered world." In Joan C. Chrisler, Carla Golden, and Patricia D. Rozee (eds.), *Lectures on the Psychology of women*. New York: McGraw-Hill.

World Health Organization. 1995. *The World Health Report 1995: Bridging the Gaps*. Geneva: World Health Organziation.

Wright, John W. 1995. *American Almanac of Jobs and Salaries*. New York: Avon.

Wright, P.H., and M.B. Scanlon 1991. "Gender role orientations and friendship: Some attenuation but gender differences still abound." *Sex Roles* 24:551-66.

Wu, Zheng. 1995. "Premarital cohabitation and postmarital cohabiting union formation." *Journal of Family Issues* 16(2):212-32.

Xu, Wu, and Ann Leffler. 1992. "Gender and race effects on occupational prestige, segregation, and earnings." *Gender & Society* 6:376-92.

Yankelovich, Daniel. 1991. "The new norms of domestic life." In Leonard Cargan (ed.), *Marriages and Families: Coping with Change*. Englewood Cliffs, NJ: Prentice Hall.

Yllo, Kersti. 1994. "The status of women, marital equality and violence against wives: A contextual analysis." *Journal of Family Issues* 5:307-20.

Yogev, Sara, and Andrea Vierra. 1983. "The state of motherhood among professional women." *Sex Roles* 9(3):391-96.

Young, Gay, Vidymali Samarasinghe, and Ken Kusterer (Eds). 1993. *Women at the Center: Development Issues and Practices for the 1990s*. West Hartford, CT: Kumarian.

Young, Jake. 1994. "Anthropological research on patterns of sexual behavior in Sub-Saharan Africa: Implications for HIV/AIDS interventions." *Journal of the Steward Anthropological Society* 22(1):1-12.

Young, Katherine K. 1987. "Introduction." In Arvind Sharma (ed.), *Women in World Religions*. Albany: State University of New York.

Young, Kevin, Philip White, and William McTeer. 1994. "Body talk: Male athletes reflect on sport, injury, and pain." *Sociology of Sport Journal* 11(2):175-94.

Young, Rosalie F., and Eve Kahana. 1993. "Gender, recovery from late life heart attack and medical care." *Women and Health* 20(1):11-31.

Yu, Lucy C., Yanju Yu, and Phyllis Kernoff Mansfield. 1990. "Gender and changes in support of parents in China: Implications for the one-child policy." *Gender & Society* 4(1):83-89.

Zakaria, Fouad. 1986. "The standpoint of contemporary Muslim fundamentalists." In Nahid Toubia (ed.), *Women of the Arab World: The Coming Challenge*. London: Zed.

Zambrana, Ruth E. 1994. "Puerto Rican families and social well-being." In Maxine Baca Zinn and Bonnie Thornton Dill (eds.), *Women of Color in U.S. Society*. Philadelphia: Temple University.

Zappert, L. T., and Stansbury, K. 1984. "In the pipeline: A comparative study of men and women in graduate programs in science, engineering, and medicine at Stanford University." Working Paper No. 20, Institute for Research on Women and Gender. Stanford, CA: Stanford University.

Zeng, Yi et al. 1993. "Causes and implications of the recent increase in the reported sex ratio at birth in China." *Population and Development Review* 19:283-302.

Zenie-Ziegler, Wedad. 1988. *In Search of Shadows: Conversations with Egyptian Women.* London: Zed.

Zi, Lian. 1995. "Marriages and families." *Fortnightly Review.* Special Issue to the Fourth World Conference on Women: 86-88.

Zimmerman, Mark K. 1987. "The women's health movement: A critique of medical enterprise and the position of women." In Beth B. Hess and Myra Marx Ferree (eds.), *Analyzing Gender: A Handbook of Social Science Research.* Newbury Park, CA: Sage.

Zinn, Maxine Baca. 1989. "Chicano men and masculinity." In Michael S. Kimmel and Michael A. Messner (eds.), *Men's Lives.* New York: Macmillan.

Zinn, Maxine Baca, and D. Stanley Eitzen. 1990. *Diversity in Families.* New York: Harper & Row.

Zuckerman, Diana M., and Donald H. Sayre. 1982. "Cultural sex-role expectations and children's sex-role concepts." *Sex Roles* 8:853-62.

NAME INDEX

SUBJECT INDEX